YE GODS!

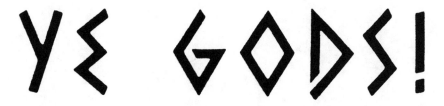

YE GODS!

AN INTRODUCTION TO CLASSICAL MYTHOLOGY

BY

HELEN BRITT

The Branson School
Ross, California

DRAWINGS BY STEPHANIE LANG

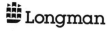 Longman

0-88334-196-4

01 02 03 04 19 18 17 16

Table of Contents

PART TWO: BRIGHT MYTHS

PART THREE: DARK MYTHS

Foreword

The purpose of this text is to introduce students to their classical heritage, the mythology of ancient Greece and Rome. For the sake of clarity, I have followed these procedures:

- Like the ancient storytellers, I have chosen from several versions of a myth the one most appealing and credible to me. A list of sources follows the text on page 141.

- Because Greek is the original mythology, Greek names are used throughout. When appropriate, the Roman name follows in parentheses. Exceptions are the Cupid and Psyche myth and the list of original Roman deities.

- In spelling mythological names, the more familiar Roman *c* and *u*, rather than the Greek *k* and *o*, are used. Accordingly, the Greek hero is referred to as *Heracles,* not *Hercules* or *Herakles;* the father of Zeus is *Cronus,* not *Kronos.*

- Each of the four sections includes study questions, vocabulary lists, and suggested topics for class discussion and writing. There is a glossary on page 143.

I am indebted to so many people that I cannot name them all. Special thanks must go to Coreen and Weston Hester, who generously put their word processor at my disposal; to Joan Robins, who edited the first draft; to John Hall, who supplied the title and edited subsequent drafts; to Margery Crawford, who patiently trudged through Greece with me; to Stephanie Lang, who illustrated the text; and to the Board of Trustees of The Branson School, and two Headmasters—Leonard Richardson and Thomas Hudnut—who gave me the gift of time.

Helen Britt
Ross, California

Introduction

Greece pulls away from the southernmost tip of Europe, bound to that continent on only one side and surrounded by hundreds of islands that look on the map like random-sized stepping-stones to Asia and Africa. Though these islands are actually the peaks of drowned mountains, legend says that the god who formed the nations of the world forgot to give a special gift to Greece. So he took all he had left—a bag full of rocks—dumped them in the bluest sea, and created the most beautiful of all nations.

The ancient Greeks had a story to explain almost everything. Imaginative and curious, they wondered about the origin of their world, the causes of natural phenomena (like wind and rain), the nature of man, and the meaning of life. In searching for answers, they created a pantheon of anthropomorphic deities who could be held responsible for everything in the world. Then these inventive people told an infinite variety of stories about their deities and their legendary heroes. Taken altogether, these stories form the body of literature we know as Greek mythology. Passed along by word of mouth from generation to generation, the myths were eventually written down in the form of plays, narrative verse, and prose. The facts were limited only by the imagination of the writer; that is why there are often many versions of the same myth.

This mythology was the religion of ancient Greece. Yet, unlike the Hebrews, the Greeks never had one book, one clear-cut body of dogma, one creed. As they were invaded over the centuries, their tolerant religion gradually changed and evolved from the worship of an earth-goddess to the worship of Zeus and the Olympians. When Greece was conquered by the Romans, the names of the deities were changed. When mythology was outlawed as a religion, worship of the Olympians faded away, but Greek mythology as literature lived on.

Two thousand years later, interest in classical mythology is growing rather than lessening. A student about to embark on the study of Greek mythology might well search for the reasons. The roots of Western civilization are in Greece. Ancient Greece produced some of the world's finest dramatists, historians, orators, philosophers, and poets. The ancient Greeks were among the first to study botany, geometry, medicine, physics, and zoology on a scientific basis. They held the first organized athletic games. Their system of government was the basis for our democracy. It was the Greeks who named the stars and planets. Without knowledge of this heritage from the past, modern man cannot hope to comprehend the present and prepare for the future. Further, the truths about human nature that the ancient Greeks explored 2,000 years ago are as valid today as they were then. Because of this, psychiatrists and philosophers from Freud to Camus have pondered the meanings of these ancient stories. Writers from Shakespeare to Shaw make frequent allusions to classical myths, even basing entire works on them. Robinson Jeffers' *Medea* is an example. No modern reader can truly appreciate these later authors unless he or she has some knowledge of Greek mythology. Finally, Greek myths were created not only to instruct but to entertain, and they remain a source of delight to modern readers.

The classical writers to whom modern readers are most indebted are listed below:

> *Homer* (ninth century B.C.)—the Greek poet who is credited with writing *The Iliad* and *The Odyssey*, concerning the Trojan War, which had occurred almost 400 years earlier. Homer is the earliest known Greek author.

Hesiod (eighth century B.C.)—the Greek poet who was especially interested in the creation and the gods. His famous poem is *Works and Days.*

Pindar (sixth century B.C.)—the Greek poet who wrote to glorify athletic contests. His famous work is *Odes.*

Sophocles, Aeschylus, Eurypides (fifth century B.C.)—three famous Greek tragedians, whose plays are still frequently performed (see list of their plays, p. 129).

Aristophanes (fourth century B.C.)—Greek dramatist noted for comedy. His most famous play is *The Birds.*

Apollodorus (probably second century B.C.)—A Greek prose writer whose *Bibliotheca* (*Library*) is the most complete source of mythology.

Ovid (first century B.C.)—the Roman poet whose beautiful, entertaining stories are found in one of the most famous mythology books, *Metamorphoses.*

Virgil (first century B.C.)—the Roman poet whose famous *Aeneid* gives additional information about the Trojan War.

Greek myths naturally divide into three kinds:

- *Etiological* These are myths that explain causes for natural phenomena—why does the sun rise and set each day? What are thunder and lightning? What causes that irrational feeling called love?

- *Entertaining* Lively, passionate, and imaginative, Greek myths are never dull. Many of them were written for the sole purpose of entertainment.

- *Historical* Many myths are based on fact, though the actual events occurred so long ago and are so shrouded in mystery that it is impossible to separate fact from myth. For many years it was thought that Homer's story of the Trojan War was pure fantasy, until in 1871 Heinrich Schliemann, armed only with a copy of *The Iliad,* discovered the site of the ancient city that Homer described.

Now you are about to step into the magical world of classical mythology—a world where horses fly, trees talk, and gods walk the earth in search of entertainment. Before you enter this world, you must do very much the same thing you do before entering the theatre: suspend your disbelief. Only then can you truly enjoy these stories of a vanished world that still lives on in literature.

PART ONE

SETTING
THE SCENE

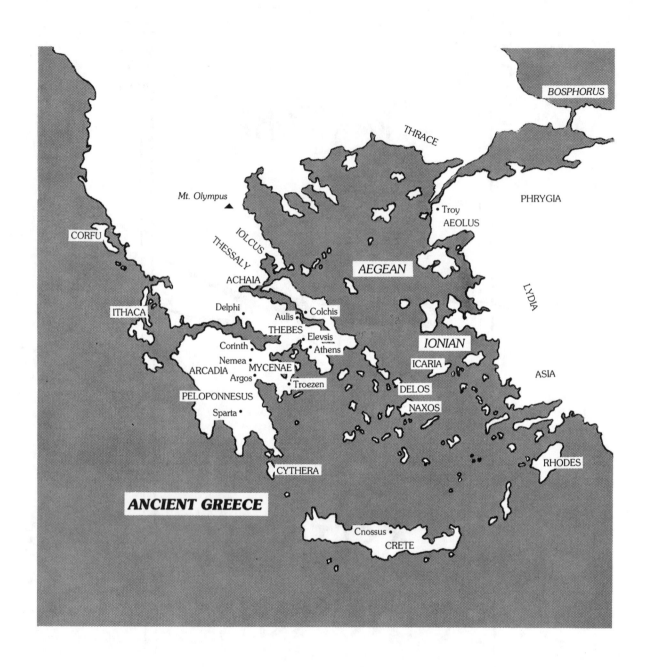

ANCIENT GREECE

BOSPHORUS

THRACE

PHRYGIA

Mt. Olympus

• Troy
AEOLUS

IOLCUS

CORFU

THESSALY

AEGEAN

LYDIA

ACHAIA

Delphi •

Aulis • • Colchis

THEBES

IONIAN

ITHACA

Elevsis

Corinth •

• Athens

ICARIA

Nemea •

ASIA

ARCADIA

MYCENAE

Argos •

• Troezen

DELOS

PELOPONNESUS

NAXOS

Sparta •

CYTHERA

RHODES

Cnossus •

CRETE

Chapter I

THE CREATION OF THE WORLD

The ancient Greeks believed that the world developed from formless, infinite space. Incredibly, modern scientists have come to the same conclusion. According to the ancient Greeks, the universe created the gods, who in turn created man. Like us, the Greeks referred to "Mother Earth"; Gaea, or the Earth Mother, was the first goddess to be worshipped in ancient times. It was not until centuries later that a male god, Zeus, became the principal deity in a pantheon of gods and goddesses.

In the beginning there was Chaos, a void of infinite space. The Greek word means "an open gulf." Out of this infinite space came Gaea—the Earth; Tartarus—the region under the earth; Eros—Love; and Erebus and Nyx—both gods of darkness. Erebus was the darkness of underground, and Nyx was the darkness of the night above the earth. Nyx and Erebus joined together to form two kinds of light: Aether, the Light of the Heavens, and Hemera, the Day. Night (Nyx) also brought forth three famous daughters, called the Moirae, or the Three Fates, who controlled the course of the universe. Clotho spun the threads of life, Lachesis measured the length of thread, and Atropos (later called "Morta" by the Romans) cut the thread.

Gaea, the Earth, gave birth to Uranus, the starry Heaven, and to the Mountains and Pontus, the Sea. Then the transformed Earth Mother, Gaea, was joined to her son Uranus, and from their union were born twelve large, strong, and handsome children called Titans.

THE TWELVE TITANS

Oceanus and *Tethys* were parents of all the river gods and of Eurynome, who (by Zeus) bore the Three Graces, incarnations of grace and beauty and companions of the Nine Muses. The Greeks believed that Oceanus encircled the world.

Coeus and *Phoebe* are best known as the parents of Leto, mother of Artemis and Apollo. From Phoebe's name comes the other part of Apollo's name, Phoebus.

Hyperion and *Theia* were the parents of Helios, the Sun God, Selene, the Moon, and Eos, the Dawn.

Mnemosne, or Memory, is most famous as the mother of the Nine Muses.

Themis was the goddess of Justice.

Iapetus is remembered because of his sons, Prometheus, Atlas, and Epimetheus.

Crius fathered the Four Winds.

Rhea became the wife of her brother, *Cronus.*

Gaea and Uranus also became the parents of hideous monsters: three giants, the Hecatonchires, each with a hundred hands and fifty heads, and three massive Cyclopes (The Greek name means "goggle-eyes"), each with only one eye in his head. Uranus loathed all these hideous sons, and as soon as they were born, he cast them into dark Tartarus. Though Gaea was filled with rage and anguish, she was powerless against the fearsome Uranus. In desperation she called upon her other children, the Titans, to rebel against their father. All but one were afraid of his terrible rage. Only her youngest son, Cronus, dared. "Mother," he said, "I shall take it upon myself to accomplish this deed. I hate my father, for he plotted shameless deeds from the first." So when Uranus came and lay over Gaea with the longing of love, Cronus stretched out his left hand from ambush. Grasping a huge, jagged sickle in his right hand, he quickly cut the genitals from his father's body and cast them behind him. Thus were connections between Earth and Heaven severed for all time.

As Uranus groaned in pain, drops of his blood fell upon the Earth Mother, Gaea, and she later bore nymphs called the Meliae, as well as another race of giants, and the Erinyes or Eumenides, also known as the Furies. They were horrible winged creatures who had writhing snakes for hair and cried tears of blood. They would pursue relentlessly with whips any man who had shed blood. Erinyes literally means "kindly ones" in Greek. The Greeks called them that to appease them, hoping they would act more mercifully to mankind. Later, the more realistic Romans called them the Furies.

A happy outcome of this violent incident was the birth of Aphrodite, the goddess of Love. Uranus' organs landed in the sea and were taken by the waves to Cythera and Cyprus. A white foam formed from the immortal flesh, and from this foam a beautiful maiden came into being. This was Aphrodite, literally "daughter of the foam," sometimes called "Cytheran Venus," from her birthplace and her Roman name. The Romans later said that Uranus fled to Asia and began the Golden Age. They called him Saturn.

Cronus now took his father's place as ruler of the world, and he married his sister, Rhea. Having been warned by his father, Uranus, that he, too, would feel the wrath of a traitorous son, Cronus used violent means to avoid his destiny. He swallowed each of his five children as each was born! Rhea was so distressed that she determined not to let Cronus swallow her sixth child. With the aid of her mother, Gaea, she secretly fled to Crete and gave birth to Zeus. When she returned to Cronus, she presented him with a stone wrapped in swaddling clothes, which he promptly swallowed. Meanwhile, deep within a hidden cave, Zeus was tended by the Meliae nymphs and nourished on goat's milk. At the entrance to the cave stood armed guards who clashed their weapons together like cymbals whenever the baby cried, so that Cronus would not become suspicious. Under these unusual conditions, the baby grew strong and sturdy.

As her mother Gaea had done before her, Rhea decided to enlist her child's help. Together, Rhea and Zeus concocted a potion to feed to Cronus, a potion that made him so sick he vomited forth the stone and the five older children he had swallowed many years before. Miraculously alive and full-grown, they were later to become famous as Olympian deities: Hestia, Demeter, Hera, Hades, and Poseidon.

Understandably feeling no love for their father, the six offspring declared war on him. This terrible war, which lasted ten years, was waged from two mountaintops: Cronus and the Titans on Mt. Othrys, Zeus and his companions on Mt. Olympus. Prometheus, the son of the Titan Iapetus, at first was loyal to Cronus. But when Cronus would not follow his strategies, Prometheus despaired of peace and went over to Zeus' side. First he suggested to Zeus that he free the three Cyclopes, who were still prisoners in Tartarus. Zeus agreed. The Cyclopes were so grateful to be freed that they gave Zeus and his brothers invaluable gifts. To Zeus they gave thunder, lightning, and the thunderbolt; to Poseidon, the trident, a three-pronged spear; and to Hades, a helmet to make him invisible when he wore it. At Prometheus' urging, Zeus also freed his uncles, the Hundred-handers. Using his gifts of thunder, lightning, and thunderbolts, Zeus set the earth afire while the Hundred-handers threw huge boulders. The earth was in flames; the rivers boiled; even the skies were scorched. The Titans were finally forced to flee Mt. Othrys and retreat to dark Tartarus, where they still remain under heavy guard. Only Prometheus, who had aided Zeus; Epimetheus, his brother; and Atlas, the strongest Titan, escaped eternal imprisonment in Tartarus. Atlas' punishment was unique: he was required to hold up the world (his name in Greek means "to support"). He continues to do so to this day. Thus, in trying to escape his fate, Cronus only brought it about, and once again a son turned against his father, urged on by a determined mother.

After order was finally restored to the world, the three victorious brothers drew lots for the division of the universe. Zeus became the king of Heaven; Poseidon, king of the Sea; and Hades, king of the Underworld. Earth belonged to all of them.

CHAPTER I: STUDY QUESTIONS

1. What is the meaning of these words?

   mythology

   pantheon

   deity

   classical

   etiological

   allusion

   anthropomorphic

2. Where is Greece?

3. Why do we study mythology?

4. Who are the following writers; what is their nationality and their century; what are they famous for?

   Aeschylus

   Apollodorus

   Eurypides

   Hesiod

   Homer

   Ovid

   Pindar

   Sophocles

   Virgil

5. What are the three kinds of myths?

6. What was the Greek idea of Chaos?

7. Who were Gaea and Uranus?

8. Who were Eros, Erebus, Nyx, Aether, Hemera, the Moirae, Pontus?

9. Who were the Titans? Who were the Cyclopes?

10. What did Uranus do to the Cyclopes and the Hundred-handers?

11. How did Cronus help Gaea?

12. Who were the Erinyes or Eumenides? What was their other name?

13. How was Aphrodite born? What does her name mean?

14. What did the ancient Greeks believe about Fate?

15. How would you contrast Gaea and Uranus? Rhea and Cronus? What are the similarities between Gaea and Rhea? Between Uranus and Cronus?

16. What did Cronus do to avoid his fate? Who outwitted him? How?

17. Why is Father Time shown with a scythe or sickle?

18. Where was Zeus born?

19. What are the names of Rhea's children?

20. Why did the Titan Prometheus aid Zeus? How did he aid Zeus?

21. What was the outcome of the war? How long did it last?

22. What is Tartarus?

23. What happened to Atlas after the war? to Prometheus? to Epimetheus? to the other Titans?

24. What gifts did the Cyclopes give to Zeus? Hades? Poseidon?

25. Three brothers drew lots after the war. Who were the brothers, and what was the outcome?

Chapter II

THE OLYMPIAN AGE

With the defeat and imprisonment of the Titans, a new age came into being, and the victorious gods became known as the Olympians. Hades lived permanently in the Underworld, but his five brothers and sisters lived on Mt. Olympus, the highest mountain in Greece, in Thessaly. Each god and goddess had a dwelling on Mt. Olympus, fashioned of gold and silver. Life there was idyllic: beyond a gate of clouds, kept by the Four Seasons, the immortal gods dined on ambrosia and nectar while being entertained by beautiful music under perpetually cloudless skies. The ethereal fluid ichor, rather than blood, coursed through their veins, so they could never grow old and die.

Although the gods and goddesses of Mt. Olympus seemed to have everything that anyone could desire, they were still not contented. Prey to all the passions that affect mankind, like love, jealousy, ambition, and greed, the Olympians often bickered with one another and, bored with life on Mt. Olympus, roamed the Earth in search of diversion.

THE TWELVE OLYMPIANS

The twelve gods and goddesses who lived on Mt. Olympus were the children of Cronus and Rhea—Zeus, Poseidon, Demeter, Hera, and Hestia—and their offspring, Apollo, Hermes, Ares, Hephaestus, Athena, Aphrodite, and Artemis. Later, Hestia was replaced by Dionysus.

Zeus (Roman name: Jupiter or Jove)

Zeus was the acknowledged leader of the Olympians. Usually portrayed as a handsome, bearded man in his prime, he carries the thunderbolt and often the aegis, a shield. He is also associated with the oak tree and the eagle and is the god of Hospitality. To the ancient Greeks, Zeus, the god with a voice of thunder, was a symbol of justice and order. Yet they delighted in telling stories of Zeus' infidelity, particularly when he used trickery to get his way. Being married to his sister, Hera, never deterred Zeus from his constant search for lovely ladies, both mortal and immortal. Because he was raised in Crete, Zeus is strongly associated with that island. The most impressive temple to Zeus, however, was built in Olympia, the site of the first Olympic Games. The Romans called Zeus "Jupiter" and sometimes "Jove." His name literally means "to shine," and as you will discover, Zeus shone very brightly indeed for the Greeks.

Hera (Juno)

Hera was Zeus' sister (swallowed by Cronus at her birth and regurgitated years later), as well as his wife. Associated with marriage, she was called Juno by the Romans. June, of course, is still the most popular month for weddings. Hera was beautiful but implacable, constantly jealous of Zeus and vengeful against his conquests. The cow and peacock are both associated with Hera, as is the city of Argos. She is also associated with Iris, her petite messenger, who descended to Earth via the rainbow. In spite of Hera's bad disposition, she is usually portrayed as a serenely dignified woman, fully robed, with a crown and scepter befitting her stature as the wife of the ruler of Mt. Olympus. Her name is the feminine version of *hero*.

Together, Zeus and Hera had three children: Hebe, Ares, and Hephaestus. Hebe, the cupbearer of the gods until Zeus replaced her with the handsome youth Ganymede, later married Heracles.

Poseidon (Neptune)

Poseidon was the god of the Sea and of Horses. This strange mixture probably came about because Poseidon gave the first horse to man, and the early Greeks called whitecaps "white horses." The brother of Zeus, Poseidon is portrayed as a mature, bearded man, distinguishable from Zeus only by his trident, the three-pronged spear given to him by his uncles, the Cyclopes. With this trident, Poseidon could stir up the seas and shake the earth. His epithet was "earth-shaker." Gruff, bad-tempered, and unlucky in love, Poseidon was married to Amphitrite. His most famous offspring were Triton, the original merman, who blew on a conch shell to signal the beginning and ending of a storm; the Cyclops Polyphemus (who achieved fame in *The Odyssey*); Pegasus, the winged horse; and Orion, the constellation in the shape of a hunter. Powerful Poseidon had a home on Mt. Olympus as well as a palace beneath the sea.

Apollo (Apollo)

Second only to Zeus in the eyes of the ancient Greeks, Apollo represented sanity and light. He was handsome and virile, the greatest musician of all gods and mortals. The god of Music, Poetry, Dance, and Prophecy, as well as of Medicine, Apollo is usually shown wearing a crown of laurel and carrying a lyre or a bow. Apollo was the twin of Artemis and the son of Zeus and Leto (Roman name Latona), daughter of the Titans Coeus and Phoebe.

The fiercely jealous Hera forced pregnant Leto to wander from place to place trying to find a haven to give birth. Finally, she was accepted on the small floating island of Delos, which became famous as the birthplace of the twins Apollo and Artemis and thus the most sacred of the Greek islands. In ancient times, no one was allowed to be born or to die there. Because his grandmother was the Titan Phoebe, Apollo is often referred to as *Phoebus* Apollo. An expert archer and bringer of sudden death, Apollo was ironically called "the Healer" because the ancient Greeks believed that outbreaks of pestilence were caused by his arrows. They prayed to Apollo to stop the killings, and when the plague had run its course, he was given credit for showing mercy and gratefully called "the Healer."

Apollo's most famous offspring was Asclepius, who also became known as the god of Medicine and was worshipped at Epidaurus. There, patients sought cures by sleeping in Asclepius' temple and dreaming that the god was healing them.

Apollo's shrine was at Delphi, considered by ancient Greeks to be the center of the world. He established his shrine there by force, having taken the form of a dolphin and swum to Delphi to kill Python, a fearsome female serpent, who had established Delphi as her territory (Delphi means "dolphin" in Greek). People came from all over to consult the oracle at Delphi and were given ambiguous answers that were vague enough to apply to almost any outcome. Delphi had such a powerful influence over ancient Greece that no legislature would draw up a constitution without the aid of the Delphic Oracle. On Apollo's temple at Delphi were carved two favorite Greek sayings, "Know thyself" and "Nothing to excess." He personified the Greek ideal of moderation, "the golden mean." Perhaps because of his near-perfection, Apollo is the only Olympian whose name was not altered by the Romans.

Artemis (Diana)

The twin sister of Apollo, Artemis was an excellent archer like her brother. She was the goddess of the hunt, a liberated young woman who remained free of romantic entanglements and fiercely clung to her independence. Paradoxically, having taken a vow of chastity, Artemis was often called upon to help women in childbirth. In Asia Minor, the virgin Artemis was worshipped as a goddess of fertility. Artemis is portrayed as tall, slender, and athletic, often surrounded by nymphs, always carrying her silver bow and arrows. She is associated with the hart (young deer). In later times, Apollo was considered the Sun God, and Artemis, his twin, was called goddess of the Moon.

Athena (Minerva)

Of all the unusual births in Greek mythology, the birth of Athena, goddess of Wisdom, was one of the strangest. Warned that, like his grandfather and father before him, he would be deposed by his son, Zeus determined to avoid his fate in a novel way: he simply swallowed his pregnant first wife, the Titan Metis (whose name means "wisdom" in Greek). Subsequently Zeus suffered a horrendous headache and summoned Hephaestus, who cracked open Zeus' skull with his hammer—and out came Athena, fully grown and attired in a suit of armor! In spite of this bizarre birth, Athena became Zeus' favorite child. He entrusted her with his aegis and depended on her good judgment in all matters. Although she was expert at all domestic arts and was the world's finest weaver, Athena remained unmarried. She was sometimes called Athena Parthenos—Athena the Virgin.

It is said that Poseidon and Athena argued over the naming of a newly-founded city. Poseidon struck the ground with his trident, and the horse appeared. Athena touched the ground with her spear, and an olive tree sprang up. Athena's gift was judged more beneficial, and thus the city was named Athens. Athena became the patron goddess of Athens, and the Parthenon still stands as a tribute to her. Though Athena was skilled in the strategies of war, she much preferred harmony, and her tree, the olive, symbolizes peace. Not surprisingly for the goddess of Wisdom, the owl was her bird.

Ares (Mars)

Ares was the god of War, disliked by the Greeks and admired by the Romans. The son of Zeus and Hera, he was detested by both of his parents. Unlike his half-sister Athena, who could wage war well but preferred peace, Ares revelled in violence and bloodshed. Appropriately, his bird was the vulture. His chariot was prepared for war by Phobos (Fear) and Dermos (Terror).

Hephaestus (Vulcan)

Whereas Ares was handsome but evil, Hephaestus was ugly but admirable. There are conflicting stories of his birth. Some say he was the son of Hera and Zeus; some, that he was the son of Hera alone, born deformed and thrown off Mt. Olympus by his disgusted mother. Another version says that Zeus hurled Hephaestus from the mountain after Hephaestus intervened in a quarrel between Zeus and Hera. At any rate, he was badly crippled and physically ugly but nevertheless had great strength in his arms and the talent to fashion exquisitely beautiful objects at his mighty forge. It was Hephaestus who made all the beautiful homes of the gods and goddesses, their armor, and handsome objects of art. He was the only god who worked for a living and, ironically, the husband of the most beautiful goddess of all, Aphrodite.

Aphrodite (Venus)

Aphrodite was the goddess of Love and Beauty. One version of her birth was that she was born from the sea-foam after Uranus' castration (see p. 6). The other version was that Aphrodite was the daughter of Zeus and Dione (sister of the Titans Mnemosne and Thetis). Aphrodite had a magic belt that could make whoever wore it the object of love and desire. Associated with the rose, she rode in a chariot drawn by doves. Gold-wreathed, smiling, and lovely, Aphrodite was said to cause green grass and blooming flowers to spring up wherever she walked. In paintings, she is often shown accompanied by the Three Graces and her son, Eros (Cupid).

Hermes (Mercury)

The son of Zeus and Maia (daughter of Atlas), Hermes is familiar to contemporary readers as a handsome youth with winged hat and sandals and a distinctive staff—the caduceus, still the symbol of medicine—adorned with writhing serpents. Lighthearted and funloving, a prankster from birth, Hermes was the fleet-footed messenger of the gods. A nimble thief himself, he was the god of Thieves and of Commerce. On a more somber note, Hermes was the one who led souls to the Underworld. The Greeks, who greatly admired guile, delighted in stories about Hermes, and he is mentioned more often than any other god in Greek myths.

Hestia (Vesta)

In contrast to her nephew Hermes, gentle Hestia is the least mentioned of all the Olympians, and in later times she is said to have given her place on Mt. Olympus to Dionysus. Hestia means "hearth" in Greek, and Hestia was sacred to the Greeks as protector of the fire. Every city had a hearth dedicated to Hestia, where sacred fire burned perpetually. A virgin, Hestia is portrayed by artists as a maiden aunt rather than a vigorous young girl—content to stay at home and remain inconspicuous.

Demeter (Ceres)

Demeter, daughter of Cronus and Rhea, was the goddess of Corn and fertility of the land, who could bring forth fruits and flowers or withhold them at will. She is often portrayed smilingly holding sheaves of corn, but she is also shown as the suffering mother, grieving for her lost daughter, Persephone (Proserpina) (see p. 17).

THREE SIGNIFICANT DEITIES

Hades (Pluto)

As ruler of the Underworld, Hades did not live on Mt. Olympus with his five brothers and sisters. Because of all the rich minerals underground, Hades was also called the god of Wealth. Plutonium derives its name from Hades' Roman name. His gift from the Cyclopes was a helmet with the power to make him invisible. A pitiless and mirthless god, Hades inspired awesome fear when he drove his chariot to Earth or to Mt. Olympus. The realm Hades ruled over was bounded by water. In fact, five rivers separated the Underworld from the Earth. One of these rivers was Lethe, the river of forgetfulness; another was the Styx ("hateful" in Greek), whose water was used by the gods to swear unbreakable oaths—much as the Bible is used in court-rooms in modern times.

An old ferryman, Charon, ferried the souls of the dead to the Underworld, but only if passage money was first placed on their eyes. On guard at the gate to the Underworld was Cerberus, a dog with three heads and the tail of a dragon. He wagged his tail at all who entered but would permit no one to leave.

Persephone (Proserpina)

Persephone, sometimes called Kore (girl), was the only daughter of Demeter. Her father was said to be Zeus. Her story, full of suspense, fascinated the ancient Greeks and explained much of their mysterious world. Without the consent of Deme-ter, Zeus promised Hades that he could marry the fair Persephone when she came of age. It was a foolish promise that was destined to cause grief and disorder in the world. When the time came for Hades to claim his unsuspecting bride, he steered his gold chariot, driven by black horses, through a chasm in the earth, forced Persephone into his carriage, and disappeared into the Underworld. Fearing the wrath of Zeus, no one would tell the grieving Demeter what had happened to her missing daughter. Desper-ately, she searched far and wide for Persephone. Finally, Helios, the Sun, who sees everything from his chariot as he traverses the earth, told Demeter the bitter truth: Persephone had been kidnapped by Hades and was living with him as Queen of the Underworld. There she would remain forever.

Demeter continued to roam the earth in despair. Disguised as an old woman in a heavy veil and dark robe, she arrived one day at the little town of Eleusis. There, she became the nursemaid of a baby named Demophoön, the son of Metaneira and Celeus. Little did they suspect the identity of their baby's old nurse. Determined to make Demophoön immortal as a replacement for her lost daughter, Demeter anointed him with ambrosia by day and placed him in the heart of the fire by night. Eventually Metaneira became suspicious of her mysterious nursemaid, and she watched one night from the shadows. When she saw her son being placed in the red-hot fire, she screamed in horror. Demeter transformed herself from the black-robed old crone to the radiant goddess of Corn. Magnificently furious, she hurled the baby to the hearth. "I, Demeter, would have made your son immortal. Now, foolish woman, you have spoiled everything! He will be a mere mortal, and you must appease my great anger." Demophoön survived his accident and lived with special honor through-out his life, but, true to her vow, Demeter did not grant him immortality. In order to appease her, the villagers of Eleusis built a shrine to Demeter, and there for centuries secret fertility rites were performed in her honor. Every fall, pilgrims—as many as 30,000 at a time—would walk along the sacred way from Athens to Eleusis to participate in the nine-day-long ceremonies. Fearing the goddess' great wrath, no one ever broke the vow of secrecy, so to this day the Eleusinian rites remain a mystery.

Meanwhile, a year had gone by since Persephone's kidnapping. As Demeter mourned, the earth became bleak and barren. Nothing flowered or bore fruit, and men were dying of starvation. Finally, Zeus realized that it would be impossible to keep his promise to his brother, Hades, without destroying mankind. He sent Hermes to the Underworld to bring Persephone back to her grieving mother. The crafty Hades agreed to let Persephone return to Earth, but first he persuaded her to eat a pomegranate, the fruit of the dead. When Persephone was reunited with Demeter, their happiness was unbounded until Persephone confessed that she had eaten four pomegranate seeds. For every seed she had eaten, she would have to spend one month in the Underworld as Hades' queen. The remaining eight months, she could remain with her devoted mother. Thus it is that for eight months of the year the earth is green and fair as Demeter rejoices in her daughter's presence, while for four months the earth is brown and barren as Demeter grieves for her daughter, Persephone, the Queen of the Underworld.

Dionysus (Bacchus)

Dionysus, god of Wine, is said to have taken the place of the modest Hestia as the twelfth Olympian. A god whose worship was established later than the other Olympians, he differed in other ways as well. Dionysus had a mortal mother, Semele, though, like Athena, he was actually born out of his father, Zeus. This came about in a very strange way. Completely beguiled by Semele's charm and beauty, Zeus impregnated her and then told her she could have anything she desired. It was a foolish promise, for the jealous Hera persuaded Semele to ask for a fatal gift—that of seeing Zeus resplendent in all his armor, complete with thunderbolts. Knowing the consequence would be death for Semele, Zeus tried to persuade her to make another request instead, but she insisted. Bound to honor this Stygian oath, Zeus complied. The sight of Zeus was literally overwhelming, and Semele burned to death from the intense heat and brightness of that sight. The grieving Zeus snatched Semele's unborn baby, implanted the fetus in his thigh and, three months later, brought forth the baby Dionysus. Wishing to avoid the further wrath of his jealous wife, Zeus gave the baby to the water nymphs to nourish. Thus, like the grapevine he represented, Dionysus was brought forth in heat and nourished by moisture.

When he grew up, Dionysus much preferred the company of men to gods. He traveled all over Greece, mingling with humans and encouraging their worship of him. When they honored him, he taught them how to plant grapevines and tend them wisely; when they resisted his worship—for Hera, still holding a jealous grudge against Dionysus' mother, tried to persuade men to shun Dionysus—he showed a vicious side. He and his companions would drive men and women to madness. Dionysus' companions were maenads (the word means "madwoman" in Greek), sometimes called bacchantes—who drove men and women to frenzied actions—and satyrs, young men with animal features, who sought only sensual gratification. Dionysus' staff was the thyrsus, distinctively covered with vine leaves and topped with a pine cone.

Dionysian revels, called bacchanalia, gradually became less frenzied and more ritualized, evolving over the centuries into dramatic festivals. He thus became the god of Drama as well as the god of Wine.

Dionysus is similar to Demeter in many ways. Both of them grieved over lost relatives: Demeter for her daughter, Dionysus for his mother. Dionysus, too, journeyed to the Underworld—to bring his mother, Semele, to Mt. Olympus. He was successful, and he encouraged his followers to worship Semele as well as himself. Like Demeter, Dionysus was honored in rituals. Euripides' play *The Bacchae* is based on Dionysus' worship. The Eleusinian rituals were celebrated in September, at harvest time, to honor Demeter; the Dionysian festivals were celebrated in the spring. Both deities are associated with the mysteries of death and immortality.

Dionysus is a complete contrast to Apollo, the ideal of moderation and intellectual thought. Dionysus and his followers sneered at moderation, and they gloried in sensual gratification rather than the pleasures of the mind. The ancient Greeks acknowledged this contrast between the god of Reason and the god of Emotion. The shrine at Delphi, for nine months of the year devoted to the worship of Apollo, was given over to Dionysus for the three winter months, when Apollo was said to be visiting the Hyperboreans. During those three months, the maenads climbed up to a plateau and remained there in a trance-like state, insensitive to cold and pain. Dionysus was not the only god who possessed both positive and negative qualities, but his were the most striking. As wine in moderation can make one happy and generous, but in excess, belligerent and destructive, so was Dionysus at once man's benefactor and man's destroyer.

OTHER DEITIES

Eros (Cupid)

The ancient Greeks did not understand the powerful, unreasonable, mysterious force of love any more than does modern man. They tried to explain love by personifying it. The first explanation (see p. 5) was that Eros became the first force to come out of Chaos at the beginning of creation. Later, it was said that Eros was the son of the goddess of Love and Beauty, Aphrodite. A handsome youth, armed with bow and arrow and sometimes depicted as blindfolded, Eros (Cupid) could use his sharp gold arrows to inspire love or his blunt lead arrows to cause love to flee. As time went on, Eros became younger and younger, finally evolving into the chubby cherub familiarly portrayed on valentines.

Four Winds

Agrestus or Eurus was the east wind; Zephyrus, the west wind; Boreas, the north wind; and Notus, the south wind. They were significant and powerful deities to the seafaring Greeks.

Helios* (Sol)

Helios was the Sun God, who drove his golden chariot, pulled by four splendid horses, from east to west every day. His favorite island was Rhodes (named for his beloved nymph, Rhode), and it is thought that Helios was the inspiration for the great Colossus of Rhodes.

---

* *Helios* was sometimes interchanged with Apollo (also called Phoebus Apollo) because of Apollo's connection with light.

Hypnos (Somnus)

Hypnos was the god of Sleep, the son of Night and brother of Death. He lived in Tartarus. His son was *Morpheus,* god of Sleep and Dreams.

Muses

The offspring of Zeus and Mnemosyne, the Nine Muses represented all the arts the Greeks most prized. *Clio* was the Muse of History, *Urania* of Astronomy, *Melpomone* of Tragedy, *Thalia* of Comedy, *Terpsichore* of Dance, *Erato* of Love Poetry, *Polyhymnia* of songs to the gods, *Euterpe* of Lyric Poetry, and *Calliope* of Epic Poetry. In the first lines of *The Odyssey,* Homer calls upon Calliope to inspire him.

Nemesis

The daughter of Nyx (Night), Nemesis was the personification of divine retribution. The name comes from the Greek word meaning "to distribute." Nemesis was the goddess who saw to it that everyone was justly rewarded—or punished.

Pan

The son of Hermes, Pan was a goat-footed god with horns who lived in the forest, chased woodland nymphs, and played his pipes. He is strongly associated with Arcady, his birthplace. Strange nighttime noises in the forest were said to be made by Pan, and that is how the word *panic* originated.

Selene* (Luna)

Beautiful Selene was goddess of the Moon, wearing a golden crown and riding across the sky in a handsome chariot. She loved the attractive youth, Endymion.

ROMAN DEITIES

Although the Romans invented new names for the Greek deities (all but Apollo), they showed very little originality in creating new gods. Only a few Roman deities are significant enough to be singled out.

Janus

The spirit of the doorway, Janus is always depicted with two faces, one looking forward and one looking backward, and he is associated with hypocrisy. The month of January takes its name from this Roman god.

Morpheus

Morpheus was created by the Roman writer Ovid. The son of Somnus (Sleep), and brother of Phantasus, he was the god of Dreams.

---

* Because she was Apollo's twin, Artemis was sometimes confused with *Selene,* goddess of the Moon.

Other familiar Roman names are:

Aurora—the Dawn
Bellona—goddess of War
Fauna—goddess of the Fields
Flora—goddess of Flowers
Fortuna—goddess of Chance
Hygeia—goddess of Health
Pomona—goddess of Fruit Trees
Voluptas—goddess of Pleasure

CHAPTER II: STUDY QUESTIONS

1. Why are the Olympians known by that name?

2. How would you describe Mt. Olympus?

3. Who are the twelve Olympians? What are their Roman names? What are their attributes?

4. What is the "golden mean"? What Olympian deity personified the golden mean? What Olympian god was a complete contrast?

5. What deity has the same name in Greek and Roman mythology?

6. Which deity gave her place in Mt. Olympus to another deity?

7. Which deity was the most disliked?

8. Which deity is associated with the olive tree? the laurel? the peacock? the hart? the lyre? the trident? the forge? the eagle? the dove? the caduceus? the vulture? the owl? Are these attributes appropriate? Why or why not?

9. In what ways are Dionysus and Demeter different from the other Olympian deities? How are they similar to one another? How are they different from one another?

10. Who was Charon? Cerberus? What was Lethe? Styx?

11. What are the Eleusinian Mysteries? In whose honor were they performed? Where? Why?

12. What prevented Persephone's permanent reunion with her mother?

13. How did Dionysus, god of Wine, become associated with drama?

14. Who were Dionysus' companions?

15. Who was Nemesis?

16. What was unique about Pan's appearance?

17. What is unique about Janus?

18. What Southern California college is named after a Roman deity?

Chapter III

THE CREATION OF MAN

PROMETHEUS

The Titan son of Iapetus, Prometheus was believed by some ancient Greeks to have created man. Over the centuries he has come to symbolize bravery in the face of oppression.

Earlier, Prometheus had helped Zeus with brilliant strategies in the war against the Titans (see p. 6). Thus, when the war was over, Zeus did not punish Prometheus and his brother Epimetheus. The ingenious Prometheus did not stay idle for long.

In his poetic account of the Creation, Ovid says, "There still was lacking a being more venerable than animals such as these, one with greater powers of thought and reasoning who might be master over all living creatures. Thus man was created, and although the other animals look down upon the earth, the creator of all things gave man an uplifted countenance and caused him to look to the sky and raise his upturned face toward the stars." Many ancient Greeks believed this "creator of all things" was Prometheus, who first molded animals of clay and then devised man. Prometheus, whose name means "forethought," was a contrast to his brother, Epimetheus, whose name means "afterthought." As Prometheus created the animals, Epimetheus gave them qualities of strength, cunning, speed, and the like, trying to divide them equally so that all the animals could defend themselves. To Prometheus' horror, he discovered that his brother had neglected to save any qualities for man, Prometheus' last and favorite creation.

Weak and defenseless, man would surely have perished without Prometheus' help. Patiently and expertly, Prometheus taught man all he would need to know to have dominion over the earth—knowledge of the stars and the science of computation, the art of writing and development of mind and memory, the skills of sailing and farming, the ability to cure sickness and to interpret dreams. He even persuaded Zeus to let man borrow fire. But Prometheus went too far in his support of man: he tricked Zeus, offering the King of the Gods a choice of two piles of ox meat. One was large and tempting, glistening with fat; the other was small and covered with hide and entrails. Zeus chose the tempting pile, only to discover that the fat actually concealed bones and entrails, while under the mangy hide of the second pile were artfully concealed the best parts of the ox. From then on, man had only to offer to the gods the scent of meat from fat and bones, while they could keep the edible parts of the beef for themselves.

Furious at being tricked by the guileful Prometheus, Zeus punished him by taking fire away from man. Prometheus knew man would perish without fire, so this time he stole fire from Helios, the Sun God. Zeus was so enraged at this act of defiance that he retaliated by punishing Prometheus directly. Zeus ordered the gentle but strong Hephaestus to chain Prometheus to a rock in the Caucasus, where he was forced to endure blistering heat by day and freezing cold by night. Every day an eagle, sent by Zeus, gnawed at Prometheus' liver, and every night the liver grew back, only to have the punishment repeated the next day. Some said this punishment lasted for 30,000 years, until finally Prometheus was released by Heracles.

Zeus was furious at Prometheus for another reason, unrelated to man. Prometheus had been told by his mother, the Titan Themis, the name of the wife who would bear Zeus a son who would destroy his father. Aware of the prophecy, Zeus wanted desperately to know the name of this wife. Prometheus adamantly refused to divulge his mother's secret. (The wife was Metis, who bore Zeus no sons because she was swallowed by him before the birth of their daughter, Athena.)

The subject of Aeschylus' play *Prometheus Bound*, Prometheus has come to personify courage in the face of adversity. When he exclaims, "Although Zeus may batter my body, he cannot shatter my spirit," he is an inspiration for all people who refuse to give in to tyranny.

PANDORA, THE FIRST WOMAN

Before Prometheus was sentenced to his punishment in the Caucasus, he warned his brother, Epimetheus, not to accept any gifts from Zeus, for he knew Zeus would stop at nothing to avenge himself. Poor dim-witted Epimetheus forgot this warning, and when Hermes arrived at his door with a lovely new creature, Epimetheus greeted them both with open arms. This new creature was Pandora ("all-gifts"), the first woman, created by the gods to look beautiful and possess all charms, yet to cause man harm through her excessive curiosity. Epimetheus gladly married the lovely Pandora. He warned her not to look inside the ornate jar Prometheus had left behind with instructions that it never be opened. Curious Pandora could not resist the temptation for long. When she opened the jar, all the evils of the world flew out to plague mankind forever after—sickness, old age, hatred, jealousy, greed, lust, spite, envy, falsehood, and many more. Only one thing remained trapped inside the lid of the jar: hope.

THE FLOOD/DEUCALION AND PYRRHA

Of the Seven Deadly Sins, the sin of pride is the worst. Excessive pride—the kind that led men to think they could neglect or compete with the gods—was called hubris by the Greeks, and it was the most dangerous of all sins, inevitably leading to destruction.

Sometime during 3,000-2,000 B.C. there was a great flood in Mesopotamia that may have been the inspiration for the following myth.

Zeus became more and more disgusted with mankind, for men and women became less mindful of the gods, performing shameful acts and forgetting that they should honor the gods. Never one for halfway measures, Zeus determined to get rid of the entire human race. The question was how best to accomplish this task. If Zeus used his thunderbolts to destroy Earth, he ran the risk of setting fire to Heaven as well. Thus, during a council of the gods, it was decided to flood the earth and destroy everything on it. Poseidon, the earth-shaker, used his powerful trident and called forth all his river gods to help. Soon the earth was completely flooded. Mortals who first feared for their crops, then feared for their lives, finally perished from starvation or drowning.

Only two people had been warned of the flood: Deucalion, son of Prometheus, and Pyrrha, daughter of Epimetheus. They were a virtuous and god-fearing couple. From his prison in the Caucasus, Prometheus had gotten word to his son, Deucalion, so the prudent couple built a boat, and after floating for nine days and nine nights, they finally found dry land at the very top of Mt. Parnassus. Looking down from Mt. Olympus, Zeus saw the lonely couple and felt compassion. As the flood waters subsided, Deucalion and Pyrrha made their way to a temple and gave thanks for their deliverance to the Titan goddess, Themis. They prayed that the human race might be restored. Moved by pity, the goddess answered: "Go from this temple and cover your heads and loosen the garments you wear. Then throw the bones of your great mother behind your backs." Deucalion and Pyrrha were perplexed at these words, but finally Deucalion said, "The earth is our great mother. I believe the stones in the body of the earth are called bones. We are ordered to throw those behind our backs!" Accordingly, they left the temple and threw the stones behind them as they had been ordered to do. Gradually, the stones lost stiffness and took the form of human beings. The ones Deucalion threw became men; the ones thrown by Pyrrha became women. Thus, a new and hardier race of mankind came into being.

THE FIVE AGES OF MAN

A more widespread belief of the ancient Greeks was that man was created by the gods during the time of Cronus. Thus, the first race of man lived during his reign. This was the Golden Age, when men were rich, happy, and loved by the gods. They never grew old.

Yet this race passed, and a second race of man was created by the Olympian gods and this period was called the Silver Age. This age was inferior to the first. Men stayed with their mothers for 100 years, and when they grew up, they did not live long because they warred with one another, forgetting to honor the gods. Zeus was displeased with this race of man, and they were destroyed.

The third race of mankind was even more violent and seemingly invincible. This period was called the Bronze Age because men fought with bronze weapons, lived in bronze houses, and tilled the soil with bronze tools. This age came to a close when men destroyed one another.

The fourth race was an improvement: a godlike race of heroes called Demigods. After they died, they were allowed to go to the Isles of the Blessed (the Elysian Fields), where Cronus was king. Many of these heroes fought in the Trojan War.

The final race, living at a time called the Iron Age, was the worst. Men had to toil and suffer, even though they received some meager rewards. War and corruption were rampant. This age was destined to be destroyed.

The Roman writer, Ovid, in describing the Ages of Man, omits the fourth group, the Demigods, emphasizing the Greek worship of their heroes.

CHAPTER III: STUDY QUESTIONS

1. What has Prometheus come to symbolize? Why?

2. During the creation of man, what mistake did Epimetheus make? How did Prometheus rectify this mistake?

3. How did Prometheus trick Zeus?

4. What secret did Prometheus know about Zeus?

5. How did Zeus punish Prometheus?

6. What is the famous play about Prometheus? Who is the author?

7. Who was given Pandora? Describe Pandora.

8. Who were the only two people to survive the flood? To whom were they related and how?

9. What were "the bones of your great mother"?

10. What were the five ages of man?

11. How did the Greek and Roman versions of these ages vary? What does that indicate?

PART ONE, STUDY QUESTIONS

1. What is the meaning of these words?

aegis	deity	polytheism
attribute	epithet	thyrsus
caduceus	guile	
Chaos	hubris	

2. From what ancient words are the following words derived? What is the connection between the ancient and the present meaning of the word?

aphrodisiac	lunatic
atlas	March
aurora borealis	mercurial
calliope	morphine
cereal	mortal
cupidity	museum
erotic	music
florist	nectarine
fortunate	olympian
heliotrope	panic
helium	phantom
hygenic	phobia
hypnotic	plutonium
iridescent	saturnine
janitor	somnolent
January	terpsichorean
jovial	titanic
June	venial
lethal	volcano
lethargic	voluptuous
lunar	zephyr

3. How do the words *prologue* and *epilogue* apply to Prometheus and his brother? What other words are derived from the Greek mythology studied thus far? List five.

4. How did the following expressions originate? What do they mean?

Pandora's box	that was his nemesis
by Jove!	a stygian oath
Promethean labor	in the arms of morpheus
Venus fly trap	janus-faced
Titanic struggle	interesting flora and fauna

5. Can you think of other expressions derived from Greek mythology? List them below.

SUGGESTED ESSAY TOPICS

St. Paul said, "The invisible must be understood by the visible." What did he mean by this statement? Use specific examples to explain how this statement might apply to Greek mythology.

In writing of the Iron Age, Hesiod says, "I wish, therefore, that I did not live among the men of the fifth race, but had died earlier or been born later." If you could choose any age at all to live in, explain which one you would choose and why.

When Pandora opened the jar and all the evils flew into the air, only hope remained. What does that situation suggest?

SUGGESTED ASSIGNMENTS

Complete the charts of the Olympian deities and other deities on the following pages.

Make a list of the cities, towns, streets, restaurants, companies, and the like that are derived from or inspired by Greek or Roman mythology. Illustrate your list with appropriate clippings from newspapers and magazines. (Example: F.T.D. Florists always use a logo of Hermes, the fleet-footed messenger of the gods.)

OLYMPIAN GODS AND GODDESSES

GREEK NAME	ROMAN NAME	FUNCTIONS	ATTRIBUTES
Aphrodite			
Apollo			
Ares			
Artemis			
Athena			
Demeter			
Hephaestus			
Hera			
Hermes			
Hestia			
Poseidon			
Zeus			

THREE SIGNIFICANT DEITIES

GREEK NAME	ROMAN NAME	FUNCTIONS	ATTRIBUTES
Dionysus			
Hades			
Persephone			

PART TWO

BRIGHT
MYTHS

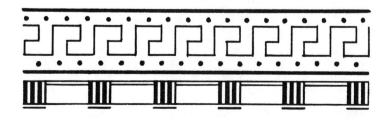

Chapter IV

APOLLO AND FRIENDS

The ancient Greeks delighted in telling stories about the Olympian deities. Like humans, their gods and goddesses were prone to jealousy and lust, to anger and trickery, to boredom and despair. They often walked the earth in search of diversion. Included here are several myths about these deities and the mortals whose lives they affected.

Lacking scientific knowledge, the ancient Greeks also used their vivid imagination to explain natural phenomena. In this section are their ingenious answers to many questions: where does the sun rise and set every day? How did spiders come into being? Why are laurel leaves perpetually green? Called etiological myths because they explain the causes of things, these stories show the light, bright, inventive side of the Greek spirit.

HERMES AND APOLLO

We begin with a lighthearted myth concerning the two most popular Greek gods. Hermes appears more often than any other god in Greek mythology, and one of the principal streets in Athens still bears his name—Ermou, Street of Hermes. The Greeks loved him because he was so carefree and clever. His half-brother, Apollo, epitomized moderation, or the "golden mean," and was in every way the Greek ideal.

The precocious son of Zeus and the fair nymph Maia, Hermes was born in a cave in Arcadia. On the very day of his birth, he left his cradle and wandered outside. At the entrance of the cave, the inquisitive baby found a tortoise, which he picked up and killed. Soon he had created from the tortoise shell the seven-string lyre, and he sang and played happily until he became bored. Next, Hermes set out for adventure. By the hills of Piera he found the sacred cattle of his older brother, Apollo. The crafty infant rounded up fifty cows and led them backward so that their tracks would be confusing. He also invented sandals that resembled snowshoes so that his footprints would be hard to follow. When Hermes reached the Alpheus River, he slaughtered two cows, cutting them into twelve equal parts to sacrifice to the Olympian gods. Hermes rubbed two sticks together—the first ever to start fire in this way—and soon a wonderful aroma filled the air. Just in time, Hermes remembered that, as one of the twelve Olympians, he could not eat any of the sacrificial meat (for because of Prometheus' trick on Zeus, the gods were to get only the savor, never the taste, of sacrificial meat). So he put out the fire with sand and, weary of adventure, returned to his cave and his cradle.

Meanwhile, Apollo had discovered that his cattle were missing, but he could not follow the confusing tracks all the way to the sea. Fortunately, he encountered an old man who told him an amazing story of seeing cows being led backward by a mere baby. Armed with this information, Apollo stormed into Maia's cave, where Hermes pretended to sleep peacefully. Seeing him there, wrapped in his baby blanket, no one would ever have believed him capable of such feats—that is, no one but Apollo. As the angry god accused him at length, the baby yawned. Finally, he protested, "How could I have done such a thing? I was born only yesterday!" Apollo did not believe Hermes for one moment. He shook his fist at his little brother and threatened to hurl him into Tartarus. It seemed there was no other solution for the problem than to go to Zeus for final arbitration. The two brothers traveled to Mt. Olympus, and there, before a solemn assembly of gods, they presented their case to Zeus.

Although Hermes was very convincing in his protestations of innocence, Zeus did not believe him either. He ordered Hermes to take Apollo to the place where he had hidden the stolen cattle. Cheerfully, the baby obeyed. When they arrived at the Alpheus River and Apollo saw that, single-handed, his little brother had slaughtered two cows, his anger turned to admiration, his frowns to laughter. The relieved Hermes brought forth his lyre and played for Apollo. "This music is worth fifty cows!" said Apollo. "The time has come for a truce, little brother." Thus it was that Hermes gave Apollo his invention, the lyre, and Apollo gave Hermes his staff, the caduceus. Apollo also gave Hermes his whip and decreed that Hermes would henceforth be the protector of cattle. They swore to one another a Stygian oath of brotherhood, which was never broken.

DAPHNE AND APOLLO

For such a handsome god, Apollo was surprisingly unlucky in love. This myth is told only by the Roman writer Ovid (43 B.C.–A.D. 17), whose most famous work is Metamorphoses.

Apollo, god of Music and Medicine, was also proud of his skill as an archer. Fresh from his recent victory at Delphi over Python, a monstrous reptile spawned by the flood, Apollo encountered Eros playing with his bow and arrow. Scornfully, Apollo said, "Why do you concern yourself with weapons that are intended for grown-ups? If you want to play at archery, just kindle little flames of love rather than trying to kill wild animals!" The insulted Eros vowed revenge against Apollo. He flew to Mt. Parnassus and drew forth from his quiver two arrows. One was gold with a bright, sharp point—the kind that causes love to be kindled. The other arrow was blunt with lead under its shaft—the kind that causes love to flee. Eros aimed his arrows carefully and then sat back to survey in amusement the damage he had done.

The lead arrow pierced Daphne, a beautiful nymph who was the daughter of the river god Peneus. As soon as she was struck by Eros' blunt arrow, she became indifferent to all men. Sought after by several suitors, she pleaded with her father to let her remain a virgin like the goddess Artemis. The old man, who would have much preferred having grandchildren, reluctantly granted his daughter's request. Meanwhile, Eros' gold arrow had pierced Apollo, and he fell helplessly in love with the first maiden he saw—Daphne. He could think of nothing and no one else, longing only to be with her, imagining what it would be like to embrace her, finally determining to marry her. Catching sight of the elusive Daphne in the forest one day, Apollo approached her gently. Daphne was repelled. Determined to escape Apollo's advances, she ran faster and faster, but she could not outrun the god, for he flew on wings of love while Daphne flew on wings of fear.

Apollo called to her as he ran, "Fair nymph, you do not know who I am, or you would not flee. I am no ordinary shepherd lad, but the great god Apollo. I love you, and I want to marry you. I cannot eat or sleep thinking of you. Though I am the god of Medicine, I cannot cure my own malady!" The terrified girl ran faster, but a nymph could never outrun a god. Finally, in desperation she pleaded with her father, Peneus. "Father, do not let me break my vow of chastity. Change my form, destroy my beauty, but do not let Apollo have me as his wife!" Daphne's prayer was answered immediately. She felt a heavy numbness in her limbs. Her soft body was encircled by bark, her hair changed to leaves, her arms to branches, her feet to rocks, her head to a treetop. Peneus had transformed her into a laurel tree. Apollo embraced the rough bark, exclaiming half in grief and half in joy, "Oh, Daphne, you cannot be my wife, but you will be my tree. I will use you as an adornment for my lyre and my quiver. Your leaves will be everlastingly green, and they will be used in wreaths to crown all victors!" Thus it is that the leaves of the laurel tree remain everlastingly green, and victors to this day wear wreaths of laurel.

CHAPTER IV: STUDY QUESTIONS

1. Who was the mother of Hermes? Where was he born?

2. What were two of Hermes' inventions?

3. What did Hermes do to anger Apollo?

4. How did Zeus get involved in the dispute?

5. Why did Apollo not remain angry?

6. What trade was made?

7. What five adjectives would you use to describe Hermes?

8. What was the ancient Greeks' theory about the cause of love?

9. What caused Eros to be angry at Apollo?

10. Who was Daphne? Who was her father?

11. Why did she flee from Apollo?

12. What is the meaning of *metamorphosis?* (Look it up in the dictionary.)

13. What was the metamorphosis of Daphne?

14. In what way is this myth etiological?

15. What five adjectives would you use to describe Apollo?

Chapter V

IMPOSSIBLE LOVE

ECHO AND NARCISSUS

Like the story of Daphne and Apollo, this myth shows the transformation of a human into a plant. It, too, deals with the subject of love. There the resemblance ends, for the myth of Echo and Narcissus teaches a moral lesson as well.

The great prophet Tiresias predicted to the mother of Narcissus that her son would live a long and happy life "if he never knows himself." As Narcissus matured, he became more and more handsome, admired by both youths and maidens. Yet he was indifferent to all of them, including the nymph Echo, who loved him wholeheartedly. A lively and talkative nymph, Echo used her conversational wiles to help her friends by diverting Hera in her attempts to find Zeus, who often dallied with one or another of the nymphs in the leafy glades. When Hera realized she was being tricked by the guileful Echo, she retaliated with a cruel punishment: Echo lost all power of speech except to repeat what others had said. This curse did not deter Echo from loving Narcissus. One day while she was following the youth admiringly, he called out, "Is anyone here?"

"Here," repeated Echo.

"Come!" he called.

"Come!" she replied.

"Here, let us meet!" shouted the impatient Narcissus.

"Let us meet," the nymph replied.

With that, she came out of the glade smiling, with outstretched arms. But the cold boy said scornfully, "Take your hands away. Do not try to embrace me. May I die before you hold me in your power!" Echo was so stunned and hurt that she ran away. From that time on she lived in deserted caves, and no one ever saw her again. Heartbroken, she stopped eating and drinking; her body wasted away until finally her bones turned to stone, and only her voice was left. It is said that she still haunts empty caves and answers all who call to her.

Undaunted by the result of his cruelty, Narcissus continued in his heartless ways until one day another one he had hurt prayed to Nemesis, "If he ever does love, may he not be able to enjoy that love!" The next day, when Narcissus returned from hunting and bent down to a silvery stream to quench his thirst, he saw his handsome image reflected in the water. Then he who had been aloof and uncaring fell in love completely—with himself. Some say Narcissus thought his reflection was another youth; some, that he knew it was his own reflection. At any rate, he was held spellbound with desire, feasting upon his image with his eyes and forgetting about food and drink and all human companionship. Gradually, like Echo before him, Narcissus

41

wasted away and was gradually consumed by the fire of love buried within him.

Echo was filled with pain, for she still loved Narcissus. It was she who heard his last words: "Alas, beloved boy, loved in vain."

"Loved in vain," echoed the heartbroken nymph.

When Narcissus was ferried to the land of the dead, he continued to stare at his image in the black waters of the River Styx. And when his former companions looked for his body, in its place they found a delicate yellow flower, circled with white petals, bending gracefully toward the stream.

PYGMALION

Like Narcissus, Pygmalion scorned the love of ordinary mortals and fell in love with a seemingly impossible object. The outcome for Pygmalion was quite different, however. Two famous modern works are based upon this myth: the play Pygmalion *by George Bernard Shaw and the musical comedy* My Fair Lady *by Lerner and Lowe.*

Pygmalion was a handsome young sculptor who lived on the island of Cyprus. He scorned the company of women and remained a bachelor, enjoying his solitude and concentrating on his art. He was attempting to sculpt one perfect ivory statue of a beautiful woman. So perfect, indeed, was the statue that it was almost impossible to tell that it was not a real woman. Pygmalion had achieved the ultimate aesthetic goal: art that conceals art. Pygmalion delighted in his beautiful statue, draping it in rich robes, festooning it with jewels, and bringing it small gifts of flowers and seashells. Soon his delight turned to misery, however, for he realized he had fallen in love with the statue, and his love could not be returned.

The island of Cyprus was sacred to Aphrodite, who was born from the seafoam there. When the time came for the annual festival in her honor, Pygmalion prayed at the shrine of the goddess of Love. "Aphrodite, please give me for my wife . . ." He could not bring himself to say, ". . . my ivory statue," so he said instead, ". . . one like my ivory statue." The altar flame leaped up three times, a sign of Aphrodite's favor.

When Pygmalion returned to his studio, he embraced the statue desperately. Much to his amazement, the cold ivory became warm to his touch, the unyielding lips parted, and the ivory statue turned into a live young woman. Aphrodite had answered his prayer! Pygmalion married his transformed statue, later named Galatea, and they had a son, Paphos, who gave his name to Aphrodite's favorite city.

CHAPTER V: STUDY QUESTIONS

1. What was the prophecy regarding Narcissus?

2. Who punished Echo? How? Why?

3. What finally happened to Narcissus?

4. How did the prophecy come true?

5. What is narcissism?

6. What is a narcissus complex?

7. What deity helped Pygmalion?

8. In what way is this appropriate?

9. How was this deity connected with Cyprus?

10. What was the name of the statue?

11. Who *and* what was Paphos?

12. Pygmalion and Narcissus are quite different, but in what ways are they alike?

Chapter VI

ETERNAL LOVE

PYRAMUS AND THISBE

This myth about young lovers was the inspiration for Romeo and Juliet. *Shakespeare also wrote an amusing burlesque of Pyramus and Thisbe for his play,* A Midsummer Night's Dream. The Fantasticks *and* West Side Story *were also inspired by this myth.*

Pyramus was the handsomest youth and Thisbe the fairest maiden in all of Babylon. Next-door neighbors all their lives, they loved one another, but their feuding parents would not allow them to see one another. Opposition only fanned the flames of their love, and they were determined to be together, come what may.

The two houses shared a common wall, and in that wall was a crack which no one ever noticed because it had been there so long. One day Pyramus and Thisbe discovered the crack, and they whispered words of endearment to one another, breathing into the crack in the wall all their hopes and dreams. As time passed, the lovers became less and less content with their limited contact. In desperation, they decided to defy their parents and run away together. They arranged to meet at nightfall of the following day by a local landmark, the Tomb of Ninus.

Thisbe, veiled and trembling with anticipation, was the first to arrive. She waited under a mulberry tree whose gleaming white berries shone near a clear spring. Suddenly a lioness, whose jaws were still bloody from a recent kill, came into view. Thisbe quickly darted into a nearby cave, but in her haste she dropped her veil. The lioness drank deeply from the stream. Then, spying the veil, she tore at it with her bloody mouth, dropping it when she left at the sound of approaching footsteps. The footsteps were those of Pyramus, who had been delayed and had run all the way to the trysting place. Seeing Thisbe's torn and bloody veil but no sign of the girl herself, he immediately assumed the worst: Thisbe had been devoured by a lion! It was all his fault; he did not deserve to live, nor did he want to live without Thisbe. Pyramus drew his sword and stabbed himself. A moment later, Thisbe emerged from the cave, thinking that the lioness had surely departed. To her horror, she discovered Pyramus lying on the ground under the mulberry tree. As she kissed his cold lips and murmured, "It is I, your Thisbe," the youth opened his eyes briefly, then fell back, dead. The distraught girl grasped her lover's sword in both hands, exclaiming, "Pyramus, I have been the cause of your death, so I shall follow you to Hades. Oh, my parents, you have kept us apart in life. May you not do so in death!" So saying, Thisbe stabbed herself, and the blood of the two lovers, mingling, stained the roots of the mulberry tree. Its ripened berries have been deep red ever since.

The grief-stricken parents regretted that they had tried to keep the lovers apart, and they allowed them to be buried in the same tomb. Thus, Pyramus and Thisbe were united in death.

PHILEMON AND BAUCIS

The ancient Greeks placed great value on hospitality; the bond between host and guest was considered sacred. This myth also portrays a different kind of love—the devotion of a married couple. Although the Greeks delighted in retelling stories of infidelity among the Olympians, they prized the ideal of fidelity.

As the god of Hospitality, Zeus liked to walk about the Earth in disguise and test its inhabitants for virtuous actions. On one such excursion—to Phrygia—he was accompanied by his son Hermes. Disguised as travelers in need of rest and refreshment, the two gods knocked on a thousand doors and were refused hospitality by a thousand cold and unfriendly people. Finally, they arrived at the door of a small thatched cottage, the home of an old married couple named Philemon and Baucis. The couple welcomed the two strangers warmly, inviting them to sit by the fire and stay to enjoy a simple supper. Baucis prepared the best food she had in the house—cabbage, bacon, olives, and fruit—while Philemon filled the wine bowl. Chatting amiably, the four sat down to enjoy the simple meal, and they all ate heartily until Philemon and Baucis noticed that no matter how often they dipped into the wine bowl, it remained miraculously full. Concluding that their guests were gods in disguise, the poor couple fell to their knees, begging the gods to have mercy on them.

"Do not fear, good people," said Zeus. "We are indeed gods, but you have treated us kindly, giving us the best that you have. Your wicked neighbors will suffer, but you will be rewarded. Come quickly with us to high ground." The bewildered couple left the house immediately with the gods, and the four climbed a nearby hill. To their amazement, Philemon and Baucis saw a large lake form, covering all the houses in Phrygia. By the side of the lake there suddenly appeared a large golden temple. Zeus broke the stunned silence. "You may have whatever you wish, good people," he said. Baucis and Philemon talked quietly for a moment; then Philemon said, "My wife and I have decided. Please let us be priests of the temple, let us die together, and may we never see one another's tomb!" Their request was honored, and the couple happily ministered as priests of the temple for many years. When they were very old, they stood one day before the temple and recalled their happy life together. Suddenly they noticed that they were both starting to sprout leaves! As they became transformed into trees, they clasped hands and called, "Farewell, dear mate." It is said that in Phrygia there are an oak and a linden tree, both growing from a double trunk. The linden tree is Baucis; the oak, Philemon, united with one another for eternity.

CHAPTER VI: STUDY QUESTIONS

1. What three plays were inspired by this myth?

2. Where did Pyramus and Thisbe live?

3. How did they manage to communicate with one another?

4. Where did they arrange to meet?

5. What caused Pyramus to think that Thisbe had perished?

6. What did he do as a result?

7. What was Thisbe's response?

8. What happened to the mulberry tree?

9. In what way does this myth have a happy ending?

10. Who were the guests of Philemon and Baucis?

11. In what way did the couple behave differently from the rest of the villagers?

12. What caused Philemon and Baucis to suspect they had divine guests?

13. What specific requests did Baucis and Philemon make?

14. How were their three requests honored?

Chapter VII

ZEUS IN LOVE

IO

This etiological myth shows three Olympians acting true to form—lustful Zeus, vengeful Hera, and guileful Hermes.

Like Daphne, Io was the beautiful daughter of a river god. Her father was Inachus, who had good reason to worry about his attractive daughter. As soon as Zeus spied Io, he could not wait to have her. Fearing the jealousy of his wife, he covered Io and himself with a thick black cloud. Hera was not fooled so easily by this ruse, and she went to Earth to investigate the mysterious cloud that had appeared so suddenly on a cloudless day. Zeus, who seemed to have a sixth sense about his wife, quickly turned Io into a cow and tried to look innocent when Hera approached. Not fooled for a moment, Hera asked for the lovely white cow as a present, and Zeus, who was powerful with all others but powerless against his wife, reluctantly gave Io to Hera. Argus, a giant with one hundred eyes, was appointed by Hera to stand guard over the new cow. He never slept, for at least two of his eyes were open at all times. Poor Io— she had no arms to raise to heaven in supplication, and she was even afraid of her own voice, which had become a pitiful moo.

In desperation, Zeus turned to his clever son Hermes for help in freeing Io. Hermes, who loved diversion, gladly agreed to trick Argus. Disguising himself as a shepherd, he charmed the giant into inviting him to sit down and play diverting music on the shepherd's pipes. Hermes played sweetly for hours, trying to lull Argus to sleep. Then he told a long and boring story. Finally, all Argus' eyes were closed in sleep. Quickly, Hermes drew his sword and cut off Argus' head. Io bounded away, and Hermes congratulated himself on his success. Hera was not so easily defeated, however. First, she took Argus' one hundred eyes and put them in her peacock's feathers, where they shine to this day. Next, she sent a stinging gadfly in pursuit of Io, still in the shape of a cow. Driven half-mad by the constant stinging, Io wandered all over the earth. She crossed the strait between Europe and Asia, which ever after has been called the Bosphorus, or "cow-crossing." She crossed a sea which has ever after been called the Ionian Sea. She even traveled to the Caucasus, where she vainly asked the aid of the chained Prometheus. Finally, she came to Egypt, where she fell down, exhausted and hopeless. Zeus had not forgotten Io, however, and he decided there was only one way to help her. He confessed all to Hera, begging her forgiveness and taking a Stygian oath that he would never see Io again if only Hera would show mercy. Hera relented. Io was transformed once more into a beautiful maiden. The only difference was that her skin was whiter than ever before.

EUROPA

Like Io, Europa gained geographical fame because Zeus fell in love with her. In this myth, however, it is Zeus, rather than the object of his affections, who is transformed into another shape.

Europa was the beautiful young princess of Sidon. After an unsettling dream—that two continents were fighting to possess her—she gathered her maidens together and suggested a picnic by the seashore. Meanwhile, looking down from Mt. Olympus, Zeus spied the pretty girls frolicking on the beach, and he was immediately smitten with Europa's charms. For this romantic exploit, Zeus disguised himself as a handsome white bull, who suddenly appeared before the carefree maidens. Unlike other bulls, this one was gentle and even sweet-smelling, allowing the girls to pet it and make flower garlands for its head. It even licked Europa's hand. "See," she said to her companions, "how tame this bull is, how gentle and loving! Let us mount his broad back and ride him for fun!"

And so she took her seat upon his back and motioned to her companions to join her. But as they ran, the bull leaped toward the sea and plunged in, lightly treading on top of the waves. The terrified Europa grasped the bull's horn with one hand, while with the other she held her skirts above the water, all the while looking longingly back to the land and her startled friends. "Do not fear, gentle maiden," said Zeus. I am no ordinary bull, but the King of all gods. I am taking you to my birthplace, Crete, where you shall become the mother of famous sons." Thus it was that Europa became the first mortal to set foot on the continent that now bears her name. She did become the mother of two famous sons, Minos and Rhadamanthus, both of whom later became judges in the Underworld. During his lifetime, Minos was the king of Crete.

CHAPTER VII: STUDY QUESTIONS

1. Why was Hera not fooled by Zeus when he dallied with Io?

2. How did Hera outsmart Zeus?

3. Who was Argus? What was unusual about him?

4. Whom did Zeus send to help Io?

5. How did this deity help?

6. What happened to Argus?

7. What strait is named for Io? Can you think of a place in England that has the same meaning?

8. What sea is named for Io?

9. What caused Hera to relent?

10. What was the change in Io at the very end?

11. Why did Europa go on a picnic?

12. How did Zeus trick Europa?

13. Where did he take her and why?

14. Who were Europa's two famous sons?

15. What land bears her name and why?

Chapter VIII

QUINTESSENTIAL LOVE

CUPID AND PSYCHE

The love story of Cupid and Psyche is one of the most universally appealing of all myths, dramatically combining extremes of love and hate, greed and unselfishness, seemingly insurmountable obstacles and the happy message that love conquers all.

Roman names are used here because the myth was written by the Roman Apuleius, adapted from a tale that first appeared in Greek mythology. Psyche means both "soul" and "butterfly" in Greek.

There once was a king and queen who had three daughters. All were beautiful, but the youngest, Psyche, so far surpassed in beauty everyone else in the kingdom that her fame spread, and people came from far and wide to pay homage to her. In their adoration of the lovely young maiden, they forgot to honor Venus, whose shrines became dusty and deserted.

The goddess of Love and Beauty was furious at Psyche, even though the girl had not sought to be so idolized. "What an upstart!" raged the goddess. "How dare she think that her beauty even approaches mine? I will give her cause to repent this hubris." Venus summoned her son, Cupid, to help her avenge herself against the innocent mortal. "I want you to use your magic arrows to make Psyche fall in love with the ugliest, most unworthy man in the world. That will teach her and all mortals not to shame me!" Obediently, the handsome, winged god of love flew to Psyche's room, where she lay asleep. As he gazed at Psyche, wondering how he could possibly obey his mother's cruel request and bring harm to such innocent beauty, Psyche stirred and murmured in her sleep. In his confusion, Cupid started, and the god of Love was pricked by one of his own arrows.

As time passed, Psyche's beauty brought her no happiness. While her sisters were courted by handsome suitors and eventually married to wealthy princes, no one sought Psyche's hand in marriage. The beautiful maiden was adored, not loved. At last, her parents, troubled at their daughter's misery and suspecting that they had incurred the anger of the gods, consulted the Oracle of Apollo. The oracle's response was terrifying:

"Psyche is destined to be the bride of no mortal lover, but of a monster whom neither gods nor men can resist. He awaits her even now at the top of the mountain."

The grief-stricken parents returned to their home in stunned silence. Following the oracle's advice, they prepared their daughter for marriage and assembled a bridal party to climb to the top of the mountain. The sombre group looked more like a funeral cortege than a wedding procession. As they walked, Psyche comforted her parents, saying, "What Fate has decreed must be, my dear parents. Do not grieve for me, but remember your daughter with love. My beauty has not brought me earthly happiness. I go with little regret, but I cannot bear your tears." At the top of the mountain, Psyche bade her parents farewell and was left alone. Trembling and pale in her wedding dress, she was more beautiful than ever before. As she stood there awaiting her horrible fate, she was suddenly lifted into the air by Zephyrus, the west wind, who gently carried her to a peaceful valley. In a meadow filled with wild flowers, the exhausted girl fell into a deep sleep.

Psyche awakened to the sound of birds and a trickling fountain. She rubbed her eyes in wonder. There, just beyond the meadow, was a magnificent golden palace, gleaming in the sunlight, surrounded by fountains and roses. As she gazed in disbelief, a voice said, "Do not be afraid, dear mistress. We are your invisible servants, here to obey your every command. Come inside the palace, please. Your husband will be here at nightfall." Scarcely believing her eyes or her ears, Psyche stepped inside the palace, which was lavishly furnished and sparkling with gold, silver, and precious jewels. After she walked throughout its many rooms, she bathed and donned a beautiful robe to replace her grass-stained dress. She ate and drank her fill, then lay down to await her fate.

At nightfall, Psyche heard a deep, melodious voice in the darkened room. "Psyche, I am your bridegroom. I will love you and give you everything you desire— on one condition. You must never try to gaze upon me. Do not ask my name, for I cannot tell you who I am." As her husband embraced her, Psyche felt passion she had only dreamed of. She gladly consented to the strange terms of her marriage. When dawn came, her husband had vanished, and she could only wait for darkness to come again, bringing with it her mysterious bridegroom.

After awhile, Psyche began to miss her sisters, and she begged her husband to let them come for a visit. "Oh, Psyche, are you not happy here with me alone? I fear that the outside world will bring us great trouble," he replied. Yet Psyche persisted in her entreaties, and finally her husband relented. One day as her two sisters stood on the top of the mountain, sadly recalling their last glimpse of their little sister, Zephyrus gently carried them to the valley, and they heard Psyche's familiar laugh.

"Dear sisters, it is indeed your little Psyche! Instead of a terrible doom, I have found perfect happiness with a wonderful husband. Instead of misery, I have found good fortune. Come, see!" As she escorted her sisters through the palace, proudly showing them all her beautiful possessions, Psyche was too happy to notice that they were strangely silent. Never having felt envy herself, she did not recognize it in others. When they pressed her for a description of her husband, Psyche finally confessed that she had never seen him—that he came to her only in the night. "Psyche, sister, have you forgotten the prophecy of Apollo's oracle? You are married to a monster! You must kill him before he devours you!" In vain did Psyche insist that her husband was no monster, but a loving bridegroom who had brought her nothing but happiness. Yet her sisters were older, and Psyche's innocence was no match for their evil envy. On their next visit, they persuaded her to accept a lamp and a knife from them, so that she could gaze upon her husband as he slept and cut off his head if he was indeed a monster.

Psyche was torn, remembering her promise to her husband, yet burning with curiosity to see him. Finally she agreed to her sisters' plan with deep misgivings. That night, as her husband lay sleeping, she lit the oil lamp with trembling hands and shone it on the sleeping form of her husband. There lay the god of Love himself—handsome beyond description, his wings dewy-white with gleaming down, moving slightly in the faint breeze. At the foot of the bed lay Cupid's bow and quiver of arrows. The curious

Psyche picked up an arrow, and as she pressed its point to her finger she pricked herself and so fell in love with Love. As she gazed adoringly at Cupid, a drop of oil fell from the lamp and burned the shoulder of the god of Love. He awakened instantly and flew to the window. "Psyche, you have betrayed me!" he said. "You have broken the one promise I extracted from you, and in so doing, you have destroyed our happiness. Love cannot live with suspicion." In vain did Psyche entreat Cupid to forgive her. It was too late. "Go to those two excellent counselors, your sisters, who have given you such wise advice. Ask their help for your future happiness. I will inflict no other punishment on you than to leave you forever!" So saying, the god of Love flew out the window, leaving Psyche to tears and bitter regret.

In the weeks to come, Psyche searched the kingdom in vain for the husband she had wronged. Meanwhile, her two sisters savored their bitter triumph and planned another visit to the palace. At the top of the mountain they waited for Zephyrus to carry them gently to the valley. When the wind came, they gave themselves eagerly, but this time Zephyrus did not carry them to the pleasant valley. Instead, they were dashed to pieces on the rocks below. In her fruitless search for Cupid, Psyche came at last to the temple of Ceres, where she busied herself sweeping and cleaning the deserted shrine. The goddess of Grain was so grateful that she took pity on the miserable girl. "You will never find Cupid," she said, "because he is locked in a room at his mother's palace, recuperating from his terrible burn." The girl groaned to think she had inflicted such pain on her beloved. "Your only hope is to gain Venus' forgiveness by throwing yourself on her mercy and offering to do anything she asks. Only through further suffering do you have the faintest hope of being reunited with your husband."

Psyche ran immediately to the palace of Venus, where she was greeted with scornful words. "So this is the mortal girl who thought she was more beautiful than the goddess of Beauty, the wretch who caused my poor son to fall in love with her and then despised that love. Go from my sight before I lose my temper and destroy you utterly!" But Psyche fell down in tears and promised to do anything the goddess asked. Venus' heart stirred with thoughts of revenge. She led Psyche to a storeroom where many grains—wheat, barley, beans, lentils, and the like—were mixed on the floor in complete disorder. "Here is fit work for you, my girl. Separate these grains by nightfall into separate piles."

After Venus left, Psyche stared at the confusing disarray. She had no idea how to begin. As she wept, feeling abandoned by both gods and men, she longed now for death. But the lowliest of creatures took pity on the beautiful maiden. An army of ants marched into the storeroom and began quietly and methodically to separate the seeds. By nightfall, the task was completed. Venus was furious. "I know you have had help with this task," said she, "and now I will give you another task that you must perform yourself. Go to the pasture of the golden rams and bring me back golden fleece from each one."

The next morning, Psyche journeyed to the place of the golden rams, and as she saw them across the river and wondered how to accomplish her task, the reeds murmured to her. "Do not try to take the fleece from the rams in the heat of the day, for they will attack any mortal who dares to enter their pasture. Rather, wait until they are full of food and calm in the cool of evening. Then you may safely cross the river and gather the golden fleece from the brambles along the riverbank." Psyche obeyed the reeds and was successful in her task. Again, Venus was furious. She pointed a long arm. "Do you see yon black waterfall? It is the source of the most hateful river of all, the River Styx. You are to go to that waterfall and fill this vial with its black water."

When Psyche saw the waterfall, she realized the extent of Venus' hatred. The sides were so steep and slimy that she would need wings to reach it. Hesitating there, she suddenly felt the vial snatched from her hand. Then she saw an eagle fly to the churning waterfall and return in an instant with the little container full of the Stygian water. Venus was not yet through with Psyche. "Proud girl, now you will have a task that will make all the others seem simple. Take this box to the Underworld and ask Queen Proserpina to fill it with some of her beauty to replace that which I have lost in caring for my son Cupid."

Psyche's heart filled with dread, for no mortal dared to venture to the Underworld and return unscathed. Carrying the box, she climbed to the top of a high tower and prepared to jump so that she could quickly enter the Underworld. The tower admonished her. "Foolish Psyche, do not jump. That is no way to enter the Underworld—not if you want to return to Earth!" The tower gave her clear instructions, including how to calm the three-headed dog, Cerberus, and the old ferryman, Charon. The tower also warned her to eat and drink nothing while she was in the Underworld, so that she could return to Earth. Above all, once back on Earth, she must under no condition open the box. Following instructions carefully, Psyche traveled to the Underworld and asked Queen Proserpina to fill the box with some of her beauty. The queen graciously complied, and soon Psyche found her way back to Earth. It was then, traveling along the road to Venus' palace, that Psyche was once more consumed by curiosity. Surely she could try just a little of the magic potion for herself; if she were more beautiful, Cupid might love her once more. She opened the box—and out came an overwhelming fragrance that caused Psyche to fall unconscious on the road.

Meanwhile, Cupid had escaped from the locked room in his mother's palace, for Love cannot be imprisoned for long. As he came upon the unconscious form of Psyche, he awakened her with the light touch of one of his arrows. "My foolish Psyche," he said. "Have you not learned your lesson? Yet, foolish or not, I do love you, and I cannot find happiness without you."

Cupid entreated Jupiter himself to grant immortality to Psyche, and even Venus begrudgingly agreed, knowing when to acknowledge defeat. The nuptials of Cupid and Psyche were joyously celebrated by all the gods, and in due time a daughter named Pleasure was born to the happy couple.

CHAPTER VIII: STUDY QUESTIONS

1. What two meanings does *psyche* have in Greek? What do these meanings imply about the heroine?

2. Why are Roman names used in telling this myth?

3. What caused Venus to become angry? Whose help did she enlist? Why?

4. What was the prophecy of the Oracle of Apollo?

5. What was Psyche's state of mind as she walked to the mountain? Why?

6. What was the promise Psyche had to make to her husband?

7. Who or what caused her to break the promise?

8. What punishment did Cupid give to Psyche?

9. What punishment befell Psyche's sisters?

10. What goddess helped Psyche? Why?

11. What tasks did Venus ask Psyche to perform? How was she aided in these tasks?

12. What trait of Psyche's caused her to make two serious mistakes? What were these mistakes?

13. What other traits (both good and bad) did Psyche possess?

14. What is the name of the daughter born to Cupid and Psyche?

15. Why is this chapter entitled "Quintessential Love"?

Chapter IX

HUBRIS

ARACHNE

Perhaps more vividly than any other myth, this story of proud Arachne underscores the dangers of hubris. It also shows another, fiercer side of Pallas Athena.

Arachne was a girl of humble birth who lived in Lydia. What distinguished her—even made her famous throughout the area—was her skill in weaving. People came from far and wide to marvel at her technique and admire her tapestries. All this attention made Arachne so conceited that she boasted she was better than the goddess of Weaving herself, Pallas Athena. This news reached Athena, who was highly displeased. She set out to see for herself the mortal girl who thought herself superior to the gods. Disguised as an old woman, Athena came to Lydia and found Arachne at her loom. "Don't you realize, foolish girl, that you are creating danger for yourself by such vain boasting? You should seek Athena's pardon before it is too late!" The girl replied scornfully, "Old woman, keep your thoughts to yourself. Perhaps your eyes are too dim to see that I am indeed the best weaver in the entire world. Athena should come to see for herself—if she dares!" Throwing off her disguise, Athena exclaimed, "She *has* come—and she dares to challenge you to a weaving contest!"

Arachne blushed crimson, then turned deathly pale. Yet she rushed headlong toward her fate. Two looms were set up for the contest, and the two weavers began creating amazing tapestries. Athena portrayed the gods and goddesses in flattering scenes, while Arachne depicted them committing brutal crimes of greed and lust. When they had finished, the spectators gasped because the results were so breathtakingly beautiful. Furious at the evil scenes that the proud girl had portrayed, Athena seized Arachne's tapestry and tore it to shreds. The astonished girl, ashamed at last, hanged herself. Then Athena turned Arachne into a spider so that she and all her descendants could weave eternally. Arachne still dangles from the gossamer thread, as though trying to hang herself.

ATALANTA

The ancient Greeks believed the two most important aspects of education to be music and gymnastics. Thus, they valued athletic competition very highly. From the first Olympic Games in 776 B.C., dedicated to Zeus, winners were heaped with honors. The events were so significant to the Greeks that they suspended all fighting during

these games, which occurred in July every four years. Even the fastest
of runners, however, was not exempt from retribution if the gods were
neglected. Handel's opera Atalanta *is based on this myth.*

Atalanta, who combined beauty and athletic ability to a high degree, had many suitors, but she was afraid to marry. As a young girl, she had consulted Apollo's oracle at Delphi, and when she asked about her future, the oracle replied, "Marriage will cause your ruin. You will strive against your fate, and although you continue to live, you will be deprived of yourself." The frightened girl determined never to marry, and in order to discourage her many suitors, she announced that any young man who lost to her in a footrace would be executed immediately. If he won, Atalanta herself would be the prize. Far from discouraging her suitors, this challenge merely spurred them on. Many young men raced against Atalanta, and all of them lost both the race and their lives.

One day a handsome young man named Hippomenes saw Atalanta. He had come to scoff, but as he watched her race, he was overcome with desire, and he determined he must marry her. He prayed to the goddess of love, Aphrodite herself, to help him. Aphrodite heeded Hippomenes' plea. She hurried to her island of Cyprus, where there grew a tree that bore apples of pure gold. Scooping up three apples, she hurried back to Hippomenes, who was about to start his fateful race. "Here," said the goddess, pressing them into his hand, "use these in the race. Your love will find a way." Meanwhile, Atalanta gazed at Hippomenes, and for the first time her heart softened. How young he was. How handsome. What a pity that he must die in his prime. If only. . . .

The race began, and though at first they appeared to be closely matched, Atalanta gradually drew ahead. Then Hippomenes drew forth the first of his golden apples, and he rolled it next to the course so that it glinted and caught Atalanta's eye. Stopping to retrieve it, she lost ground, and for awhile Hippomenes was ahead. Then Atalanta caught up and passed him. He threw out the second golden apple, and Atalanta again stopped to pick it up and lost ground. They were nearing the end of the course, and Atalanta was leading again when Hippomenes threw out his last golden apple. Again Atalanta stopped to retrieve the apple, and this time she was unable to make up the lost ground. Hippomenes had won the race and, much to her surprise, Atalanta was glad.

The two were married, but in their great happiness, they forgot to thank Aphrodite by burning incense to her. The goddess was infuriated. One night, the two lovers, overcome by desire, went into the shrine of Cybele, and there they broke the rule of chastity, one of the primary rules of the sacred shrine. To their horror, Atalanta and Hippomenes began to grow tawny manes and fur; their voices turned to roars, and soon they were completely transformed into lions. After that, they were tamed by Cybele and forced to pull her chariot through the skies. Aphrodite had accomplished her revenge, and the oracle's prophecy had at last come true.

CHAPTER IX: STUDY QUESTIONS

1. What is the Greek word for Arachne's fault?

2. What deity did she anger? How?

3. More than her skill or even her boasting, what did Arachne do to cause her severe punishment?

4. What happened to Arachne and her descendants?

5. What are the meanings of *arachnoid* and *arachnid?* How are they connected to this myth?

6. What areas of study were deemed most important by the ancient Greeks?

7. What was prophesied to Atalanta? How did she attempt to avoid her fate?

8. With whom did Atalanta fall in love? What deity helped this young man? How?

9. What angered this deity?

10. How did the prophecy come true?

Chapter X

EXTRAVAGANT WISHES

MIDAS

The two stories concerning Midas are gently humorous. Midas was not arrogant, merely foolish, and his punishment was fittingly mild.

Many centuries later in Tanglewood Tales, *Nathaniel Hawthorne embellished the first Midas myth by adding a daughter who turned to gold. A charming invention, this daughter is not in the original myth.*

Midas, King of Phrygia, was very hospitable. When Silenus, the foolish old companion of Dionysus, drank too much wine and became separated from the god of Wine, he fortunately wandered into Midas' rose garden and fell asleep. Discovered by Midas' servants, who festooned Silenus with wreaths and flowers, the confused old man was brought to King Midas, who immediately recognized him as Dionysus' companion, Silenus. King Midas wined and dined his guest lavishly for ten days; then he brought him to Dionysus, who was so delighted to see his old friend that he offered Midas any gift of his own choosing. Midas, who was more greedy than wise, immediately said, "Let whatever I touch turn to gold!" Dionysus realized that this was a foolish wish, but he honored his promise and granted Midas the golden touch.

When Midas returned to his palace, he could hardly wait to try his new gift. He was overjoyed to find that the first thing he touched—a leafy branch—immediately turned into a golden bough. Trees, ears of corn, the pillars of his house, his furniture— all turned to gleaming gold! Midas' happiness was short-lived, however. Sitting down to his lunch, he found that no matter how quickly he ate, his food and wine turned to gold as they entered his mouth. Wealthy as he was, he was doomed to starve to death! Now he hated the gift he had recently prayed for. He raised his arms to Dionysus and pleaded, "Great god, free me from this golden curse!" Dionysus was merciful. He told Midas to go to the Pactolus River and to bathe his body completely in its waters. The king did so at once, and as he washed himself in the river, the golden touch passed from his body into the water. To this day, the banks of the Pactolus River are hard with golden sand.

After this incident, Midas despised riches, and he spent most of his time away from the palace and in the forest. Unfortunately, his experience with the golden touch had not brought him wisdom. One day the Forest God Pan, who played the pipes well enough, was so carried away by the flattery of the wood nymphs that he challenged Apollo, the god of Music, to a contest to determine who was the better musician. Midas was asked to be one of the judges. Forgetting one of the first rules he should have remembered—in a contest, always side with the more powerful god—Midas honestly but foolishly preferred Pan's pipes to Apollo's lyre and gave his vote to Pan. The god of Music was righteously indignant. "You have the ears of a jackass," said Apollo. "Very well, then, you shall keep them!"

With that, he turned Midas' ears into big, floppy, hairy asses' ears. King Midas was so ashamed that he hurried home and covered his head with a large red turban. He allowed his hair to grow very long, and the only one who knew his terrible secret was the servant who trimmed his hair. Obsessed with his desire to tell the king's secret but knowing that the penalty would be death, the barber walked out into the country, far from the palace. There he dug a hole, bent down, and whispered Midas' secret. Then he returned to the palace, feeling greatly relieved. In the springtime, reeds grew out of that hole, and they spread the secret to the other reeds. Even today, if you listen very carefully when the south wind blows, you can hear the reeds whisper, "King Midas has asses' ears!"

BELLEROPHON AND PEGASUS

In this myth a mortal is again granted a wish by a god. The wish itself is not foolish, but the final outcome underscores the danger of hubris. Though humans may be favored by the gods and given the means to accomplish heroic deeds, they are not automatically entitled to godlike status.

The offspring of Poseidon and the blood of Medusa, Pegasus was a winged horse who roamed wild and free, owned by no one. Bellerophon was a handsome mortal who yearned to ride Pegasus. In Athena's temple, Bellerophon prayed that he might own the wonderful horse, and when he awoke from his night's sleep, he found a golden bridle in his hand. He quickly went in search of Pegasus, who accepted the bridle readily and was quickly tamed by Bellerophon. Together, the two experienced many adventures. Their most famous exploit was the slaying of the Chimaera, a monster with the head of a lion, the body of a goat, and the tail of a dragon. Attacking the Chimaera from the air on his winged horse, Bellerophon was able to shoot his arrows from many directions, and he quickly killed the monster.

All his victories and the praise that followed them gave Bellerophon so much confidence that he decided to fly to Mt. Olympus itself on the back of his glorious steed. As they soared higher and higher, the horse realized the folly of their undertaking, and he threw his rider, who plummeted to Earth. The fates of Pegasus and Bellerophon were very different: the horse was welcomed to Mt. Olympus and given a permanent stable there. It was he who was allowed to fetch the thunderbolts when Zeus required them, and he was the particular favorite of the Nine Muses. By contrast, Bellerophon was crippled by his fall from the sky. Wretched and friendless, he wandered the earth until at last the great adventurer died alone, mourned by no one.

CHAPTER X: STUDY QUESTIONS

1. What caused Midas to be given the golden touch?

2. Who was the donor of the golden touch?

3. What was wrong with the gift?

4. How did Midas get his life back to normal?

5. What was the effect on the Pactolus River?

6. What nineteenth-century writer changed the Midas myth? How?

7. What deity did Midas anger? How?

8. What was his punishment?

9. Who was the only one who knew Midas' secret?

10. What did he do with the secret?

11. What was the result?

12. What deity helped Bellerophon get his wish of owning Pegasus?

13. What was the Chimaera?

14. How was Bellerophon hubristic? What was the result of his hubris?

15. What finally happened to Pegasus?

16. What large company uses Pegasus as its symbol?

Chapter XI

FLYING AND FALLING

ICARUS

This myth explores the traditional differences between youth and age, but in contrast to earlier myths it also shows the deep affection of a father for his son. More than anything else, it demonstrates the Greek belief in the golden mean.

The great inventor and architect, Daedalus, fell into disfavor with King Minos of Crete, who imprisoned Daedalus and his son Icarus in the labyrinth Daedalus had designed for the minotaur, a monster that was half-man, half-bull (see p. 122). The two easily escaped from the labyrinth, but they were faced with the seemingly impossible task of avoiding King Minos' army and navy. Never one to give up easily, the inventive Daedalus decided to turn to the sky for escape. Using feathers and wax, he devised two pairs of wings so that he and his son could fly away from Crete like giant birds.

When the wings were finally attached and father and son were ready to leave, Daedalus warned Icarus, "Do not fly too high, my son, or the sun will melt the wax. Do not fly too low, or the waves will soak your feathers and make them too heavy. Remember to steer a middle course. Follow me, and you will be safe." As he kissed his son, the tears came to his eyes, for he felt a chill of fear.

When they first started, Icarus timidly obeyed his father, but as he flew, he felt more and more powerful and exultant. Overcome with the joy of flying, he soared higher and higher, as if to reach heaven, until finally he came too close to the sun's rays. Then his wings melted, and with a terrified cry he fell into the sea below. Meanwhile, Daedalus glanced anxiously behind to see whether his son was still following him. He called, "Icarus, where are you?" There was no answer. Looking down in horror, Daedalus saw feathers floating on the water. He abandoned his flight and recovered his son's drowned body for burial, lamenting the clever gifts that had brought him such sorrow. Ever after, that body of water where Icarus drowned has been called the Icarian Sea.

PHAETHON

Besides providing etiological explanations, the myth of Phaethon combines many motifs that intrigued the ancient Greeks—hubris, the golden mean, relationships between father and son, the foolish promise that cannot be broken, and the primitive fear of falling (seen also in the Icarus and Bellerophon stories). Many readers find the story of Phaethon one of the most poignant and appealing in all of Greek mythology.

The son of Helios and the nymph Clymene, Phaethon was raised by his mother as a mortal, far from the magnificent palace of the Sun God. His classmates did not believe Phaethon's boast that the mighty Helios was his father, and he himself began to doubt what his mother had told him. "I have not lied to you, Phaethon, but if you have any doubt about your parentage, travel to Helios' palace and ask him yourself," said Clymene. Thus it was that Phaethon set off on a fateful journey to the palace of Helios.

The sun god's palace had been designed by the master craftsman Hephaestus, with gold columns, ivory ceilings, and huge silver doors, beyond which sat Helios in a purple robe on an emerald throne, dazzling with a sparkling crown, the sun itself. When he saw all this splendor, Phaethon was momentarily speechless, but he soon recovered himself, introduced himself to his father, and impressed Helios with his simple dignity. Helios spoke kindly to the boy. "Yes, Phaethon, I am proud to acknowledge that I am your father, and I am glad you came to see me—so glad that I swear by the River Styx I will grant any request you ask of me. "The excited boy could think of only one wish—that he be allowed to drive the chariot of the sun across the sky for just one day. Helios' heart sank, for he realized he had made a rash promise. "Please reconsider, Phaethon. I am bound by my Stygian oath to you, but I must warn you that you have made a dangerous request. Even Zeus himself would not attempt to drive my chariot across the skies for one day! It requires far more strength and skill than you possess. The ascent is very steep, and the horses are unruly. In mid-heaven the road is very high, and even I am filled with fear when I look down on the earth below. Furthermore, the road is not without hazards. It is difficult to avoid the stars, with their jagged edges. Even if you do, you will find the descent very steep, and the horses need a steady rein throughout. Please reconsider, Phaethon, and choose more wisely. Beware, lest I be the donor of a fatal gift to you!"

The young boy would not be dissuaded, and with a heavy heart Helios prepared his chariot for Phaethon's fateful journey. The shining chariot had been fashioned by Hephaestus of silver, gold, and precious jewels. The horses, snorting, prancing, and breathing fire, were led out of the stables to be harnessed. Helios anointed Phaethon's face with sacred ointment to protect him from the searing heat. Finally, he set his shining crown on Phaethon's head, sighing deeply. "Phaethon, remember my advice. Spare the whip and use the reins with force. You must maintain full control of the horses. Follow the middle course. If you go too high, you will burn the heavens; too low, the earth. Farewell, my proud son."

Phaethon stood tall in the chariot, holding the reins with pride. The four horses started the steep ascent, breaking through the clouds with flying feet. Almost immediately they realized that the chariot was lighter than usual, and they broke away from the middle course and went their own way. In vain did Phaethon pull on the reins. In vain did he call out, for he realized with cold panic that he did not even know the names of the horses. Now at last Phaethon regretted his rash request, but it was too late. He was alone in the vast heavens, powerless with runaway horses. He dropped the reins, and the horses wandered through the heavens as their impulses took them. As they roamed wildly, dragging the sun chariot up and down, the clouds became scorched and smoky, the earth was inflamed, fields were burned, people were destroyed by fire. Even dark Tartarus became light through the cracks that were opened everywhere on earth. Phaethon himself was engulfed in thick, hot smoke, unable to see anything, almost unable to breathe.

Surveying this holocaust, Zeus realized he must take action immediately or the earth and even heaven itself would be completely destroyed. Having no clouds or rain, he took a thunderbolt and hurled it directly at Phaethon. The boy was thrown from the chariot and fell to earth, his hair aflame, leaving a long trail of fire like a shooting star. Helios' chariot was destroyed by the flames, but the horses bolted through the sky and were later caught by the Sun God and returned to their stable. Haephestus built a new chariot, even grander than the first, and Helios never again let the reins out of his hands. Some parts of the earth were never the same again. It was on that day that the skin of the Ethiopians turned black, that Libya was made a desert, and that the Nile River fled and hid his head. Many seas ran dry, never to be filled again. Phaethon's body was placed gently in a tomb by naiads, who wept for the boy who had dared so much and fallen so far.

CHAPTER XI: STUDY QUESTIONS

1. Why was it necessary for Daedalus and Icarus to escape by air? From whom were they escaping? What land?

2. How did they escape?

3. What was Daedalus' advice to his son?

4. Why did Icarus not follow the advice?

5. What caused Icarus to fall?

6. What was his father's reaction?

7. What famous body of water is named after Icarus?

8. Who were the parents of Phaethon?

9. What caused him to seek his father?

10. What was unusual about Helios' crown?

11. Why did Helios not retract his promise to Phaethon?

12. What hazards did Helios point out to Phaethon?

13. What was his advice to Phaethon?

14. What advice does this remind you of in another myth in this section?

15. Why did the horses behave differently with Phaethon? What did they do? What did Phaethon do?

16. What did Zeus do? Why?

17. What did Phaethon resemble as he fell?

18. In what ways is this myth etiological? Name three ways.

19. What finally happened to Helios' chariot? to Helios? to Phaethon?

20. What is the modern meaning of *phaethon?* (Look it up in the dictionary.)

PART TWO, STUDY QUESTIONS

The Oracle of Apollo told Psyche's parents, "She is destined to be the bride of no mortal lover but a monster whom neither gods nor men can resist." Do you agree that love is a monster that cannot be resisted? Give specific examples to support your opinion.

Listed below are some subjects that most concerned the ancient Greeks.

Fate	Hospitality
Hubris	Disguise and Revelation
The Golden Mean	Etiology
Metamorphosis	Falling
The Foolish Promise	Love (many different kinds)
Contests	

How many of these subjects or themes can you find in the myths in this section? Can you think of any more themes?

In what ways does modern society have a different idea of fate? Why?

How does the modern attitude about guile contrast with the ancient Greeks'—or does it?

"Only the good die young" was a favorite belief of the Greeks. Read the myth of Cleobis and Biton in another mythology text and see how it demonstrates this belief.

The fear of falling is a primitive fear common to all people. How did the Greeks deal with this fear?

Having read this many myths, you now can make an assessment of the Greek character. Name five traits the Greeks most admired. Support each one with an example.

SUGGESTIONS FOR OUTSIDE STUDY

Read one of the following myths and give a brief summary to the class:

Actaeon
Adonis
Callisto
Caphalus and Procris
Castor and Pollux

Cyparissus
Hero and Leander
Orion
Pan and Syrinx

Reread one of the myths in this section in at least two mythology texts in your library. You will see for yourself how many different versions there are of any one myth. Describe the differences in detail.

Read the short myth of Alcyone and Ceyx. You will find the origin of the word *halcyon*. What does it mean?

The famous twentieth-century poet W. H. Auden wrote a poem about Icarus' fall, entitled "Musee de Beaux Arts." Read this poem and discuss its meaning.

Read the novel *Till We Have Faces* by C. S. Lewis, for a modern version of the Cupid and Psyche myth, told from the point of view of one of Psyche's sisters. Report to the class on the differences in the two versions.

SUGGESTED ESSAY TOPICS

Discuss father/son, mother/son relationships in Greek myths studied in Parts I and II. How do they differ?

Based on what you have read thus far, write a character sketch of Apollo, Zeus, Hermes, Aphrodite, or Athena, discussing both positive and negative traits. Be specific! Do not simply summarize their experiences but analyze their specific character traits.

Oscar Wilde wrote, "In this world there are only two tragedies. One is not getting what one wants, and the other is getting it." Apply this statement to at least two of the myths in this section.

IN-CLASS CREATIVE WRITING

If you could have one wish, what would it be? Why?

or

The myth of Midas states, "He hated the gift he had recently prayed for." Have you ever regretted a wish that came true? Explain.

OUT-OF-CLASS CREATIVE WRITING

Write an original myth based on one of the gods or goddesses we have studied. You may invent new gods and goddesses to mingle with the old ones, as well as new people. Use your imagination!

PART THREE

DARK
MYTHS

Chapter XII

THREE DARK MYTHS

Although the ancient Greeks admired moderation and deplored violence, they were fascinated by excess. Greek mythology contains many stories of rape and murder, even cannibalism, and the punishments that inevitably followed. This section concentrates on the darker side of the Greek spirit.

AGAVE AND PENTHEUS

Agave was the mother of Pentheus, King of Thebes. When Dionysus came to Thebes to establish his worship there, he encountered opposition from Pentheus. The king thoroughly disapproved of Dionysus because he disrupted order and encouraged drunken revels. The god of Wine disguised his anger at the king's opposition, and he encouraged Pentheus to go with him to the mountain, where the women of Thebes were dancing in the god's honor. When Pentheus arrived at the ceremony, Dionysus drove the women into such a frenzy that they mistook Pentheus for a wild boar. They attacked and dismembered the king. Then his own mother, Agave, carried his head triumphantly back to Thebes. When she came to her senses, she screamed in horror at what she had done to her beloved son. Dionysus had had his revenge.

LYCAON

Lycaon, King of Arcadia, incurred Zeus' anger by violating the rule of hospitality. Zeus had visited Arcadia in disguise but then disclosed his true identity. Not quite convinced the visitor was really Zeus, Lycaon arranged to have a prisoner killed, boiled, and served to his guest. Zeus recognized at once what had happened. Flinging his plate on the ground, he cried, "You act like an animal; you shall be an animal!" He then turned Lycaon and all of his decendents into wolves.

TEREUS, PROCNE, AND PHILOMELA

The story of King Tereus, Procne, and Philomela combines three elements that most fascinated the ancient Greeks—violence, guile, and metamorphosis. T.S. Eliot refers to this myth in "The Wasteland," and Shakespeare's play Titus Andronicus *is based on the tragic tale.*

Tereus, the son of Ares, became the king of Thrace and married a young Athenian princess named Procne. Far from her home and her beloved sister, the young bride pined, and even the birth of a son could not make her happy. When Tereus offered to journey to Athens and return with Procne's sister, Philomela, Procne was overjoyed. She might better have left things as they were. The moment he saw Philomela, Tereus lusted after her, and during the return journey to Thrace, he raped her. To conceal his crime, Tereus cut out Philomela's tongue and imprisoned her in a tower not far from the palace. Then he returned home, telling his wife that Philomela had taken sick and died during the journey from Athens. He even wept with Procne over Philomela's death.

Meanwhile, Philomela devised a plan to inform her sister of her predicament. An expert weaver, she wove an intricate robe that depicted the whole story of what had happened to her. Then she persuaded an unsuspecting guard to present the robe to the queen. As soon as she examined the weaving on the robe, Procne comprehended the whole horrible story. Secretly, she arranged to free Philomela and bring her to the palace. Joyfully reunited, the two sisters were determined to avenge themselves on King Tereus—but how? Their final plan was diabolical: Procne stabbed her little boy, Itys, who was the image of his father. She had his body dismembered, cooked, and served to Tereus, who ate his dinner with gusto. Suddenly Philomela appeared with Itys' head on a platter. Grabbing an axe, the king chased the two screaming women and would have caught them had not the gods intervened. They turned Philomela into a nightingale, her voice not only restored but more beautiful than ever. Procne became a swallow, the bird that loves to nest in high places but always returns to its original home. The wicked Tereus became a lapwing, a slow-flying bird that has a shrill, wailing cry and lives in filth.

CHAPTER XII: STUDY QUESTIONS

1. Who was Pentheus?

2. Why did he disapprove of Dionysus?

3. What did Agave do? Why?

4. Whom did Lycaon anger? Why?

5. What was the result?

6. Who were Tereus, Procne, and Philomela?

7. What was Tereus' crime?

8. How did Philomela communicate with her sister?

9. What became of Itys, Procne, Philomela, Tereus?

10. In what ways were the metamorphoses of Tereus, Procne, and Philomela fitting?

Chapter XIII

STORIES OF THE UNDERWORLD

The Underworld of the ancient Greeks was not like the modern, fiery conception of hell, but a pale, sad, and dismal place where there was neither pleasure nor pain. There was, however, a part of the underworld, called Tartarus or the Land of the Damned, that was reserved for those who had committed serious crimes offending the gods.

It was said by the Greek writer Hesiod that a bronze anvil falling for nine nights and nine days from heaven would reach the earth on the tenth, and, in turn, a bronze anvil falling for nine nights and nine days from earth would reach Tartarus on the tenth. It was a dark, gloomy place from which there was no possible escape.

The three most famous sinners were Tantalus (see p. 91), Ixion, and Sisyphus. Apparently the Greeks believed that perpetual frustration was the worst punishment imaginable.

IXION

Though wicked Ixion had killed his father-in-law to avoid giving him an expensive present, Zeus forgave him for that brutal crime and even invited him to Mt. Olympus to sup with the gods. Ixion repaid this hospitality by lusting after Hera. To test Ixion's loyalty, Zeus created a cloud with Hera's shape so that Ixion would be tricked into thinking the cloud was Hera herself. The unscrupulous Ixion was tricked, and he made love to the cloud. From that union came Centaurus, the father of the half-man, half-horse centaurs. Ixion compounded his crime by boasting to his friends about his romantic conquest of Hera. The furious Zeus decreed an eternal punishment in Tartarus. Ixion was lashed to a fiery wheel and doomed to revolve without ceasing through all eternity.

SISYPHUS

The son of Aeolus, Sisyphus was the King of Corinth, who betrayed Zeus by telling the river god Asopus that Zeus, in the guise of an eagle, had stolen Asopus' daughter Aegina and had become her lover. Zeus was so incensed at this betrayal that he sentenced Sisyphus to eternal punishment in Tartarus. Sisyphus had to push a huge rock up a steep hill, and as soon as he was almost at the top of the hill, the rock would slip back and roll down to the bottom. Then Sisyphus must begin his labor again—and again—and again—never quite succeeding in getting the rock to the top of the hill. This tale inspired the great twentieth-century writer, Albert Camus, to write *The Myth of Sisyphus.*

ORPHEUS

Of all the myths involving the Underworld, this is the most poignant, combining as it does tenderness and violence, love and vengeance, hope and despair. Orpheus was the center of a mystery religion, and rites in his honor continued long after his death. Among other restrictions, Orphics had to abstain from eating meat.

The son of Apollo, god of Music, and Calliope, muse of Epic Poetry, Orpheus was fittingly the world's greatest musician. At the sound of his lyre and his voice, wild animals became tame, trees moved to listen, and even rocks became soft. Orpheus married the lovely maiden Eurydice, but their happiness was short-lived. Soon after their wedding day, a viper bit Eurydice's foot and she died of the venom. Orpheus was so overcome with grief that he even dared to go to the Underworld in search of his bride. As he journeyed there, he played and sang so movingly that Charon willingly rowed him across the River Styx, Cerberus wagged his tail, and Orpheus was granted an audience with the god of the Underworld, grim Hades himself. Orpheus begged in song that Eurydice be allowed to return to Earth with him, and his pleading moved even Hades to tears. The King of the Underworld granted Orpheus' request conditionally: that he walk ahead of Eurydice on the path to Earth, and that he not look back during the journey. Orpheus readily agreed, and the shade of Eurydice, still limping from her snake bite, followed him silently along the steep, dark path to Earth. At last Orpheus could see dim light in the distance. Impulsively, he turned back to be sure Eurydice was still behind him. She was, but as he watched in horror, Eurydice sank back to the Underworld, arms still outstretched, murmuring, "Farewell, my husband."

In vain did Orpheus try to rejoin her. This time Charon would not ferry him across, and Cerberus growled menacingly, showing his teeth in a snarl. Now Orpheus was totally dejected. Shunning the company of all men and women, he played and sang only sad songs. One day as he sat alone in the forest, a group of Thracian women, returning from the rites of Dionysus, saw him from a hilltop. "See," said one, pointing her finger menacingly, "There is the one who scorns us!" So saying, she threw a rock at Orpheus, but the rock softened and landed harmlessly. Then her companions joined her in throwing rocks, dirt, and branches. Soon they were shouting so loudly in their mad frenzy that the sweet sounds of Orpheus' music were drowned out, and his music no longer had the power to charm. As the Bacchantes became more and more excited, they surrounded Orpheus and tore at his limbs until finally he was dead. After the mad women had left, the Muses silently gathered up Orpheus' dismembered limbs and placed them in a tomb at the base of Mt. Olympus. There, it is said, nightingales sing more sweetly than anywhere else in the world.

CHAPTER XIII: STUDY QUESTIONS

1. What was the Greek conception of the Underworld?

2. What was the name for the part reserved for sinners?

3. Who are the three most famous sinners?

4. What were the crimes of Ixion and Sisyphus? What were their punishments?

5. Who were the famous parents of Orpheus?

6. What special talents did Orpheus possess?

7. Who was Orpheus' wife?

8. What special mission did Orpheus undertake?

9. What is the special meaning of *shade* here? Look in the dictionary.

10. What were the two conditions made by Hades?

11. What mistake did Orpheus make during his mission?

12. In what manner did Orpheus die?

13. What was special about Orpheus' burial ground?

14. In what way is the Orpheus myth similar to Pyramus and Thisbe? to Baucis and Philomen? In what ways is it different?

Chapter XIV

GREEK TRAGEDY

Any discussion of tragic myths should include Greek drama—specifically, Greek tragedy. All of the surviving Greek dramas are based on mythology, and they are among the best sources of information we possess about Greek myths.

Greek drama evolved from rural religious festivals honoring Dionysus, during which masks were carried on poles. As time passed, these celebrations became more formalized, and presentations were moved to large outdoor amphitheatres. The most famous festival was the Dionysia, a five-day celebration held every spring. Dramatists submitted their best works in competition with one another, and the winner was given a crown of ivy. During the festival all business ceased; prisoners were even released from jail and allowed to view the plays. Because the first drama prize (in 534 B.C.) was won by the dramatist Thespis, actors have been known as thespians even since. In the absence of formal church services and an ecclesiastical book like the Bible, the great dramatists of ancient Greece served as the religious thinkers. The greatest of the tragic poets were Aeschylus, Sophocles, and Euripides.

The word *drama* means "to do," and Greek plays contained much action. Plays were performed outdoors with no curtain. The permanent backdrop was usually the exterior of a Greek palace or temple. Men (no women performed) wore masks and headdresses, and no more than three characters appeared on stage at one time. Violence occurred offstage, although it was reported in gory detail to the audience. Plots were austere and short with no sub-plots to detract from the concentration. Some speeches were sung, and a chorus of 12-15 men danced and sang on the stage (called the *orchestra*), emphasizing the moral of the play with their actions. Orchestra means "dancing place" in Greek. Dramatists treated the same subject in different ways. That is one reason we have so many different versions of the same myth. The plots were familiar to the audience, so there were no surprises in the story itself, only in the way it unfolded and proceeded to its inevitable conclusion. The tragic hero could not escape his ultimate destiny, but he could make free choices during his lifetime and was expected to accept responsibility for his actions. The audience experienced both pity and terror in watching the drama, and afterwards felt a sense of relief, called catharsis.

Thirty-one plays by Aeschylus, Sophocles, and Euripides are extant, and many of these ancient plays are still performed; they retain the power to move modern man. The Greek dramatists dealt with human nature, human emotions, and basic moral problems that face people in all ages, and thus the plays that they wrote are timeless. The story that follows, concerning Oedipus, is the subject of a famous play by Sophocles.

OEDIPUS

The tragic tale of Oedipus underscores the ancient Greeks' beliefs that man could never escape his fate and that no man could be counted happy until the end of his life was known. The inspiration for dramatists throughout the centuries, the Oedipus myth is also the basis for a familiar psychiatric term, "Oedipus complex," first used by Sigmund Freud to describe the mother-son relationship. The fate of Oedipus and his four children has been the subject of three famous dramas by Sophocles.

Upon the tragic death of his brother Amphion, husband of Niobe (see p. 92), Laius became king of Thebes. Soon afterward, King Laius was warned by an oracle that his newborn son would be a danger to Laius' throne and his life if allowed to live. The frightened king gave his newborn child to a servant with orders to tie him to a tree so that he would die of exposure. The baby's ankles were pierced and bound together so that he could be left hanging from the branch of a tree. The servant could not bring himself to commit such a heartless act, and he gave the baby to shepherds from the neighboring kingdom of Corinth, who brought him to the childless rulers of that land. They named their adopted son Oedipus, meaning "swollen-footed," and he grew up assuming that his parents were Polybus and Merope. In Thebes, meanwhile, King Laius and Queen Jocasta assumed that their son had perished from exposure on Mt. Cythera.

When Oedipus grew to young manhood, he heard rumors that he was not the true son of Polybus, and he determined to consult the priestess at Delphi to find out the truth. Instead of answering Oedipus' question about his parentage, the oracle told him that he was fated to kill his father and commit incest with his mother. To avoid this horrifying fate, Oedipus determined not to return to Corinth; instead he set out for Thebes. At a junction of three roads near Delphi, Oedipus was ordered off the narrow thoroughfare by an arrogant man in a chariot. When Oedipus refused to step aside, he was stung by a whip, and the hot-tempered young man retaliated by striking the man in the chariot and killing him and all but one of his attendants, who fled in terror. The man in the chariot was King Laius of Thebes, Oedipus' father. In attempting to avoid his fate, Oedipus had all unknowingly walked to it.

Continuing his journey, Oedipus came upon a beast that had been terrorizing the countryside. This beast, called the Sphinx, had the body of a lion, the wings of a bird, and the face of a woman. It demanded of *every* traveler the answer to a riddle and devoured all those who could not answer. Everyone thus far had failed and perished. The riddle was, "What goes on four feet in the morning, two feet at midday, and three in the evening?" Oedipus answered correctly, "Man! He crawls as a baby, walks upright as an adult, and uses a cane in old age." The Sphinx was so mortified to hear the correct answer that she killed herself. Oedipus became an instant hero, who could claim a seemingly wonderful prize, the crown of Thebes. Creon, the brother of Jocasta, who had been acting as Regent of Thebes since the death of Laius, was so overjoyed at the death of the Sphinx that he made Oedipus the king of Thebes with Jocasta as his queen. Thus, all unwittingly, Oedipus had not only killed his father but married his mother.

The couple had four children: Polyneices, Eteocles, Ismene, and Antigone. For a few years they were all very happy. Then Thebes was afflicted by famine and pestilence. Crops were failing, citizens were dying, and no one knew why. The concerned king sent his brother-in-law, Creon, to the Delphic Oracle, who said that the pestilence would not end until the murderer of Laius was punished. Oedipus dedicated himself completely to unraveling the old murder mystery, little suspecting that the murderer he sought was himself. As the clues were amassed and Jocasta realized the true identity of Oedipus, she hanged herself. Oedipus, finally facing the truth and acknowledging his guilt, blinded himself with Jocasta's brooches and was again exiled to the barren countryside.

CHAPTER XIV: STUDY QUESTIONS

1. What does the word *drama* mean?

2. What is the origin of the word *thespian?*

3. How did Greek drama evolve?

4. What is the *orchestra* literally?

5. In the fifth century B.C., how were plays performed? Where? When?

6. How were playwrights reimbursed?

7. What are ten characteristics of the Greek theatre?

8. What is catharsis?

9. Who were the three greatest Greek dramatists?

10. Why are their plays still performed?

11. Who was Laius? Jocasta?

12. What did the oracle tell Laius?

13. What did this prophecy cause him to do?

14. How did Oedipus get his name?

15. Who were Polybus and Merope? In what kingdom did they live?

16. What did the priestess at Delphi tell Oedipus?

17. What did that cause him to do?

18. What happened at the crossroad?

19. What was the Sphinx?

20. What was the riddle of the Sphinx?

21. What was the answer to the riddle?

22. What was Oedipus' reward?

23. Who was Creon?

24. What caused Oedipus to send Creon to the oracle?

25. What did the oracle say?

26. What was the irony in Oedipus' response?

27. What did Jocasta do when she learned the truth? What did Oedipus do?

Chapter XV

THE HOUSE OF ATREUS

The ancient Greeks believed a curse could have such immense power that several generations could suffer the results. Five generations of the House of Atreus were affected by a curse—guilty and innocent alike sharing in tragedy and horror—all starting with the crime of Tantalus, whose hubris ended in suffering and death.

In this story, history and mythology intertwine. The period is known to historians as the Mycenean Age. The Kingdom of Mycenae was so rich and powerful that it dominated Greece for several centuries, including the time of the Trojan War (about 1250 B.C.).

Tantalus

Tantalus, King of Lydia, was a son of Zeus and a great favorite of all the gods. They invited him to their feasts of nectar and ambrosia on Mt. Olympus, and he reciprocated with lavish hospitality of his own. While it is true that one is not always automatically grateful for the generosity of superiors and that one may even become resentful of patronage, the full reasons for Tantalus' heinous crime are not known. As a son of Zeus, he may have been resentful that he was not as well accepted as Dionysus. For whatever the reason, he invited the Olympian gods to a magnificent feast and tried to humiliate them by boiling, cutting into pieces, and serving to the gods his son, Pelops.

Tantalus' hubris was so great that he thought he could outsmart the gods, but they immediately recognized the strange dish and refused to eat it. Only Demeter, distracted because of Persephone's absence in the Underworld, ate Pelops' shoulder. Tantalus was immediately put to death, and it was decreed that he should suffer eternal punishment in Tartarus. There he stands in a pool of water with fruit trees overhead. When he bends to drink, the water recedes so that he can never reach it with his thirsty lips. When he stretches to pick a piece of the luscious fruit, the wind tosses the branches just out of reach. So Tantalus is doomed to be forever hungry and thirsty while surrounded by food and drink.

Pelops

The gods restored Pelops to life, and Hephaestus fashioned an ivory shoulder to replace the part that had been eaten by Demeter. Pelops later sought the hand of Hippodamia, the daughter of King Oenomaus. Warned by an oracle that his son-in-law would destroy him, Oenomaus decreed that all suitors must first win a chariot race against the King. All unsuccessful suitors were beheaded and their heads nailed to the palace to discourage future suitors. It was impossible to win a race against the King, for he had unbeatable horses, a gift from Ares.

Pelops bribed the King's charioteer to replace the lynch-pins in the royal chariot with waxen ones. Thus, the wheels flew off midway through the race, the King was flung to his death, and Pelops won both the race and the hand of the beautiful Hippodamia. Pelops did not honor his agreement with the King's charioteer—to be the first to sleep with the virgin princess. Instead, he tossed him into the sea. As the charioteer fell to his death, he proclaimed a curse on Pelops and all of his family. The House of Atreus now was doubly doomed. The curse did not affect Pelops during his lifetime, for, through his marriage to Hippodamia, he became ruler of the large territory that still bears his name—the Peloponnesus.

Niobe

The daughter of Tantalus, Niobe, married the famous musician Amphion, and they became the rulers of Thebes. With seven handsome sons and seven beautiful daughters, Niobe seemed to have everything one could desire, but she, like her father, was guilty of hubris. When it came time to burn incense to Leto, the mother of Apollo and Artemis, the Thebans willingly went to Leto's shrine. This obedience irritated Niobe, who said scornfully, "What has Leto done that is so wonderful? She has only two children. I have fourteen. My grandfather is Zeus himself, and my father, Tantalus, supped with the gods on Mt. Olympus. My beauty is that of a goddess. There is no doubt that I shall always be blessed. It is I—not Leto—who should be honored."

Foolish Niobe! Leto heard her words and angrily summoned her children, Apollo and Artemis, asking them to avenge her honor. The two expert archers immediately killed the seven sons of Niobe and Amphion. The grief-stricken father killed himself in despair, but Niobe continued to defy the gods. So Apollo and Artemis killed Niobe's seven daughters as well. Alone and defeated, the stunned Niobe wandered, weeping unconsolably, throughout the countryside. Finally, on Mt. Sipylus in Boetia, the gods took pity on her and turned her into a stone that still remains wet as if from eternal weeping.

Atreus and Thyestes

Niobe's brother Pelops had two famous sons, Atreus and Thyestes. Bitter rivals from childhood, the brothers fell in love with the same woman and struggled for the same kingdom, Mycenae. Atreus succeeded in winning both the crown and the beautiful Aerope, but after they were married, she had an affair with Thyestes. To avenge this insult, Atreus killed three of Thyestes' sons and had them cooked and served to their father. Horrified when he discovered that he had eaten his own children (Atreus had carefully preserved the hands and feet as evidence of his crime) but powerless to do anything against the king, Thyestes fled Mycenae, vowing eventual revenge.

Aegisthus

Thyestes raped his daughter, Pelopia, on the advice of an oracle, who told him that he must do the horrid deed in order to regain his power. The child of this incestuous union was Aegisthus. As soon as he was old enough, Aegisthus traveled to Mycenae and assassinated Atreus. He then seized the throne for his father, Thyestes.

Agamemnon and Menelaus

Agamemnon and Menelaus, the sons of Atreus, fled for their lives after their father was assassinated. Traveling to Sparta, they enlisted the aid of King Tyndareus, who helped the two sons of Atreus gain back the throne of Mycenae. Tyndareus and his wife Leda had two daughters. Helen, the most beautiful woman in the world, whose true father was said to be Zeus, was given to Menelaus, who then became King of Sparta. The other daughter, Clytemnestra, was already married, but that did not deter Agamemnon. He killed her first husband and first-born child, then married her against her will. Agamemnon thus became ruler of the richest, most powerful kingdom in Greece.

THE TROJAN WAR

Background

> *These events occurred before the Trojan War. The curse of the House of Atreus extended far after that war, and Atreus' sons, Agamemnon and Menelaus, were principals in the Trojan War. The events leading to that war follow.*

Hecuba, Queen of Troy, was troubled by a dream that the child she was about to bear turned into a burning torch that destroyed the whole city. King Priam consulted a seer about this strange dream, and he was advised that the dream meant the son about to be born to Hecuba would cause the destruction of Troy. Thus, when the baby was born, Hecuba and Priam left him in the countryside to die of exposure. The child survived, however. Rescued by shepherds, he was raised simply, far away from the royal palace. Many years later, through the rattle he had with him when he was taken by the shepherds, he was recognized as the king's son and joyfully reunited with his parents. This handsome prince was Paris, who did indeed cause the destruction of Troy.

About the time that Paris was reunited with his parents in Troy, there was another joyful event—a lavish party to celebrate the wedding of Thetis, a beautiful nymph loved by both Zeus and Poseidon, and the mortal Peleus. All the gods and goddesses had been invited except—by an oversight—Eris, goddess of Discord. Furious at the slight, Eris suddenly appeared at the height of the festivities and tossed down a golden apple with the message, "For the fairest." Hera, Athena, and Aphrodite fought over the apple, each claiming that she was the fairest. The only solution was a contest, and chosen as judge of this fateful contest was none other than the young prince of Troy, Paris.

The three goddesses attempted to bribe the judge. Hera promised him power and riches. Athena promised to make him a famous warrior, and Aphrodite promised him the most beautiful woman in the world. Paris proclaimed Aphrodite the winner, preferring her gift to those of the others. Undeniably the most beautiful woman in the world was Helen, the wife of Menelaus, son of Atreus. So beautiful was she, indeed, that her father had made all Helen's suitors sign a pact promising to aid whatever man she married if she were even taken from him. Honoring her promise, Aphrodite arranged for Paris to visit Sparta, where he was entertained royally by the unsuspecting Menelaus. Completely violating the sacred bond between host and guest, Paris, with Aphrodite's help, beguiled Helen into falling in love with him and leaving her husband. The couple fled to Troy.

The enraged Menelaus demanded his wife's return, but King Priam refused. Now Menelaus, whose honor was at stake, called upon his brother Agamemnon and former suitors of Helen's, including Odysseus, to attack Troy and bring back his wayward wife. After many delays, the Greek troops, called the Achaeans, finally assembled at Aulis with eighty ships, ready to sail to Troy and make a quick end to the war. They were completely frustrated at Aulis because there was no wind. It was said that Artemis was enraged because one of her sacred deer had been butchered, and she demanded a human sacrifice in return. This was to be no ordinary sacrifice, however, but a beautiful young princess—Iphigenia, the daughter of Agamemnon and Clytemnestra. The son of Atreus was loath to sacrifice his daughter and to incur the wrath of his wife, but he felt that he had no choice. He tricked Iphigenia into traveling to Aulis with the promise of marriage to the great warrior Achilles. The sacrifice was accomplished, the wind rose, and the troops sailed jubilantly to Troy. Behind was a fiercely grieving Clytemnestra, who vowed revenge on her husband.

The Trojan War lasted for ten years, and its story has been immortalized by Homer in *The Iliad* (*Ilium* is the Greek word for Troy). By the end of it, almost all of the Trojans and many famous Greek heroes were dead, including Achilles. His mother, Thetis, had attempted to grant him immortality by dipping him in the River Styx. She had held onto the baby by the heel, and that was the only vulnerable spot on Achilles' body, mortally struck by one of Paris' arrows.

The Curse Continues

The Greeks ultimately won the war. Menelaus was reunited with his errant wife, Helen, and they resumed their relatively uneventful life together as King and Queen of Sparta. Agamemnon's fate was not as mild. Taking as his mistress/slave Cassandra, the proud daughter of King Priam, he sailed back to Mycenae in triumph. Cassandra had been loved by Apollo and spurned his advances. In frustrated spite, Apollo had given Cassandra the gift of prophecy and the curse of never being believed. As they approached Agamemnon's palace, Cassandra shrieked that she saw bloody destruction just ahead, but Agamemnon ignored her ravings. For ten years Clytemnestra had nursed her hatred for her husband and plotted her revenge. She had even become the mistress of Agamemnon's hated cousin, Aegisthus, son of Thyestes, who had killed Agamemnon's father, Atreus. Masking her true feelings, Clytemnestra greeted her husband warmly and brought him into the palace for the traditional ceremonial bath. Aegisthus stabbed the unsuspecting Agamemnon to death, and Clytemnestra cut off his head with an axe, then turned to the terrified Cassandra and murdered her as well.

Agamemnon and Clytemnestra had two children besides Iphigenia. The boy, Orestes, was smuggled out of the palace amidst fears for his life. The girl, Electra, stayed on, hating her mother and Aegisthus for what they had done to her father. Modern psychiatrists still refer to the strong bond between father and daughter as an "Electra complex." After he had grown to young manhood, Orestes consulted the Delphic Oracle, who told him he must avenge his father's death by murdering his mother and her lover. The ancient Greeks considered matricide (killing one's mother) the worst crime of all—so horrible that it could never be atoned for. Reluctantly, Orestes returned home and, encouraged by his sister Electra, he killed the unsuspecting Clytemnestra and Aegisthus, and thus avenged his father's death. Pursued by the Furies (Eumenides), Orestes finally expiated his guilt after many unhappy years through the intervention of Athena. Later forgiven when he acknowledged his guilt, Orestes ultimately married his cousin, Hermione, daughter of Helen and Menelaus. With this peaceful resolution, the curse of the House of Atreus finally came to an end.

Afterward

In the late nineteenth century, Heinrich Schliemann, following his successful excavations at Troy, was equally successful at Mycenae. In one of the royal graves he found a gold mask. When he lifted it, for a brief moment he saw the face of an ancient king before it crumbled to dust. Schliemann triumphantly telegraphed the King of Greece, "I have gazed upon the face of Agamemnon!"

CHAPTER XV: STUDY QUESTIONS

1. Who was the father of Tantalus?

2. How did he reciprocate the gods' hospitality?

3. Which deity absentmindedly ate the wrong thing at the banquet?

4. What was the punishment decreed for Tantalus?

5. What crime did Pelops commit?

6. What was the prize he gained?

7. What was his punishment?

8. What territory in Greece is named for Tantalus' son?

9. In what way was Niobe related to Tantalus?

10. What goddess did Niobe offend? How?

11. What specifically was her punishment?

12. What do you call this kind of punishment?

13. Who were two famous grandsons of Tantalus?

14. Who was Aerope?

15. What was Atreus' crime?

16. What was Thyestes' crime? What was the outcome of his crime?

17. Who were two famous sons of Atreus?

18. What kingdoms did they rule? Who were their wives?

19. Who was Hecuba? What dream did she have?

20. What action did she and her husband take because of that dream?

21. How did their plan go wrong?

22. Who were Peleus and Thetis?

23. Who was not invited to the wedding?

24. What was the revenge for this oversight?

25. Who was in the contest? Who was the judge? What were the bribes?

26. Who was the winner? Who was the prize?

27. What pact were Helen's suitors required to sign?

28. Who were the Achaeans?

29. Who was Iphigenia? What happened to her? Why?

30. What were two results of the incident you just described?

31. How long did the Trojan War last?

32. What happened to Achilles during that war?

33. What is the Homeric name for Troy? What famous work did Homer write about the Trojan War?

34. Who was Cassandra? What special talent did she possess?

35. How had she received that talent? How was it also a curse?

36. What happened to Menelaus after the war? to Helen?

37. What happened to Agamemnon? to Cassandra? to Clytemnestra? to Aegisthus?

38. In what way are any of the above connected to the House of Atreus?

39. What psychiatric term did Electra's feeling inspire?

40. What ultimately happened to Orestes? What goddess aided him?

41. Who was Hermione?

42. What was so special about Mycenae?

PART THREE, STUDY QUESTIONS

What is the derivation of the following phrases?

"tantalizing aroma"

"Oedipus complex"

"Achilles' heel"

"She's (he's) a real Cassandra!"

"Electra complex"

"He was a real trojan in the doctor's office."

"the face that launched a thousand ships"

QUESTIONS FOR THOUGHT AND DISCUSSION

Discuss the Greek idea of Fate. How did it differ from the prevalent belief today?

The Greeks believed in the power of curses. Do we? Can you think of any famous modern-day curses?

The Greeks also believed in the power of dreams. Do we? Give examples.

The Greeks evidently believed that the worst kind of punishment was eternal frustration. Do you agree? Why or why not?

SUGGESTIONS FOR OUTSIDE STUDY

There are many other famous sinners in mythology. Read one of the myths below and report to the class briefly:

Glaucis
Phineus
Salmoneus

Read about the House of Troy or the House of Labdacus. Give a brief report to the class.

SUGGESTED ESSAY TOPICS

The Greek thinker Solon once said, "Until he is dead, do not yet call a man happy, but only lucky." Apply this statement to one of the people you have read about in this section.

The contemporary writer Pamela Hansford Johnson once wrote, "Gratitude is not an emotion—only the expectation of gratitude." Apply this statement to someone you have read about in this section.

Aeschylus once wrote, "What is pleasanter than the bond between host and guest?" Give three examples from your reading thus far of Greek hospitality, used well or misused. (You may cite examples from previous sections of the text if you like.)

PART FOUR

HEROES

Chapter XVI

"Wonders are many, and none is more wonderful than man."
Sophocles in Antigone

The ancient Greeks believed in the nobility of man. They told and retold the exploits of the heroes so often that these adventures eventually took on magical qualities, and it was difficult to remember that these mythical heroes, or demigods, had actually once lived on earth. The heroes even had a special section reserved for them in the Underworld: the Elysian Fields, or the Islands of the Blessed—a place like Camelot, where the weather was always temperate and golden blossoms opened perpetually.

PERSEUS

The story of Perseus contains more magical elements than those of the other Greek heroes in this section. Very prominent in this myth, also, is the belief in the power of destiny. Try as we may, we cannot escape our fate.

The Birth of Perseus

King Acrisius of Argos had a beautiful daughter, Danae, but no sons to inherit his hard-won crown. Thus he traveled to Delphi to ask the oracle whether he would have sons. Often the oracle's answers were ambiguous, but there was no mistaking this prediction: Acrisius would have no sons, and his daughter would bear a son who would one day destroy him. Dumbfounded by this bad news and determined to avoid his fate, Acrisius devised a way to do so without incurring the wrath of the gods by directly killing his daughter. Acrisius' solution was to confine Danae in a bronze house, which was then buried underground. The only light came from the ceiling, part of which was open to the sky. Day after day the lovely daughter of Acrisius sat alone in her bronze prison, until Zeus saw her from the sky and was smitten with her beauty. He turned himself into a shower of gold, rushed in through the open ceiling, and impregnated Danae.

When King Acrisius discovered that Danae had borne a baby, he was both furious and frustrated. Again avoiding direct murder, he put mother and son in a sealed chest and had it thrown into the open sea. He was confident that they could not survive. Acrisius had not reckoned with the interference of Zeus, who protected the chest containing his child from the buffeting of the waves. Instead of perishing in the Aegean Sea, Danae and her baby, safely dry inside the chest, washed ashore on the island of Seriphus and were rescued almost immediately by a kindly fisherman, Dictys, brother of the island's ruler. He immediately took the mother and her child to his wife, and now it seemed that Danae and her son were safe at last. She named her baby Perseus, which in Greek means "the Destroyer."

Perseus' Maturation

Under the nurturing care of his mother and his two benefactors, Perseus grew to young manhood. Danae's beauty became a disadvantage once more, for when Dictys' brother, King Polydectes, saw her, he was determined to have her at all costs. Polydectes knew that he would have to win Danae through trickery, for the young Perseus was now strong, proud, and intelligent. It was the custom that when the king married, all the men of the island presented fine gifts to him. So Polydectes falsely announced his engagement to the princess of a neighboring island, correctly guessing that he could shame Perseus into committing a rash act. As all the men of the island presented their finest horses and gold, Perseus, who for the first time was ashamed of his poverty, promised instead to fulfill a dangerous mission for the king. Thus it was that Perseus was tricked into facing almost certain death.

Perseus and Medusa

At that time there were three gorgons, whom all men both loathed and feared. With huge teeth, wings, bird claws, and writhing snakes for hair, these women were so ugly that they turned anyone who looked at them to stone. Two of the gorgons were immortal and thus invincible, but the third, Medusa, had once been a beautiful maiden. So proud had she been of her long, lustrous hair, constantly brushing her locks and admiring herself, that she incurred the wrath of Athena, who inflicted the worst punishment she could devise—she turned Medusa into a gorgon, and her beautiful hair was now a writhing mass of vipers.

Perseus' mission for Polydectes was to slay Medusa and bring back her head as proof—a mission everyone thought impossible. Polydectes had not reckoned on Perseus' dedication and the aid he would receive from the gods as the son of Zeus. The two deities chosen by Perseus' father to help him were Athena and Hermes. With their aid, Perseus was able to find the home of the gorgons. Hermes lent Perseus winged sandals, a cap that could make him invisible, a sack that could become any size, and a sharp sword. Athena lent him her shining bronze aegis and explained how to use it as a mirror so that he would not have to look at Medusa directly and thus be turned to stone. Following the advice of Hermes and Athena, Perseus finally discovered the remote home of the gorgons and was able to surprise Medusa. He attacked her with Hermes' razor-sharp sword, never looking at her directly but using Athena's mirrorlike shield and flying with Hermes' winged sandals. When he had finally decapitated Medusa, he carried his prize off in the magic pouch, which had become just the right size to accommodate that fearsome head. The invisible cap helped Perseus to escape the two immortal gorgons, who flew after him, hurling threats and curses, yet unable to see anything but the empty air.

Perseus and Andromeda

While flying back to the island of Seriphus with Medusa's head, Perseus saw from the air a surprising sight. A beautiful maiden sat motionless, chained to a rock, as the sea churned all around her. Moved by the sight of this helpless girl, Perseus swooped down, introduced himself, and asked her why she was in such a strange predicament. "I am Andromeda, the daughter of King Cepheus and Queen Cassiopeia, rulers of Ethiopia," she said with simple dignity. Andromeda related her tragic story above the crashing of the waves. Queen Cassiopeia, her mother, had incurred the wrath of

Nereus' daughter by claiming that she was more beautiful than all the sea nymphs. Nereus' daughter prevailed upon her father, the sea god, to send a giant serpent to terrorize the sea coast. In order to rid themselves of this monster, the king and queen were told that they would have to sacrifice their daughter, Andromeda, to the sea monster. Thus it was that the innocent Andromeda was chained to a rock, doomed to be devoured by the giant reptile at the next high tide. Nearby, awaiting their daughter's doom, were the distraught parents. Perseus quickly struck a bargain with them: he would kill the monster if they would promise that Perseus could marry Andromeda. Without hesitation and with no time to spare—for it was almost high tide—they agreed.

When the monstrous reptile rose out of the water, Perseus was ready. Using his sword and his winged shoes, he attacked the beast from all directions. Some say he turned the monster to stone by displaying the head of Medusa. With the death of the sea serpent, Andromeda was freed from her rocky perch, and the happy couple was married. Perseus returned his borrowed gifts to Hermes and Athena with profuse thanks. Then he traveled back to Seriphus with a sense of triumph. His mission to kill Medusa had been a success, and he had a beautiful bride as well.

The Rest of Perseus' Story

Perseus' euphoria was short-lived. When he returned to Seriphus, he found that in his absence Danae and Dictys had been forced to flee from the lecherous Polydectes and were hiding in a cave, having long since given up hope that Perseus was still alive. Meanwhile, Polydectes and his courtiers were having a drunken celebration in the palace. To the rioters' amazement, Perseus strode into the banquet hall, carrying the head of Medusa in his sack. "Polydectes, here is the prize you sent me all over the world to seek. Look and see!" With that, Perseus brandished the loathsome head, and all who gazed upon it turned to stone, their expressions of horror and amazement fixed forever.

With Polydectes dead, Dictys became the ruler of the island, and order was restored. It was time for Danae, Perseus, and Andromeda to return to Argos. After all those years, mother and son wanted to see their homeland once more. Alerted by a messenger that Perseus was on his way, the terrified King Acrisius hurriedly left the palace and fled to far-away Larissa. Ironically, he feared the vengeance of Perseus, while Perseus wanted only to be reunited with his grandfather. When the three travelers reached Larissa, they stopped to enjoy the athletic contests there, and Perseus could not resist joining in the discus throw. The discus he hurled somehow swerved and hit a spectator in the stands. That spectator was King Acrisius, who had sought for so long to avoid the oracle's prophecy and now, far from home, had finally met his fate.

Afterward

Perseus could not bring himself to take the throne of Argos, but instead he exchanged kingdoms with a cousin and became the ruler of Tiryns. Perseus gave the head of Medusa to Athena, who proudly displayed it in the center of her aegis.

CHAPTER XVI: STUDY QUESTIONS

1. What did the Delphic Oracle tell King Acrisius?

2. How did he try to avoid this prophecy?

3. What made Acrisius furious and frustrated?

4. What did he do?

5. How did Acrisius' second plan go awry?

6. Who was Dictys? Polydectes?

7. What trick did Polydectes use to get Perseus to leave the island? Why did he want Perseus to go?

8. What or who were the gorgons? Describe them.

9. In what way was Medusa different from the other gorgons?

10. What deities helped Perseus? In what way?

11. Why was Andromeda chained to a rock?

12. What bargain did Perseus strike with Andromeda's parents?

13. Where did Andromeda live?

14. Where did she first go with Perseus?

15. What did Perseus find there?

16. How did he handle the situation?

17. For a third time, King Acrisius attempted to avoid his fate. How?

18. What was the outcome?

19. What happened to the head of Medusa? to Perseus?

20. What kingdom did Perseus rule?

Chapter XVII

JASON

Like Perseus, Jason undertook a seemingly impossible mission and was aided by magical powers. Yet Jason himself remains a curiously colorless hero, and it is Medea who emerges as the real protagonist. Euripides made Medea, not Jason, the subject of his tragedy, and the modern poet Robinson Jeffers entitled his powerful play Medea.

This myth is thought to be based on actual history. The quest of the Argonauts was probably the first major maritime expedition, occurring between 1300 and 1200 B.C. *The historical Argonauts were more piratical than idealistic, however, and the gold they sought was not fleece.*

Jason's Early Life

Two brothers, Aeson and Pelias, aspired to rule the Thessalonian kingdom of Iolcus. They finally agreed that Pelias would rule until Aeson's son, Jason, came of age. When Pelias became king, Aeson had the baby smuggled out of the country so that he would not be killed by his wicked uncle. While Jason was being raised by the wise centaur Chiron, who later raised Achilles, King Pelias was advised by an oracle to "beware of a person wearing only one shoe." Thus, when a young man suddenly appeared before him one day, wearing one sandal (the other had been lost in a muddy riverbank), Pelias was struck with fear. The young man with one shoe was Jason, grown tall and handsome, who had come to claim his rightful accession to the throne. Masking his unwillingness to give up his power, King Pelias suggested that Jason first undertake an exciting adventure to prove himself worthy of such high office. The adventure Pelias proposed was appealing to Jason: it was to sail to the far-off land of Colchis and to bring back the fleece of the golden ram that had transported Phrixus and Helle across the sea from Thebes to Colchis many years before. Pelias did not mention that this quest was almost certain to end in death for any who undertook it.

Jason spread the word throughout Greece that he was looking for brave young men to undertake the adventure of a lifetime. He employed the shipbuilder Argus to build a craft larger than any ship ever built before. Called the *Argo* in his honor, the ship held fifty-four sailors, called the Argonauts. These adventurers included all the outstanding young men of Greece—Hercules, Theseus, Nestor, Peleus (the father of Achilles), Laertes (the father of Odysseus), and Orpheus, whose music was to be an invaluable help during the voyage. After many adventures on their way to the kingdom of the golden fleece, the Argonauts finally arrived at Colchis. King Aetes greeted his guests with traditional hospitality (the Greek word *Xenos* means both guest and stranger), bathing and feeding them before he asked the reason for their visit. When he realized who they were, his heart hardened, for he had no desire to give the golden fleece to this young stranger. Masking his feelings, Aetes agreed to give Jason the golden fleece if Jason could prove his bravery by accomplishing the task of yoking to a plough two fire-breathing bulls with feet of bronze and then sowing the teeth of a dragon in a field. Only Aetes knew that as soon as the dragon's teeth were sown, an army of armed men would immediately spring up and use their weapons against the person who sowed the deadly crop. Never dreaming the full extent of the danger he was facing, Jason agreed to perform these tasks the following day, and Aetes smiled to himself.

The Meeting of Jason and Medea

Unobtrusively watching this exchange was the darkly beautiful daughter of the king—Medea. Like her sister, Circe, Medea was a witch, possessing mysterious magical powers beyond the understanding of mankind. Some say that Aphrodite, desiring to help Jason, ordered her son Eros to strike Medea with a golden arrow. In any event, she fell instantly and completely in love with the handsome adventurer. Everything Medea did from then on, good or evil, was done for Jason alone. Medea knew that what her father proposed for Jason would end in certain death if she did not intervene immediately. Therefore, she sent a messenger to the *Argo* to arrange a meeting with Jason late that night. Then, trembling and pale but resolute, Medea warned Jason about the ferocity of the bulls and the armed men who would spring from the dragon's teeth. She gave him a magic ointment to soothe the rage of the savage bulls, told him a trick to use on the armed men, and gave him a magic potion to rub on his body so that he would be invincible for one day. Jason was so affected by the wild beauty of this rash young woman, who was risking everything to help him, that he impulsively offered to take her away from Colchis and to marry her. Embracing her, Jason passionately declared, "Nothing but death will ever come between us!" It was a statement he would later regret.

Jason Procures the Golden Fleece

The next day, using the magic potions Medea had given him, Jason tamed the wild bulls and easily yoked them to the plow. When he sowed the dragon's teeth, the armed men who sprang up attacked Jason in vain, and they finally turned upon one another in confusion and destroyed themselves when Jason, following Medea's advice of the previous night, threw large rocks in their midst. Watching all of this, the Argonauts cheered Jason while Aetes was filled with blind fury. He suspected that his daughter had aided Jason and was determined to kill all the Argonauts at the first opportunity. Medea knew her father well, and she realized that the Argonauts were in grave danger. There was no time to lose in pursuit of the golden fleece. Using another magic potion, Medea caused the sleepless dragon who was guarding the golden fleece to close his eyes. Jason snatched up the golden fleece, and they hurried back to the *Argo* to set sail for Greece.

The Flight From Colchis

As soon as he realized that the *Argo* was sailing away, Aetes sent his son Absyrtis in hot pursuit. Medea allowed her brother to overtake the *Argo*; then she coolly murdered Absyrtis, dismembered his body, and had his limbs strewn in the sea. Aetes, in a swift and closely-following ship, would have overtaken the *Argo*, but he stopped to gather his son's limbs so that proper burial rites could be performed. Thus, cursing his daughter and mourning his son, Aetes returned to Colchis without the golden fleece.

Jason and Pelias

Jason and Medea were married during the journey back to Greece. When the Argonauts returned in triumph to Iolcus, Jason found to his horror that the wicked King Pelias had ordered Jason's father, Aeson, put to death. Medea not only restored Aeson to vigorous life, but she tricked Pelias' daughters into killing their father. Demonstrating her powers, Medea threw an old ram into a steaming cauldron, and soon out jumped a frisky lamb. The daughters of the king were so impressed that they begged Medea to use this rejuvenation process on their aging father. She agreed, and they threw the protesting King Pelias into a kettle of boiling water—only this time the magic was not magical. King Pelias was boiled to death. Medea had her revenge for Jason's sake.

Jason and Medea in Corinth

Fleeing the wrath of Pelias' daughters, Jason and Medea went to Corinth, where they raised a family and lived in quiet harmony for several years. Then, motivated by either ambition or love, but certainly forgetting his impassioned vow to Medea, Jason determined to marry the young princess Glauce, daughter of King Creon of Corinth. He announced to Medea that she and their children must leave Corinth forever. In all those tranquil years of marriage, Medea's passion for Jason had never waned. Now that all-consuming love turned to all-consuming hate, and she sent the young princess a golden cloak which she had rubbed with poisonous ointment. As soon as Glauce donned the cloak, she was consumed by fire, dying a horrible death. This punishment was not enough for Medea. She stabbed Jason's two beloved children to death, set fire to the palace, and escaped in a chariot drawn by dragons. Her last words to the stunned Jason were, "I loathed you more than I loved them."

Afterward

Medea fled to Athens, where she became the consort of King Aegeus, father of the hero Theseus. Jason either killed himself in grief and despair or was killed when a rotting plank from the *Argo* fell on him. The golden fleece disappeared. Like so many golden treasures, this one, too, turned out to be not worth the cost.

CHAPTER XVII: STUDY QUESTIONS

1. What agreement did Aeson and Pelias make?

2. What was Pelias advised by the oracle?

3. How did he attempt to avoid his fate?

4. What was the name of Jason's ship? its sailors? How many were there? Who were three famous heroes on the voyage?

5. What was their destination?

6. What did King Aetes propose that Jason do?

7. Why did Medea agree to help Jason? How did she help him?

8. For what did Jason use large rocks?

9. How did Jason get the golden fleece?

10. What did Medea do to avoid being overtaken by her father?

11. In Jason's absence from Iolcus, what had happened?

12. In what two ways did Medea help this situation?

13. Where did Jason and Medea then flee?

14. What caused Medea's rage?

15. What double revenge did she take?

16. Where did she go?

17. Afterwards, what happened to Medea, to Jason, to the golden fleece?

18. What was the final irony?

19. What three adjectives best describe Jason?

20. What three adjectives best describe Medea?

Chapter XVIII

HERACLES (HERCULES)

More than any other hero, Heracles captured the imagination of the ancient Greeks. In many ways he represented the opposite of what they professed to believe. Their ideal was moderation; Heracles was excessive in everything he did. They had high regard for music; Heracles murdered his music teacher by bashing in his head with a lyre. They disliked hubris; Heracles once shot at the sun god Helios because he was shining too brightly. Yet Heracles possessed many qualities that appealed not only to the ancient Greeks but to modern man as well.

Heracles' Early Life

Alcmene, the granddaughter of Perseus, was married to Amphitryon, a famous general of Thebes, when she caught the eye of Zeus. Determined to have a child by this beauty, Zeus disguised himself as her husband and visited her bedchamber. Thus it was that Alcmene gave birth to twins—Iphicles, fathered by Amphitryon, and Heracles, fathered by Zeus. Heracles first demonstrated his immense strength when he was only eight months old. Hera had somehow discovered Zeus' latest infidelity, and she determined to destroy the baby her husband had recently fathered. As the twins lay asleep in their cradles, Hera sent two serpents to destroy them. Iphicles screamed in terror, but Heracles simply strangled the serpents and smiled gleefully when his alarmed parents appeared at the nursery door.

As he grew to young manhood, Heracles became famous as a strong, bold, good-natured fellow with an unpredictable temper. He married and had three children, but in a fit of madness (some say caused by his implacable enemy, Hera), he killed his wife and children and the children of Iphicles as well. When he came to his senses and realized the enormity of his crime, Heracles was inconsolable. He wanted desperately to atone for his sin and rid himself of his blood guilt. At Delphi, the oracle advised Heracles to become a servant to his cousin, Eurystheus of Tiryns, and to do whatever he asked for a period of twelve years. Heracles readily agreed, and in all that time he performed uncomplainingly whatever impossible tasks Eurystheus could devise.

The Labors of Heracles

Eurystheus first asked Heracles to kill the Nemean Lion, an animal that had such a thick hide it could not be wounded. When Heracles realized that the lion was invulnerable to his arrows, he strangled it and carried it back to Tiryns over his shoulder. Eurystheus was so aghast at this display of strength that he told Heracles to stay outside the walls of the city henceforth. From that time on, Heracles wore the Nemean lion skin as a kind of shield.

The second labor was to kill the Hydra, a monster with nine heads, one of which was immortal. All would grow back doubly if they were chopped off. Heracles finally burned all the stumps of the heads to keep them from growing back, burying the still-snapping immortal head under a rock. He then dipped his arrows in the blood of the Hydra to make them poisonous. Many years later, Heracles had cause to regret this act.

The third labor was to capture a stag with horns of gold and to bring it back to Eurystheus still alive. After chasing the animal for a whole year, Heracles finally succeeded in capturing it and bringing it back to Mycenae.

Heracles' next labor was to capture alive the Erymanthian Boar. He finally chased the boar into deep snow, trapped it in a net, and carried it off to show Eurystheus.

The fifth labor was to clean in one day the filthy stables of King Augeas. They housed 3,000 oxen and had not been cleaned in thirty years. This task was relatively easy for Heracles: he simply tore away the foundations of the stables and diverted two rivers so that their waters flowed through and thoroughly cleansed the stables.

Heracles' sixth labor was lightened by the assistance of Athena. Ordered to drive off the Stymphalion Birds from their nests because they were so numerous and noisy, Heracles used huge bronze rattles crafted by Hephaestus and lent to him by Athena. He frightened the birds so that they flew up and were easy targets for his arrows.

Heracles' seventh labor was to bring to Eurystheus a special golden bull from Crete. Heracles simply caught it, took it to the gates of the city to show to Eurystheus, then set it free. This bull was later to cause trouble for Athens.

The eighth labor was to bring back the man-eating mares of Diomedes. Heracles accomplished this task with dispatch.

The ninth labor was to bring back the warrior's belt of Hippolyta, Queen of the Amazons. Although Heracles had foreseen difficulty, the queen was surprisingly cooperative, and she was about to present the belt to him when his old enemy, Hera, intervened. She caused Hippolyta's fierce warriors to think that Heracles intended to harm their queen. They attacked him, and in the confusion that followed, Heracles killed the queen, seized the belt, and fled with his prize.

Heracles' tenth labor was to bring the cattle of Geryon back from the island of Erythea. Again, Hera impeded his progress by setting a gadfly upon the cattle so that they stampeded. Nevertheless, Heracles finally succeeded in bringing them to Tiryns for Eurystheus to view.

The eleventh labor was to bring back the golden apples of the Hesperides. This labor differed from the others in that Heracles did not know exactly where to find the apples. The Hesperides were the daughters of Atlas, who was holding up the heavens. Heracles accordingly asked Atlas to get the apples while Heracles temporarily took up Atlas' task. Atlas readily agreed, but when he returned with the apples, he announced to Heracles that he, Atlas, would take the apples to Eurystheus. In a rare display of guile, Heracles pretended to go along with Atlas' idea, but realizing that he might inherit permanently this boring and back-breaking task, he asked Atlas to hold the heavens for just a moment while Heracles adjusted his shoulder pads. The trick worked. Atlas took back the heavens, and Heracles went on his way with the apples of the Hesperides. During this labor, Heracles came across Prometheus in the Caucasus, killed the eagle who was eating his liver, and freed Prometheus from his bondage.

Eurystheus thought the twelfth labor would be the most difficult of all. That was to bring the three-headed dog, Cerberus, back from the Underworld. Heracles walked imperturbably through Hades, where he saw his cousin Theseus and rescued him. He easily found the vicious dog, got a stranglehold on him, hoisted him on his shoulder, brought him to Tiryns to show to Eurystheus, and then took the dog back to Hades, where Cerberus was no doubt very relieved to return!

The Strange Death of Heracles

More tales have been told about Heracles than about any other Greek hero. They all emphasize his superhuman strength, his hearty impulsiveness, his temper, and his bold courage. Yet of all the tales about Heracles, the most intriguing concerns the manner in which he died. Heracles had killed his first wife, Megara, in a fit of madness. After a brief second marriage, he was married to a woman named Deianera. The couple was very much in love. When they had been married only a short time, they experienced an unpleasant incident that had a far-reaching effect. While on a journey together, they had to cross a river where the centaur Nessus acted as ferry-man. Heracles strode across the river unaided, but Nessus carried Deianera, and halfway across he became so aroused by her beauty that he attempted to rape the young wife. When Deianera screamed, Heracles drew forth his bow and fatally shot Nessus with an arrow that had been poisoned with the Hydra's blood. As the centaur lay dying, he apologized to Deianera for his shameful behavior and told her that if ever Heracles should cease to love her, the vial of blood he was about to give her would revive her husband's love. Deianera took the vial gratefully, although it was unimaginable to her that she would ever need to use it.

Several years later, it seemed to Deianera that Heracles was much too interested in a young maiden named Iole. Some say Heracles' old enemy Hera gave Deianera this idea. Remembering the vial of centaur's blood, she sprinkled the contents on a ceremonial robe and had it delivered to Heracles. When the hero proudly tried on the robe, he was consumed by fire. He had never felt such agony. He burned, but he did not die. As he tore off the robe, his skin came off with it. Still the fiery agony persisted. In blind rage, Heracles threw into the sea the messenger who had delivered the robe. The horrified Deianera realized that Nessus had finally avenged himself on Heracles through her foolishness. Nessus had been poisoned with the arrow dipped in the Hydra's blood, and now this poison was worse than death to her beloved husband. In shame and despair, she hanged herself. In his agony, Heracles begged to be killed, but no one would kill him. He then built his own funeral pyre and lay in it, finally persuading the warrior Philoctetes to light the brands. In gratitude, Heracles bequeathed his bow and arrow to Philoctetes, who later used them in the Trojan War.

Afterward

No trace of Heracles' body was ever found, and it was said that he was accepted by the Olympians as the true son of Zeus, and that even the vengeful Hera became reconciled, and in token of that reconciliation, she gave Heracles her daughter Hebe as a bride. Thus, Heracles, who possessed emotions stronger than his intellect, who was both arrogant and humble, who was impulsive but strangely gentle, became the only Greek hero to live on Mt. Olympus, his troubled heart and wracked body finally at peace.

CHAPTER XVIII: STUDY QUESTIONS

1. In what ways was Heracles a strange hero for the Greeks?

2. Who was the great-grandfather of Heracles? the mother? the brother?

3. What deity remained Heracles' enemy throughout his life?

4. What amazing thing did Heracles do when he was still a baby?

5. What horrible act did Heracles commit when a young man? Why?

6. What was his reaction?

7. What did the Delphic Oracle advise Heracles to do?

8. During his first labor, Heracles acquired what famous "trademark"?

9. Describe the Hydra. How did killing the Hydra affect Heracles afterwards?

10. How did Heracles clean the stables of King Augeas?

11. Who was Hippolyta? What happened to her? Who caused that incident?

12. Why did Heracles ask Atlas to help him? How? When?

13. How did Heracles trick Atlas?

14. During this labor, what good deed did Heracles perform?

15. Heracles went to the Underworld for what purpose on his last labor?

16. Who was Heracles' third wife?

17. What is a centaur?

18. What secret did Nessus give to Heracles' wife?

19. What was in the vial? What did it cause?

20. Sophocles said in *Antigone*, "Nobody likes the man who brings bad news." How does that saying apply to the Heracles myth?

21. How did Heracles finally die?

22. What special honor was given to Heracles after his death?

Chapter XIX

THESEUS

The young Theseus greatly admired his older cousin Heracles and tried to emulate him. The two heroes remained friends throughout their lives even though they were very different. Theseus used his intellect fully as much as his muscles, and he was more analytical than emotional.

In 500 B.C. the poet Pindar wrote, "O bright and violet-crowned and famed in song, bulwark of Greece, famous Athens, divine city." It is not surprising, therefore, that Athens—then as now the center of Greek culture—should take Theseus as its own special hero.

Although he was not resurrected as a mythical hero until the fifth century B.C., the real Theseus probably lived about 1450 B.C. Ruins of the labyrinth and the palace of Cnossus in Crete still stand.

Young Theseus

The parentage of Theseus is shrouded in mystery. Aethra, the daugher of the King of Troezen, gave birth to Theseus after King Aegeus of Athens had visited Troezen. Some say, however, that Poseidon was the true father of Theseus, and Theseus himself grew up believing this story because his grandfather had told him that Poseidon was his father. Theseus was raised in Troezen by his mother, who had been advised by Aegeus to follow certain instructions. Before returning to Athens, Aegeus had buried a sword and a pair of sandals in the ground and covered them with a heavy stone. When the child was strong enough, Aethra was to tell him the location of the stone so that he could attempt to lift it and uncover the sword and the sandals. If he was successful, only then should he be told that Aegeus was his father. He should then journey to Athens to be welcomed by the king as his true son and rightful heir.

Under the watchful eyes of his mother, Theseus grew strong and intelligent. Slight and wiry, he was an expert wrestler. When Theseus became sixteen, Aethra decided it was time for him to attempt to lift the stone. Theseus succeeded on the first try, and Aethra told him that King Aegeus was his true father. Discarding the idea of traveling to Athens by sea as too easy, Theseus chose instead to go by the dangerous overland route, where all travelers were in mortal danger from robbers and highwaymen. Theseus welcomed the challenge. Alone and unaided, he was able to rid the road of many criminals, using both his wits and his skill as a warrior. During his first violent encounter, Theseus won as a trophy a huge bronze club, which ever after was associated with him. Perhaps his most bizarre adventure on the road to Athens was with the villain Procrustes, "the stretcher," a sinister innkeeper who kept two special beds for his unsuspecting guests. If a traveler was short, Procrustes put him in the long bed and stretched his limbs until he fit. Tall travelers were put in the short bed, and their extremities were hacked off until there was a perfect fit. Using the short bed, Theseus gave Procrustes a fatal dose of his own medicine.

121

Theseus in Athens

When Theseus arrived in Athens, he was exhausted but triumphant, having rid the road between Troezen and Athens of all the villains en route. Yet his troubles were by no means over. Medea had flown to Athens after leaving Corinth, and she was now the consort of King Aegeus. With her powers of divination, she knew that Theseus was the son of Aegeus, even though he did not identify himself, and she was determined that he not usurp any of her power. She warned Aegeus that this young stranger meant to do him harm, and she proposed that Aegeus allow Medea to poison the young man's cup of wine at dinner. As the unsuspecting Theseus reached for the poisoned cup, he exposed the sword his father had buried many years before. Aegeus dashed the cup from Theseus' hand and welcomed his son with tears of joy and relief. Then, turning to the treacherous Medea, he expelled her from the kingdom.

Aegeus and Theseus in Athens

For a while everything went well for father and son. Theseus rid Athens of the bull that had been terrorizing the countryside (the same bull Heracles had brought back to show Eurystheus and then let loose), he helped his father wage a victorious war against Aegeus' wicked brother, and he was accepted joyfully by the Athenians as Aegeus' rightful heir to the throne. The happiness of this reunion was short-lived, however, for one day a black-sailed ship in the harbor awaited its grim cargo.

Many years before, the beloved son of King Minos of Crete had been killed by a wild bull while in Athens, and Minos had blamed King Aegeus for the loss of his son. Minos himself had done a foolish thing: having promised to sacrifice to Poseidon a bull that had been a gift from the god of the Sea, Minos had instead sacrificed an inferior bull. The Earth-shaker was so furious that he took devilish revenge against the king. He caused Queen Pasiphae to fall in love with the bull and, by him, to conceive a monster, half man, half bull, called the minotaur. King Minos was so revolted by this monster that he commissioned the famous architect, Daedalus (see p. 67) to design a labyrinth where the minotaur could live. Because of Minos' son's death, every nine years Minos demanded a deadly tribute from King Aegeus of Athens: seven youths and seven maidens had to sail to Crete to be thrown into the labyrinth, where, unable to find their way out, they would eventually be devoured by the minotaur. Against his father's wishes, Theseus volunteered to sail to Crete as one of the young people. He was determined to survive and to destroy the minotaur as well, using both strength and guile. Theseus was so confident that he took along a white sail and told his father that he would hoist it on the return voyage if all went well.

Theseus in Crete

As soon as the black-rigged ship arrived in Crete and the beautiful young daughter of Minos, Ariadne, saw Theseus, she was determined that such a brave and handsome youth should not be the victim of the minotaur. First, Ariadne enlisted the aid of the labyrinth's designer, Daedalus, who told her to give Theseus a spool of thread, which he should attach to the entrance of the labyrinth and unwind as he traveled through the intricate passages of the maze. In this way, he could retrace his footsteps when he wanted to return to daylight. With this aid, Ariadne extracted Theseus' promise that he would take her back to Athens and marry her after the successful accomplishment of his mission. Theseus surprised the sleeping monster and, using his wrestling skills coupled with his ingenuity, was able to kill it with his bare hands. Then carefully following the trail of the thread, he found his way back to the entrance of the labyrinth and rejoined the Athenian youths and maidens. Together with Ariadne, they set sail for the island of Naxos, their first stopover on the return voyage to Athens.

Two Misfortunes

Two unfortunate events occurred on the return voyage to Athens. Whatever the reason (and some say Theseus tired of Ariadne; some, that Ariadne joined in the mad revels of the Maenads), Theseus left Ariadne on the island of Naxos, where she later became the bride of Dionysus. As he finally approached the harbor of Athens, Theseus inexplicably did not raise the white sail, the prearranged sign of victory. Watching from the Acropolis, Aegeus was so grief-stricken at the sight of the black sail signifying his son's death that he hurled himself into the sea. Henceforth, that body of water was called the Aegean Sea.

King Theseus

Theseus became King of Athens upon his father's death, although he rejected the title. Under his wise rule, Athens became a democracy, where for the first time citizens were allowed to vote. Theseus was kind as well as wise; he received the exiled, blinded Oedipus, he helped in the war against tyranny in Thebes, and he comforted his cousin Heracles after he had murdered his wife and children. Still adventurous, Theseus sailed on the expedition for the golden fleece and aided Heracles in his tenth labor. In gratitude, Heracles gave Theseus the beautiful Amazon, Antiope, as a bride. (It is this wedding that is celebrated in Shakespeare's *Midsummer Night's Dream*.) Theseus was a loyal friend. His friends on more than one occasion caused him trouble, but none more than the time he journeyed to the underworld with his friend Pirithous to steal Persephone away from Hades to be Pirithous' bride. The King of the Underworld simply invited Theseus and Pirithous to sit down, knowing they would be unable ever to rise again. It was here, in the Chairs of Forgetfulness, that Heracles found his cousin Theseus, during his twelfth labor, and released him. Pirithous still sits on his chair.

Theseus, Phaedra, and Hippolytus

After the death of his Amazon wife Antiope, Theseus married a much younger woman named Phaedra, the sister of Ariadne. The son of Theseus and Antiope, Hippolytus was much closer to Phaedra's age and much more attractive to her than her own husband, but Hippolytus coolly scorned her advances. In passionate desperation, Phaedra killed herself, but not without seeking vengeance on the indifferent Hippolytus. She left a suicide note in which she accused Hippolytus of attempted rape. Nothing the young man could say would convince his father of the truth. Theseus banished his son from the country, and on his way from Athens, Hippolytus was attacked by a sea monster sent by Poseidon. Hippolytus was brought dying to his father, who finally realized that Hippolytus had been telling the truth. Grief-stricken and lonely, Theseus spend his final years a chastened man. While on the island of Scyros, governed by his friend King Lycomedes, Theseus either fell or was pushed from a precipice to his death.

Afterward

Many years later, Theseus' body was brought back to Athens and buried in a tomb built in his honor. Buried with him were his bronze staff and the sword of Aegeus. The ruins of Cnossos, King Minos' palace, still stand as a reminder of the Minoan civilization that dominated Greece from 2400 B.C. until about 1400 B.C. The oldest palace excavated in Europe (by Sir Arthur Evans), it contains mute evidence of bull-leaping, labyrinthine passages, and the high artistic and cultural level of Minoan civilization.

CHAPTER XIX: STUDY QUESTIONS

1. In what way were Theseus and Heracles related?

2. Theseus was never quite sure who was his father. Who were the two possibilities?

3. What task did Theseus perform when he was fifteen years old?

4. Why did he decide to go to Athens at all? Why by the inland route rather than by sea?

5. Who was Procrustes? What was his fate?

6. Who in Athens was an enemy of Theseus, and what did this person do?

7. How did Theseus' father recognize him?

8. What did Theseus do to endear himself to the citizens of Athens?

9. Why was King Minos angry at King Aegeus?

10. Who was the famous mother of King Minos' father?

11. Why was Poseidon angry at Minos? What revenge did he take?

12. What was the labyrinth? Who built it?

13. What special agreement did Theseus make with King Aegeus before leaving Athens for Crete?

14. Who helped Theseus? Why?

15. How did Theseus destroy the minotaur and escape the labyrinth?

16. What happened to Ariadne?

17. How did the Aegean Sea get its name?

18. What good things did Theseus do as king?

19. How did he become a prisoner in the Underworld? Who freed him?

20. What cruel act did Phaedra commit? to whom? What was the result?

21. How did Theseus die?

22. What happened after his death?

23. What two articles was buried with Theseus?

24. What was the Minoan civilization?

Chapter XX

ODYSSEUS (ULYSSES)

Called "the great tactician" by Homer, Odysseus embodied all the traits the ancient Greeks most admired. Not only crafty and diplomatic, Odysseus was also brave, handsome, steadfast, and well-spoken. Like the other Greek heroes in this section, Odysseus achieved fame by traveling far from home and doing brave deeds. Yet, unlike them, Odysseus always learned from his mistakes, and a considerable part of his appeal is his ability to change and mature.

This legendary hero may actually have lived many centuries before Homer sang of his exploits. Thanks to the excavations of Heinrich Schliemann, we know that Troy did exist; Odysseus' rocky island kingdom still stands and still bears the name of Ithaca.

Odysseus' Early Years

The red-haired son of King Laertes and Queen Anticlea of Ithaca, Odysseus became king of that rocky island on the west coast of Greece as a young man while his parents were still alive. He was one of many suitors for the hand of Helen (see p. 93). As you remember, Helen's father required all of her suitors to sign a pact agreeing to come to the aid of her husband if she were ever abducted. After Menelaus was chosen to be Helen's husband, Odysseus married Penelope, daughter of King Icarus, and the happiness of the young couple was crowned by the birth of a son, Telemachus.

When Telemachus was less than a year old, Helen fled to Troy with Paris, and Menelaus required all of Helen's former suitors to honor their agreement. Odysseus was loath to leave his wife and son to fight in a distant land for a woman he no longer desired. He thus devised a crafty plan: when Menelaus' friend Palamedes arrived in Ithaca to exhort Odysseus to join the battle, Odysseus pretended to be mad. He yoked an ass and an ox to a plow and sowed salt. Suspecting a trick, Palamedes seized the toddler Telemachus and threw him in the path of the plow. Odysseus immediately turned the plow aside and admitted to Palamedes that he had been feigning madness to avoid going to war. Odysseus never forgave Palamedes for outsmarting him. He later tricked the Greeks into thinking that Palamedes was a traitor, and they stoned him to death outside the walls of Troy.

Odysseus and the Trojan War

Once committed to fight in the Trojan War, Odysseus became one of its greatest heroes. Besides being valiant in battle, he was valued by Agamemnon, the general of the Achaeans (Greeks) for his diplomacy and military strategy. One of Odysseus' greatest adventures involved bringing the Palladium out of Troy.

Said to have fallen from heaven, the Palladium was a statue of Pallas Athena that symbolized good fortune. The Trojans believed that their city could never fall to the Greeks as long as the Palladium remained safe inside the walls of Troy. Odysseus and his friend Diomedes disguised themselves as Trojans and during one dark night scaled the walls of Troy and stole the sacred statue. This was a great psychological blow to the Trojans.

It was Odysseus who conceived the idea for the Trojan horse, the fatal gift that resulted in the ultimate destruction of Troy. The war had gone on for ten weary years, and while the Greeks had won many battles, they had still not been able to storm the walled city of Troy. Many famous heroes had died in battle—including Prince Hector of Troy and the great Achaean Achilles—and the Greeks were eager to be done with fighting and return to their homeland. Following Odysseus' scheme, the Greeks pretended to abandon the long siege of Troy, and they withdrew many ships to a nearby island. There, hidden from the Trojans, they constructed a huge wooden horse, which they then filled with men and left on the beach in front of Troy. The Greeks who were not in the horse went to their ships and pretended to sail away in final departure. Having watched all this from within the walls, the curious Trojans finally emerged, feeling safe for the first time in ten years. They marveled at the huge horse and wondered whether it was a peace offering from the departed Greeks. The priest Laocoon warned, "I fear the Greeks, even when they bear gifts." Cassandra, King Priam's daughter, echoed his warning.

As the people debated what to do with the horse, a man appeared on the beach, shouting, "My name is Sinon. I am a Greek. Through the treachery of that foul Odysseus, I was left behind when my countrymen sailed for home. I beg your mercy." The Trojans brought him before King Priam, who asked him about the strange wooden horse. "It is an offering to Athena, made so large by the Greeks that it cannot be easily carried into Troy. Odysseus hopes that the Trojans will instead destroy the horse and thus incur the wrath of Athena." "Don't believe this villainous spy!" shouted Laocoon. "Can't you see what he is trying to do? This is a trick that will bring destruction to Troy!" The Trojans hesitated, and as they did so, two immense sea serpents rode in on the water and advanced directly to Laocoon and his two sons. As the crowd gasped in horror, the serpents strangled the three and then retreated to the sea. The terrified Trojans took this act as a sign from the gods that Sinon, not Laocoon, had been telling the truth. They opened the gates of their city and triumphantly dragged in the huge, heavy wooden horse.

As Odysseus and the other Greek warriors crouched inside the belly of the horse, the Trojans celebrated far into the night. Finally, exhausted from their revelry, they staggered off to bed. It was then that the Greeks, led out by the traitor Sinon, emerged from the horse, opened the gates of Troy to their companions, who had been hiding outside the city in the dark, slaughtered all the Trojans, and set fire to the once-impregnable city. Thanks to "the great tactician" Odysseus, the Trojan War was finally over.

The Long Voyage Home

Odysseus' long journey from Troy to Ithaca is the subject of Homer's *The Odyssey*. With the total destruction of Troy, the Greeks had accomplished their mission and were ready to board their ships and return to their various city-states. Menelaus and Helen were fated to be delayed in Egypt; Agamemnon was to be slain by his wife and her lover as soon as he arrived home; Odysseus would have to wait another ten years before seeing his wife and son again. But these things were not known to the Greeks as they eagerly set sail for home.

Odysseus' first stop was the island of Ismarus, where he and his men, fresh from the horrors of war, behaved like pirates, ruthlessly plundering and taking captives until they were stopped by the men of the island. Odysseus lost six men from each ship before fleeing, and he never again behaved in such a barbaric way.

The next stop was the island of the Lotus-Eaters. Just one taste of the lotus plant, and men would forget all thoughts of home as they were lulled into pleasant inertia. Some of Odysseus' men tasted the plant, and Odysseus had to drag them to their ship and tie them to their benches in order to make them leave that beguiling island.

The next adventure was on the island of the Cyclopes, where the giant cannibal Polyphemus held Odysseus and several of his men captive in a cave as he devoured them meal by meal. Odysseus and his men blinded the one-eyed giant with a fiery poker they had fashioned from a tree stump, and they escaped from the cave by harnessing themselves to the bellies of the Cyclops' rams. But in a foolish show of hubris, Odysseus shouted out his name to Polyphemus, who begged his father Poseidon to take revenge on the man who had blinded him. The god of the Sea made Odysseus' life miserable for the next ten years.

Sailing to the island of Aeolus, keeper of the winds, Odysseus found warm hospitality and was given a leather bag full of winds so that he could get home safely. After nine days at the helm without sleep, Odysseus sighted Ithaca and gratefully sank into an exhausted sleep. His crew, greedy and curious, opened the bag of winds, expecting to find treasure. Instead, all manner of gale-force winds were released, and the ships were blown back to the island of Aeolus. This time, the king was completely disgusted with Odysseus and refused to help him further.

At the next island, a deceptively peaceful land-locked harbor hid the fierce Laestrygonians, who hurled rocks and destroyed all the ships in Odysseus' company except his own, which he had prudently moored outside the harbor.

Mourning many lost companions, the ever-dwindling group came to Aiaia, island of the alluring sorceress Circe, who had many magic powers. Here, with the help of Hermes, Odysseus outsmarted Circe, who had already turned some of Odysseus' men into swine and intended to do the same to their captain. Odysseus did not altogether escape Circe's magic, however, for he remained on her island more than two years, until his men finally persuaded him to resume his voyage home. Circe directed Odysseus to the Underworld so that he could receive further instructions from the blind prophet Tiresias. In that desolate place, Odysseus encountered many shades of those he had known, including his mother, who had died of a broken heart during his long absence; Agamemnon, murdered by his wife, who warned Odysseus never to trust a woman; and the great warrior Achilles, who told Odysseus that the humblest life was preferable to dreary death. Odysseus was grateful to leave the Underworld, but he still faced many dangers.

Circe had warned him about the sirens—sea nymphs who charmed men with their songs and lured them to their death on the jagged rocks where the sirens sang. Odysseus filled the ears of his men with wax so that they would avoid temptation, but he bade them lash him to the mast so that he could hear the sirens' hauntingly beautiful music.

Circe had also warned Odysseus about Scylla and Charybdis, twin perils he and his men must pass on their journey. On one side of the narrow passage (some say the Strait of Messina) was Scylla, a six-headed monster with an insatiable appetite. On the other was Charybdis, a deadly whirlpool that sucked whole ships to the bottom of the sea. In avoiding Charybdis, Odysseus came too close to Scylla, and the monster stretched out her long necks and seized six of Odysseus' men, one in each mouth.

Circe had warned that when Odysseus and his companions arrived at the island of the sun god, Helios, they must not eat the sacred cattle. But Odysseus' starving men disobeyed their captain's order, and while Odysseus slept, they tried to slaughter Helios' immortal cattle. As the apparently slain animals lowed and writhed on the spit, Odysseus and his men fled in horror from the island, but they were overtaken by a fierce storm that destroyed Odysseus' ship and all of his men. Fashioning a raft from the wreckage, Odysseus drifted to the island of Ogygia, ruled over by the lovely sea nymph Calypso. For almost seven years Odysseus remained on Calypso's island, unable to escape from the beautiful jailor who had fallen in love with him and wished to grant him immortality. Although Odysseus had never stopped loving Penelope and longing for home, he had now all but given up hope of seeing Ithaca again.

Odysseus had a strong ally, determined to help him no matter how great the wrath of Poseidon. This ally was Athena, goddess of Wisdom, who admired Odysseus for the very qualities she herself possessed. While Poseidon was on a visit to far-off lands, Athena pleaded with Zeus to aid Odysseus on his trip home, and Zeus somewhat reluctantly agreed to send Hermes to Calypso with the order to let Odysseus go. Gracious in defeat, the lovely nymph assembled the materials for Odysseus to make a boat so that he could sail home to Ithaca. All went well for Odysseus until Poseidon, returning from his trip, saw the man he had vowed to harm, and he furiously brought forth a violent storm. This time, Odysseus was forced to swim for his life to the island of Scheria, an idyllic spot that some scholars identify with present-day Corfu. There, under the protection of the gracious princess Nausicaa, Odysseus was treated regally. After hearing his adventures, the Scherians, full of admiration and pity, gave Odysseus valuable presents and took him home to Ithaca.

Odysseus' troubles were by no means over, however. In his absence, young aristocrats from all over Ithaca had sought the hand of Penelope, and Telemachus, now about 20 years old, was too dispirited to combat the more than 100 suitors who demanded that Penelope choose a husband from their ranks. Penelope played a trick on them. Weaving by day, she promised to marry as soon as her project was completed. Every night she unwove the portion she had woven during the day. When the suitors eventually discovered her trick through an unfaithful maidservant, they were furious and demanded an immediate decision. Meanwhile, Athena inspired Telemachus' bravery and engineered a reunion between father and son. Disguised as a beggar, Odysseus was now forced to be humble before the suitors in his own home as he plotted their destruction. When Penelope decreed an archery contest for her hand, using Odysseus' giant bow that none of the suitors was able to string, the suitors reluctantly gave the disguised Odysseus a turn. This was the opportunity he had been awaiting. With the aid of Athena, Telemachus, and two faithful servants, Odysseus slaughtered all the suitors and was happily reunited with the faithful Penelope.

Afterward

Unlike most Greek heroes, Odysseus lived on to old age. Long before he died, following family custom, he relinquished his crown to Telemachus, who ruled Ithaca prudently. Sitting on a crag of his rocky island, old and idle, perhaps Odysseus thought of his many adventures and yearned to be young once more.

CHAPTER XX: STUDY QUESTIONS

1. Who immortalized Odysseus? What two famous works did he create?

2. What is Odysseus' greatest appeal?

3. Why was Odysseus forced to go to the Trojan War against his wishes? What trick did he play to avoid going?

4. What was the Palladium, and how did it figure in Odysseus' story?

5. Why did the Trojans allow the wooden horse in their city?

6. When the Trojan War ended, how long had Odysseus been away from home?

7. What were Odysseus' adventures on his long voyage home? List them.

8. How did Odysseus' adventures change him?

9. What is the name of Jacques Cousteau's ship? Why is this an appropriate (or inappropriate) name?

10. There are two modern meanings of the word *siren*. What are they? What is their connection with the sirens in Odysseus' story?

11. What traits do Athena and Odysseus have in common?

12. "Penelope's web" refers to a project that is always underway and never finished. What is the allusion to the Odysseus story?

13. How many years did it take Odysseus to get home from the Trojan War?

14. How did Odysseus overcome the suitors—by guile or strength or a combination? Who helped him?

15. What action on behalf of Telemachus did Odysseus take that was similar to what his father had done for him?

16. Why did Homer call Odysseus "the great tactician"? In what ways is this epithet appropriate? Be specific.

17. What other attributes—both good and bad—did Odysseus possess?

PART FOUR, STUDY QUESTIONS

What is the derivation of the following words or phrases?

"Herculean task"	"Penelope's web"
"on a par with cleaning the Augean stables"	"between Scylla and Charybdis"
"a stare like the Gorgon's"	odyssey
Medusa (biological term)	"siren's song"
"Procrustean puzzle"	"beware of Greeks bearing gifts"
"She's a real Amazon"	"an elysian summer"

SUGGESTIONS FOR DISCUSSION

What is different between the way Theseus accomplished his deeds and the way Heracles accomplished his?

What traits do all of these heroes have in common? In what ways are they different?

What traits do the women in these stories have in common? In what ways are they different?

Judging from these stories, what traits would you say the Greeks most admire? dislike?

What values do we most prize in our heroes today? Or do we have any heroes?

EXTRA READING AND REPORTS

Charles Dickens' *A Tale of Two Cities* contains a reference to Medusa. If you have read that novel, share the allusion with the class.

In another mythology text, read about the background of the golden fleece. How did it get to Colchis? Why? Report to the class.

Research the other adventures of the Argonauts and give a brief report to the class.

One adventure of the Argonauts involved the Harpies. What were Harpies, and how does the ancient meaning relate to the modern meaning?

Read the story of another hero, such as Achilles, Hector, or Aeneas, and report to the class.

Heracles gave his arrows to Philoctetes. Find out what eventually happened to these powerful arrows. Report to the class.

Read Euripides' play *Alcestis* or read an account of Alcestis in another mythology text. What hero is strongly associated with this story? Report to the class.

Laocoon and his sons being strangled by the sea serpents is the subject of a famous statue, the original of which is in the Vatican in Rome. Look in your library for a book containing a reproduction of this statue. Can you find any other statues or paintings based on the Trojan War?

Read Somerset Maugham's short story, "The Lotus-Eater." What connection does this modern story have with the ancient myth?

Read Tennyson's poem, "Ulysses." It concerns the latter life of Odysseus. What does it add to your understanding of Odysseus? Explain.

Richard Strauss' opera *Ariadne and Naxos* is based on Greek mythology. Read the libretto and report to the class on its story.

SUGGESTED ESSAY TOPICS

In the play *Medea,* Euripides states, "When love is in excess, it brings a man nor honor nor any worthiness." Apply this statement to the story of Jason and Medea.

Write a character analysis of one of the following. Discuss their three outstanding traits (at least one should be negative). Be specific in your examples.

Heracles	Perseus
Jason	Theseus
Medea	Odysseus

Write another adventure for Odysseus, in which he behaves in keeping with his character.

SUGGESTED ORAL REPORTS AT THE CONCLUSION OF GREEK MYTHOLOGY STUDY

Mythology Not Studied (Egyptian, American Indian, Norse, etc.)

Ancient Greek Arts, for example
   Architecture
   Music
   Painting

The Constellations and How They Were Named

The Oracle at Delphi and Other Ancient Greek Shrines

Botany and Ancient Greece
   How trees and flowers figured in mythology

History of the Olympic Games

Greek Topography and Climate

Everyday Life in Ancient Greece

The Role of Women in Ancient Greece

The Bull from the Sea by Mary Renault (Theseus)

The Greek Treasure by Irving Stone (H. Schliemann)

Titus Andronicus by Shakespeare (Procne and Philomela)

A Play by Sophocles, Aeschylus, or Euripides (see following list)

Alphabetical List of Greek Tragedies That Deal with Subjects in This Text

Antigone	Sophocles
Electra	Euripides
Electra	Sophocles
Helen	Euripides
Hippolytus	Euripides
Iphigenia in Aulis	Euripides
Iphigenia in Tauris	Euripides
Medea	Euripides
Oedipus at Colonus	Sophocles
Oedipus Rex	Sophocles
Orestes	Euripides
Prometheus Bound	Aeschylus
Seven against Thebes	Aeschylus
The Agamemnon	Aeschylus
The Bacchae	Euripides
The Eumenides	Aeschylus
The Libation Bearers	Aeschylus

APPENDIX A

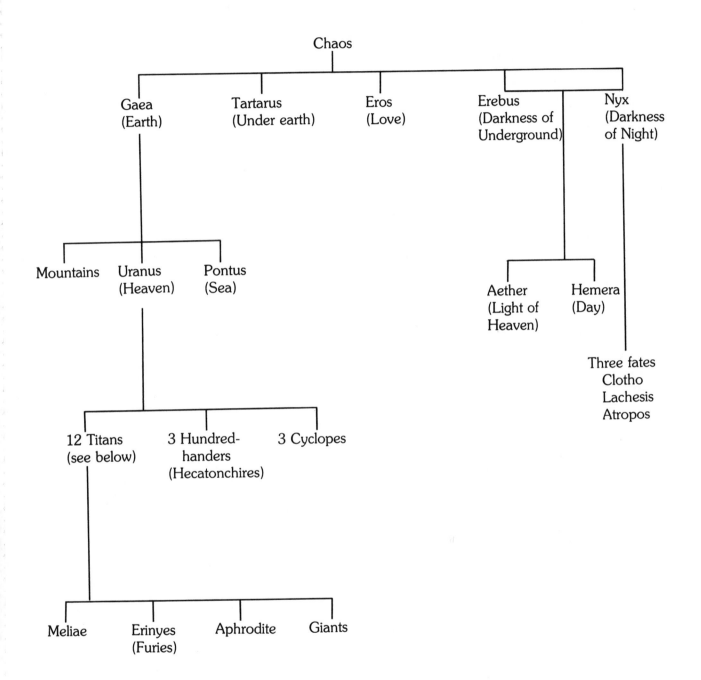

APPENDIX B

Genealogy of the House of Atreus

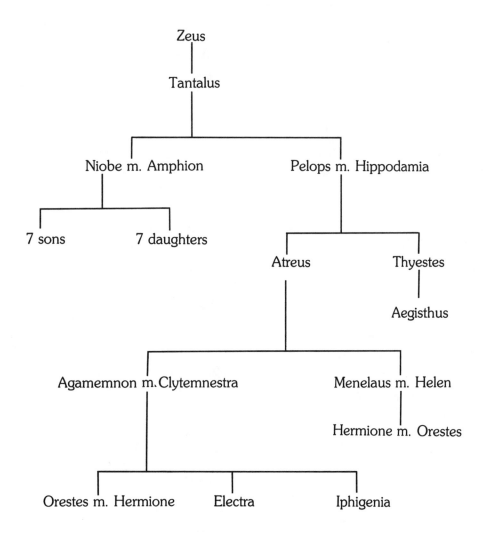

BIBLIOGRAPHY

Asimov, Isaac. *Words from the Myths.* New York: New American Library (Signet), 1969.

Bullfinch, Thomas. *Bullfinch's Mythology.* New York: Avenal Books, 1978.

Carpenter, Thomas H. and Gula, Robert J. *Mythology.* Wellesley Hills: Independent School Press, 1977.

Durrell, Lawrence. *The Greek Islands.* New York: Penguin, 1980.

Frazer, Sir James George. *The Golden Bough.* New York: MacMillan, 1963.

Grant, Michael. *The Birth of Western Civilization.* New York: McGraw-Hill, 1964.

Graves, Robert. *Greek Gods and Heroes.* Garden City: Doubleday (Dell), 1978.

Hamilton, Edith. *Mythology.* New York: New American Library (Mentor), 1969.

Hendricks, Rhoda A. *Classical Gods and Heroes.* New York: William Morrow & Company, Inc., 1974.

Herzberg, Max J. *Myths and Their Meaning.* Boston: Allyn and Bacon, 1960.

Lewis, Richard. *Muse of the Round Sky.* New York: Simon and Schuster, 1969.

Patrick, Richard. *Greek Mythology.* New York: Crescent (Crown), 1972.

Pinsent, John. *Greek Mythology.* New York: Hamlyn, 1973.

Rosenberg, Donna and Baker, Sorelle. *Mythology and You.* Skokie: National Textbook Company, 1981.

Rouse, W.H.D. *Gods, Heroes and Men of Ancient Greece.* New York: New American Library (Mentor), 1957.

Scherer, Margaret R. *Myths of Greece and Rome.* New York: Metropolitan Museum of Art, 1960.

Taylor, William M. *Athenian Odyssey.* Corte Madera: Omega Books, 1977.

Watts, A.C. *Metamorphoses of Ovid.* San Francisco: North Point Press, 1980.

Glossary of Names

A

Absyrtis—the brother of Medea

Achaeans—Homer's name for Greeks

Achilles—hero of the Trojan War

Acrisius—Perseus' grandfather and Danae's father

Acropolis—the upper fortified part of an ancient Greek city

Aegean Sea—sea arm of the Mediterranean between Asia Minor and Greece; named after King Aegeus

Aegeus—father of Theseus; King of Athens

aegis—shield, associated with Zeus and Athena

Aegisthus—Clytemnestra's lover; killed by Orestes

Aeolus—god of the Winds; tried to help Odysseus

Aerope—wife of Atreus

Aeschylus—one of three greatest Greek tragic dramatists

Aetes—King of Colchis; father of Medea

Agamemnon—ruler of Mycenae; brother of Menelaus

Agave—follower of Dionysus; mother of Pentheus

Aiaia—Circe's island

Amazons—women warriors

Amphion—husband of Niobe and a famous musician

Amphitrite—wife of Poseidon

Andromache—Queen of Troy; mother of Paris

Andromeda—Ethiopian princess who married Perseus

Antigone—daughter of Oedipus and Jocasta

Aphrodite (Venus)—goddess of Love and Beauty

Apollo—god of Music, Healing, Light

Apollodorus—Greek writer, second century B.C.

Apples of Hespirides (golden)—object of Heracles' 11th labor

Arachne—mortal girl turned to a spider by Athena

Arcady—Greek region associated with Pan

Ares (Mars)—god of War

Argo—Jason's ship; used in the quest for the Golden Fleece

Argonauts—Jason's sailors

Argos—builder of Argo

Argus—giant with 100 eyes who guarded Io

Ariadne—daughter of King Minos of Crete

Aristophanes—greatest Greek writer of comedy

Artemis (Diana)—virgin goddess of the hunt

Asclepius—son of Apollo; god of Medicine

Atalanta—athletic girl; turned to lion

Athena (Minerva)—goddess of Wisdom

Atlas—Titan son of Iapetus

Atreus—father of Agamemnon and Menelaus

Atropos (Morta)—one of the Moirae (Three Fates); cut the thread of life

Augean Stables—connected with Heracles' 5th labor

Aulis—port of embarcation for Trojan War

Aurora—Roman goddess of the Dawn

B

Bacchantes—women who wildly followed Dionysus

Bacchus—another name for Dionysus, god of Wine

Baucis—faithful wife of Philemon

Bellerophon—owner of Pegasus

Bosphorus—passage between Asia and Europe; named for Io

C

caduceus—the staff of Hermes; also associated with Asclepius

Calliope—Muse of epic poetry; daughter of Zeus and Mnemosne

Calypso—Sea nymph; kept Odysseus on Ogygia for seven years

Cassandra—Princess of Troy; mistress of Agamemnon

Centaurs—mythical creatures, half-man and half-horse

Cerberus—three-headed dog who guarded the entrance to the Underworld

Ceres—Roman name for Demeter

Chaos—the void before Creation

Charon—the old man who ferried people to the Underworld

Charybdis—deadly whirlpool, facing the sea monster Scylla

Chiron—a wise centaur

Circe—beautiful sorceress who turned men to swine

Clio—Muse of History

Clotho—one of the Moirae (Three Fates); spun the cloth of life

Clymene—mother of Phaethon

Clytemnestra—wife of Agamemnon

Cnossus—King Minos' palace on Crete

Coeus—Titan father of Leto, thus grandfather of Apollo and Artemis

Colchis—kingdom of the Golden Fleece

Corinth—kingdom associated with Jason and Medea

Creon—regent of Thebes; Oedipus' uncle and brother-in-law

Crete—largest island in Greece

Cronus—father of Zeus; husband of Rhea

Cupid—Roman name for Eros

Cybele—deity associated with Rhea; had a lion-driven chariot

Cyclopes—monsters with only one eye; sons of Gaea and Uranus

Cyprus—island of Aphrodite

Cythera—island associated with Aphrodite

D

Daedalus—architect of the labyrinth; father of Icarus

Danae—mother of Perseus

Daphne—loved by Apollo; turned to laurel

Deianera—wife of Heracles

Delos—birthplace of Apollo and Artemis

Delphi—site of shrine sacred to Apollo

Demeter (Ceres)—goddess of Corn

Demophoön—baby Demeter intended to make immortal

Dermos (Terror)—one of Ares' helpers

Deucalion—husband of Pyrhha and son of Prometheus

Diana—Roman name for Artemis

Dictys—rescuer of Perseus and Danae
Diomedes—friend of Odysseus; helped steal the Palladium
Dione—mother of Aphrodite, according to one version
Dionysus (Bacchus)—god of Wine
dolphin—associated with Apollo and Delphi
dove—bird associated with Aphrodite

E
Echo—nymph who loved Narcissus
Electra—daughter of Agamemnon and Clytemnestra
Eleusinian Mysteries—rites associated with the worship of Demeter at Eleusis
Elysian Fields—heaven for heroes
Endymion—youth beloved by Selene
Epimetheus—"afterthought"; brother of Prometheus; son of Iapetus
Erato—Muse of Love Poetry
Erinyes—"the kindly ones"; another name for the Furies
Eris—goddess of Discord; caused the Trojan War
Eros (Cupid)—god of Love; son of Aphrodite
Euripides—one of three greatest Greek tragic dramatists
Europa—maiden kidnapped by Zeus when disguised as a bull
Eurydice—wife of Orpheus
Eurystheus—cousin of Heracles, for whom Heracles performed twelve labors
Euterpe—Muse of Lyric Poetry

F
Fates—see *Moirae*
Fauna—Roman goddess of Animals
Flora—Roman goddess of Plants
Fortuna—Roman goddess of Chance
Furies—women who relentlessly pursued evil-doers

G
Gaea—"Mother Earth"; sister and wife of Uranus
Galatea—the statue loved by Pygmalion
Ganymede—handsome youth who became cup-bearer to the Gods
Glauce—princess murdered by Medea with a poisoned robe
Golden Age—fifth century B.C.
Golden Fleece—Jason's quest
Gorgons—three dreadful women; Medusa is the most famous
Graces—three divinities of festivity and happiness

H
Hades (Pluto)—god of the Underworld
Harpies—evil creatures, part woman, part bird
Hebe—daughter of Zeus and Hera; cup-bearer to the Gods
Hecatonchires—the Hundred-handers; sons of Gaea and Uranus

Hector—King of Troy during the Trojan War; father of Paris
Hecuba—Queen of Troy during the Trojan War; mother of Paris
Helen—wife of Menelaus; ran away with Paris
Helios—Sun God
Hephaestus—smith of the gods
Hera (Juno)—wife and sister of Zeus
Heracles—favorite Greek hero
Hercules—*see Heracles*
Hermes—messenger of the gods
Hermione—daughter of Helen and Menelaus
Hesiod—Greek writer of the eighth century B.C.
Hestia (Vesta)—goddess of the Hearth
Hippolytus—son of Theseus
Hippomenes—lover of Atalanta
Homer—Greek writer of *The Iliad* and *The Odyssey*
Hydra—nine-headed monster killed by Heracles
Hygeia—Roman goddess of Health
Hypnus (Somnus)—god of Sleep

I

Iapetus—Titan father of Prometheus, Epimetheus, and Atlas
Icarus—son of Daedalus
Iliad—Homer's epic about the Trojan War
Ilium—Troy
Io—maiden turned into a heifer by Hera
Ionian Sea—arm of the Mediterranean Sea between Italy and Greece; named for Io
Iphicles—brother of Heracles
Iphigenia—daughter of Agamemnon and Clytemnestra; sacrificed at Aulis
Iris—Hera's pretty messenger; associated with the rainbow
Ismene—daughter of Oedipus and Jocasta; sister of Antigone
Ithaca—rocky island on the west coast of Greece; ruled by Odysseus
Itys—son of Tereus and Procne
Ixion—famous sinner lashed to wheel in Tartarus

J

Janus—two-faced god (Roman)
Jason—adventurer who sought the golden fleece
Jocasta—wife and mother of Oedipus
Jove—Roman name for Zeus
Juno—Roman name for Hera
Jupiter—Roman name for Zeus

K

Kore—another Greek name for Persephone

L

Labyrinth—home of the Minotaur; built by Daedalus
Lachesis—one of the Moirae (Three Fates); measured the thread of life
Laestrygonians—fierce warriors who battled Odysseus and his men
Laius—King of Thebes; father of Oedipus
Laocoon—priest who warned his countrymen of the danger of the Trojan horse
Latona—Roman name for Leto; mother of Apollo and Artemis
laurel—tree sacred to Apollo (see Daphne)
Lethe—the River of Forgetfulness in the Underworld
Leto (Latona)—mother of Apollo and Artemis
Luna—Roman name for Selene
Lycaon—sinner turned into a wolf by Zeus

M

Maenads (Bacchantes)—mad followers of Dionysus
Maia—nymph mother of Hermes
Mars—Roman name for Ares
Medea—wife of Jason
Medusa—gorgon slain by Perseus
Melpomene—Muse of Tragedy
Menelaus—King of Sparta; husband of Helen
Mercury—Roman name for Hermes
Merope—wife of Polybus; foster-mother to Oedipus
Metaneira—wife of Heracles
Metis—Wisdom; mother of Athena, swallowed by Zeus
Midas—King of Phrygia; received the golden touch from Dionysus
Minerva—Roman name for Athena
Minos—King of Crete
Minotaur—half-man and half-bull; slain by Theseus
Mnemosyne—Memory; mother of the Nine Muses
Moirae—the Three Fates
Morpheus—god of Sleep and Dreams
Morta—see *Atropos*
Muses (Nine)—embodiments of the arts
mulberry—tree associated with Pyramus and Thisbe
Mycenae—Agamemnon's kingdom

N

Naiads—water nymphs
Narcissus—young man who fell in love with his reflection
Nausicaa—princess of Scheria; aided Odysseus
Naxos—island where Theseus and Ariadne parted
Nemea, Lion of—captured by Heracles
Nemesis—goddess of Retribution
Neptune—Roman name for Poseidon
Nereids—sea nymphs
Nessus—centaur killed by Heracles
Ninus, Tomb of—meeting place of Pyramus and Thisbe

147

Niobe—proud woman turned to stone
Nymphs—beautiful maidens dwelling in forests, meadows, mountains, and waters
Nyx—Night

O

oak—tree associated with Zeus
Oceanus—Titan who encircled the world
Odysseus—hero of Homer's *The Odyssey*
Oedipus—King of Thebes, who unknowingly killed his father and married his mother
Ogygia—Calypso's island
olive—associated with Athena
Olympians—the twelve deities who lived on Mt. Olympus
Olympus—Mountain home of the Olympians
oracle—a person through whom a deity was believed to speak
Orestes—son of Agamemnon, who killed his mother, Clytemnestra
Orpheus—famous musician; husband of Eurydice
Ovid—Roman writer of *Metamorphoses*
owl—bird associated with Athena

P

Palamedes—Greek warrior who persuaded Odysseus to join the Trojan War
Palladium—statue of Pallas Athena considered a good luck symbol by the Trojans
Pallas Athena—see *Athena*
Pandora—the first woman
Paphos—the son of Pygmalion and Galatea
Paris—Prince of Troy; Helen's lover
Pasiphae—Queen of Crete; mother of the Minotaur
peacock—Hera's attribute
Pegasus—Bellerophon's winged horse
Peleus—father of Achilles
Pelops—son of Tantalus
Penelope—Odysseus' faithful wife
Peneus—father of Daphne; a river god
Pentheus—son of Agave; killed by his mother
Persephone (Proserpina)—daughter of Demeter
Perseus—hero savior of Andromeda and slayer of Medusa
Phaedra—wife of Theseus
Phaethon—son of Helios and Clymene
Phantasus—Roman god of strange dreams
Philemon—kind husband of Baucis
Philoctetes—Heracles' friend
Philomela—sister of Procne; turned into nightingale
Phobos (Fear)—one of Ares' helpers
Phoebe—Titan mother of Leto; grandmother of Apollo
Phoebus Apollo—see *Apollo*
Pindar—Greek poet, sixth century B.C.
Pleasure—the daughter of Cupid and Psyche
Pluto—Roman name for Hades

Polybus—foster-father of Oedipus
Polydectes—wicked king who lusted after Danae
Polyhymnia—Muse of Songs to the Gods
Polyphemus—Cyclops son of Poseidon, tricked by Odysseus
Pomona—Roman goddess of Fruit Trees
Pontus—the Sea; son of Gaea and Uranus
Poseidon (Neptune)—god of the Sea and Horses
Priam—King of Troy; father of Paris
Procne—wife of King Tereus; changed to a swallow
Procrustes—villainous innkeeper killed by Theseus
Prometheus—"forethought"; Titan son of Iapetus; punished by Zeus
Proserpina—Roman name for Persephone
Psyche—heroine of Cupid and Psyche myth
Pygmalion—sculptor who fell in love with his statue
Pyramus—Thisbe's lover
Pyrrha—wife of Deucalion; daughter of Epimetheus
Python—monster killed by Apollo at Delphi

R

Rhadamanthus—son of Europa; judge in Underworld
Rhea—wife of Cronus; mother of Zeus

S

Saturn—Roman name for Cronus
Satyrs—companions of Dionysus
Scylla—six-headed monster, facing the whirlpool Charybdis
Selene—goddess of the Moon
Semele—mortal mother of Dionysus
Silenus—drunken old friend of Dionysus
Sinon—Greek spy who persuaded the Trojans to accept the Trojan horse
Sisyphus—sinner condemned to pushing a heavy stone uphill in Tartarus
Sol—Roman name for Helios
Somnus—Roman god of Sleep
Sophocles—Greek Tragedian, author of *Oedipus,* fifth century B.C.
Sphinx—monster who killed herself when Oedipus answered her riddle
Stymphalion birds—the object of Heracles' sixth labor
Styx—river in the Underworld

T

Tantalus—favorite of the gods; sinned and is eternally hungry and thirsty
Tartarus—worst part of the Underworld
Telemachus—son of Odysseus and Penelope
Tereus—wicked king turned into a lapwing
Terpsichore—Muse of Dance
Tethys—wife and sister of Oceanus
Thalia—Muse of Comedy
Thebes—Oedipus' city

Themis—goddess of Justice
Theseus—hero of Athens; slayer of the Minotaur
Thetis—mother of Achilles
Thisbe—Pyramus' sweetheart
Thracian women—mad followers of Dionysus
Thyestes—son of Pelops; father of Aegisthus
thyrsus—staff of Dionysus
Tiresias—blind prophet
Tiryns—city ruled by Perseus; near Mycenae; home of Heracles' cousin Eurystheus
Titans—twelve offspring of Gaea and Uranus
Triton—son of Poseidon and Amphitrite
Troezen—birthplace of Theseus
Troy—site of Trojan War; discovered by H. Schliemann in 1871

U

Ulysses—Roman name for Odysseus
Underworld—region under the Earth ruled by Hades
Urania—Muse of Astronomy
Uranus—Heaven; brother and husband of Gaea

V

Venus—Roman name for Aphrodite
Vesta—Roman name for Hestia
Virgil—famous Roman writer, first century B.C.
Voluptus—Roman goddess of Pleasure
Vulcan—Roman name for Hephaestus
vulture—bird associated with Ares

Z

Zephyrus—the west wind
Zeus (Jupiter; Jove)—King of the Gods

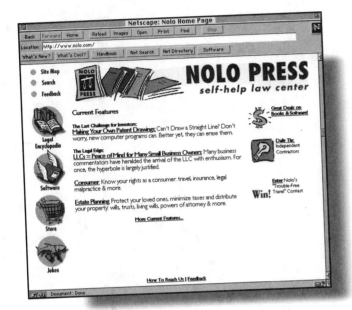

SEVENTH EDITION

How to File for
BANKRUPTCY

BY ATTORNEYS STEPHEN ELIAS,
ALBIN RENAUER & ROBIN LEONARD

16496

NOLO PRESS BERKELEY

Your Responsibility When Using a Self-Help Law Book

We've done our best to give you useful and accurate information in this book. But laws and procedures change frequently and are subject to differing interpretations. If you want legal advice backed by a guarantee, see a lawyer. If you use this book, it's your responsibility to make sure that the facts and general advice contained in it are applicable to your situation.

Keeping Up to Date

To keep its books up to date, Nolo Press issues new printings and new editions periodically. New printings reflect minor legal changes and technical corrections. New editions contain major legal changes, major text additions or major reorganizations. To find out if a later printing or edition of any Nolo book is available, call Nolo Press at 510-549-1976 or check the catalog in the *Nolo News,* our quarterly newspaper. You can also contact us on the Internet at www.nolo.com.

To stay current, follow the "Update" service in the *Nolo News.* You can get a free one-year subscription by sending us the registration card in the back of the book. In another effort to help you use Nolo's latest materials, we offer a 25% discount off the purchase of the new edition your Nolo book when you turn in the cover of an earlier edition. (See the "Special Upgrade Offer" in the back of the book.)

This book was last revised in: **January 1998**.

Seventh Edition	JANUARY 1998
Illustrations	MARI STEIN
Cover Design	TONI IHARA
Book Design	TERRI HEARSH
Production	NANCY ERB
Proofreading	ROBERT WELLS
Index	SAYRE VAN YOUNG
Printing	CUSTOM PRINTING COMPANY

Elias, Stephen.
   How to file for bankruptcy / by Stephen Elias, Albin Renauer &
Robin Leonard. — 7th ed.
     p.   cm.
  Includes index.
  ISBN 0-87337-420-7
  1. Bankruptcy—United States—Popular works.   I. Renauer, Albin.
II. Leonard, Robin.   III. Title
KF1524.6.E4 1997
346.7307'8—dc21
                                     97-30142
                                        CIP

Quantity sales: For information on bulk purchases or corporate premium sales, please contact the Special Sales department. For academic sales or textbook adoptions, ask for Academic Sales. 800-955-4775, Nolo Press, Inc., 950 Parker St., Berkeley, CA, 94710.

Acknowledgments

The authors gratefully acknowledge the following people for their support and creative contributions.

Ralph "Jake" Warner, founder and owner of Nolo Press. Without Jake's willingness to produce quality products no matter what the cost, this book would never have been written.

Mary Randolph, Senior Legal Editor at Nolo Press. Mary's cheerful and tireless editing turned a camel designed by a committee into a world-class race horse.

Terri Hearsh, Toni Ihara, Amy Ihara and Nancy Erb, superb graphic designers and wonderful people who, along with the rest of their department, produce the best looking books in the world, in our humble opinion.

Lisa Goldoftas, former editor at Nolo Press.

Marguerite Kirk, a bankruptcy attorney in Fort Worth, Texas. Marguerite focuses on helping clients deal with the emotional trauma of bankruptcy.

Susan Levinkind, formerly a Massachusetts bankruptcy lawyer, who now lives in California. Susan is co-author of Nolo's *Legal Research: How to Find and Understand the Law* and is law librarian for the Santa Clara County Municipal Court.

Mike Mansel of Insurance Associates, Herb Kristal, Kim Wislee at National Underwriter Co., Jess Glidewell at Equitable Life Insurance Company in San Francisco, Les Peat, Director of Vermont Law School Law Library, and Bobbe Powers, bankruptcy specialist in Bakersfield.

Virginia Simons of TLC Typing Services 805-322-3742. TLC has helped people do their own bankruptcies since 1981.

Jim Snyder of Legal Help, SR 3, Box 4250-31, Tehachapi, California 93561, 805-821-6740. Jim is a bankruptcy expert who educated the authors about what this book should include.

We would also like to acknowledge A. Richard Anton for his invaluable help in the development of this book. Richard died in October of 1991.

Dedications

To mom and dad, who gave me what money can't buy, and to whom I'm forever indebted.

—A.R.

To everyone who uses this and other Nolo books, for their courage and for having the good sense to take the law into their own hands.

—S. R. E., R. L. and A. R.

Table of Contents

4 Handling Your Case in Court

5 Life After Bankruptcy

6 Your House

7 Secured Debts

8 Nondischargeable Debts

9 Help Beyond the Book

Appendices

A1 Appendix 1: State and Federal Exemption Tables

A2 Appendix 2: Exemption Glossary

A3 Appendix 3: Addresses of Bankruptcy Courts

A4 Appendix 4: Tear-Out Forms

I

How to Use This Book

This book shows you how to file for bankruptcy, which will cancel your debts and let you start fresh. Usually, this type of bankruptcy (known as Chapter 7 bankruptcy) is a routine process that requires no special courtroom or analytical skills. All you must do is pay careful attention to the instructions in this book and use common sense. Usually, you won't need to hire a lawyer to handle your case.

There are several ways to use this book. The more assets you own and debts you owe, and the more concerned you are with keeping property through the bankruptcy process, the more you'll want to read. But if you have few assets and want to put your indebtedness behind you as quickly as possible, reading two chapters and referring to two appendices at the back of the book should do the job. (See Section B, below.)

A. Quick Answers to Your Bankruptcy Concerns

This section is designed to focus your attention on some preliminary concerns you may want to address before deciding to file for Chapter 7 bankruptcy. If you've already decided to file because of advice you've been given or material you've read, proceed directly to Ch. 3, where we tell you how to fill in and file the bankruptcy forms.

- **I need help in deciding whether my economic situation justifies filing a Chapter 7 bankruptcy.**

    Read Ch. 1, *Should You File for Chapter 7 Bankruptcy*, Sections B and D.

- **I want an overview of Chapter 7 bankruptcy.**

    Read Ch. 1, *Should You File for Chapter 7 Bankruptcy*, Section A.

- **I want information on Chapter 13 bankruptcy.**

    Read Ch. 1, *Should You File for Chapter 7 Bankruptcy*, Section E.4.

- **I want information on the most common alternatives to filing for bankruptcy.**

    Read Ch. 1, *Should You File for Chapter 7 Bankruptcy*, Section E.

- **I want to know which items of property I own are subject to the bankruptcy court's control when I file for Chapter 7 bankruptcy.**

    Read Ch. 2, *Your Property and Bankruptcy*, Section A.

- **I want to know what will happen to my car if I file for bankruptcy.**

    If it is all paid off, read Ch. 2, *Your Property and Bankruptcy*, Section B.6.

    If you still owe money on the car, read Ch. 7, *Secured Debts*, Section B.

- **I want to know what will happen to my house if I file for bankruptcy.**

    Read Ch. 6, *Your House*, Sections A and C.

- **I want to know what property I am at risk of losing if I file for bankruptcy.**

    Read Ch. 2, *Your Property and Bankruptcy*, Section B.6, and Appendix 1.

- **I want information on how to protect property I might lose in bankruptcy.**

    Read Ch. 2, *Your Property and Bankruptcy*, Section C.

- **I want to know which of my debts cannot be canceled (discharged) in Chapter 7 bankruptcy.**

    Read Ch. 8, *Non-Dischargeable Debts*, Section A.

- **I specifically want to know if my student loan can be canceled (discharged) in Chapter 7 bankruptcy.**

    Read Ch. 8, *Non-Dischargeable Debts*, Section B.2.

- **I specifically want to know if my tax debt can be canceled (discharged) in Chapter 7 bankruptcy.**

    Read Ch. 8, *Non-Dischargeable Debts*, Section B.3.

- **I want to know whether or not I need an attorney to file for Chapter 7 bankruptcy.**

    Read Section D, below.

- **I have a cosigner for a debt and want to know the effect that filing for Chapter 7 bankruptcy will have on that person.**

    Read Ch. 1, *Should You File for Chapter 7 Bankruptcy*, Section B.3.

- **I want to know what will happen in a Chapter 7 bankruptcy if I give away property to friends or relatives just before filing or I don't list certain property on my bankruptcy papers.**

    Read Ch. 2, *Your Property and Bankruptcy*, Section A.3, and Ch. 3, *Filling In and Filing the Bankruptcy Forms*, Section D.

- **I want information on how a Chapter 7 bankruptcy will affect debts owed because of a divorce.**

  Read Ch. 8, *Non-Dischargeable Debts*, Sections B.4 and C.4.

B. What This Book Doesn't Cover

This book explains routine bankruptcy procedures. If your situation is complicated, you may need help beyond this book. (See Ch. 9, *Help Beyond the Book*.) This book doesn't cover the following situations:

- **Bankruptcies for people in business partnerships**

  If you're a partner in a business, filing for personal (not business) bankruptcy will affect your business; we don't address that situation in this book.

- **Bankruptcies for people who own stock in privately held corporations**

  If you own stock in a privately held corporation, filing for bankruptcy could affect the corporation's legal and tax status. This book doesn't cover those bankruptcies.

- **Business reorganizations**

  This book doesn't cover procedures under Chapter 11 of the bankruptcy laws, which allow a business to continue operating while paying off all or a portion of its debts under court supervision.

- **Farm reorganizations**

  A special set of bankruptcy statutes called Chapter 12 lets farmers continue farming while paying off their debts over time. This book doesn't cover Chapter 12 bankruptcies or the sometimes complicated question of whether a farmer is better off filing for a Chapter 7 or a Chapter 12 bankruptcy. If you're a farmer, check with a bankruptcy professional. If you decide to file for Chapter 7 bankruptcy, this book should do the job.

- **Chapter 13 bankruptcies (repayment plans)**

  Chapter 13 allows people to repay a portion of their debts, with court supervision, over a three- to five-year period. This book doesn't tell you how to file a Chapter 13 bankruptcy. It does, however, help you decide whether Chapter 7 bankruptcy (the kind covered by this book) or Chapter 13 is better for you. Most people opt for Chapter 7. Some people file for Chapter 13, find they are unable to complete the three- or five-year plan, and then ask the court to convert the case to Chapter 7.

C. Icons

We do our best to steer you toward the parts of the book you need and away from the parts that don't apply.

 When you see the "fast track" icon, you'll be alerted to a chance to skip some material you may not need to read.

 Information following this icon is for married couples only.

 This icon cautions you about potential problems.

Suggested references for additional information follow this icon.

D. Getting Professional Help

If you need help with your bankruptcy, get it. Getting help may be as simple as using a bankruptcy typing service to help you prepare and file your forms. It may involve consulting a bankruptcy attorney for advice or representation. Or it may involve hitting the law library and figuring things out for yourself. We do our best to point out where you may need assistance, although only you can judge when you're in over your head. Ch. 9, *Help Beyond the Book*, discusses how to find the kind of help you need.

> ### GEOGRAPHICAL VARIATION IN BANKRUPTCY LAW
>
> Bankruptcy law comes from the federal Congress and is meant to be uniform across the country. But when disputes arise about the bankruptcy laws, bankruptcy courts must make the decisions—and they don't all decide the issues in the same way. The result is that bankruptcy law and practice vary significantly from court to court and from region to region. This book can't possibly address every variation. When you need a bankruptcy professional, find someone who's familiar with your local bankruptcy court.

Here are some common problems that may require professional help:

- You want to hold on to a house or motor vehicle.

- You want to discharge (wipe out) a student loan, income taxes or a debt arising from your intoxicated driving, a marital settlement agreement or divorce decree, your fraudulent behavior, an intentional tort (such as libel, slander, battery or intentionally causing another person emotional harm).
- You have debts such as back child support and court fines, and could be imprisoned or fined if you don't pay them.
- A creditor files an objection to the discharge of a large debt that you believe should be discharged.
- You've recently given away or sold property because you wanted to hide it from the bankruptcy court.
- You want help negotiating with a creditor or the bankruptcy court, and the amount involved justifies hiring a bankruptcy professional to assist you.

 BANKRUPTCY LAWS MAY CHANGE

On October 20, 1997, the National Bankruptcy Review Commission (NBRC) submitted a 1,300-page report to Congress suggesting 172 changes to the U.S. Bankruptcy Code. The NBRC worked for two years reviewing every provision of the Code, hearing testimony and receiving input from thousands of people and organizations who have something to say about the U.S. bankruptcy system.

The NBRC's work and report have not been without controversy. The commission itself was deeply divided on its consumer recommendations. Many creditors believe the suggestions don't do enough to stem the current tide of consumer filings, which have been over one million for the second consecutive year. The main response to the NBRC's report has been a swift introduction of bills into the Congress. These bills cover a wide range of issues, but essentially would make it more difficult for a consumer to file for bankruptcy.

To find out if any of these bills have become law, please visit Nolo's Web site at www.nolo.com. ■

Should You File for Chapter 7 Bankruptcy?

Skip Ahead

If you've already decided to file for bankruptcy, skip ahead to Ch. 2, *Your Property and Bankruptcy*.

Americans learn almost from birth that it's a good thing to buy all sorts of goods and services. A highly paid army of persuaders surrounds us with thousands of seductive messages each day that all say "buy, buy, buy." Easily available credit makes living beyond one's means easy and resisting the siren sounds of the advertisers difficult. But we're also told that if we fail to pay for it all right on time, we're miserable deadbeats. In short, much of American economic life is built on a contradiction.

If for some reason, such as illness, loss of work or just plain bad planning, our ability to pay for the goods or services we need is interrupted, fear and guilt are often our first feelings. We may even feel we've fundamentally failed as human beings.

Nonsense. There's lots more to life than an A+ credit rating, and lots of better things to feel guilty about than the failure to pay for a snowmobile or a summer vacation on time. The importance we have for our families, friends and neighbors should never be forgotten. Nor should the fact that the American economy is based on consumer debt. In the age of $50-billion bailouts for poorly managed financial institutions, you really shouldn't feel too guilt-ridden about the debts you've run up. Remember that large creditors expect defaults and bankruptcies and treat them as a cost of doing business. The reason so many banks issue credit cards is that it is a very profitable business, even with so many bankruptcies.

Fortunately, for thousands of years it's been recognized that debts can get the better of even the most conscientious among us. From Biblical times to the present, sane societies have discouraged debtors from falling on their swords and have provided sensible ways for debt-oppressed people to start new economic lives. In the United States, this is done through bankruptcy.

Bankruptcy is a truly worthy part of our legal system, based as it is on forgiveness rather than retribution. Certainly, it helps keep families together, reduces suicide and keeps the ranks of the homeless from growing even larger.

If you suddenly find yourself without a job, socked with huge, unexpected medical bills you can't pay or simply snowed under by an impossible debt burden, bankruptcy provides a chance for a fresh start and a renewed positive outlook on life.

Bankruptcy can also have its down sides—economically, emotionally and in terms of your future credit rating. So before you race into bankruptcy court, take some time to understand what bankruptcy is all about and what your alternatives are.

A. An Overview of Chapter 7 Bankruptcy

This book explains how to file for "Chapter 7" bankruptcy. Its name comes from the chapter of the federal statutes (the Bankruptcy Code) that contains the bankruptcy law. Chapter 7 bankruptcy is sometimes called "straight" bankruptcy. This bankruptcy cancels most of your debts; in exchange, you might have to surrender some of your property.

The whole Chapter 7 bankruptcy process takes about three to six months, costs $130 in filing fees and $45 in administrative fees, and commonly requires only one trip to the courthouse.

To file for bankruptcy, you fill out a two-page petition and several other forms. Then you file the petition and forms with the bankruptcy court in your area. Basically, the forms ask you to describe:

- your property
- your current income and its sources
- your current monthly living expenses
- your debts
- property you claim the law allows you to keep through the bankruptcy process (exempt property)
- property you owned and money you spent during the previous two years, and
- property you sold or gave away during the previous two years.

WHAT CAN YOU KEEP IF YOU FILE FOR BANKRUPTCY?

If you're thinking about bankruptcy, you probably want to know what property you'll be able to keep if you file. Most states let you keep clothing, household furnishings, Social Security payments you haven't spent and other basic items. These items are called "exempt property," and the laws that specify what property is exempt are called "exemption laws." Ch. 2, *Your Property and Bankruptcy,* explains exemptions in more detail, and Appendix 1 contains a list of exempt property for each state.

Filing for bankruptcy puts into effect something called the "automatic stay." The automatic stay immediately stops your creditors from trying to collect what you owe them. So, at least temporarily, creditors cannot legally grab (garnish) your wages, empty your bank account, go after your car, house or other property, or cut off your utility service or welfare benefits.

Until your bankruptcy case ends, your financial problems are in the hands of the bankruptcy court. It assumes legal control of the property you own (except your exempt property, which is yours to keep) and the debts you owe as of the date you file. Nothing can be sold or paid without the court's consent. You have control, however, with a few exceptions, of property and income you acquire after you file for bankruptcy.

The court exercises its control through a court-appointed person called a "bankruptcy trustee." The trustee is mostly interested in what you own and what property you claim as exempt. This is because the trustee's primary duty is to see that your creditors are paid as much as possible on what you owe them. And the more assets the trustee recovers for creditors, the more the trustee is paid.

The trustee goes through the papers you file and asks you questions at a short hearing, called the "creditors' meeting," which you must attend. Creditors may attend, too, but rarely do.

After this meeting, the trustee collects the property that can be taken from you (your nonexempt property) to be sold to pay your creditors. You can surrender the property to the trustee, pay the trustee its fair market value or, if the trustee agrees, swap some exempt property of equal value for the nonexempt property. If the property isn't worth very much or would be cumbersome for the trustee to sell, the trustee can "abandon" the property—which means that you get to keep it. Very few people actually lose property in bankruptcy.

If you've pledged property as collateral for a loan, the loan is called a secured debt. The most common examples of collateral are houses and motor vehicles. In most cases, you'll either have to surrender the collateral to the creditor or make arrangements to pay for it during or after bankruptcy. (Ch. 7, *Secured Debts*, explains how to do this.) If a creditor has recorded a lien against your property, that debt is also secured. You may be able to wipe out the lien in bankruptcy. (This is explained in Ch. 7.)

If you're a party to a contract or lease, and you or the other party still has obligations under it, the trustee may cancel it unless the contract will produce assets for the creditors. If it's canceled, you and the other party to the contract are cut loose from any contractual obligations.

If, after you file for bankruptcy, you change your mind, you can ask the court to dismiss your case. As a general rule, a court will dismiss a Chapter 7 bankruptcy case as long as the dismissal won't harm the creditors. (See Ch. 4,

Handling Your Case in Court, Section E.) Usually, you can file again if you want to, although you may have to wait 180 days. (See Section B.1, below.)

At the end of the bankruptcy process, most of your debts are wiped out (discharged) by the court. You no longer legally owe your creditors. You can't file for Chapter 7 bankruptcy again for another six years from the date of your filing.

If you're deeply in debt, bankruptcy may seem like a magic wand. But there are drawbacks. First, bankruptcy can get intrusive. You are required to disclose your financial activities during the previous two years, as well as your current property holdings, looking for anything of value that the law allows to be taken and sold to pay your creditors. Having your property and previous activities made public in this way can be depressing, especially if you're forced to surrender property you badly want to keep. And to people who would rather struggle along under mountains of debt than acquire the label of bankrupt, bankruptcy represents a substantial failure.

B. When Chapter 7 Bankruptcy May Not Help You

Filing for Chapter 7 bankruptcy is one way to solve debt problems—but, it's not the only way. In several common situations, bankruptcy is either unwise or legally impossible.

1. You Previously Received a Bankruptcy Discharge

You cannot file for Chapter 7 bankruptcy if you obtained a discharge of your debts under Chapter 7 or Chapter 13 in a case begun within the past six years. (11 U.S.C. § 727.) If, however, you obtained a Chapter 13 discharge in good faith after paying at least 70% of your unsecured debts, the six-year bar does not apply. The six-year period runs from the date you filed for the earlier bankruptcy, not the date you received your discharge.

Chapter 13 bankruptcy has no such restriction; you can file for it at any time. So if you are barred from filing Chapter 7, and you want to file for bankruptcy quickly (for instance, to stop creditors' collection efforts), Chapter 13 is an option if you have enough income to make payments toward your debts. (See Section E, below.)

Also, you cannot file for Chapter 7 bankruptcy if a previous Chapter 7 or Chapter 13 case was dismissed within the past 180 days because:

- you violated a court order, or
- you requested the dismissal after a creditor asked for relief from the automatic stay.

2. You Want to Stop Bill Collector Abuse and Harassment

Usually, it isn't necessary to file for bankruptcy just to get annoying collection agencies off your back. Under federal law, they cannot threaten you, lie about what they can do to you or invade your privacy. Under this law, you can also legally force collection agencies to stop phoning or writing you simply by demanding that they stop, even if you owe them a bundle and can't pay a cent.

Creditors collecting their own debts (except those that create their own collection agencies and operate them under a different name) are not governed by this law. While they cannot harass you, they don't have to stop contacting you because you write them a letter demanding that they leave you alone.

> **Help When Debt Collectors Call**
> For information on your rights when creditors and collection agencies try to collect from you, see *Money Troubles: Legal Strategies to Cope With Your Debts*, by Robin Leonard (Nolo Press).

3. A Friend or Relative Cosigned a Loan

A friend, relative or anyone else who cosigns a loan or otherwise takes on a joint obligation with you can be held wholly responsible for the debt if you can't pay it. If you file for Chapter 7 bankruptcy, you will no longer be liable for the debt, but the cosigner will be left on the hook. If you don't want to subject a cosigner to this liability, explore one of the alternatives outlined in Section E, below. By arranging to pay the debt over time, you can keep creditors from going after the cosigner for payment.

4. You Could Pay Your Debts Over Three to Five Years

A bankruptcy judge who decides that you have enough assets or income to repay your debts can dismiss your Chapter 7 bankruptcy petition or convert your case to a Chapter 13 bankruptcy. To figure out if you have enough property to pay what you owe, see Ch. 2, *Your Property and Bankruptcy*, Section B.6.b. If the value of your nonexempt property exceeds the amount of your debt (Section D, below), you're at risk of having your case dismissed or converted if you file.

A judge may seriously consider dismissing or converting your case if all of the following are true:

- a substantial majority of your debts are consumer (not business) debts
- you have an adequate and steady income or other property, and
- with little modification of lifestyle, you could pay off all or most of your debts over three to five years.

Even if a bankruptcy judge wouldn't throw out your case, if you can repay your debts over time you may be better off negotiating with your creditors or filing for Chapter 13 bankruptcy than filing for Chapter 7 bankruptcy.

5. You Want to Prevent Seizure of Wages or Property

You may not need to file for bankruptcy to keep creditors from seizing all your property and wages.

Normally, a creditor's only legal means of collecting a debt is to sue you, win a court judgment and then try to collect the amount of the judgment out of your property and income. A lot of your property, however, including food, clothing, personal effects and furnishings, is probably protected by law (exempt) from being taken to pay the judgment. And, quite likely, your nonexempt property is not worth enough to tempt a creditor to go after it, as the costs of seizure and sale can be quite high.

Creditors usually first go after your wages and other income. Here too, however, laws protect you. Only 25% of your net wages can be taken to satisfy a court judgment (up to 50% for child support and alimony). And often, you can keep more than 75% of your wages if you can demonstrate that you need the extra amount to support yourself and your family. Income from a pension or other retirement benefit is usually treated like wages. Creditors cannot touch public benefits such as welfare, unemployment insurance, disability insurance or Social Security.

6. You Defrauded Your Creditors

Bankruptcy is geared towards the honest debtor who got in too deep and needs the help of the bankruptcy court to get a fresh start. A bankruptcy court does not want to help someone who has played fast and loose with creditors or tries to do so with the bankruptcy court.

Certain activities are red flags to the courts and trustees. If you have engaged in any of them during the past year, do not file for bankruptcy until you consult a bankruptcy lawyer. These no-nos are:

- unloading assets to your friends or relatives to hide them from creditors or from the bankruptcy court (Ch. 2, *Your Property and Bankruptcy,* shows you how to legally convert nonexempt property to exempt property)
- incurring debts for non-necessities when you were clearly broke
- concealing property or money from your spouse during a divorce proceeding, and
- lying about your income or debts on a credit application.

For more information on creditor claims of fraud, see Ch. 4, *Handling Your Case in Court,* Section D.3.

7. You Recently Incurred Debts for Luxuries

If you've recently run up large debts for a vacation, hobby or entertainment, filing for bankruptcy probably won't help you. Most luxury debts incurred just before filing are not dischargeable if the creditor objects. And running up unnecessary debts shortly before filing casts a suspicion of fraud over your entire bankruptcy case.

Last-minute debts presumed to be nondischargeable include:

- debts of $1,000 or more to any one creditor for luxury goods or services made within 60 days before filing, and
- debts for cash advances in excess of $1,000 obtained within 60 days of filing for bankruptcy

To discharge luxury debts, you will have to prove that extraordinary circumstances required you to make the charges and that you really weren't trying to put one over on your creditors. It's an uphill job. Judges often assume that people who incur last-minute charges for luxuries were on a final buying binge before going under and had no intention of paying.

Creditors, too, are getting aggressive about crying "fraud." Visa and MasterCard lose an estimated $1.5 billion a year from people who file for bankruptcy, and Visa claims that 30% to 40% of the losses come from fraudulent debts. In an effort to minimize the number of last-minute debts that may be discharged, Visa challenges nearly one-half of all bankruptcy cases filed by people who made large luxury charges or cash advances shortly before filing for bankruptcy.

8. You Expect Debts for Necessities

If you expect to incur more debts for necessities, you should consider delaying filing for bankruptcy. Most debts you incur before you file will be discharged, but debts incurred after you file will not. Waiting until after you incur these debts to file will let you include them in your bankruptcy petition.

A go-slow approach works best in the case of debts for necessities, such as additional medical costs you anticipate because of an existing illness, the cost of buying your children new school clothes or substantial heating costs during the upcoming winter.

C. Emergency Filings

As mentioned above, when you file for bankruptcy, the automatic stay immediately stops any lawsuit filed against you and virtually all actions against your property by a creditor, collection agency or government entity. Especially if you are at risk of being evicted or foreclosed on, being found in contempt for failure to pay child support or losing such basic resources as utility services, welfare or unemployment benefits, your driver's license or your job (because of a raft of wage garnishments), the automatic stay may provide a powerful reason for filing for bankruptcy.

Here is how the automatic stay affects some common emergencies:

- **Utility disconnections.** If you're behind on a utility bill and the company is threatening to disconnect your water, electric, gas or telephone service, the automatic stay will prevent the disconnection for at least 20 days. Bankruptcy will probably discharge the past due debts for utility service. Although the amount of a utility bill itself rarely justifies a bankruptcy filing, preventing electrical service cutoff in January in New England might be justification enough.
- **Foreclosure.** If your home mortgage is being foreclosed on, the automatic stay temporarily stops the proceedings, but the creditor will often be able to proceed with the foreclosure sooner or later. If you are facing foreclosure, Chapter 13 bankruptcy is always a better remedy than Chapter 7 bankruptcy, if you want to keep your house. (See Section E.4, below.)

- **Eviction.** If you are being evicted from your home, the automatic stay can usually buy you a few days or a few weeks. But if the landlord asks the court to lift the stay and let the eviction proceed—which landlords usually do—the court will probably agree, reasoning that eviction won't affect the bankruptcy. Despite the attractiveness of even a temporary delay, it is seldom a good idea to file for bankruptcy solely because you're being evicted. You'll probably be better off looking for a new place to live or fighting the eviction in state court, if you have a defense.

- **Enforcement of child support or alimony.** If you owe child support or alimony, bankruptcy will not interrupt your obligation to make current payments. And the automatic stay does not stop proceedings to establish, modify or collect back support. Also, these debts will survive bankruptcy intact and will have to be paid once the case is closed. In Chapter 13 bankruptcy, you can include the back support in your repayment plan.

- **Public benefit overpayments.** If you receive public benefits and were overpaid, normally the agency is entitled to collect the overpayment out of your future checks. The automatic stay prevents this collection; furthermore, the debt (the overpayment you owe) is dischargeable unless the agency convinces the court it resulted from fraud on your part. Whether or not the threatened collection of an overpayment justifies bankruptcy depends on how severely you'll be affected by the proposed reduction in benefits.

- **Loss of driver's license because of liability for damages.** In some states, your driver's license may be suspended until you pay a court judgment for damages resulting from an automobile accident. The automatic stay can prevent this suspension if it hasn't already occurred. If you are absolutely dependent on your ability to drive for your livelihood and family support, keeping your driver's license can be a powerful reason to file for bankruptcy.

- **Multiple wage garnishments.** Although no more than 25% of your wages may be taken to satisfy a court judgment (up to 50% for child support and alimony), many people file for bankruptcy if more than one wage garnishment is threatened. For some people, any loss of income is devastating; also, some employers get angry at the expense and hassle of facilitating a succession of garnishments and take it out on their employees. Although federal law prohibits you from being fired for one garnishment, an employer can fire you for multiple garnishments. (15 U.S.C. § 1674 (a).) Filing for bankruptcy stops garnishments dead in their

tracks. Not only will you take home a full salary, but also you may be able to discharge the debt in bankruptcy.

If the primary reason you file is to get the benefit of the automatic stay, you don't need to file all of your papers at once; you can file just the two-page petition and a mailing list of your creditors. If you don't file the rest of your papers within 15 days, however, the case will be dismissed. Ch. 3, *Filling In and Filing the Bankruptcy Forms*, Section J, explains emergency filings.

D. Does Bankruptcy Make Economic Sense?

If you are inclined to file for Chapter 7 bankruptcy, take a moment to decide whether it makes economic sense. You need to consider two questions:
- Will bankruptcy discharge enough of your debts to make it worth your while?
- Will you have to give up property you desperately want to keep?

Married Couples

If you are married and filing jointly, consider the debts and property of both spouses as you read this section.

Most married couples are better off filing for bankruptcy together. If, however, you are in a relatively new marriage, have not accumulated any joint (marital) property and want to get rid of separate (premarital) debts, you are probably safe filing alone. In addition, you may want to file alone if:
- you live in a community property state (see Ch. 2, Section A.6) and your debts are primarily community in nature (virtually all debts incurred during marriage are considered community)
- your spouse owns separate, valuable property, such as a second home
- you and your spouse own a house in tenancy by the entirety (look at your deed), or
- you and your spouse have separated.

1. Will Bankruptcy Discharge Enough of Your Debts?

Certain categories of debts cannot be discharged in Chapter 7 bankruptcy. These are called nondischargeable debts, and it doesn't make much sense to file for Chapter 7 bankruptcy if your primary goal is to get rid of them. Ch. 8, *Nondischargeable Debts*, covers these debts in detail. For the purpose of deciding whether or not to file for bankruptcy, the main ones are:

- back child support and alimony obligations, and debts considered in the nature of support, such as an obligation to pay attorney's fees for a child support hearing, or an obligation to pay marital debts in lieu of alimony
- student loans that first became due fewer than seven years ago (plus any time you received a deferment or forbearance or were in a previous bankruptcy case)
- court-ordered restitution owed to either a court or a victim and fee imposed by a court to file a case, motion, complaint or appeal
- income taxes less than three years past due, and
- court judgments for injuries or death to someone arising from your intoxicated driving.

The bankruptcy judge may rule any of the following debts nondischargeable if the creditor objects in the bankruptcy court:

- Debts incurred on the basis of fraud, such as lying on a credit application or writing a bad check.
- Debts from willful and malicious injury to another or another's property, including assault, battery, false imprisonment, libel and slander.
- Debts from larceny (theft), breach of trust or embezzlement.
- Debts arising out of a marital settlement agreement or divorce decree (that aren't otherwise automatically nondischargeable as support or alimony), such as credit card debts you agree to pay or payments you owe to an ex-spouse to even up the property division. The court won't let you discharge these debts unless you prove that you need the money for basic support or to continue the operation of a business or that the benefit you'd receive by the discharge outweighs any detriment to your ex-spouse or children.

As a general rule, if more than 50% of your debts are nondischargeable, Chapter 7 bankruptcy's disadvantages probably outweigh the advantages. If you can discharge more than 50% of your debts, however, Chapter 7 bankruptcy may make sense; after your discharge, you should be in a better position than before to pay off the nondischargeable debts.

Even if the bulk of your indebtedness is from debts that are nondischargeable only if the creditor files an objection with the court, it may still make sense to file for bankruptcy and hope your creditors don't object.

Worksheet 1, below, helps you total all of your debts, including your nondischargeable ones. Detailed instructions follow the worksheet, and a tear-out copy is in Appendix 4.

TIPS ON FILLING OUT THE WORKSHEET

- Make several photocopies before you mark it up, in case you need to redo your work.
- Use a pencil or erasable pen.
- Feel free to estimate; you don't need exact numbers.

Column 1: Description of Debt/Name of Creditor. The first column lists common categories of debts to remind you of what you owe. Fill in your specific ones. If you are married, indicate if the debt is owed by the husband (H), wife (W) or jointly (J). Even if you are married and filing alone, list your spouse's debts as well as your own. This will guarantee that your liability, if any, for your spouse's debts will be discharged in your bankruptcy.

Column 2: Total Amount of Debt. Enter the amount of each debt. If you are uncertain, put your best estimate and a question mark. You can figure it out later if it's important.

If you're making payments on a debt, enter the entire amount owed, not the amount you are behind or the amount of your monthly payments. For instance, if you owe $10,000 on a car, make monthly payments of $300, and are three months behind, enter $10,000.

Even if you think you don't owe a particular debt— perhaps because you were billed for something you never received, or a product or service was no good—be sure to include the debt on your worksheet now and on your bankruptcy forms if you file. By listing the debt you are not admitting that you owe it, but you are guaranteeing that if the creditor attempts to collect it after your bankruptcy, you won't have to pay. If you don't list the debt, it may not be discharged.

If you need more space or have debts that aren't listed, use the blank lines at the bottom of the form. After you have listed all your debts, add them up and enter the total at the bottom. This is your total indebtedness.

Column 3: Is Debt Dischargeable? To determine which of your debts will be discharged in bankruptcy and which will not, refer to the discussion at the beginning of this section on nondischargeable debts or Ch. 8, *Nondischargeable Debts.* If the debt isn't dischargeable, write "no" and enter the amount. When you've filled in all the amounts, total them and enter the number at the bottom of the column. This is the amount you'll still owe after bankruptcy if you choose to file.

WORKSHEET 1: YOUR DEBTS

1 Description of debt/name of creditor If married, indicate if owned by husband (H), wife (W) or jointly (J)	2 Total amount of debt	3 Is Debt Dischargeable? yes/no If no, enter amount of debt	4 Is Debt Secured? If yes, enter amount secured and collateral
Mortgages and home equity loans			
Motor vehicle loans			
Personal and consolidation loans			
Student loans			
Medical (doctor, dentist and hospital) bills			
Lawyers' and accountants' bills			
Totals this page $ _____		$ _____	$ _____

WORKSHEET 1: YOUR DEBTS (CONTINUED)

1 Description of debt/name of creditor If married, indicate if owned by husband (H), wife (W) or jointly (J)	2 Total amount of debt	3 Is Debt Dischargeable? yes/no	If no, enter amount of debt	4 Is Debt Secured? If yes, enter amount secured and collateral
Totals from previous page	$		$	$
Credit and charge card				
Department store and gasoline credit cards				
Alimony and child support				
Unpaid taxes				
Unpaid utility bills (gas, electric, water, phone, cable)				
Back rent				
Liens (other than tax liens)				
Other debts				
GRAND TOTALS	$		$	$

Most debts are dischargeable if you list them on the papers you file with the bankruptcy court. If a debt is dischargeable, write "Yes" in Column 3 and don't enter an amount.

Column 4: Is the Debt Secured? When deciding whether or not to file for bankruptcy, it is crucial that you know the difference between secured and unsecured debts.

Secured debts. A debt is secured if you stand to lose specific property if you don't make your payments to the creditor. A debt is also secured if a creditor has filed a lien against your property. To completely eliminate a secured debt in bankruptcy, you may have to give up the property that is security for the debt (called collateral) or pay its market value. In a few situations, you may be able to wipe out the lien in bankruptcy. If you truly need the item (for instance, a car or expensive work tools), bankruptcy may not be the best remedy for you.

EXAMPLE: Ken buys a car for $10,000, to be paid off in four years. While still owing $7,000, he files for Chapter 7 bankruptcy. Ken can discharge the $7,000 debt, but he will have to either surrender the car to the creditor or make new arrangements to pay for it. (How to make those arrangements is explained in Ch. 7, *Secured Debts.*)

Unsecured debts. An unsecured debt is any debt for which you haven't pledged collateral or for which the creditor has not recorded a lien. The debt is not related to any particular property you possess, and failure to repay the debt will not entitle the creditor to repossess property (although the creditor could sue you, get a court judgment on the debt and then take some of your property to satisfy the judgment). Most debts are unsecured, including bank credit card debts, medical and legal bills, utility bills and most store revolving charge accounts. Most unsecured debts are simply canceled by bankruptcy.

Put a "yes" (for secured debts) or "no" (for unsecured debts) for each debt. For each "yes," briefly identify the property you pledged as collateral for the debt or to which the lien attaches. If you used a loan to buy the collateral, the debt is called a "purchase-money secured debt." For example, if a car dealer gave you a loan to buy a car, and the car is the collateral that secures the loan (which means the dealer can repossess it if you don't pay back the loan), it's a purchase-money secured debt. If you pledged something you already owned as collateral, the debt is a non-purchase-money secured debt. A lien may be referred to as an involuntary secured debt.

Handling secured debts in bankruptcy can get complicated. Following Worksheet 1 are several general rules to help you with the task at hand—deciding whether or not to

file for bankruptcy. If you want a more detailed discussion of your options for dealing with secured debts, read Ch. 7, *Secured Debts.*

Rule 1: Collateral for a purchase-money secured debt will have to be given back to the creditor to get the debt completely eliminated. If you want to keep the property, you will either have to agree to let the debt survive your bankruptcy or pay the creditor the market value (not the total you still owe) of the property up front. If you really don't want to give up some or all of this property, consider one of the alternatives to Chapter 7 bankruptcy outlined in Section E, below.

Rule 2: You can keep certain property that is collateral for a non-purchase-money secured debt or which has a lien from a lawsuit attached to it. These items are limited to a few specific exemptions—furniture, clothing, tools of a trade, personal effects and appliances. See Ch. 7, *Secured Debts,* for more details.

Rule 3: If your home is collateral for a debt (including a mortgage), read Ch. 6, *Your House,* before deciding whether or not to file for bankruptcy.

2. How Much Property Will You Have to Give Up?

Whether or not you decide to file for bankruptcy may depend on what property will be taken to pay your creditors (nonexempt property) and what property you will keep (exempt property).

Certain kinds of property are exempt in almost every state, while others are almost never exempt. The following are items you can typically keep (exempt property):

- motor vehicles, to a certain value
- reasonably necessary clothing (no mink coats)
- reasonably needed household furnishings and goods (the second TV may have to go)
- household appliances
- jewelry, to a certain value
- personal effects
- life insurance (cash or loan value, or proceeds), to a certain value
- pensions
- part of the equity in your home
- tools of your trade or profession, to a certain value
- portion of unpaid but earned wages, and
- public benefits (welfare, Social Security, unemployment compensation) accumulated in a bank account.

Items you must typically give up (nonexempt property) include:

- expensive musical instruments (unless you're a professional musician)
- stamp, coin and other collections

- family heirlooms
- cash, bank accounts, stocks, bonds and other investments
- second car or truck, and
- second or vacation home.

If it appears that you have a lot of nonexempt property, read Ch. 2, *Your Property and Bankruptcy,* before deciding whether or not to file for bankruptcy. That chapter helps you determine exactly how much of your property is not exempt and suggests ways to preserve its value by selling some of it and buying exempt property before you file.

If you want to keep your nonexempt property, consider filing for Chapter 13 bankruptcy or using one of the other alternatives discussed in Section E, below.

EXAMPLE 1: Several years ago, John and Louise inherited a genuine Chinese jade vase. It's their most prized possession and is worth $2,000. They don't want to give it up, but are in desperate financial shape, with debts of more than $40,000.

If they file for Chapter 7 bankruptcy, their debts will be discharged, but they will probably lose the vase because it's not exempt in their state. In Chapter 13 bankruptcy, they could keep the vase and pay their debts out of their income over the next three years. After several anguished days, John and Louise decide to file for Chapter 7 bankruptcy and give up the vase.

(John and Louise might be tempted to hide the vase and hope the trustee doesn't discover it. That would be a crime (perjury), for which they could be fined or jailed. It's also an abuse of the bankruptcy process that could get their petition dismissed and prevent them from filing again for six months. A much safer alternative would be to sell the vase and use the proceeds to buy exempt property before they file. See Ch. 2, *Your Property and Bankruptcy.*)

EXAMPLE 2: Over the years, Connie has carefully constructed an expensive computer system which she uses primarily for hobbies, but also as a work tool for her marginal desktop publishing business. Connie has also amassed a debt of $100,000, consisting primarily of ten bank credit cards, medical bills and department store charge accounts.

Connie discovers that if she files for bankruptcy, she can discharge all of the debts if she surrenders most of the computer equipment (though she can keep the pieces essential to her desktop publishing business) to the trustee to pay her creditors. Connie decides that canceling her debts is far more important to her than hanging on to the entire system, and proceeds to file for Chapter 7 bankruptcy.

E. Alternatives to Chapter 7 Bankruptcy

In some situations, filing for Chapter 7 bankruptcy is the only sensible remedy for debt problems. In many others, however, another course of action makes better sense. This section outlines your main alternatives.

1. Do Nothing

Surprisingly, the best approach for some people deeply in debt is to take no action at all. If you're living simply, with little income and property, and look forward to a similar life in the future, you may be what's known as "judgment proof." This means that anyone who sues you and obtains a court judgment won't be able to collect simply because you don't have anything they can legally take. (As a famous song of the 1970s said, "freedom's just another word for nothing left to lose.") Remember, except in unusual situations (being a tax protester or willfully failing to pay child support) you can't be thrown in jail for not paying your debts. Nor can a creditor take away such essentials as basic clothing, ordinary household furnishings, personal effects, food, Social Security, unemployment or public assistance.

So, if you don't anticipate having a steady income or property a creditor could grab, bankruptcy is probably not necessary. Your creditors probably won't sue you, because it's unlikely they could collect the judgment. Instead, they'll simply write off your debt and treat it as a deductible business loss for income tax purposes. In several years, it will become legally uncollectible under state law (called the statute of limitations). And in seven years, it will come off your credit record.

2. Negotiate With Your Creditors

If you have some income, or you have assets you're willing to sell, you may be a lot better off negotiating with your creditors than filing for bankruptcy. Negotiation may simply buy you some time to get back on your feet, or you and your creditors may agree on a complete settlement of your debts for less than you owe.

Negotiating With Creditors
How to negotiate with your creditors is covered in detail in *Money Troubles: Legal Strategies to Cope With Your Debts,* by Robin Leonard (Nolo Press). That book covers how to deal with creditors when you owe money on credit cards, student loans, mortgage loans, car loans, child support and alimony, among other debts.

3. Get Outside Help to Design a Repayment Plan

Many people can't do a good job negotiating with their creditors. Inside, they feel that their creditors are right to insist on full payment. Or, their creditors are so hard-nosed or just plain irrational that the process is too unpleasant to stomach. In any case, the ability to negotiate is an art, and involves a number of skills.

If you don't want to negotiate with your creditors, you can turn to a lawyer, a non-lawyer bankruptcy typing service or a nonprofit credit counselor. Again, their services are detailed in *Money Troubles.*

4. Pay Over Time With Chapter 13 Bankruptcy

Chapter 13 bankruptcy lets you discharge most debts by paying all or a portion of them over a three- to five-year period. In most situations, Chapter 7 bankruptcy is a better approach to debt problems than is Chapter 13.

If you have steady income and think you could squeeze out a steady amount each month to make payments on your debts, Chapter 13 bankruptcy may be a good option for you. Instead of having your nonexempt assets sold to pay creditors (which is what happens in Chapter 7 bankruptcy), you keep your property and use your income to pay all or a portion of the debts over three to five years. The minimum amount you must pay is roughly equal to the value of your nonexempt property. In addition, you must pledge your disposable income (net income less reasonable expenses) over the life of your plan. The income you use to repay creditors need not be wages. You can use benefits, investment income or receipts as an independent contractor or businessperson.

To file for Chapter 13 bankruptcy, you fill out the same forms as in a Chapter 7 bankruptcy, listing your money, property, expenses, debts and income, and then file them with the bankruptcy court. In addition, you must file with the court a workable plan to repay your debts, given your income and expenses. You make payments under the plan directly to the bankruptcy trustee, who in turn distributes the money to your creditors. As in Chapter 7 bankruptcy, the act of filing immediately stops your creditors from taking further action against you.

Usually, the plan is designed so that you make regular payments on your secured debts and reduced payments on your unsecured debts for three years, at which time any remaining unpaid balance on the unsecured debts is wiped out. In some cases, a five-year repayment period is allowed.

You can file for Chapter 13 bankruptcy at any time, even if you wound up a Chapter 7 bankruptcy the day before or just completed another Chapter 13 repayment plan. If you file more than once, however, you'll be required to pay back a large percentage of your debts. You cannot file for Chapter 13 bankruptcy, however, if your secured debts exceed $750,000 or your unsecured debts exceed $250,000.

If for some reason you cannot finish a Chapter 13 repayment plan—for example, you lose your job six months into the plan and can't make the payments—the trustee may modify your plan. The trustee may give you a grace period (if the problem looks temporary), reduce your total monthly payments or extend the repayment period. As long as it looks like you're acting in good faith, the trustee will try to be accommodating and help you across rocky periods. If it's clear that there's no way you'll be able to complete the plan because of circumstances beyond your control, the court might let you discharge your debts on the basis of hardship. Examples of hardship would be a sudden plant closing in a one-factory town or a debilitating illness.

If the bankruptcy court won't let you modify your plan or give you a hardship discharge, you have two options:

- You can convert your case to a Chapter 7 bankruptcy unless you received a Chapter 7 discharge within the previous six years.
- You can have the bankruptcy court dismiss your Chapter 13 petition, which would leave you in the same position as you were in before you filed your petition, except you'll owe less because of the payments you made. Also, if your Chapter 13 bankruptcy is dismissed, your creditors may add to their debts any interest that was abated during your Chapter 13 petition case.

Filing for Chapter 13 Bankruptcy
For information on Chapter 13 bankruptcy—including instructions on completing the forms—see *Chapter 13 Bankruptcy: Repay Your Debts*, by Robin Leonard (Nolo Press). ∎

Your Property and Bankruptcy

This chapter is about what happens to your property when you file for Chapter 7 bankruptcy. Section A explains what property is subject to the reach of the bankruptcy court. Section B introduces Worksheet 2, which helps you inventory your property and determine which of it is exempt—that is, which of it you can keep through bankruptcy. Happily, most people find that they can keep virtually all their property through the bankruptcy process. There is one major exception: property that is collateral (security) for a debt may usually be taken even if it is exempt. Ch. 7, *Secured Debts*, explains more about collateral.

USING THE INFORMATION IN THIS CHAPTER

- **Deciding if bankruptcy is appropriate.** If you haven't decided whether or not to file for Chapter 7 bankruptcy, knowing what you own and how much you can get for it will help you decide. It may be easier simply to sell off some property (especially property that you would have to give up anyway if you file for bankruptcy) and pay creditors directly rather than to go through bankruptcy.
- **Determining what property you can keep.** Often, whether or not you can keep property through bankruptcy depends on what it is worth. For instance, many states allow you to keep a car, but only if it is worth less than $1,200. If it is worth significantly more, you will have to turn it over to the trustee to be sold. After the sale, you'll get $1,200 from the proceeds and your creditors will get the rest.
- **Summarizing information about your property before you file.** If you decide to file for bankruptcy, you'll need to fill out forms that ask what property you own, how much it's worth and what you claim as exempt. The work you do in this chapter can be transferred to those forms.

Once you have figured out what property you can keep through bankruptcy, you may be able, before you file for bankruptcy, to reduce the amount of nonexempt property you own and increase the amount of exempt items. Section C offers suggestions—and important cautions—if you want to try this strategy.

A. Property in Your Bankruptcy Estate

When you file for bankruptcy, everything you own as of that date becomes subject to the bankruptcy court's authority. This property is collectively called your "bankruptcy estate." With a very few exceptions (discussed below), property you acquire after you file for bankruptcy isn't included in your bankruptcy estate. If you filed for Chapter 13 bankruptcy first and now want to convert your case to Chapter 7 bankruptcy, everything you owned as of the date you filed your Chapter 13 petition is the property of your Chapter 7 estate. (11 U.S.C. § 348(f)(1)(A).)

Five categories of property make up your bankruptcy estate.

1. Property You Own and Possess

Probably, the property that comes to mind first is what you have in your possession—for example, clothing, books, TV, stereo system, furniture, tools, car, real estate, boat, artworks and stock certificates. All these things are included in your bankruptcy estate.

Property you have control of but that belongs to someone else is not part of your bankruptcy estate, because you don't have the right to sell it or give it away. Here are examples of property not considered part of your bankruptcy estate:

EXAMPLE 1: A parent establishes a trust for her child and names you as trustee to manage the money in the trust until the child's 18th birthday. You possess and control the money, but it's solely for the child's benefit and cannot be used for your own purposes. It isn't part of your bankruptcy estate.

EXAMPLE 2: Your sister has gone to Zimbabwe for an indefinite period and has loaned you her TV while she's gone. Although you might have use of the set for years to

come, you don't own it. It isn't part of your bankruptcy estate.

EXAMPLE 3: You are making monthly payments to lease a car. You will possess the car as long as you make the monthly payments, but you don't own it. It is not part of your bankruptcy estate.

2. Property You Own But Don't Possess

Any property you own, even if you don't have physical possession of it, is part of your bankruptcy estate. For instance, you may own a share of a vacation cabin in the mountains, but never go there yourself. Or you may own furniture or a car that someone else is using. Other examples include a deposit held by a stockbroker or a security deposit held by your landlord or the utility company.

3. Property You've Recently Given (or Had Taken) Away

People contemplating bankruptcy are often tempted to unload their property on friends and relatives or pay favorite creditors before they file. Don't bother. Property given away or paid out shortly before you file for bankruptcy is still part of your bankruptcy estate, and the trustee has legal authority to take it back. Be sure to include this property on Worksheet 2 in Section B, below.

a. Giving Away Property

You might be thinking about signing over the title certificate to an item of property to a relative or the person you live with, and then not listing it in your bankruptcy papers. This is both dishonest and foolhardy. On your bankruptcy forms, you must list all property transactions within the previous year. Failure to report a transaction is perjury—a felony. If the transfer is discovered, which it often is (trustees pay close attention to all financial transactions), the trustee can take the item and sell it to pay your creditors if:

- the transfer occurred within a year before you filed
- you didn't receive a reasonable amount for the item— giving something away or selling it for less than it's worth is the same thing for bankruptcy purposes, or
- the transfer either left you insolvent or greatly pushed you towards that state.

b. Paying Off a Favorite Creditor

You can't pay a favorite creditor, such as a relative or friend, and then file for bankruptcy, leaving your other creditors to get little or nothing. Similarly, a secured creditor who repossessed collateral shortly before you file might not get to keep it if the collateral is worth considerably more than the debt. The trustee would want to sell the collateral, pay off the debt and give the balance to other creditors.

Bankruptcy law calls payments and repossessions shortly before filing for bankruptcy "preferences." The trustee can sue the creditor for the amount of the preference and make it a part of the bankruptcy estate, so that it can be distributed among your creditors. If the collateral is exempt, you may be able to get it back.

In general, a preference exists when you pay or transfer property worth more than $600 to a creditor:

- within 90 days before filing for bankruptcy, or
- within one year before filing if the creditor was close to you—for example, a friend, relative, corporation owned by you or business partner.

4. Property You Are Entitled to Receive But Don't Yet Possess When You File

Property that you have a legal right to receive but haven't yet received when you file for bankruptcy is included in your bankruptcy estate. The most common examples are wages you have earned but have not yet been paid and a tax refund that is legally due you but which you haven't yet received. Here are some other examples:

- Vacation or termination pay you earned before filing for bankruptcy but which hasn't been paid.
- Property you've inherited, but not yet received, from someone who has died. If you're a beneficiary in the will or trust of someone who is alive, you're not yet entitled to receive the property, because he could change his will before he dies. If he has died, however, you have a legal right to receive the property left you.
- Property you will receive from a trust. If you receive periodic payments from a trust, but aren't entitled to the full amount of the trust yet, the full amount of the trust is considered property of your bankruptcy estate, and should be listed on Worksheet 2 and your bankruptcy papers. Although the bankruptcy trustee may not be able to get the money, you don't want to be accused of hiding it.
- Proceeds of an insurance policy, if the death, injury or other event that gives rise to payment has occurred. For example, if you were the beneficiary of your father's life insurance policy, and your father has died but you haven't received your money yet, the amount you're entitled to is part of your bankruptcy estate.

- Compensation you're legally entitled to receive for an injury, even if the amount hasn't yet been determined. If you have a valid claim against someone who injured you, you have a legal right to be compensated even though the amount you're entitled to hasn't been determined in a lawsuit or agreement.
- Accounts receivable (money owed you for goods or services you've provided). Even if you're pretty certain you won't be paid, that money is considered part of your bankruptcy estate. It's the trustee's job to go after the money, and leaving it off the bankruptcy forms can get you into trouble.
- Money earned before you filed for bankruptcy from property in your bankruptcy estate, but which you haven't received. This includes, for example, rent from commercial or residential real estate, royalties from copyrights or patents and dividends earned on stocks.

5. Certain Property Acquired Within 180 Days After You File for Bankruptcy

Most property you acquire—or become entitled to acquire—after you file for bankruptcy isn't included in your bankruptcy estate. But there are exceptions. If you acquire (or become entitled to acquire) certain items within 180 days after you file, you are required to report the acquisition to the bankruptcy court, and you may lose the items to the bankruptcy trustee. (11 U.S.C. § 541(a)(5).) The properties subject to the 180-day rule are:

- property you inherit
- property from a marital settlement agreement or divorce decree, and
- death benefits or life insurance policy proceeds.

You will have to report the acquisition of any of these items to the bankruptcy court on a supplemental form, even if your bankruptcy case is over. Instructions for filing the supplemental form are in Ch. 4, *Handling Your Case in Court*, Section B.

6. Your Share of Marital Property

IF YOU'RE MARRIED AND FILING JOINTLY All marital property that fits into any of the above five categories is property of your bankruptcy estate. If you're single and filing alone, however, this section tells you which marital property is part of your bankruptcy estate and which is beyond the trustee's reach.

There are two types of state marital property laws: community property and common law property.

COMMUNITY PROPERTY STATES		
Arizona	Louisiana	Texas
California	Nevada	Washington
Idaho	New Mexico	Wisconsin

a. Community Property States

In community property states, as a general rule, all property either spouse earns or receives during the marriage is community property and is owned jointly by both spouses. Exceptions are gifts and inheritances received specifically by one spouse, and property owned by one spouse before the marriage or acquired after permanent separation.

If you're married and file for bankruptcy, all the community property you and your spouse own is considered part of your bankruptcy estate, even if your spouse doesn't file. The technical rule is that community property is included in the bankruptcy estate if the spouse who files for bankruptcy has sole or joint legal authority to control or manage it, or if the filing spouse's creditors could reach it under state law. As a practical matter, this includes all community property except (in a few states) community property businesses that are solely managed by the filing spouse.

EXAMPLE: Paul and Sonya live in Arizona, a community property state. They own a house and a savings account as community property. Under Arizona law, both Paul and Sonya have equal management responsibilities over their community property. If Paul files for bankruptcy, both the bank account and house are in Paul's bankruptcy estate, even though Sonya hasn't filed.

The separate property of the spouse filing for bankruptcy is also part of the bankruptcy estate. But your spouse's separate property isn't part of your bankruptcy estate if you file alone.

EXAMPLE: Paul owns an airplane as his separate property (he owned it before he married Sonya), and Sonya came to the marriage owning a grand piano. Because only Paul is filing for bankruptcy, Paul's airplane will be part of his bankruptcy estate, but Sonya's piano won't be.

You may need to do some research into your state's property laws to make sure you understand which of your property is separate and which is community. See Ch. 9, *Help Beyond the Book*, for tips on research.

b.   Common Law Property States

When only one spouse files for bankruptcy in a common law property state, that spouse's separate property and half of the couple's jointly owned property, go into the bankruptcy estate.

The general rules of property ownership in common law states are:

- Property that has only one spouse's name on a title certificate (car, house, stocks), even if bought with joint funds, belongs to that spouse separately.
- Property that was purchased or received as a gift or inheritance jointly for the use of both spouses is jointly owned, unless a title slip has only one spouse's name on it (which means it belongs to that spouse separately, even if both spouses use it).
- Property that one spouse buys with separate funds or receives as a gift or inheritance for that spouse's separate use is that spouse's separate property (unless, again, a title certificate shows differently).

B.   Property You Can Keep

Completing Worksheet 2 below (a blank copy is in Appendix 4) will give you a good idea of what property you own, how you own it, what it is worth and how much of it you can keep if you file for Chapter 7 bankruptcy. Instructions and a list of property that may fit into the various listed categories follow the Worksheet.

1.   Your Property

This checklist of commonly owned property items should help you list, under the appropriate category on Column 1, the property you own. If you're married, enter all property owned by you or your spouse, and indicate whether the property is owned by husband (H), wife (W) or jointly (J).

For cash on hand and deposits of money, indicate the source of each, such as wages or salary, insurance policy proceeds or the proceeds from the sale of an item of property. Although cash on hand is usually not exempt, you may be able to exempt all or some of it if you can show it came from an exempt source, such as unemployment insurance.

1.   Real Estate

- ☐ Residence
- ☐ Condominium or cooperative apartment
- ☐ Mobile home
- ☐ Mobile home park space
- ☐ Rental property
- ☐ Vacation home or cabin
- ☐ Business property
- ☐ Undeveloped land
- ☐ Farm land
- ☐ Boat/marina dock space
- ☐ Burial site

After listing the real estate you own, specify your ownership interest.

There are many ways to own real estate. The most common, outright ownership, is called "fee simple." Even if you owe a bank, as long as you have the right to sell the house, leave it to your heirs and make alterations, your ownership is fee simple. A fee simple interest may be owned by one person or by several people jointly. Normally, when people are listed on deeds as the owners—even if they own the property as joint tenants, tenants in common or tenants by the entirety—the ownership interest is in fee simple.

Other kinds of ownership are more complicated. But if this material makes your head spin, don't worry about it. Just leave this blank. Later, if you file for bankruptcy, the trustee can help you sort it out.

- **Life estate.** This is your right to possess and use property only during your lifetime. You can't sell the property, give it away or leave it to someone when you die. Instead, when you die, the property passes to whomever was named in the instrument (trust, deed or will) that created your life estate. This type of ownership is usually created when the sole owner of a piece of real estate wants his surviving spouse to live on the property for her life, but then have the property pass to his children. The surviving spouse has a life estate. Surviving spouses who are beneficiaries of A-B, spousal or marital by-pass trusts, have life estates.
- **Future interest.** This is your right to own property sometime in the future. A common future interest is owned by a person who—under the terms of a deed, will or trust—will own the property when its current possessor dies. This type of ownership is often referred to as "beneficial" ownership. The beneficial owner has a right to make the person or trustee currently in charge of the property preserve it for the beneficial owner's future benefit. Note that until the person who signed the will or living trust dies, you have no future ownership interest in the property, because the person making the will or living trust can easily amend the document to cut you out.
- **Contingent interest.** This ownership interest depends upon one or more conditions being fulfilled before it comes into existence. Wills sometimes leave property

WORKSHEET 2: YOUR PROPERTY

1 Your property	2 Value of property (actual dollar or garage sale value)	3 Your ownership share (%, $)	4 Amount of liens	5 Amount of your equity	6 Exempt? If not, enter non- exempt amount
1. Real estate					
2. Cash on hand (state source of money)					
3. Deposits of money (indicate sources of money)					
4. Security deposits					
5. Household goods, supplies and furnishings					
6. Books, pictures, art objects; stamp, coin and other collections					

WORKSHEET 2: YOUR PROPERTY (CONTINUED)

1 Your property	2 Value of property (actual dollar or garage sale value)	3 Your ownership share (%, $)	4 Amount of liens	5 Amount of your equity	6 Exempt? If not, enter non- exempt amount
7. Apparel					
8. Jewelry					
9. Firearms, sports equipment and other hobby equipment					
10. Interests in insurance policies					
11. Annuities					
12. Pension or profit-sharing plans					
13. Stocks and interests in incorporated and unincorporated companies					

WORKSHEET 2: YOUR PROPERTY (CONTINUED)

1 Your property	2 Value of property (actual dollar or garage sale value)	3 Your ownership share (%, $)	4 Amount of liens	5 Amount of your equity	6 Exempt? If not, enter non-exempt amount
14. Interests in partnerships					
15. Government and corporate bonds and other investment instruments					
16. Accounts receivable					
17. Family support					
18. Other debts owed you where the amount owed is known and definite					
19. Powers exercisable for your benefit, other than those listed under real estate					
20. Interests due to another person's death					

WORKSHEET 2: YOUR PROPERTY (CONTINUED)

1 Your property	2 Value of property (actual dollar or garage sale value)	3 Your ownership share (%, $)	4 Amount of liens	5 Amount of your equity	6 Exempt? If not, enter non- exempt amount
21. All other contingent claims and claims where the amount owed you is not known					
22. Patents, copyrights and other intellectual property					
23. Licenses, franchises and other general intangibles					
24. Automobiles and other vehicles					
25. Boats, motors and accessories					
26. Aircraft and accessories					
27. Office equipment, furnishings and supplies					
28. Machinery, fixtures, equipment and supplies used in business					

WORKSHEET 2: YOUR PROPERTY (CONTINUED)

1 Your property	2 Value of property (actual dollar or garage sale value)	3 Your ownership share (%, $)	4 Amount of liens	5 Amount of your equity	6 Exempt? If not, enter non- exempt amount
29. Business inventory					
30. Livestock, poultry and other animals					
31. Crops—growing or harvested					
32. Farming equipment and implements					
33. Farm supplies, chemicals and feed					
34. Other personal property					

Subtotal (column 6): _____

Wild Card Exemption − _____

Total Value of NONEXEMPT Property _____

to people under certain conditions. If the conditions aren't met, the property passes to someone else. For instance, Emma's will leaves her house to John provided that he takes care of her until her death. If John doesn't care for Emma, the house passes to Emma's daughter Jane. Both John and Jane have contingent interests in Emma's home.

- **Lienholder.** If you are the holder of a mortgage, deed of trust, judgment lien or mechanic's lien on real estate, you have an ownership interest in the real estate.
- **Easement holder.** If you are the holder of a right to travel on or otherwise use property owned by someone else, you have an easement.
- **Power of appointment.** If you have a legal right, given to you in a will or transfer of property, to sell a specified piece of someone's property, indicate it.
- **Beneficial ownership under a real estate contract.** This is the right to own property by virtue of having signed a binding real estate contract. Even though the buyer doesn't yet own the property, the buyer does have a "beneficial interest"—that is, the right to own the property once the formalities are completed.

2. Value of Your Property

In Column 2, enter a value for each item of property listed in Column 1. It's easy to enter a dollar amount for your cash on hand, deposits of money, bonds, investment instruments, insurance, annuities, pensions, stock and interest in corporations, interest in partnerships, rights or powers and property transferred under assignment.

For your other property, estimate its market value—that is, what you could sell it for at a garage sale or through a classified ad. As long as your estimates are reasonable, the lower the value you place on property, the more of it you will probably be allowed to keep through the bankruptcy process. Trustees have years of experience and a pretty good sense of what real property is worth. Be honest. It's okay to be wrong as long as you do your best to estimate the fair market value and briefly explain any uncertainties. If you can't estimate—for example, you have an unusual asset such as a future interest, life estate or a lease, leave this column blank.

If you own an item jointly, put the value of the entire asset here. In Column 3, you will enter your share.

Here are some suggestions for valuing specific items:

- **Real estate.** If your interest is ownership of a house, get an estimate of its market value from a local real estate agent or appraiser. If you own another type of real estate—such as land used to grow crops—put the amount it would bring in at a forced sale. As a general rule, the lower the fair market value of your property, the better off you'll be in bankruptcy. But your estimate must be close to real market conditions to stand up in court.

- **Cars.** Start with the low *Kelley Blue Book* price. If the car needs substantial repair, reduce the value by the amount it would cost you to fix the car. If the car's worth is below the *Blue Book* value, be prepared to show why. You can find a copy of the *Blue Book* at the public library. If you have Internet access, visit their site at http://www.kbb.com. Select "Used Cars" and either "Goin' Shoppin'" for the retail or "What's My Car Worth" for the trade-in value.

- **Older goods.** Want ads in a local flea market or pennysaver newspaper are a good place to look for prices. If the item isn't listed, use the garage sale value—that is, begin with the price you paid and then deduct about 20% for each year you've owned the item. For example, if you bought a camera for $400 three years ago, subtract $80 for the first year (down to $320), $64 for the second year (down to $256) and $51 for the third year (down to $205).

- **Life insurance.** Put the current cash surrender value. (Call your insurance agent to find out.) Term life insurance has a cash surrender value of zero. Don't put the amount of benefits the policy will pay, unless you're the beneficiary of an insurance policy and the insured person has died.

- **Stocks, bonds, etc.** Check the listing in a newspaper business section. If you can't find the listing, or the stock isn't traded publicly, call your broker and ask. If you have a brokerage account, use the value from your last statement.

- **Jewelry, antiques and other collectibles.** Any valuable jewelry or collection should be appraised.

Total Column 2 and enter the figure in the space provided.

Personal Property (Schedule B)

2. Cash on hand (include sources)
- ☐ In your home
- ☐ In your wallet
- ☐ Under your mattress

3. Deposits of money (include sources)
- ☐ Bank account
- ☐ Brokerage account (with stockbroker)
- ☐ Certificates of deposit (CD)
- ☐ Credit union deposit
- ☐ Escrow account
- ☐ Money market account
- ☐ Money in a safe deposit box deposit
- ☐ Savings and loan deposit

4. Security deposits
- ☐ Electric
- ☐ Gas
- ☐ Heating oil
- ☐ Security deposit on a rental unit
- ☐ Prepaid rent
- ☐ Rented furniture or equipment
- ☐ Telephone
- ☐ Water

5. Household goods, supplies and furnishings
- ☐ Antiques
- ☐ Appliances
- ☐ Carpentry tools
- ☐ China and crystal
- ☐ Clocks
- ☐ Dishes
- ☐ Food (total value)
- ☐ Furniture (list every item; go from room to room so you don't miss anything)
- ☐ Gardening tools
- ☐ Home computer (for personal use)
- ☐ Iron and ironing board
- ☐ Lamps
- ☐ Lawn mower or tractor

- ☐ Microwave oven
- ☐ Patio or outdoor furniture
- ☐ Radios
- ☐ Rugs
- ☐ Sewing machine
- ☐ Silverware and utensils
- ☐ Small appliances
- ☐ Snow blower
- ☐ Stereo system
- ☐ Telephone and answering machines
- ☐ Televisions
- ☐ Vacuum cleaner
- ☐ Video equipment (VCR, Camcorder)

6. Books, pictures and other art objects; stamp, coin and other collections
- ☐ Art prints
- ☐ Bibles
- ☐ Books
- ☐ Coins
- ☐ Collectibles (such as political buttons, baseball cards)
- ☐ Family portraits
- ☐ Figurines
- ☐ Original art works
- ☐ Photographs
- ☐ Records, CDs, audiotapes
- ☐ Stamps
- ☐ Video tapes

7. Apparel
- ☐ Clothing
- ☐ Furs

8. Jewelry
- ☐ Engagement and wedding rings
- ☐ Gems
- ☐ Precious metals
- ☐ Watches

9. Firearms, sports equipment and other hobby equipment
- ☐ Board games
- ☐ Bicycle
- ☐ Camera equipment

- ☐ Electronic musical equipment
- ☐ Exercise machine
- ☐ Fishing gear
- ☐ Guns (rifles, pistols, shotguns, muskets)
- ☐ Model or remote cars or planes
- ☐ Musical instruments
- ☐ Scuba diving equipment
- ☐ Ski equipment
- ☐ Other sports equipment
- ☐ Other weapons (swords and knives)

10. Interests in insurance policies
- ☐ Credit insurance
- ☐ Disability insurance
- ☐ Health insurance
- ☐ Homeowner's or renter's insurance
- ☐ Term life insurance
- ☐ Whole life insurance

11. Annuities

12. Pension or profit-sharing plans
- ☐ IRA
- ☐ Keogh
- ☐ Pension or retirement plan
- ☐ 401(k) plan

13. Stock and interests in incorporated and unincorporated companies

14. Interests in partnerships
- ☐ Limited partnership interest
- ☐ General partnership interest

15. Government and corporate bonds and other investment instruments
- ☐ Corporate bonds
- ☐ Municipal bonds
- ☐ Promissory notes
- ☐ U.S. savings bonds

16. Accounts receivable
- ☐ Accounts receivable from business
- ☐ Commissions already earned

17. Family support
- ☐ Alimony (spousal support, maintenance) due under court order
- ☐ Child support payments due under court order
- ☐ Payments due under divorce property settlement

18. Other debts owed you where the amount owed is known and definite
- ☐ Disability benefits due
- ☐ Disability insurance due
- ☐ Judgments obtained against third parties you haven't yet collected
- ☐ Sick pay earned
- ☐ Social Security benefits due
- ☐ Tax refund due under returns already filed
- ☐ Vacation pay earned
- ☐ Wages due
- ☐ Worker's compensation due

19. Powers exercisable for your benefit, other than those listed under real estate
- ☐ Right to receive, at some future time, cash, stock or other personal property placed in an irrevocable trust
- ☐ Current payments of interest or principal from a trust
- ☐ General power of appointment over personal property

20. Interest due to another person's death
- ☐ Beneficiary of a living trust, if the trustor has died
- ☐ Expected proceeds from a life insurance policy where the insured has died
- ☐ Inheritance from an existing estate in probate (the owner has died and the court is overseeing the distribution of the property) even if the final amount is not yet known

- ☐ Inheritance under a will that is contingent upon one or more events occurring, but only if the owner has died

21. All other contingent claims and claims where the amount owed you is not known, including tax refunds, counter-claims and rights to setoff claims (claims you think you have against a person, government or corporation, but haven't yet sued on)
- ☐ Claims against a corporation, government entity or individual
- ☐ Potential tax refund but return not yet filed

22. Patents, copyrights and other intellectual property
- ☐ Copyrights
- ☐ Patents
- ☐ Trade secrets
- ☐ Trademarks
- ☐ Trade Names

23. Licenses, franchises and other general intangibles
- ☐ Building permits
- ☐ Cooperative association holdings
- ☐ Exclusive licenses
- ☐ Liquor licenses
- ☐ Nonexclusive licenses
- ☐ Patent licenses
- ☐ Professional licenses

24. Automobiles and other vehicles
- ☐ Car
- ☐ Mini bike or motor scooter
- ☐ Mobile or motor home if on wheels
- ☐ Motorcycle
- ☐ Recreational vehicle (RV)
- ☐ Trailer
- ☐ Truck
- ☐ Van

25. Boats, motors and accessories
- ☐ Boat (canoe, kayak, rowboat, shell, sailboat, pontoon, yacht, etc.)

- ☐ Boat radar, radio or telephone
- ☐ Outboard motor

26. Aircraft and accessories
- ☐ Aircraft
- ☐ Aircraft radar, radio and other accessories

27. Office equipment, furnishings and supplies
- ☐ Artwork in your office
- ☐ Computers, software, modems, printers
- ☐ Copier
- ☐ Fax machine
- ☐ Furniture
- ☐ Rugs
- ☐ Supplies
- ☐ Telephones
- ☐ Typewriters

28. Machinery, fixtures, equipment and supplies used in business
- ☐ Military uniforms and accoutrements
- ☐ Tools of your trade

29. Business inventory

30. Livestock, poultry and other animals
- ☐ Birds
- ☐ Cats
- ☐ Dogs
- ☐ Fish and aquarium equipment
- ☐ Horses
- ☐ Other pets
- ☐ Livestock and poultry

31. Crops—growing or harvested

32. Farming equipment and implements

33. Farm supplies, chemicals and feed

34. Other personal property of any kind not already listed
- ☐ Church pew
- ☐ Health aids (for example, wheelchair, crutches)
- ☐ Hot tub or portable spa
- ☐ Season tickets

3. Your Ownership Share

In Column 3, enter two amounts:
- the percentage of your separate ownership interest in the property listed in Column 1, and
- the value of your separate ownership interest in the property listed in Column 1.

EXAMPLE: You and your brother jointly bought a music synthesizer worth $10,000. Although you still owe $3,000 (which means that you and your brother have $7,000 equity in the synthesizer), your ownership share is one-half (50%), or $5,000, which is what you list in Column 3.

IF YOU ARE MARRIED

If you're filing jointly with your spouse, or if you're filing alone and live in a community property state, put your combined share here. If you live in a common law property state and are filing alone, enter only your share here.

Total Column 3 and enter the figure in the space provided.

4. Value of Liens

In Column 4, put the value of any legal claim (lien) someone else has made against the property. Even if you own only part of the property, enter the full value of the lien.

Liens must be paid off before property can be transferred to a new owner free and clear. The amount of any liens will have to be subtracted from the property's value so the trustee can know how much would be left for unsecured creditors if the property were sold. Even if the value of the lien exceeds the property's value, include it here. That lets the trustee know there won't be anything for the unsecured creditors.

Include:
- Liens held by secured creditors. For instance, if you owe on a mortgage, the mortgage-holder has a lien on your property. The mortgage must be paid off before the property can be transferred to someone else. Similarly, if you owe on a car note, the holder of the note has a lien on your car.
- Liens placed by the IRS or other taxing authority after you failed to pay a tax bill.
- In the case of real estate, a lien placed by a contractor who worked on the house without getting paid (a mechanic's or materialman's lien).
- A judgment lien recorded against your property by someone who won a lawsuit against you, if it was filed

in the public records more than 90 days before you filed for bankruptcy.

Total Column 4 and enter the figure in the space provided.

5. Amount of Your Equity

Your equity is the amount you would get to keep if you sold the property. If you own the property alone (or if you and your spouse own the property and are filing jointly), calculate your equity by subtracting the amount in Column 4 from the property's total value (Column 2). Put this amount in Column 5. If you get a negative number, enter "0."

If you co-own the property with someone other than your spouse, the calculation of Column 5 is a little more complex.

1. If the liens in Column 4 are from debts jointly incurred by you and the other owner of the property, figure the total equity (Column 2 less Column 4). Then multiply that number by your ownership share (the percentage you figured in Column 3) and enter that amount.
2. If the liens in Column 4 are from debts incurred solely by you, then deduct the total amount of the lien from the amount in Column 2. Only your assets—not a co-owner's—can be taken to pay your creditors in bankruptcy.

Total Column 5 and enter the figure in the space provided.

6. Is the Property Exempt?

Figuring out exactly what property you're legally entitled to keep if you file for bankruptcy takes some work, but this information is crucial. It's your responsibility—and to your benefit—to claim all exemptions to which you're entitled. If you don't claim property as exempt, you could lose it to your creditors.

a. An Overview of Exemptions

Exempt property is the property you may keep during and after bankruptcy. Nonexempt property is the property you must surrender to the bankruptcy trustee, who will use it to pay your creditors. The more you can claim as exempt, the better off you are. You don't literally have to surrender the property if you pay the trustee the property's value in cash, or the trustee is willing to accept exempt property of roughly equal value instead. But the value of your non-exempt property belongs to your creditors, not to you.

Each state has its own list of what items of property are exempt in bankruptcy. Some types of property are exempt regardless of value. For instance, many states exempt all "personal effects" (things such as electric shavers and hair dryers), ordinary household furniture and clothing without regard to their value.

Other kinds of property are exempt up to a limit. For instance, cars are often exempt up to a certain amount—usually between $1,200 and $2,500. An exemption limit means that any equity above the limit is considered nonexempt. The trustee can take the property and sell it, give you the exemption amount (theoretically, so you can replace the property that is sold), and distribute the remainder to your creditors.

Many states also provide a general-purpose exemption, called a "wild card" exemption, which you can apply to any type of property or split among several items. You can use the wild card exemption to increase the exemption amount of a partially exempt item or to exempt some nonexempt property. For example, Washington has a $1,000 wild card exemption. You could add it to Washington's $2,500 vehicle exemption and exempt up to $3,500 equity in a car. Or you could use it to exempt up to $1,000 of any other property.

Bankruptcy law allows married couples filing jointly to each claim a full set of exemptions; this is called "doubling." Some states, however, expressly prohibit doubling certain exemptions, usually the homestead exemption, which exempts equity in a residence. If a court decision or statute clearly says that doubling is allowed or prohibited, we've indicated it in Appendix 1, which lists all state exemptions. For most items, the chart doesn't say. In that case, go ahead and double.

EXEMPTING TENANCY BY THE ENTIRETY PROPERTY

"Tenancy by the entirety" is a property ownership form available only to married couples in certain common law property states. To find out how you and your spouse own your house, you'll probably have to look at your deed. One advantage of tenancy by the entirety is that when one spouse dies, her share goes automatically to the survivor.

In bankruptcy, only 15 states and the District of Columbia exempt all property held as tenancy by the entirety, but with limitation. You can exempt tenancy by the entirety property only if you are filing alone and only to discharge debts incurred by you alone. If you try to discharge debts incurred with your spouse, the tenancy by the entirety property is no longer exempt. States that exempt tenancy by the entirety property are Delaware, Florida, Hawaii, Indiana, Maryland, Massachusetts, Michigan, Minnesota, North Carolina, Ohio, Pennsylvania, Tennessee, Vermont, Virginia and Wyoming.

b. Determining Which of Your Property Is Exempt

To determine which of your property is exempt, carefully follow the steps set out below. As you go through the lists of exempt property, give yourself the benefit of the doubt. If it appears that a particular exemption covers all or part of a property item, claim it.

Step 1: Choose an exemption system.

The states listed below require that their residents choose between two sets of exemptions. If your state isn't listed, only your state's exemption system is available to you. Skip to Step 2.

States where you must choose your bankruptcy exemption system:

Arkansas	Massachusetts	Pennsylvania
California	Michigan	Rhode Island
Connecticut	Minnesota	South Carolina
District of	New Hampshire	Texas
Columbia	New Jersey	Vermont
Hawaii	New Mexico	Washington
		Wisconsin

If your state is listed above (except California), you must choose between your state's exemptions and a list of federal bankruptcy exemptions. You can't mix and match, however—if you pick your state's exemption system, you may use only its exemptions, and the same goes if you pick the federal exemptions. If you and your spouse jointly file for bankruptcy, both of you must select the same system.

CALIFORNIA NOTE

Californians, too, must choose between two sets of exemptions. But these are two different systems enacted by the state—not a state system and a federal system. The discussion on choosing between two exemption systems assumes you will be comparing a state system to a federal system. Follow that discussion, but substitute "California System 1" for "your state exemptions" and "California System 2" for "the federal exemptions."

If you must choose between two exemption systems, look in Appendix 1 for:

- your state's exemptions plus the federal non-bankruptcy exemptions, and
- the federal bankruptcy exemptions list (it appears after all the state lists).

Compare the federal bankruptcy exemptions list to your state's list plus the federal non-bankruptcy exemptions to see how each treats valuable items, such as your home and car.

- **Your home.** If the equity in your home is your major asset, your choice may be dictated by the homestead exemption alone. Compare your state's homestead exemption to the $15,000 federal exemption. In several states (Arkansas, California System 1, Connecticut, Hawaii, Massachusetts, Minnesota, New Hampshire, New Mexico, Texas, Vermont, Washington and Wisconsin), the homestead exemption is $20,000 or more, so choosing your state exemptions will keep more of your property exempt. In California System 2, District of Columbia, Michigan, New Jersey, Pennsylvania, Rhode Island and South Carolina, the state homestead exemption is $15,000 or less, and you may be able to lower the value of your nonexempt property by selecting the federal exemptions.
- **Other valuable property.** If the equity in your home isn't a factor in your decision, identify the most valuable items you own. Look at the federal bankruptcy exemptions and your state and the federal non-bankruptcy exemptions. Which helps you bring down the value of your nonexempt property?
- **Your pension.** If your pension is covered by the federal law called ERISA, it isn't considered part of your bankruptcy estate and has no effect on the value of your nonexempt property.

  If your pension is not covered by ERISA, it is exempt only if you use your state's exemptions and the

pension is listed in either your state exemption list or the federal non-bankruptcy exemption list.

Step 2: Decide which items you listed on Worksheet 2 might be exempt under the exemption system you're using.

Use the notes at the beginning of Appendix 1 and Appendix 2: *Exemption Glossary* if you need more information or an explanation of terms. In evaluating whether or not your cash on hand and deposits of money are exempt, look to the source of the money, such as welfare benefits, insurance proceeds or wages.

Step 3: Decide which items you listed on Worksheet 2 might be exempt under the federal non-bankruptcy exemptions, if available.

If you use your state exemptions—this includes all Californians—you may also select from a list of federal non-bankruptcy exemptions, mostly military and other federal benefits, as well as 75% of wages you have earned but have not yet been paid. You cannot, however, combine your exemptions if the federal non-bankruptcy exemptions duplicate your state's exemptions.

EXAMPLE: You're using your state's exemptions. Both your state and the federal non-bankruptcy exemptions let you exempt 75% of unpaid wages. You cannot combine the exemptions to claim 100% of your wages; 75% is all you can exempt.

Step 4: Double your exemptions if you're married and state law allows it.

If you are married and filing jointly, you can double all exemptions unless your state expressly prohibits it. Look in your state's listing in Appendix 1. If your state's chart doesn't say doubling is prohibited, go ahead and double. If you're using the federal bankruptcy exemptions, you may double all exemptions.

Step 5: Determine the value of all nonexempt items. If an item (or group of items) is exempt to an unlimited amount, put "0" in Column 6.

If an item (or group of items) is exempt to a certain amount (for example, household goods to $4,000), total up the value of all items that fall into the category using the values in Column 5. Subtract from the total the amount of the exemption. What is left is the nonexempt value. Enter that in Column 6.

If an item (or group of items) is not exempt at all, copy the amount from Column 5 to Column 6.

EFFICIENCY SUGGESTION

While you're determining which of your property is exempt, write down in Column 6 the numbers of the statutes that authorize each exemption. (These are in Appendix 1.) You will need this information when you fill out Schedule C of your bankruptcy papers.

Step 6: Look at all the items for which you entered an amount more than "0" in Column 6.

These are the items—or their values—you stand to lose in bankruptcy. If there are a lot, you may still seriously consider bankruptcy if:

- you can sell some nonexempt property before you file (Section C, below)
- your debts are so high you're willing to give up some property in exchange for their discharge
- you can raise enough cash to buy the nonexempt property you want back from the trustee (see Ch. 4, Section A.4), or
- the property will be difficult or expensive for the trustee to sell and he is likely to abandon it (give it back to you).

SPECIAL EXEMPTION RULES FOR PENSIONS

If your pension is covered by the federal law called ERISA (Employee Retirement Income Security Act— ask the pension plan administrator, benefits coordinator or personnel manager at your job), pay special attention to these rules.

Rule 1: Your ERISA pension is exempt if you use the federal bankruptcy exemption system.

Rule 2: Your ERISA pension is yours to keep if you use a state exemption system, even if your state exemption list doesn't refer to ERISA pensions. The reason is somewhat complex, involving both ERISA law and bankruptcy law. But the upshot for you is that you don't even need to list your ERISA pension in Schedule C, because it's not considered to be part of your bankruptcy estate. (*Patterson v. Shumate*, 504 U.S. 753 (1992).)

If your pension is not covered by ERISA, it is exempt only if:

- you use your state's exemptions, and
- the pension is listed in either your state exemption list or the federal non-bankruptcy exemption list.

If it looks like you might lose your pension in bankruptcy, see a lawyer before filing.

C. Selling Nonexempt Property Before You File

If you have an asset that is not exempt, you may want to sell it before you file for bankruptcy. You can use the proceeds to buy exempt property that will help you make a fresh financial start or to pay debts that won't be discharged by the bankruptcy. If you choose to pay some debts, and you pay any unsecured ones, you must delay filing for bankruptcy at least 90 days after making the payment, or one year if it was to a relative, close friend or company in which you are an officer. (See Section A.3, above.)

EXAMPLE: Jan owns a piano worth $1,000. Under her state's laws, the piano is nonexempt. That means if she files for bankruptcy, the bankruptcy trustee will take the piano, sell it and distribute the proceeds among her creditors. But Jan can sell the piano before she files for bankruptcy and use the $1,000 to buy exempt property, such as tools for her business, or to pay a nondischargeable debt, such as a tax bill. If she does the latter, she must wait at least 90 days before filing for bankruptcy.

⚠️ **CONSULT A LOCAL BANKRUPTCY ATTORNEY**
Your local bankruptcy court may consider these kinds of transfers an attempt to defraud your creditors. (See Section 2, below.) The only sure way to find out in advance what is and isn't permissible in your area is to ask people familiar with local bankruptcy court practices.

1. How to Proceed

There are two ways to reduce your nonexempt property. You can replace nonexempt property with exempt property or use your nonexempt property to pay debts.

a. Replace Nonexempt Property With Exempt Property

There are several ways to replace your nonexempt property holdings with exempt property.

- Sell a nonexempt asset and use the proceeds to buy an asset that is completely exempt. For example, you can sell a nonexempt coin collection and purchase clothing, which in most states is exempt without regard to value.
- Sell a nonexempt asset and use the proceeds to buy an asset that is exempt up to the amount received in the sale. For example, you can sell a nonexempt coin collection worth $1,200 and purchase a car that is exempt up to $1,200 in value.
- Sell an asset that is only partially exempt and use the proceeds to replace it with a similar asset of lesser

value. For example, if typewriters are only exempt up to a value of $200, you could sell your $500 typewriter and buy a workable second-hand one for $200, putting the remaining cash into other exempt assets such as clothing or appliances.

- Use cash (which isn't exempt in most states) to buy an exempt item, such as furniture or tools.

b. Pay Debts

If you choose to reduce your nonexempt property by using the money from the sale of your nonexempt property to pay debts, keep the following points in mind:

- **Don't pay off a debt that could be discharged in bankruptcy.** Dischargeable debts such as credit card bills can be completely discharged in bankruptcy. The only reason to pay a dischargeable debt would be if you want to:
  - keep good relations with a valued creditor, such as a doctor who you rely on for necessary medical treatment, or
  - pay a debt for which a relative or friend is a cosigner, because the friend or relative will be stuck with paying the whole debt if you get it discharged.

  In either case, if the payment is more than $600, you must wait at least 90 days after you pay that creditor before filing for bankruptcy. Otherwise, the payment is considered a "preference," and the trustee can set it aside and take back the money for your other creditors. (11 U.S.C. §§ 547(b),(c)(7), (f).)

  You can, however, pay regular monthly bills right up until bankruptcy. So keep paying monthly phone bills, utilities, rent and mortgage payments.

- **Be careful when paying secured debts.** If you want to use the proceeds from nonexempt property to pay off a debt secured by collateral, first read Ch. 7, *Secured Debts*. If the collateral for the debt isn't exempt, paying off the debt will accomplish little, because the trustee will take the collateral when you file for bankruptcy. If the collateral is exempt, you may be able to keep the collateral without paying off the debts before you file for bankruptcy.

2. Fraudulent Transactions

There's one major limitation on selling nonexempt property and using it to purchase exempt property: you can't do it to defraud your creditors. If a creditor or the trustee complains about a pre-bankruptcy transaction, and the court concludes that your primary motive was greed rather than gaining a fresh start, the court may let the trustee take the new property and sell it to pay your creditors. In extreme cases, the court may even deny you a bankruptcy discharge.

The two main factors a judge looks at are:

- **Your motive.** The bankruptcy court will probably go along with your sale and purchase if the exempt property you end up with is a necessity, or clearly designed to help you make a fresh start. For example, it's probably fine to sell a second (and usually nonexempt car) and buy some tools needed for your cabinet-making business, or school clothing or books for your children. But if you sell your second car and buy a $3,000 diamond ring with the proceeds, a court might consider it a greedy attempt to cheat your creditors, even if the ring is exempt under your state's laws. Put a little differently, if the court thinks that you're trying to preserve the value of your nonexempt property for use after bankruptcy rather than really acquiring useful property, your conversion attempt will probably fail.

- **The amount of property involved.** If the amount of nonexempt property you get rid of before you file is enough to pay most of your debts, the court may dismiss your case.

Here are five important guidelines for staying out of trouble when you're making these kinds of pre-bankruptcy transactions.

1. **Be honest.** Accurately report all your transactions on Form 7, the Statement of Financial Affairs. If the subject comes up with the trustee, creditors or the court, freely admit that you tried to arrange your property holdings before filing for bankruptcy so that you could better get a fresh start. Courts see frankness about your pre-bankruptcy activities as a sign you had honorable intentions. If you lie about or attempt to conceal what you did or why you did it, the bankruptcy trustee or court may conclude you had fraudulent intentions and either disallow the transaction or—even worse—deny you a bankruptcy discharge.

2. **Sell and buy for equivalent value.** If you sell a $500 nonexempt item and purchase an exempt item obviously worth $500, you shouldn't have a problem. If, however, you sell a $500 nonexempt item and purchase a $100 exempt item, be prepared to account for the $400 difference. Otherwise, the court will probably assume that you're trying to cheat your creditors and either force you to cough up the $400 (if you still have it) or, possibly, dismiss your bankruptcy case.

MOVING TO A STATE WITH MORE GENEROUS EXEMPTIONS MAY NOT BE ALLOWED

Some debtors take a look at the list of exemptions for their state in Appendix 1 and are horrified at how short the list is or how low the value of the items are. Their state isn't merely ungenerous—it seems downright cruel.

One couple tried to get around this problem by selling their assets, moving to Florida, buying a new house with the cash (Florida has an unlimited homestead exemption) and then filing for bankruptcy over a year after buying the house. The bankruptcy court, however, declared the purchase fraudulent and denied them the homestead exemption. (*In re Coplan*, 156 B.R. 88 (M.D. Fla. 1993).)

So be careful if you plan to move to improve your lot.

3. **Sell and buy property at reasonable prices.** When you sell nonexempt property with a mind to purchasing exempt property, make the price as close to the item's market value as possible. This is especially true if the sale is made to a friend or relative. If you sell your brother a $900 stereo system for $100, a creditor or the trustee may cry foul, and the judge may agree.

At the other end of the transaction, if you pay a friend or relative significantly more for the exempt property than it is apparently worth, suspicions may be raised that you're just trying to transfer your assets to relatives to avoid creditors.

4. **Don't make last-minute transfers or purchases.** The longer you can wait to file for bankruptcy after making these kinds of property transfers, the less likely it is the judge will disapprove. For example, judges frequently rule that a hasty transaction the night before filing shows an intent to cheat creditors. The open, deliberate and advance planning of property sales and purchases, however, is usually considered evidence that you didn't intend to defraud; however, one court ruled that the debtor's deliberate planning (over a year before filing) was evidence of an intent to cheat creditors. This conflict illustrates our earlier warning that you must find out your bankruptcy court's approach. (See *In re Swift*, 72 B.R. 563 (W.D. Okla. 1987) and *In re Krantz*, 97 B.R. 514 (N.D. Iowa 1989).)

If it's at all possible, don't file for bankruptcy until at least 90 days after using the proceeds from nonexempt property to buy exempt property or making a payment on a nondischargeable unsecured debt. If there is nonexempt property that belongs in your bankruptcy estate but that you haven't yet received, you should consider putting off filing until you get the property and have an opportunity to sell it and buy exempt property.

5. **Don't merely change the way you hold title to property.** Merely changing the way property is held from a nonexempt form to an exempt form usually arouses suspicion.

EXAMPLE: Jeff owns a house as his separate property. Although he's married, Jeff incurred virtually all of his debts alone, and so he plans to file for bankruptcy alone. In Jeff's state, the homestead exemption is only $7,500; Jeff's equity in his home is nearly $30,000. Jeff's state also exempts property held in tenancy by the entirety, so Jeff transfers ownership of the house to himself and his wife as tenants by the entirety. That exempts the house from all debts Jeff incurred solely. Because Jeff didn't create a new exemption to give himself a fresh start, but merely changed ownership form, the bankruptcy court would probably rule the transfer fraudulent, and take Jeff's house. (Jeff would get his $7,500 exemption.)

COMMUNITY PROPERTY

If you're married and live in a community property state (Arizona, California, Idaho, Louisiana, Nevada, New Mexico, Texas, Washington or Wisconsin), when you file for bankruptcy the trustee can usually take both your share of community property and your spouse's, even if your spouse doesn't file. So you might be tempted to change all or a portion of the community property into your spouse's separate property. Beware: Creditors or the trustee are apt to cry fraud, and the trustee is likely to take the property anyway.

To give you an idea of what judges consider out-of-bounds behavior on the eve of or shortly before filing for bankruptcy, here are some transactions courts decided were fraudulent:

- A debtor bought goods on credit but never paid for them. He then sold those goods and bought property that he tried to exempt.
- A debtor with nonexempt property was forced into involuntary bankruptcy by a creditor. The debtor

convinced the creditor to drop the forced bankruptcy. Then the debtor sold the nonexempt property, purchased exempt property, and filed for Chapter 7 bankruptcy.

- A debtor sold nonexempt property that was worth enough to pay off all her debts.
- A debtor sold nonexempt items for amounts well below what they were worth.
- A debtor sold valuable property to a non-filing spouse for one dollar.
- A debtor transferred nonexempt property the day after a creditor won a lawsuit against him, and then filed for bankruptcy.
- A debtor in a state with an "unlimited" homestead exemption sold all her nonexempt property and used the proceeds to pay off a large portion of her mortgage.
- A debtor bought a piano and harpsichord and a whole life insurance policy, which were all exempt in his state. He didn't play either instrument, and he had no dependents who needed insurance protection.

TAKING OUT LOANS TO PAY NONDISCHARGEABLE DEBTS

Some people are tempted to borrow money to discharge debts that aren't dischargeable—for instance a student loan—and then list the loan as a dischargeable unsecured debt. Be careful if you do this. A court could consider your actions fraudulent and dismiss your bankruptcy. If the court doesn't dismiss your case, the creditor may ask the court to declare the debt nondischargeable. If you take out the loan while you're broke and file for bankruptcy soon thereafter, you probably will be penalized. And if you borrow money or use your credit card to pay off a nondischargeable tax debt, you will not be able to discharge the loan or credit card charge. (11 U.S.C. § 523(a)(14).)

This chapter shows you how to fill out and file the forms for a Chapter 7 bankruptcy. For the most part, it's very simple—just a matter of putting the right information in the right blanks and shipping the papers off to the right bankruptcy court.

A. Finding the Right Bankruptcy Court

Because bankruptcy is a creature of federal, not state, law, you must file for bankruptcy in a special federal court. There are federal bankruptcy courts all over the country.

The federal court system divides the country into judicial districts. Every state has at least one judicial district; most have more. Normally, you file in the bankruptcy court for the federal judicial district where you've lived during the greater part of the previous 180 days (six months). You'll probably file in the nearest sizable city. If you run a business, you can instead file in the district where your principal place of business has been located during the previous 180 days, or where the business's principal assets have been located during that period.

Appendix 3 lists the addresses and phone numbers of all federal bankruptcy courts. If you live in a state with more than one district, call the court in the closest city and ask whether you live in its district. Chances are you do. While we do our best to keep Appendix 3 up-to-date, locations and phone numbers of bankruptcy courts change. If information in Appendix 3 is wrong, look in the government listings in your white pages or call directory assistance.

> **EXAMPLE:** For the past two months, you've lived in San Luis Obispo, which is in California's central judicial district. Before that you lived in Santa Rosa, in California's northern judicial district. Because during the past six months you lived longer in the northern district than the central, you should file in the bankruptcy court in the northern district. If it's too inconvenient to file there, you could wait another month, when you would qualify to file in the central district court.

➡ EMERGENCY FILING
Although people usually file all their bankruptcy forms at once, you don't have to. If you need to stop creditors quickly, you can simply file the two-page Voluntary Petition, together with a list of the name, address and zip code of each of your creditors. The automatic stay, which stops collection efforts and lawsuits against you, will then go into effect. You have 15 days to file the rest of the forms. (Bankruptcy Rule 1007(c).) See Section J, below, for instructions.

B. Before You Begin: Get Some Information From the Court

Although bankruptcy courts operate similarly throughout the country, every bankruptcy court has its own requirements for filing bankruptcy papers. If your papers don't meet these local requirements, the court clerk may reject them. So before you begin preparing your papers, write or go to your bankruptcy court to find out its requirements.

In urban areas especially, you may get no response to a letter or phone call. You may need to visit the court and get the information in person.

1. Fees

Currently, the fee for filing for a Chapter 7 bankruptcy is $130. The court also charges a $45 administrative fee. Fees change, however, so make sure you verify them with the court.

In general, you must pay the fees regardless of your income. If you can't come up with the full amount, you can ask the court for permission to pay the filing fee in installments. (Instructions for making this request are in Section J, below.) You can pay in up to four installments over 120 days. You can't pay an attorney or typing service until you've fully paid your fees—the court is entitled to its money first.

2. Local Forms

In addition to the official forms which must be filed in every bankruptcy court (they are in Section C, below), your local bankruptcy court may require you to file one or two forms that it has developed. People filing in southern California in particular must get local forms

You must get all local forms from your local bankruptcy court or a local stationery store. We can't, of course, include all local forms in this book, or tell you how to fill them out. Most, however, are self-explanatory. If you need help in obtaining or understanding them, see a local bankruptcy lawyer or typing service. (See Ch. 9, *Help Beyond the Book*.)

3. Local Court Rules

Most bankruptcy courts publish local rules that govern the court's procedures. These rules seldom apply to Chapter 7 bankruptcy cases; instead, they primarily concern Chapter 11 business bankruptcies and adversarial bankruptcy actions. But occasionally, a rule does affect a Chapter 7 bankruptcy.

You can get your local rules from the bankruptcy court—but be prepared to comb through reams of material to find the one or two rules that might apply in your case. Our recommendation is that you not bother unless you have the time and patience to pluck the few kernels of wheat you might find from the tons of chaff.

4. Number of Copies

Before filing your papers, be sure you know how many copies your court requires.

A sample letter that you can send to the court to gather this and other useful information is below. (A tear-out copy is in Appendix 4.) Include a large, self-addressed envelope. Call and ask the court if you need to affix return postage; many, but not all, courts can mail without charge.

LETTER TO BANKRUPTCY COURT

Sandra Smith
432 Oak Street
Cincinnati, OH 45219
(123) 456-7890

July 2, 19XX

United States Bankruptcy Court
735 U.S. Courthouse
100 E. 5th Street
Cincinnati, OH 45202

Attn: COURT CLERK
TO THE COURT CLERK:

Please send me the following information:

1. Copies of all local forms required by this court for an individual (not corporation) filing a Chapter 7 bankruptcy and for making amendments.
2. The number of copies or sets required.
3. The order in which forms should be submitted.
4. Complete instructions on this court's emergency filing procedures and deadlines.

I would also appreciate answers to two other questions:

1. Do you require a separate creditor mailing list (matrix)? If so, do you have specific requirements for its format?
2. Is the filing fee still $130? Is the administrative fee still $45? If either have changed, please advise.

I've enclosed a self-addressed envelope for your reply. Thank you.

Sincerely,

Sandra Smith

Sandra Smith

C. Bankruptcy Forms Checklist

You must file:

- ☐ Form 1—Voluntary Petition, in which you ask the bankruptcy court to discharge your debts.
- ☐ Form 6, which consists of:
    - ☐ Schedule A—Real Property
    - ☐ Schedule B—Personal Property
    - ☐ Schedule C—Property Claimed as Exempt
    - ☐ Schedule D—Creditors Holding Secured Claims
    - ☐ Schedule E—Creditors Holding Unsecured Priority Claims
    - ☐ Schedule F—Creditors Holding Unsecured Nonpriority Claims
    - ☐ Schedule G—Executory Contracts and Unexpired Leases
    - ☐ Schedule H—Codebtors
    - ☐ Schedule I—Current Income
    - ☐ Schedule J—Current Expenditures
    - ☐ Summary Schedules A through J
    - ☐ Declaration Concerning Debtor's Schedules, in which you declare under penalty of perjury that the information you put in the schedules is true and correct.
- ☐ Form 7—Statement of Financial Affairs, in which you provide information about your economic affairs during the past several years.
- ☐ Form 8—Chapter 7 Individual Debtor's Statement of Intention, in which you tell the court and your secured creditors what you plan to do with your property listed as collateral for a secured loan.
- ☐ Mailing matrix—a form on which you list your creditors and their addresses. The court uses this form to prepare mailing labels and mail notice of your bankruptcy filing to your creditors.
- ☐ Required local forms.

Note: Forms 2, 4 and 5 aren't used in Chapter 7 voluntary bankruptcy filings. Form 3 is the application to pay the filing fee in installments.

All together, these forms are usually called your "bankruptcy petition," although technically your petition is only Form 1. Appendix 4 contains a tear-out copy of each form, except for required local forms. As mentioned, you'll have to get these forms from the court, a local bankruptcy lawyer or a typing service.

USING THE NOLO PRESS FORMS

The content and numbering of the forms are set by the official Bankruptcy Rules, a set of rules issued by the United States Supreme Court. Private publishers, however, are free to modify the format of official forms, as long as each form asks the same questions in the same order. (Bankruptcy Rule 9009.)

Courts must accept all forms that:

- contain the questions and answers prescribed by the official forms
- are printed on one side only
- have adequate top margins, and
- have two pre-punched holes in the top margin. (Bankruptcy Rules 5005 and 9029.)

Under the Bankruptcy Rules, all courts must accept the forms in this book, even if the court is used to seeing forms published by a different company, with its own unique format. Our forms meet all of the official Bankruptcy Rule requirements, except that they don't have holes punched in the top—you'll have to do that yourself. (See Section J, below.)

D. Tips for Completing Forms

Here are some tips to make filling in your forms easier and the whole bankruptcy process smoother. A sample completed form accompanies each form's instructions. Refer to it while you fill in your bankruptcy papers.

Use your worksheets. If you've completed the worksheets in Chs. 1 and 2, you've already done a lot of the work. It will save you lots of time when you prepare your bankruptcy forms; keep them handy. If you skipped those chapters, refer to Worksheet 2 and the accompanying instructions (Ch. 2) for help in identifying what property you should list in your bankruptcy forms.

Photocopy the forms before you start. You can't tear out and file the forms in Appendix 4 because they are slightly smaller than regulation size, due to bookbinding requirements. Good photocopies of the forms on 8½" by 11" paper will work fine, however. Make at least two photocopies of all the forms in the Appendix. Keep the originals (taken from Appendix 4) for additional copies if you need more.

Start with drafts. First enter the information in pencil, so you can make corrections along the way. Prepare final forms to file with the court only after you've double-checked your drafts.

Type your final forms. Although you are not required to type your forms, many courts prefer that they be typed. But even if your court doesn't, the court clerk is likely to be friendlier if you show up with neatly typed forms. If you don't have access to a typewriter, many libraries have typewriters available to the public (for a small rental fee), or you can hire a bankruptcy form preparation service to prepare your forms with the information you provide. (See Ch. 9, *Help Beyond the Book.*)

Be ridiculously thorough. Always err on the side of giving too much information rather than too little. If you leave information off the forms, the bankruptcy trustee or court may become suspicious of your motives. If you leave creditors off the forms, the debts you owe these creditors probably won't be discharged—hardly the result you want. If you intentionally or carelessly fail to list all your property, or fail to accurately describe your recent property transactions, the court may rule that you acted with fraudulent intent. It may deny your bankruptcy discharge altogether, and you may lose some property that you might otherwise have kept.

Put a response to every question that calls for one. Most of the forms have a box to check if your answer is "none." If a question doesn't have a "none" box and the question doesn't apply to you, type in "N/A" for "not applicable." This will let the trustee know that you didn't overlook the question. Occasionally, a question that doesn't apply to you will have a number of blanks. Put "N/A" in only the first blank if it is obvious that this applies to the other blanks as well. If it's not clear, put "N/A" in every blank.

Don't worry about repetition. Sometimes different forms— or different questions on the same form—may ask for the same or overlapping information. Don't worry about providing the same information multiple times—too much information is never a sin in bankruptcy.

Explain uncertainties. If you can't figure out which category on a form to use for a debt or item of property, list the debt or item in what you think is the appropriate place and briefly note next to your entry that you're uncertain. The important thing is to disclose the information somewhere. The bankruptcy trustee will sort it out, if necessary.

Be scrupulously honest. You must swear, under penalty of perjury, that you've been truthful on your bankruptcy forms. The most likely consequence for failing to be scrupulously honest is a dismissal of your bankruptcy case, but you could be prosecuted for perjury if it's evident that you deliberately lied.

Use continuation pages if you run out of room. The space for entering information is sometimes skimpy, especially if you're filing jointly. Most of the forms come with pre-formatted continuation pages if you need more room. But if there is no continuation form in Appendix 4, prepare one yourself, using a piece of regular white 8½" by 11" paper. Put "see continuation page" next to the question you're working on and enter the additional information on the continuation page. Label the continuation pages with your name, the form name and indicate "Continuation Page 1," "Continuation Page 2" and so on. Be sure to attach all continuation pages to their appropriate forms when you file your bankruptcy papers.

Get help if you need it. If your situation is complicated, you're unsure about how to complete a form or you run into trouble when you go to file your papers, consult a bankruptcy attorney or bankruptcy form preparer, or do some legal research before proceeding. (See Ch. 9, *Help Beyond the Book.*)

SAMPLE CONTINUATION PAGE

In re: Joshua and Alice Milton, Debtors.

Form 7, Statement of Financial Affairs

Continuation Page 1

11. Closed Financial Accounts: Bank of Iowa, 150 Broadway, Cedar Rapids, IA 52407; Savings Account No. 1-23-567-890, final balance of $3,446.18; closed September 11, 19XX.

SEEK EMOTIONAL SUPPORT IF YOU NEED IT

Many people who file for bankruptcy feel a sense of loss. It may be a loss of an old comfortable lifestyle, a loss of identity or a loss of property. They grieve for the way things used to be or could have been.

If you feel this sense of loss, focus on the future before you. Many who have filed for bankruptcy before you are now prosperous.

It may be important for you to discuss your experience with someone who you feel can help you: a counselor, a clergy member, your spouse or another loved one.

E. Form 1—Voluntary Petition

Filing your voluntary petition gets your bankruptcy started and puts the automatic stay into effect, stopping creditors from trying to collect from you.

EMERGENCY FILING

If you want to file as quickly as possible, without filling in all the bankruptcy forms, go to Section J for instructions.

SAMPLE FORMS

Throughout this chapter, we have the completed sample forms of Molly and Jonathan Maytag, who live in Ohio. Bear in mind that these are examples only. Even if you live in Ohio, your completed forms will look very different.

A completed sample two-page Voluntary Petition and line-by-line instructions follow.

First Page

Court Name. At the top of the first page, fill in the first two blanks with the name of the judicial district you're filing in, such as the "Central District of California." If your state has only one district, type XXXXXX in the first blank. If your state divides its districts into divisions, type the division after the state name, such as "Northern District of Ohio, Eastern Division." See Appendix 3 for the bankruptcy courts in your state.

Name of Debtor. Enter your full name (last name first), in capital letters, as used on your checks, driver's license and other formal documents.

ARE YOU MARRIED AND FILING WITH YOUR SPOUSE?

If you and your spouse are filing jointly, you'll have to designate one of you as the debtor and one of you as the spouse. In some states, if a couple has lived together for a period of time and have held themselves out as husband and wife, they may be legally married. Such common law marriages can be created in Alabama, Colorado, Idaho, Iowa, Kansas, Montana, Ohio, Oklahoma, Pennsylvania, Rhode Island, South Carolina, Texas, Utah and the District of Columbia. If you live in one of these states (or did at a time when you believed that you had a common law marriage), you may be married for purposes of the bankruptcy laws. If you are unsure of your marital status, see a lawyer.

Name of Joint Debtor (Spouse). If you are married and filing jointly with your spouse, put your spouse's name (last name first) in the joint debtor box. Again, use the name that appears on formal documents. If you're filing alone, type "N/A" anywhere in the box.

All Other Names. If you have been known by any other name in the last six years, list it here. If you've operated a business as an individual proprietor during the previous six years, include your trade name (fictitious or assumed business name). But don't include minor variations in spelling or form. For instance, if your name is John Lewis Odegard, don't put down that you're sometimes known as J.L. But if you've used the pseudonym J.L. Smith, list it. If you're uncertain, list the name if you think you may have used it with a creditor. It can't hurt, because the purpose of this box is to make sure that when your creditors receive notice of your bankruptcy filing, they'll know who you are. Do the same for your spouse (in the box to the right) if you are filing jointly. If you're filing alone, type "N/A" anywhere in the box to the right.

Soc. Sec./Tax I.D. No. Enter your Social Security number. If you have a taxpayer's I.D. number, enter it as well. Do the same for your spouse (in the box to the right) if you are filing jointly. If you're filing alone, type "N/A" anywhere in the box to the right.

Street Address of Debtor. Enter your current street address. Even if you get all of your mail at a post office box, list the address of your personal residence.

Street Address of Joint Debtor. Enter your spouse's current street address (even if it's the same as yours) if you are filing jointly—again, no post office boxes. If you're filing alone, type "N/A" anywhere in the box.

County of Residence. Enter the county in which you live. Do the same for your spouse if you're filing jointly. Otherwise type "NA" in the box.

FORM 1. VOLUNTARY PETITION

UNITED STATES BANKRUPTCY COURT __Northern__ DISTRICT OF __Ohio, Eastern Division__	**Voluntary Petition**

Name of Debtor (if individual, enter Last, First, Middle): MAYTAG, MOLLY MARIA	Name of Joint Debtor (Spouse) (Last, First, Middle): MAYTAG, JONATHAN
All Other Names used by the Debtor in the last 6 years (include married, maiden, and trade names): Johnson, Molly Maria	All Other Names used by the Joint Debtor in the last 6 years (include married, maiden, and trade names): Maytag Delicatessen
Soc. Sec./Tax I.D. No. (if more than one, state all): 999-99-9999	Soc. Sec./Tax I.D. No. (if more than one, state all): 000-00-0000
Street Address of Debtor (No. & Street, City, State & Zip Code): 21 Scarborough Road South Cleveland Heights, OH 41118	Street Address of Joint Debtor (No. & Street, City, State & Zip Code): 21 Scarborough Road South Cleveland Heights, OH 41118
County of Residence or of the Principal Place of Business: Cuyahoga	County of Residence or of the Principal Place of Business: Cuyahoga
Mailing Address of Debtor (if different from street address): N/A	Mailing Address of Joint Debtor (if different from street address): N/A

Location of Principal Assets of Business Debtor
(if different from street address above):

N/A

Information Regarding the Debtor (Check the Applicable Boxes)

Venue (Check any applicable box)

☒ Debtor has been domiciled or has had a residence, principal place of business, or principal assets in this District for 180 days immediately preceding the date of this petition or for a longer part of such 180 days than in any other District.

☐ There is a bankruptcy case concerning debtor's affiliate, general partner, or partnership pending in this District.

Type of Debtor (Check all boxes that apply)		**Chapter or Section of Bankruptcy Code Under Which the Petition is Filed** (Check one box)	
☒ Individual(s) ☐ Railroad ☐ Corporation ☐ Stockbroker ☐ Partnership ☐ Commodity Broker ☐ Other _____		☒ Chapter 7 ☐ Chapter 11 ☐ Chapter 13 ☐ Chapter 9 ☐ Chapter 12 ☐ Sec. 304 – Case ancillary to foreign proceeding	

Nature of Debts (Check one box)	**Filing Fee** (Check one box)
☒ Consumer/Non-Business ☐ Business	☒ Full Filing Fee attached ☐ Filing Fee to be paid in installments. (Applicable to individuals only.) Must attach signed application for the court's consideration certifying that the debtor is unable to pay fee except in installments. Rule 1006(b). See Official Form No. 3.
Chapter 11 Small Business (Check all boxes that apply) ☐ Debtor is a small business as defined in 11 U.S.C. § 101 N/A ☐ Debtor is and elects to be considered a small business under 11 U.S.C. §1121(e) (Optional)	

Statistical/Administrative Information (Estimates only)	THIS SPACE FOR COURT USE ONLY
☒ Debtor estimates that funds will be available for distribution to unsecured creditors. ☐ Debtor estimates that, after any exempt property is excluded and administrative expenses paid, there will be no funds available for distribution to unsecured creditors.	

Estimated Number of Creditors	1-15	16-49	50-99	100-199	200-999	1000-over
	☐	☒	☐	☐	☐	☐

Estimated Assets	$0 to $50,000	$50,001 to $100,000	$100,001 to $500,000	$500,001 to $1 million	$1,000,001 to $10 million	$10,000,001 to $50 million	$50,000,001 $100 million	More than $100 million
	☐	☐	☒	☐	☐	☐	☐	☐

Estimated Debts	$0 to $50,000	$50,001 to $100,000	$100,001 to $500,000	$500,001 to $1 million	$1,000,001 to $10 million	$10,000,001 to $50 million	$50,000,001 $100 million	More than $100 million
	☐	☐	☒	☐	☐	☐	☐	☐

Voluntary Petition
(This page must be completed and filed in every case.)

Name of Debtor(s): **Maytag, Molly & Jonathan**   Form 1, Page 2

Prior Bankruptcy Case Filed Within Last 6 Years (If more than one, attach additional sheet)

Location Where Filed: N/A	Case Number:	Date Filed:

Pending Bankruptcy Case Filed by any Spouse, Partner or Affiliate of this Debtor (If more than one, attach additional sheet)

Name of Debtor: N/A	Case Number:	Date Filed:
District:	Relationship:	Judge:

Signatures

Signature(s) of Debtor(s) (Individual/Joint)

I declare under penalty of perjury that the information provided in this petition is true and correct.

[If petitioner is an individual whose debts are primarily consumer debts and has chosen to file under chapter 7] I am aware that I may proceed under chapter 7, 11, 12 or 13 of title 11, United States Code, understand the relief available under each such chapter, and choose to proceed under chapter 7.

I request relief in accordance with the chapter of title 11, United States Code, specified in this petition.

X *Molly Maytag*
Signature of Debtor

X *Jonathan Maytag*
Signature of Joint Debtor

(216) 555-7373
Telephone Number (If not represented by attorney)

July 13, 19XX
Date

Signature of Debtor (Corporation/Partnership)

I declare under penalty of perjury that the information provided in this petition is true and correct and that I have been authorized to file this petition on behalf of the debtor.

The debtor requests relief in accordance with the chapter of title 11, United States Code, specified in this petition.

X _____N/A_____
Signature of Authorized Individual

_____
Printed Name of Authorized Individual

_____
Title of Authorized Individual

_____
Date

Signature of Attorney

X _____N/A_____
Signature of Attorney for Debtor(s)

_____
Printed Name of Attorney for Debtor(s)

_____
Firm Name

_____
Address

_____

_____
Telephone Number

_____
Date

Signature of Non-Attorney Petition Preparer

I certify that I am a bankruptcy petition preparer as defined in 11 U.S.C. § 110, that I prepared this document for compensation, and that I have provided the debtor with a copy of this document.

_____N/A_____
Printed Name of Bankruptcy Petition Preparer

_____
Social Security Number

_____
Address

_____

Names and Social Security numbers of all other individuals who prepared or assisted in preparing this document:

N/A

If more than one person prepared this document, attach additional sheets conforming to the appropriate official form for each person.

Exhibit A

(To be completed if debtor is required to file periodic reports (e.g., forms 10K and 10Q) with the Securities and Exchange Commission pursuant to Section 13 or 15(d) of the Securities Exchange Act of 1934 and is requesting relief under chapter 11.)

☐ Exhibit A is attached and made a part of this petition.

Exhibit B

(To be completed if debtor is an individual whose debts are primarily consumer debts.)

I, the attorney for the petitioner named in the foregoing petition, declare that I have informed the petitioner that [he or she] may proceed under chapter 7, 11, 12, or 13 of title 11, United States Code, and have explained the relief available under each such chapter.

X _____N/A_____
Signature of Attorney for Debtor(s)   Date

X _____
Signature of Bankruptcy Petition Preparer

_____
Date

A bankruptcy petition preparer's failure to comply with the provisions of title 11 and the Federal Rules of Bankruptcy Procedure may result in fines or imprisonment or both. 11 U.S.C. § 110; 18 U.S.C. § 156.

Mailing Address of Debtor. Enter your mailing address if it is different from your street address. If it isn't, put "N/A." Do the same for your spouse—in the box to the right—if you are filing jointly.

Location of Principal Assets of Business Debtor. If you—or your spouse if you are filing jointly—have been self-employed or operated a business as a sole proprietor within the last two years, you'll be considered a "business debtor." This means you will have to provide additional information on Form 7 (Section G, below). If your business owns any assets—such as machines or inventory—list their primary location. If they are all located at your home or mailing address, enter that address.

Venue. Check the top box. Here is where you state why you're filing in this particular bankruptcy court. Remember, your selection of the court in which to file must be based on your residence (for the longer part of the previous 180 days), the principal place of your business, or the location of the principal assets of your business (Section A, above).

Type of Debtor. Check the first box—"Individual(s)"—even if you have been self-employed or operated a sole proprietorship during the previous two years. If you are filing as a corporation, partnership or other type of business entity, you shouldn't be using this book. (See Introduction, *How to Use This Book,* Section A.)

Nature of Debts. Check "Consumer/Non-Business" if you aren't in business and haven't been for the previous two years. Even if you're self-employed or in business as a sole proprietor, if most of your debts are owed personally—not by your business—check "Consumer/Non-Business." If, however, the bulk of your indebtedness is owed by your business, check "Business." If you are in doubt, check "Business."

Chapter 11 Small Business. Type "N/A" anywhere in the box.

Chapter or Section of Bankruptcy Code Under Which the Petition Is Filed. Check "Chapter 7."

Filing Fee. If you will attach the entire fee, check the first box. If you plan to ask the court for permission to pay in installments, check the second box. (Instructions for applying to the court are in Section J, below.) If you will apply for a fee waiver, type "N/A."

Statistical/Administrative Information. Here you estimate information about your debts and assets. If you completed Worksheets 1 and 2 in Chs. 1 and 2, you may be able to fill in these sections now. If you didn't complete those worksheets, wait until you've completed the other forms before providing this information. But remember to come back and check the appropriate boxes before filing.

If you plan to make an emergency filing (Section J, below), use Worksheets 1 and 2 to arrive at your best estimates.

Second Page

Name of Debtor(s). Enter your name and your spouse's, if you are filing jointly.

Prior Bankruptcy Case Filed Within Last 6 Years. If you haven't filed a bankruptcy case within the previous six years type "N/A" in the first box. If you—or your spouse, if you're filing jointly—have, enter the requested information. A previous Chapter 7 bankruptcy bars you from filing another one until six years have passed. And, if a previously filed Chapter 7 bankruptcy case was dismissed for cause within the previous 180 days, you may have to wait and be limited as to the debts you can discharge. (See Ch. 1, *Should You File for Chapter 7 Bankruptcy?*, Section B. If either situation applies to you, see a bankruptcy lawyer before filing.)

Pending Bankruptcy Case Filed by any Spouse, Partner or Affiliate of This Debtor. The term affiliate refers to a related business under a corporate structure and partner refers to a business partnership. If your spouse has a bankruptcy case pending anywhere in the country, enter the requested information. Otherwise, type "N/A" in the first box.

Signature(s) of Debtor(s) (Individual/Joint). You—and your spouse, if you are filing jointly—must sign where indicated. If you are filing singly, type "N/A" on the joint debtor signature line. Include your telephone number and the date. You—and your spouse if you are filing jointly—declare that you are aware that you may file under other sections of the bankruptcy code and that you still choose to file for Chapter 7 bankruptcy.

Signature of Debtor (Corporation/Partnership). Type "N/A" on the first line.

Signature of Attorney. Type "N/A" on the first line.

Exhibit B. Type "N/A" on the signature line.

Signature of Non-Attorney Petition Preparer. If a Bankruptcy Petition Preparer typed your forms, have that person complete this section. Otherwise, type "N/A" on the first line.

OTHER BANKRUPTCY OPTIONS

Chapter 13 bankruptcy lets you pay off all or a portion of your debts over a three- to-five-year period without giving up any property. To qualify, you must have steady income in an amount sufficient to pay your unsecured creditors at least the value of your non-exempt property. Most Chapter 13 filings either are abandoned (the debtor stops making the payments) or end up converting to Chapter 7 bankruptcy. Thus, many bankruptcy lawyers recommend filing a Chapter 7 bankruptcy at the outset. If you have adequate income left after expenses to pay all or a major portion of your debts over time, however, you may be forced by the court to choose Chapter 13 bankruptcy. For more information on Chapter 13 bankruptcy, see Ch. 1, *Should You File for Chapter 7 Bankruptcy?*, Section E.4.

Chapter 12 bankruptcy, which is very similar to Chapter 13, is specially designed for family farmers and provides a way to keep the farm while paying off debts over time. If you are a farmer, we recommend you speak with a bankruptcy attorney about Chapter 12 bankruptcy before choosing to file a Chapter 7 bankruptcy.

Chapter 11 bankruptcy is usually reserved for corporations and partnerships. Individuals occasionally file for Chapter 11 bankruptcy, however, if their secured debts exceed $750,000, their unsecured debts exceed $250,000 and they think they'll have enough steady income to pay off a portion of their debts over a several year period. This book doesn't cover Chapter 11 bankruptcies and few bankruptcy attorneys recommend them for individuals.

F. Form 6—Schedules

"Form 6" refers to a series of schedules that provides the trustee and court with a picture of your current financial situation. Most of the information needed for these schedules was asked for in Worksheets 1 and 2 which—we hope—you completed earlier. Completed sample forms and instructions follow.

1. Schedule A—Real Property

Here you list all the real property you own as of the date you'll file the petition. Don't worry about whether a particular piece of property is exempt. In Schedule C you claim your exemptions. If you filled in Worksheet 2 in Ch. 2, *Your Property and Bankruptcy*, get it out. Much of that information goes on Schedule A.

A completed sample of Schedule A and line-by-line instructions follow. Even if you don't own any real estate, you still must complete the top of this form.

REAL PROPERTY DEFINED

Real property—land and things permanently attached to land—includes more than just a house. It can also include unimproved land, vacation cabins, condominiums, duplexes, rental property, business property, mobile home park spaces, agricultural land, airplane hangars and any other buildings permanently attached to land.

You may own real estate even if you can't walk on it, live on it or get income from it. This might be true, for example, if:

- you own real estate solely because you are married to a spouse who owns real estate and you live in a community property state, or
- someone else lives on property that you are entitled to receive in the future under a trust agreement.

Leases and Time-Shares: If you hold a time-share lease in a vacation cabin or property, lease a boat dock or underground portions of real estate for mineral or oil exploration, or otherwise lease or rent real estate of any description, don't list it on Schedule A. All leases should be listed on Schedule G. (See Section 7, below.)

In re. Type your name and the name of your spouse, if you're filing jointly.

Case No. If you made an emergency filing, fill in the case number assigned by the court. Otherwise, leave this blank.

Description and Location of Property. List the type of property—for example, house, farm or undeveloped lot—and street address of every piece of real property you own. You don't need to include the legal description (the description on the deed) of the property.

In re ___Maytag, Molly and Jonathan___,   Case No._____
                    Debtor   (If known)

SCHEDULE A—REAL PROPERTY

Except as directed below, list all real property in which the debtor has any legal, equitable, or future interest, including all property owned as a co-tenant, community property, or in which the debtor has a life estate. Include any property in which the debtor holds rights and powers exercisable for the debtor's own benefit. If the debtor is married, state whether husband, wife, or both own the property by placing an "H," "W," "J," or "C" in the column labeled "Husband, Wife, Joint, or Community." If the debtor holds no interest in real property, write "None" under "Description and Location of Property."

Do not include interests in executory contracts and unexpired leases on this schedule. List them in Schedule G—Executory Contracts and Unexpired Leases.

If an entity claims to have a lien or hold a secured interest in any property, state the amount of the secured claim. See Schedule D. If no entity claims to hold a secured interest in the property, write "None" in the column labeled "Amount of Secured Claim."

If the debtor is an individual or if a joint petition is filed, state the amount of any exception claimed in the property only in Schedule C—Property Claimed as Exempt.

DESCRIPTION AND LOCATION OF PROPERTY	NATURE OF DEBTOR'S INTEREST IN PROPERTY	HUSBAND, WIFE, JOINT, OR COMMUNITY	CURRENT MARKET VALUE OF DEBTOR'S INTEREST IN PROPERTY WITHOUT DEDUCTING ANY SECURED CLAIM OR EXEMPTION	AMOUNT OF SECURED CLAIM
Residence at 21 Scarborough Road South, Cleveland Heights, OH 44118	Fee Simple	J	$95,000	$75,000 mortgage $12,000 second mortgage $2,000 judgment lien
Unimproved lot at 244 Highway 50, Parma, OH 44000	Fee Simple	H	$5,000	none

Total ➡ $ $100,000

(Report also on Summary of Schedules.)

➡ IF YOU DON'T OWN REAL ESTATE
Type "N/A" anywhere in the first column and move
on to Schedule B.

Nature of Debtor's Interest in Property. In this column, you
need to give the legal term of the interest you (or you and
your spouse) have in the real estate. Ch. 2, *Your Property
and Bankruptcy,* Section B.1, contains descriptions of the
most common types of ownership interests in real estate. If
your ownership interest sounds like it's one of the categories described, enter that category. If you have no idea
which label describes your interest, put "Don't know."

Husband, Wife, Joint or Community. If you're not married,
put "N/A." If you are married, indicate whether the real
estate is owned:

- by the husband (H)
- by the wife (W)
- jointly by husband and wife in a common law property state (J), or
- jointly by husband and wife as community property
  (C)—a form of joint ownership that applies to property acquired by couples living in Arizona, California,
  Idaho, Louisiana, Nevada, New Mexico, Texas, Washington or Wisconsin. California also includes any real
  property acquired by a couple in another state that
  they own when they move to California.

**Current Market Value of Debtor's Interest in Property Without
Deducting Any Secured Claim or Exemption.** Enter the current
fair market value of your real estate ownership interest. If
you filled in Worksheet 2 (Ch. 2, *Your Property and Bankruptcy*), use the amount you entered in Column 2.

Don't figure in homestead exemptions or any mortgages
or other liens on the property. Just put the actual current
market value as best you can compute it. See Ch. 2, *Your
Property and Bankruptcy,* Section B.2, for information on
valuing real estate.

If you own the property with someone else who is not
filing for bankruptcy, put only your ownership share in this
column. For example, if you and your brother own a home
as joint tenants (each owns 50%), split the current market
value in half.

If your interest is intangible—for example, you are a
beneficiary of real estate held in trust that won't be distributed for many years—provide an estimate or put "don't
know," and explain why you can't be more precise.

Total. Add the amounts in the fourth column and enter
the total in the box at the bottom of the page.

Amount of Secured Claim. Here is where you list mortgages and other debts secured by the property. If there is no
secured claim of any type on the real estate, enter "None."

If there is, enter separately the amount of each outstanding
mortgage, deed of trust, home equity loan or lien (judgment lien, mechanic's lien, materialman's lien, tax lien or
the like) that is claimed against the property. If you don't
know the balance on your mortgage, deed of trust or home
equity loan, call the lender. To find out the values of liens,
visit the land records office in your county and look up the
parcel in the records; the clerk can show you how. Or you
can order a title search through a real estate attorney or title
insurance company. If you own several pieces of real estate
and there is one lien on file against all the real estate, list the
full amount of the lien for each separate property item.
Don't worry if, taken together, the value of the liens on a
property item is higher than the value of the property; it's
quite common.

How you itemize liens in this schedule won't affect how
your property or the liens will be treated in bankruptcy.
The idea here is to notify the trustee of all possible liens that
may affect your equity in your real estate.

If you can't afford to pay a lawyer or title insurance
company to find out any of this information, enter "unknown."

2. Schedule B—Personal Property

Here you must list and evaluate all of your personal property, including property that is security for a debt and property that is exempt. If you didn't fill in Worksheet 2, turn to
Ch. 2, *Your Property and Bankruptcy,* for explanations and
suggestions about property for each of the schedule's categories.

⚠ BE HONEST AND THOROUGH
Probably the single biggest temptation to cheat in the
bankruptcy process arises with your personal property
schedule, because once you list an item, the whole world—
including the bankruptcy trustee—knows about it. And, if
it's nonexempt, it may be sold for the benefit of your
creditors. Don't give in to temptation and try to hide an
asset. If your omission is discovered, your bankruptcy will
most likely be dismissed, and you won't be able to discharge
your debts in any subsequent bankruptcy you might file.
Even include assets you think are worthless. The failure to
disclose worthless assets has been used as grounds for
denying a bankruptcy discharge. (See *In re Calder,* 912 F.2d
454 (10th Cir. 1990).)

A completed sample and line-by-line instructions follow. If you need more room, use an attached continuation
page or type up a continuation page yourself. (See Section
D, above.)

In re and **Case No.** Follow the instructions for Schedule A.

Type of Property. The form lists general categories of personal property. You leave this column as is.

None. If you own no property that fits in a category listed in the first column, enter an "X" in this column next to the category.

Description and Location of Property. List specific items that fall in each general category. See the checklist following Worksheet 2 (Ch. 2, *Your Property and Bankruptcy*) for some prompts on property to list here. The checklist categories correspond exactly; however, some categories are described slightly differently than on the form. (That's because we translated the form into English.)

Separately list all items worth $50 or more. Combine small items into larger categories whenever reasonable. For example, you don't need to list every spatula, colander, garlic press and ice cream scoop; instead, put "kitchen cookware." If you list numerous items in one category (as is likely for household goods and furnishings), you may need to attach a continuation sheet.

When listing cash on hand or describing deposit accounts, try to explain the source of the funds (for instance, from wages, Social Security payments or child support). This may help you later when you decide whether any of your money qualifies as exempt property.

Most of your personal property is probably at your residence. If so, write a sentence at the top of the form or column to that effect: "All property is located at my/our residence unless otherwise noted." Indicate specifically when the facts are different. If someone else holds property for you (for example, you loaned your aunt your color TV), put that person's name and address in this column. The idea is to tell the trustee where all your property is located so that it can be taken and sold to pay your creditors if it isn't exempt.

A few categories ask you to "give particulars." This is what you should do:

Question 16—List all child support or alimony arrears— that is, money that should have been paid to you but hasn't been. Specify the dates the payments were due and missed, such as "$250 monthly child support payments for June, July, August and September 19XX."

Question 17: List all money owed to you and not yet paid other than child support and alimony. If you've obtained a judgment against someone but haven't been paid, list it here. State the defendant's name, the date of the judgment, the court that issued the judgment, the amount of the judgment and the kind of case (such as car accident).

Question 21: State what the patent, copyright, trademark or the like is for. Give the number assigned by the issuing

agency and length of time the patent, copyright, trademark or the like will last.

Question 22: List all licenses and franchises, what they cover, the length of time remaining, who they are with and if you can transfer them to someone else.

Question 30: For your crops, list whether or not they've been harvested, whether or not they've been sold, and if so to whom and for how much, if you've taken out any loan against them and if they are insured.

Husband, Wife, Joint, or Community. If you're not married, put "N/A" at the top of the column.

If you are married and own all or most of your personal property jointly with your spouse, put one of the following on the top or bottom of the form:

- **If you live in a common law property state:** "All property is owned jointly unless otherwise indicated." Then note when a particular item is owned by only H or W.
- **If you live in a community property state:** "All property is owned jointly as community property unless otherwise indicated." Then note when a particular item is owned by only H or W.

If you are married and own many items separately, for each item specify:

- husband (H)
- wife (W)
- jointly by husband and wife (J), or
- jointly by husband and wife in a community property state (C).

For more information on ownership of property by married couples, see Ch. 2, *Your Property and Bankruptcy*, Section A.6.

Current Market Value of Debtor's Interest in Property, Without Deducting Any Secured Claim or Exemption. You can take the information requested here from Worksheet 2. Put the current market value of the property, without regard to any

In re ____Maytag, Molly and Jonathan____,   Case No._____
                    Debtor   (If known)

SCHEDULE B—PERSONAL PROPERTY

Except as directed below, list all personal property of the debtor of whatever kind. If the debtor has no property in one or more of the categories, place an "X" in the appropriate position in the column labeled "None." If additional space is needed in any category, attach a separate sheet properly identified with the case name, case number, and the number of the category. If the debtor is married, state whether husband, wife, or both own the property by placing an "H," "W," "J," or "C" in the column labeled "Husband, Wife, Joint, or Community." If the debtor is an individual or a joint petition is filed, state the amount of any exemptions claimed only in Schedule C—Property Claimed as Exempt.

Do not include interests in executory contracts and unexpired leases on this schedule. List them in Schedule G—Executory Contracts and Unexpired Leases.

If the property is being held for the debtor by someone else, state that person's name and address under "Description and Location of Property."

TYPE OF PROPERTY	NONE	* All property is located at our residence unless otherwise noted. DESCRIPTION AND LOCATION OF PROPERTY	HUSBAND, WIFE, JOINT, OR COMMUNITY	CURRENT MARKET VALUE OF DEBTOR'S INTEREST IN PROPERTY, WITHOUT DEDUCTING ANY SECURED CLAIM OR EXEMPTION
1. Cash on hand.		Cash from wages	J	100
2. Checking, savings or other financial accounts, certificates of deposit, or shares in banks, savings and loan, thrift, building and loan, and homestead associations, or credit unions, brokerage houses, or cooperatives.		Checking account #12345, Ameritrust, 10 Financial Way, Cleveland Hts, OH 44118 (from wages)	J	250
		Savings account #98765, Shaker Savings, 44 Trust Street, Cleveland Hts, OH 44118 (from wages)	J	400
		Checking account #058-118061, Ohio Savings, 1818 Lakeshore Dr., Cleveland, OH 44123	H	100
3. Security deposits with public utilities, telephone companies, landlords, and others.	X			
4. Household goods and furnishings, including audio, video, and computer equipment.		Stereo system	J	300
		Washer/Dryer set	J	150
		Refrigerator	J	250
		Stove	J	150
		Household furniture	J	600
		Minor appliances	J	75
		Antique desk	J	250
		Vacuum	J	30
		Bed & bedding	J	500
		Television	J	135
		VCR	J	75
		Lawnmower	J	100
		Swingset, children's toys	J	180
		Snowblower	J	100
		Oriental rug	J	2,500

In re ___Maytag, Molly and Jonathan___,   Case No._____
Debtor   (If known)

SCHEDULE B—PERSONAL PROPERTY
(Continuation Sheet)

TYPE OF PROPERTY	NONE	DESCRIPTION AND LOCATION OF PROPERTY	HUSBAND, WIFE, JOINT, OR COMMUNITY	CURRENT MARKET VALUE OF DEBTOR'S INTEREST IN PROPERTY, WITHOUT DEDUCTING ANY SECURED CLAIM OR EXEMPTION
5. Books, pictures and other art objects, antiques, stamp, coin, record, tape, compact disc, and other collections or collectibles.		Books Stamp collection	J J	50 75
6. Wearing apparel.		Clothing	J	625
7. Furs and jewelry.		Wedding rings Diamond necklace Watches	J W J	225 325 50
8. Firearms and sports, photographic, and other hobby equipment.		Mountain bike Camera Sword collection	J J W	165 125 1,485
9. Interests in insurance policies. Name insurance company of each policy and itemize surrender or refund value of each.		Life insurance policy, Lively Ins. Co., 120 Manhattan Street, NY, NY 10012 Policy #14-171136 Life insurance policy, Live-a-long-time Co. 52 Mitchell Ave., Hartford, CT 06434. Policy #33-19195WY17	H W	120 65
10. Annuities. Itemize and name each issuer.	X			
11. Interests in IRA, ERISA, Keogh, or other pension or profit sharing plans. Itemize.		Cleveland Builder's Pension, 100 Chester Way, Cleveland, OH 44114 IRA, Basic Bank, 9712 Smitco Creek Blvd., Columbus, OH 45923	H J	6,612 3,400
12. Stock and interests in incorporated and unincorporated businesses. Itemize.		Trusso Corp. stock, #3711. 50 shares @ $20 each Investco Ltd. stock, #1244711, 5 shares @ $100 each Rayco Co. stock, #RC53, 20 shares @ $40 each All certificates at Ameritrust, 10 Financial Way, Cleveland Hts, OH 44118	J J J	1,000 500 800
13. Interests in partnerships or joint ventures. Itemize.	X			

In re ___Maytag, Molly and Jonathan_____,   Case No._____
　　　　　　　　　Debtor　　　　　　　　　　　　　　　　　　　(If known)

SCHEDULE B—PERSONAL PROPERTY
(Continuation Sheet)

TYPE OF PROPERTY	NONE	DESCRIPTION AND LOCATION OF PROPERTY	HUSBAND, WIFE, JOINT, OR COMMUNITY	CURRENT MARKET VALUE OF DEBTOR'S INTEREST IN PROPERTY, WITHOUT DEDUCTING ANY SECURED CLAIM OR EXEMPTION
14. Government and corporate bonds and other negotiable and non-negotiable instruments.		US Savings Bonds, located at Ameritrust, 10 Financial Way, Cleveland Hts, OH 44118	J	1,000
		Promissory note from Jonathan Maytag's sister, Trini Maytag Ellison, dated 11/3/XX	J	500
15. Accounts receivable.	X			
16. Alimony, maintenance, support, and property settlements to which the debtor is or may be entitled. Give particulars.	X			
17. Other liquidated debts owing debtor including tax refunds. Give particulars.		Wages for 6/XX from Cleveland Builder	H	1,900
		Wages for 6/1/XX to 6/30/XX from Typing Circles	W	100
18. Equitable or future interest, life estates, and rights or powers exercisable for the benefit of the debtor other than those listed in Schedule of Real Property.	X			
19. Contingent and noncontingent interests in estate of a decedent, death benefit plan, life insurance policy, or trust.	X			
20. Other contingent and unliquidated claims of every nature, including tax refunds, counterclaims of the debtor, and rights to setoff claims. Give estimated value of each.	X			
21. Patents, copyrights, and other intellectual property. Give particulars.	X			
22. Licenses, franchises, and other general intangibles. Give particulars.	X			

In re ___Maytag, Molly and Jonathan___,   Case No._____

Debtor   (If known)

SCHEDULE B—PERSONAL PROPERTY
(Continuation Sheet)

TYPE OF PROPERTY	NONE	DESCRIPTION AND LOCATION OF PROPERTY	HUSBAND, WIFE, JOINT, OR COMMUNITY	CURRENT MARKET VALUE OF DEBTOR'S INTEREST IN PROPERTY, WITHOUT DEDUCTING ANY SECURED CLAIM OR EXEMPTION
23. Automobiles, trucks, trailers, and other vehicles and accessories.		1988 Honda Motorcycle	W	1,000
24. Boats, motors, and accessories.		Sailboard, docked at Lake Erie Dock, Cleveland, OH	J	1,250
25. Aircraft and accessories.	X			
26. Office equipment, furnishings, and supplies.		Computer (for business)	J	1,100
		Typewriter (for business)	J	125
		Fax Machine (for business)	J	500
27. Machinery, fixtures, equipment, and supplies used in business.		Carpentry tools	J	150
28. Inventory.	X			
29. Animals.		Poodles (2)	J	200
30. Crops—growing or harvested. Give particulars.	X			
31. Farming equipment and implements.	X			
32. Farm supplies, chemicals, and feed.	X			
33. Other personal property of any kind not already listed, such as season tickets. Itemize.	X			

Total ➡ $ 29,692

___0___ continuation sheets attached

(Include amounts from any continuation sheets attached. Report total also on Summary of Schedules.)

secured interests or exemptions. For example, if you own a car worth $6,000, still owe $4,000 on the car note and your state's motor vehicle exemption is $1,200, put down $6,000 for the market value of the car.

EVALUATING PERSONAL PROPERTY

As long as your estimates are reasonable, the lower the value you place on property, the more of it you will probably be allowed to keep through the bankruptcy process. Enter the actual values for cash on hand, deposit accounts and assets with actual cash values, such as insurance, annuities, pensions, stocks, partnerships, bonds, accounts receivable and support to which you are entitled. For interests that are difficult to assess, perhaps because their value depends upon future events, seek the help of a property appraiser or state that you can't estimate the value.

Other suggestions for valuing specific items are at Chapter 2, *Your Property and Bankruptcy*, Section B.2.

Total. Add the amounts in this column and put the total in the box at the bottom of the last page. If you used any continuation pages in addition to the preprinted form, remember to attach those pages and include the amounts from those pages in this total.

3. Schedule C—Property Claimed as Exempt

This is possibly your most important form. It's where you claim all property you think is legally exempt from being taken to pay your creditors. In the overwhelming majority of Chapter 7 bankruptcies filed by individuals, all—or virtually all—of the debtor's property is exempt.

⚠️ **IF YOU OWN A HOME**
Be sure to read Ch. 6, *Your House,* before completing Schedule C.

When you work on this form, you'll need to refer frequently to several other documents. Have in front of you:
- Worksheet 2 (from Ch. 2)
- your drafts of Schedules A and B
- the list of state or federal bankruptcy exemptions you'll be using, provided in Appendix 1, and
- if you're using your state's exemptions, the additional non-bankruptcy federal exemptions, provided in Appendix 1.

Set out below is a sample completed Schedule C and line-by-line instructions.

GIVE YOURSELF THE BENEFIT OF THE DOUBT

When you claim exemptions, give yourself the benefit of the doubt: if an exemption seems to cover an item of property, claim it. You may find that you're legally entitled to keep much of the property you're deeply attached to, such as your home, car and family heirlooms. In fact, in the overwhelming majority of Chapter 7 bankruptcies filed by individuals, all—or virtually all—of the debtor's property is exempt.

Your exemption claims will be examined by the trustee and possibly a creditor or two, although few creditors monitor bankruptcy proceedings. In close cases, bankruptcy laws require the trustee to honor rather than dishonor your exemption claims. In other words, you're entitled to the benefit of the doubt.

If the trustee doesn't allow the exemption, or a creditor successfully challenges it, you've lost nothing by trying. You simply may need to amend Schedule C, an easy process described in Ch. 4, *Handling Your Case in Court,* Section B.

In re and **Case No.** Follow the instructions for Schedule A.

Debtor elects the exemptions to which the debtor is entitled under. If you're using the federal exemptions, check the top box. If you're using your state exemptions or live in California (where you must use one of two state systems), check the lower box. See Ch. 2, *Your Property and Bankruptcy,* Section B.6, for how to choose between the federal and state exemption systems.

The following instructions cover one column at a time. But rather than listing all your exempt property in the first column and then completing the second column before moving on to the third column, you might find it easier to list one exempt item and complete all columns for that item before moving on to the next exempt item.

Description of Property. To describe the property you claim as exempt, take these steps:

Step 1: Turn to Ch. 2, *Your Property and Bankruptcy*, Section B.7, to find out which exemptions are available to you and which property to claim as exempt (if you have already used Worksheet 2 to identify your exempt property, skip this step).

In re   Maytag, Molly and Jonathan   ,   Case No._____
             Debtor   (If known)

SCHEDULE C—PROPERTY CLAIMED AS EXEMPT

Debtor elects the exemptions to which debtor is entitled under:

(Check one box)

☐ 11 U.S.C. § 522(b)(1):   Exemptions provided in 11 U.S.C. § 522(d). **Note: These exemptions are available only in certain states.**

☒ 11 U.S.C. § 522(b)(2):   Exemptions available under applicable nonbankruptcy federal laws, state or local law where the debtor's domicile has been located for the 180 days immediately preceding the filing of the petition, or for a longer portion of the 180-day period than in any other place, and the debtor's interest as a tenant by the entirety or joint tenant to the extent the interest is exempt from process under applicable nonbankruptcy law.

DESCRIPTION OF PROPERTY	SPECIFY LAW PROVIDING EACH EXEMPTION	VALUE OF CLAIMED EXEMPTION	CURRENT MARKET VALUE OF PROPERTY WITHOUT DEDUCTING EXEMPTIONS
Real Property Residence at 21 Scarborough Road South, Cleveland Hts, OH 44118	2329.66(A)(1)	10,000	95,000
Cash on hand Cash from wages	2329.66(A)(13)	100	100
Money deposits Ameritrust checking account #12345	2329.66(A)(4)(a)	250	250
Shaker Savings account #98765	2329.66(A)(4)(a)	400	400
Ohio Savings account #058-118061	1775.24(A)(4)(a)	100	100
Household goods			
Stereo System	2329.66(A)(17) (wildcard)	300	300
Washer/Dryer set	2329.66(A)(4)(b)	150	150
Refrigerator	2329.66(A)(3)	250	250
Stove	2329.66(A)(3)	150	150
Household furniture	2329.66(A)(4)(b)	600	600
Minor appliances	2329.66(A)(4)(b)	75	75
Antique desk	2329.66(A)(4)(b)	250	250
Vacuum	2329.66(A)(4)(b)	30	30
Beds & bedding	2329.66(A)(3)	500	500
Television	2329.66(A)(4)	135	135
VCR	2329.66(A)(4)	75	75
Lawnmower	2329.66(A)(4)	100	100
Swingset, children's toys	2329.66(A)(4)	180	180
Snowblower	2329.66(A)(4)	100	100
Books, pictures, etc.			
Stamp collection	2329.66(A)(4)(b)	75	75
Lithograph	2329.66(A)(4)(b)	50	50

Because we are married, we each claim a full set of exemptions to the extent permitted by law. All references are to Ohio Revised Code unless otherwise noted.

In re <u>Maytag, Molly and Jonathan</u>

SCHEDULE C—PROPERTY CLAIMED AS EXEMPT

(Continuation Sheet)

DESCRIPTION OF PROPERTY	SPECIFY LAW PROVIDING EACH EXEMPTION	VALUE OF CLAIMED EXEMPTION	CURRENT MARKET VALUE OF PROPERTY WITHOUT DEDUCTING EXEMPTIONS
<u>Wearing Apparel</u>			
Clothing	2329.66(A)(3)	625	625
<u>Furs & jewelry</u>			
Wedding rings	2329.66(A)(4)(c)	225	225
Diamond necklace	2329.66(A)(4)(c)	325	325
Watches	2329.66(A)(4)(c)	50	50
<u>Insurance</u>			
Lively Insurance Co., life insurance policy #14-171136	3911.12	120	120
Live-a-long-time Co., life insurance policy #33-19195WY17	3911.14	65	65
<u>IRA, Pensions, Etc.</u>			
Cleveland Builder Pension	2329.66(A)(10)(a)	6,612	6,612
IRA	2329.66(A)(10)(b)	3,400	3,400
<u>Firearms, sports equipment</u>			
Mountain bike	2329.66(A)(4)(b)	165	165
Camera	2329.66(A)(4)(b)	125	125
<u>Other liquidated debts</u>			
Wages from Cleveland Builder	2329.66(A)(13)	1,900	1,900
Wages from Typing Circles	2329.66(A)(13)	100	100
<u>Vehicles</u>			
1988 Honda motorcycle	2329.66(A)(2)	1,000	1,000
<u>Animals</u>			
2 Poodles	2329.66(A)(4)(b)	200	200
<u>Office equipment</u>			
Computer (for business)	2329.66(A)(5)	1,100	1,100
Typewriter (for business)	2329.66(A)(5)	125	125
Fax (for business)	2329.66(A)(17) (wildcard)	500	500
<u>Tools of trade</u>			
Carpentry tools	2329.66(A)(5)	150	150

Step 2: Decide which of the real estate you listed on Schedule A, if any, you want to claim as exempt. Use the same description you used in the Description and Location of Property column of Schedule A.

Step 3: Decide which of the personal property you listed on Schedule B you want to claim as exempt. For each item identified, list both the category of property (preprinted in the Types of Property column) and the specific item, from the Description and Location of Property column.

Specify Law Providing Each Exemption. Citations to the specific laws that create exemptions are in the state and federal exemption lists provided in this book.

You can simplify this process by typing, anywhere on the form, the name of the statutes you are using. The name is noted at the top of the exemption list you use. For example, you might type "All law references are to the Florida Statutes Annotated unless otherwise noted."

For each item of property, enter the citation (number) of the specific law that creates the exemption, as set out on the exemption list. If you are combining part or all of a "wild card" exemption with a regular exemption, list both citations. If the wild card and the regular exemption have the same citation, list the citation twice and put "wild card" next to one of the citations. If you use any reference other than one found in your state statutes, such as a federal non-bankruptcy exemption or a court case, list the entire reference for the exempt item.

Value of Claimed Exemption. Claim the full exemption amount allowed, up to the value of the item. The amount allowed is listed in Appendix 1.

Bankruptcy rules allow married couples to double all exemptions unless the state expressly prohibits it. That means that each of you can claim the entire amount of each exemption, if you are both filing. If your state's chart in Appendix 1 doesn't say your state forbids doubling, go ahead and double. If you are married and doubling your exemptions, put a note to this effect on the form. (See sample Schedule C.)

If you are using part or all of a wild card exemption in addition to a regular exemption, list both amounts. For example, if the regular exemption for an item of furniture is $200, and you plan to exempt it to $500 using $300 from your state's wild card exemption, list $200 across from the citation you listed for the regular exemption, and the $300 across from the citation you listed for the wild card exemption (or across from the term "wild card").

⚠️ **LIMITS ON EXEMPTIONS**
Don't claim more than you need for any particular item if you face an overall limitation on the amount that can be claimed for a group of items. For instance, if you're allowed household furniture up to a total amount of $2,000, don't inflate the value of each item of furniture, simply to get to $2,000. Use the values as stated on Schedule B.

Current Market Value of Property Without Deducting Exemption. Enter the fair market value of the item you are claiming as exempt. This information may already be listed on Schedule A or Schedule B. If it isn't, look back at Worksheet 2 in Ch. 2, *Your Property and Bankruptcy*.

EXAMPLE: The federal exemptions let you exempt household goods and furnishings up to $400 an item. To use the federal exemptions, you must itemize each household good and furnishing on Schedule C and assign each a separate fair market value. If on Schedule B you used a total value for a group of items that includes a smaller item for which you need a separate value, get the separate value from Worksheet 2, if you filled it in.

4. Schedule D—Creditors Holding Secured Claims

In this schedule you list all creditors who hold claims secured by your property. This includes:

- holders of a mortgage or deed of trust on your real estate
- creditors who have won lawsuits against you and recorded judgment liens against your property
- doctors or lawyers to whom you have granted a security interest in the outcome of a lawsuit, so that the collection of their fees would be postponed (the expected court judgment is the collateral)
- contractors who have filed mechanics' or material-man's liens on your real estate
- taxing authorities, such as the IRS, that have obtained tax liens against your property
- creditors with either a purchase-money or non-purchase-money security agreement (for definitions, see Ch. 7, *Secured Debts*, Section C), and
- all parties who are trying to collect a secured debt, such as collection agencies and attorneys.

CREDIT CARD DEBTS

Most credit card debts, whether the card is issued by a bank, gasoline company or department store, are unsecured and should be listed on Schedule F. Some department stores, however—most notably Sears—retain a security interest in all durable goods, such as furniture, appliances, electronics equipment and jewelry, bought using the store credit card. Also, if you were issued a bank or store credit card as part of a plan to restore your credit, you may have had to post property or cash as collateral for debts incurred on the card. If either of these exceptions apply to you, list the credit card debt on Schedule D.

Line-by-line instructions and a completed sample of Schedule D follow. If you completed Worksheet 1, the information in it may be of help here.

In re and **Case No.** Follow Instructions for Schedule A.

☐ **Check this box if debtor has no creditors holding secured claims to report on this Schedule D.** Check the box at the bottom of the Schedule's instructions if you have no secured creditors and skip ahead to Schedule E.

Creditor's Name and Mailing Address. Here you list all secured creditors, preferably in alphabetical order. For each,

fill in the account number, if you know it, the name and the complete mailing address, including zip code (call the creditor or the post office and get it if you don't have it).

If you have more than one secured creditor for a given debt, list the original creditor first and then immediately list the other creditors. For example, if you've been sued or hounded by a collection agency, list the information for the attorney or collection agency after the original creditor.

If, after typing up your final papers, you discover that you've missed a few creditors, don't retype your papers to preserve perfect alphabetical order. Simply add the creditors at the end. If your creditors don't all fit on the first page of Schedule D, make as many copies of the preprinted continuation page as you need to fit them all.

Codebtor. If someone else can be legally forced to pay your debt to a listed secured creditor, enter an "X" in this column and list the codebtor in the creditor column of this Schedule. You'll also need to list the codebtor as a creditor in Schedule F and on Schedule H. If there is no codebtor, type "N/A."

The most common codebtors are:

- cosigners
- guarantors (people who guarantee payment of a loan)
- ex-spouses with whom you jointly incurred debts before divorcing
- joint owners of real estate or other property, if a lien was filed against the property
- co-parties in a lawsuit, if a judgment lien has been recorded against both co-parties
- non-filing spouses in a community property state (most debts incurred by a non-filing spouse during marriage are considered community debts, making that spouse equally liable with the filing spouse for the debts), and
- non-filing spouses in states other than community property states, for debts incurred by the filing spouse for basic living necessities such as food, shelter, clothing and utilities.

Husband, Wife, Joint, or Community. Follow the instructions for Schedule A.

Date Claim Was Incurred, Nature of Lien, and Description and Market Value of Property. This column calls for a lot of information for each secured debt. If you list two or more creditors on the same secured claim (such as the lender and a collection agency), simply put ditto marks (") in this column for the second creditor. Let's take these one at a time.

Date Claim Incurred. Enter the date the secured claim was incurred. For most claims, this is the date you signed the security agreement. If you didn't sign a security agreement with the creditor, the date is most likely the date a contractor or judgment creditor recorded a lien against your

In re ___Maytag, Molly and Jonathan___, Case No._____
Debtor (If known)

SCHEDULE D—CREDITORS HOLDING SECURED CLAIMS

State the name, mailing address, including zip code, and account number, if any, of all entities holding claims secured by property of the debtor as of the date of filing of the petition. List creditors holding all types of secured interest such as judgment liens, garnishments, statutory liens, mortgages, deeds of trust, and other security interests. List creditors in alphabetical order to the extent practicable. If all secured creditors will not fit on this page, use the continuation sheet provided.

If any entity other than a spouse in a joint case may be jointly liable on a claim, place an "X" in the column labeled "Codebtor," include the entity on the appropriate schedule of creditors, and complete Schedule H—Codebtors. If a joint petition is filed, state whether husband, wife, both of them, or the marital community may be liable on each claim by placing an "H," "W," "J," or "C" in the column labeled "Husband, Wife, Joint, or Community."

If the claim is contingent, place an "X" in the column labeled "Contingent." If the claim is unliquidated, place an "X" in the column labeled "Unliquidated." If the claim is disputed, place an "X" in the column labeled "Disputed." (You may need to place an "X" in more than one of these three columns.)

Report the total of all claims listed on this schedule in the box labeled "Total" on the last sheet of the completed schedule. Report this total also on the Summary of Schedules.

☐ Check this box if debtor has no creditors holding secured claims to report on this Schedule D.

CREDITOR'S NAME AND MAILING ADDRESS INCLUDING ZIP CODE	CODEBTOR	HUSBAND, WIFE, JOINT, OR COMMUNITY	DATE CLAIM WAS INCURRED, NATURE OF LIEN, AND DESCRIPTION AND MARKET VALUE OF PROPERTY SUBJECT TO LIEN	CONTINGENT	UNLIQUIDATED	DISPUTED	AMOUNT OF CLAIM WITHOUT DEDUCTING VALUE OF COLLATERAL	UNSECURED PORTION, IF ANY
ACCOUNT NO. 64-112-1861 Ameritrust 10 Financial Way Cleveland Hts, OH 44118		J	9/12/XX; purchase-money secured debt; mortgage on residence VALUE $ 95,000				75,000	-0-
ACCOUNT NO. 64-112-8423 Ameritrust 10 Financial Way Cleveland Hts, OH 44118		J	8/9/XX; nonpurchase-money secured debt; second mortgage on residence VALUE $ 95,000				12,000	-0-
ACCOUNT NO. N/A Computers for Sale P.O. Box 1183 San Ramon, CA 94000		J	8/12/XX; purchase-money secured interest, computer VALUE $ 1,100				2,000	900
ACCOUNT NO. 521129 Quality Collection Agency 21 Main Drive West Cleveland Hts, OH 44115	"		" VALUE $				"	"

___1___ continuation sheets attached

Subtotal ➡ $ 89,000
(Total of this page)

Total ➡ $ N/A
(Use only on last page)

(Report total also on Summary of Schedules)

In re ___Maytag, Molly and Jonathan___ ,　　　　　　　Case No._____
　　　　　　　　　　Debtor　　　　　　　　　　　　　　　　　　　　(If known)

SCHEDULE D—CREDITORS HOLDING SECURED CLAIMS
(Continuation Sheet)

CREDITOR'S NAME AND MAILING ADDRESS INCLUDING ZIP CODE	CODEBTOR	HUSBAND, WIFE, JOINT, OR COMMUNITY	DATE CLAIM WAS INCURRED, NATURE OF LIEN, AND DESCRIPTION AND MARKET VALUE OF PROPERTY SUBJECT TO LIEN	CONTINGENT	UNLIQUIDATED	DISPUTED	AMOUNT OF CLAIM WITHOUT DEDUCTING VALUE OF COLLATERAL	UNSECURED PORTION, IF ANY
ACCOUNT NO. 5514 Fanny's Furniture 14–4th Street Cleveland, OH 44114		J	6/4/XX; purchase-money secured interest, children's bedroom furniture VALUE $ 450				1,000	500
ACCOUNT NO. N/A Bonnie Johnson 40 Mayfield University Hts, OH 44118	X	"	" VALUE $				"	"
ACCOUNT NO. 834-19-77381 Ohio Savings 100 Chester Way Cleveland, OH 44115		J	9/1/XX; judgment lien on all real property in Cuyahoga county VALUE $ 100,000				2,200	-0-
ACCOUNT NO. N/A George Money, Attorney 10 Main Drive Street Cleveland, OH 44112		"	" VALUE $				"	"
ACCOUNT NO. VALUE $								
ACCOUNT NO. VALUE $								

Subtotal ➡ (Total of this page) $ 3,200

Total ➡ (Use only on last page) $ 92,200

Sheet no. __1__ of __1__ continuation sheets attached to
Schedule of Creditors Holding Secured Claims

(Report total also on Summary of Schedules)

property, or the date a taxing authority notified you of a tax liability or assessment of taxes due.

Nature of Lien. Here are the possibilities:

- **Purchase-money security interest**—if the debt was incurred to purchase the property, as with a mortgage or car note.
- **Nonpossessory nonpurchase-money security interest**—if the debt was incurred for a purpose other than buying the collateral, as with home equity loans or loans from finance companies.
- **Possessory nonpurchase-money security interest**—if you own property that has been pledged to a pawnshop.
- **Judgment lien**—if the creditor sued you, obtained a court judgment and recorded a lien against your property.
- **Tax lien**—if a taxing authority placed a lien on your property.
- **Child support lien**—if you owe child support and your child's other parent has recorded a lien against your property.
- **Mechanic's or materialman's liens**—if someone performed work on real property, a vehicle or other property, wasn't paid and recorded a lien.
- If you don't know what kind of lien you are dealing with, put "Don't know nature of lien" after the date. The bankruptcy trustee will help you figure it out later.

See Ch. 7, *Secured Debts,* Section D, for complete definitions of the different types of liens.

Description of property. Describe each item of real estate and personal property that is collateral for the secured debt you owed the creditor listed in the first column. Use the same description you used on Schedule A for real property, or Schedule B for personal property. If a creditor's lien covers several items of property, list all items effected by the lien.

Market Value. The amount you put here must be consistent with what you put on Schedule A or B. If you put only the total value of a group of items on Schedule B, you must now get more specific. For instance, if a department store has a secured claim against your washing machine, and you listed your "washer/dryer set" on Schedule B, now you must provide the washer's specific market value. This may be on Worksheet 2; if it isn't, see the instructions for the "Current Market Value" of Schedule B.

Contingent, Unliquidated, Disputed. Indicate whether the creditor's secured claim is contingent, unliquidated or disputed. Check all categories that apply. If you're uncertain of which to choose, check the one that seems closest. If none applies, leave them blank. Briefly, these terms mean:

Contingent. The claim depends on some event that hasn't yet occurred and may never occur. For example, if you cosigned a secured loan, you won't be liable unless the principal debtor defaults. Your liability as cosigner is contingent upon the default.

Unliquidated. This means that a debt apparently exists, but the exact amount hasn't been determined. For example, say you've sued someone for injuries you suffered in an auto accident, but the case isn't over. Your lawyer has taken the case under a contingency fee agreement—he'll get a third of the recovery if you win, and nothing if you lose—and has a security interest in the final recovery amount. The debt to the lawyer is unliquidated because you don't know how much, if anything, you'll win.

Disputed. There's a dispute over the existence or amount of the debt. For instance, the IRS says you owe $10,000 and has put a lien on your property, and you say you owe $500.

> **YOU'RE NOT ADMITTING YOU OWE THE DEBT**
> You may think a contingent, unliquidated or disputed debt is no debt at all, or you may not want to "admit" that you owe the debt. By listing a debt here, however, you aren't admitting anything. You are assuring that any debt you do owe gets discharged (assuming it's otherwise dischargeable).

Amount of Claim Without Deducting Value of Collateral. For each secured creditor, put the amount it would take to pay off the secured claim, regardless of what the property is worth. The lender can tell you the amount.

> **Example:** Your original loan was for $13,000 plus $7,000 in interest (for $20,000 total). You've made enough payments so that $15,000 will cancel the debt; you would put $15,000 in this column.

If you have more than one creditor for a given secured claim (for example, the lender and a collection agency), list the debt only for the lender and put ditto marks (") for each subsequent creditor.

Subtotal/Total. Total the amounts in the Amount of Claim column for each page. Do not include the amounts represented by the ditto marks if you listed multiple creditors for a single debt. On the final page of Schedule D (which may be the first page or a preprinted continuation page), enter the total of all secured claims.

Unsecured Portion, If Any. If the market value of the collateral is equal to or greater than the amount of the claim, enter "0," meaning that the creditor's claim is fully secured. If the market value of the collateral is less than the amount of the claim(s) listed, enter the difference here.

For instance, if the market value of the collateral is $5,000, but you still owe $6,000 on it and a judgment creditor filed a $2,000 lien against it, then the claims against the property total $8,000. Therefore, put $3,000 ($8,000 – $5,000) in this column.

5. Schedule E—Creditors Holding Unsecured Priority Claims

Schedule E identifies certain creditors who may be entitled to be paid first—by the trustee—out of your nonexempt assets.

Set out below are a sample completed Schedule E and line-by-line instructions.

In re and **Case No.** Follow the instructions for Schedule A.

☐ **Check this box if debtor has no creditors holding unsecured priority claims to report on this Schedule E.** Priority claims are claims that must be paid first in your bankruptcy case. The most common examples are unsecured income tax debts and past due alimony or child support. There are several other categories of priority debts, however. Read further before assuming whether or not you can check this box.

Examine each of the following categories. Check a box if you owe a debt in that category.

☐ **Extensions of credit in an involuntary case.** Don't check this box. You are filing a voluntary, not an involuntary, case.

☐ **Wages, salaries and commissions.** If you owe a current or former employee of your business wages, vacation pay or sick leave which was earned within 90 days before you file your petition or within 90 days of the date you ceased your business, check this box. If you owe money to an independent contractor who did work for you which was earned within 90 days before you file your petition or within 90 days of the date you ceased your business, check this box if in the 12 months before you file for bankruptcy, this independent contractor earned at least 75% of his or her total independent contractor receipts from you. Only the first $4,000 owed per employee or independent contractor is a priority debt.

☐ **Contributions to employee benefit plans.** Check this box only if you owe contributions to an employee benefit fund for services rendered by an employee of your business within 180 days before you file your petition or within 180 days of the date you ceased your business.

☐ **Certain farmers and fishermen.** Check this box only if you operate or operated a grain storage facility and owe a grain producer, or you operate or operated a fish produce or storage facility and owe a U.S. fisherman for fish or fish products. Only the first $4,000 owed per person is a priority debt.

☐ **Deposits by individuals.** If you took money from people who planned to purchase, lease or rent goods or services from you which you never delivered, you may owe a priority debt. For the debt to qualify as a priority, the goods or services had to have been put to personal, family or household use. Only the first $1,800 owed (per person) is a priority debt.

☐ **Alimony, maintenance or support.** Check this box if you are behind on your payments to a spouse, former spouse or child for alimony or child support pursuant to a marital settlement agreement or court order, such as a divorce decree or paternity order.

☐ **Taxes and certain other debts owed to governmental units.** Check this box if you owe unsecured back taxes or if you owe any other debts to the government, such as fines imposed for driving under the influence of drugs or alcohol. Not all tax debts are unsecured priority claims. For example, if the IRS has recorded a lien against your real property, and the equity in your property fully covers the amount of your tax debt, you debt is a secured debt. It should be on Schedule D, not on this schedule.

☐ **Commitments to maintain the capital of an insured depository institution.** Don't check this box. It is for business bankruptcies.

If you checked none of the priority debt boxes, go back and check the first box, showing you have no unsecured priority claims to report. Then go on to Schedule F.

If you checked any of the priority debt boxes, make as many photocopies of the continuation page as the number of priority debt boxes you owe. You will need to complete a separate sheet for each debt. Here is how to complete a continuation page for each type of debt.

In re and **Case No.** Follow the instructions for Schedule A.

Type of Priority. Identify one of the types of priority you checked in page 1.

Creditor's Name and Mailing Address, Including Zip Code. List the name and complete mailing address (including zip code) of each priority creditor, as well as the account number if you know it. You may have more than one priority creditor for a given debt. For example, if you've been sued or hounded by a collection agency, list the attorney or collection agency in addition to the original creditor.

Codebtor. If someone else can be legally forced to pay your debt listed to a priority creditor, enter an "X" in this column and list the codebtor in the creditor column of this schedule. You'll also need to list the codebtor as a creditor

In re __Maytag, Molly and Jonathan__ ,   Case No._____
               Debtor   (If known)

SCHEDULE E—CREDITORS HOLDING UNSECURED PRIORITY CLAIMS

A complete list of claims entitled to priority, listed separately by type of priority, is to be set forth on the sheets provided. Only holders of unsecured claims entitled to priority should be listed in this schedule. In the boxes provided on the attached sheets, state the name and mailing address, including zip code, and account number, if any, of all entities holding priority claims against the debtor or the property of the debtor, as of the date of the filing of the petition.

If any entity other than a spouse in a joint case may be jointly liable on a claim, place an "X" in the column labeled "Codebtor," include the entity on the appropriate schedule of creditors, and complete Schedule H—Codebtors. If a joint petition is filed, state whether husband, wife, both of them, or the marital community may be liable on each claim by placing an "H," "W," "J," or "C" in the column labeled "Husband, Wife, Joint, or Community."

If the claim is contingent, place an "X" in the column labeled "Contingent." If the claim is unliquidated, place an "X" in the column labeled "Unliquidated." If the claim is disputed, place an "X" in the column labeled "Disputed." (You may need to place an "X" in more than one of these three columns.)

Report the total of all claims listed on each sheet in the box labeled "Subtotal" on each sheet. Report the total of all claims listed on this Schedule E in the box labeled "Total" on the last sheet of the completed schedule. Repeat this total also on the Summary of Schedules.

☐   **Check this box if debtor has no creditors holding unsecured priority claims to report on this Schedule E.**

TYPES OF PRIORITY CLAIMS (Check the appropriate box(es) below if claims in that category are listed on the attached sheets)

☐   **Extensions of credit in an involuntary case**

Claims arising in the ordinary course of the debtor's business or financial affairs after the commencement of the case but before the earlier of the appointment of a trustee or the order for relief. 11 U.S.C. § 507(a)(2).

☐   **Wages, salaries, and commissions**

Wages, salaries, and commissions, including vacation, severance, and sick leave pay owing to employees and commissions owing to qualifying independent sales representatives up to $4,000* per person, earned within 90 days immediately preceding the filing of the original petition, or the cessation of business, whichever occurred first, to the extent provided in 11 U.S.C. § 507(a)(3).

☐   **Contributions to employee benefit plans**

Money owed to employee benefit plans for services rendered within 180 days immediately preceding the filing of the original petition, or the cessation of business, whichever occurred first, to the extent provided in 11 U.S.C. § 507(a)(4).

☐   **Certain farmers and fishermen**

Claims of certain farmers and fishermen, up to a maximum of $4,000* per farmer or fisherman, against the debtor, as provided in 11 U.S.C. § 507(a)(5).

☐   **Deposits by individuals**

Claims of individuals up to a maximum of $1,800* for deposits for the purchase, lease, or rental of property or services for personal, family, or household use, that were not delivered or provided. 11 U.S.C. § 507(a)(6).

☐   **Alimony, Maintenance, or Support**

Claims of a spouse, former spouse, or child of the debtor for alimony, maintenance, or support, to the extent provided in 11 U.S.C. § 507(a)(7).

☒   **Taxes and Certain Other Debts Owed to Governmental Units**

Taxes, customs, duties, and penalties owing to federal, state, and local governmental units as set forth in 11 U.S.C. § 507(a)(8).

☐   **Commitments to Maintain the Capital of an Insured Depository Institution**

Claims based on commitments to the FDIC, RTC, Director of the Office of Thrift Supervision, Comptroller of the Currency, or Board of Governors of the Federal Reserve system, or their predecessors or successors, to maintain the capital of an insured depository institution. 11 U.S.C. § 507 (a)(9).

* Amounts are subject to adjustment on April 1, 1998, and every three years thereafter with respect to cases commenced on or after the date of adjustment.

__1__ continuation sheets attached

In re _Maytag, Molly and Jonathan_____,   Case No._____
                    Debtor   (If known)

SCHEDULE E—CREDITORS HOLDING UNSECURED PRIORITY CLAIMS
(Continuation Sheet)

_Taxes_____

TYPE OF PRIORITY

CREDITOR'S NAME AND MAILING ADDRESS INCLUDING ZIP CODE	CODEBTOR	HUSBAND, WIFE, JOINT, OR COMMUNITY	DATE CLAIM WAS INCURRED AND CONSIDERATION FOR CLAIM	CONTINGENT	UNLIQUIDATED	DISPUTED	TOTAL AMOUNT OF CLAIM	AMOUNT ENTITLED TO PRIORITY
ACCOUNT NO. N/A IRS Cincinnati, OH 42111		J	April 15, 19XX, Tax Liability				2,200	2,200
ACCOUNT NO. N/A Ohio Dept. of Tax P.O. Box 1460 Cincinnati, OH 43266-0106		J	April 15, 19XX, Tax Liability				800	800
ACCOUNT NO.								
ACCOUNT NO.								
ACCOUNT NO.								

Sheet no. __1__ of __1__ sheets attached to
Schedule of Creditors Holding Unsecured Priority Claims

Subtotal ➡ (Total of this page) $ 3,000

Total ➡ (Use only on last page) $ 3,000

(Report total also on Summary of Schedules)

in Schedule F and in Schedule H. Common codebtors are listed in the instructions for Schedule D.

Husband, Wife, Joint or Community. Follow the instructions for Schedule A.

Date Claim Was Incurred and Consideration for Claim. State the date the debt was incurred—a specific date or a period of time—and brief details about why you owe (or might owe) the debt.

Contingent, Unliquidated, Disputed. Follow the instructions for Schedule D.

Total Amount of Claim. For each priority debt being addressed on this page, put the amount it would take to pay off the debt in full, even if it's over the priority limit. (This applies only if you owe wages, salaries, commissions, debts for operating a grain or fish facility, or deposits.) For taxes, list only the amount that is unsecured (and therefore a priority) if part of your tax debt is secured and included on Schedule D. If the amount isn't determined, write "not yet determined" in this column.

Subtotal/Total. Total the amounts in the Total Amount of Claim column on each page. If you use continuation pages for additional priority debts, enter the total of all priority debts on the final page.

Amount Entitled to Priority. If the priority claim is larger than the maximum indicated on the first page of Schedule E (for example, $4,000 of wages owed to each employee), put the maximum here. If the claim is less than the maximum, put the amount you entered in the Total Amount of Claim column.

6. Schedule F—Creditors Holding Unsecured Nonpriority Claims

In this schedule, list all creditors you haven't listed in Schedules D or E. For purposes of completing Schedule F, it doesn't matter that the debt might be nondischargeable—such as a student loan. It also doesn't matter that you believe that you don't owe the debt. It's essential that you list every creditor to whom you owe, or possibly owe, money.

If you want to repay a particular creditor, list the debt and get it discharged anyway. You can always voluntarily pay the debt out of property or income you receive after you file for bankruptcy, even though the creditor is legally barred from trying to collect the debt.

EXAMPLE: Peter owes his favorite aunt $8,000. When Peter files for bankruptcy he lists the debt, which is discharged when Peter's bankruptcy is over. Peter can voluntarily pay off the $8,000 out of his wages after his bankruptcy discharge. Peter's aunt, however, couldn't sue him or enforce payment of the debt.

Inadvertent errors or omissions on this schedule can come back to haunt you. A debt you owe to a creditor you forget to list might not be discharged in bankruptcy if the creditor doesn't otherwise learn of your bankruptcy filing.

Below are a sample completed Schedule F and line-by-line instructions. Refer to Worksheet 1 (Ch. 1, *Should You File for Chapter 7 Bankruptcy?*) for help if you completed it. Use as many preprinted continuation pages as you need.

In re and **Case No.** Follow the instructions for Schedule A.

☐ **Check this box if debtor has no creditors holding unsecured nonpriority claims to report on this Schedule F.** Check this box if you have no unsecured nonpriority debts (this would be very rare).

Creditor's Name and Mailing Address, Including Zip Code. List, preferably in alphabetical order, the name and complete mailing address of each unsecured creditor, as well as the account number if you know it. If you have more than one unsecured creditor for a given debt, list the original creditor first and then immediately list the other creditors. For example, if you've been sued or hounded by a collection agency, list the attorney or collection agency in addition to the original creditor. When you are typing your final papers, if you get to the end and discover that you left a creditor off, don't redo the whole list in search of perfect alphabetical order. Just add the creditors at the end.

EASY-TO-OVERLOOK CREDITORS

One debt may involve several different creditors. Remember to include:

- your ex-spouse, if you are still obligated under the terms of a divorce decree or settlement agreement to pay alimony or child support, to pay joint debts, to turn any property over to your ex or to make payments as part of your property division
- anyone who has cosigned a promissory note or loan application signed by you
- any holder of a loan or promissory note that you cosigned for someone else
- the original creditor, anybody to whom the debt has been assigned or sold by the original creditor and any other person (such as a bill collector or attorney) trying to collect the debt, and
- anyone who may sue you because of a car accident, business dispute or the like.

In re ___Maytag, Molly and Jonathan___ ,   Case No._____
                    Debtor   (If known)

SCHEDULE F—CREDITORS HOLDING UNSECURED NONPRIORITY CLAIMS

State the name, mailing address, including zip code, and account number, if any, of all entities holding unsecured claims without priority against the debtor or the property of the debtor as of the date of filing of the petition. Do not include claims listed in Schedules D and E. If all creditors will not fit on this page, use the continuation sheet provided.

If any entity other than a spouse in a joint case may be jointly liable on a claim, place an "X" in the column labeled "Codebtor," include the entity on the appropriate schedule of creditors, and complete Schedule H—Codebtors. If a joint petition is filed, state whether husband, wife, both of them, or the marital community may be liable on each claim by placing an "H," "W," "J," or "C" in the column labeled "Husband, Wife, Joint, or Community."

If the claim is contingent, place an "X" in the column labeled "Contingent." If the claim is unliquidated, place an "X" in the column labeled "Unliquidated." If the claim is disputed, place an "X" in the column labeled "Disputed." (You may need to place an "X" in more than one of these three columns.)

Report the total of all claims listed on this schedule in the box labeled "Total" on the last sheet of the completed schedule. Report this total also on the Summary of Schedules.

☐ Check this box if debtor has no creditors holding unsecured nonpriority claims to report on this Schedule F.

CREDITOR'S NAME AND MAILING ADDRESS INCLUDING ZIP CODE	CODEBTOR	HUSBAND, WIFE, JOINT, OR COMMUNITY	DATE CLAIM WAS INCURRED AND CONSIDERATION FOR CLAIM. IF CLAIM IS SUBJECT TO SETOFF, SO STATE	CONTINGENT	UNLIQUIDATED	DISPUTED	AMOUNT OF CLAIM
ACCOUNT NO. N/A Alan Accountant 5 Green St. Cleveland, OH 44118		J	4/XX, tax preparation				250
ACCOUNT NO. 4189000026113 American Allowance P.O. Box 1 New York, NY 10001		J	1/XX to 4/XX, VISA credit card charges			X	5,600
ACCOUNT NO. Patricia Washington, Esq. Washington & Lincoln Legal Plaza, Suite 1 Cleveland, OH 44114		"	"		"		"
ACCOUNT NO. 845061-86-3 Citibank 200 East North Columbus, OH 43266		J	19XX , student loan charges				10,000

___2___ continuation sheets attached

Subtotal ➡ (Total of this page) $ 15,850

Total ➡ (Use only on last page) $ N/A

(Report total also on Summary of Schedules)

In re __Maytag, Molly and Jonathan__ ,
Debtor

Case No._____
(If known)

SCHEDULE F—CREDITORS HOLDING UNSECURED NONPRIORITY CLAIMS
(Continuation Sheet)

CREDITOR'S NAME AND MAILING ADDRESS INCLUDING ZIP CODE	CODEBTOR	HUSBAND, WIFE, JOINT, OR COMMUNITY	DATE CLAIM WAS INCURRED AND CONSIDERATION FOR CLAIM. IF CLAIM IS SUBJECT TO SETOFF, SO STATE	CONTINGENT	UNLIQUIDATED	DISPUTED	AMOUNT OF CLAIM
ACCOUNT NO. 9816-12HH Cleveland Hospital 19–1st Avenue Cleveland, OH 44115		J	12/XX, surgery and medical treatment				17,450
ACCOUNT NO. Jane Jackson, Esq. 50–2nd Avenue Cleveland, OH 44115		"	"				"
ACCOUNT NO. 4401 Dr. Dennis Dentist 4 Superior Way Cleveland Hts, OH 44118		W	12/XX to 6/XX; dental work				1,050
ACCOUNT NO. 222387941 Illuminating Co. 55 Public Square Cleveland, OH 44115		J	3/XX to 7/XX; electrical work				750
ACCOUNT NO. N/A Bonnie Johnson 40 Mayfield University Hts, OH 44118		W	8/XX; personal loan				5,500

Subtotal ➡ (Total of this page) $ 24,750

Total ➡ (Use only on last page) $ N/A

Sheet no. __1__ of __2__ continuation sheets attached to
Schedule of Creditors Holding Unsecured Nonpriorty Claims

(Report total also on Summary of Schedules)

In re ___Maytag, Molly and Jonathan___,   Case No._____

Debtor   (If known)

SCHEDULE F—CREDITORS HOLDING UNSECURED NONPRIORITY CLAIMS
(Continuation Sheet)

CREDITOR'S NAME AND MAILING ADDRESS INCLUDING ZIP CODE	CODEBTOR	HUSBAND, WIFE, JOINT, OR COMMUNITY	DATE CLAIM WAS INCURRED AND CONSIDERATION FOR CLAIM. IF CLAIM IS SUBJECT TO SETOFF, SO STATE	CONTINGENT	UNLIQUIDATED	DISPUTED	AMOUNT OF CLAIM
ACCOUNT NO. N/A Dr. Helen Jones 11 Marks Way Cleveland, OH 44112		J	4/XX to 8/XX, pediatric care				2,000
ACCOUNT NO. 11210550 Ohio Gas Company East 1717 East 9th St. Cleveland, OH 44115		J	12/XX to 6/XX, gas service				800
ACCOUNT NO. N/A Ellen Rogers 900 Grand View Jackson, WY 83001		H	6/XX to 8/XX, child support				1,800
ACCOUNT NO. 487310097 Sears P.O. Box 11 Chicago, IL 60619		J	19XX to 19XY; dept. store and catalogue charges				3,800
ACCOUNT NO. 6007 John White, Esq. 21 Main Street Cleveland, OH 44114		W	2/XX to 6/XX; represented us in lawsuits against us for unpaid bills				3,450

Sheet no. __2__ of __2__ continuation sheets attached to
Schedule of Creditors Holding Unsecured Nonpriorty Claims

Subtotal ➡ (Total of this page) $ 11,850

Total ➡ (Use only on last page) $ 52,450

(Report total also on Summary of Schedules)

Codebtor. If someone else can be legally forced to pay your debt to a listed unsecured creditor, enter an "X" in this column and list the codebtor as a creditor in this schedule. Also list the codebtor in Schedule H. Common codebtors are listed at Schedule D.

Husband, Wife, Joint or Community. Follow the instructions for Schedule A.

Date Claim Was Incurred and Consideration for Claim. If Claim Is Subject to Setoff So State. State when the debt was incurred. It may be one date or a period of time. With credit card debts, put the approximate time over which you ran up the charges unless the unpaid charges were made on one or two specific dates. Then state what the debt was for. You can be general ("clothes" or "household furnishings") or specific ("refrigerator" or "teeth capping").

If you are entitled to a setoff against the debt—that is, the creditor owes you some money, too—give the amount and why you think you are entitled to the setoff. If there is more than one creditor for a single debt, put ditto marks (") in this column for the subsequent creditors.

Contingent, Unliquidated, Disputed. Follow the instructions for Schedule D.

Amount of Claim. List the amount of the debt claimed by the creditor, even if you dispute the amount. That way, it will all be wiped out if it's dischargeable. If there's more than one creditor for a single debt, put the debt amount across from the original creditor and put ditto marks (") across from each subsequent creditor you have listed.

Subtotal/Total. Total the amounts in the last column for this page. Do not include the amounts represented by the ditto marks if you listed multiple creditors for a single debt. On the final page (which may be the first page or a preprinted continuation page), enter the total of all unsecured nonpriority claims. On the first page in the bottom lefthand corner, note the number of continuation pages you are attaching.

7. Schedule G—Executory Contracts and Unexpired Leases

In this form, you list every executory contract or unexpired lease to which you're a party. "Executory" means the contract is still in force—that is, both parties are still obligated to perform important acts under it. Similarly, "unexpired" means that the contract or lease period hasn't run out—that is, it is still in effect. Common examples of executory contracts and unexpired leases are:

- car leases
- residential leases or rental agreements
- business leases or rental agreements
- service contracts

- business contracts
- time-share contracts or leases
- contracts of sale for real estate
- copyright and patent license agreements
- leases of real estate (surface and underground) for the purpose of harvesting timber, minerals or oil
- future homeowners' association fee requirements
- agreements for boat docking privileges, and
- insurance contracts.

CONTRACT DELINQUENCIES

If you are delinquent in payments that were due under a lease or executory contract, the delinquency should be listed as a debt on Schedule D, E or F. The sole purpose of this schedule is to identify existing contractual obligations that you still owe or that someone owes you.

Below are a sample completed Schedule G and line-by-line instructions.

In re and **Case No.** Follow the instructions for Schedule A.

☐ **Check this box if debtor has no executory contracts or unexpired leases.** Check this box if it applies; otherwise, complete the form.

Name and Mailing Address, Including Zip Code, of Other Parties to Lease or Contract. Provide the name and full address (including zip code) of each party—other than yourself—to each lease or contract. These parties are either people who signed agreements or the companies for whom these people work. If you're unsure about whom to list, include the person who signed an agreement, any company whose name appears on the agreement, and anybody who might have an interest in having the contract or lease enforced. If you still aren't sure, put "don't know."

Description of Contract or Lease and Nature of Debtor's Interest. State Whether Lease Is for Nonresidential Real Property. State Contract Number of Any Government Contract. For each lease or contract, give:

- a description of the basic type (for instance, residential lease, commercial lease, car lease, business obligation, copyright license)
- the date the contract or lease was signed
- the date the contract is to expire (if any)
- a summary of each party's rights and obligations under the lease or contract, and
- the contract number, if the contract is with any government body.

It's up to the trustee to decide whether a contract or lease should be continued in force or terminated (rejected). Unless the lease or contract will produce assets for the creditors, the trustee is likely to terminate it. This means

In re _Maytag, Molly and Jonathan_____ ,
Debtor

Case No._____
(If known)

SCHEDULE G—EXECUTORY CONTRACTS AND UNEXPIRED LEASES

Describe all executory contracts of any nature and all unexpired leases of real personal property. Include any timeshare interests.

State nature of debtor's interest in contract, i.e., "Purchaser," "Agent," etc. State whether debtor is the lessor or lessee of a lease.

Provide the names and complete mailing addresses of all other parties to each lease or contract described.

NOTE: A party listed on this schedule will not receive notice of the filing of this case unless the party is also scheduled in the appropriate schedule of creditors.

☐ Check this box if debtor has no executory contracts or unexpired leases.

NAME AND MAILING ADDRESS, INCLUDING ZIP CODE, OF OTHER PARTIES TO LEASE OR CONTRACT	DESCRIPTION OF CONTRACT OR LEASE AND NATURE OF DEBTOR'S INTEREST. STATE WHETHER LEASE IS FOR NONRESIDENTIAL REAL PROPERTY. STATE CONTRACT NUMBER OF ANY GOVERNMENT CONTRACT
Scarborough Road South Homeowners Association 1 Scarborough Road South Cleveland Hts, OH 41118	Homeowner's Association Contract for residential property, signed 10/XX, expires 12/XX. Provides for maintenance, gardening and repairs of property.

you and the other parties to the agreement are cut loose from any obligations unless you agree otherwise, and any monetary damages that the creditor has suffered as a result will be discharged in your bankruptcy, even if they are suffered after your filing date.

For example, assume that you are leasing a car when you file for bankruptcy. The creditor who owns the lease cannot repossess the car until the trustee exercises her right to assume or reject the lease, which normally must occur within 60 days of when you file. (If the trustee fails to assume the lease within the 60-day period, it is deemed rejected.) During that 60-day period, you can use the car without paying for it. The accrued payments will be discharged as if they were incurred prior to your bankruptcy.

As a general rule, people filing Chapter 7 bankruptcies are not parties to leases or executory contracts that would likely add value to their bankruptcy estates. But this is not always the case. For instance, assume that just before you filed for bankruptcy, you signed a five-year residential lease at very favorable terms. Because the trustee might be able to sell the lease to someone else for a profit—to be turned over to your creditors—the trustee might well assume the lease and then sell it.

Bankruptcy law has special rules for executory contracts related to intellectual property (copyright, patent, trademark or trade secret), real estate and time-share leases. If you are involved in one of these situations, see a lawyer.

8. Schedule H—Codebtors

In Schedules D, E and F, you identified those debts for which you have codebtors—usually, a cosigner, guarantor, ex-spouse, non-filing spouse in a community property state, non-filing spouse for a debt for a necessity, nonmarital partner or joint contractor. You must also list those codebtors here.

In Chapter 7 bankruptcy, your codebtors will be wholly responsible for your debts, unless they, too, declare bankruptcy.

Below are a sample completed Schedule H and line-by-line instructions.

In re and **Case No.** Follow instructions for Schedule A.

☐ **Check this box if debtor has no codebtors.** Check this box if it applies; otherwise, complete the form.

Name and Address of Codebtor. List the name and complete address (including zip code) of each codebtor. If the codebtor is a non-filing current spouse, put all names by which that person was known during the previous six years.

Name and Address of Creditor. List the name and address of each creditor (as listed on Schedule D, E or F) to which each codebtor is indebted.

EXAMPLE: Tom Martin cosigned three different loans—with three different banks—for debtor Mabel Green, who is filing for bankruptcy. In the first column, Mabel lists Tom Martin as a codebtor. In the second, Mabel lists each of the three banks.

IF YOU ARE MARRIED AND FILING ALONE

If you live in a community property state, your spouse may be a codebtor for most of the debts you listed in Schedules D, E and F. This is because in these states, most debts incurred by one spouse are owed by both spouses. In this event, don't relist all the creditors in the second column, simply write "all creditors listed in Schedules D, E and F, except:" and then list any creditors whom you owe solely.

9. Schedule I—Current Income of Individual Debtor(s)

The bankruptcy trustee screens each filing for possible abuse of the bankruptcy system. The amount of your income and the type of expenditures you're making are the primary factors the trustee considers. If you can afford to repay your debts in a reasonable period of time, the bankruptcy court will probably dismiss your bankruptcy petition.

Chapter 7 bankruptcy petitions are rarely dismissed because the debtor's income is too high or because expenditures are too low. But high income and low expenses guarantee trouble. You should be concerned if you clearly have enough disposable income to pay a substantial majority (roughly 70% or more) of your unsecured debts back over a three- to five-year period.

Below are a sample completed Schedule I and line-by-line instructions. If you're married and filing jointly, you must fill in information for both spouses. If you are married but filing alone, only fill in the information for debtor.

In re and **Case No.** Follow the instructions for Schedule A.

Debtor's Marital Status. Enter your marital status. Your choices are single, married, separated (you aren't living with your spouse and plan never to again), widowed or divorced. You are divorced only if you have received a final judgment of divorce from a court.

Dependents of Debtor and Spouse. List the names, ages and relationships of all persons for whom you and your spouse provide at least 50% of support. This may include your children, your spouse's children, your parents, other relatives and domestic partners. It does not include your spouse.

In re ___Maytag, Molly and Jonathan___ ,   Case No._____
                    Debtor   (If known)

SCHEDULE H—CODEBTORS

    Provide the information requested concerning any person or entity, other than a spouse in a joint case, that is also liable on any debts listed by debtor in the schedules of creditors. Include all guarantors and co-signers. In community property states, a married debtor not filing a joint case should report the name and address of the nondebtor spouse on this schedule. Include all names used by the nondebtor spouse during the six years immediately preceding the commencement of this case.

    ☐ Check this box if debtor has no codebtors.

NAME AND ADDRESS OF CODEBTOR	NAME AND ADDRESS OF CREDITOR
Bonnie Johnson 40 Mayfield University Hts, OH 44118	Fanny's Furniture 14–4th Street Cleveland, OH 44114

In re ___Maytag, Molly and Jonathan_____,
    _____Debtor_____

Case No._____
                    (If known)

SCHEDULE I—CURRENT INCOME OF INDIVIDUAL DEBTOR(S)

The column labled "Spouse" must be completed in all cases filed by joint debtors and by a married debtor in a Chapter 12 or 13 case whether or not a joint petition is filed, unless the spouses are separated and a joint petition is not filed.

DEBTOR'S MARITAL STATUS:	DEPENDENTS OF DEBTOR AND SPOUSE		
	NAMES	AGE	RELATIONSHIP
Married	Sara Maytag	14	daughter
	Harold Maytag	12	son

Employment:	DEBTOR	SPOUSE
Occupation	Clerk/typist	Construction Worker
Name of Employer	Typing Circles	Cleveland Builder
How long employed	1 1/2 years	4 years
Address of Employer	40 Euclid Drive Cleveland, OH 44112	100 Chester Way Cleveland, OH 44114

INCOME: (Estimate of average monthly income)		DEBTOR		SPOUSE
Current monthly gross wages, salary, and commissions (pro rate if not paid monthly)		$ 1,450	$	3,000
Estimated monthly overtime		$ 0	$	0
SUBTOTAL		$ 1,450	$	3,000
LESS PAYROLL DEDUCTIONS				
a. Payroll taxes and Social Security		$ 350	$	600
b. Insurance		$ N/A	$	250
c. Union dues		$ N/A	$	50
d. Other (Specify: _____)		$ N/A	$	N/A
SUBTOTAL OF PAYROLL DEDUCTIONS		$ 350	$	900
TOTAL NET MONTHLY TAKE HOME PAY		$ 1,100	$	2,100
Regular income from operation of business or profession or farm (attach detailed statement)		$ N/A	$	N/A
Income from real property		$ N/A	$	N/A
Interest and dividends		$ 100	$	100
Alimony, maintenance or support payments payable to the debtor for the debtor's use or that of dependents listed above		$ N/A	$	N/A
Social Security or other government assistance (Specify:_____)		$ N/A	$	N/A
Pension or retirement income		$ N/A	$	N/A
Other monthly income		$ N/A	$	N/A
(Specify:_____)		$ N/A	$	N/A
_____		$ N/A	$	N/A
TOTAL MONTHLY INCOME		$ 1,200	$	2,200

TOTAL COMBINED MONTHLY INCOME $ _____3,400_____   (Report also on Summary of Schedules)

Describe any increase or decrease of more than 10% in any of the above categories anticipated to occur within the year following the filing of this document:

N/A

Employment. Provide the requested employment information. If you have more than one employer, enter "See continuation sheet" just below the box containing the employment information and then complete a continuation sheet. If you are retired, unemployed or disabled, put when and what you did when you last worked.

Income. Enter your estimated monthly gross income from regular employment, before any payroll deductions are taken. In the second blank, put your estimated monthly overtime pay. Add them together and enter the subtotal in the third blank.

If you are self-employed or an independent contractor, use the blank below labeled "Regular income from operation of business or profession or farm." Also attach a sheet of paper. Call it "Attachment to Schedule I" and include your name (and spouse's name if you're filing jointly) and list your average gross monthly receipts and average monthly expenses.

Payroll Deductions. In the four blanks, enter the deductions taken from your gross salary. The deductions listed are the most common ones, but you may have others to report. Other possible deductions are state disability taxes, wages withheld or garnished for child support, credit union payments or perhaps payments on a student loan or a car.

Subtotal of Payroll Deductions. Add your payroll deductions and enter the subtotal.

Total Net Monthly Take Home Pay. Subtract your payroll deductions subtotal from your income subtotal.

Regular income from operation of business or profession or farm. If you are self-employed or operate a sole proprietorship, enter your monthly income from that source here. If it's been fairly steady for at least one calendar year, divide the amount you entered on your most recent tax return (IRS Schedule C) by 12 for a monthly amount. If your income hasn't been steady for at least one calendar year, enter the average net income from your business or profession for the past three months. In either case you must attach a statement of your income. Use your most recent IRS Schedule C filed with the IRS.

Income from real property. Enter the monthly income from real estate rentals, leases or licenses (such as mineral exploration, oil and the like).

Interest and dividends. Enter the average estimated monthly interest you receive from bank or security deposits and other investments, such as stocks.

Alimony, maintenance or support payments payable to the debtor for the debtor's use or that of dependents listed above. Enter the average monthly amount you receive for your support (alimony, spousal support or maintenance) or your children (child support).

Social Security or other government assistance. Enter the total monthly amount you receive in Social Security, AFDC, SSI, public assistance, disability payments, veterans' benefits, unemployment compensation, worker's compensation or any other government benefit. If you receive food stamps, include their monthly value. Specify the source of the benefits.

Pension or retirement income. Enter the total monthly amount of all pension, annuity, IRA, Keogh or other retirement benefits you currently receive.

Other monthly income. Specify any other income (such as royalty payments or payments from a trust) you receive on a regular basis and enter the monthly amount here. You may have to divide by 3, 6 or 12 if you receive the payments quarterly, semi-annually or annually.

Total Monthly Income. Add all additional income to the Total Net Monthly Take Home Pay amount and enter the grand total in this blank.

Total Combined Monthly Income. If you are filing jointly, add your total income to your spouse's total income and enter the result here.

Describe any increase or decrease of more than 10% in any of the above categories anticipated to occur within the year following the filing of this document. Identify any changes in your pay or other income—in excess of 10%—that you expect in the coming year. For instance, if recent layoffs at your place of employment mean you probably won't be working overtime, which will reduce your net monthly income by more than 10%, say so.

10. Schedule J—Current Expenditures of Individual Debtor(s)

In this form, you must list your family's total monthly expenditures, even if you're married and filing alone. Be complete and accurate. Your disposable income is computed by subtracting your reasonable expenditures from your net income (on Schedule I). Expenditures for items the trustee considers luxuries won't be considered reasonable, and will be disregarded for the purpose of figuring your disposable income. For instance, payments on expensive cars or investment property may be disregarded by the trustee. Reasonable expenditures for housing, utilities, food, medical care, clothing, education and transportation will be counted. Be ready to prove high amounts with bills, receipts and canceled checks.

EXAMPLE 1: Joe owes $100,000 (excluding his mortgage), earns $4,000 a month and spends $3,600 a month, primarily for necessities, including mortgage payments on a moderately priced family home. Joe would be

In re ___Maytag, Molly and Jonathan___ ,   Case No._____
                      Debtor   (If known)

SCHEDULE J—CURRENT EXPENDITURES OF INDIVIDUAL DEBTOR(S)

Complete this schedule by estimating the average monthly expenses of the debtor and the debtor's family. Pro rate any payments made bi-weekly, quarterly, semi-annually, or annually to show monthly rate.

☐ Check this box if a joint petition is filed and debtor's spouse maintains a separate household. Complete a separate schedule of expenditures labeled "Spouse."

Rent or home mortgage payment (include lot rented for mobile home)	$ 650
Are real estate taxes included? Yes __X__ No _____	
Is property insurance included? Yes __X__ No _____	
Utilities: Electricity and heating fuel	$ 245
Water and sewer	$ 40
Telephone	$ 85
Other ___garbage___	$ 15
Home maintenance (repairs and upkeep)	$ 175
Food	$ 550
Clothing	$ 125
Laundry and dry cleaning	$ 50
Medical and dental expenses	$ 400
Transportation (not including car payments)	$ 80
Recreation, clubs and entertainment, newspapers, magazines, etc.	$ 30
Charitable contributions	$ 50
Insurance (not deducted from wages or included in home mortgage payments)	
Homeowner's or renter's	$ 120
Life	$ N/A
Health	$ N/A
Auto	$ 60
Other _____	$ N/A
Taxes (not deducted from wages or included in home mortgage payments)	
(Specify: ___income taxes to IRS & Ohio Dept. of Tax___)	$ 200
Installment payments: (In Chapter 12 and 13 cases, do not list payments to be included in the plan)	
Auto	$ N/A
Other ___credit card accounts___	$ 400
Other ___loans___	$ 550
Alimony, maintenance, and support paid to others	$ 600
Payments for support of additional dependents not living at your home	$ N/A
Regular expenses from operation of business, profession, or farm (attach detailed statement)	$ N/A
Other _____	$ N/A
TOTAL MONTHLY EXPENSES (Report also on Summary of Schedules)	$ 4,425

[FOR CHAPTER 12 AND CHAPTER 13 DEBTORS ONLY]
Provide the information requested below, including whether plan payments are to be made bi-weekly, monthly, annually, or at some other regular interval.

A. Total projected monthly income	N/A	$ _____
B. Total projected monthly expenses		$ _____
C. Excess income (A minus B)		$ _____
D. Total amount to be paid into plan each _____		$ _____
	(interval)	

allowed to proceed with a Chapter 7 bankruptcy because his monthly disposable income ($400) wouldn't let him pay off 70% or more of his debts over three to five years.

EXAMPLE 2: Same facts, except that Joe spends $2,200 a month. In this case, the court might rule that because Joe has $1,800 a month in disposable income, he could pay off most of his debts either informally or under a Chapter 13 repayment plan. The court could dismiss Joe's Chapter 7 bankruptcy petition or pressure him to convert it to Chapter 13 bankruptcy.

EXAMPLE 3: Same facts as Example 2, but Joe is incurably ill and will soon quit working. The court may allow him to proceed with a Chapter 7 bankruptcy.

Below are a sample completed Schedule J and some guidelines for filling it out.

⚠ ONCE AGAIN, BE ACCURATE

Creditors sometimes try to use the information on these forms to prove that you committed fraud when you applied for credit. If a creditor can prove that you fraudulently filled in a credit application, the debt may survive bankruptcy. See Ch. 8, *Nondischargeable Debts*. If accuracy on this form will substantially contradict information you previously gave a creditor, see a bankruptcy attorney before filing.

In re and **Case No.** Follow the instructions for Schedule A.

☐ **Check this box if a joint petition is filed and debtor's spouse maintains a separate household. Complete a separate schedule of expenditures labeled "Spouse."** If you and your spouse are jointly filing for bankruptcy, but maintain separate households (for example, you've recently separated), check this box and make sure that you each fill out a separate Schedule J.

Expenditures. For each listed item, fill in your monthly expenses. If you make some payments biweekly, quarterly, semi-annually or annually, prorate them to show your monthly payment. Here are some pointers:

- Do not list payroll deductions you listed on Schedule I.
- Include payments you make for your dependents' expenses in your figures as long as those expenses are reasonable and necessary for the dependents' support.
- Utilities—Other: This includes garbage and cable TV service.
- Installment payments—Other: Write "credit card accounts" on one line and enter your total monthly payments for them. Put the average amount you actually pay, even if it's less than it should be. On the

other line put "loans" (except auto loans) and enter your total payments.

Total Monthly Expenses. Total up all your expenses.

For Chapter 12 and 13 Debtors Only. Type "N/A" anywhere in this section.

11. Summary of Schedules

This form helps the bankruptcy trustee and judge get a quick look at your bankruptcy filing. Below is a completed Summary; line-by-line instructions follow it.

Court name. Copy this information from Form 1— Voluntary Petition.

In re and **Case No.** Follow the instructions for Schedule A.

Name of Schedule. This lists the schedules. Don't add anything.

Attached (Yes/No). You should have completed all of the schedules, so type "Yes" in this column for each schedule.

Number of Sheets. Enter the number of pages you completed for each schedule. Remember to count continuation pages. Enter the total at the bottom of the column.

Amounts Scheduled. For each column—Assets, Liabilities and Other—copy the totals from Schedules A, B, D, E, F, I and J and enter them where indicated. Add up the amounts in the Assets and Liabilities columns and enter their totals at the bottom.

Now, go back and fill in the statistical-administrative information on Form 1—Voluntary Petition.

United States Bankruptcy Court

__Northern__ District of __Ohio, Eastern Division__

In re __Maytag, Molly and Jonathan__ , Case No._____
　　　　　Debtor　　　　　　　　　　　　　　　　　　　　　　　　　　　(If known)

SUMMARY OF SCHEDULES

Indicate as to each schedule whether that schedule is attached and state the number of pages in each. Report the totals from Schedules A, B, D, E, F, I and J in the boxes provided. Add the amounts from Schedules A and B to determine the total amount of the debtor's assets. Add the amounts from Schedules D, E and F to determine the total amount of the debtor's liabilities.

NAME OF SCHEDULE		ATTACHED (YES/NO)	NUMBER OF SHEETS	AMOUNTS SCHEDULED		
				ASSETS	LIABILITIES	OTHER
A	Real Property	Yes	1	$ 100,000		
B	Personal Property	Yes	4	$ 37,402		
C	Property Claimed as Exempt	Yes	2			
D	Creditors Holding Secured Claims	Yes	2		$ 92,200	
E	Creditors Holding Unsecured Priority Claims	Yes	2		$ 3,000	
F	Creditors Holding Unsecured Nonpriority Claims	Yes	3		$ 52,450	
G	Executory Contracts and Unexpired Leases	Yes	1			
H	Codebtors	Yes	1			
I	Current Income of Individual Debtor(s)	Yes	1			$ 3,400
J	Current Expenditures of Individual Debtor(s)	Yes	1			$ 4,425
Total Number of Sheets of All Schedules ➡			18			
Total Assets ➡				$ 137,402		
Total Liabilities ➡					$ 147,650	

12. Declaration Concerning Debtor's Schedules

In this form, you are required to swear that everything you have said on your schedules is true and correct. Deliberate lying is a major sin in bankruptcy, and could cost you your bankruptcy discharge, a fine of up to $500,000 and up to five years in prison.

Below is a completed Declaration and instructions.

In re and **Case No.** Follow the instructions for Schedule A.

Declaration Under Penalty of Perjury by Individual Debtor. Enter the total number of pages in your schedules (the number on the Summary plus one). Enter the date and sign the form. Be sure that your spouse signs and dates the form if you are filing jointly.

Certification and Signature of Non-Attorney Bankruptcy Petition Preparer. If a BPP typed your forms, have that person complete this section. Otherwise, type "N/A" anywhere in the box.

Declaration Under Penalty of Perjury on Behalf of Corporation or Partnership. Enter an "N/A" anywhere in this blank.

G. Form 7—Statement of Financial Affairs

Congratulations—you're almost through. This form gives information about your recent financial transactions such as payments to creditors, sales or other transfers of property and gifts. Under certain circumstances, the trustee may be entitled to recapture property that you transferred to others prior to filing for bankruptcy, and sell it for the benefit of your unsecured creditors.

The questions on the form are, for the most part, self-explanatory. Spouses filing jointly combine their answers and complete only one form.

If you have no information for a particular item, check the "None" box. If you fail to answer a question and don't check "None," you will have to amend your papers—that is, file a corrected form—after you file. Add continuation sheets if necessary.

⚠ BE HONEST AND COMPLETE
Don't give in to the temptation of leaving out a transfer or two, assuming that the trustee won't find or go after the property. Not only must you sign this form under penalty of perjury, but if the trustee or a creditor discovers that you left information out, your bankruptcy could be dismissed.

A completed Statement of Financial Affairs and detailed information about questions that are not self-explanatory follow.

Court name. Copy this information from Form 1—Voluntary Petition.

In re and **Case No.** Follow the instructions for Schedule A.

1. Income from employment or operation of business. Enter your gross income for this year and for the previous two years. This means the total income before taxes and other payroll deductions or business expenses are removed.

2. Income other than from employment or operation of business. Include interest, dividends, royalties, worker's compensation, other government benefits and all other money you have received from sources other than your job or business during the last two years. Provide the source of each amount, the dates received and the reason you received the money so that the trustee can verify it if he desires.

3. Payments to creditors. Here you list payments you've recently made to creditors. There are two kinds of creditors—arm's-length and insiders. An insider—defined on the first page of the Statement of Financial Affairs—is essentially a relative or close business associate. All other creditors are arm's-length creditors.

In re _____Maytag, Molly and Jonathan_____,   Case No._____
                     Debtor   (If known)

DECLARATION CONCERNING DEBTOR'S SCHEDULES

DECLARATION UNDER PENALTY OF PERJURY BY INDIVIDUAL DEBTOR

I declare under penalty of perjury that I have read the foregoing summary and schedules consisting of _____19_____ sheets, and that they are true and correct to the best of my knowledge, information, and belief.

(Total shown on summary page plus 1)

Date___July 3, 19XX___   Signature___*Molly Maytag*___
                                                              Debtor

Date___July 3, 19XX___   Signature___*Jonathan Maytag*___
                                                              (Joint Debtor, if any)

[If joint case, both spouses must sign.]

CERTIFICATION AND SIGNATURE OF NON-ATTORNEY BANKRUPTCY PETITION PREPARER (See 11 U.S.C. § 110)

I certify that I am a bankruptcy petition preparer as defined in 11 U.S.C. § 110, that I prepared this document for compensation, and that I have provided the debtor with a copy of this document.

N/A

_____   _____
Printed or Typed Name of Bankruptcy Petition Preparer   Social Security No.

_____

_____
Address

Names and Social Security numbers of all other individuals who prepared or assisted in preparing this document:

If more than one person prepared this document, attach additional signed sheets conforming to the appropriate Official Form for each person.

X_____   _____
Signature of Bankruptcy Petition Preparer   Date

A bankruptcy petition preparer's failure to comply with the provisions of Title 11 and the Federal Rules of Bankruptcy Procedure may result in fine or imprisonment or both. 11 U.S.C. § 110; 18 U.S.C. § 156.

DECLARATION UNDER PENALTY OF PERJURY ON BEHALF OF CORPORATION OR PARTNERSHIP
N/A

I, the _____ [the president or other officer or an authorized agent of the corporation or a member or an authorized agent of the partnership] of the _____ [corporation or partnership] named as debtor in this case, declare under penalty of perjury that I have read the foregoing summary and schedules, consisting of _____ sheets, and that they are true and correct to the best of my knowledge, information, and belief.
(Total shown on summary page plus 1)

Date_____   Signature_____

_____
[Print or type name of individual signing on behalf of debtor]

[An individual signing on behalf of a partnership or corporation must indicate position or relationship to debtor.]

Penalty for making a false statement or concealing property: Fine of up to $500,000, imprisonment for up to 5 years, or both. 18 U.S.C. §§ 152 and 3571.

a. **List any payment over $600 made to an arm's-length creditor,** if the payment was made:
- to repay a loan, installment purchase or other debt, and
- during the 90 days before you file your bankruptcy petition.

b. **List any payment made to an insider creditor,** if the payment was made within one year before you file your bankruptcy petition. Include alimony and child support payments.

The purpose of these questions is to discover if you have preferred any creditor over others. If you have paid an arm's-length creditor during the 90 days before you file or an insider during the year before you file, the trustee can demand that the creditor turn over the amount to the court, so the trustee can use it to pay your other unsecured creditors. (See Ch. 2, *Your Property and Bankruptcy*, Section A.3.) The trustee may ask you to produce written evidence of any payments you list here, such as copies of canceled checks, check stubs or bank statements.

4. **Suits, executions, garnishments and attachments.**

a. Include all court actions that you are currently involved in or which you were involved in during one year before filing. Court actions include personal injury cases, small claims actions, contract disputes, divorces, paternity actions, support or custody modification actions and the like. Include:

Caption of the suit and case number. The caption is the case title (such as *John Jones v. Ginny Jones*). The case number is assigned by the court clerk and appears on the first page of any court-filed paper.

Nature of the proceeding. A phrase, or even a one-word description, is sufficient. For example, "suit by debtor for compensation for damages to debtor's car caused by accident," or "divorce."

Court and location. This information is on any Summons you received or prepared.

Status or disposition. State whether the case is awaiting trial, is pending a decision, is on appeal or has ended.

b. If, at any time during the year before you file for bankruptcy, your wages, real estate or personal property was taken from you under the authority of a court order to pay a debt, enter the requested information. If you don't know the exact date, put "on or about" the approximate date.

5. **Repossessions, foreclosures and returns.** If, at any time during the year before you file for bankruptcy, a creditor repossessed or foreclosed on property you had bought and were making payments on, or had pledged as collateral for a loan, give the requested information. For instance, if your car, boat or video equipment was repossessed because you defaulted on your payments, describe it here. Also, if you voluntarily returned property to a creditor because you couldn't keep up the payments, enter that here.

6. Assignments and receiverships.

a. If, at any time during the 120 days (four months) before you file for bankruptcy, you assigned (legally transferred) your right to receive benefits or property to a creditor to pay a debt, list it here. Examples include assigning a percentage of your wages to a creditor for several months or assigning a portion of a personal injury award to an attorney. The assignee is the person to whom the assignment was made, such as the creditor or attorney. The terms of the assignment should be given briefly—for example, "wages assigned to Snorkle's Store to satisfy debt of $500."

b. Identify all of your property that has been in the hands of a court-appointed receiver, custodian or other official during the year before you file for bankruptcy. If you've made child support payments directly to a court, and the court in turn paid your child's other parent, list those payments here.

7. **Gifts.** Provide the requested information about gifts you've made in the past year. The bankruptcy court and trustee want this information to make sure you haven't improperly unloaded any property before filing for bankruptcy. List all charitable donations over $100 and gifts to family members over $200.

You don't have to list gifts to family members that are "ordinary and usual," but there is no easy way to identify such gifts. The best test is whether someone outside of the family might think the gift was unusual under the circumstances. If so, list it. Forgiving a loan is also a gift, as is charging interest substantially below the market rate. Other gifts include giving a car or prepaid trip to a business associate.

8. **Losses.** Provide the requested information. If the loss was for an exempt item, most states let you keep the insurance proceeds up to the limit of the exemption. (See Appendix 1.) If the item was not exempt, the trustee is entitled to the proceeds. In either case, list any proceeds you've received or expect to receive.

9. **Payments related to debt counseling or bankruptcy.** If you paid an improperly high fee to an attorney, bankruptcy form preparer, debt consultant or debt consolidator, the trustee may try to get some of it back to be distributed to

your creditors. Be sure to list all payments made by someone else on your behalf as well as payments you made directly.

10. Other transfers. List all real and personal property that you've sold or used as collateral for a secured debt during the year before you file for bankruptcy. Some examples are selling or abandoning (junking) a car, pledging your house as security (collateral) for a loan, granting an easement on real estate or trading property.

Don't include any gifts you listed in Item 7. Also, don't list property you've parted with as a regular part of your business or financial affairs. For example, if you operate a mail order book business, don't list the books you sold during the past year. Similarly, don't put down payments for regular goods and services, such as your phone bill, utilities or rent. The idea is to disclose transfers of property that legally belongs in your bankruptcy estate.

11. Closed financial accounts. Provide information for each account in your name or for your benefit that was closed during the past year or transferred to someone else.

12. Safe deposit boxes. Provide information for each safe deposit box you've had within the past year.

13. Setoffs. A setoff is when a creditor, often a bank, uses money in a customer's account to pay a debt owed to the creditor by that customer. Here, list any setoffs your creditors have made during the last 90 days.

14. Property held for another person. Describe all property you've borrowed from, are storing for or hold in trust for someone. Examples are funds in an irrevocable trust controlled by you and property you're holding as executor or administrator of an estate.

If you list valuable items, the trustee will likely want more details. Some people have described all of their property as being in trust or otherwise belonging to someone else, hoping to escape giving it to the trustee. The tactic doesn't work. Include only property you truly hold for others.

➡ **BUSINESS DEBTORS**

Only business debtors must complete questions 16–21. A business debtor is anyone who operated a profession or business, or who was otherwise self-employed, anytime during the two years before filing for bankruptcy. If you are not a business debtor, type "N/A" right before question 16 and skip ahead to just after question 21.

16. Nature, location and name of business. Provide the information requested in question "a." If question "b" or "c" applies to you, you should not be using this book.

17. Books, records and financial statements.

a. Identify every person other than yourself—usually a bookkeeper or accountant—who was involved in the accounting of your business during the previous six years. If you were the only person involved in your business's accounting, check "None."

b. If your books weren't audited during the past two years, check "None." Otherwise, fill in the requested information.

c. Usually, you, your bookkeeper, accountant, ex-business associate or possibly an ex-mate will have business records. If any are missing, explain. The more the loss of your records was beyond your control, the better off you'll be.

d. You may have prepared a financial statement if you applied to a bank for a loan or line of credit for your business or in your own name. If you're self-employed and applied for a personal loan to purchase a car or house, you probably submitted a financial statement as evidence of your ability to repay. Financial statements include:
   - balance sheets (compares assets with liabilities)
   - profit and loss statements (compares income with expenses)
   - financial statements (provides an overall financial description of a business).

18. Inventories. If your business doesn't have an inventory because it's a service business, check "None." If your business does deal in products, but you were primarily the middle person or original manufacturer, put "no inventory required" or "materials purchased for each order as needed." If you have an inventory, fill in the information requested in items "a" and "b."

19. Current partners, officers, directors and shareholders. Check "None" for "a" and "b."

20. Former partners, officers, directors and shareholders. Check "None" for "a" and "b."

21. Withdrawals from a partnership or distributions by a corporation. Check "None."

If completed by an individual or individual and spouse. Sign and date this section. If you're filing jointly, be sure your spouse dates and signs it as well.

Certification and Signature of Non-Attorney Bankruptcy Petition Preparer. If a BPP typed your forms, have that person complete this section. Otherwise, type "N/A" anywhere in the box.

If completed on behalf of a partnership or corporation. Type "N/A."

Be sure to insert the number of continuation pages, if any, you attached.

FORM 7. STATEMENT OF FINANCIAL AFFAIRS

UNITED STATES BANKRUPTCY COURT

<u>Northern</u> DISTRICT OF <u>Ohio, Eastern Division</u>

In re: <u>Maytag, Molly and Jonathan</u> ,   Case No. _____
                      (Name)   (If known)
                                    Debtor

STATEMENT OF FINANCIAL AFFAIRS

This statement is to be completed by every debtor. Spouses filing a joint petition may file a single statement on which the information for both spouses is combined. If the case is filed under Chapter 12 or Chapter 13, a married debtor must furnish information for both spouses whether or not a joint petition is filed, unless the spouses are separated and a joint petition is not filed. An individual debtor engaged in business as a sole proprietor, partner, family farmer, or self-employed professional, should provide the information requested on this statement concerning all such activities as well as the individual's personal affairs.

Questions 1–15 are to be completed by all debtors. Debtors that are or have been in business, as defined below, also must complete Questions 16–21. **Each question must be answered. If the answer to any question is "None," or the question is not applicable, mark the box labeled "None."** If additional space is needed for the answer to any question, use and attach a separate sheet properly identified with the case name, case number (if known), and the number of the question.

DEFINITIONS

"In business." A debtor is "in business" for the purpose of this form if the debtor is a corporation or partnership. An individual debtor is "in business" for the purpose of this form if the debtor is or has been, within the two years immediately preceding the filing of this bankruptcy case, any of the following: an officer, director, managing executive, or person in control of a corporation; a partner, other than a limited partner, of a partnership; a sole proprietor or self-employed.

"Insider." The term "insider" includes but is not limited to: relatives of the debtor; general partners of the debtor and their relatives; corporations of which the debtor is an officer, director, or person in control; officers, directors, and any person in control of a corporate debtor and their relatives; affiliates of the debtor and insiders of such affiliates; any managing agent of the debtor. 11 U.S.C. § 101(30).

1.   Income from employment or operation of business

None

☐   State the gross amount of income the debtor has received from employment, trade, or profession, or from operation of the debtor's business from the beginning of this calendar year to the date this case was commenced. State also the gross amounts received during the **two years** immediately preceding this calendar year. (A debtor that maintains, or has maintained, financial records on the basis of a fiscal rather than a calendar year may report fiscal year income. Identify the beginning and ending dates of the debtor's fiscal year.) If a joint petition is filed, state income for each spouse separately. (Married debtors filing under Chapter 12 or Chapter 13 must state income of both spouses whether or not a joint petition is filed, unless the spouses are separated and a joint petition is not filed.)

AMOUNT	SOURCE (If more than one)
$6,000 (1/1/XX–7/3/XX)	Wife's employment
$18,000 (1/1/XX–7/3/XX)	Husband's employment
$14,000 (19XY)	Wife's employment
$29,000 (19XY)	Husband's employment
$11,000 (19XZ)	Wife's employment
$16,000 (19XZ)	Husband's employment

2. **Income other than from employment or operation of business**

None

State the amount of income received by the debtor other than from employment, trade, profession, or operation of the debtor's business during the **two years** immediately preceding the commencement of this case. Give particulars. If a joint petition is filed, state income for each spouse separately. (Married debtors filing under Chapter 12 or Chapter 13 must state income for each spouse whether or not a joint petition is filed, unless the spouses are separated and a joint petition is not filed.)

AMOUNT	SOURCE
$300	19XX, stock dividends (J)
$740	19XY, stock dividends (J)
$4,000	19XX, worker's comp benefits (H)

3. **Payments to creditors**

None a. List all payments on loans, installment purchases of goods or services, and other debts, aggregating more than $600 to any creditor, made within **90 days** immediately preceding the commencement of this case. (Married debtors filing under Chapter 12 or Chapter 13 must include payments by either or both spouses whether or not a joint petition is filed, unless the spouses are separated and a joint petition is not filed.)

NAME AND ADDRESS OF CREDITOR	DATES OF PAYMENTS	AMOUNT PAID	AMOUNT STILL OWING
Ameritrust	4/17/XX	$650	$87,000
10 Financial Way	5/17/XX	$650	
Cleveland Hts, OH 44118	6/17/XX	$650	

None b. List all payments made within **one year** immediately preceding the commencement of this case, to or for the benefit of, creditors who are or were insiders. (Married debtors filing under Chapter 12 or Chapter 13 must include payments by either or both spouses whether or not a joint petition is filed, unless the spouses are separated and a joint petition is not filed.)

NAME AND ADDRESS OF CREDITOR; RELATIONSHIP TO DEBTOR	DATES OF PAYMENTS	AMOUNT PAID	AMOUNT STILL OWING
Ellen Rogers	8/XX to 5/XY	$600/month	$600/month since 6/XY
900 Grand View			
Jackson, WY 83001			
(ex-wife, mother of husband's			
2 children)			

4. **Suits, executions, garnishments and attachments**

None a. List all suits to which the debtor is or was a party within **one year** immediately preceding the filing of this bankruptcy case. (Married debtors filing under Chapter 12 or Chapter 13 must include information concerning either or both spouses whether or not a joint petition is filed, unless the spouses are separated and a joint petition is not filed.)

CAPTION OF SUIT AND CASE NUMBER	NATURE OF PROCEEDING	COURT AND LOCATION	STATUS OR DISPOSITION
Cleveland Hospital v. Jonathan Maytag (H)	Suit for doctor's fee and medical bills	Cleveland Municipal Ct., Cleveland, OH	trial set 9/7/XX
Dennis Dentist v. Molly M. Maytag, #91-8080 (W)	Suit for dentist's fees	Cleveland Hts Small Claims Court, Cleveland, OH	open
Freedom Financial v. Jonathan & Molly Maytag #90-9101 (J)	Suit for unpaid American Express bill	Cleveland Municipal Ct., Cleveland, OH	open
American Allowance v. Jonathan & Molly Maytag #90-7400 (J)	Suit for unpaid VISA bill	Cleveland Municipal Ct., Cleveland, OH	open

None □ b. Describe all property that has been attached, garnished or seized under any legal or equitable process within **one year** immediately preceding the commencement of this case. (Married debtors filing under Chapter 12 or Chapter 13 must include information concerning property of either or both spouses whether or not a joint petition is filed, unless the spouses are separated and a joint petition is not filed.)

NAME AND ADDRESS OF PERSON FOR WHOSE BENEFIT PROPERTY WAS SEIZED	DATE OF SEIZURE	DESCRIPTION AND VALUE OF PROPERTY
Quality Collection Agency 21 Main Street Cleveland, OH 44115	on or about 2/XX	(J) bank account levy – $650
Quality Collection Agency 21 Main Street Cleveland, OH 44115	4/10/XX to 6/30/XX	(H) wage garnishment $850

5. Repossessions, foreclosures and returns

None □ List all property that has been repossessed by a creditor, sold at a foreclosure sale, transferred through a deed in lieu of foreclosure or returned to the seller within **one year** immediately preceding the commencement of this case. (Married debtors filing under Chapter 12 or Chapter 13 must include information concerning property of either or both spouses whether or not a joint petition is filed, unless the spouses are separated and a joint petition is not filed.)

NAME AND ADDRESS OF CREDITOR OR SELLER	DATE OF REPOSSESSION, FORECLOSURE SALE, TRANSFER OR RETURN	DESCRIPTION AND VALUE OF PROPERTY
Ameritrust 10 Financial Way Cleveland Hts, OH 44118	6/18/XX repossessed	(J) 1987 Honda Civic, approximate value $4,500
Shaker Savings 44 Trust St. Cleveland Hts, OH 44118	6/30/XX repossessed	(J) 1985 Buick Skylark, approximate value $3,000

6. Assignments and receiverships

None ☒ a. Describe any assignment of property for the benefit of creditors made within **120 days** immediately preceding the commencement of this case. (Married debtors filing under Chapter 12 or Chapter 13 must include any assignment by either or both spouses whether or not a joint petition is filed, unless the spouses are separated and a joint petition is not filed.)

NAME AND ADDRESS OF ASSIGNEE	DATE OF ASSIGNMENT	TERMS OF ASSIGNMENT OR SETTLEMENT

None
[X]
b.   List all property which has been in the hands of a custodian, receiver, or court-appointed official within **one year** immediately preceding the commencement of this case. (Married debtors filing under Chapter 12 or Chapter 13 must include information concerning property of either or both spouses whether or not a joint petition is filed, unless the spouses are separated and a joint petition is not filed.)

NAME AND ADDRESS OF CUSTODIAN	NAME AND LOCATION OF COURT; CASE TITLE & NUMBER	DATE OF ORDER	DESCRIPTION AND VALUE OF PROPERTY

7.   Gifts

None
[X]
List all gifts or charitable contributions made within **one year** immediately preceding the commencement of this case except ordinary and usual gifts to family members aggregating less than $200 in value per individual family member and charitable contributions aggregating less than $100 per recipient. (Married debtors filing under Chapter 12 or Chapter 13 must include gifts or contributions by either or both spouses whether or not a joint petition is filed, unless the spouses are separated and a joint petition is not filed.)

NAME AND ADDRESS OF PERSON OR ORGANIZATION	RELATIONSHIP TO DEBTOR, IF ANY	DATE OF GIFT	DESCRIPTION AND VALUE OF GIFT

8.   Losses

None
[ ]
List all losses from fire, theft, other casualty or gambling within **one year** immediately preceding the commencement of this case **or since the commencement of this case.** (Married debtors filing under Chapter 12 or Chapter 13 must include losses by either or both spouses whether or not a joint petition is filed, unless the spouses are separated and a joint petition is not filed.)

DESCRIPTION AND VALUE OF PROPERTY	DESCRIPTION OF CIRCUMSTANCES AND, IF LOSS WAS COVERED IN WHOLE OR IN PART BY INSURANCE, GIVE PARTICULARS	DATE OF LOSS
Mountain bike; $165	Daughter Sara's bicycle was stolen. Insurance covered replacement. We purchased new bike on 12/17/XY.	10/5/XX

9. Payments related to debt counseling or bankruptcy

None
☐

List all payments made or property transferred by or on behalf of the debtor to any person, including attorneys, for consultation concerning debt consolidation, relief under the bankruptcy law or preparation of a petition in bankruptcy within **one year** immediately preceding the commencement of this case.

NAME AND ADDRESS OF PAYEE	DATE OF PAYMENT; NAME OF PAYOR IF OTHER THAN DEBTOR	AMOUNT OF MONEY OR DESCRIPTION AND VALUE OF PROPERTY
John White, Esq. 21 Main St. Cleveland, OH 44114	2/11/XX	(J) $500 retainer fee paid

10. Other transfers

None
X

a. List all other property, other than property transferred in the ordinary course of the business or financial affairs of the debtor, transferred either absolutely or as security within **one year** immediately preceding the commencement of this case. (Married debtors filing under Chapter 12 or Chapter 13 must include transfers by either or both spouses whether or not a joint petition is filed, unless the spouses are separated and a joint petition is not filed.)

NAME AND ADDRESS OF TRANSFEREE; RELATIONSHIP TO DEBTOR	DATE	DESCRIBE PROPERTY TRANSFERRED AND VALUE RECEIVED

11. Closed financial accounts

None
☐

List all financial accounts and instruments held in the name of the debtor or for the benefit of the debtor which were closed, sold, or otherwise transferred within **one year** immediately preceding the commencement of this case. Include checking, savings, or other financial accounts, certificates of deposit, or other instruments; shares and share accounts held in banks, credit unions, pension funds, cooperatives, associations, brokerage houses and other financial institutions. (Married debtors filing under Chapter 12 or Chapter 13 must include information concerning accounts or instruments held by or for either or both spouses whether or not a joint petition is filed, unless the spouses are separated and a joint petition is not filed.)

NAME AND ADDRESS OF INSTITUTION	TYPE AND NUMBER OF ACCOUNT AND AMOUNT OF FINAL BALANCE	AMOUNT AND DATE OF SALE OR CLOSING
Ohio Savings 1818 Lakeshore Avenue Cleveland, OH 44123	(H) Checking account #058-118061 final balance $84.12	12/2/XY

12. Safe deposit boxes

None ☐

List each safe deposit or other box or depository in which the debtor has or had securities, cash, or other valuables within **one year** immediately preceding the commencement of this case. (Married debtors filing under Chapter 12 or Chapter 13 must include boxes or depositories of either or both spouses whether or not a joint petition is filed, unless the spouses are separated and a joint petition is not filed.)

NAME AND ADDRESS OF BANK OR OTHER DEPOSITORY	NAMES AND ADDRESSES OF THOSE WITH ACCESS TO BOX OR DEPOSITORY	DESCRIPTION OF CONTENTS	DATE OF TRANSFER OR SURRENDER, IF ANY
Ameritrust 10 Financial Way Cleveland Hts., OH 44118	Molly Maytag Jonathan Maytag 21 Scarborough Rd. So. Cleveland Hts, OH 41118	stock certificates for Trusso Corp., Investco Ltd., and Rayco Co.	N/A

13. Setoffs

None ☒

List all setoffs made by any creditor, including a bank, against a debt or deposit of the debtor within **90 days** preceding the commencement of this case. (Married debtors filing under Chapter 12 or Chapter 13 must include information concerning either or both spouses whether or not a joint petition is filed, unless the spouses are separated and a joint petition is not filed.)

NAME AND ADDRESS OF CREDITOR	DATE OF SETOFF	AMOUNT OF SETOFF

14. Property held for another person

None ☐

List all property owned by another person that the debtor holds or controls.

NAME AND ADDRESS OF OWNER	DESCRIPTION AND VALUE OF PROPERTY	LOCATION OF PROPERTY
Paul & Bonnie Johnson 40 Mayfield University Hts, OH 44118	Poodle – Binkie $100	residence
Felicia Maytag 8 Superior Rd Cleveland, OH 44114	19XW Ford Pickup $750	residence

15. Prior address of debtor

None ☒

If the debtor has moved within the **two years** immediately preceding the commencement of this case, list all premises which the debtor occupied during that period and vacated prior to the commencement of this case. If a joint petition is filed, report also any separate address of either spouse.

ADDRESS	NAME USED	DATES OF OCCUPANCY

The following questions are to be completed by every debtor that is a corporation or partnership and by any individual debtor who is or has been, within the **two years** immediately preceding the commencement of this case, any of the following: an officer, director, managing executive, or owner of more than 5 percent of the voting securities of a corporation; a partner, other than a limited partner, of a partnership; a sole proprietor or otherwise self-employed.

*(An individual or joint debtor should complete this portion of the statement **only** if the debtor is or has been in business, as defined above, within the two years immediately preceding the commencement of this case.)*

N/A

16. Nature, location and name of business

None
☐
a. If the debtor is an individual, list the names and addresses of all businesses in which the debtor was an officer, director, partner, or managing executive of a corporation, partnership, sole proprietorship, or was a self-employed professional within the **two years** immediately preceding the commencement of this case, or in which the debtor owned 5 percent or more of the voting or equity securities, within the **two years** immediately preceding the commencement of this case.

b. If the debtor is a partnership, list the names and addresses of all businesses in which the debtor was a partner or owned 5 percent or more of the voting securities, within the **two years** immediately preceding the commencement of this case.

c. If the debtor is a corporation, list the names and addresses of all businesses in which the debtor was a partner or owned 5 percent or more of the voting securities, within the **two years** immediately preceding the commencement of this case.

NAME	ADDRESS	NATURE OF BUSINESS	BEGINNING AND ENDING DATES OF OPERATION

17. Books, records and financial statements

None
☐
a. List all bookkeepers and accountants who within the **six years** immediately preceding the filing of this bankruptcy case kept or supervised the keeping of books of account and records of the debtor.

NAME AND ADDRESS	DATES SERVICES RENDERED

None
☐
b. List all firms or individuals who within the **two years** immediately preceding the filing of this bankruptcy case have audited the books of account and records, or prepared a financial statement of the debtor.

NAME AND ADDRESS	DATES SERVICES RENDERED

None c. List all firms or individuals who at the time of the commencement of this case were in possession of the books of account and records of the debtor. If any of the books of account and records are not available, explain.

NAME   ADDRESS

None d. List all financial institutions, creditors and other parties, including mercantile and trade agencies, to whom a financial statement was issued within the **two years** immediately preceding the commencement of this case by the debtor.

NAME AND ADDRESS   DATE ISSUED

18. Inventories

None a. List the dates of the last two inventories taken of your property, the name of the person who supervised the taking of each inventory, and the dollar amount and basis of each inventory.

                                                 DOLLAR AMOUNT OF INVENTORY

DATE OF INVENTORY   INVENTORY SUPERVISOR   (Specify cost, market or other basis)

None b. List the name and address of the person having possession of the records of each of the two inventories reported in a., above.

                                               NAME AND ADDRESSES OF

DATE OF INVENTORY   CUSTODIAN OF INVENTORY RECORDS

19. Current partners, officers, directors and shareholders

None a. If the debtor is a partnership, list the nature and percentage of partnership interest of each member of the partnership.

NAME AND ADDRESS   NATURE OF INTEREST   PERCENTAGE OF INTEREST

None b. If the debtor is a corporation, list all officers and directors of the corporation, and each stockholder who directly or indirectly owns, controls, or holds 5 percent or more of the voting securities of the corporation.

☐

NAME AND ADDRESS	TITLE	NATURE AND PERCENTAGE OF STOCK OWNERSHIP

20. Former partners, officers, directors and shareholders

None a. If the debtor is a partnership, list each member who withdrew from the partnership within **one year** immediately preceding the commencement of this case.

☐

NAME	ADDRESS	DATE OF WITHDRAWAL

None b. If the debtor is a corporation, list all officers or directors whose relationship with the corporation terminated within **one year** immediately preceding the commencement of this case.

☐

NAME AND ADDRESS	TITLE	DATE OF TERMINATION

21. Withdrawals from a partnership or distributions by a corporation

None If the debtor is a partnership or corporation, list all withdrawals or distributions credited or given to an insider, including compensation in any form, bonuses, loans, stock redemptions, options exercised and any other perquisite during **one year** immediately preceding the commencement of this case

☐

NAME AND ADDRESS OF RECIPIENT; RELATIONSHIP TO DEBTOR	DATE AND PURPOSE OF WITHDRAWAL	AMOUNT OF MONEY OR DESCRIPTION AND VALUE OF PROPERTY

[If completed by an individual or individual and spouse]

I declare under penalty of perjury that I have read the answers contained in the foregoing statement of financial affairs and any attachments thereto and that they are true and correct.

Date _____ July 3, 19XX _____   Signature of Debtor _____ *Molly Maytag* _____

Date _____ July 3, 19XX _____   Signature of Joint Debtor (if any) _____ *Jonathan Maytag* _____

CERTIFICATION AND SIGNATURE OF NON-ATTORNEY BANKRUPTCY PETITION PREPARER (See 11 U.S.C. § 110)

I certify that I am a bankruptcy petition preparer as defined in 11 U.S.C. § 110, that I prepared this document for compensation, and that I have provided the debtor with a copy of this document.

N/A

_____   _____
Printed or Typed Name of Bankruptcy Petition Preparer   Social Security No.

_____

_____
Address

Names and Social Security numbers of all other individuals who prepared or assisted in preparing this document:

If more than one person prepared this document, attach additional signed sheets conforming to the appropriate Official Form for each person.

X_____   _____
Signature of Bankruptcy Petition Preparer   Date

A bankruptcy petition preparer's failure to comply with the provisions of title 11 and the Federal Rules of Bankruptcy Procedure may result in fine or imprisonment or both. 11 U.S.C. § 110; 18 U.S.C. § 156.

[If completed by or on behalf of a partnership or corporation]   N/A

I declare under penalty of perjury that I have read the answers contained in the foregoing statement of financial affairs and any attachments thereto and that they are true and correct to the best of my knowledge, information and belief.

Date _____   Signature _____

_____
Print Name and Title

[An individual signing on behalf of a partnership or corporation must indicate position or relationship to debtor.]

_____ 0 _____ *continuation sheets attached*

Penalty for presenting fraudulent claim: Fine of up to $500,000 or imprisonment for up to 5 years, or both. 18 U.S.C. §§ 152 and 3571.

H. Form 8—Chapter 7 Individual Debtor's Statement of Intention

This form is very important if you owe any secured debts. All property that is security for a debt will end up in the creditor's hands, even if it's exempt, unless you use one of the specific remedies the bankruptcy laws provide. Your Statement of Intention tells your creditors which approach you plan to take—whether you want to keep an item and pay for it in one of the ways permitted by the bankruptcy laws, or whether you choose to surrender the property in exchange for cancellation of the debt.

Ch. 7, *Secured Debts,* describes each option available regarding your secured debts—read it carefully before completing this form.

IF YOU ARE MARRIED

If you're filing jointly, complete only one form, even though it says "Individual Debtor's Statement of Intention."

Below is a completed Statement of Intention and instructions.

Court name. Copy this information from Form 1—Voluntary Petition.

In re and **Case No.** Follow the instructions for Schedule A.

Chapter. Type in "7."

If you have no secured debts, type "N/A" after statement 1 and skip ahead to the signature section of the form.

Section a, Property to Be Surrendered. If you've decided to give up any (or all) property you've pledged as collateral for a secured debt, or the property has already been taken and you don't want to get it back, complete Section a. (If you need more space, use a continuation page.) If you plan to retain all property tied to your secured debts, type "N/A."

Section b, Property to Be Retained. If you will surrender all property tied to your secured debts, type "N/A." If you want to hold on to any of the property you've pledged as collateral for a secured debt, read Ch. 7, *Secured Debts,* to understand your options. Then come back to this form and fill in Section b as follows:

Description of Property. Identify the collateral, such as "19XX Volvo" or "house at 316 Maiden Lane, Miami Beach, Florida."

Creditor's Name. List on a separate line, the name of each creditor with a lien on the property listed in the first column.

Property is claimed as exempt; Property will be redeemed; Debt will be reaffirmed. Check the appropriate column, for each creditor with a lien, based on what you read in Ch. 7,

Secured Debts. Also, if you own a home, read Ch. 6, *Your House.*

If your district lets you retain property by keeping your payments current (without reaffirming or redeeming) and you want to use this method (it's described in Ch. 7), fill in a description of the property in the first column. In the second column, fill in the creditor's name, followed by the words, "intend to retain property by keeping payments current on contract with creditor." Do not check any of the last three columns. If your district doesn't specifically allow this method but the creditor has informally agreed to let you retain the property by keeping your payments current, complete Section 2a, *Property to Be Surrendered*, by following the above instructions.

Credit Card Debts

If you owe on a bank or department store credit card and want to keep the card through bankruptcy, contact the bank or store before you file. If you offer to "reaffirm" the debt, some banks or store may let you keep the credit card. If you do reaffirm it, list it on the Statement of Intention, even though technically it isn't a secured debt.

Signature. Date and sign the form. If you're married and filing jointly, your spouse must also date and sign the form.

Certification of Non-Attorney Bankruptcy Petition Preparer. If a BPP typed your forms, have that person complete this section. Otherwise, type "N/A" anywhere in the box.

Form 8. CHAPTER 7 INDIVIDUAL DEBTOR'S STATEMENT OF INTENTION

UNITED STATES BANKRUPTCY COURT

_____ Northern _____ DISTRICT OF __Ohio, Eastern Division__

In re ___Maytag, Molly and Jonathan___ ,
(Name)
Debtor

Case No. _____
(If known)

Chapter ___7___

1. I have filed a schedule of assets and liabilities which includes consumer debts secured by property of the estate.

2. I intend to do the following with respect to the property of the estate which secures those consumer debts:

   a. *Property to be surrendered.*

	Description of Property	Creditor's Name
1.	N/A	
2.		
3.		

   b. *Property to be retained.*

[*Check any applicable statement.*]

	Description of property	Creditor's name	Property is claimed as exempt	Property will be redeemed pursuant to 11 U.S.C. § 722	Debt will be reaffirmed pursuant to 11 USC § 524(c)
1.	Residence	Ameritrust (mortgage)	X		
2.		Ameritrust (2nd mortgage)	X		
3.		Ohio Savings (judgment lien)			X
4.	Computer	Computers for Sale		X	
5.	Bedroom furniture	Fanny's Furniture		X	

Date: ___July 3, 19XX___

Molly Maytag/ Jonathan Maytag
Signature of Debtor

CERTIFICATION OF NON-ATTORNEY BANKRUPTCY PETITION PREPARER (See 11 U.S.C. § 110)

I certify that I am a bankruptcy petition preparer as defined in 11 U.S.C. § 110, that I prepared this document for compensation, and that I have provided the debtor with a copy of this document.

___N/A___

Printed or Typed Name of Bankruptcy Petition Preparer   Social Security No.

Address

Names and Social Security numbers of all other individuals who prepared or assisted in preparing this document:

If more than one person prepared this document, attach additional signed sheets conforming to the appropriate Official Form for each person.

X _____

Signature of Bankruptcy Petition Preparer   Date

A bankruptcy petition preparer's failure to comply with the provisions of title 11 and the Federal Rules of Bankruptcy Procedure may result in fine or imprisonment or both. 11 U.S.C. § 110; 18 U.S.C. § 156.

I. Mailing Matrix

When you file for bankruptcy, you may need to include a sheet called a "mailing matrix." The mailing matrix is a blank page divided into approximately 30 boxes. You type in the names and addresses of your creditors, and the trustee photocopies the page to create mailing labels. Some courts don't require a mailing matrix, while other courts have their own forms or require a specific type face or spacing. If you need to provide a matrix, but your court doesn't have its own, you can use the form in Appendix 4. Here's how to fill it out:

Step 1: On a separate piece of paper, make a list of all your creditors, in alphabetical order. You can copy them off of Schedules D, E, F and H. Be sure to include cosigners and joint debtors. If you and your spouse jointly incurred a debt and are filing jointly, however, don't include your spouse. Also, include collection agencies or attorneys, if you've been sued. And if you're seeking to discharge marital debts you assumed during a divorce, include both your ex-spouse and the creditors.

Step 2: Make several copies of the mailing matrix form.

Step 3: In the top left-hand box on the form, enter your name and address. Then enter the names and addresses of each creditor, one per box and in alphabetical order (or in the order required by your local bankruptcy court). Use as many sheets as you need.

J. How To File Your Papers

Filing your papers should be simple. Here's how to do it.

1. Basic Filing Procedures

Step 1: Make sure you have the following information (you may need to check with the bankruptcy court clerk—see Section B, above):
- the amount of the filing and administrative fees
- the specific order in which documents should be layered, and
- the number of copies of each document needed.

Step 2: Put all your bankruptcy forms, except Form 8—Chapter 7 Individual Debtor's Statement of Intention—in the order required by the bankruptcy court or in the order we present them in this book.

Step 3: Check that you, and your spouse if you're filing a joint petition, have signed each form where required.

Step 4: Make the number of copies required by the court, plus:
- two additional copies of all forms (except the Statement of Intention)—one set for the clerk to file-stamp and give or send back to you when you file the papers, and one set in the event your papers are lost in the mail (if you file by mail)
- one extra copy of the Statement of Intention for each person listed on that form, and
- one extra copy of the Statement of Intention for the trustee.

Step 5: Use a standard two hole punch (copy centers have them) to punch the top/center of all your bankruptcy papers. Don't staple together any forms.

Step 6: If you plan to mail your documents to the court, address a 9 x 12 inch envelope to yourself. Although most people prefer to file by mail, you can take your papers to the bankruptcy court clerk. Going to the court will let you correct minor mistakes on the spot.

Step 7: If you can pay the filing and administrative fees when you file, clip or staple a money order, payable to "U.S. Bankruptcy Court," to your original set of papers. If you want to pay in installments, attach a filled-in application and order for payment in installments, plus any additional papers required by local rules. Although you can pay the filing fee ($130) in installments, the administrative fee ($45) must be paid in full when you file your petition. Instructions for paying in installments are in Section 2, just below. In certain parts of the country, you can apply to the court to have the filing fee waived. (See sidebar, below.)

Step 8: Take or mail the original and copies of all forms (except the Statement of Intention) to the correct bankruptcy court (see Section A, above) accompanied by the payment or an application and order for payment in installments.

Step 9: Ask the court clerk the name and address of the trustee assigned to your case. Then have a friend or relative (other than your spouse if you are filing jointly) over the age of 18 mail by first class, a copy of your Statement of Intention to the bankruptcy trustee and to all the creditors listed on that form. Be sure to keep the original. You must do this within 30 days of filing your papers, but you should do it sooner.

Step 10: On a Proof of Service by Mail (a copy is in Appendix 4), enter the name and complete address of the trustee and all creditors to whom your friend or relative sent your Statement of Intention. Have that person sign and date the Proof of Service.

Step 11: Make a copy of the original Statement of Intention and of the Proof of Service your friend or relative signed. Staple the original Proof of Service to the original Statement of Intention, and send or take the originals to the bankruptcy clerk.

2. Paying in Installments

You must pay the $45 administrative fee in full when you file your petition. You can pay the $130 filing fee in up to four installments over 120 days. (Bankruptcy Rule 1006(b)(1).) To do so, you must file a completed Application to Pay Filing Fee in Installments when you file your petition. A blank copy of this form is in Appendix 4.

You cannot apply for permission to pay in installments if you've paid an attorney to help you with your bankruptcy. This rules does not apply to Bankruptcy Petition Preparers—that is, you can pay a BPP and request permission to pay the filing fee in installments. (Rule 1006.)

The Application is easy to fill out. At the top, fill in the name of the court (this is on Form 1—Voluntary Petition), your name and your spouse's name if you're filing jointly, and "7" following the blank "Chapter." Leave the Case No. space blank. Then enter:

- the total filing fee you must pay: $130 (item 1)
- the amount you propose to pay when you file the petition (item 4, first blank)
- the number of additional installments you need (three maximum), and
- the amount and date you propose for each installment payment (item 4, second, third and fourth blanks).

You (and your spouse, if you're filing jointly) must sign and date the Application. If you use a BPP, have that person complete the second section. Leave the bottom section entitled "Order" blank for the judge to fill out. The judge will either approve the application as submitted, or will modify it. You'll be informed of the judge's decision.

Getting The Filing Fee Waived

On October 1, 1997, an experimental program to allow low-income debtors in the Southern District of Illinois, the District of Montana, the Eastern District of New York, the Eastern District of Pennsylvania, the Western District of Tennessee and the District of Utah to file for bankruptcy without paying the filing fee came to an end. A report on the experiment is due in Congress on March 1, 1998. Congress is expected to enact legislation allowing low-income debtors throughout the country to file for bankruptcy without paying the filing fee. If you will file for bankruptcy before this becomes law and cannot afford the fee, you'll need the help of a legal aid lawyer.

---

3. Emergency Filing

If you want to file for bankruptcy in a hurry to get an automatic stay to stop your creditors, in most places you can accomplish that by filing Form 1—Voluntary Petition and a mailing matrix. Some courts also require that you file a cover sheet and an Order Dismissing Chapter 7 Case, which will be processed if you don't file the rest of your papers within 15 days. (Bankruptcy Rule 1007(c).) If the bankruptcy court for your district requires this form, you can get it from the court, a local bankruptcy attorney or typing service.

If you don't follow up by filing the additional documents within 15 days, your bankruptcy case will be dismissed. You can file again, if necessary, although if your case was dismissed when you opposed a creditor's request to lift the stay, you'll have to wait 180 days to refile.

For an emergency filing:

Step 1: Check with the court to find out exactly what forms must be submitted for an emergency filing.

Step 2: Fill in Form 1—Voluntary Petition. (See Section E, above.)

Step 3: On a mailing matrix (or whatever other form is required by your court), list all your creditors, as well as collection agencies, sheriffs, attorneys and others who are seeking to collect debts from you. (See Section I, above.)

Step 4: Fill in any other papers the court requires.

Step 5: File the originals and required number of copies, accompanied by your fee (or an application for payment of fee in installments) and a self-addressed envelope with the bankruptcy court. Keep copies of everything for your records.

Step 6: File all other required forms within 15 days. If you don't, your case will probably be dismissed.

K. Effect of Filing

Once you file your bankruptcy papers, your property is under the supervision of the bankruptcy court. Don't throw out, give away, sell or otherwise dispose of any property unless and until the bankruptcy trustee says otherwise. You can however, make day-to-day purchases such as groceries, personal effects and clothing with the income you earn after filing. If you have any questions about this, ask the bankruptcy trustee. ■

CHAPTER

4

Handling Your Case In Court

For most people, the Chapter 7 bankruptcy process is straightforward and proceeds pretty much on automatic. The bankruptcy trustee decides whether or not your papers pass muster and if not, what amendments you need to file. Ordinarily, you have few decisions to make.

This chapter tells you how to handle the routine procedures that move your bankruptcy case along, and how to deal with unexpected complications that may arise because:

- you discover an error in your papers
- a creditor asks the court to lift the automatic stay
- you object to a creditor's claim
- a creditor objects to the discharge of a particular debt or your claim that an item of property is exempt, or
- you decide to dismiss your case.

Some of these problems—fixing a simple error in your papers, for example—you can handle yourself. For more complicated problems, such as fighting a creditor in court about the discharge of a large debt, you'll need a lawyer's help.

A. Routine Bankruptcy Procedures

A routine Chapter 7 bankruptcy case takes three to six months from beginning to end and follows a series of predictable steps.

1. The Court Schedules the Meeting of Creditors

Shortly after you file for bankruptcy, a bankruptcy trustee appointed by the court reads the forms you filed. The trustee decides, based on your papers, whether you have enough nonexempt property to sell to raise cash to pay your creditors. If you don't have enough nonexempt property for this purpose—most people don't—your bankruptcy is called a "no-asset case." If you do have enough nonexempt property to produce cash for your creditors, your bankruptcy is called an "asset case."

After reviewing your papers, the trustee sends a notice of your bankruptcy filing to all the creditors you listed. The notice tells the creditors whether or not they should file claims—that is, request to be paid. In no-asset cases, they don't need to bother. The notice also sets a date for the meeting of creditors, usually several weeks later. This is a very important date. Within 60 days after the meeting, your creditors must file their claims or, if they want to contest the discharge of a debt, file an objection.

2. You Notify Problem Creditors

When the trustee mails your creditors official notice of your filing, the automatic stay goes into effect. The automatic stay prohibits virtually all creditors from taking any action directed toward collecting the debts you owe them until the court says otherwise. In general, creditors cannot:

- undertake any collection activities (writing letters or calling, for example)
- file lawsuits
- terminate utilities or public benefits (such as welfare or food stamps)
- proceed with a pending lawsuit (all lawsuits are put on hold pending the outcome of your bankruptcy case)
- withhold money in their possession as a setoff for a debt (creditor can freeze your account, however, thereby shutting off your access to the money), or
- record liens against property.

In general, a creditor who undertakes any of these activities is considered in contempt of court and can be fined by the bankruptcy court.

There are some notable exceptions to the automatic stay, however. Even if you file bankruptcy, the following proceedings can continue:

- a criminal case against you
- a case to establish paternity or to establish, modify or collect child support or alimony, and
- a tax audit, the issuance of a tax deficiency notice, a demand for a tax return, the issuance of a tax assessment and the demand for payment of such an assessment—the IRS cannot, however, record a lien or seize your property after you file for bankruptcy.

In addition, the bankruptcy court can annul the automatic stay—that is, retroactively lift the stay from the moment it was imposed—and allow a creditor to continue collection efforts. (Lifting the automatic stay is covered in Section D.1, below.)

Creditors won't know to stop their collection efforts until they receive notice of your bankruptcy filing. The notice sent by the court may take several weeks to reach your creditors. If you want quicker results, send your own notice to creditors (and bill collectors, landlords or sheriffs) who you want to stop harassing you. A sample letter notifying your creditors is shown below. A tear-out form notice, which you can adapt to your own situation, is in Appendix 4.

HOW A ROUTINE BANKRUPTCY PROCEEDS

Step	Description	When It Happens
1. You notify problem creditors of your bankruptcy filing.	You should send your own notice immediately to any creditors you want to stop bothering you. A tear-out copy of such a notice is in Appendix 4.	As soon as you file your initial papers.
2. The court appoints a trustee.	The court appoints a trustee to examine your papers and manage your property.	Within a week or two after you file.
3. The court sets a date for the meeting of creditors.	The court sets a date for the meeting of creditors. The trustee notifies your creditors, whose names and addresses you gave in your bankruptcy papers.	Shortly after you file.
4. You attend the meeting of creditors.	The meeting of creditors is the only court appearance most people make. The judge is almost never there, and creditors seldom attend. The trustee and any creditors who show up can ask you about the information in your papers.	20–40 days after you file. (Bankruptcy Rule 2003; however, in many districts, the meetings are routinely held 45–90 days after you file.)
5. You and the trustee deal with your nonexempt property.	The trustee may collect your nonexempt property and sell it to pay your creditors. Or you may keep the property if you pay the court its market value in cash or give up exempt property of the same value.	Shortly after the meeting of creditors.
6. You deal with secured property.	If, on your Statement of Intention, you said you would surrender or redeem the collateral securing a debt, or reaffirm a secured debt, you must do so now.	Within 45 days of the date you file the Statement of Intention. (It is usually filed with your initial papers.)
7. The court grants your discharge.	The court may schedule a brief final court appearance called a "discharge hearing." It doesn't require preparation on your part. If there's no discharge hearing, you'll be mailed formal notice of your discharge.	Three to six months after you file.
8. Your case is closed.	Trustee distributes any remaining property to your creditors.	A few days or weeks after the discharge.

Notice to Creditor of Filing for Bankruptcy

Lynn Adams
18 Orchard Park Blvd.
East Lansing, MI 48823

June 15, 19xx

Cottons Clothing Store
745 Main Street
Lansing, MI 48915

Dear Cottons Clothing:

On June 14, 19XX, I filed a voluntary petition under Chapter 7 of the U.S. Bankruptcy Code. The case number is 43-6736-91. I filed my case *in pro per*, no attorney is assisting me. Under 11 U.S.C. § 362(a), you may not:

- take any action against me or my property to collect any debt
- enforce any lien on my real or personal property
- repossess any property in my possession
- discontinue any service or benefit currently being provided to me, or
- take any action to evict me from where I live.

A violation of these prohibitions may be considered contempt of court and punished accordingly.

Very truly yours,

Lynn Adams

Lynn Adams

If a creditor tries to collect a debt in violation of the automatic stay (including an IRS intercept to pay your student loan debt), you can ask the bankruptcy court to hold the creditor in contempt of court and to award you money damages. How to make this request is beyond the scope of this book.

3. Attend the Meeting of Creditors

For most people, the creditors' meeting is brief. Very few, if any, creditors show up, and the trustee asks some questions about information in your forms.

If you don't show up, you may be fined by the judge. Even worse, your case may be dismissed. If you know in advance that you can't attend the creditors' meeting as scheduled by the court, call or visit the court clerk and try to reschedule the meeting.

IF YOU'RE MARRIED AND FILING JOINTLY

Both you and your spouse must attend the meeting of the creditors.

Because the meeting of creditors is the place where the trustee gets information from the debtor, some trustees may question a debtor more closely about items in the bankruptcy papers than others.

a.   Preparing for the Creditors' Meeting

Before the meeting, call or visit the bankruptcy court clerk. Explain that you're proceeding without a lawyer ("in pro per") and ask what records you're required to bring. You should take a copy of every paper you've filed with the bankruptcy court. Also, bring copies of all documents that describe your debts and property, such as bills, deeds, contracts and licenses. Some courts—not most—also require you to bring financial records, such as tax returns and checkbooks.

If the clerk refuses to tell you what documents to bring, get the clerk's name. If you bring the wrong documents to the creditors' meeting, explain to the bankruptcy trustee what happened. Remember, you have a right to represent yourself. Although the clerks can't give legal advice, they're required to give you general information about the court's requirements.

Some people become anxious at the prospect of answering a trustee's questions and consider having an attorney accompany them. But if you were forthright with your creditors and honest in preparing your bankruptcy papers, there's no reason to have an attorney with you at the creditors' meeting. If you think you've been dishonest with a creditor or the court, or you have specific questions, see a lawyer before you go to court—or better yet, before you file. You can visit the bankruptcy court and watch other meetings of creditors if you think that might help alleviate some anxiety. Just call the clerk and ask when these meetings are held.

The night before the creditors' meeting, thoroughly review the papers you filed with the bankruptcy court. If you discover mistakes, make careful note of them. You'll probably have to correct your papers after the meeting, an easy process. (Instructions are in Section B, below.)

After reviewing your papers, go over the list below of questions the trustee is likely to ask you. Be sure you can answer them by the time of the meeting.

b.   The Routine Creditors' Meeting

Most creditors' meetings are quick and simple. You appear in the bankruptcy courtroom at the date and time stated on the bankruptcy notice. A number of other people who have filed for bankruptcy will be there too, for their own creditors' meetings. When your name is called, you'll be asked to sit or stand near the front of the courtroom. The court clerk will swear you in and ask your name, address and other identifying information. Then the trustee will briefly go over your forms with you, asking many of the questions listed below. Your answers to all questions should be both truthful and consistent with your bankruptcy papers. The trustee is likely to be most interested in:

- anticipated tax refunds
- any possible right that you have to sue someone because of a recent accident or business loss, and
- recent large payments to creditors or relatives.

If you caught any errors in your papers in your review, bring them to the attention of the trustee before you start answering questions. If you don't admit mistakes voluntarily, and they're discovered during questioning, the trustee may suspect that you're hiding something. If you discover while you're being questioned that your papers were in error, give the correct answer in your testimony and immediately point out to the trustee that your papers are incorrect and need to be amended.

When the trustee is finished, any creditors who showed up are given a chance to question you. Usually, only secured creditors come—creditors who have the right to repossess property pledged as collateral for a debt. They may seek clarification of anything unclear on your Statement of Intention or propose terms of a reaffirmation agreement if you selected the option to "reaffirm" a debt. Representatives of department stores where your debt is secured, such as Sears, are apt to attend. They'll be there to make sure you've reaffirmed the debt. If you've proposed a redemption, be ready to negotiate.

A creditor might also ask for explanations if information in your bankruptcy papers differs from what was on your credit application. (See Ch. 3, *Filling in and Filing the Bankruptcy Forms.*) When the creditors are through asking questions, you're dismissed.

IF YOU USED A BANKRUPTCY PETITION PREPARER

Many bankruptcy trustees are lawyers who either practice bankruptcy law or belong to a law firm that does. The fact that trustees and bankruptcy petition preparers (BPP) are often competitors leads some trustees to look for ways to harass local BPPs. One way they do this is to ferret out any instance of a BPP providing "legal advice," which by law a lawyer may provide but a BPP may not.

If you used a BPP to help you with your bankruptcy papers (see Ch. 9, *Help Beyond the Book*), the trustee may question you about the help you received. You may be asked any or all of the following questions:

- Is the name of the BPP on this form the name of the person who prepared your petition?
- Did the BPP give you a copy of your bankruptcy papers?
- Are the signatures on the bankruptcy papers yours, or were your papers signed by someone else?
- Did you file your bankruptcy papers with the clerk, or did the BPP do it for you?

The more responsibility you assumed for getting the necessary information from this book and making important decisions such as which property to claim as exempt, the better off you will be.

Answer the trustee's questions truthfully. The information you provide won't affect your bankruptcy. If your response indicates that the BPP has provided legal advice, however, the trustee may attempt to recapture the fee you paid the BPP and use the money to pay other creditors. It may be helpful to ask the BPP whether the trustees in your area are likely to question you, and if so, what suggestions she has for your appearance at the creditors' meeting.

COMMON QUESTIONS AT THE CREDITORS' MEETING

1. What are your full name and current address?
2. Do you own or rent your home?
3. What is your spouse's name?
4. When were you married?
5. What was your (your wife's) maiden name?
6. Did you ever have another name?
7. Have you made any voluntary or involuntary transfers of real or personal property within the last year?
8. Are any of your debts from credit card use?
9. Have you returned or destroyed your credit cards?
10. Is Schedule A a complete list of all your real property?
11. Is Schedule B a complete list of your personal property?
12. Is Schedule C a complete list of all property you claim as exempt?
13. Is Schedule D a complete list of your creditors having security?
14. Is Schedule E a complete list of your creditors having priority?
15. Is Schedule F a complete list of your unsecured creditors?
16. Are you suing anyone?
17. Is anyone suing you?
18. Are you currently expecting a tax refund?
19. Did you receive a tax refund last year?
20. Are you currently employed and, if so, by whom?
21. What caused your financial difficulties?
22. Have those difficulties ended?
23. Have you paid the filing fees for your bankruptcy case?
24. Did anyone help you prepare your bankruptcy papers? If so, who?
25. How much did that person charge?
26. Have you included on your papers the amount of the charge? (If a lawyer or bankruptcy petition preparer (BPP) assisted you, you'll probably be required to submit a "Statement by Debtor's Attorney of Fees Charged" or a "Statement by Debtor's Attorney of No Fees Charged." The lawyer or BPP who helped you should fill it out for you and give it to you to submit.)
27. Do you understand the potential consequences of seeking a discharge in bankruptcy, including the effects on your credit history?
28. Are you aware that there are other types of bankruptcy cases? Did you consider any of them before deciding on Chapter 7 bankruptcy?
29. Do you understand the effect of receiving a discharge of your debts in bankruptcy?
30. If you plan to reaffirm any debts (this is covered in Ch. 7, *Secured Debts*, Section C.4), do you understand the effect of such a reaffirmation?

HOLD YOUR HEAD HIGH

No matter how well you prepare for the creditors' meeting, you may feel nervous and apprehensive about coming face to face with the trustee and your creditors, to whom you've disclosed the intimate details of your finances over the last several years. You may feel angry with yourself and your creditors at having to be there. You may be embarrassed. You may think you're being perceived as a failure.

Nonsense. It takes courage to face your situation and deal firmly with it. Bankruptcy, especially when you're handling your own case without a lawyer, isn't an easy out. Let yourself see this as a turning point at which you're taking positive steps to improve your life. Go to the creditors' meeting proud that you've chosen to take control over your life and legal affairs.

c. Potential Problems at the Creditors' Meeting

If you or your papers give any indication that you own valuable nonexempt property, the trustee may question you vigorously. Or a creditor who's owed a lot of money may grill you about the circumstances of the debt, hoping to show that you incurred the debt without intending to pay it or by lying on a credit application, and that therefore it should survive bankruptcy. (See Ch. 8, *Nondischargeable Debts*.)

You may also be closely questioned about why you claimed certain property as exempt. For some reason, some bankruptcy trustees (who are usually attorneys) believe that claiming exemptions requires legal expertise. If this happens to you, simply describe the process you went through in selecting your exemptions from Appendix 1. All the trustee can do if he or she disagrees is to object to your exemptions. (See Section D.2, below.)

If the trustee or a creditor becomes abusive, say so and refuse to answer more questions until you're treated civilly. You can even stop the meeting simply by telling the trustee you want a hearing before the bankruptcy court judge to clear up the scope of the trustee's authority. For instance, some trustees demand that debtors surrender their credit cards on the spot. The bankruptcy law doesn't authorize that, and the best response is to refuse, telling the trustee to take it up with the judge.

Don't be afraid to assert your rights, as you perceive them, at the creditors' meeting. And don't be afraid of expressing your views to the bankruptcy judge if it comes to that. No harm comes from appearing before the judge, as long as you obey the judge's decisions and treat the judge respectfully.

4. Deal With Nonexempt Property

After the meeting of creditors, the trustee is supposed to collect all of your nonexempt property and have it sold to pay off your creditors. Normally, the trustee accepts the exemptions you claim (on Schedule C) and goes after only property you haven't claimed as exempt. If, however, the trustee or a creditor disagrees with an exemption you claimed and files a written objection with the bankruptcy court, the court will schedule a hearing. After listening to both sides, the judge will decide the issue. (See Section D, below.)

If you really want to keep certain nonexempt items and can borrow money from friends or relatives, or you've come into some cash since you filed for bankruptcy, you may be able to trade the trustee cash for the item. The trustee, whose sole responsibility at this stage is to maximize what your creditors get paid, is interested simply in what cash your property can produce, not in any particular item. So the trustee shouldn't mind taking cash in place of nonexempt property you want to hang onto.

EXAMPLE: Maura files for Chapter 7 bankruptcy and claims her parlor grand piano as exempt. The trustee disagrees, and the judge rules the piano to be nonexempt. To replace the piano on the open market might cost Maura $7,000. The trustee determines that the piano would probably sell for $4,500 at an auction, and is willing to let Maura keep the piano for that amount. Maura is somewhat bothered by having to pay for her own property, but she knows that what she pays will be distributed to her creditors in lieu of the proceeds that the piano would bring were it sold.

The trustee may also be willing to let you keep nonexempt property if you volunteer to trade exempt property of equal value. For instance, the trustee might be willing to let Maura keep her nonexempt piano if she gives up her car, even though Maura could claim it as exempt in her state. Again, the trustee is interested in squeezing as many dollars as possible from the estate, and usually won't care whether the money comes from exempt or nonexempt assets.

5. Deal With Secured Property

When you filed your Statement of Intention, you told the trustee and your creditors whether you wanted to keep property that is security for a debt or give it to the creditor

in return for cancellation of the debt. (Ch. 7, *Secured Debts*, discusses your options.) The law says you must carry out your intentions within 45 days of the date you filed the Statement.

For instance, if you have photography equipment that's security for a debt, and on the Statement of Intention you said that you wanted to redeem it by paying its fair market value to the creditor, the payment is supposed to be made within the 45-day period. Similarly, if you stated your intention to reaffirm a car note (by agreeing to have the debt survive bankruptcy and continue making payments as before), you're supposed to sign a reaffirmation agreement within 45 days. If you planned to file a motion to avoid a lien on the property, the motion should be filed within 45 days.

Courts, however, have no practical way to enforce the 45-day deadline and generally will let you and the creditor work matters out. This means that you have some flexibility in dealing with your secured property. For instance, if you stated your intention to reaffirm a car note, but later discover that you can raise the cash to redeem the car, you can change your mind, amend your Statement of Intention and then arrange the redemption. Or, if you stated your intention to redeem property but the 45-day period passes because you're having some difficulty raising the cash, you'll still be able to redeem the property if the creditor agrees to hold off.

But if you don't honor your intentions within the 45-day period, the creditor can ask the court for permission to take the collateral. The court will probably grant it.

To avoid a sticky situation, do your best to honor the 45-day deadline. This means you should:

- sign a reaffirmation agreement if you said you were going to reaffirm the debt
- pay a creditor the property's fair market value if you want to redeem the property, or
- file the necessary court papers to eliminate the lien, or reduce it and informally pay it off.

Instructions for all these procedures are in Ch. 7, *Secured Debts*.

6. Attend the Discharge Hearing

You may have to attend a brief court hearing, called a discharge hearing. At the hearing, the judge explains the effects of discharging your debts in bankruptcy and lectures you about staying clear of debt. You should receive a discharge order from the court within four weeks of the hearing. If you don't, call the trustee.

Most courts, however, don't schedule a discharge hearing unless you stated on your Statement of Intention that you intended to reaffirm a debt. At the hearing, the judge warns you of the consequences of reaffirmation: you'll continue to owe the full debt, you may lose the collateral and the creditor can sue you if you default on your payments.

Whether or not you must attend a discharge hearing, you'll receive a copy of your discharge order from the court. The order does not specify which debts were discharged. It simply says that those debts which qualified for discharge were discharged. Nevertheless, make several photocopies of the order and keep them in a safe place. If it's necessary, be ready to send copies to creditors who attempt to collect their debt after your case is over or to credit bureaus that still list you as owing a discharged debt. A sample discharge order is below.

B. Amending Your Bankruptcy Papers

One of the outstanding aspects of bankruptcy procedure is that you can amend any of your papers at any time before your final discharge. This means that if you made a mistake on papers you've filed, you can correct it easily.

There may be a few exceptions to this rule. For instance, some courts may not let you amend your exemption schedule after the deadline for creditors to object to the exemptions you claimed. Bankruptcy rules state clearly, however, that you have a right to amend any time before your case is closed. (Bankruptcy Rule 1009.) If you run into a judge who rules to the contrary, consult a bankruptcy attorney.

If your mistake means that notice of your bankruptcy filing must be sent to one or more additional creditors (for instance, if you inadvertently left off a creditor who must be notified), you'll have to pay a filing fee of $20. If your mistake doesn't require new notice (for example, you add information about property you owned when you filed or about an income tax refund you expect to receive soon), you do not have to pay an additional filing fee.

If you amend your schedules to add creditors before the meeting of creditors, you'll usually be required to provide the newly listed creditors with notice of the meeting as well as with notice of your amendment. (Instructions are in Section B.2, below.)

If you become aware of debts or property that you should have included in your papers, amending your petition will avoid any suspicion that you're trying to conceal things from the trustee. Failing to amend your papers after discovering this kind of information, however, may doom your bankruptcy petition to dismissal or one or more of your debts to nondischargeable status.

Even if your bankruptcy case is already closed, you may be allowed to amend your papers to add an omitted creditor who tries to collect the debt. (See Ch. 5, *Life After Bankruptcy*.)

⚠️ **DON'T OVER-AMEND YOUR PAPERS**

It's important to make changes, corrections, additions and deletions in as few amendments as possible. If you file amendments too many times, the court may not let you back into court until you get help from an attorney. (The court's action may be illegal, but unchallengeable as a practical matter.)

1. Common Amendments

Even a simple change in one form may require changes in several other forms. Here are some of the more common reasons for amendments and the forms that you may need to amend. Exactly what forms you'll have to change depends on your court's rules. (Instructions for making the amendments are in Section B.2, below.)

a. Add or Delete Exempt Property on Schedule C

If you want to add or delete property from your list of exemptions, you must file a new Schedule C. You may also need to change:

- Schedule A, if the property is real estate and not listed there
- Schedule B, if the property is personal property and not listed there
- Schedule D and Form 8—Chapter 7 Individual Debtor's Statement of Intention, if the property is collateral for a secured debt and isn't already listed
- Form 7—Statement of Financial Affairs, if any transactions regarding the property weren't described on that form, as required
- Mailing matrix (if your court requires one), if the exempt item is tied to a particular creditor.

b. Add or Delete Property on Schedules A or B

You may have forgotten to list some of your property on your schedules. And the following property must be reported to the bankruptcy trustee if you receive it, or become entitled to receive it, within 180 days after filing for bankruptcy:

- property you inherit or become entitled to inherit
- property from a marital settlement agreement or divorce decree, or
- death benefits or life insurance policy proceeds.

(See Ch. 2, *Your Property and Bankruptcy*, Section A.5.)

Form 18. DISCHARGE OF DEBTOR
IN A CHAPTER 7 CASE

UNITED STATES BANKRUPTCY COURT

_____ DISTRICT OF _____

In re _____ ,   Case No. _____
     (Name)   (If known)

                  Debtor

                                        Chapter _____

DISCHARGE OF DEBTOR

It appearing that the debtor is entitled to a discharge, **IT IS ORDERED**: The debtor is granted a discharge under section 727 of title 11, United States Code (the Bankruptcy Code).

Dated: _____

BY THE COURT

_____
United States Bankruptcy Judge

SEE THE BACK OF THIS ORDER FOR IMPORTANT INFORMATION.

EXPLANATION OF BANKRUPTCY DISCHARGE
IN A CHAPTER 7 CASE

This court order grants a discharge to the person named as the debtor. It is not a dismissal of the case and it does not determine how much money, if any, the trustee will pay to creditors.

Collection of Discharged Debts Prohibited

The discharge prohibits any attempt to collect from the debtor a debt that has been discharged. For example, a creditor is not permitted to contact a debtor by mail, phone, or otherwise, to file or continue a lawsuit, to attach wages or other property, or to take any other action to collect a discharged debt from the debtor. *[In a case involving community property:]* [There are also special rules that protect certain community property owned by the debtor's spouse, even if that spouse did not file a bankruptcy case.] A creditor who violates this order can be required to pay damages and attorney's fees to the debtor.

However, a creditor may have the right to enforce a valid lien, such as a mortgage or security interest, against the debtor's property after the bankruptcy, if that lien was not avoided or eliminated in the bankruptcy case. Also, a debtor may voluntarily pay any debt that has been discharged.

Debts That are Discharged

The chapter 7 discharge order eliminates a debtor's legal obligation to pay a debt that is discharged. Most, but not all, types of debts are discharged if the debt existed on the date the bankruptcy case was filed. (If this case was begun under a different chapter of the Bankruptcy Code and converted to chapter 7, the discharge applies to debts owed when the bankruptcy case was converted.)

Debts that are Not Discharged.

Some of the common types of debts which are not discharged in a chapter 7 bankruptcy case are:

a.　Debts for most taxes.

b.　Debts that are in the nature of alimony, maintenance, or support.

c.　Debts for most student loans.

d.　Debts for most fines, penalties, forfeitures, or criminal restitution obligations.

e.　Debts for personal injuries or death caused by the debtor's operation of a motor vehicle while intoxicated.

f.　Some debts which were not properly listed by the debtor.

g.　Debts that the bankruptcy court specifically has decided or will decide in this bankruptcy case are not discharged.

h.　Debts for which the debtor has given up the discharge protections by signing a reaffirmation agreement in compliance with the Bankruptcy Code requirements for reaffirmation of debts.

This information is only a general summary of the bankruptcy discharge. There are exceptions to these general rules. Because the law is complicated, you may want to consult an attorney to determine the exact effect of the discharge in this case.

If you have new property to report for either of these reasons, you may need to file amendments to:

- Schedule A, if the property is real estate
- Schedule B, if the property is personal property
- Schedule C, if the property was claimed as exempt or you want to claim it as exempt
- Schedule D and Form 8—Chapter 7 Individual Debtor's Statement of Intention, if the property is collateral for a secured debt
- Form 7—Statement of Financial Affairs, if any transactions regarding the property haven't been described as required by that form, or
- Mailing matrix (if your court requires one), if the item is tied to a particular creditor.

If your bankruptcy case is already closed, see Ch. 5, *Life After Bankruptcy*, Section A.

c. Change Your Plans for Secured Property

If you've changed your plans for dealing with an item of secured property, you must file an amended Form 8—Chapter 7 Individual Debtor's Statement of Intention.

d. Correct Your List of Creditors

To correct your list of creditors, you may need to amend:

- Schedule C, if the debt is secured and you plan to claim the collateral as exempt
- Schedule D, if the debt is a secured debt
- Schedule E, if the debt is a priority debt (as defined in Ch. 3, *Filling In and Filing the Bankruptcy Forms*)
- Schedule F, if the debt is unsecured
- Form 7—Statement of Financial Affairs, if any transactions regarding the property haven't been described as required by that form, or
- Mailing matrix (if your court uses it), which contains the names and addresses of all your creditors.

If your bankruptcy case is already closed, see Ch. 5, *Life After Bankruptcy*.

e. Add an Omitted Payment to a Creditor

If you didn't report, on your forms, a payment to a creditor made within the year before you filed for bankruptcy, you must amend your Form 7—Statement of Financial Affairs.

2. How to File an Amendment

To make an amendment, take these steps:

Step 1: Fill out the Amendment Cover Sheet in Appendix 4, if no local form is required. Otherwise, use the local form.

Step 2: Make copies of the forms affected by your amendment.

Step 3: Check your local court rules or ask the court clerk whether you must retype the whole form to make the correction or if you can just type the new information on another blank form. If you can't find the answer, ask a local bankruptcy lawyer or forms preparer. If it's acceptable to just type the new information, precede the information you're typing with "ADD:," "CHANGE:" or "DELETE:" as appropriate. At the bottom of the form, type "AMENDED" in capital letters.

Step 4: If your amendment involves adding a creditor, follow these special instructions (otherwise, go on to Step 5).

If the creditors' meeting hasn't yet been held, include with the amended papers you are preparing, a copy of the Notice of the Meeting of Creditors you received from the court.

If the creditors' meeting has already been held, you must ask the court to schedule a second Meeting of Creditors and issue a new Notice of the Meeting of Creditors. You must send out the notice to the new creditor and to every creditor listed in Schedules D, E and F. Ask the court clerk whether it will notify the other creditors, or whether you must. If you must, you can include the Notice when you send the amended papers. (See Step 8, below.)

Step 5: Call or visit the court and ask what order it requires the papers in and how many copies it requires.

Step 6: Make the required number of copies, plus one copy for yourself, one for the trustee and one for any creditor affected by your amendment.

Step 7: Have a friend or relative mail, first class, a copy of your amended papers to the bankruptcy trustee and to any creditor affected by your amendment.

Step 8: Enter the name and complete address of every new creditor affected by your amendment on the Proof of Service by Mail (a copy is in Appendix 4). Also enter the name and address of the bankruptcy trustee. Then have the person who mailed the Amendment to the trustee and new creditors sign and date the Proof of Service.

Step 9: Mail or take the original Amendment and Proof of Service and copies to the bankruptcy court. Enclose or take a money order for the filing fee, if required. If you use the mail, enclose a prepaid self-addressed envelope so the clerk can return a file-stamped set of papers to you.

C. Filing a Change of Address

If you move while your bankruptcy case is still open, you must give the court, the trustee and your creditors your new address. Here's how to do it:

Step 1: Make one or two photocopies of the blank Notice of Change of Address and Proof of Service forms in Appendix 4.

Step 2: Fill in the Change of Address form.

Step 3: Make one photocopy for the trustee, one for your records and one for each creditor listed in Schedules D, E and F (or use the list of creditors on your Mailing Matrix, if you prepared one).

Step 4: Have a friend or relative mail a copy of the Notice of Change of Address to the trustee and to each creditor.

Step 5: Have the friend or relative complete and sign the Proof of Service by Mail form, listing the bankruptcy trustee and the names and addresses of all creditors the Notice was mailed to.

Step 6: File the original Notice of Change of Address and original Proof of Service with the bankruptcy court.

D. Special Problems

If complications crop up during your bankruptcy, you may need to go to court yourself or get an attorney to help you. This section briefly describes some of the more common problems. Complications will most likely take the form of a motion or objection filed with the court. In such a situation, you will receive a notice from the court outlining your rights. (See copy, below).

1. A Creditor Asks the Court to Lift the Automatic Stay

The automatic stay lasts for the length of your bankruptcy case unless the court lifts the stay for a particular creditor. To get the stay lifted, a creditor must convince the court that lifting the stay won't interfere with the bankruptcy process.

A creditor who wants the court to lift the stay must make the request in writing, in a document called a motion. The court will schedule a hearing, and you'll be notified. You may not need to prepare any papers in response. The bankruptcy rules state that no response is necessary unless a court orders otherwise. (Bankruptcy Rule 9014.) Unfortunately, some courts have done just this in their local rules, which means that unless you respond, you lose automatically. Check your local rules on this point. If a response is required, you may need to consult a bankruptcy attorney.

If no response is required, simply show up at the hearing (the date, place and time will be set out in the notice you receive) and explain your side of things to the judge. If you don't show up, you have little chance, if any, of winning. At the hearing, the judge will either decide the matter on the spot or "take it under submission" and mail out a decision in a few days. The stay can be lifted within a week or two after you file, but several weeks to several months is more common.

a. Grounds for Lifting the Stay

The bankruptcy court may lift the automatic stay for several reasons:

• The activity being stayed is not a legitimate concern of the bankruptcy court. For instance, the court may let a child custody proceeding proceed, because its outcome won't affect your economic situation.

• The activity being stayed will inevitably happen regardless of what the bankruptcy court does. For instance, if a lender shows the court that a mortgage foreclosure will ultimately occur, regardless of the bankruptcy filing, the court will usually lift the stay and let the foreclosure proceed. (If you want to keep your house, you are better off filing for Chapter 13 bankruptcy.)

• The creditor's interest in property owned or possessed by you is being harmed by the stay. For instance, if you've stopped making payments on a car and it's losing value, the court may lift the stay. That would allow the creditor to repossess the car now, unless you're willing and able to periodically pay the creditor an amount equal to the ongoing depreciation until your case is closed.

• You have no ownership interest in property sought by the creditor. If you don't own some interest in property that a creditor is seeking, the court isn't interested in protecting the property under the stay, and will lift the stay.

There are many kinds of ownership interests. You can own property outright. You can own the right to possess it sometime in the future (but not now). You can co-own it with any number of other owners. You can own the right to possess it while someone else owns legal title (for example, tenant and landlord, or new car owner and finance company).

For most kinds of property, there's an easy way to tell if you have an ownership interest: If you would be entitled to receive any cash if the property were sold, you have an ownership interest.

For intangible property (property you can't see or touch), however, it may be harder to show your ownership interest. For instance, if you have a long-term lease (a year or more) on your home, most bankruptcy courts would consider it an ownership interest in the property and would not lift the stay to let a landlord go ahead with eviction. But if the lease has expired, a court would probably rule that you have no ownership interest in the property and would lift the stay, allowing the eviction to go forward.

Another example of an unlikely ownership interest is the rights an insured person has under an insurance policy, which means the automatic stay prevents insurance companies from canceling insurance policies.

b.   Opposing a Request to Lift the Stay

Generally, a court won't lift the stay if you can establish that it's necessary either to preserve your property (for yourself if it's exempt or for the benefit of your creditors if it's not), or to preserve your general economic condition. You may also need to convince the court that the creditor's investment in the property will be protected while the bankruptcy is pending.

Here are some possible responses you may make if a creditor tries to get the stay lifted.

- **Repossession of cars or other personal property:** If the stay is preventing a creditor from repossessing property pledged as collateral (your car, furniture, jewelry or other personal property), the creditor will probably argue that the stay should be lifted because you might damage the collateral, or because the property is depreciating (declining in value) while your bankruptcy case is pending. Your response depends on the facts. If the property is still in good shape, be prepared to prove it to the judge.

  If the property is worth more than you owe on it, you can argue that depreciation won't hurt the creditor, because the property could be repossessed or foreclosed on later and sold for as much or more than the amount of the debt. But if, as is common, you have little or no equity in the property, you'll need to propose a way to protect the creditor's interest while you keep the property—assuming you want it. One way to do this is to agree with the creditor on the amount of a cash security deposit that would be sufficient to offset the expected depreciation.

  If you intend to keep secured property (see Ch. 7, *Secured Debts*), you can argue that lifting the stay would deprive you of your rights under the bankruptcy laws. For example, if you intend to redeem a car by paying its fair market value, the court should deny the motion to lift the stay until you have an opportunity to do so.

- **Utility disconnections:** For 20 days after you file your bankruptcy petition, a public utility (electric, gas, telephone or water) may not alter, refuse or discontinue service to you, or discriminate against you in any other way, solely on the basis of an unpaid debt or your bankruptcy filing. (11 U.S.C. § 366(a).) If your service was disconnected before you filed, the utility company must restore it within 20 days after you file for bankruptcy—without requiring a deposit—if you so request it.

  After 20 days, the utility is entitled to discontinue service unless you provide adequate assurance that your future bills will be paid. (11 U.S.C. § 366(b).) Generally, that means you'll have to come up with a security deposit.

  If you and the utility can't agree on the size of the deposit, the utility may cut off service, which means you'll need to get a lawyer and go to the bankruptcy court to have it reinstated. If the utility files a motion to lift the stay, argue at the hearing that your deposit is adequate.

- **Evictions:** If you rely on the automatic stay to stop an eviction, expect the landlord to come barreling into court to have the stay lifted. Filing for bankruptcy has become a favorite tactic for some eviction defense clinics, who file a bare-bones bankruptcy petition to stop evictions even if the tenant's debts don't justify bankruptcy. In response, many bankruptcy courts are willing to grant landlords immediate relief from the stay without looking too closely at the case. This is true even if you have a legitimate bankruptcy.

CALIFORNIA LANDLORDS MIGHT IGNORE THE AUTOMATIC STAY ALTOGETHER

A California law allows a landlord who has sued for eviction and has won a judgment for possession (but not a money judgment for back rent) to enforce the judgment—that is, to let the marshal or sheriff evict—even if you file for bankruptcy. (Code of Civil Procedure § 715.050.)

This California law probably violates the federal bankruptcy law and is unenforceable. Bankruptcy law is under the power of the federal legislative body—Congress—and states are generally unable to make laws pertaining to bankruptcy. Nevertheless, California landlords may very well ignore your bankruptcy if you file just to stop the sheriff from throwing you out on the street.

About the only times you can argue that bank-ruptcy should stop an eviction are if you have a long-term lease or you have a month-to-month tenancy in a city with rent control. Your argument against the stay being lifted should concentrate on the fact that the value of the tenancy is an asset of the bankruptcy estate, and lifting the stay would unfairly award it to the landlord.

2. The Trustee or a Creditor Disputes a Claimed Exemption

After the meeting of creditors, the trustee and creditors have 30 days to object to the exemptions you claimed. If the deadline passes and the trustee wants to challenge an exemption, he is out of luck, even if the claimed exemption isn't supported by the exemption statutes. (*Taylor v. Freeland and Kronz*, 503 U.S. 638 (1992).) The objections must be in writing and filed with the bankruptcy court. Copies must be served on (personally handed or mailed to) the trustee, you and, if you have one, your lawyer. (Bank-ruptcy Rule 4003.)

a. Reasons for Objecting

The most common grounds for the trustee or a creditor to object are:

- The claimed item isn't exempt under the law. For example, a plumber who lives in New Jersey and selects his state exemptions might try to exempt his plumbing tools under the "goods and chattels" exemption. The trustee and creditors are likely to object on the ground that these are work tools, and New Jersey has no "tools of trade" exemption.
- Shortly before you filed for bankruptcy, you sold non-exempt property and purchased exempt property to cheat your creditors. (How to avoid this accusation is discussed in Ch. 2, *Your Property and Bankruptcy*.)
- Property you claimed as exempt is worth more than you say it is. If the property's true value is higher than the exemption limit for that item, the item should be sold and the excess over the exemption limit distributed to your creditors.

  EXAMPLE: In Connie's state, clothing is exempted to a total of $2,000. Connie values her mink coat at $1,000 and her other clothes at $1,000, bringing her within the $2,000 exemption. A creditor objects to the $1,000 valuation of the coat, claiming that such mink coats routinely sell for $3,000 and up. If the creditor prevails, Connie would have to surrender the coat to the trustee. She'd get the first $1,000 (the

exempt amount). Or, Connie could keep the coat if she gave the trustee $2,000 or its equivalent in other property.

- You and your spouse have doubled an exemption where doubling isn't permitted.

  EXAMPLE: David and Marylee, a married couple, file for bankruptcy using California's System 1 exemptions. Each claims a $1,900 exemption in their family car, for a total of $3,800. California bars a married couple from doubling the System 1 automobile exemption.

b. Responding to Objections

When objection papers are filed, the court schedules a hearing. The creditor or trustee must prove to the bankruptcy court that the exemption is improper. You don't have to prove anything. In fact, you don't have to respond to the objection or even show up unless the bankruptcy court orders—or local rules require—you to. Of course, you can—and probably should—either file a response or show up at the hearing to defend your claim of a legitimate exemption.

3. A Creditor Objects to the Discharge of a Debt

There are two possible reasons that a creditor may object to the discharge of a debt:

- The creditor claims that the debt is not dischargeable.
- The creditor claims that the debt is secured and that you must reaffirm the debt, redeem the property or abandon the property.

a. Claims That the Debt Is Nondischargeable

Several types of debts can survive bankruptcy. (See Ch. 8, *Nondischargeable Debts*). Most of these debts are automatically nondischargeable. Others, however, survive bankruptcy only if the creditor successfully raises an objection in the bankruptcy court within 60 days after the meeting of creditors. Briefly, they are:

- debts incurred on the basis of fraud, such as lying on a credit application
- debts from willful or malicious injury to another or another's property, including assault, battery, false imprisonment, libel and slander
- debts from larceny, breach of trust or embezzlement, and
- debts arising from a marital settlement agreement or divorce decree other than child support or alimony.

To object formally to the discharge of a debt, the creditor must file a document termed a Complaint to Determine Dischargeability of a Debt. A copy of the complaint must be served on (delivered to) you and the trustee.

To defend against the objection, you'll need to file a written response and be prepared to argue your case in a court hearing. If the creditor files a Complaint on any of the first three grounds, you'll need to provide evidence countering your alleged "bad acts." If the creditor is your ex-spouse or a creditor you and your ex-spouse owe money to, you will have to provide evidence of either of the following:

- Based on your assets, income and other obligations, you will not be able to pay the debt after your bankruptcy case is over.
- Even if you can afford to pay the debt after your bankruptcy case, the benefit you'd receive by the discharge outweighs any detriment to your ex-spouse or child.

Increasingly, the creditors most likely to object to the discharge of a debt are credit card issuers. Except for the situations outlined in Ch. 8, *Nondischargeable Debts*, Sections C.1.c and C.1.d, there's no specific rule about what constitutes credit card fraud in bankruptcy. But courts are increasingly looking to the following factors to determine fraud:

- short time between incurring the charges and filing for bankruptcy
- consulting an attorney before incurring more debt
- recent charges over $1,000
- many charges under $50 (to avoid pre-clearance of the charge by the credit card issuer) when you've reached your credit limit
- charges after the card issuer has ordered you to return the card or sent several "past due" notices
- changes in your pattern of use of the card (for instance, much travel after a sedentary life)
- charges after you're obviously insolvent (no job, income or savings); you could probably defeat a claim of fraud because of no job if you diligently sought employment
- charges for luxuries, and
- multiple charges on the same day.

Credit card recovery programs are quite aggressive. Visa brags that while only 30% of its members challenged any bankruptcies five years ago, today 99% of its members do so. Visa and MasterCard employees typically review bankruptcy filings (as well as a customer's file with the bank that issued the credit) to discern the date of insolvency, and then challenge all charges made after that date. The banks claim that insolvency is evidenced by any of the following:

- A notation in the customer's file that the customer has met with an attorney.

- A rapid increase in spending, quickly followed by 60–90 days of quiet.
- The date noted on any attorney's fee statement, if the customer consults a lawyer for help with a bankruptcy. Thus, if you pay a bankruptcy professional for help and submit a fee statement, be sure to put the date of your filing on that form. If you put an earlier date, your creditors may claim you knew you were insolvent at that earlier date and that all subsequent purchases should be declared nondischargeable.

Of course, because a creditor challenges your discharge of a credit card debt doesn't mean the creditor is right. In virtually every case, the creditor files a standard 15- to 20-paragraph form complaint, that makes boldface conclusions with no supporting facts. The creditor rarely attaches statements for the account, but only a printout of the charges to which it is objecting.

Most of the time, credit card issuers rarely win these cases when they go before a judge. Judges are finding that credit card issuers usually send pre-approved cards without doing an adequate credit check. Judges also discover that cards are issued to all applicants, no matter what number is entered into the household income blank on the credit application. Finally judges are finding that debtors are using the cards for the precise reasons the creditors encouraged them to use the cards—"when you're short on cash," "to take that much-deserved vacation," "to consolidate other debts" or "to buy expensive gifts." Ultimately, judges rule that credit card issuers must assume responsibility for their own neglectful behavior and cannot claim fraud when someone on the financial edge uses a card for precisely the reasons anticipated by the issuer.

To fight this kind of case, you may need to hire an attorney. (See Ch. 9, *Help Beyond the Book,* for information on finding a lawyer.) You can certainly represent yourself, if you have the time and patience to file the response papers and fight it out in court. In a few courts, including the District of Oregon and the Southern District of New York, you can request that the dispute be sent to court-sponsored mediation. The creditor does not have to agree, nor does the judge have to send your case, however, if everyone agrees, mediation can provide an informal, quick and inexpensive resolution of the dispute.

If you decide to defend yourself, you'll want to get a copy of *Represent Yourself in Court,* by Paul Bergman and Sara Berman-Barret (Nolo Press). That book shows you how to file and serve papers, gather evidence through a formal procedure called discovery, make and respond to motions and try your own case. Engaging in formal discovery can be very helpful in this kind of case. For example, if you were to send the credit card issuer a set of questions (called

Form 20A. Notice of Motion or Objection

UNITED STATES BANKRUPTCY COURT

_____ DISTRICT OF _____

In re _____ ,   Case No. _____
                              (Name)   (If known)
                                      Debtor
                                                                              Chapter _____

NOTICE OF [MOTION TO   ] [OBJECTION TO   ]

_____ has filed papers with the court to [relief sought in motion or objection].

Your rights may be affected. You should read these papers carefully and discuss them with your attorney, if you have one in this bankruptcy case. (If you do not have an attorney, you may wish to consult one.)

If you do not want the court to [relief sought in motion or objection], or if you want the court to consider your views on the [motion] [objection], then on or before (date), you or your attorney must:

File with the court a written request for a hearing [or, _if the court requires a written response_, an answer, explaining your position] at:

[address of the bankruptcy clerk's office]

If you mail your [request] [response] to the court for filing, you must mail it early enough so the court will **receive** it on or before the date stated above.

You must also mail a copy to:

[movant's attorney's name and address]

[names and addresses of others to be served]

Attend the hearing scheduled to be held on (date) , (year) , at ___ a.m./p.m. in Courtroom _____, United States Bankruptcy Court, [address].

Other steps required to oppose a motion or objection under local rule or court order.

If you or your attorney do not take these steps, the court may decide that you do not oppose the relief sought in the motion or objection and may enter an order granting that relief.

Date: _____   Signature: _____

                                                        Name:_____

                                                        Address: _____

interrogatories) to answer under oath, you will want to ask the following:

- You have alleged that the debtor obtained funds from you by false pretenses and false representations. Please state with particularity the nature of the false pretenses and false representations.
- State all steps taken by you to determine the creditworthiness of the debtor.
- Identify all means you used to verify the debtor's income, expenses, assets or liabilities. Identify any documents obtained in the verification process.
- Identify your general policies concerning the decision to grant credit and how those policies were applied to the debtor.
- You have alleged that at the time the debtor obtained credit from you he/she did not intend to repay it. State all facts in your possession to support this allegation.
- Identify all credit policies you allege were violated by the debtor. State how such policies were communicated to the debtor and identify all documents which contained those policies.
- Identify the dates on which you claim any of the following events occurred:
  — The debtor consulted a bankruptcy attorney.
  — The debtor had a reduction in income.
  — The debtor formed the intent not to repay this debt.
  — The debtor violated the terms of the credit agreement.
- State whether you believe that every user of a credit card who does not later repay the debt has committed fraud on you.
- If the answer to the preceding question is no, state all facts that give rise to fraud in this debtor's use of the card.

After receiving a list of questions such as the above, the credit card issuer is likely to see that you are serious about defending yourself. There is a good chance that it will withdraw its complaint.

If you want to read cases supporting the debtor's position in cases claiming fraudulent use of a credit card, visit a law library or search the Internet for any of the following:

- *In re Christensen*, 193 B.R. 863 (N.D. Ill. 1996)
- *In re Duplante*, 204 B.R. 49 (S.D. Cal. 1996)
- *In re Stansel*, 203 B.R. 339 (M.D. Fla. 1996)
- *In re Chinchilla*, 202 B.R. 1010 (S.D. Fla. 1996)
- *In re Grayson*, 199 B.R. 397 (W.D. Mo. 1996)
- *In re Vianese*, 195 B.R. 572 (N.D.N.Y. 1995).

b. Claims That the Debt Is Secured

Increasing numbers of creditors object to the discharge of a debt claiming that the debt is secured and that the debtor must reaffirm the debt, redeem the property or abandon the property. (These options are discussed in Ch. 7, *Secured Debts.*) Many creditors, rather than file a formal motion or objection in court, will send a debtor a reaffirmation agreement after the debtor files for bankruptcy. Accompanying the agreement is a letter in which the creditor promises to reinstate the debtor's credit if the debtor agrees to repay the debt, despite filing for bankruptcy.

Consumer bankruptcy attorneys estimate that 50% of creditors send reaffirmation agreements to debtors, usually to harass or frighten. It's *never* a good idea to sign a reaffirmation agreement in such a situation. Why saddle yourself with debts you know you can't pay? You filed for bankruptcy to get a fresh start, not to still owe money. Don't be lured by the promise of restored credit. Creditors don't restore credit until *after* the outstanding debt is paid in full. Besides, you can apply for a new credit card after your bankruptcy case is over. (See Ch. 5, *Life After Bankruptcy*, Section G.4.) Throw the reaffirmation agreement in the garbage, or send it back after writing "Decline" across it.

The creditor may persist—that is, file a formal objection with the court. You may need an attorney to assist you. If your claim is that the debt is not secured, you will need to put the burden on the creditor to prove that it is. If the debt is secured, you will have to show that the value of the collateral is much less than what you owe. This means that the debt is either no longer secured or nominally secured and should be wiped out in bankruptcy.

If the debt is truly secured, then the creditor may be entitled to have it reaffirmed. Still, if you are not represented by a lawyer, the reaffirmation agreement *must be approved by a judge.* If you agree to sign an agreement, be sure to call the court clerk to find out how you schedule a hearing before the judge. In addition, a reaffirmation agreement is valid only if it is filed with the court. So if you sign one and have the court approve it, don't make any payments on it until the creditor provides you with a court file-stamped copy.

4. You Want to Get Back Exempt Property Taken by a Creditor

You may have decided to file bankruptcy after a creditor repossessed or legally seized some of your property. You may be entitled to get the property back from the creditor if:

- the property was taken less than one year before your bankruptcy filing

- the property can be claimed as exempt, and
- you weren't trying to conceal the property when it was taken.

To get property back, you must file a formal complaint against the creditor and prove that the property belongs in the bankruptcy estate where you can claim it as exempt. You'll probably need an attorney's help.

Given the cost of attorneys, it's seldom worth your while to go after this type of property unless it's valuable or an irreplaceable family heirloom. Keep in mind that most property is only exempt up to a certain value—for example, a car may be exempt up to $1,200, furnishings up to $1,000. Thus, even if you get the property back, it may still be sold by the trustee, in which case you'll receive only the exempt amount from the proceeds.

E. You Want to Dismiss Your Case

If you change your mind after you file for bankruptcy, you can ask the court to dismiss your case. As a general rule, a court will dismiss a Chapter 7 bankruptcy case as long as the dismissal won't harm your creditors.

Common reasons for dismissing your case include the following:

- You discover an omitted creditor; you want to dismiss your case to refile it and include the omitted creditor.

- You discover that a major debt you thought was dischargeable isn't. You don't have enough other debts to justify your bankruptcy case.
- You realize that an item of property you thought was exempt isn't. You don't want to lose it in bankruptcy.
- You come into a sum of money and can afford to pay your debts.
- Your bankruptcy case turns out to be more complex than you originally thought. You need a lawyer, but you don't have the money to hire one.
- The emotional stress of bankruptcy is too much for you.

You will probably need to draft two forms. Sample forms are below.

Step 1: Refer to your court's local rules for time limits, format of papers and other details of voluntary dismissals. If you can't find the precise information from reading your local rules, ask the court clerk, the trustee assigned to your case, a local bankruptcy petition preparer or a bankruptcy lawyer.

Step 2: Make at least three copies of the blank, line-numbered legal paper in Appendix 4 (to allow for mistakes). Type from line number 1 to line 13 as follows (see samples, below):

Line 1: Your name, and that of your spouse if you're filing jointly.

Line 1.5: Your address.

Line 2: Your city, state and zip code.

Line 2.5: Your phone number.

Line 3: Type: Debtor in Pro Per.

Line 7: Center and type UNITED STATES BANKRUPTCY COURT, in capital letters.

Line 8: Center and type the judicial district and state you are in. Get this information from your bankruptcy petition.

Lines
9-12:   Type as shown in the example.

Step 3: Make a few photocopies of the page with the information you have typed so far. This will save you typing later, because you can use this same heading for both forms.

Step 4: Using one of the copies that you just made, start typing again at line 14. Prepare a PETITION FOR VOLUNTARY DISMISSAL, as shown in the sample.

Petition for Voluntary Dismissal

1	John Doe
2	1111 Any Street Berkeley, CA 94700
3	(510) 555-1223 Debtor in Pro Per

1

2

3

4

5

6

7

8 UNITED STATES BANKRUPTCY COURT

9 NORTHERN DISTRICT OF CALIFORNIA

10

11 In re:)   Case No. 12-34567 NS
    John Doe,   )
12   )   PETITION FOR VOLUNTARY DISMISSAL
)
13   )
)
14   Debtor(s)   )

15

16   The debtor in the above-mentioned case hereby moves to dismiss his bankruptcy case for the following reasons:

17   1. Debtor filed a voluntary petition under Chapter 7 of the Bankruptcy Code on September 12, 19xx.

18   2. No complaints objecting to discharge or to determine the dischargeability of any debts have been filed in

19 the case.

20   3. Debtor realizes that filing a Chapter 7 bankruptcy petition was erroneous. Debtor now realizes that a

21 particular debt may not be dischargeable. Debtor would have to litigate this matter, and Debtor does not feel he has

22 the ability to do so on his own nor the resources to hire an attorney to do it for him. Debtor intends to pursue other

23 means of taking responsibility for his debts.

24   4. No creditor has filed a claim in this case.

25   WHEREFORE, Debtor prays that this bankruptcy case be dismissed without prejudice.

26 Date: _____   _____

27   Signature of Debtor

28 Date: _____   _____

    Signature of Debtor's Spouse

ORDER GRANTING VOLUNTARY DISMISSAL

1 John Doe
1111 Any Street
2 Berkeley, CA 94700
(510) 555-1223
3 Debtor in Pro Per

4

5

6

7

8   UNITED STATES BANKRUPTCY COURT

9   NORTHERN DISTRICT OF CALIFORNIA

10

11 In re:) Case No. 12-34567 NS
 John Doe,   )
12   ) ORDER GRANTING VOLUNTARY DISMISSAL
13   )
)
14   Debtor(s)   )

15

16

17   AND NOW, this _____ day of _____, 19____, the Court having found that the

18 voluntary dismissal of this case is in the best interests of the debtor and does not prejudice the rights of any of his

19 creditors, it is hereby ordered that the petition for voluntary dismissal is approved.

20

21 Dated: _____ _____

22   U.S. Bankruptcy Judge

23

24

25

26

27

28

Step 5: Using another of your copies, start typing again at line 14. This time, prepare an ORDER GRANTING VOLUNTARY PETITION, as shown in the sample.

Step 6: Make at least three copies of each form.

Step 7: Take your originals and copies to the bankruptcy court clerk. When you get to the court clerk, explain that you are filing a petition to dismiss your case. The clerk will take your originals and one or more of your copies. Ask the clerk the following:
- If there is a problem, will you be contacted? If not, how will you learn of the problem?
- If the judge signs the Order, when can you expect to get it?
- Once you have a signed order, who sends copies to your creditors—you or the court? If you send the copies, do you also have to file a proof of service?

Step 8: Once you receive the signed order, put it away for safe keeping if you don't have to notify your creditors. If you do, make copies and send one to each.

Step 9: If you have to file a proof of service, follow the instructions in Ch. 8, *Nondischargeable Debts*, Section B.2.b.ii, Step 6. ■

CHAPTER

5

Life After Bankruptcy

Congratulations! After you receive your final discharge and your case is closed, you can get on with your life and enjoy the fresh start that bankruptcy offers. You may, however, want to rebuild your credit, and you may still need to deal with one or more of the following events:

- You receive or discover new nonexempt property.
- A creditor tries to collect a nondischargeable debt.
- A creditor tries to collect a debt that has been discharged.
- A creditor or the trustee asks the court to revoke your discharge.
- A government agency or private employer discriminates against you because of your bankruptcy.

A. Newly Acquired or Discovered Property

If you omit property from your bankruptcy papers, or you acquire certain kinds of property soon after you file, the trustee may reopen your case after your discharge. The trustee probably won't reopen it, however, unless the property is nonexempt and is valuable enough to justify the expense of reopening the case, seizing and selling the property and distributing the proceeds among your creditors. If the after-discharge property you acquire or discover is of little value, however, tell the trustee, even if you think the assets don't justify reopening the case. That is the trustee's decision, not yours.

1. Notifying the Trustee

It's your legal responsibility to notify the bankruptcy trustee if you:

- receive or become entitled to receive, within 180 days of filing for bankruptcy, property that belongs in your bankruptcy estate, or
- failed to list some of your nonexempt property in your bankruptcy papers.

a. Newly Acquired Property

If you receive or become entitled to receive certain property within 180 days after your bankruptcy filing date, it must be reported to the trustee, even if you think the property is exempt or your case is already closed. If you don't report it and the trustee learns of your acquisition, the trustee could ask the court to revoke the discharge of your debts. (See Section E, below.) Property that must be reported is:

- an inheritance
- property from a divorce settlement, or
- proceeds of a life insurance policy or death benefit plan.

These categories of property are discussed in more detail in Ch. 2, *Your Property and Bankruptcy*, Section A.

To report this property to the trustee, use the form called Supplemental Schedule for Property Acquired After Bankruptcy Discharge. A blank copy is in Appendix 4. The form is self-explanatory. When you've filled it out, follow these steps:

Step 1: Photocopy a Proof of Service by Mail (a blank copy is in Appendix 4) and fill it out, but don't sign it.

Step 2: Make two photocopies of the Supplemental Schedule and the Proof of Service.

Step 3: Have a friend or relative mail the original Supplemental Schedule and a copy of the Proof of Service to the trustee and then sign the original Proof of Service.

Step 4: File a copy of the Supplemental Schedule and the original Proof of Service with the bankruptcy court. No additional filing fee is required.

Step 5: Keep a copy of the Supplemental Schedule and the Proof of Service for your records.

In some areas, the court may require you to file amended bankruptcy papers. If that happens, follow the instructions in Ch. 4, *Handling Your Case in Court*, Section B.

b. Nonexempt Property Not Listed in Your Papers

If, after your bankruptcy case is closed, you discover some nonexempt property that you should have listed in your bankruptcy papers but didn't, you don't need to file any documents with the court. You must, however, notify the trustee. A sample letter is shown below.

LETTER TO TRUSTEE

1900 Wishbone Place
Wilkes-Barre, PA 18704

October 22, 19XX

Francine J. Chen
Trustee of the Bankruptcy Court
217 Federal Building
197 S. Main St.
Wilkes-Barre, PA 18701

Dear Ms. Chen:

I've just discovered that I own some property I didn't know of while my bankruptcy case was open. Apparently, when I was a child I inherited a bank account from my uncle, the proceeds of which were supposed to be turned over to me when I turned 21. Although I turned 21 eight years ago, for some unknown reason I never got the money.

The account, #2424 5656-08 in the Bank of New England, 1700 Minuteman Plaza, Boston, MA 02442, has a balance of $4,975.19. Please let me know how you intend to proceed.

Sincerely,

Ondine Wallace

Ondine Wallace

2. Reopening Your Bankruptcy Case

If any of the new property or newly discovered property is valuable and nonexempt, the trustee may try to reopen your case, grab the property and have it sold to pay your creditors. If the property could be sold for a profit, given the expense of reopening the case and conducting an auction, the trustee will probably reopen the case.

To reopen a case, the trustee files a complaint with the court, asking for authorization to sell the new assets and distribute the proceeds. The request will be refused if the bankruptcy judge believes too much time has passed or that the assets aren't worth enough to justify reopening the case. But it's almost impossible to predict how a judge will decide. In two cases involving the same type of property with approximately the same value, one judge reopened a case 14 months after the discharge, while the other refused to reopen a case just eight months after the discharge,

stating that too much time had passed. (*In re Podgorski,* 18 B.R. 889 (N.D. Ind. 1982) and *In re Tyler,* 27 B.R. 289 (E.D. Va. 1983).)

GET HELP IF THE SITUATION MERITS IT
If the trustee reopens your case, and either your bankruptcy discharge or valuable property is at stake, find a bankruptcy lawyer to defend your interests in court. If, however, the amount at stake is something you can stand to lose, you'll probably be better off by simply consenting to what the trustee wants. A third alternative is to oppose the reopening in court, but to represent yourself rather than hire a lawyer. For this you'll need to do a heap of legal research. (See Ch. 9, *Help Beyond the Book.*)

B. Newly Discovered Creditors

Debts you didn't list in your bankruptcy papers are not discharged unless the creditor actually knew you filed for bankruptcy and had an opportunity to file a claim with the court or object to the discharge. If, after your bankruptcy is closed, you discover that you left a creditor off your papers who wasn't otherwise notified of your bankruptcy case, you may be able to reopen your case, amend your papers and discharge the debt.

The key is whether your bankruptcy case was an asset case or a no-asset case.

- Asset cases are ones that produced nonexempt assets which were sold to pay your unsecured creditors at least part of what they were owed.
- No-asset cases are ones that produced no nonexempt assets for your unsecured creditors.

If your case was a no-asset one, you may be able to reopen your case, amend your papers and discharge the omitted debt. But this is the judge's decision, and some refuse to allow no-asset cases to be reopened to add an omitted creditor.

If your case was an asset one, you probably won't be allowed to reopen it. It would be unfair to the creditor who was omitted to allow the case to be reopened and the omitted debt discharged because the trustee would have already distributed your nonexempt assets to the listed creditors. But in no-asset cases, allowing you to reopen the case and discharge the debt isn't unfair to the creditor, because no assets were distributed in the first place.

If you think you may be able to discharge a debt this way, simply follow the steps outlined in Ch. 4, *Handling Your Case in Court,* Section B, on amending your bankruptcy papers.

C. Attempts to Collect Nondischargeable Debts

After bankruptcy, creditors whose debts haven't been discharged are entitled to be paid; creditors whose debts have been discharged are not. But it isn't always clear into which category a creditor falls. The reason there's room for argument about which debts have been discharged is that the bankruptcy court doesn't give you a list of your discharged debts. Your final discharge merely says all debts that are legally dischargeable have been discharged.

How do you know which debts have been discharged and which debts must still be paid? Here's the general rule: All the debts you listed in your bankruptcy papers are discharged unless a creditor successfully objected to the discharge of a particular debt in the bankruptcy court, or the debt falls in one of the following categories:

- student loan that became due fewer than seven years ago (be sure to add in the time you received any deferment or forbearance)
- taxes that became due within the past three years
- child support or alimony
- fines and penalties or court fees
- debts related to intoxicated driving, or
- debts not discharged in a previous bankruptcy because of fraud or misfeasance.

Ch. 8, *Nondischargeable Debts,* discusses all of these categories.

In addition, if only one spouse files in a community property state, the other spouse's share of the community debts (debts incurred during the marriage) is also discharged. The community property states are Arizona, California, Idaho, Louisiana, New Mexico, Nevada, Texas, Washington and Wisconsin.

Even if you think some of your debts weren't discharged in bankruptcy, the creditors may never try to collect. Many believe that bankruptcy cuts off their rights, period; even attorneys often don't understand that some debts can survive bankruptcy.

If a creditor does try to collect a debt after your bankruptcy discharge, write to the creditor and state that your debts were discharged. Unless you're absolutely certain that the debt wasn't discharged—for example, a student loan where the first payment became due just a year ago and you did not attempt to discharge it on hardship grounds—this is a justifiable position for you to take. It's up to the creditor to establish that a given debt wasn't discharged in your bankruptcy. You're not required to roll over and play dead, even if it's more likely than not that the creditor is right. A sample letter is shown below.

LETTER TO CREDITOR

388 Elm Street
Oakdale, WY 95439

March 18, 19XX

Bank of Wyoming
18th and "J" Streets
Cheyenne, WY 98989

To Whom It May Concern:

I've received numerous letters from your bank claiming that I owe $6,000 for student loans borrowed between September of 1985 and September of 1987. I received a bankruptcy discharge of my debts on February 1, 19XX. I enclose a copy of the discharge for your reference.

Sincerely,
Brenda Woodruff
Brenda Woodruff

If the creditor ignores your letter and continues collection efforts, there are other ways to respond.

- **Amend your bankruptcy papers.** If a debt wasn't discharged simply because you forgot to list it on your bankruptcy papers, you may be able to get it discharged after your case is closed by amending your papers to include the debt. See Section B, above.

- **Do nothing.** The creditor knows you've just been through bankruptcy, have little or no nonexempt property and probably have no way to pay the debt, especially all at once. Thus, if you don't respond to collection efforts, the creditor may decide to leave you alone, at least for a while. But if the creditor has sued you and won a court judgment, in most states that judgment may be collected for 10 or 20 years, and usually may be renewed indefinitely.

- **Negotiate.** Try to negotiate for a lower balance or a payment schedule that works for you. Again, the creditor knows you've just been through bankruptcy and may be willing to compromise.

- **Defend in court.** If the creditor sues you for the debt, you can raise any defenses you have to the debt itself.

EXAMPLE: Edna was sued by the Department of Education for failing to pay back a student loan she received. Edna refused to make the payments because the trade school she gave the money to went out of business before classes even began. This is a grounds recognized by the Department of Education for forgiving a student loan.

- **Protest a garnishment or other judgment collection effort.** A creditor who has sued you and won a court judgment is likely to try to take (garnish) your wages or other property to satisfy the judgment. But the creditor can't take it all. What was exempt during bankruptcy is still exempt. (Appendix 1 lists exempt property.) Nonetheless, the creditor can still request that 25% of your wages be taken out of each paycheck.

Soon after the garnishment—in some states, before—the state court must notify you of the garnishment, tell you what's exempt under your state's laws and how you can protest. Grounds for protest are that the garnishment isn't justified or that it causes you hardship. To protest, you'll have to file a document in the state court; it goes by different names in different states. In New York, for example, it's called a Discharge of Attachment; in California it's a Claim of Exemption. If you do protest, the state court must hold a hearing, within a reasonable time, where you can present evidence of why the court should nullify the garnishment. The court may not agree, but it's certainly worth a try.

Protesting a wage garnishment is usually a relatively straightforward procedure. Because states are required to tell you how to proceed, you'll prob-

ably be able to handle it without the assistance of a lawyer.

Most states also have procedures for objecting to other types of garnishments, such as a garnishment of a bank account. You'll have to do a bit of research at a law library to learn the exact protest procedure, which is similar to the one for protesting a wage garnishment. (See Ch. 9, *Help Beyond the Book.*)

HELP IN DEALING WITH YOUR DEBTS AFTER BANKRUPTCY

With some debts, such as taxes, child support or alimony, exempt property may be taken, and a garnishment protest will do little good. Don't be surprised if the U.S. Treasury Department garnishes nearly 100% of your wages to pay back federal income taxes. The best strategy here is to attempt to negotiate the amount down. If the government refuses, you could quit your job in disgust and the government won't get a penny.

If you quit your job to avoid paying child support, however, you could end up in jail.

For tips on "doing nothing," negotiating with your creditors, defending in court or protesting a garnishment, see *Money Troubles: Legal Strategies to Cope With Your Debts*, by Robin Leonard (Nolo Press). For specific help in dealing with tax debts, see *Stand Up to the IRS*, by Frederick W. Daily (Nolo Press).

D. Attempts to Collect Clearly Discharged Debts

If a creditor tries to collect a debt that clearly was discharged in your bankruptcy, you should respond at once with a letter like the one shown below. Again, you can assume a debt was discharged if you listed it in your bankruptcy paper, the creditor didn't successfully object to its discharge and it isn't in one of the nondischargeability categories cited in Section C, above. Also, if you live in a community property state and your spouse filed singly, your share of the community debts is also discharged.

If a debt was discharged, the law prohibits creditors from filing a lawsuit, sending you collection letters, calling you, withholding credit or threatening to file or actually filing a criminal complaint against you. (11 U.S.C. § 524.)

LETTER TO CREDITOR

1905 Fifth Road
N. Miami Beach, FL 35466

March 18, 19XX

Bank of Miami
2700 Finances Hwy
Miami, FL 36678

To Whom It May Concern:

I've been contacted once by letter and once by phone by Rodney Moore of your bank. Mr. Moore claims that I owe $4,812 on Visa account number 1234 567 890 123.

As you're well aware, this debt was discharged in bankruptcy on February 1, 19XX. Thus, your collection efforts violate federal law, 11 U.S.C. § 524. If they continue, I won't hesitate to pursue my legal rights, including bringing a lawsuit against you for harassment.

Sincerely,

Dawn Schaffer

Dawn Schaffer

If the collection efforts don't immediately stop, you'll likely need the assistance of a lawyer to write the creditor again and, if that doesn't work, to sue the creditor for harassment. If the creditor sues you over the debt, you'll want to raise the discharge as a defense and sue the creditor yourself to stop the illegal collection efforts. The court has the power to hold the creditor in contempt of court. The court may also fine the creditor for the humiliation, inconvenience and anguish caused you and order the creditor to pay your attorney's fees. (See, for example, *In re Barbour*, 77 B.R. 530 (E.D. N.C. 1987), where the court fined a creditor $900 for attempting to collect a discharged debt.)

You can bring a lawsuit to stop collection efforts in state court or in the bankruptcy court. The bankruptcy court should be more familiar with the prohibitions against collection and more sympathetic to you. If the creditor sues you (almost certainly in state court), you or your attorney can file papers requesting that the case be transferred (removed) to the bankruptcy court.

E. Attempts to Revoke Your Discharge

In rare instances, a trustee or creditor asks the bankruptcy court to revoke a discharge. If the trustee or a creditor attempts to revoke your discharge, consult a bankruptcy attorney. (See Ch. 9, *Help Beyond the Book.*)

Your discharge can be revoked only if it's proved that:

- you obtained the discharge through fraud that the trustee or creditor discovered after your discharge
- you intentionally didn't tell the trustee you acquired property from an inheritance, a divorce settlement or a life insurance policy or death benefit plan within 180 days after you filed for bankruptcy, or
- before your case was closed, you refused to obey an order of the bankruptcy court, or, for a reason other than the privilege against self-incrimination, you refused to answer a question, important to your bankruptcy, asked by the court.

For the court to revoke your discharge on the basis of fraud, the trustee or creditor must file a complaint within one year of your discharge. For the court to revoke your discharge on the basis of your fraudulent failure to report property or your refusal to obey an order or answer a question, the complaint must be filed either within one year of your discharge or before your case is closed, whichever is later. You're entitled to receive a copy of the complaint, and the court must hold a hearing on the matter before deciding whether to revoke your discharge.

If your discharge is revoked, you'll owe your creditors. Any payment your creditors received from the trustee, however, will be credited against what you owe.

F. Post-Bankruptcy Discrimination

You may be afraid that after your bankruptcy, you'll have trouble getting or keeping a job or finding a place to live or will suffer other discrimination. There are, however, laws against discrimination by government and by private employers.

1. Government Discrimination

All federal, state and local governmental units are prohibited from denying, revoking, suspending or refusing to renew a license, permit, charter, franchise or other similar grant solely because you filed for bankruptcy. (11 U.S.C. § 525(a).) Judges interpreting this law have ruled that the government cannot:

- deny you a job or fire you
- deny you or terminate your public benefits, even if you discharged a debt to the government for overpayment of public benefits
- deny you or evict you from public housing, even if you discharged a debt for public housing back rent

- deny you or refuse to renew your state liquor license
- exclude you from participating in a state home mortgage finance program
- withhold your college transcript
- deny you a driver's license
- deny you a contract, such as a contract for a construction project, or
- exclude you from participating in a government-guaranteed student loan program.

In general, once any government-related debt has been discharged, all acts against you that arise out of that debt also must end. If, for example, you lost your driver's license because you didn't pay a court judgment that resulted from a car accident, once the debt is discharged, you must be granted a license. (If your license was also suspended because you didn't have insurance, however, you may not get your license back until you meet the requirements set forth in your state's financial responsibility law.)

If, however, the judgment wasn't discharged, you can still be denied your license until you pay up. If you and the government disagree about whether or not the debt was discharged, see Section C, above.

Keep in mind, however, that only post-bankruptcy government denials based on your bankruptcy are prohibited. You may be denied a loan, job or apartment for reasons unrelated to the bankruptcy (for example, because you earn too much to qualify for public housing), or for reasons related to your future creditworthiness (for example, because the government concludes you won't be able to repay a Small Business Administration loan).

2. Non-Government Discrimination

Private employers may not terminate you or otherwise discriminate against you solely because you filed for bankruptcy. (11 U.S.C. § 525(b).) While the Bankruptcy Act expressly prohibits employers from firing you, it is unclear whether or not the act prohibits employers from not hiring you because you went through bankruptcy.

Unfortunately, however, other forms of discrimination in the private sector aren't illegal. If you seek to rent an apartment and the landlord does a credit check, sees your bankruptcy and refuses to rent to you, there's not much you can do other than try to show that you'll pay your rent and be a responsible tenant. Or, if an employer refuses to hire you because of a poor credit history—not because you filed for bankruptcy—you may have little recourse.

If you suffer illegal discrimination because of your bankruptcy, you can sue in state court or in the bankruptcy court. You'll probably need the assistance of an attorney.

G. Rebuilding Credit

Although a bankruptcy filing can remain on your credit record for up to ten years from the date of your discharge, in about three years, you can probably rebuild your credit to the point that you won't be turned down for a major loan. Most creditors look for steady employment and a history, since bankruptcy, of making and paying for purchases on credit. And many creditors disregard a bankruptcy completely after about five years.

REBUILDING YOUR CREDIT
For more information on rebuilding your credit, see *Credit Repair*, by Robin Leonard (Nolo Press).

SHOULD YOU REBUILD YOUR CREDIT?

Habitual overspending can be just as hard to overcome as excessive gambling or drinking. If you think you may be a compulsive spender, one of the worst things you might do is rebuild your credit. Instead, you need to get a handle on your spending habits.

Debtors Anonymous is a 12-step support program similar to Alcoholics Anonymous and has programs nationwide. If a Debtors Anonymous group or a therapist recommends that you stay out of the credit system for a while, follow that advice. Even if you don't feel you're a compulsive spender, paying as you spend may still be the way to go.

Debtors Anonymous meets all over the country. To find a meeting close-by, call directory assistance or send a self-addressed stamped envelope to Debtors Anonymous, General Services Board, P.O. Box 400, New York, NY 10163-0400. Or call and leave a message at 212-642-8220.

---

1. Create a Budget

To start rebuilding your credit, the first step is to create a budget. Making a budget will help you control impulses to overspend and help you start saving money—an essential part of rebuilding your credit.

Before you put yourself on a budget that limits how much you spend, take some time to find out exactly how much money you spend now. Make copies of the Daily Expenses form in Appendix 4 and fill it out for 30 days.

Write down every cent you spend—50¢ for the paper, $2 for your morning coffee and muffin, $5 for lunch, $3 for the bridge or tunnel toll, and so on. If you omit any money spent, your picture of how much you spend, and your budget, will be inaccurate.

At the end of the 30 days, review your sheets. Are you surprised? Are you impulsively buying things, or do you tend to buy the same types of things consistently? If the latter, you'll have an easier time planning a budget than if your spending varies tremendously from day to day.

Think about the changes you need to make to put away a few dollars at the end of every week. Even if you think there's nothing to spare, try to set a small goal—even $5 a week. It will help. If you spend $2 per day on coffee and a muffin, that adds up to $10 per week and at least $40 per month. Eating breakfast at home might save you most of that amount. If you buy the newspaper at the corner store every day, consider subscribing. (A subscription doesn't involve extending credit; if you don't pay, they simply stop delivering.)

Once you understand your spending habits and identify what changes you need to make, you're ready to make a budget. At the top of a sheet of paper, write down your monthly net (after taxes and other mandatory deductions) income. At the left, list everything you spend money on in a month. Include any bank or other deposit accounts you do, or plan to, deposit money into, and any nondischarged, reaffirmed or other debts you make payments on. To the

right of each item, write down the amount of money you spend, deposit or pay each month. Finally, total up the amount. If it exceeds your monthly income, make some changes (eliminate or reduce expenditures for non-necessities) and start over. Once your budget is final, stick to it.

AVOIDING FINANCIAL PROBLEMS

These nine rules, suggested by people who have been through bankruptcy, will help you stay out of financial hot water.

1. Create a realistic budget and stick to it.
2. **Don't impulse buy.** When you see something you hadn't planned to purchase, go home and think it over. It's unlikely you'll return to the store and buy it.
3. **Avoid sales.** Buying a $500 item on sale for $400 isn't a $100 savings if you didn't need the item in the first place. It may be spending $400 unnecessarily.
4. **Get medical insurance.** You can't avoid medical emergencies, but living without medical insurance is an invitation to financial ruin.
5. **Charge items only if you could pay for them now.** Don't charge based on future income—sometimes future income doesn't materialize.
6. **Avoid large house payments.** Obligate yourself only for what you can now afford and increase your mortgage payments only as your income increases. Again, don't obligate yourself based on future income that you might not have.
7. **Think long and hard before agreeing to cosign or guarantee a loan for someone.** Your signature obligates you as if you were the primary borrower. You can't be sure that the other person will pay.
8. **Avoid joint obligations with people who have questionable spending habits**—even your spouse or significant other. If you incur a joint debt, you're probably liable for it all if the other person defaults.
9. **Avoid high-risk investments,** such as speculative real estate, penny stocks and junk bonds. Invest conservatively in things such as certificates of deposit, money market funds and government bonds. And never invest more than you can afford to lose.

DAILY EXPENSES

Date:

Item	Cost

Date:

Item	Cost

Date:

Item	Cost

Date:

Item	Cost

2. Keep Your Credit File Accurate

Rebuilding your credit involves keeping incorrect information out of your credit file.

Start by obtaining a copy of your file from one of the "big three" credit reporting agencies:

- Experian, National Consumer Assistance Center, P.O. Box 949, Allen, TX 75002-0940; 800-682-7654 or 800-422-4879
- Equifax, P.O. Box 105873, Atlanta, GA 30348; 404-612-3321
- Trans Union, P.O. Box 390, Springfield, PA 19064; 610-933-1200

You will need to send the agency your name and any previous names, addresses for the last two years, telephone number, year or date of birth, employer and Social Security number. If you're married, enclose the same information for your spouse.

You are entitled to a free copy of your report if you were denied credit because of an item in your report. You must request your file within 60 days of being denied credit. Also, you are entitled to a free copy of your report if you receive public assistance, you are unemployed and plan to look for work in the next 60 days or you believe your file contains errors due to someone's fraudulent use of your name, credit history, Social Security number or the like. Finally, you are entitled to an annual free copy of your report if you live in Colorado, Georgia, Maryland, Massachusetts or Vermont. If you are not entitled to a free copy of your report, expect to pay $8 for a copy.

In addition to your credit history, your credit report will contain the sources of the information and the names of people who have received your file within the last year, or within the last two years if those people sought your file for employment reasons.

You can dispute any item in your credit file. For example, if the file shows you owing $3,500 on your Visa bill and being 120 days late on payments, but the loan was discharged and you owe nothing, the item should be removed from your credit file or changed.

Credit files can contain negative information for up to seven years, except for bankruptcy filings, which can stay for ten. You will want to challenge outdated, as well as incorrect or incomplete information. The bureau must investigate the accuracy of anything you challenge within 30 days, and either correct it, or if it can't verify the item, remove it.

If, after the investigation, the bureau keeps information in your file you still believe is wrong, you are entitled to write a statement of up to 100 words giving your version, to be included in your file. It's a good idea to include a statement tied to a particular item in your file. When the item eventually is removed from your file, so will the statement be. If you write a general "my life was a mess and I got into debt" statement, however, it will stay for a full seven years from the date you place it, even if the negative items come out sooner. An example of a statement is shown below.

LETTER TO CREDIT BUREAU

74 Ash Avenue
Hanover, NH 03222

March 18, 19XX

Credit Reporters of New England
4118 Main Blvd.
Manchester, NH 03101

To Whom It May Concern:

Your records show that I am unemployed. That's incorrect. I am a self-employed cabinet maker and carpenter. I work out of my home and take orders from people who are referred to me through various sources. My work is known in the community and that's how I earn my living.

Sincerely,

Denny Porter

Denny Porter

The statement, or a summary of it, must be given to anyone who's given your credit file. In addition, if you request it, the bureau must pass on a copy or summary of your statement to any person who received your report within the past year, or two years if it involved employment.

You also want to keep new negative information out of your file. To do this, remain current on your bills. What you owe, as well as how long it takes you to pay, are in that file.

Finally, you want to modify public records to reflect what occurred in the bankruptcy, so wrong information won't appear in your credit file. For example, if a court case was pending against you at the time you filed for bankruptcy, and, as part of the bankruptcy, the potential judgment against you was discharged, be sure the court case is formally dismissed. You may need the help of an attorney. (See Ch. 9, *Help Beyond the Book*.)

CREDIT REPAIR AGENCIES

You've probably seen ads for companies that claim they can fix your credit, qualify you for a loan and get you a credit card. Stay clear of these companies—many of their practices are illegal. Some steal the credit files or Social Security numbers of people who have died or live in places like Guam or the U.S. Virgin Islands and replace your file with these other files. Others create new identities for debtors by applying to the IRS for a taxpayer I.D. number and telling debtors to use it in place of their Social Security number.

But even the legitimate companies can't do anything for you that you can't do yourself. If items in your credit file are correct, these companies cannot get them removed. If items are incorrect, they follow the same steps outlined above. About the only difference between using a legitimate credit repair agency and doing it yourself is saving a few thousands of dollars those agencies charge.

3. Negotiate With Some Creditors

If you owe any debts that show up as past due on your credit file (perhaps the debt wasn't discharged in bankruptcy, was reaffirmed in bankruptcy or was incurred after you filed), you can take steps to make them current. Contact the creditor and ask that the item be removed in exchange for either full or partial payment. On a revolving account (such as a department store), ask the creditor to "re-age" the account that is to be shown as current.

4. Get a Secured Credit Card

Once you have your budget and some money saved, you can begin to get some positive information in your credit file. One way is to get a secured credit card.

Some banks will give you a credit card and a line of credit if you deposit money into a savings account. In exchange, you are barred from removing the money from your account. Because it's difficult to guarantee a hotel reservation or rent a car without presenting at least one major credit card, get such a card if you truly believe you'll control any impulses to overuse—or even use—it.

Another reason to have these cards is that in a few years, banks and other large creditors will be more apt to grant you credit if, since your bankruptcy, you've made and paid for purchases on credit. A major drawback with these cards, however, is that the interest rate often nears 22%. So use the card only to cash checks or to buy inexpensive items you can pay for when the bill arrives. Otherwise, you're going to pay a bundle in interest.

CREDIT CARDS

If you've hung onto a bank credit card, or department store or gasoline credit card by reaffirming the debt or not listing the creditor on your bankruptcy paper, judicious use of that card can help rebuild your credit. If you discharged the credit card debt, it may still be possible to get your card back if you voluntarily pay what was discharged.

⚠ AVOID CREDIT CARD LOOK ALIKES
These are cards that allow you to make purchases only from the issuing company's own catalogues. The items in the catalogue tend to be overpriced and of mediocre (if not poor) quality. And your use of the card isn't reported to credit bureaus so you won't be rebuilding your credit.

5. Work With a Local Merchant

Another step to consider in rebuilding your credit is to approach a local merchant (such as a jewelry or furniture store) about purchasing an item on credit. Many local stores will work with you in setting up a payment schedule, but be prepared to put down a deposit of up to 30%, to pay a high rate of interest or to find someone to cosign the loan.

6. Borrow From a Bank

Bank loans provide an excellent way to rebuild credit A few banks offer something called a passbook savings loan. But in most cases, you'll have to apply for a standard bank loan. You probably won't qualify for a standard bank loan unless you bring in a cosigner, offer some property as collateral or agree to a very high rate of interest.

The amount you borrow depends on how much the bank requires you to deposit (in the case of a passbook loan) or its general loan term limits.

Banks that offer passbook loans typically give you one to three years to repay the loan. But don't pay the loan back too soon—give it about six to nine months to appear on your credit file. Standard bank loans are paid back on a monthly schedule.

Before you take out any loan, be sure to understand the terms:

- **Interest rate.** The interest rate on the loan is usually between two and six percentage points over what the bank charges its customers with the best credit.
- **Prepayment penalties.** Usually, you can pay the loan back as soon as you want without incurring any pre-payment penalties. Prepayment penalties are fees banks sometimes charge if you pay back a loan early and the bank doesn't collect as much interest from you as it had expected. The penalty is usually a small percentage of the loan amount.
- **Whether the bank reports the loan to a credit bureau.** This is key; the whole reason you take out the loan is to rebuild your credit. You may have to make several calls to find a bank that reports the loan. ■

CHAPTER

6

Your House

f you own a home, chapter 7 bankruptcy may not be the best strategy to deal with your debts. Before you decide to file, you must be aware of two important points:

- Chapter 7 bankruptcy won't stop a mortgage foreclosure. If you want to keep your home, you must keep making your mortgage payments before, during and after bankruptcy. If you've already missed mortgage payments, you'll have to make them up to prevent foreclosure. (See Section B, below.)
- If you have nonexempt equity in your home, you will lose your home if you file for Chapter 7 bankruptcy. (Exempt property is discussed in Ch. 2, *Your Property and Bankruptcy*, Section B.6, and Section C of this chapter.) Even if your mortgage payments are current, if you have equity in your home that isn't exempt, the bankruptcy court will take your home and sell it to pay off your creditors. (See Sections C and D, below.)

This chapter explains how Chapter 7 bankruptcy, and some alternative strategies, affect your chances of keeping your home. Of course, your home isn't your only consideration in deciding whether or not to file for bankruptcy, so read Ch. 1, *Should You File for Chapter 7 Bankruptcy?*, as well, before making the decision. If you're still uncertain about what to do after reading these chapters, see a bankruptcy lawyer. Chances are, your home is valuable enough to justify the extra expense to save it.

BE AWARE OF THE FOLLOWING:

- Some of the procedures discussed in this chapter are complex and require a lawyer. We don't provide step-by-step instructions. If you try to handle them yourself, a mistake could cost you your home.
- If you own two homes, or you want to protect equity in a home you aren't living in, see a bankruptcy lawyer.

A. How Bankruptcy Affects a Typical Homeowner

Here's an overview of how bankruptcy would affect you as a homeowner.

1. Mortgage Payments

You must keep making mortgage payments. As you probably know too well, you don't really "own" much of your home—a bank or other lender that has a mortgage or deed of trust on the home probably owns most of it. (In some states, a mortgage takes the form of a "deed of trust." The

practical effect is the same. Throughout this chapter, "mortgage" includes deeds of trust.)

Until the mortgage is paid off, the lender has the right to foreclose if you miss mortgage payments. Chapter 7 bankruptcy doesn't change this. (See Section B, below.)

2. Liens on Your House

Bankruptcy won't eliminate most liens on your home. If you've pledged your home as security for loans other than your mortgage—for example, you took out a home equity loan—or a creditor such as the IRS has recorded a lien, those creditors, too, have claims against your home. Their claims are generally called "liens."

Most lienholders have a right to foreclose (force a sale of your house) if the lien isn't paid off within a specified time.

WHO GETS WHAT FROM THE SALE OF A HOME IN BANKRUPTCY

Mortgage lenders and priority lienholders get paid first...

...then you get the amount of your homestead exemption...

...then other lienholders (if any proceeds are left over)...

...then unsecured creditors (if any proceeds are left over).

If there is a judicial (judgment) lien on your home—a creditor sued you, obtained a court judgment and recorded a lien at the land records office—however, you may be able to get rid of the lien entirely without paying a cent to the lienholder. And in some states, if your home is sold in bankruptcy, you get your homestead amount ahead of secured creditors holding judicial liens.

You can get rid of the lien by filing a motion to avoid a judicial lien. We describe this procedure in Ch. 7, *Secured Debts*, Sections B.1 and C.2.

3. Keeping Your House

You may lose your house unless a homestead exemption protects your equity. The difference between what your house is worth and what you owe the mortgage lender and all lienholders is called your equity. If you were to sell your home today, without filing for bankruptcy, the money raised by the sale would go first to the mortgage lender to pay off the mortgage and then to lienholders to pay off the liens. If anything was left over, you'd get it.

If you file for bankruptcy, and the trustee has your house sold, the creditors will get paid in pretty much the same order, with one big difference. In a bankruptcy sale, whatever is left after the mortgages and liens have been paid goes not to you, but to your unsecured creditors—unless a homestead exemption entitles you to some or all of it.

As a practical matter, if there's nothing left over for your unsecured creditors, the trustee won't bother to sell your house. Thus, the amount of your homestead exemption often determines whether or not you'll lose your home in bankruptcy.

If the bankruptcy trustee calculates that there would be leftover proceeds from a sale of your home to give to your unsecured creditors, the trustee will, without a doubt, take your home and sell it to get those proceeds.

Section C of this chapter explains how to determine whether a homestead exemption will prevent the trustee from selling your home.

B. If You're Behind on Your Mortgage Payments

If you're behind on your house payments and looking for a solution, your first strategy should be to negotiate with the lender and try other non-bankruptcy alternatives discussed in this section. (This section deals only with secured debts created by agreements. For a discussion of eliminating judicial liens on your home, see Ch. 7, *Secured Debts*, Sections B.1 and C.2.)

Chapter 7 bankruptcy's automatic stay won't prevent foreclosure if you fall behind on your mortgage payments. At most, it will postpone foreclosure for a month or so.

About the only way Chapter 7 bankruptcy can help you hang on to your home is by discharging your other debts, so that after bankruptcy you can more easily make your mortgage payments.

⚠ IF FORECLOSURE IS A REAL POSSIBILITY

If you think foreclosure is a real possibility, immediately see a lawyer experienced in debt problems. Don't wait until the last minute. The lawyer may need several months to negotiate with the lender or plan for an eventual bankruptcy so that you get the most out of it.

HOW A HOMESTEAD EXEMPTION WORKS: AN EXAMPLE

This chart applies only to those states that use dollar-amount homestead exemptions. If your state bases the homestead exemption on acreage, your lot size will determine whether or not you keep your home . (See Section C, below.)

This example is based on a $100,000 home with a $35,000 homestead exemption.

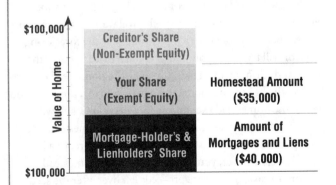

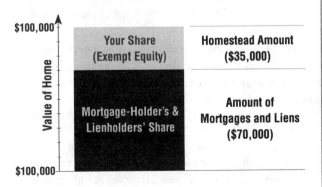

If the total equity in your home is more than your homestead exemption ($35,000 in this example), the trustee will sell your house to get the nonexempt equity.

If your total equity is less than the homestead amount, the trustee won't sell your house because there is no nonexempt equity.

1. Negotiating With the Lender

If you've missed a few mortgage payments, most lenders are willing to negotiate. What the lender agrees to will depend on your credit history, the reason for your missed payments and your financial prospects.

EXAMPLE: Doug misses a few house payments because he had a car accident and couldn't work for two months. It looks like he'll soon be back to work. The bank will probably work out a deal with Doug rather than immediately move to foreclose.

Here are the possible options your lender might agree to:

- Spread out the repayment of the missed payments over a few months. For example, if your monthly payment is $1,000 and you missed two months ($2,000), the lender might let you add $500 on to your monthly payment for four months.
- Reduce or suspend your regular payments for a specified time and then add a portion of your overdue amount to your regular payments later on.
- Extend the length of your loan and add the missed payments at the end.
- Suspend the principal portion of your monthly payment for a while and have you pay only interest, taxes and insurance.
- Refinance your loan to reduce future monthly payments.
- Let you sell the property for less than you owe the lender and waive the rest. This is called a "short sale."

2. If the Lender Starts to Foreclose

If your debt problems look severe or long-lasting, the lender may take steps toward foreclosure. Again, if you're faced with foreclosure and want to keep your house, consult a lawyer who specializes in debt problems to work out a strategy to save your home.

In most cases, before foreclosure actually occurs the lender will "accelerate" the debt or "call the loan." This means you must pay the entire balance immediately. If you don't, the lender will foreclose.

EXAMPLE: Don and Louise bought a $100,000 home by putting $20,000 down and getting an $80,000 mortgage. Their monthly house payments are $900. After paying on the mortgage for several years, they've recently missed three consecutive payments. The bank accelerated the loan and is now demanding the entire $76,284 balance. Because they can't pay it, the bank begins foreclosure proceedings.

Foreclosure takes from 90 days to 18 months, depending on the state you live in and the type of loan. During this time, you have several options:

- Sell your house. Again, if you don't get any offers that will cover what you owe your lender, a short sale may be possible.
- Get another lender to give you a loan that pays off all or part of the first loan and puts you on a new schedule of monthly payments. If the original lender has accelerated the loan, you'll need to refinance the entire balance of the loan to prevent foreclosure. If the lender hasn't accelerated the loan, however, you can prevent foreclosure simply by paying the missed payments, taxes and insurance, plus interest.
- File for Chapter 13 bankruptcy, if you can't come up with the needed money in a lump sum right away. Chapter 13 bankruptcy allows you to "cure the default"—make up missed payments—and make the regular payments. (See Section D.2, below.)
- Use what some bankruptcy attorneys have nicknamed a "Chapter 20." First, file for Chapter 7 to get rid of dischargeable debts and your personal liability for your mortgage. Foreclosure is staved off during this period by your making payments. Then, immediately after the Chapter 7 discharge, or on the day you get your discharge, file for Chapter 13 bankruptcy to pay off the liens on your home and any remaining (non-dischargeable) debts.

3. If Foreclosure Is Unavoidable

If you've exhausted the suggestions described in Section B.2, above, and it looks like foreclosure is inevitable, you should be aware that losing your home in bankruptcy will often be a better deal than losing it in a foreclosure sale. There are two reasons.

First, a forced sale of your home in bankruptcy is supervised by the bankruptcy trustee, who will want to sell the house for as much as possible. In a foreclosure sale, the foreclosing creditor will try to get only a high enough price to cover the amount due on the mortgage. If you have a homestead exemption on the house, the more the house is sold for, the more you get for the homestead exemption. (See Section C, below.)

Second, debtors are rarely entitled to the homestead exemption if the house is sold through foreclosure. In a bankruptcy sale, however, you are entitled to your homestead amount in cash, if there are proceeds left over after the secured creditors have been paid off.

In short, if your only choices are losing your home in foreclosure and losing your home in bankruptcy, bankruptcy is generally a better deal. But again, consult a lawyer about alternatives before you act.

C. If Your Equity Is More Than Your Homestead Exemption

If you file for Chapter 7 bankruptcy, the fact you've kept up on your house payments may not prevent you from losing it. The trustee will have your house sold if the sale will produce some cash to pay your unsecured creditors. If the sale won't produce cash, the trustee will not take the house.

The outcome depends on two facts:
- whether you have any equity in your home, and
- whether that equity is exempt.

If you haven't yet figured out the equity in your home in Worksheet 2 in Ch. 2, *Your Property and Bankruptcy,* the worksheet a few pages ahead will help you do that. Once you've determined your equity, you can figure out whether or not that equity is exempt under the homestead exemption. If your equity is fully protected, you won't lose your home by filing for bankruptcy.

Before you fill out the worksheet, find out what kind of homestead exemption system your state uses by looking at the lists below. If your state bases the exemption on lot size, or exempts an unlimited amount of equity, you don't need the worksheet to figure out whether or not your equity is exempt.

HOMESTEAD EXEMPTION BASED ON LOT SIZE

Arkansas	Kansas	Texas
Florida	Oklahoma	
Iowa	South Dakota	

In these states, you can easily determine whether your home is exempt. The homestead exemption is based simply on acreage.

Look in Appendix 1 for the acreage limitation in your state. If your property is less than the maximum, your home is fully protected. If your property exceeds the maximum allowable acreage, your home will be sold by the trustee if you have any equity in the property.

HOMESTEAD EXEMPTION BASED ON LOT SIZE AND EQUITY

Alabama	Michigan	Nebraska
Hawaii	Minnesota	Oregon
Louisiana	Mississippi	

These states use the size of your lot and the amount of your equity to determine whether your home is exempt. First look in Appendix 1 for the acreage limitation in your state. If your property exceeds the maximum allowable acreage, your home will be sold by the trustee if you have any equity in the property, even if that equity is within the exemption dollar limit.

If your lot size is within the allowed acreage, your exemption is determined by the equity amount limit. Use the worksheet below to see if your equity is fully protected.

HOMESTEAD EXEMPTION BASED ON EQUITY ALONE

All Other States with Homestead Exemptions (see Appendix 1)

Federal Exemptions

If your state isn't listed in either of the lists above, but has a homestead exemption, or if you are using the federal exemptions, your homestead exemption is a fixed dollar amount and isn't based on lot size. Use the worksheet below to determine if your equity exceeds the exemption limit.

⚠️ **THIS WORKSHEET IS FOR ESTIMATE PURPOSES ONLY**
The trustee can challenge the value you claim, and may determine that your house is worth more than you think. Depending on your homestead amount, this difference could mean the difference between keeping your home and losing it. Thus, if you discover that the difference between line 6 and 7 of this worksheet is less than 10% of the value of your home, there is some risk that you might lose your home if you file for Chapter 7 bankruptcy. Seek the advice of an experienced bankruptcy practitioner in your area.

Worksheet Instructions

Line 1: Estimated market value of your home

If you've already filled out Worksheet 2 in Ch. 2, *Your Property and Bankruptcy,* take the home value from that worksheet.

If you haven't filled out Worksheet 2, estimate how much your home could be sold for in a bankruptcy sale. In a bankruptcy sale, a typical home goes for 10%–30% less than what it would bring in a normal sale. The trustee knows this and will probably take it into account when deciding whether or not to go after your home.

The trustee, however, is not required to use this discounted value. He may use the full market value of your home in deciding whether to take it. To be on the safe side, you may want to put the full market value of your home on this line.

To get a rough idea of what your home is worth, ask a realtor what comparable homes in your neighborhood have sold for. Or look in newspapers real estate sections.

Line 2: Costs of sale

Costs of sale vary, but tend to be about 5% of the sales price. The trustee does not have to subtract the costs of sale in determining whether to take your home, but many do. If you want to err on the side of caution, for the purposes of this estimate, put "0" in this blank.

Line 3: Amount owed on mortgages and other loans

Enter the amount needed to pay off your mortgage and any other loans that are secured by the home as collateral. If you can't come up with a reasonably reliable estimate, contact each lender and ask how much is necessary to cancel the debt.

Line 4: Amount of liens

Enter the amount of all liens recorded against your home. If you've already figured this amount in Worksheet 2 of Ch. 2, you can use those figures.

If you haven't yet filled out Worksheet 2, here's what to do. Liens are claims against your home which have been recorded with the land records office. The three most common types of liens are tax liens, mechanic's liens and judgment liens. Tax liens can be recorded against your home by the county, state or federal government for failure to pay property, income or other taxes. Mechanic's liens can be recorded by people who do work on your home and who aren't paid what they're owed. And judgment liens can be recorded by anyone who has sued you and won.

If you think there might be liens on your home but you're not sure, visit the county land records office. Tell the clerk you'd like to check your title for liens against it. The clerk should direct you to an index (often on microfiche) that lists all property in the county by the owner's last name. Next to your home should be a list of any liens recorded against it.

Line 5: Total of lines 2, 3 and 4

Line 6: Equity

Subtract line 5 from line 1, and put the amount on line 6. For bankruptcy purposes, this is your equity in the property—that is, the amount the house will sell for, less what must be paid to others from the proceeds.

📖 **LEGAL RESEARCH NOTE**
If you do legal research in this area, pay attention to how reported bankruptcy court decisions use the term "equity." Courts occasionally divide a homeowner's equity into two types: "encumbered" and "unencumbered." Encumbered equity is your home's value less only the mortgage. Unencumbered equity is your home's value less the mortgage and liens. We use equity to mean unencumbered equity. But some courts use equity to mean encumbered equity. The term often appears in cases discussing whether a state's homestead exemption allows the debtor to be paid before certain lienholders.

Line 7: Homestead exemption

On this line, put the amount of your state's homestead exemption (or the federal exemption if your state allows it and you plan to use it). Not every state has a homestead exemption. To find out what your homestead exemption is, check Appendix 1.

If you're married, bankruptcy law allows each spouse to claim the full value of the exemption (called "doubling"). Some states expressly prohibit this, however, as noted in Appendix 1. A few other states expressly allow it, and they, too, are noted in Appendix 1. If your state is silent, go ahead and double.

WORKSHEET 3

Determining Your Nonexempt Equity: Homestead Exemption Based on Equity

1. Estimated market value of your home $ _____

2. Costs of sale (approx. 5% of sale price) $ _____

3. Amount owed on mortgages and other loans $ _____

4. Amount of liens $ _____

5. Total of lines 2, 3 and 4 $ _____

6. Equity (line 1 minus line 5) $ _____

7. Homestead exemption
   (see Appendix 1) $ _____

8. Nonexempt equity (line 6 minus line 7) $ _____

HOMESTEAD DECLARATION NOTE
If you're going to claim a homestead exemption when you file for bankruptcy, pay attention to whether you must file a "declaration of homestead" before the homestead exemption will take effect. Appendix 1 has this information.

Line 8: Nonexempt equity

Subtract line 7 from line 6 and enter the total on line 8. If the amount is less than zero, all of your equity is exempt. But remember, this is only an estimate. If your estimate is correct, the trustee won't have your home sold, because the proceeds would go to you and the mortgage-holders and lienholders, not your unsecured creditors.

But if the amount on line 8 is greater than zero—that is, your equity (line 6) exceeds the homestead exemption amount (line 7)—the bankruptcy trustee can force the sale of your home to pay off your creditors. (If you can raise the cash, most trustees will let you pay them the difference between your equity and your homestead exemption, and allow you to keep your home. See Section D.2, below.)

From the proceeds of the sale, your secured creditors are paid the amounts of their mortgages, liens and so forth. You get cash in the amount of the homestead exemption and your unsecured creditors get the rest.

If you find, after using this worksheet, that you have nonexempt equity in your home, don't file for Chapter 7 bankruptcy if you can help it. You'll almost certainly lose your home. You'll probably fare better, and hold on to your home longer, by using your equity to help pay off your debts. Some of these methods are discussed in Section D.

IS A MOBILE HOME REAL PROPERTY?

Some states specifically include mobile homes in their homestead exemptions. Other states include any "real or personal property used as a residence." This would include a trailer, mobile home or houseboat, so long as it's your residence. Some states don't say. To find out if a mobile home fits within the homestead exemption in those states, you'll have to do some legal research to determine if the mobile home is considered a homestead or a motor vehicle. (See Ch. 9, *Help Beyond the Book*.)

D. Ways to Prevent the Loss of Your House in Bankruptcy

If you have nonexempt equity in your home and would lose it if you filed for bankruptcy, you probably want to explore options other than bankruptcy. We outline some of them here, but you should see an experienced bankruptcy lawyer to help you.

1. Reduce Your Equity Before Filing for Bankruptcy

If you can reduce your nonexempt equity before you file for bankruptcy, you may be able to pay off your other debts and avoid bankruptcy. And if you later file for bankruptcy, you may be able to save your home. But you'll probably have to act at least 91 days to one year before you file.

There are two ways to reduce your equity:
- borrow against the equity, or
- sell part ownership of your house.

You can use the proceeds to buy exempt property or to pay off other debts.

 CONSULT A LOCAL BANKRUPTCY LAWYER BEFORE REDUCING YOUR EQUITY
If you do file for bankruptcy, the bankruptcy court in your area might view your actions as an abuse of the bankruptcy process and dismiss your bankruptcy petition. How to stay out of trouble is discussed in Ch. 2, *Your Property and Bankruptcy,* Section C.

a. Borrow Against Your Equity

If you borrow against your equity, you won't reduce your overall debt burden. You may be able to lower your overall monthly bills, however, if you can get a lower interest rate or a longer term equity loan to pay off short-term, high-interest debts. You can also fully deduct the interest you pay on home equity loans (unlike other loans) from your income taxes. Also, some lenders will work out a plan where you pay very little now, but pay a big balloon payment later on. This will give you an instant drop in your monthly bills. Later, when you're better off financially, you may be able to refinance again, and do away with the balloon payment. But be warned: If you can't refinance, you may lose your home when the balloon payment comes due.

b. Sell Some of Your Equity

Another way to protect your equity may be to sell some of it. By owning your home jointly with someone else, your equity is reduced.

Selling a portion of your equity may appeal to you because what you need now is more cash, not another monthly bill. Perhaps a friend or a relative would be willing to buy a half share in your home. If you pursue this strategy, you may need to wait a year after the sale before filing for bankruptcy. Otherwise the sale might be voided by the bankruptcy trustee, especially if it appears that you gave your friend or relative a bargain on the price.

Even a year may not be sufficient in some courts if the judge views your actions as defrauding your creditors. (See Ch. 2, *Your Property and Bankruptcy,* Section C.2.) These standards vary widely from court to court. Be sure to consult a local bankruptcy attorney who is aware of local practice before you try this.

Also, think long and hard about whether you want to share ownership of your home. A co-owner can sell his interest, force a sale of the property, die and leave it to someone else, and so on. Again, consult a bankruptcy lawyer before you sell. It can be fraught with complications and traps for the uninformed.

2. If You File for Bankruptcy

If you do file for Chapter 7 bankruptcy, you may be able to keep the trustee from selling your house through one of the following methods:

- **Offer to substitute cash for the amount of nonexempt equity.** You may be able to convince the trustee not to sell your house if you can come up with as much cash as would be available from the proceeds to pay unsecured creditors. You may be able to raise the cash by selling exempt property or using income you earn after you file.

  EXAMPLE: The Robertsons have approximately $5,000 of nonexempt equity in their home. All of their home furnishings are exempt. After discussing the matter with the trustee, they sell three pieces of furniture and a camera for a total of $1,800, and scrape together $2,700 extra cash from income earned since they filed for bankruptcy. They offer the cash to the trustee as a substitute for the nonexempt equity. The trustee accepts the money, because the creditors get close to the same amount and the trustee need not sell the home.

- **Increase your homestead exemption with a wild card exemption.** In several states, you can add a wild card exemption amount to the amount of your homestead exemption. Although these amounts are usually small,

they may be enough to make a difference. (See Ch. 2, *Your Property and Bankruptcy,* Section B.6).

WILD CARD EXEMPTIONS THAT CAN BE APPLIED TO REAL ESTATE	
California, System 2	$800
Connecticut	$1,000
Georgia	$400
Indiana	$4,000
Kentucky	$1,000
Maine	$400
Maryland (this is the only exemption you can use on your home; there is no homestead exemption)	$5,500
Missouri	$1,250
New Hampshire	$8,000
Ohio	$400
Pennsylvania	$300
Vermont	$400
Virginia (if you're a disabled veteran)	$2,000
West Virginia	$800
Federal	$800

A number of other states have wild card exemptions, but these apply only to personal property.

- **File for or convert to Chapter 13 bankruptcy.** Chapter 13 bankruptcy lets you pay your debts out of your income, rather than by selling your property. Thus, if you file for Chapter 13 bankruptcy, you won't give up your home, even if you have nonexempt equity. Chapter 13 bankruptcy also permits you to spread out repayments of missed installments, taxes and late charges on a mortgage. Furthermore, if your lender has begun foreclosure proceedings, Chapter 13 bankruptcy can halt them as long as your house hasn't yet been sold. (See Ch. 1, *Should You File for Chapter 7 Bankruptcy?*)

  You can convert to Chapter 13 bankruptcy at any time during a Chapter 7 bankruptcy proceeding. If you miss mortgage payments after you filed for your Chapter 7 bankruptcy, however, some courts won't let you include them in your Chapter 13 repayment plan. So try to make all payments due after you file for Chapter 7. If the lender won't accept them (because it wants to proceed with foreclosure), save the money so you can make up the payments later. ■

CHAPTER

7

Secured Debts

Secured debts are debts linked to specific items of property (sometimes called collateral or security). The property guarantees payment of the debt; if the debt isn't paid, the creditor can take the property or force its sale to pay off the debt. Some secured debts you incur voluntarily—such as a mortgage or car loan. Others are imposed against your will—like tax liens and liens imposed on property to enforce a judgment. If you've ever had property repossessed when you failed to pay a bill or had a creditor force the sale of an item after suing you, obtaining a judgment and recording a lien, you've had some experience with secured debts.

This chapter explains what happens to secured debts in bankruptcy and helps you decide whether or not to try to keep property that is collateral for a debt.

➡️ **YOU MAY BE ABLE TO SKIP THIS CHAPTER**

If you have no property that is collateral for a debt, no liens recorded against your property, or if all such property has been taken by your creditors more than 90 days before you file for bankruptcy, you don't need to read this chapter.

A. The Statement of Intention Form

When you file for bankruptcy, you must inform the bankruptcy court and your affected creditors what you plan to do about the property that secures your debts. You tell them by filing a form called the "Chapter 7 Individual Debtor's Statement of Intention" and mailing a copy of the form to each creditor you list on it.

There are line-by-line instructions in Ch. 3, *Filling in and Filing the Bankruptcy Forms,* Section H, but read this chapter first to gain the necessary background to make the decisions requested on the form.

Although the Statement of Intention is not due until 30 days after you file for bankruptcy, it's commonly filed right after you file the other papers. Thus, you should make your decisions as to what to do with each item of secured property before you file.

The law says you must carry out your stated intentions within 45 days of the date you file the form. There are no apparent penalties, however, if you don't.

If you change your mind after you file, you can amend the form easily using the instructions in Ch. 4, *Handling Your Case in Court,* Section B.

HOW TO USE THIS CHAPTER

This chapter explains what happens to secured debts in bankruptcy, and your options regarding those debts. You'll learn about the advantages and disadvantages of each option listed on the Statement of Intention, as well as suggested strategies for keeping specific items of property such as automobiles.

To get the most out of this chapter, you should proceed as follows:

Step 1: Read Section B to learn about what happens to secured debts in bankruptcy. A clear understanding of this material is crucial to understanding the rest of the chapter and the options listed on the Statement of Intention.

Step 2: Read or skim Section C to learn about your options.

Step 3: Once you understand how these options work, Section D helps you decide whether a particular item of property is worth keeping and, if so, the best option for keeping it.

Step 4: Once you decide what procedures to use, Section E gives you step-by-step, do-it-yourself instructions for the simple procedures. If you opt for one of the complex procedures, you'll need the help of a lawyer, but Section E explains the basics.

SECURED DEBTS AND BANKRUPTCY

Bankruptcy eliminates your personal liability for secured debts, but the creditor's lien remains. Sometimes you can take further steps in bankruptcy to eliminate or reduce a lien.

B. What Bankruptcy Does to Secured Debts

Bankruptcy's effect on secured debts is different than on other kinds of debts, because a secured debt consists of two parts:

- The first part is no different than an unsecured debt: it is personal liability for the debt, and it is what obligates you to pay the debt to the creditor. Bankruptcy wipes out your personal liability if the debt is dischargeable. (See Ch. 8, *Nondischargeable Debts.*) Once your personal liability is eliminated, the creditor cannot sue you to collect the debt.

- The second part of a secured debt is the creditor's legal claim (lien or security interest) on the property that is collateral for the debt. A lien gives the creditor the right to repossess the property or force its sale if you do not pay the debt. Bankruptcy, by itself, does not eliminate liens. But during bankruptcy you may be able to eliminate, or at least reduce, liens on secured property.

    EXAMPLE: Mary buys a couch on credit from a furniture store. She signs a contract that states she must pay for the couch over the next year. The contract also states that the creditor (the store) has a security interest in the couch and can repossess it if any payment is more than 15 days late. In this type of secured debt, Mary's obligation to pay the debt is her personal liability, and the store's right to repossess the couch is the lien.

1. Eliminating Liens in Bankruptcy

As mentioned above, there are several procedures you can invoke during bankruptcy to eliminate or reduce liens. But these procedures are neither automatic nor required—you have to request them.

The most powerful of these procedures lets you eliminate (avoid) some types of liens on certain kinds of exempt property without paying anything to the creditor. (See Ch. 2, *Your Property and Bankruptcy,* for a definition of exempt property.) With the lien eliminated, you get to keep the property free and clear without paying anything more to the creditor.

Other procedures let you eliminate a creditor's lien (and keep the property) by paying the creditor either the amount of the lien or the current value of the property, whichever is less.

Finally, you can rid yourself of a lien by simply surrendering the property to the creditor.

The choice of which procedure to use on each item of secured property is up to you.

2. If You Don't Eliminate Liens

If you take no steps to eliminate a lien during bankruptcy, the lien survives bankruptcy intact. The creditor will be free to take the property or force its sale.

EXAMPLE: Mary (from the example above) successfully goes through bankruptcy and receives her discharge. Her personal liability for the purchase price of her couch is eliminated, but the creditor's lien on her couch remains. The creditor has the right to repossess the couch as soon as the automatic stay is lifted, or possibly even sooner.

If the property is valuable and easily resold (an automobile, for example), the creditor will surely repossess the item at the first opportunity unless you agree to keep making payments. (See Sections C.4 and C.5.a, below.) If, however, the property is of little value and not worth the cost of repossessing (such as Mary's couch), the creditor may do nothing.

If the property is of the type with a "title" or ownership document, such as a house or car, and the creditor does nothing, the lien simply remains on the property until you sell it. At that time, the lien must be paid out of the proceeds of the sale. If the property has no ownership document, the creditor has no practical way to enforce it.

In some cases, if the property is declining in value and it is clear that you aren't going to take steps to keep it, the creditor might request the bankruptcy court's permission to take the property even before the bankruptcy case is over.

C. Ways to Deal With Secured Debts in Bankruptcy

There are seven ways to deal with secured debts in bankruptcy. Some options are on the Statement of Intention form; others are not. All but the first option allow you to keep property.

You may want to skim through these options for now, and refer back to them as you read Section D. That section indicates which option is best for specific kinds of property, including houses and cars.

1. Surrender Property

Description: Surrendering secured property simply means allowing the creditor to repossess or take the item or foreclose on the lien. It completely frees you from the debt—the lien is satisfied by your surrender of the property and your personal liability is discharged by the bankruptcy.

Advantage: A quick and easy way to completely rid yourself of a secured debt.

Disadvantage: You lose the property.

Restrictions: None. You can surrender any kind of property to get rid of any kind of lien.

When to use it: For property that you don't need or want, or would cost too much to keep.

How it works: You simply list the property as surrendered on your Statement of Intention, and send a copy of the form to the creditor. It's then up to the creditor to contact you to arrange a time to pick up the property. If the creditor never takes the property, it's yours to keep. Section E.1 contains step-by-step instructions.

2. Avoid (Eliminate) Liens

Description: Lien avoidance is a procedure by which you ask the bankruptcy court to "avoid" (eliminate or reduce) liens on your exempt property.

How much of a lien is avoided depends on the value of the property and the amount of the exemption. If the property is entirely exempt or worth less than the legal exemption limit, the court will eliminate the entire lien and you'll get to keep the property without paying anything. If the property is worth more than the exemption limit, the lien is reduced to the difference between the exemption limit and either the property's value or the amount of the debt, whichever is less. (11 U.S.C. § 522(f)(2).)

> **EXAMPLE:** A creditor has a $500 lien on Harold's guitar, which is worth $300. In Harold's state, the guitar is exempt only to $200. He could get the lien reduced to $100. The other $400 of the lien is eliminated (avoided).

($500 lien) $300 = value of item
  – 200 = exemption amount
  $100 = amount of lien remaining after lien avoidance

Advantages: Lien avoidance costs nothing, involves only a moderate amount of paperwork, and allows you to keep property without paying anything. It is the best and most powerful tool for getting rid of liens.

Disadvantage: Some paperwork is involved.

Restrictions: Lien avoidance has several important restrictions:

- You must have owned the property before the lien was "fixed" on it. Exactly when a lien is fixed on property depends on vague state law. For purposes of your bankruptcy filing, assume that if the property had a lien on it when you acquired it, you can't avoid that lien. (See *Farrey v. Sanderfoot*, 500 U.S. 291 (1991).)
- The property must be claimed as exempt.
- The lien must be either:
  - a *judicial lien*, which can be removed from any exempt property, including real estate and automobiles, or
  - a *nonpossessory nonpurchase-money security interest*, which can be avoided only on the following exempt property:
- household furnishings, household goods, clothing, appliances, books and musical instruments or jewelry that are primarily for your personal, family or household use
- health aids professionally prescribed for you or a dependent
- animals or crops held primarily for your personal, family or household use—but only the first $5,000 of the lien can be avoided (11 U.S.C. § 522(f)(3).), or
- implements, professional books or tools used in a trade (yours or a dependent's)—but only the first $5,000 of the lien can be avoided. (11 U.S.C. § 522(f)(3).)

Until October 1994, any nonpossessory nonpurchase-money security interest on exempt animals, crops and implements, professional books or tools used in a trade could be avoided without limit. Section 310 of the Bankruptcy Reform Act of 1994, however, added a limitation on your ability to avoid these liens. The new language states:

The debtor may not avoid the fixing of a lien on an interest of the debtor or a dependent of the debtor in property…to the extent the value of such implements, professional books, tools of the trade, animals, and crops exceeds $5,000.

We do not know exactly what Congress meant by "to the extent the value…exceeds $5,000." Our interpretation is above—that only the first $5,000 of the lien can be avoided. It is possible, however, that a court will interpret this new section to mean that you cannot avoid a nonpossessory nonpurchase-money security interest on any exempt animals, crops, or implements, professional books or tools used in a trade which exceed $5,000 in value. Nonpossessory nonpurchase-money security interests cannot be removed from real estate or from motor vehicles unless they are a tool of your trade. Generally, a motor vehicle is not considered a tool of trade unless you use it as an integral part of your business—for example, you do door-to-door sales or delivery work. It is not considered a tool of trade if you simply use it to get to and from your workplace, even if you have no other means of getting there. (See Exemption Glossary for definitions and examples of tools of the trade.)

creditor agrees to it. Many creditors refuse to take installment payments after their liens have been reduced.

How it works: You request lien avoidance by checking the column "Property is claimed as exempt" on the Statement of Intention and typing and filing a document called a "motion." (Complete instructions for preparing and filing a motion to avoid a lien are in Section E.2, below.) Although it may sound complicated, lien avoidance is a routine procedure that involves just a little time.

ELIMINATING JUDICIAL LIENS ON REAL ESTATE

As explained in Ch. 6, your homestead exemption protects your equity—that is, the extent to which the value of the property exceeds the total of any consensual liens (mortgages) on the property.

> EXAMPLE: Zoe and Bud own a $100,000 house with an $80,000 mortgage; their equity is $20,000. The homestead exemption in their state is $30,000. Although Credo-check has recorded a $200,000 judgment (judicial) lien against Zoe and Bud's home, their equity is fully protected because it's less than the homestead exemption amount.

If your equity is fully protected by an exemption—that is, no equity remains after the consensual liens and homestead exemption are deducted, as is the case in the example—you can entirely eliminate the judicial liens on the property. (11 U.S.C. § 522(f).) Thus, Zoe and Bud could eliminate the entire $200,000 lien.

When to use it: Use lien avoidance whenever possible, especially if a lien can be completely wiped out. Even if you don't need the property, you can avoid the lien, sell the property and use the money for things you do need.

To keep things simple, you may want to avoid liens only on property completely exempt. Then the lien will be eliminated entirely and you'll own the property free and clear, without paying anything to the creditor.

In theory, even partial lien avoidance can be beneficial, but you'll have to pay the remaining amount of the lien to the creditor either in a lump sum, or in installments if the

---

SPECIAL RULES FOR LIENS ARISING FROM DIVORCE

Because courts place a high priority on protecting the interests of children and former spouses, the Bankruptcy Code prohibits you from avoiding a judicial lien that secures a debt to your ex-spouse or children for alimony or child support. (11 U.S.C. § 522(f)(1)(A).) In some divorces, however, it's not always clear if a lien is for support or is just to pay marital bills. In the latter case, the lien may be avoided.

Also, a Supreme Court case limits your right to avoid liens arising out of a division of property that takes place during a divorce. For example, if you get sole ownership of your marital home at the same time that your ex-spouse gets a security interest (such as a promissory note) in the home, the court may not let you avoid the lien. The determining issues are when you *alone* acquired title to the property and when your ex-spouse's lien affixed. Consult with a bankruptcy practitioner to determine how this case—and subsequent cases—may affect you if you intend to avoid a lien arising from a divorce. (The main case is *Farrey v. Sanderfoot*, 500 U.S 291 (1991).)

3. Redeem Property

Description: You have the right to "redeem" property—buy it back from the creditor rather than have it taken by the creditor and sold to someone else. You pay the creditor the property's current market value, usually in a lump sum, and in return the lien is eliminated. You then own the property free and clear.

> EXAMPLE: Susan and Gary owe $500 on some household furniture now worth $200. They can keep the furniture and eliminate the $500 lien by paying the creditor the $200 within 45 days of filing their Statement of Intention.

IMPORTANT DEFINITIONS: TYPES OF LIENS CREATED BY SECURED DEBTS

Various types of liens are created by secured debts. The type of lien on your property often determines which lien-reduction or lien-eliminating procedures you can use.

You may want to skip this list of definitions for now and refer to it when we describe a specific kind of lien.

Security Interests—Liens You Agree to

If you voluntarily pledge property as collateral—that is, as a guarantee that you will pay a debt—the lien on your property is called a security interest. Many written security agreements give the creditor the right to take the property after you miss a payment.

The most common types of security interests are:

Purchase-Money Security Interests: If you purchase an item on credit and pledge it as collateral for the debt, the lien on the collateral is called a purchase-money security interest. Typical purchase-money secured debts are automobile loans and debts for large furniture purchases.

These kinds of liens cannot be eliminated in bankruptcy. You will have to either honor the original contract and continue making payments, or pay the value of the property up front to keep the property. (See Section B.2, above.)

Nonpurchase-Money Security Interests: If you pledge property you already own as collateral for a loan, the lien is called a nonpurchase-money security interest. If you retain possession of the property, for example you borrow from a lending company or credit union, and pledge your car or stereo equipment as security for the loan, the loan is called **nonpossessory.**

These kinds of liens can be eliminated in bankruptcy if the collateral is exempt and meets the criteria described in Section C.2.

If you don't retain possession of the property, for instance, if you turn property over to a pawnshop, the loan is called **possessory.** These liens cannot be eliminated in bankruptcy as described in Section C.2.

Liens Created Without Your Consent

If a creditor gets a lien on your property without your consent, it is termed a non-consensual lien. There are three major types of non-consensual liens.

Judicial Liens: A judicial lien is created against your property by somebody who wins a money judgment in a lawsuit against you, and then takes the additional steps necessary to record a lien against your property.

If a judicial lien is on exempt property, you can probably eliminate it in bankruptcy unless it arose out of a mortgage foreclosure. (See Section C.2.)

Statutory Liens: Non-consensual liens can also be created automatically by law. For example, in most states when you hire someone to work on your house, the worker or supplier of materials automatically gets a mechanic's lien or "materialman's lien" on the house if you don't pay. Liens like these are called statutory liens.

A statutory lien can be eliminated in bankruptcy if it:

- did not become effective 90 days or more prior to the date you filed for bankruptcy
- was not perfected (made official by filing the applicable documents with the land records office) before you filed for bankruptcy, or
- is for rent you owe.

These liens can be eliminated only as "preferences." There is no specific provision in the bankruptcy code for eliminating these kinds of liens.

> **EXAMPLE:** Sam's home suffered severe water damage after a pipe burst in the upstairs bathroom. He had the damage repaired at a cost of $4,000. Now, because of unexpected medical bills, he can't pay the plumber and carpenter the last $2,000 he owes them for the work done on the house. The carpenter and plumber have a statutory lien on his house for $2,000.

Tax Liens: Federal, state and local governments have the authority to impose liens on your property if you owe delinquent taxes. Tax liens are usually impossible to eliminate in bankruptcy.

Advantage: Redemption is a great option if you owe more than the property is worth. The creditor must accept the current value of the item as payment in full.

Disadvantage: Generally, redemption requires immediate lump-sum payment of the value of the item; it may be difficult to come up with that much cash on short notice. You can try to get the creditor to accept your redemption payments in installments, but few courts require a creditor to accept installment payments.

Restrictions: You can redeem property only if all of the following are true:

- The debt is a consumer debt. This means it was incurred "primarily for a personal, family or household purpose." This includes just about everything except business debts.
- The property is tangible personal property. Tangible property is anything you can touch. For instance, a car, furniture, boat, computer, jewelry and furs are all examples of tangible property. Stocks are intangible. The property must also be personal property, which simply means it can't be real estate.
- The property is either:
  - claimed as exempt (exempt property is explained in Ch. 2, *Your Property and Bankruptcy*), or
  - abandoned by the trustee. A trustee will abandon property that has little or no nonexempt value beyond the amount of the liens. If property is abandoned, you'll receive notice in the mail. You can then redeem the property by paying the secured creditor its current market value. You may have to amend your Statement of Intention if you follow this course. Call the trustee and find out. (See Ch. 4, *Handling Your Case in Court*, Section B, for how to amend a form.)

When to use it: Use redemption only if you owe more than the property is worth and lien avoidance is not available.

Redemption usually makes sense for keeping small items of household property, where raising money for the lump-sum payment will not be that difficult and the cost of replacing the property would be much greater.

Redemption can also be used for automobiles, which are not eligible for lien avoidance and are likely to be repossessed if a lien remains after bankruptcy and you don't agree to keep making payments. If the creditor won't agree to installment payments, however, raising the cash necessary to redeem an automobile may be difficult.

How it works: You and the creditor must agree on the value of the property, and then draft and sign a redemption agreement. Agreeing on the value may take a little negotiation. Also, sometimes you can get the creditor to agree to accept payments in installments by agreeing to a higher value. Whatever you agree to, put it in the redemption agreement. See Section E.3, below, for sample agreements and full instructions.

4. Reaffirm a Debt

Description: When you reaffirm a debt, both the creditor's lien on the collateral and your personal liability survive bankruptcy intact—as if you never filed for bankruptcy. You and the creditor draw up an agreement which sets out the amount you owe and the terms of the repayment. In return, you get to keep the property as long as you keep current on your payments.

If you default on your payments, the creditor can repossess the collateral. You can also be held liable for the difference between what the property is resold for and the unpaid amount of the agreement. This is called a "deficiency balance." Nearly all states permit deficiency balances for most types of property. About half of the states, however, don't allow them on repossessed personal property if the original purchase price was under a few thousand dollars.

You can cancel a reaffirmation agreement by notifying the creditor before either of the following, whichever occurs later:

- the date of your discharge, or
- 60 days after you filed the reaffirmation agreement with the bankruptcy court (this often happens at the discharge hearing).

If your case is already closed, however, you will not be able to switch to the other options listed in this chapter.

Advantages: Reaffirmation can be used when lien avoidance or redemption is unavailable or impractical. It provides a sure way to keep property, as long as you abide by the terms of the reaffirmation agreement.

Disadvantages: Because reaffirmation leaves you personally liable, there is no way to "walk away" from the debt, even if the property becomes worthless or you simply decide you no longer want it. You'll still be legally bound to pay the agreed-upon amount even if the property is damaged or destroyed. And because you can't file for Chapter 7 bankruptcy again until six years from the date of your discharge, you'll be stuck with the debt.

EXAMPLE: Tasha owns a computer worth $900. She owes $1,500 on it. She reaffirms the debt for the full $1,500. Two months after bankruptcy, she spills a soft drink into the disk drive and the computer is a total loss. Now, she has not only lost the computer, but because she reaffirmed the debt, she still must pay the creditor the $1,500.

Restrictions: Reaffirmation can be used on any kind of property and any kind of lien, but the creditor must agree to the terms of the reaffirmation and the court must approve it. The court can disapprove the agreement if it appears that the creditor is giving you a bum deal, or if you've failed to exercise other options that would be more in your favor.

When to use it: Because of the disadvantages of reaffirmation, it should be used only if redemption and lien avoidance are unavailable or impractical. Use it primarily for property you can't be without and only if you have good reason to believe you'll be able to pay off the balance.

For some types of property, such as automobiles or your home, reaffirmation may be the only practical way to keep the item. Also, reaffirmation can be a sensible way to keep property worth significantly more than what you owe on it.

If you do decide to reaffirm, try to get the creditor to accept less than the full amount you owe as full payment of the debt. (This doesn't apply when you reaffirm your mortgage.) As a general rule, you should never reaffirm a debt for more than the property is worth. A creditor will often accept a lower amount because that's all the creditor would get for the property if it were repossessed.

How it works: You and the creditor agree to the terms of the reaffirmation in a written "reaffirmation agreement" which is submitted and approved by the court at the discharge hearing. Generally, if you know you want to reaffirm a debt, keep current on your payments to stay on the good side of the creditor. If you're behind, the creditor has the right to demand that you get current before agreeing to a reaffirmation contract, but you usually have some room to negotiate. Complete instructions and sample reaffirmation agreements are in Section E.4, below.

NEGOTIATION NOTE

Negotiating with a creditor can be an intimidating experience. If you want help in negotiating a reaffirmation agreement and you think negotiation could save you a significant amount, consider hiring a good negotiator to deal with the creditor. (See Ch. 9, *Help Beyond the Book*.)

5. Retain Property Without Reaffirming or Redeeming

Description: Some bankruptcy courts allow you to keep secured property as long as you remain current on your payments under your contract with the creditor. If you fall behind, the creditor can take the property, but your personal liability for the debt is wiped out by the bankruptcy.

EXAMPLE: Jill owes $1,200 on her computer which was pledged as security when she bought it. One month after the close of her bankruptcy case, her computer slides off her desk and breaks into a million pieces. If Jill simply continued to pay off the lien without reaffirming, she could let the creditor repossess the now-useless property and be free of any liability.

Other courts limit your options for retaining property to surrendering or redeeming the property or reaffirming the debt. In those districts, if you do not use these methods, the creditor may repossess the property at any time, regardless of whether you are current on your payments. It is up to you to discuss with the creditor whether it would be willing to voluntarily forego repossessing the property as long as you keep current on the contract.

If your court has not ruled on this matter, consult a bankruptcy practitioner as to the local custom in your area. But because this is an unsettled and changing area of the law, even if your state or district is listed above, you may want to consult a bankruptcy practitioner to see if there's been a change.

Advantages: Informal repayment can be used when lien avoidance or redemption is not available and allows for payments in installments rather than a lump sum. Unlike reaffirmation, it also leaves you the option of walking away from a debt without being personally liable for the balance owed.

Disadvantage: Unless the court prohibits it (see above), a creditor can take property at any time—and probably will if the property can be easily resold.

Restrictions: Because informal repayment requires an agreement between you and the creditor, it can be used on any kind of property and any kind of lien. Some courts that have formally recognized this tactic, however, require the debtor to fully comply with the original terms of the contract, including any requirements to insure the collateral and pay interest on the principal due.

CAN YOU KEEP SECURED PROPERTY WITHOUT REAFFIRMING OR REDEEMING?

If your state (or district) is not listed below, your bankruptcy court has not yet ruled on whether
or not you can keep secured property by simply staying current on your payments.

STATE OR DISTRICT	YES	NO	MAYBE	CASE
Alabama		✔		*Taylor v. AGE Federal Credit Union*, 3 F.3d 1512 (11th Cir. 1993)
Arkansas (Eastern District)		✔		*In re Kennedy*, 137 B.R. 302 (E.D. Ark, 1992)
Arkansas (Western District)	✔			*In re Parker*, 142 B.R. 327 (W.D. Ark. 1992)
California (Central District)			✔	*In re Dever*, 164 B.R. 132 (C.D. Cal. 1994)
California (Eastern District)			✔	*In re Weir*, 173 B.R. 682 (E.D. Cal. 1994)
California (Southern District)			✔	*In re Bracamortes*, 166 B.R. 160 (S.D. Cal. 1994)
Colorado	✔			*Lowery Federal Credit Union v. West*, 882 F.2d 1543 (10th Cir. 1989)
Connecticut	✔			*In re Boodrow*, ___ F.3d ___ (2nd Cir. 1997)
Florida		✔		*Taylor v. AGE Federal Credit Union*, 3 F.3d 1512 (11th Cir. 1993)
Georgia		✔		*Taylor v. AGE Federal Credit Union*, 3 F.3d 1512 (11th Cir. 1993)
Idaho		✔		*In re Chavarria*, 117 B.R. 582 (D. Idaho 1990)
Illinois		✔		*In re Edwards*, 901 F.2d 1383 (7th Cir. 1990)
Indiana		✔		*In re Edwards*, 901 F.2d 1383 (7th Cir. 1990)
Kansas	✔			*Lowery Federal Credit Union v. West*, 882 F.2d 1543 (10th Cir. 1989)
Maryland	✔			*In re Belanger*, 962 F.2d 345 (4th Cir. 1992)
Massachusetts	✔			*In re Ogando, No. 96-42722-JFQ*
Michigan (Western District)		✔		*In re Schmidt*, 145 B.R. 543 (W.D. Mich. 1992)
Missouri (Western District)		✔		*In re Gerling*, 175 B.R. 295 (W.D. Mo. 1994)
New Mexico	✔			*Lowery Federal Credit Union v. West*, 882 F.2d 1543 (10th Cir. 1989)
New York	✔			*In re Boodrow*, ___ F.3d ___ (2nd Cir. 1997)
North Carolina	✔			*In re Belanger*, 962 F.2d 345 (4th Cir. 1992)
Ohio (Northern District)	✔			*In re Laubacher*, 150 B.R. 200 (N.D. Ohio 1992)
Oklahoma	✔			*Lowery Federal Credit Union v. West*, 882 F.2d 1543 (10th Cir. 1989)
Pennsylvania (Eastern District)	✔			*In re McNeil*, 128 B.R. 603 (E.D. Penn. 1991)
Pennsylvania (Western District)	✔			*In re Stefano*, 134 B.R. 824 (W.D. Penn. 1991)
South Carolina	✔			*In re Belanger*, 962 F.2d 345 (4th Cir. 1992)
Tennessee (Eastern District)		✔		*In re Whitaker*, 85 B.R. 788 (E.D. Tenn. 1992)
Tennessee (Western District)	✔			*In re Barriger*, 61 B.R. 506 (W.D. Tenn. 1986)
Texas (Western District)	✔			*In re Harper*, 143 B.R. 682 (W.D. Tex. 1992)
Utah	✔			*Lowery Federal Credit Union v. West*, 882 F.2d 1543 (10th Cir. 1989)
Vermont	✔			*In re Boodrow*, ___ F.3d ___ (2nd Cir. 1997)
Virginia	✔			*In re Belanger*, 962 F.2d 345 (4th Cir. 1992)
Washington (Western District)	✔			*In re Rosenow*, 22 B.R. 99 (W.D. Wash. 1982)
West Virginia	✔			*In re Belanger*, 962 F.2d 345 (4th Cir. 1992)
Wisconsin		✔		*In re Edwards*, 901 F.2d 1383 (7th Cir. 1990)
Wyoming	✔			*Lowery Federal Credit Union v. West*, 882 F.2d 1543 (10th Cir. 1989)

When to use it: Use this option if lien avoidance or redemption is not available, and you don't want to reaffirm the debt.

If your district does not force creditors to agree to this arrangement and you are worried about losing the property, contact the creditor to see if it will forego repossession as long as your payments are current. If losing the property would not be a major inconvenience, you might simply keep sending payments and gamble that the creditor won't bother to repossess as long as the checks keep coming.

Keep in mind that, because this option leaves the creditor in a vulnerable position, the creditor may be eager to repossess and resell the collateral before it declines in value any further. This is especially true for automobiles, which depreciate fast and can be easily resold. In such cases, your only options may be to reaffirm or redeem.

On the other hand, a creditor probably won't be eager to repossess property that isn't worth much or would be hard to resell. For this kind of property, you can probably get the creditor to agree to your paying off the lien in installments after bankruptcy without having to reaffirm the debt.

How it works: In the districts that allow it, you indicate on your Statement of Intention that you plan to retain the property by keeping current on your obligations—which may include monthly payments, insurance coverage and more—under the contract.

In the districts that do not allow it, ask the creditor to informally let you keep the property as long as you keep current on the contractual obligations. On the Statement of Intention, however, you indicate that you are surrendering the property—which means that the creditor doesn't have to wait for you to default to repossess. Complete instructions are in Section E.5, below.

6. Pay Off the Lien Later in a Follow-Up Chapter 13 Bankruptcy

Description: You can file what some bankruptcy practitioners call a "Chapter 20" bankruptcy—that is, filing for Chapter 13 bankruptcy immediately after completing a Chapter 7 bankruptcy. The Chapter 13 bankruptcy is used to pay off any liens remaining after your Chapter 7 case has wiped out your personal liability. And if the lien exceeds the value of the property, you can often get the lien fully discharged by simply paying the current value of the item, rather than the full amount of the lien.

Because this book covers Chapter 7 bankruptcies only, space does not permit us to give a full explanation of how to do a successful follow-up Chapter 13 case. For more infor-

mation, see *Chapter 13 Bankruptcy: Repay Your Debts*, by Robin Leonard (Nolo Press).

Advantage: Filing a follow-up Chapter 13 case allows you to pay off remaining liens over time, even if the creditor is demanding immediate payment.

Disadvantage: This strategy requires that you file for Chapter 13 bankruptcy, which means you must fill out another set of bankruptcy forms and pay another filing fee. This strategy also requires that you give up all of your disposable income over the next three to five years to the bankruptcy trustee. Staying involved in the bankruptcy system for three to five more years means that it may take that much longer before you can begin to rebuild your credit.

Restrictions: There are no restrictions on the use of the Chapter 20 technique. To file for Chapter 13 bankruptcy, however, your unsecured debts cannot exceed $250,000 and your secured debts cannot exceed $750,000.

When to use it: This remedy makes sense only if lien avoidance is not available or redemption is not practical. It can be particularly useful for dealing with liens on property you need to keep, but cannot raise the lump sum necessary to redeem the property.

How it works: You file your Chapter 13 petition as soon as you get your Chapter 7 discharge. This keeps the automatic stay in effect and prevents the creditor from taking steps to take your property. Then you work with the bankruptcy court trustee to set up your three- to five-year Chapter 13 payment plan.

7. Lien-Eliminating Techniques Beyond the Scope of This Book

Deep in the recesses of the bankruptcy code are other procedures for eliminating certain kinds of "non-consensual" liens. (11 U.S.C. § 522(h) gives a debtor the power to use a wide range of lien avoidance techniques available to the bankruptcy trustee. The techniques are found in §§ 545, 547, 548, 549, 553 and 724(a).) These liens include:

- liens securing the payment of penalties, fines or punitive damages, but which are not judicial liens, and
- non-consensual liens that were recorded or perfected while you were already insolvent or within the 90 days before you filed for bankruptcy.

Eliminating these liens requires the aid of an experienced bankruptcy professional.

D. Choosing the Best Options

Now it's time pick the best option for each of your secured debts. If an item has more than one lien on it, you might use different procedures to deal with each lien. For example, you might eliminate a judicial lien on exempt property through lien avoidance, and redeem the property to satisfy a purchase-money security interest.

The chart, below, summarizes the strategies discussed in this section.

No Matter Which Option You Choose Remember This Rule

If the option you're considering requires paying more than the current market value of the property you want to keep, it's a bad deal. There are usually ways you or a lawyer can keep any item of secured property by paying no more than the current value of the property.

---

1. What Property Should You Keep?

Be realistic about how much property you will be able to afford to keep after bankruptcy. Face the fact that you may not be able to keep everything, and decide which items you can do without.

These questions will help you decide whether an item is worth keeping:

- How important is the property to you?
- Will you need the property to help you make a fresh start after bankruptcy?
- How much would it cost to keep the property? (This will depend on what procedure you use.)
- Which would be more expensive: to redeem the property or to replace it?
- If you're considering installment payments, will you realistically be able to make the payments after bankruptcy?
- If you're considering surrendering your property and buying a replacement item, will you need a loan to purchase it and if so, will you be able to get such a loan after bankruptcy?

EXAMPLE 1: Fran bought a sports car two years ago for $16,000. Now Fran is unemployed, but is about to start a new job. She still owes $13,000 on the car, and it is currently worth $10,000. Although she likes the car, she can't come up with the $10,000 in cash to redeem it, and she doesn't want to remain personally liable for the $13,000 debt. If Fran is willing to lower her standards a little, she can buy a reliable used car to get her to work and back for about $3,000. She decides to surrender the car. Now she will have to buy the new, lower-priced car, but she may have difficulty getting a loan for it.

EXAMPLE 2: Joe owns a six-year-old Toyota worth $2,000. It is security for a debt of $2,500. If Joe files for bankruptcy, he will probably be able to keep the car by paying the secured creditor only $2,000 (the value of the car). Joe decides it's worth paying that amount. He knows the car is reliable and will probably last another six years. He also believes it would be a hassle to find a car of comparable quality at that price, and it's his only means of getting to work. And, after some realistic budgeting, Joe concludes that making the payments after bankruptcy will not wreck his budget. He has probably made the right decision.

OPTIONS FOR DEALING WITH SECURED PROPERTY

How to Use This Chart: Answer the questions in columns 1 through 4 to narrow down your options. After you've answered all the questions, follow across from your answer in column 4 to find your options. Read all sections listed in *italics* for more information about each option. (N/A = Not Applicable)

1 Do you want to keep the property?	2 Is the property exempt?	3 Is the property an auto-mobile? (If yes, but it is a tool of your trade, choose "No")	4 What kind of lien is on the property?	Your options
No	N/A	N/A	N/A	Surrender *(Section C.1)*
Yes	No	No *(Section D.4)*	Any Kind	Informally repay—continue to pay off the lien, but do not reaffirm debt *(Section C.5)* Redeem if the trustee abandons the property *(Section C.3)* Reaffirm *(Section C.4)* Surrender and buy replacement property *(Section C.1)*
	Yes	Yes *(Section D.2)*	Any Kind	Redeem if the trustee abandons the property *(Section C.3)* Reaffirm *(Section C.4)* Surrender and buy replacement property *(Section C.1)*
		No *(Section D.3)*	Purchase-Money Security Interest	Redeem *(Section C.3)* Reaffirm if property is worth more than debt (Section C.4) Informally repay—continue to pay off the lien, but do not reaffirm debt *(Section C.5)* File a follow-up Chapter 13 bankruptcy *(Section C.5.b)*
			Non-purchase-Money Security Interest	Avoid lien *(Subject to limitations described in Section C.2)* Redeem *(Section C.3)* Informally repay—continue to pay off the lien, but do not reaffirm debt *(Section C.5)* File a follow-up Chapter 13 bankruptcy *(Section C.5.b)* Reaffirm *(Section C.4)*
			Judicial Lien	Avoid lien *(Section C.2)* Redeem *(Section C.3)* Informally repay—continue to pay off the lien, but do not reaffirm debt *(Section C.5)* File a follow-up Chapter 13 bankruptcy *(Section C.5.b)* Reaffirm *(Section C.4)*
			Statutory Lien	Redeem *(Section C.3)* Reaffirm if property is worth more than debt *(Section C.4)* Informally repay—continue to pay off the lien, but do not reaffirm debt *(Section C.5)* File a follow-up Chapter 13 bankruptcy *(Section C.5.b)*
		Yes *(Section D.2)*	Security Interest	Redeem *(Section C.3)* Reaffirm if property is worth more than debt *(Section C.4)* Surrender and buy replacement property *(Section C.1)*
			Judicial Lien	Avoid lien *(Section C.2)* Redeem *(Section C.3)* Reaffirm if property is worth more than debt *(Section C.4)*
			Statutory Lien	Redeem *(Section C.3)* Reaffirm if property is worth more than debt *(Section C.4)* Surrender and buy replacement property *(Section C.1)*

⚠️ **KEEP UP WITH YOUR PAYMENTS**
If you are thinking of using reaffirmation, paying off a lien outside of bankruptcy or redeeming property by paying in installments, being current on your payments will make negotiations go more smoothly, and may persuade the creditor to cut you some slack.

2. Motor Vehicles or Real Estate

Liens on cars or real estate involve special considerations.

a. Your Home

Filing for bankruptcy when you own a house is discussed in Ch. 6, *Your House,* but a few words about eliminating liens are appropriate here. If you own a home and want to file for bankruptcy, Chapter 13 bankruptcy is almost always the better option. Mortgage liens cannot be eliminated or reduced in Chapter 7 bankruptcy, and Chapter 7 bankruptcy won't stop a foreclosure if you are behind on payments.

If you are current on your mortgage, however, Chapter 7 bankruptcy might help you eliminate other liens on your house. To determine if any liens can be eliminated, total up the amount of your mortgage(s), applicable homestead exemption and other liens on your home. If the total exceeds the value of your home, you can probably eliminate some of the liens.

You can use lien avoidance to get rid of judicial liens if they conflict with your homestead exemption. And this can be done without a lawyer's help. (Lien avoidance is explained in Section C.2, above; the forms necessary to carry it out are in Section E.2, below.)

Liens on your home that might be eliminated with the help of a lawyer are "unrecorded" tax liens and liens for penalties, fines or punitive damages from a lawsuit. (See Section C.6, above.)

b. Your Car

Because repossessed motor vehicles can easily be resold, it is likely that if a lien remains on your car, the creditor will act quickly to either repossess it or force its sale. For this reason, if you intend to keep your car, you should deal with liens on it during bankruptcy.

If your automobile is exempt, any judicial liens on it can be eliminated through lien avoidance. (See Section C.2, above.)

The purchase-money security interest held by the seller can be dealt with only through redemption or reaffirmation. Raising the lump-sum amount necessary for a redemption is your best option. (See Section C.3, above.) If

that is not possible, your only realistic option is to reaffirm the debt. (See Section C.4, above.) Proposals for informal repayment are likely to be rejected by the creditor. (See Section C.5, above.)

If your automobile falls within the "tool of trade" exemption, you can use lien avoidance for any non-purchase-money liens on the vehicle. (See Section C.2, above.)

3. Exempt Property

Liens on exempt property can be dealt with in four different ways:

- lien avoidance
- redemption
- informal payment of the lien, or
- reaffirmation.

Lien avoidance should be used whenever possible to eliminate judicial liens and nonpurchase-money security interests. Use redemption whenever the lien exceeds the value of the property and you can raise the lump sum amount necessary to buy the property back at its current market value.

If you can't raise the lump sum necessary for redemption, you'll have to either reaffirm the debt or pay off the lien outside of bankruptcy. Which option you choose depends on how anxious the creditor is to repossess the item. If the property is of little value you can probably get away with informally paying off the lien. Property of greater value, however, may require reaffirmation. Remember to never agree to pay more than the property is currently worth.

Bear in mind that, even if you can get liens wiped out, you still may not get to keep the property, if the property is worth more than your exemption amount. The trustee will want to sell the property, pay you your exemption amount in cash, and distribute the remaining portion among your unsecured creditors.

In this situation, the only way to hold on to the property is to buy it back from the trustee. How much you have to pay depends on several factors, but keep in mind this basic rule: The amount you offer to the trustee has to leave your secured and unsecured creditors no worse off than they would have been had the trustee sold the property to somebody else.

> **EXAMPLE:** Mindy has a $1,000 asset on which she can claim a $500 exemption. There is a $200 judicial lien on the asset. Mindy cannot avoid the lien because it does not "impair" her exemption. If the trustee sold the property, Mindy would get her $500 exemption, the lienholder would get his $200, and the remaining $300 would go to Mindy's unsecured creditors. If Mindy wanted to buy the property from the trustee, she'd have to offer him $500: $200 for the lienholder, and $300 for her unsecured creditors.

As you can see, the amount you have to offer the trustee will vary from case to case, depending on the amount of the liens, the amount of your exemption, and whether you or the trustee can eliminate the liens on the asset. You can consult with the trustee to work out the particulars.

4. Nonexempt Property

If you want to keep nonexempt property, your options are limited. You can:

- redeem the property if the trustee "abandons" it (abandoning property means that the trustee releases it from the bankruptcy estate; a trustee will abandon property when there is not enough value in it to justify selling it to raise money for the unsecured creditors)
- reaffirm the debt, or
- pay off the lien informally outside of bankruptcy.

a. Property Worth More Than the Debt

If your nonexempt property is worth more than the liens on it, you probably won't have a chance to keep it. The trustee is likely to sell the property, pay off the liens and distribute the rest of the proceeds to your unsecured creditors.

> **EXAMPLE:** Elena pledges her $4,000 car as security for a $900 loan. The $900 lien is the only lien on her car, and only $1,200 of the $4,000 is exempt. If Elena files for bankruptcy, the trustee will take the car, sell it, pay off the $900 lien, give Elena her $1,200 exemption and distribute the rest of the proceeds to Elena's creditors.

If the trustee does not take the property, and you want to keep it, your best bet is probably to reaffirm the debt. This will keep the creditor from taking the property. (See Sections C.4, above and E.4, below, for complete instructions.)

b. Property Worth Less Than the Debt

If the property is worth less than the liens on it, the trustee will probably abandon the property.

> **EXAMPLE:** When Stan bought his $500 sofa on credit from the Reliable Furniture Co., he pledged the sofa as security. Since then, the sofa has declined in value to only $100, but he still owes $250 on it. The trustee will abandon the property because its sale would yield no proceeds for the unsecured creditors.

The trustee might also abandon property if the collateral has more than one lien on it, and the combined total of all the liens exceeds the value of the collateral. In this case, the creditors with the lowest priority liens are called "undersecured" creditors. (The priority of liens is determined by state and federal law. Generally, the most recent lien is the lowest priority lien, but certain types of liens always have priority over others.)

> **EXAMPLE:** Aaron's car is currently worth $3,000. He pledged his car as collateral for the loan he used to buy it. That loan has a remaining balance of $2,200. He later pledged his car for two personal loans on which he owes $500 each. In addition, there is a judgment lien against his car for $1,000. The total balance of all liens is $4,200.
>
> In this situation, the original $2,200 purchase-money loan is fully secured, and so is the first personal loan for $500. The other $500 loan is secured only by the remaining $300 in equity, and so it is an undersecured claim. And there is nothing securing the $1,000 judgment, so it is undersecured.

When the trustee abandons the property, you have the right to buy it back (redeem it) at its current market value. This is your best option, if you can come up with the lump sum payment or if the creditor will accept redemption in installments. Redemption eliminates all liens on the property. (See Section C.3, above.)

If you can't come up with the lump sum necessary to redeem the property, and the creditor won't agree to installment payments, reaffirmation is the only sure way to keep the property. If you are willing to gamble that the creditor won't take the property as long as you keep up your payments, you always have the option of simply continuing paying off the lien outside of bankruptcy. Whatever option you choose, just remember not to pay more than the property is worth.

GETTING BACK EXEMPT PROPERTY REPOSSESSED JUST BEFORE BANKRUPTCY

If, during the 90 days before you filed for bankruptcy, a secured creditor took exempt property that would qualify for either lien avoidance or redemption, you may be able to get the property back. But you must act quickly—before the creditor resells the property. If the creditor has already resold the property, you probably can't get it back. Repossessed cars are usually resold very quickly, but used furniture may sit in a warehouse for months.

Legally, the creditor must give back such property because the repossession is an illegal "preference," and the property is still part of the bankruptcy estate. (11 U.S.C. §§ 542, 543, 547; see Ch. 2, *Your Property and Bankruptcy,* Section A.3.) In practice, however, the creditor won't give it back unless the court orders it (which usually means you'll need the help of a lawyer) or unless you make a reasonable offer of cash.

Assuming you don't want to hire a lawyer, you probably won't be able to get an item back unless you talk the creditor into allowing you to redeem it or re-affirm. The creditor might prefer to have cash in hand rather than used property sitting in a warehouse. If you plan to avoid the lien on the exempt item and not pay anything, however, the creditor probably won't turn over the property unless forced to by court order.

Whether it's worth the expense of a court order to get back an exempt item so you can avoid the lien depends on how badly you need the property and how much you'll save through lien avoidance. Compare how much it would cost to redeem the property or buy replacement property. If those options are cheaper, or you decide you can get along without the property, don't bother with the court order.

PLANNING REMINDER
Once you've filed for bankruptcy, a creditor cannot legally take your property. And, as you now know, it's much easier to keep property than it is to get it back after the creditor repossesses it. So if you have some exempt property that a creditor is about to take, and you haven't filed for bankruptcy yet, you may want to file right away to prevent the seizure.

E. Step-by-Step Instructions

Once you decide what to do with each item of secured property, you must list your intentions on your Statement of Intention, file that form and then carry out the procedures within 45 days. (See Ch. 3, *Filling in and Filing the Bankruptcy Forms,* for instructions.)

1. How to Surrender Property

If you plan to surrender any secured property, here's how to proceed.

Step 1: When you fill out your Statement of Intention, state that you are surrendering the property that secures the debt. (Instructions are in Ch. 3.)

Step 2: The creditor, who will receive a copy of the Statement of Intention, must make arrangements to pick up the property. It's not your responsibility to get the property back to the creditor. If the creditor never comes to pick it up, so much the better for you. If the creditor does pick it up, get a receipt. (See sample receipt, below.)

RECEIPT FOR SURRENDER OF PROPERTY

1. This receipt certifies that _____ name of repossessor (print) _____ took the following item(s): (List items)

_____
_____
_____

on _date_, 19__, because of debt owed to _name of creditor (print)_.

2. _Name of repossessor (print)_ is an authorized agent of _name of creditor (print)_.

Signed: _Your signature_ Dated: _____

Signed: _Repossessor's signature_ Dated: _____

2. How to Avoid Liens on Exempt Property

To avoid a lien, you claim the property as exempt on your Statement of Intention, and file a separate request (motion) with the bankruptcy court. Filing a motion to avoid a lien is quite simple and can be done without a lawyer.

What goes on your motion papers depends on the kind of lien you're trying to get eliminated. Read Subsection a, below, if you're dealing with a nonpossessory nonpurchase-money security interest, and Subsection b, below, if you want to avoid a judicial lien.

a. Eliminating Nonpossessory Nonpurchase-Money Security Interests

Before you file a motion to avoid a lien, be sure:

- you have a nonpossessory nonpurchase-money secured debt (defined in Section C.1, above), and
- the secured property qualifies for lien avoidance (see Section C.2, above).

In most courts, you must file your motion with the court within 30 days after you file for bankruptcy. But some courts require it to be filed before the creditors' meeting. Check your local rules.

You will need to fill out one complete set of forms for each affected creditor—generally, each creditor holding a lien on that property. Sample forms are at the end of this section. Some courts have their own forms; if yours does, use those forms and adapt these instructions to fit them.

Step 1: If your court publishes local rules, refer to them for time limits, format of papers and other details of a motion proceeding.

Step 2: Make at least five copies of the blank, line-numbered legal paper in Appendix 4 (to allow for mistakes). Use those sheets to type your motion to avoid the lien. Type from line number 1 to line 13 as follows (see samples, below):

    Line 1: Your name, and that of your spouse if you're filing jointly.

    Line 1.5: Your address.

    Line 2: Your city, state and zip code.

    Line 2.5: Your phone number.

    Line 3: Type: Debtor in Pro Per.

    Line 7: Center and type UNITED STATES BANKRUPTCY COURT, in capital letters.

    Line 8: Center and type the judicial district and state you are in. Get this information from your local bankruptcy court or from your bankruptcy petition.

Lines
    9-12: Type as shown in the example.

Note: Not all courts have separate "AL" (avoid lien) numbers. Leave that space blank until you file your papers with the court.

Step 3: Make a dozen photocopies of the page with the information you have typed so far. This will save you typing later, because you can use this same heading for all the forms mentioned in this section.

Step 4: Using one of the copies that you just made, start typing again at line 14. Prepare a Motion to Avoid Nonpossessory, Nonpurchase-Money Security Interest, as shown in the example, below.

Step 5: Call the court clerk and give your name and case number. Say you'd like to file a motion to avoid a lien and need to find out when and where the judge will hear arguments on your motion. The clerk will give you a hearing date; ask for one at least 31 days in the future, because you must mail notice of your motion at least 30 days before the hearing (unless local rules state differently). Write down the information.

If the clerk will not give you this information over the phone, go to the federal courthouse with a copy of your Motion to Avoid Nonpossessory, Nonpurchase-Money Security Interest form filled out. You can file that form alone and schedule a hearing. Be sure to write down the information about when and where your motion will be heard by the judge.

Step 6: Prepare a proposed Order to Avoid Nonpossessory, Nonpurchase-Money Security Interest for the judge to sign, granting your request. (See sample, below.) Specify exactly what property the creditor has secured, in the space indicated in the sample. You can get this information from the security agreement you signed, which should also match what you put on Schedule B. Make two extra copies, and take them with you to the hearing.

The court's local rules may require you to file the proposed order with the rest of your motion papers.

Step 7: Prepare a Notice of Motion putting the place, date and time of the hearing in the places indicated on the sample.

Step 8: Prepare at least two Proofs of Service by Mail, as shown in the sample; one for each affected creditor and one for the trustee. These forms state that a friend or relative of yours, who is at least 18 years old and not a party to the bankruptcy, mailed your papers to the creditor(s) or the trustee. Fill in the blanks with your friend's name, county, state, address and zip code as indicated. Put the creditor's (or trustee's) name on line 22. On line 25, put the city or town of the post office that your friend will mail your papers from.

Have your friend sign and date the form at the end as indicated on the sample.

Step 9: Make at least three extra copies of all forms.

Step 10: Keep both copies of the Proof of Service. Put one copy of the Motion, Notice of Motion and proposed Order in a stamped envelope with sufficient postage, and have your friend mail them to the affected creditor(s) and the trustee.

Step 11: File the original copy of the Notice of Motion, Motion, (proposed Order, if required in your area) and Proof of Service with the bankruptcy court. There is no fee.

Step 12: The trustee or creditors affected by your motion may submit a written response. In most areas they are not required to respond in writing and can simply show up in court to argue their side. In some courts, however, if the trustee or a creditor doesn't file a written response to your motion, it may be automatically granted. Consult your local rules.

Step 13: Attend the hearing. The hearing is usually very short, ten minutes or less. Because you filed the motion, you argue your side first. Explain briefly how your property falls within the acceptable categories of exempt property listed in 11 U.S.C. § 522(f)(2) (see Section B.2, above), that the lien on it is a nonpossessory nonpurchase-money security interest and that the lien impairs your exemption.

The Bankruptcy Code states that a lien on exempt property can be eliminated to the extent the lien "impairs" the exemption. Impairs is defined in 11 U.S.C. § 522(f)(2).

Then the trustee or creditor (or an attorney) responds. The judge either decides the matter and signs your proposed order, or "takes it under advisement" and mails you the order in a few days.

There is rarely a penalty if you lose. If, however, a judge believes that you had no reasonable basis for your motion, or if you don't show up for the hearing, you may be required to pay the creditor's costs and reasonable attorney's fees associated with defending against your motion—often $200 to $300.

b.   Eliminating a Judicial Lien

To have a judicial lien eliminated, follow the procedure for filing a motion in Subsection a, above, but use the Motion to Avoid Judicial Lien and Order to Avoid Judicial Lien forms. Samples are shown below.

If you are eliminating a judicial lien on your home, use the Motion to Avoid Judicial Lien (on Real Estate) and Order to Avoid Judicial Lien (on Real Estate) in this chapter as samples.

MOTION TO AVOID NONPOSSESSORY, NONPURCHASE-MONEY SECURITY INTEREST

John Doe
1111 Any Street
Berkeley, CA 00000
(510) 000-0000
Debtor in Pro Per

UNITED STATES BANKRUPTCY COURT

[name of district]   DISTRICT OF   [your state]

[name of division, if any] DIVISION

In re:
[your name(s)]

Case No. [Copy from your petition]

Chapter 7

AL [This no. may be assigned by the clerk]
(No.)

Debtor(s)

MOTION TO AVOID NONPOSSESSORY, NONPURCHASE-MONEY SECURITY INTEREST

1. Debtors [your name(s)] , filed a voluntary petition for relief under Chapter 7 of Title 11 of the United States Code on [date you filed for bankruptcy] .

2. This court has jurisdiction over this motion, filed pursuant to 11 U.S.C. § 522(f), to avoid a nonposses-sory nonpurchase-money security interest held by [name of lienholder] on property held by the debtor.

3. On or about [date you incurred the debt] , debtors borrowed $ [amount of loan] from [name of creditor] . As security for loan, [name of creditor] insisted upon, and the debtors executed, a note and security agreement granting to [name of creditor] a security interest in and on the debtor's personal property, which consisted of [items held as security as they are listed in your loan agreement] which are held primarily for the family and household use of the debtors and their dependents.

4. All such possessions of debtors have been claimed as fully exempt in their bankruptcy case.

5. The money borrowed from [name of creditor] does not represent any part of the purchase money of any of the articles covered in the security agreement executed by the debtors, and all of the articles so covered remain in the possession of the debtors.

6. The existence of [name of creditor] 's lien on debtor's household and personal goods impairs exemptions to which the debtors would be entitled under 11 U.S.C. § 522(b).

WHEREFORE, pursuant to 11 U.S.C. § 522(f), debtors pray for an order avoiding the security interest in their personal and household goods, and for such additional or alternative relief as may be just and proper.

Dated: _____

Dated: _____

_____
Debtor in Propria Persona

_____
Debtor in Propria Persona

Address

ORDER TO AVOID NONPOSSESSORY, NONPURCHASE-MONEY SECURITY INTEREST & NOTICE OF MOTION TO AVOID NONPOSSESSORY, NONPURCHASE-MONEY SECURITY INTEREST

John Doe
1111 Any Street
Berkeley, CA 00000
(510) 000-0000
Debtor in Pro Per

UNITED STATES BANKRUPTCY COURT

_____ [name of district] DISTRICT OF _____ [your state]

_____ [name of division, if any] DIVISION

In re:
[your name(s)]

Case No. _____ [Copy from your petition]

Chapter 7

AL _____ [This no. may be assigned by the clerk]
(No.)

_____ Debtor(s)

ORDER TO AVOID NONPOSSESSORY, NONPURCHASE-MONEY SECURITY INTEREST

The motion of the above-named debtor(s) _____ [your name(s)], to avoid the lien of the respondent, _____ [name of creditor] is sustained.

The lien is a nonpossessory, nonpurchase-money lien that impairs the debtor's exemptions in the following property: _____ [list all items held as security as listed in your loan agreement]

Unless debtor's bankruptcy case is dismissed, the lien of the respondent is hereby extinguished and the lien shall not survive bankruptcy or affix to or remain enforceable against the aforementioned property of the debtor. _____ [name of creditor] shall take all necessary steps to remove any record of the lien from the aforementioned property of the debtor.

Dated: _____ _____ U.S. Bankruptcy Judge

John Doe
1111 Any Street
Berkeley, CA 00000
(510) 000-0000
Debtor in Pro Per

UNITED STATES BANKRUPTCY COURT

_____ [name of district] DISTRICT OF _____ [your state]

_____ [name of division, if any] DIVISION

In re:
[your name(s)]

Case No. _____ [Copy from your petition]

Chapter 7

AL _____ [This no. may be assigned by the clerk]
(No.)

_____ Debtor(s)

NOTICE OF MOTION TO AVOID NONPOSSESSORY, NONPURCHASE-MONEY SECURITY INTEREST

Please take notice of motion is set for a hearing on: _____ [leave blank] 19___, at

___ o'clock ___ .m. at _____ [leave blank—location of bankruptcy court] in

courtroom _____ [leave blank].

MOTION TO AVOID JUDICIAL LIEN

John Doe
1111 Any Street
Berkeley, CA 00000
(510) 000-0000
Debtor in Pro Per

UNITED STATES BANKRUPTCY COURT

[Name of district]   DISTRICT OF   _[your state]_

[name of division, if any] DIVISION

In re:
[your name(s)]

               Debtor(s)

Case No. _[Copy from your petition]_

Chapter 7

AL _[This no. may be assigned by the clerk]_
(No.)

MOTION TO AVOID JUDICIAL LIEN

1. Debtor(s) _[your name(s)]_ commenced this case on _[date you filed for bankruptcy]_ by filing a voluntary petition for relief under Chapter 7 of Title 11 of the United States Code.

2. This court has jurisdiction over this motion, filed pursuant to 11 U.S.C. § 522(f) to avoid and cancel a judicial lien held by _[name of judicial lienholder]_ on property held by the debtor.

3. On _[date judicial lien was recorded]_, creditors recorded a judicial lien against the following items of debtor's property:

     [list all exempt property affected by lien]

This judicial lien is entered of record as follows:

     [list judicial lien including date of the lien, amount and court case number]

4. All such possessions of debtor(s) have been claimed as fully exempt in their bankruptcy case.

/ / /

5. The existence of _[name of creditor]'s_ lien on debtor's household and personal goods impairs exemptions to which the debtor(s) would be entitled under 11 U.S.C. § 522 (b).

WHEREFORE, debtor(s) pray for an order against _[name of lienholder]_, avoiding and cancelling the judicial lien in the above-mentioned property, and for such additional or alternative relief as may be just and proper.

Dated: _____

        _____
        Debtor in Propria Persona

Dated: _____

        _____
        Debtor in Propria Persona

        Address

NOTICE OF MOTION TO AVOID JUDICIAL LIEN & ORDER TO AVOID JUDICIAL LIEN

John Doe
1111 Any Street
Berkeley, CA 00000
(510) 000-0000
Debtor in Pro Per

UNITED STATES BANKRUPTCY COURT

[name of district] DISTRICT OF _[your state]_

[name of division, if any] DIVISION

In re:
[your name(s)]   Case No. ___ _[Copy from your petition]_

    Chapter 7

    AL ___ _[This no. may be assigned by the clerk]_
    (No.)

    Debtor(s)

NOTICE OF MOTION TO AVOID JUDICIAL LIEN

Please take notice of motion set for a hearing on: ___ _[leave blank]_ , 19___

at ___ o'clock ___ .m. at ___ _[leave blank—location of bankruptcy court]_

in courtroom ___ _[leave blank]_

John Doe
1111 Any Street
Berkeley, CA 00000
(510) 000-0000
Debtor in Pro Per

UNITED STATES BANKRUPTCY COURT

[name of district] DISTRICT OF _[your state]_

[name of division, if any] DIVISION

In re:
[your name(s)]   Case No. ___ _[Copy from your petition]_

    Chapter 7

    AL ___ _[This no. may be assigned by the clerk]_
    (No.)

    Debtor(s)

ORDER TO AVOID JUDICIAL LIEN

The motion of the above-named debtor(s), ___ _[your name(s)]_ , to avoid the lien of

the respondent, ___ _[name of creditor]_ , is sustained.

The lien is a judicial lien that impairs the exemption as follows:

___ _[list all exempt property subject to the judicial lien]_

Unless debtor's bankruptcy case is dismissed, the lien of the respondent is hereby extinguished and the lien shall not survive bankruptcy or affix to or remain enforceable against the aforementioned property of the debtor.

___ _[name of creditor]_ shall take all necessary steps to remove any record of the lien from the aforementioned property of the debtor.

Dated: ___

___ U.S. Bankruptcy Judge

MOTION TO AVOID JUDICIAL LIEN (ON REAL ESTATE)

```
 1   John Doe
 2   1111 Any Street
 3   Berkeley, CA 00000
     (510) 000-0000
     Debtor in Pro Per
 4
 5
 6
 7
 8
 9                    UNITED STATES BANKRUPTCY COURT

10          [name of district]   DISTRICT OF   [your state]
                  [name of division, if any]   DIVISION
11   In re:
12   [your name(s)]                   Case No.  [Copy from your petition]
13                                    Chapter 7
14                                    AL  [This no. may be assigned by the clerk]
15                Debtor(s)               (No.)
16
17           MOTION TO AVOID JUDICIAL LIEN ON REAL ESTATE
18       1.  Debtor(s)  [your name(s)] , commenced this case on  [date you filed for
19   bankruptcy]   by filing a voluntary petition for relief under Chapter 7 of Title 11 of the United States Code.
20       2.  This court has jurisdiction over this motion, filed pursuant to 11 U.S.C. § 522(f) to avoid and cancel a
21   judicial lien held by  [Name of judicial lienholder]  on real property used as the debtor's residence, under 28
22   U.S.C. § 1334.
23       3.  On  [date judicial lien was recorded] , creditors recorded a judicial lien against debtor's residence
24   at  [your address, city, state, zip code] . This judicial lien is entered of record as follows:
25           [list judicial lien including date of the lien, amount and court case number]
26       4.  The debtor's interest in the property referred to in the preceding paragraph and encumbered by the lien
27   has been claimed as fully exempt in their bankruptcy case.
28       ///
```

```
 1       5.  The existence of  [name of judicial lienholder]  's lien on debtor's real property impairs exemptions
 2   to which the debtor(s) would be entitled under 11 U.S.C. §555(b).
 3       WHEREFORE, debtor(s) request an order against  [name of judicial lienholder] , avoiding and cancelling
 4   the judicial lien in the above-mentioned property, and for such additional or alternative relief as may be just and
 5   proper.
 6   Dated: _____
 7                                               Debtor in Propria Persona
 8   Dated: _____
 9                                               Debtor in Propria Persona
10                                               Address
11
12
13
14
15
16
17
18
19
20
21
22
23
24
25
26
27
28
```

NOTICE OF MOTION TO AVOID JUDICIAL LIEN & ORDER TO AVOID JUDICIAL LIEN (ON REAL ESTATE)

John Doe
1111 Any Street
Berkeley, CA 00000
(510) 000-0000
Debtor in Pro Per

UNITED STATES BANKRUPTCY COURT

[name of district]   DISTRICT OF   _[your state]_

[name of division, if any]   DIVISION

In re:
[your name(s)]

Case No. ___ _[Copy from your petition]_

Chapter 7

AL ___ _[This no. may be assigned by the clerk]_
(No.)

Debtor(s)

ORDER AVOIDING JUDICIAL LIEN

The motion of the above-named debtor(s), ___ _[your name(s)]_ ___, to avoid the lien

of the respondent, ___ _[name of judicial lienholder]_ ___ is sustained.

It is hereby ORDERED AND DECREED that the judicial lien held by ___ _[Name of judicial lienholder]_ ___,

in debtor's residential real estate at ___ _[your address, city, state and zip]_ ___, entered of record at

___ _[describe the lien exactly as it appears on the public record]_ ___ be hereby canceled.

It is further ORDERED that unless debtor's bankruptcy case is dismissed, ___ _[name of judicial_

lienholder] ___ shall take all steps necessary and appropriate to release the judicial lien and remove it from the

local judgment index.

Dated: _____

_____
U.S. Bankruptcy Judge

John Doe
1111 Any Street
Berkeley, CA 00000
(510) 000-0000
Debtor in Pro Per

UNITED STATES BANKRUPTCY COURT

[name of district]   DISTRICT OF   _[your state]_

[name of division, if any]   DIVISION

In re:
[your name(s)]

Case No. ___ _[Copy from your petition]_

Chapter 7

AL ___ _[This no. may be assigned by the clerk]_
(No.)

Debtor(s)

NOTICE OF MOTION TO AVOID JUDICIAL LIEN

Please take notice of motion set for a hearing on: ___ _[leave blank]_ ___, 19 ___

at ___ o'clock ___ .m. at ___ _[leave blank—location of bankruptcy court]_

in courtroom ___ _[leave blank]_

PROOF OF SERVICE BY MAIL

1 | John Doe
1111 Any Street
2 | Berkeley, CA 00000
(510) 000-0000
3 | Debtor in Pro Per

4

5

6

7

8   UNITED STATES BANKRUPTCY COURT

9 | _____ *[name of district]* _____ DISTRICT OF _____ *[your state]* _____

10 | _____ *[name of division, if any]* _____ DIVISION

11 | In re:)
[your name(s)]   )
12 |)   Case No.___ *[Copy from your petition]* ___
)
13 |)   Chapter 7
)
14 | _____ Debtor(s) _____)   AL __*[This no. may be assigned by the clerk]*__
)   (No.)

15   PROOF OF SERVICE BY MAIL

16 | I, ___ *[friend's name]* ___ , declare that : I am a resident or employed in the County of ___*[the county*

17 | *where friend lives or works]* ___ , State of ___*[state where friend lives or works]* ___ . My residence/business

18 | address is ___*[friend's address]* ___ . I am over the age of eighteen years and not a party to this case.

19 | On ___*[leave blank]* ___ , 19___ . I served the Notice of Motion and Motion to Avoid Judicial Lien on

20 | *[creditor's name]* , by placing true and correct copies thereof enclosed in a sealed envelope with postage thereon

21 | fully prepaid in the United States Mail at ___*[city of post office where papers will be mailed]*___ , address as

22 | follows:

23 | *[address of affected creditor's and trustee]*

24 | I declare under penalty of perjury that the foregoing is true and correct, and that this declaration was

25 | executed on.

26 | Dated:___*[leave blank]*___ , 19_____ at ___*[leave blank]*_____
                                               (City and State)

27 | ___*[leave blank]*_____

28 | (Signature)

3. How to Redeem Property

If you want to redeem exempt or abandoned property, list the property on your Statement of Intention as property to be retained and check the column that says property will be redeemed. (More instructions are in Ch. 3, *Filling in and Filing the Bankruptcy Forms.*) You must pay the creditor the current market value of the property within 45 days after you file.

⚠ EXPLORE LIEN AVOIDANCE FIRST
If lien avoidance (Section C.2, above) is available, you may be able to get rid of a lien on exempt property without paying anything.

a. Agreeing on the Value of the Property

Before you can redeem property, you and the creditor must agree on what the property is worth. If you believe the creditor is setting too high a price for the property, tell the creditor why you think the property is worth less—it needs repair, it's falling apart, it's damaged or stained, or whatever. If you can't come to an agreement, you can ask the bankruptcy court to rule on the matter. But you will probably need an attorney to help you make this request, so it is not worth your while unless you and the creditor are very far apart.

You and the creditor should sign a redemption agreement, stating the terms of your agreement and the amount you are going to pay, in case there is a dispute later. (See the sample forms, Subsection d, below.)

b. If the Creditor Won't Cooperate

The creditor may refuse to let you redeem property, claiming that it isn't one of the types of property described in Section C.3 above or because you can't agree on the value. If so, you will need to file a formal complaint in the bankruptcy court to have a judge resolve the issue. You will need an attorney to help you, so think twice about whether you really want to redeem the property. It may be better just to let the creditor have it.

c. Paying in Installments

If you can't raise enough cash to pay the creditor within 45 days, try to get the creditor to let you pay in installments. Some creditors will agree if the installments are big enough and if you agree to pay interest on the installments. But a creditor is not required to accept installments and can demand the entire amount in cash.

If the creditor refuses to accept installments, you can ask the bankruptcy court to delay the time required for you to make the payment for a month or two. But to do so, you will need to file a formal complaint in the bankruptcy court. Again, you will need an attorney to help you, so it may not be worth it.

d. Paperwork

Below are two sample redemption agreements you can use to type up your agreement with the creditor. Form 1 is for installments, and Form 2 is for a lump sum payment. Type the form on legal paper (the blank paper in Appendix 4 with numbers down the left side) and put your bankruptcy case number on it in case you need to file it later. You should fill out one for every item of property you want to redeem. Have the creditor sign it.

There is no need to file these agreements with the trustee. Keep them with your other bankruptcy papers, in case the trustee or the judge wants to see them.

AGREEMENT FOR INSTALLMENT REDEMPTION OF PROPERTY

1	John Doe
	1111 Any Street
2	Berkeley, CA 00000
	(510) 000-0000
3	Debtor in Pro Per
4	
5	
6	
7	

8

UNITED STATES BANKRUPTCY COURT

9

_____ *[name of district]* _____ DISTRICT OF _____ *[your state]* _____

10

11 In re:
[your name(s)]   )   Case No._____ *[Copy from your petition]* _____
)
12   )   Chapter 7
)
13   )
)   AL __*[This no. may be assigned by the clerk]*__
14   Debtor(s)   )   (No.)

15

16 AGREEMENT FOR INSTALLMENT REDEMPTION OF PROPERTY

17 _____, (Debtor), and _____, (Creditor) agree that

18 1. Creditor owns a security interest in _____ (Collateral).

19 2. The value of Collateral is $_____.

20 3. Creditor's security interest is valid and enforceable despite the debtor's bankruptcy case.

21 4. If Debtor continues to make payments of $_____ a month on Creditor's security interest,

Creditor will take no action to repossess or foreclose its security.

22 5. Debtor's payments will continue until the amount of $_____, plus interest (to be computed at

23 the same annual percentage rate as in the original contract between the parties) is paid.

24 6. Upon being fully paid as specified in paragraph 5, Creditor will take all steps necessary to terminate its

25 security interest in Collateral.

26 Dated: _____   _____

27   Signature

28 Dated: _____   _____
                                      Signature

AGREEMENT FOR LUMP SUM REDEMPTION OF PROPERTY

1   John Doe
     1111 Any Street
2   Berkeley, CA 00000
     (510) 000-0000
3   Debtor in Pro Per

4

5

6

7

8   UNITED STATES BANKRUPTCY COURT

9   _____ *[name of district]* _____ DISTRICT OF _____ *[your state]* _____

10

11 In re:
     [your name(s)]   )   Case No. _____ *[Copy from your petition]* _____

12   )   Chapter 7

13

14   _____ Debtor(s) _____)

15

16   AGREEMENT FOR REDEMPTION OF PROPERTY

17 _____, (Debtor), and _____, (Creditor) agree that:

18   1. Creditor owns a security interest in _____ (Collateral).

19   2. The value of Collateral is $_____.

20   3. Creditor's security interest is valid and enforceable despite the debtor's bankruptcy case.

21   4. Debtor agrees to pay the full value of the collateral no later than _____.

22   5. Upon receiving the payment specified in paragraph 4, Creditor will take all steps necessary to terminate its

23 security interest in Collateral.

24

25

26 Dated: _____   _____
                                  Debtor in Propria Persona

27 Dated: _____   _____
                                  Debtor in Propria Persona

28

4. How to Reaffirm a Debt

If you decide to reaffirm a debt, you must list it as such on your Statement of Intention. Then, within 45 days of filing your Statement of Intention, you must:

- type and sign a Reaffirmation Agreement (a sample is below)
- prepare an Application for Approval of Reaffirmation Agreement and an Order Approving Reaffirmation Agreement (samples are below), and
- attend the discharge hearing, where the judge will probably warn you against reaffirmation and give you a chance to back out.

In the reaffirmation agreement, put the fair market value of the property as well as the amount you actually owe. The form agreement on the following page lets you reaffirm the debt only for an amount equal to or less than the value of the collateral. It also contains a written promise from the creditor not to take the item in return for your promise to pay the creditor a fixed amount equal to the current value of the property.

⚠ MAKE SURE YOUR REAFFIRMATION AGREEMENT ISN'T FOR TOO MUCH

If the creditor requires you to reaffirm for the full amount owed on the collateral (an amount that is greater than the current market value of the collateral), select another option unless you really, really want the property and won't otherwise be able to get similar property after bankruptcy. In general, you should try to avoid staying on the hook for a debt larger than the current value of the property you want to keep.

Your right to cancel reaffirmation agreements. The Bankruptcy Code gives you the right to cancel any reaffirmation agreement by notifying the creditor at any time:

- before you receive your discharge, or
- within 60 days after the reaffirmation agreement is filed with the bankruptcy court,

whichever is later. (11 U.S.C. § 524(c)(2).)

Notice to the creditor should be by certified mail, return receipt requested. This precludes the creditor from later claiming it was not notified.

Canceling your reaffirmation will leave your debt in the same condition as if you had never filed the reaffirmation agreement. That is, your personal liability for debt will be discharged (assuming the debt is dischargeable), and the creditor will be able to enforce its lien on your property, by either repossessing it or foreclosing on it. If your bankruptcy case is still open, you can still try other options discussed in this chapter.

Bankruptcy courts frown on reaffirmation agreements because they obligate debtors to make payments after bankruptcy, which contradicts bankruptcy's purpose. If you elect to reaffirm a debt, the trustee will question you about it at the meeting of the creditors. (See Ch. 4, *Handling Your Case in Court*, Section A.3.) In addition, your reaffirmation agreement must include a statement that you understand that bankruptcy law does not require you to reaffirm a debt. The agreement must also include a statement that you either were advised by a lawyer of the consequence of reaffirming a debt or were not represented by a lawyer in negotiating the reaffirmation agreement.

REAFFIRMATION AGREEMENT

John Doe
1111 Any Street
Berkeley, CA 00000
(510) 000-0000
Debtor in Pro Per

UNITED STATES BANKRUPTCY COURT

[name of district] DISTRICT OF _[your state]_

[name of division, if any] DIVISION

In re:
[your name(s)]

Case No. _[Copy from your petition]_

Chapter 7

_____
Debtor(s)

REAFFIRMATION AGREEMENT

[Your name(s)] the debtor in the above-captioned bankruptcy case, and _[name of creditor]_ hereby agree that:

1. _[Your name(s)]_, subject to the approval of the bankruptcy court and the statutory right to rescind, reaffirms _[his/her/their]_ debt of _[amount of debt]_ to _[name of creditor]_, secured by _[describe secured property]_, currently valued at _[current value of the secured item]_.

2. This debt will be paid in installments of _[amount per month]_ per month, at _[interest rate]_ simple interest, until it has been paid in full.

3. _[Name of creditor]_ agrees to waive all previous and current defaults on this debt.

4. _[Name of creditor]_ further agrees that it will not act to repossess the _[describe secured property]_ securing this debt unless the debtor is more than thirty days in default under this agreement.

///

5. _[Name of creditor]_ further agrees that, in the event of any deficiency judgment arising out of this transaction, it will not execute against the debtor's wages.

THIS AGREEMENT MAY BE CANCELLED BY THE DEBTOR ANY TIME BEFORE _[date 60 days after filing with the court]_ OR THE DATE OF THE BANKRUPTCY DISCHARGE IF THAT IS AFTER _[same date as above]_ BY GIVING NOTICE TO _[name of creditor]_.

Debtor is aware that reaffirming this debt is not required by the Bankruptcy Act, by nonbankruptcy law or by any agreement.

Debtor was not represented by an attorney during the course of negotiating this agreement.

Dated: _____ _____
[sign your name here]
[type your name here]

Dated: _____ _____
[creditor's signature]
for _[type creditor's name here]_

APPLICATION FOR APPROVAL OF REAFFIRMATION AGREEMENT PURSUANT TO 11 U.S.C. § 524(C)

```
 1   John Doe
 2   1111 Any Street
 3   Berkeley, CA 00000
     (510) 000-0000
     Debtor in Pro Per




               UNITED STATES BANKRUPTCY COURT

     _____ DISTRICT OF _____
     [name of district]            [your state]

     _____ DIVISION
     [name of division, if any]

     In re:
     [your name(s)]
                                   Case No. _____
                                            [Copy from your petition]
                                   Chapter 7

                    Debtor(s)

          APPLICATION FOR APPROVAL OF REAFFIRMATION
          AGREEMENT PURSUANT TO 11 U.S.C. § 524(C)

     TO THE HONORABLE _____ BANKRUPTCY JUDGE:

     The debtor(s) in this case, ___[your name(s)]___, hereby apply for approval of their reaffirmation
     agreement with ___[name of creditor]___. In support of this application we hereby aver that:

     1.   ___[Your name(s)]___, wish to reaffirm ___[his/hers/their]___ debt
          with ___[name of creditor]___, to the extent it is secured by ___[describe secured
          property]___.

     2.   The ___[describe secured property]___ is presently worth ___[current value of secured property]___.

     3.   The reaffirmation agreement, signed by the parties and providing for the payment of ___[current value
          of secured property]___ at ___[interest rate]___ interest, in ___[number of payments]___ monthly install-
          ments, is attached to this application.

     ///
```

```
 1   4.   The agreement does not impose a hardship on _____ ___[name(s) of debtor's]___
 2        ___[for our/my dependents, if any]___ because the debtor(s)' current income is $_____ per
 3        month, and expenses are $_____ per month.
 4
 5        WHEREFORE, the debtors pray that the reaffirmation of the aforesaid debt be approved.
 6
 7   Dated: _____     _____ [sign your name here]
 8                                [type your name here]
```

ORDER APPROVING REAFFIRMATION AGREEMENT

1 | John Doe
1111 Any Street
2 | Berkeley, CA 00000
(510) 000-0000
3 | Debtor in Pro Per

4

5

6

7

8 | UNITED STATES BANKRUPTCY COURT

9 | _____ *[name of district]* _____ DISTRICT OF _____ *[your state]* _____

10 | _____ *[name of division, if any]* _____ DIVISION

11 | In re:
[your name(s)]) Case No. _____ *[Copy from your petition]* _____
12 |)
) Chapter 7
13 |)
)
14 |)
)
Debtor(s))
15 | _____)

16

17 | ORDER APPROVING REAFFIRMATION AGREEMENT

18 | AND NOW, this _____ day of _____, 19___ the court having found that the reaffirma-

19 | tion agreement proposed by the debtors is in the best interest of the debtor and does not pose a hardship on the

20 | debtor or the debtor's dependents, it is hereby ordered that the reaffirmation with ____ *[name of creditor]* ____ is

21 | approved.

22

23 | Dated: _____   _____

24 | U.S. Bankruptcy Judge

25

26

27

28

5. How to Retain Property Without Reaffirming or Redeeming

In the districts that allow retention of property without reaffirming or redeeming (noted in Section C.5, above), in the second column after typing the creditor's name, write on your Statement of Intention the following: "I plan to retain the property by keeping current on my obligations under the contract." Be sure you understand that your obligation may include monthly payments, insurance coverage and more.

In the districts that do not allow this method of retaining property, ask the creditor to informally let you keep the property as long as you keep current on your contractual obligations. On the Statement of Intention, indicate that you are surrendering the property. If you default, the creditor's only recourse is to repossess the property.

But the creditor doesn't have to wait for you to default. Because you indicated that you are surrendering your property on the Statement of Intention, the creditor can repossess at any time. Keep making payments and keep a copy of every check or money order you send in.

If the lien was reduced during the bankruptcy, you can stop paying when your payments total the reduced lien amount plus interest. Unless the creditor takes steps to have the lien removed from the property, however, it will remain on public record. If you will never sell the property, this won't be a problem. But you might have problems several years down the road if you need clear title to the property in order to sell it. You may have to go to court to prove you've paid off the lien.

6. How to Pay Off Liens in a Follow-Up Chapter 13 Bankruptcy (the "Chapter 20" Strategy)

The subject of how to file for Chapter 13 bankruptcy is beyond the scope of this book. The process is fairly similar to filing for Chapter 7, and even uses most of the same forms. You have to pay another filing fee, and submit to the court a three- to five-year plan that spells out how you plan to pay off your remaining debts. To be approved, your plan must pay off each secured debt in an amount at least equal to the value of the property that secures the debt. Also, you must devote all of your disposable income over the course of the plan to the repayment of your debts. For a further discussion of Chapter 13, see Ch. 1, *Should You File for Chapter 7 Bankruptcy?*, Section E.4. ■

Nondischargeable Debts

Not all debts can be discharged in a Chapter 7 bankruptcy. Some debts survive the bankruptcy process and are as valid and collectable as they were before you filed for bankruptcy. Obviously, to understand exactly what bankruptcy will do for you, you need to know which, if any, of your debts are likely to survive bankruptcy.

When granting your final discharge, the bankruptcy court won't specify which of your debts have been discharged. All you'll get from the court is a paper called a final discharge, which states that:

- you're released from "all dischargeable debts"
- you aren't liable for debts that have been automatically discharged or have been ruled dischargeable by the bankruptcy court, and
- you aren't liable for certain categories of debts unless the court ruled them to be nondischargeable.

This chapter helps you figure out exactly which of your debts will be discharged and which debts may survive.

A. Overview of Nondischargeable Debts

Under the bankruptcy laws, 13 major categories of debts may turn out to be nondischargeable. Debts in nine of these categories are never discharged unless you prove that the debt fits within a narrow exception to the general rule. Debts in the other four categories are always discharged unless the creditor files an objection in the bankruptcy court and convinces the court to rule that the debt isn't discharged.

1. Debts Not Discharged Unless an Exception Applies

The debts in these categories aren't discharged unless you show the bankruptcy court that the debt comes within an exception to the rule:

- Debts you don't list in your bankruptcy papers (11 U.S.C. § 523(a)(3)).
- Recent student loans (11 U.S.C. § 523(a)(8)).
- Most federal, state and local taxes (11 U.S.C. § 523(a)(1)) and any money borrowed or charged on a credit card to pay those taxes (11 U.S.C. § 523(a)(14)).
- Child support and alimony and debts in the nature of support (11 U.S.C. §§ 523(a)(5) and 523(a)(18)).
- Fines or restitution (to the court or victim) imposed in a criminal-type proceeding (11 U.S.C. § 523(a)(7); 18 U.S.C. § 3613).
- Fees imposed by a court for the filing of a case, motion, complaint or appeal or for other costs and

expenses assessed with such filling (11 U.S.C. § 523(a)(17)).
- Debts resulting from intoxicated driving (11 U.S.C. § 523(a)(9)).
- Debts you couldn't discharge in a previous bankruptcy that was dismissed due to fraud or misfeasance (11 U.S.C. § 523(a)(10)).

To get a debt in any of these categories discharged, you can take one of two courses of action:

- **Get a lawyer and ask the bankruptcy court, while your case is open, to rule that a particular debt should be discharged.** You'll have to file a Complaint to Determine Dischargeability of a Debt with the bankruptcy court and then show, in court, that your debt isn't covered by the general rule that says these kinds of debts aren't dischargeable. (The grounds for getting such debts discharged are discussed in detail in Section B, below.) If you prove the exception, the court will rule that the debt is discharged, and the creditor won't be allowed to collect it after bankruptcy.

  Filing a Complaint to Determine Dischargeability requires an attorney's help; procedures vary considerably among courts. In a few courts, including the District of Oregon and the Southern District of New York, you can request that the dispute be sent to court-sponsored mediation. The creditor does not have to agree, nor does the judge have to send your case; however, if everyone agrees, mediation can provide an informal, quick and inexpensive resolution of the dispute.

- **Don't take any action during bankruptcy, and if the creditor attempts to collect after your case is closed, argue that the debt was discharged.** If you don't do anything while your bankruptcy is pending, your next chance to make such an argument is when a creditor sues you over the debt, or if you've already lost a lawsuit, when the creditor sets out to collect. You'll argue, simply, that the debt was discharged by the bankruptcy. Usually, the creditor must then reopen the bankruptcy case to get a ruling that the debt wasn't discharged.

  (One court has ruled, however, that to discharge a Health Education Assistance Loan (HEAL), you must file a complaint to determine dischargeability. You cannot argue that it was discharged when the holder of the loan tries to collect after your bankruptcy case is over. *U.S. v. Wood*, 925 F.2d 1580 (7th Cir. 1991).) It isn't uncommon for a creditor to drop rather than pursue the matter. But even if the creditor does reopen your case, you'll have a chance to argue your side in the bankruptcy court. If you fail to persuade the court that you come within an exception, the court will rule that the debt survived the bankruptcy and the creditor can collect it. (Ch. 5, *Life After Bankruptcy,* discusses what to do if a creditor tries to collect a debt after your bankruptcy.)

2. Debts Discharged Unless the Creditor Objects

The other four categories of nondischargeable debts are in fact discharged if:
- you list them on your bankruptcy petition, and
- the creditor doesn't formally object within the time allowed.

If the creditor doesn't file an objection, the debt will be discharged and the creditor barred from trying to collect. The reason a creditor must object for these debts to be nondischargeable is that a court must examine the circumstances closely to determine whether or not the debt should be legally discharged.

These four categories of nondischargeable debts are:
1. Debts incurred on the basis of fraudulent acts, including using a credit card when payment is impossible (11 U.S.C. § 523(a)(2)).

> EXAMPLE: Joe obtains a bank loan by lying about his income on the loan application. Before the loan is paid off, Joe files for bankruptcy and lists the loan on his bankruptcy petition. The bank receives notice of the bankruptcy but fails to file an objection to the discharge of the debt within the required period. The debt will be discharged.
>
> If, however, the bank filed an objection in time and proved that Joe gave false information, the bankruptcy court would rule that the debt would survive the bankruptcy.

2. Debts from willful and malicious injury to another or another's property (11 U.S.C. § 523(a)(6)).
3. Debts from embezzlement, larceny or breach of trust (fiduciary duty) (11 U.S.C. § 523(a)(4)).
4. Debts arising from a marital settlement agreement or divorce decree (11 U.S.C. § 523(a)(15)).

If you have a debt of this type, your best approach is to do nothing and hope the creditor doesn't come forward. If the creditor does object, you should respond if you want the debt to be discharged. If the debt is large enough to justify the fees you'll have to pay, hire a bankruptcy attorney to handle it. If the judge rules in your favor after a creditor has accused you of fraud, the court should make the creditor pay your attorneys' fees. See Section C.1, below.

If you can't afford an attorney or don't want to hire one, you'll have to do some legal research yourself. See Ch. 9, *Help Beyond the Book.*

B. Debts Not Discharged Unless an Exception Applies

This section discusses each category of debt that, under the bankruptcy laws, isn't dischargeable in a Chapter 7 bankruptcy unless an exception applies.

1. Debts or Creditors You Don't List

For a debt to be discharged in bankruptcy, the creditor must know of the bankruptcy proceeding in time to object to the discharge. Creditors usually hear of a bankruptcy from the court, which sends a notice to all creditors listed in your bankruptcy papers. If the official notice fails to reach the creditor for some reason beyond your control—because the post office errs, or the creditor moved without leaving a forwarding address, for example—the debt will be discharged.

But if you forget to list a creditor on your bankruptcy papers or carelessly misstate a creditor's identity or address, the creditor won't be notified by the court. If that happens, the debt won't be discharged unless the creditor knew of your bankruptcy through other means, such as a letter or phone call from you. (See Ch. 4, *Handling Your Case in Court,* Section A.2.)

If at any time during the bankruptcy process you discover that you left a creditor or debt off your bankruptcy papers, you should file an amendment. It's a simple process. See Ch. 4, *Handling Your Case in Court,* Section B, for instructions. If you discover the omission after your case ends, you may be able to return to court and get the omitted creditor added. (See Chapter 5, *Life After Bankruptcy,* Section B.)

2. Student Loans

Most student loans are nondischargeable—you'll still have to repay them after bankruptcy. But the bankruptcy court may let you discharge a student loan if:
- the loan is guaranteed by a private company, not the government (very few loans fall into this category)
- payments on the loan first became due more than seven years before you filed for bankruptcy, or
- it would cause you undue hardship to repay the loan.

Even if you are a non-student cosigner of a student loan (such as the parent or sibling of the student debtor), you, too, may not be able to discharge the loan. Courts, however, are split on the issue. (The trend is not to allow cosigners to discharge the loans.) You will want to check with a bankruptcy practitioner or do some legal research if this affects you.

GETTING YOUR TRANSCRIPT

If you don't pay back loans obtained directly from your college, the school can withhold your transcript. But if you file for bankruptcy and receive a discharge of the loan, the school can no longer withhold your records. (*In re Gustafson,* 111 B.R. 282 (9th Cir. BAP 1990).)

In addition, while your bankruptcy case is pending, the school cannot withhold your transcript even if the court eventually rules your school loan nondischargeable.

a.   Payments First Due Over Seven Years Ago

Normally, you can discharge a student loan if your first installment payment became due over seven years before you filed for bankruptcy.

> **EXAMPLE:** Albert borrowed $15,000 in student loans between 1985 and 1989; his first installment on his ten-year repayment schedule was due in March 1990. If Albert files for bankruptcy any time before March of 1997, he won't be able to discharge the loan.

If you received any deferment or forbearance of your repayment obligation during the seven years before you file for bankruptcy or your payments were suspended while you were in a different bankruptcy case, the seven-year period is extended for the length of the deferment, forbearance, or other bankruptcy case. So if Albert returned to graduate school from September of 1990 to August of 1991 (12 months) and the lending institution allowed him to suspend paying back his loan during that time, the loan can't be discharged until March of 1998, not March of 1997.

b.   Undue Hardship

If the first installment on your loan was not due at least seven years before you file for bankruptcy, you'll have to repay the loan unless you can show the bankruptcy court that it would cause undue hardship for you to do so.

Courts rarely allow student loans to be discharged on hardship grounds. They take the position that Congress wants student loans to be repaid absent exceptional circumstances. And sometimes, even if a court finds that it would be a hardship to repay the entire debt, the court allows only a portion of it to be discharged.

i. Factors Courts Use in Determining Undue Hardship

In determining undue hardship, bankruptcy courts look to the three factors discussed below. Only if you can show that all of these factors are present will the court grant an undue hardship discharge of your student loan. (The main case establishing these factors is *Brunner v. New York State Higher Education Services Inc.*, 831 F.2d 395 (2nd Cir. 1987).)

- **Poverty.** Based on your current income and expenses, you cannot maintain a minimal living standard and repay the loan. The court must consider your current and future employment and income (or employment and income potential), education, skills and the marketability of your skills, health and family support obligations.
- **Persistence.** It is not enough that you can't currently pay your loan. You must also demonstrate to the

court that your current financial condition is likely to continue indefinitely—that is, your situation is hopeless.

- **Good Faith.** The court must conclude that you've made a good-faith effort to repay your debt. Someone who files for bankruptcy immediately after getting out of school or after the pay-back period begins will not fall into good favor with the court. Nor will someone who hasn't looked extensively for employment. And if you haven't made any payments, you should be able to show the court that you thought enough about your obligation to obtain a deferment or forbearance.

SPECIAL RULES FOR HEAL, PLUS AND CONSOLIDATED LOANS

HEAL. The dischargeability of Health Education Assistance Loans (HEAL loans) is governed by the federal HEAL Act, not bankruptcy law. Under the HEAL Act, to discharge a loan, you must show that the loan became due more than seven years past, and that repaying it would not merely be a hardship, but would impose an unconscionable burden on your life. (42 U.S.C. § 292f(g).)

PLUS. Parental Loans for Students (PLUS Loans) are granted to a parent to finance a child's education. Even though the parent does not receive the education, if the parent files for bankruptcy, the loan is treated like any other student loan. The parents must meet the seven-year or undue hardship test to discharge the loan. (See, for example, *In re Wilcon*, 143 B.R. 4 (D. Mass. 1992).)

Consolidated. Consolidated loans result when a lender combines multiple student loans into one, with one interest rate and payment schedule, or refinances one loan at a lower interest rate. If the first payment on your consolidated loan became due fewer than seven years ago, the bankruptcy court probably will not let you discharge any of the consolidated loan even if some of the original loans are older than seven years. (See for example, *In re Menendez*, 151 B.R. 972 (M.D. Fla. 1993).)

---

ii. Filing a Complaint to Determine Dischargeability

To seek a discharge of your student loan on the ground of undue hardship, you must file a formal complaint with the bankruptcy court—at a current cost of $120. This is considered an "adversarial proceeding" in bankruptcy, and you

should look at your local rules to see if any apply to complaints or adversarial proceedings.

In general, you can file your complaint with the court any time after you file for bankruptcy. Some courts may require that adversarial proceedings be filed at a certain time, however, so check your local rules.

You will need to fill out two forms, depending on your court's requirements. Sample completed forms are below.

Step 1: Refer to your court's local rules for time limits, format of papers and other details of an adversarial proceeding.

Step 2: Make at least three copies of the blank, line-numbered legal paper in Appendix 4 (to allow for mistakes). Type from line number 1 to line 13 as follows (see samples, below):

    Line 1: Your name, and that of your spouse if you're filing jointly.

    Line 1.5: Your address.

    Line 2: Your city, state and zip code.

    Line 2.5: Your phone number.

    Line 3: Type: Debtor in Pro Per.

    Line 7: Center and type UNITED STATES BANKRUPTCY COURT, in capital letters.

    Line 8: Center and type the judicial district and state you are in. Get this information from your bankruptcy petition.

    Lines 9-15: Type as shown in the example.

Step 3: Make a few photocopies of the page with the information you have typed so far. This will save you typing later, because you can use this same heading for both forms.

Step 4: Using one of the copies that you just made, start typing again at line 16. Prepare a COMPLAINT TO DETERMINE DISCHARGEABILITY OF STUDENT LOAN, as shown in the example, below. When you are done, make at least four copies of the Complaint.

Step 5: Call the bankruptcy court clerk and ask the following:

- Is the fee for filing a Complaint to Determine Dischargeability still $120?
- How much does it cost to make photocopies of papers at the courthouse?
- What is the mailing address of the trustee in your case (if you don't already have it)?

• What is the mailing address of the U.S. trustee? (The U.S. trustee oversees all bankruptcy matters in your district.)

Step 6: Prepare a Proof of Service by Mail, as shown in the sample. This form states that a friend or relative of yours, who is at least 18 years old and not a party to the bankruptcy, mailed your papers. Fill in the blanks with your friend's name, county, state, address and zip code as indicated. On line 23, put the city or town of the post office that your friend will mail your papers from. Starting at line 25, put the names and addresses of the creditor, the trustee in your case and the U.S. trustees'.

Step 7: Take your Complaint to the bankruptcy court for filing. (Remember to bring your checkbook to pay the filing fee and change to make photocopies.) When you get to the court clerk, ask for a Summons, which you will have to fill out before you file your Complaint. (A Summons is a paper which lets the creditor know you've filed a Complaint.) You can use your pen—you don't have to type the information on the Summons. It asks for your name, the name of the creditor, your case number and some other identifying information. Ask the clerk for help if you don't know what to put in any blank.

In many districts, the court clerk will give you a "status conference date"—a date you'll meet with the creditor and bankruptcy judge. The date will probably be in a few weeks or months, depending how busy the judge is. The clerk either will tell you to write the date on the Summons or will give you a separate paper, called an Order, which contains the date.

Step 8: Ask the clerk where a copy machine is located; make four copies of the Summons and any Order.

Step 9: Get back in line and file your Complaint and Summons.

Step 10: Put one copy of the Complaint, any Order and Summons in a stamped envelope with sufficient postage; have your friend mail them to the creditor, your trustee and the U.S. trustee. (The creditor gets the original Summons; your trustee and the U.S. trustee each get a copy; keep another for your records.)

Step 11: The creditor affected by your Complaint will submit a written response within 30 days.

Step 12: Get a copy of *Represent Yourself in Court: How to Prepare and Try a Winning Case*, by Paul Bergman and Sara Berman-Barrett (Nolo Press). It contains all the information you need to handle your own case, start to finish, without a lawyer. Because your case is fairly straightforward—a medical or similar condition is keeping you from working or working enough to pay your student loan—you should have no problem proceeding on your own.

Step 13: From here, your case proceeds like any other trial. If your district requires you to attend a status conference, go. The bankruptcy judge will try to settle the matter. If you can't settle it, the judge will see what plans each side has. Will anyone be filing motions or doing discovery? (All of this is explained in *Represent Yourself in Court*.) The judge will probably also set a trial date.

COMPLAINT TO DETERMINE DISCHARGEABILITY OF STUDENT LOAN

1 John Doe

2 1111 Any Street
    Berkeley, CA 00000

3 (510) 000-0000
    Debtor in Pro Per

4

5

6

7

8 UNITED STATES BANKRUPTCY COURT

9 _____[name of district]_____ DISTRICT OF _____[your state]_____

10 _____[name of division, if any]_____ DIVISION

11 [your name(s)]

12 Case No. _____ [Copy from your petition]

13   v.   Chapter 7

14

15 [name of creditor]

16

17 COMPLAINT TO DETERMINE DISCHARGEABILITY OF STUDENT LOAN

18 1. Debtor(s) filed this case under Chapter 7 of the Bankruptcy Code on _insert the date you filed your

19 petition_. This Court thus has jurisdiction over this action under 28 U.S.C. § 1334. This proceeding is a core

20 proceeding.

21 2. One of the unsecured debts owing by the Debtor(s) and listed on Schedule F—Creditors Holding

22 Unsecured Nonpriority Claims— is a student loan owing to _insert the name of the holder of your loan_.

23 3. This loan was incurred to pay expenses at _insert the name of the school(s) you attended_.

24 4. Based on the Debtor(s)' current income and expenses, the Debtor(s) cannot maintain a minimal living

25 standard and repay off loan. _insert information about your current and future employment, your income

26 and income potential, education, skills and the marketability of your skills, health, and family support

27 obligations_.

28 5. The Debtor(s)' current financial condition is likely to continue for a significant portion of the repayment

---

1 period of the loan. _insert information about your health including any life–threatening, debilitating or

2 chronic conditions you have_.

3 6. The Debtor(s) have made a good-faith effort to repay their debt.

4 7. The Debtor(s) have filed for bankruptcy for reasons other than just to discharge their student loan.

5

6 Dated: _____ Debtor in Propria Persona

7 Dated: _____ Debtor in Propria Persona

8 Address

9

10

11

12

13

14

15

16

17

18

19

20

21

22

23

24

25

26

27

28

PROOF OF SERVICE BY MAIL

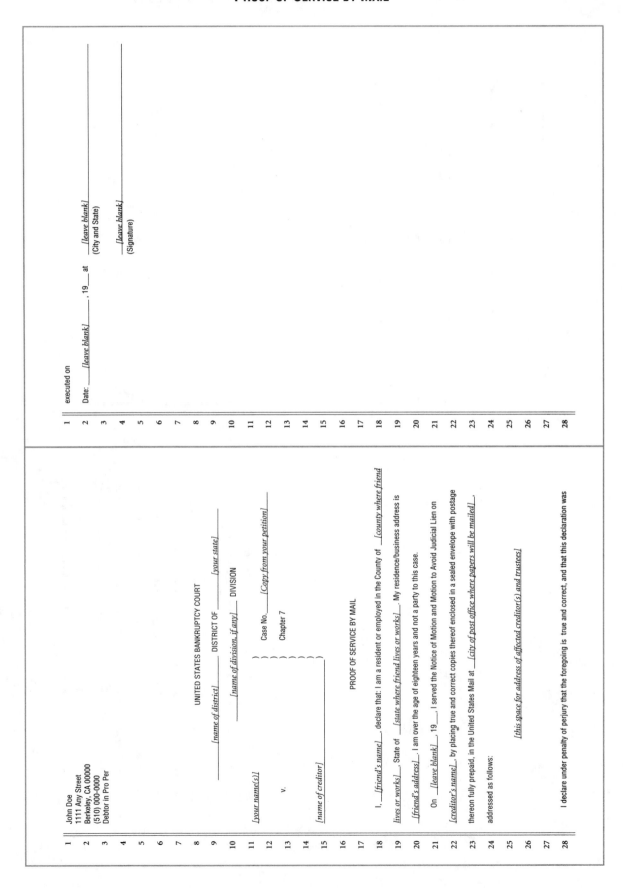

John Doe
1111 Any Street
Berkeley, CA 00000
(510) 000-0000
Debtor in Pro Per

UNITED STATES BANKRUPTCY COURT

_____ [name of district] _____ DISTRICT OF _____ [your state] _____

_____ [name of division, if any] _____ DIVISION

[your name(s)]

                                        Case No. _____ [Copy from your petition]

v.   Chapter 7

[name of creditor]

PROOF OF SERVICE BY MAIL

I, [friend's name] , declare that: I am a resident or employed in the County of [county where friend lives or works] , State of [state where friend lives or works] . My residence/business address is [friend's address] . I am over the age of eighteen years and not a party to this case.

On [leave blank] , 19 ___ , I served the Notice of Motion and Motion to Avoid Judicial Lien on [creditor's name] by placing true and correct copies thereof enclosed in a sealed envelope with postage thereon fully prepaid, in the United States Mail at [city of post office where papers will be mailed] , addressed as follows:

                    [this space for address of affected creditor(s) and trustees]

I declare under penalty of perjury that the foregoing is true and correct, and that this declaration was executed on

Date: _____ [leave blank] _____ , 19 ___ at _____ [leave blank] _____
                                                  (City and State)

                                        _____ [leave blank] _____
                                                  (Signature)

3. Taxes

As a general rule, recent federal, state and local taxes aren't dischargeable in Chapter 7 bankruptcy. (They can, however, be included in a Chapter 13 bankruptcy repayment plan.) Although there are some exceptions, these exceptions seldom apply in practice. And even if they do, the taxing authority will probably be able to enforce any tax lien that has been placed on your property. Before automatically assuming your tax debt does not qualify for discharge, do some research or see an attorney. One book we recommend is *Stand Up to the IRS,* by Frederick W. Daily (Nolo Press).

Income taxes. Federal, state and local income taxes aren't dischargeable unless they were first owed at least three years before you file for bankruptcy and you properly filed your tax return for the years in question at least two years prior to filing for bankruptcy. If the IRS completes a Substitute for Return on your behalf which you neither sign nor consent to, your return is not considered filed. (See *In re Bergstrom,* 949 F.2d 341 (10th Cir. 1991).)

There's one exception, so if you've recently been negotiating with the IRS or state tax agency or have been in a tax court case, and the three-year period has elapsed, don't get too excited. Any income or property tax assessed within 240 days of filing for bankruptcy is nondischargeable. This means that once your negotiation or case is over and your tax liability set, you must wait at least 240 days before filing if you want a chance at having your taxes discharged.

Also, if you borrowed money or used your credit card to pay taxes that would otherwise be nondischargeable, you cannot eliminate the loan or credit card debt in bankruptcy. In other words, you can't turn your nondischargeable tax debt into a dischargeable tax debt by paying it on your credit card.

⚠️ **UNDERSTAND THE ASSESSMENT DATE**

If you're unsure of the assessment date, consider seeing a tax lawyer—but don't ask the IRS for the date. If the IRS gives you the wrong date—telling you that the 240 days have elapsed, the IRS won't be held to it if it turns out to be wrong. That is, you won't be able to discharge the taxes. (See, for example, *In re Howell,* 120 B.R. 137 (9th Cir. BAP 1990).)

Penalties on taxes that are dischargeable are also dischargeable. Penalties imposed on unpaid taxes that are more than three years old are dischargeable, even if the taxes themselves are not. (See, for example, *In re Roberts,* 906 F.2d 1440 (10th Cir. 1990).) The IRS disagrees with this interpretation of the bankruptcy law, and will probably continue to argue in other courts that all penalties on nondischargeable taxes are themselves nondischargeable.

EXAMPLE: Jill failed to file a tax return for 1989. In 1995, the IRS discovers Jill's failure and in January 1996 assesses tax of $5,000 and penalties and interest of $12,000. Jill files for bankruptcy in January 1997. Because Jill didn't file a return for 1989, she can't discharge the tax, even though it became due more than three years past (and more than 240 days have elapsed since the taxes were assessed). Jill can discharge the penalty for failure to file and the penalties for failure to pay the tax from 1990–1993, although she should be prepared for the IRS to come into court and argue otherwise. Jill can't discharge the penalties for the unpaid taxes for years 1994–1996, the three years immediately preceding her bankruptcy filing.

Property taxes. Property taxes aren't dischargeable unless they became due more than a year before you file for bankruptcy. But even if your personal liability for paying the property tax out of your pocket is discharged, the tax lien on your property is unaffected. From a practical standpoint, this discharge is no discharge at all, because you'll have to pay off the lien before you can transfer clear title to the property.

Other taxes. Other types of taxes that aren't dischargeable are business-related: payroll taxes, excise taxes and customs duties. Sales, use and poll taxes are also probably not dischargeable. If you have any of these types of taxes, see a bankruptcy attorney.

4. Child Support and Alimony

Alimony (also called spousal support or maintenance) and child support obligations are usually not dischargeable, but there are a few exceptions.

a. Dischargeable Alimony and Child Support

Two kinds of alimony or child support debts can be discharged.

- **Support paid under an agreement between unmarried persons.** If an unmarried couple enters into an agreement about their obligations to each other, as many do, the agreement often covers support (who pays whom) in the event the couple separates. In most states, these agreements are enforceable—the recipient can sue if the other person doesn't pay. But unlike alimony or child support ordered by a court, if the person who must pay files for bankruptcy, the obligation can be discharged unless the recipient sues and wins a court judgment against the other person.

- **Support owed someone other than a spouse, ex-spouse or child.** If a parent or a child has given (assigned, in legal terms) the right to receive the support to someone else, or a creditor has garnished the payments, the debt is dischargeable (unless it's owed to the welfare department or another government agency or office, such as a court child support collections unit).

  Be aware, however, that courts are increasingly characterizing debts to people other than parents, but for the benefit of children—such as attorney's fees incurred in a child custody case or hospital delivery costs—as nondischargeable child support. (See, for example, *In re Poe*, 118 B.R. 809 (N.D. Okla. 1990); *In re Jones*, 9 F.3d 878 (10th Cir. 1993); *In re Seibert*, 914 F.2d 102 (7th Cir. 1990).)

b. Nondischargeable Alimony and Child Support

An obligation called child support, alimony or something similar is clearly nondishargeable. Some other debts, however, may also be considered nondischargeable child support or alimony. The most common are marital debts—the debts a spouse was ordered to pay when the couple divorced.

Often, the spouse who's paying alimony or child support agreed at the time of the divorce to pay more than half of the marital debts, in exchange for a lower support obligation. If that spouse later files for bankruptcy, a portion of the debt is really support. Consequently, it's considered a nondischargeable debt owed to the other spouse. Similarly, one spouse may have agreed to pay some of the other spouse's or children's future living expenses (shelter, clothing, health insurance, transportation) in exchange for a lower support obligation. The obligations for the future expenses are treated as support owed to the other spouse and aren't dischargeable.

EXAMPLE: When Erica and Tom divorced, they had two young children. Tom offered to pay most of the marital debts in exchange for low child support payments; Erica agreed because she had a good income of her own and felt able to support the children without too much help from Tom. If Tom files for bankruptcy before paying off the marital debts, the bankruptcy judge won't grant a discharge for all the marital debts.

Obligations that are generally considered support and aren't dischargeable include debts that:

- are paid to a spouse who is maintaining the primary residence of the children while there is a serious imbalance of incomes
- terminate on the death or remarriage of the recipient spouse
- depend on the future income of either spouse, or
- are paid in installments over a substantial period of time. (See, for example, *In re Goin*, 808 F.2d 1391 (10th Cir. 1987); *In re Calhoun*, 10 B. Ct. D. 1402 (6th Cir. 1983).)

Bankruptcy courts in Kentucky, Michigan, Ohio and Tennessee add another consideration—if the child or recipient spouse needs support, then the debt may be considered support. (*In re Stone*, 79 B.R. 633 (D. Md. 1987).)

5. Fines, Penalties and Restitution

You cannot discharge fines, penalties or restitution that a federal, state or local government has imposed to punish you for violating a law. Examples include:

- fines imposed for infractions (most traffic tickets, for example), misdemeanors (petty offenses) or felonies (serious crimes)
- fines imposed by a judge for contempt of court
- fines imposed by a government agency for violating agency regulations (for example, a fine imposed for fraudulently obtaining public benefits)
- some penalties for underpaying taxes or filing a late tax return (see Section 3, above)
- surcharges for court or agency enforcement of a law; it's common for courts (and some government agencies) to order people to pay, above the basic fine or penalty, the costs associated with enforcing the law, and
- restitution (payment to an economically injured victim) imposed in criminal cases—in some criminal cases, judges give a convicted defendant probation, provided he makes restitution to the victim; restitution is nondischargeable because it's imposed against the defendant, as rehabilitation, rather than to compensate the victim. (18 U.S.C. § 3613).

6. Court Fees

You cannot discharge a fee imposed by a court for the filing of a case, motion, complaint or appeal, or for other costs and expenses assessed with respect to such court filing. The law targets prisoners who attempt to discharge court fees, especially fees related to appeals, but its scope is much greater.

7. Intoxicated Driving Debts

Debts for the death of, or personal injury to, someone resulting from your driving while illegally intoxicated by alcohol or drugs (under the intoxicated driving laws of your state) aren't dischargeable.

Even if you are sued and the judge or jury finds you liable but doesn't specifically find that you were intoxicated, the judgment against you may nevertheless be declared nondischargeable if the creditor convinces the bankruptcy court that you were in fact intoxicated.

Debts for property damage resulting from your intoxicated driving are dischargeable.

EXAMPLE: Christopher was in a car accident in which he caused both property damage and personal injury to Ellen. Several months later Christopher filed for bankruptcy and listed Ellen as a creditor. After the bankruptcy case was over, Ellen sued Christopher, claiming that the debt wasn't discharged because Christopher was driving while intoxicated. If Ellen shows that Christopher was illegally intoxicated under his state's laws, she will be able to pursue her personal injury claim against him. She is barred, however, from trying to collect for any property damage.

8. Debts You Couldn't Discharge in a Previous Bankruptcy

If a bankruptcy court dismissed a previous bankruptcy case because of your fraud or other bad acts (misfeasance), you cannot discharge any debts that would have been discharged in the earlier bankruptcy. This rule doesn't affect debts incurred since the date you filed the earlier bankruptcy case.

C. Debts Discharged Unless the Creditor Objects

Four types of nondischargeable debts are in fact discharged unless the creditor objects during the bankruptcy proceedings. Again, the four types of debts are:

- debts incurred by fraudulent acts, including using a credit card when you know you won't be able to pay
- debts from willful or malicious injury to a person or property
- debts from embezzlement, larceny or breach of trust (fiduciary duty), and
- debts other than alimony or child support that arise from a marital settlement agreement or divorce decree including a promise to pay marital debts or payments owed an ex-spouse to even up a property division.

To object to the discharge of this kind of debt, a creditor must file a written complaint with the bankruptcy court and prove in court that the debt fits in one of the categories. The complaint must be filed within 60 days of the first date set by the court for the meeting of creditors. If a creditor gets late notice of the bankruptcy and files a late claim, the court will extend the 60-day period for filing objections.

Because filing a complaint usually requires the help of an attorney, it's expensive. Creditors tend to object only when the debt is substantial—about $500 or more. You'll probably need to hire an attorney yourself if you want to respond to the creditor in court. (See Ch. 9, *Help Beyond the Book*.)

1. Debts From Fraud

This category has several sub-categories; to be nondischargeable, a debt must fit within at least one.

If a creditor challenges discharge of a debt by claiming you engaged in fraud, but the judge finds in your favor, the judge may order the creditor to reimburse you for the money you spent on attorney's fees.

a. Debts From Intentionally Fraudulent Behavior

If a creditor can show that a debt arose because of your dishonest act, and that the debt wouldn't have arisen had you been honest, the court will probably not let you discharge the debt. These are common examples:

- You wrote a check for something and stopped payment on it after changing your mind and deciding not to pay.
- You wrote a check against insufficient funds but assured the merchant that the check was good.
- You rented or borrowed an expensive item and claimed it was yours to get a loan.

- You got a loan by telling the lender you'd pay it back, when you had no intention of doing so.

The dishonest act (fraud) can be oral, or written. A debt arising from a false written statement about your financial condition is also nondischargeable under another section of the bankruptcy code discussed immediately below.

Sometimes even silence can be fraudulent rather than golden. For example, one woman obtained an extension of a loan from her mother-in-law without mentioning that she planned to divorce her husband. A court ruled that the omission was fraudulent and the loan nondischargeable. (*In re Verdon*, 95 B.R. 877 (N.D. N.Y. 1989).)

For a debt to be nondischargeable under this section, your deceit must be intentional, and the creditor must have relied on your deceit in extending credit. Courts may judge your intent by looking at your actions. For example, if you loaded up your credit cards when you obviously couldn't pay the debt, the court may conclude that you committed fraud. Some courts have ruled that the creditor's reliance must have been reasonable under the circumstances, but other courts have ruled that the reliance need not have been reasonable.

It isn't fraud if when you made a promise to pay you intended to keep it. For example, if to obtain credit you promise (and intend) to pay back a minimum amount each month, but are unable to pay it, you aren't guilty of fraud even if the creditor relied on your promise in extending you credit. The debt will be dischargeable. But if the evidence shows that when you made the promise you didn't intend to perform it, the debt will probably be ruled nondischargeable.

b. Debts From a False Written Statement About Your Financial Condition

If a creditor proves that you incurred a debt because of a false written statement you made, it isn't dischargeable. Here are the rules:

- The false statement must be written—for instance, made in a credit application, rental application or resume.
- The false statement must have been "material"—that is, a potentially significant factor in the creditor's decision to extend you credit. Misspelling a reference's name isn't material. Claiming that you resided somewhere for ten years when you only lived there ten months, however, might be, because stability is an important factor in deciding whether or not to grant credit. The two most common materially false statements are omitting debts and overstating income.

- The false statement must relate to your financial condition or the financial condition of "insiders"—people close to you or a business entity with which you're associated. Specifically, an insider is a relative, someone you're in partnership with, a partnership in which you're a general partner or a corporation in which you're a director, officer or in control.
- The creditor must have relied on the false statement, and the reliance must have been reasonable. A creditor is presumed to have relied on any statement you make in a credit application or financial statement. And reliance is normally considered reasonable if the creditor performed a credit check or had other valid reasons for relying on your statements, such as a previous business relationship with you.
- You must have intended to deceive the creditor. This is hard to prove, so most courts look at the disparity between what's on the application and the truth. For instance, if you wrote that you make $150,000 a year, but you only make $10,000, the court will conclude you intended to deceive. If, on the other hand, you establish that the error came from genuine carelessness, you may get the debt discharged.

c. Recent Debts for Luxuries

Bankruptcy law presumes that if you ran up debts of more than $1,000 to one creditor for luxury goods or services within 60 days before filing for bankruptcy, you intended to cheat the creditor or subvert the bankruptcy process. So don't take a trip to Japan, charge it on your American Express card and file for bankruptcy right after returning.

If you've recently run up credit charges for luxuries but haven't yet filed for bankruptcy, wait a while if you can. See Ch. 1, *Should You File for Chapter 7 Bankruptcy?*

d. Recent Cash Advances

If you obtained cash advances totaling more than $1,000 under an open-ended consumer credit plan fewer than 60 days before you filed for bankruptcy, the debt is nondischargeable. "Open-ended" means there's no date when the debt must be repaid, but rather, as with most credit cards, you may take forever to repay the debt as long as you pay a minimum amount each month.

2. Debts From Willful and Malicious Acts

If the act that caused a debt was willful and malicious (an intentional wrongful act which necessarily produces harm and is without just cause), the debt isn't dischargeable if the creditor successfully objects. Most creditors don't.

Generally, crimes that injure people or property are considered willful and malicious acts. An example is stabbing someone with a knife because you're angry. Your liability for the injury or damage caused the victim will probably be ruled nondischargeable.

An example of an act that isn't willful and malicious is driving slightly over the speed limit on an interstate highway. You may intend to speed, but driving a bit above 65 doesn't necessarily produce harm. On the other hand, if you're driving 110 miles an hour and get in an accident, some courts would rule that harm was an obvious consequence of your actions, and that your actions were therefore willful and malicious.

Willfulness and malice are commonly raised by secured creditors when the collateral securing a loan has been destroyed. For example, if you bought a car on credit and junk it rather than return it when you file for bankruptcy, the creditor (the legal owner of the car) may claim that you willfully and maliciously destroyed the collateral, and that you still owe the value of the car. If, however, you can show that you junked the car because you thought you owed no more money, you thought the car had no value or you desperately needed money for necessities, then you may be able to discharge the debt, because your actions did not necessarily produce harm.

Some other acts that are sometimes considered to be willful and malicious include:

- false imprisonment (unlawfully restraining someone)
- intentional infliction of emotional distress (deliberately or recklessly causing extreme anxiety, fear or shock)
- medical or legal malpractice involving the deliberate or reckless delivery of incompetent professional services
- libel or slander (making false and derogatory statements about someone to a third person)
- forcible entry and detainer (activities of a landlord to evict a tenant, such as removing a door or changing the locks), and
- conversion of personal property (taking someone's property or cash), such as hiding assets from your spouse during a divorce proceeding or destroying collateral.

> ### COPYRIGHTS AND PATENTS
>
> Debts from an infringement of a creditor's trademark, copyright or patent are nondischargeable if the infringement was willful, not accidental. Infringement is generally considered willful if the infringer knew of the trademark, copyright or patent, or if the trademark or copyright was registered with the appropriate federal agency before the infringement.

3. Debts From Embezzlement, Larceny or Breach of Fiduciary Duty

A debt incurred as a result of embezzlement, larceny or breach of fiduciary duty is nondischargeable if the creditor successfully objects to its discharge.

Embezzlement is taking property entrusted to you for another and using it for yourself. Examples of embezzlement are when a trustee misappropriates trust funds or a bank clerk takes money from the bank.

Larceny is another word for theft. If you owe a debt because you stole property or services, you can't discharge the debt if the victim goes to court and proves the larceny.

Breach of fiduciary duty is the failure to live up to a duty of trust you owe someone, based on a relationship where you're required to manage property or money for another, or where your relationship is a close and confidential one. In general, common fiduciary relationships are:

- agent and principal
- among partners
- attorney and client
- bailor and bailee (a bailor is someone who stores property for someone else, the bailee)
- bank officer and customer
- broker and customer
- estate executor and beneficiary
- guardian and ward
- husband and wife, and
- landlord and tenant.

Many bankruptcy courts, however, limit the definition of fiduciary. Many require the relationship to have been formed by a technical or express trust (such as an estate executor and beneficiary), not just by the general laws of a state (such as among partners). They don't consider agents and principals, bailors and bailees, bank officers and customers or brokers and customers to be fiduciaries.

4. Debts From a Divorce Decree or Marital Settlement Agreement

Any debt arising from a separation agreement or divorce, or in connection with a marital settlement agreement, divorce decree or other court order, can be considered dischargeable. Your ex-spouse or child must challenge the discharge of the debt in the bankruptcy court by filing a nondischargeability complaint. Once the challenge is raised, the court will allow the debt to be discharged unless:

- you have the ability to pay the debt from income or property not reasonably necessary for your support and not reasonably necessary for you to continue, preserve and operate a business, or

- discharging the debt would result in a detriment to your former spouse or child that would outweigh the benefit you would receive by the discharge.

The majority of courts have held that the burden of proving the debtor's ability/inability to pay or proving who would be harmed more by the discharge/nondischarge is on the debtor. (See, for example, *In re Hill*, 184 B.R. 750 (N.D. Ill. 1995).) A few courts, however, have held that the burden is on the non-filing ex-spouse.

Decisions interpreting this provision of the Bankruptcy Code include the following:

- A debtor could not prove that the benefit he would receive by the discharge of a property equalizing payment would outweigh the detriment to his ex-wife. The court therefore focused on his ability to pay and determined that it would be a hardship for him to pay it all (nearly $19,000) at once. The court ordered him to pay $10,000 of it at a rate of $200 per month. (*In re Comisky*, 183 B.R. 883 (N.D. Cal. 1995).)

- A debtor proved that she could not afford to pay the marital debts she agreed to pay in her divorce because most of her assets were tied up by her ex-husband (she'd get her share of the marital property if and when he decided to sell the property). The court further found that the benefit she'd receive by the discharge would outweigh the detriment to her ex-husband (who would have to pay the debts) because he held most of the marital property, was receiving child support payments from her and earned approximately $2,000 per month. (*In re Becker*, 185 B.R. 567 (W.D. Mo. 1995).)

- A court concluded that a debtor clearly could not afford to pay the debts he agreed to pay in his divorce, and that the benefit to him in discharging the debts was substantial—he'd receive a necessary fresh start. But the court also found that the detriment to his ex-wife in having to pay the debts was significant—that she might be forced to file for bankruptcy, too. The court concluded that this wasn't so bad, allowed the ex-husband to discharge the debts and suggested that a "discharge of the debts by both parties...[was] the most sensible solution to the combined problems." (*In re Hill*, 184 B.R. 750 (N.D. Ill. 1995).)

DEBTS YOUR CREDITORS CLAIM ARE NONDISCHARGEABLE

Some of your creditors may be claiming that the debts you owe them cannot be wiped out in bankruptcy. In fact, computer leases—software and hardware—often contain clauses stating that if you're unable to complete the lease period, you can't eliminate the balance of the debt in bankruptcy.

Hogwash. The only debts you can't discharge in bankruptcy are the ones the Bankruptcy Code lists as nondischargeable—and we've described them in this chapter. Don't let your creditors intimidate you into thinking otherwise.

Help Beyond the Book

Although this book covers routine bankruptcy procedures in some detail, it doesn't come close to covering everything. That would require a 1,000-page treatise, most of which would be irrelevant for nearly all readers. That said, here are some suggestions if you need more information or advice than this book provides.

The major places to go for follow-up are:

- **Bankruptcy Petition Preparers:** When you're ready to file for bankruptcy, but need typing assistance in filling out the forms.
- **Lawyers:** When you want information, advice or legal representation.
- **Law Libraries:** When you want more information on an issue raised in the course of your bankruptcy.

Before we discuss each of these approaches in more detail, here's a general piece of advice: Keep control of your case whenever possible. By getting this book and filing for Chapter 7 bankruptcy, you've taken responsibility for your own legal affairs. If you decide to get help from others, shop around until you find someone who respects your efforts as a self-helper and at least recognizes your right to participate in the case as a valuable partner.

A. Bankruptcy Petition Preparers

Even though you should be able to handle routine bankruptcy procedures yourself, you may want someone familiar with the bankruptcy courts in your area to:

- type your forms
- help you over any rough spots you encounter when filling in the forms
- provide some basic information about local procedures and requirements, or
- help you prepare for negotiations with your creditors.

For this level of assistance—routine form preparation and basic, general information rather than specific advice on a course of action—consider employing a bankruptcy petition preparer (BPP). BPPs will type your bankruptcy papers for about $100 to $250. In 1994, Congress created the BPP designation for the specific purpose of regulating non-lawyers who assist people filing for bankruptcy with completing their forms. (11 U.S.C. § 110(g)(1).)

On its face, the law is meant to protect consumers. For instance, the law makes it difficult for a BPP to charge an unreasonable fee—that is, a fee not reasonably related to the amount of service the BPP was authorized to provide. The law also permits a bankruptcy court to fine a BPP up to $500 for:

- failing to put the BPP's name, address and Social Security number on a bankruptcy petition
- failing to give the customer a copy of the documents at the time the documents are signed
- using the word "legal" or any similar term in advertisements or advertising under a category that includes such terms, or
- accepting court filing fees from the person filing for bankruptcy—that is, you must pay the filing fee to the court yourself or give the BPP a cashier's check made out to the court.

The most controversial provision of the new law is its $1,000 "bounty"—collectible by the trustee or a creditor—against a BPP who:

- commits a fraudulent, unfair or deceptive act
- violates any of the technical rules listed above, or
- causes a case to be dismissed by failing to file the papers, acting negligently, violating the bankruptcy statutes or regulations, or intentionally disregarding the law or procedural rules.

In addition to the bounty, the BPP must also pay you any actual monetary loss, plus $2,000, or twice the amount you paid to the BPP, whichever is greater. The trustee will, no doubt, use this money to pay your creditors.

INFORMATION FOR BANKRUPTCY PETITION PREPARERS

Bankruptcy Petition Preparer Tom Binford and attorney Richard Lubetzky publish a kit for Bankruptcy Petition Preparers who want to know how to comply with the bankruptcy code requirements for this new profession, and deal with enforcement efforts by courts and trustees. The price is $34.95, which includes shipping and handling. To order, call 800-400-2534 (in California) or 209-434-2534 (outside of California), or write to Tom Binford, 319 Everglade, Fresno, CA 93720-1604.

BPPs are very different from lawyers. They can't give legal advice or represent you in court—only lawyers are allowed to do those things. When you use a BPP, you remain responsible for the decision-making in your case. You must decide what information to put in the forms and what property to claim as exempt. You cannot, legally, pass this responsibility on to a BPP.

BPPs are springing up all over the country to help people who don't want or can't afford to hire a lawyer, but you're still more likely to find a BPP if you live on the West Coast. A recommendation from someone who has used a particular BPP is the best way to find a reputable one in your area.

BPPs often advertise in classified sections of local newspapers and in the Yellow Pages. You may have to look hard to find BPPs, however, because the Bankruptcy Code bars them from using the term "legal" or any similar term in their advertisements or from advertising under any category which contains the word "legal" or a similar term. A local legal aid office may provide a reference, as will the occasional court clerk. And many BPPs have display ads in local throwaway papers like the Classified Flea Market or Giant Nickel.

⚠️ **BEWARE OF LAWYERS' WARNINGS ABOUT BPPS**
In many parts of the country, bankruptcy attorneys are extremely unhappy with BPPs that compete with them. Often, the attorneys charge that BPPs are practicing law (something the law allows only licensed attorneys to do) or that they're incompetent.

Because "practicing law" is never defined clearly, it's almost impossible to say whether or not BPPs sometimes do it. And some BPPs probably are incompetent, just as some lawyers are. But the paperwork you'll get from a BPP is probably prepared just as competently as what you'd get from a bankruptcy lawyer's office; most routine bankruptcy work in a lawyer's office is done by non-lawyer personnel anyway. How to fill out bankruptcy forms isn't taught in law school and doesn't involve any skill that lawyers (as opposed to others) necessarily possess.

So if you choose to go to a BPP, and a lawyer or the bankruptcy trustee (who's almost always a bankruptcy lawyer) finds out, you may be advised that you've made a terrible mistake and that you should instantly contact a lawyer. Don't let this rattle you.

B. Bankruptcy Lawyers

If you need to prepare custom-made court papers, to show up at a court hearing to argue your side of a dispute during your bankruptcy or negotiate with a creditor or the trustee, you may need to consult a bankruptcy lawyer. You can't use a BPP because BPPs cannot represent you in court. Nor can they legally give you guidance on how to handle the matter yourself. Also, non-routine bankruptcy procedures often require a knowledge of federal court procedure and the ability to engage in legal analysis. An experienced lawyer should have expertise in these areas. A bankruptcy lawyer can also provide valuable assistance in negotiating with a creditor or trustee.

You may be able to hire an attorney to handle only a specific procedure while handling the main part of the bankruptcy yourself. As a general rule, you should bring an attorney into the case whenever a dispute involves something of sufficient value to justify the attorney's fees. If a creditor objects to the discharge of a $500 debt, and it will cost you $400 to hire an attorney, you may be better off trying to handle the matter yourself, even though this increases the risk that the creditor will win. If, however, the dispute is worth $1,000 and the attorney will cost you $200, hiring the attorney makes sense.

1. How To Find a Bankruptcy Lawyer

Where there's a bankruptcy court, there are bankruptcy lawyers. They're listed in the Yellow Pages under attorneys and often advertise in newspapers. You should use an experienced bankruptcy lawyer, not a general practitioner, to advise you or handle matters associated with bankruptcy.

There are several ways to find the best bankruptcy lawyer for your job:

- **Personal Referrals:** This is your best approach. If you know someone who was pleased with the services of a lawyer, call that lawyer first. If that lawyer doesn't handle bankruptcies or can't take on your case, he or she may recommend someone else who's experienced, competent and available.
- **Bankruptcy Petition Preparers:** If there's a BPP in your area, chances are she works closely with bankruptcy attorneys who are both competent and sympathetic to self-helpers.
- **Group Legal Plans:** Some unions, employers and consumer action organizations offer group plans to their members or employees, who can obtain comprehensive legal assistance free or for low rates. If you're a member of such a plan, and the plan covers bankruptcies, check with it first for a lawyer.
- **Prepaid Legal Insurance:** Prepaid legal insurance plans offer some services for a low monthly fee and charge more for additional or different work. That means that participating lawyers may use the plan as a way to get clients, who are attracted by the low-cost basic services, and then sell them more expensive services. If the lawyer recommends an expensive course of action, get a second opinion before you agree.

  But if a plan offers extensive free advice, your initial membership fee may be worth the consultation you receive, even if you use it only once. You can always join a plan for a specific service and then not renew. For bankruptcy purposes, however, a plan won't be much help unless it offers the services of bankruptcy attorneys.

There's no guarantee that the lawyers available through these plans are of the best caliber; sometimes they aren't. As with any consumer transaction, check out the plan carefully before signing up. Ask about the plan's complaint system, whether you get to choose your lawyer and whether or not the lawyer will represent you in court.

- **Lawyer Referral Panels:** Most county bar associations will give you the names of some bankruptcy attorneys who practice in your area. But bar associations usually provide only minimal screening for the attorneys listed, which means those who participate may not be the most experienced or competent. You may find a skilled attorney willing to work for a reasonable fee this way, but take the time to check out the credentials and experience of the person to whom you're referred.

LEGAL ADVICE OVER THE TELEPHONE

If you are seeking legal advice on a specific issue, consider using Tele-Lawyer, a company that offers legal advice over the phone. You can talk to a lawyer who specializes in the subject area you're concerned about for $3 a minute. The average call to Tele-Lawyer lasts about 14 minutes and costs about $42.

If the lawyer can't answer a question, he or she will research it—for free—and get back to you. But most questions can be answered immediately because Tele-Lawyer provides its lawyers with a large database specially designed to help them answer common questions.

You can reach Tele-Lawyer at:

800-835-3529 (charge to Visa or MasterCard)
900-370-7000 (charge appears on your phone bill)
900-446-4529 (charge appears on your phone bill)
900-654-3000 (charge appears on your phone bill).

---

2. What to Look for in a Lawyer

No matter what approach you take to finding a lawyer, here are three suggestions on how to make sure you have the best possible working relationship.

First, fight the urge you may have to surrender your will and be intimidated by a lawyer. You should be the one who decides what you feel comfortable doing about your legal and financial affairs. Keep in mind that you're hiring the lawyer to perform a service for you; shop around if the price or personality isn't right.

Second, it's important that you be as comfortable as possible with any lawyer you hire. When making an appointment, ask to talk directly to the lawyer. If you can't, this may give you a hint as to how accessible he or she is. Of course, if you're told that a paralegal will be handling the routine aspects of your case under the supervision of a lawyer, you may be satisfied with that arrangement.

If you do talk directly, ask some specific questions. Do you get clear, concise answers? If not, try someone else. If the lawyer says little except to suggest that he or she handle the problem (with a substantial fee, of course), watch out. You're talking with someone who doesn't know the answer and won't admit it (common), or someone who pulls rank on the basis of professional standing. Don't be a passive client or hire a lawyer who wants you to be one.

Also, pay attention to how the lawyer responds to your considerable knowledge. If you've read this book, you're already better informed about the law than most clients. Many lawyers are threatened when the client knows too much (in some cases, anything).

Finally, once you find a lawyer you like, make an hour-long appointment to discuss your situation fully. Your goal at the initial conference is to find out what the lawyer recommends and how much it will cost. Go home and think about the lawyer's suggestions. If they don't make complete sense or you have other reservations, call someone else.

3. What Bankruptcy Attorneys Charge

Fees charged by bankruptcy attorneys vary from about $350 to $1,000 (plus the $175 filing and administrative fees) and up for a routine Chapter 7 bankruptcy case. Most bankruptcy attorneys let you pay in installments.

Fortunately, there are some limitations on what a bankruptcy attorney can charge. Because every penny you pay a bankruptcy lawyer is a penny not available to your creditors, the attorney must report the fee to the bankruptcy court. The court has the legal authority to call the attorney in to justify the fee. This rarely happens, because attorneys know what local bankruptcy judges will allow and set their fees accordingly.

Commonly, bankruptcy attorneys charge a basic fee for a routine case and then charge set amounts for extra procedures if they're necessary. For instance, the basic fee may be $750, but it will cost you $150 more to respond to a motion brought by a creditor and $250 more to file a motion to establish the fair market value of secured property.

C. The Law Library

Often, you can handle a problem yourself if you're willing to do some research in a law library. The trick is in knowing what types of information you can find there. Sometimes, what you need to know isn't written down. For instance, if you want to know whether the local bankruptcy judge is strict or lenient when it comes to pre-bankruptcy planning, you can't find out by going to the law library. You'll probably have to talk to a typing service or bankruptcy lawyer.

The library can help you, however, if your question involves a legal interpretation, such as how the judge is likely to rule if the trustee objects to one of your exemption claims. You can find out in the law library how similar questions have been decided by bankruptcy courts and courts of appeal.

Here's what you should find in the average law library:
- books and articles by bankruptcy experts on almost every aspect of bankruptcy law and practice, including many of the local procedures peculiar to each court
- federal bankruptcy statutes, which govern the bankruptcy process
- federal bankruptcy rules, which govern bankruptcy court procedure in more detail
- published decisions of bankruptcy court judges and appellate courts that interpret the bankruptcy statutes and rules
- specific instructions for handling routine and non-routine bankruptcy procedures, and
- cross-reference tools to help you get from one statute, rule or case to another and to help you find out whether the material you find is up-to-date.

Here, briefly, are the basic steps of researching bankruptcy questions.

1. Find the Law Library

To do legal research, you need to find a law library that's open to the public. Public law libraries are often found in county courthouses, public law schools and state capitals. If you can't find one, ask a public library reference librarian, court clerk or lawyer.

2. Use a Good Legal Research Resource

If you want to find the answer to a legal question, rather than simply look up a statute or case to which you already have the citation, you need some guidance in basic legal research techniques. Good resources that may be available in your law library include:
- *Legal Research: How to Find and Understand the Law,* by Steve Elias and Susan Levenkind (Nolo Press)
- *Legal Research Made Easy: A Roadmap Through the Law Library Maze,* by Nolo Press and Robert Berring (Nolo Press/Legal Star Video)
- *The Legal Research Manual: A Game Plan for Legal Research and Analysis,* by Christopher and Jill Wren (A-R Editions)
- *Introduction to Legal Research: A Layperson's Guide to Finding the Law,* by Al Coco (Want Publishing Co.)
- *How to Find the Law,* by Morris Cohen, Robert Berring and Kent Olson (West Publishing Co.).

3. Use *Collier on Bankruptcy*

It's a good idea to get an overview of your subject before trying to find a precise answer to a precise question. The best way to do this is to find a general commentary on your subject by a bankruptcy expert. For example, if you want to find out whether a particular debt is nondischargeable, you should start by reading a general discussion about the type of debt you're dealing with. Or, if you don't know whether you're entitled to claim certain property as exempt, a good overview of your state's exemptions would get you started on the right track.

The most complete source of this type of background information is a multi-volume treatise known as *Collier on Bankruptcy,* by Lawrence P. King, et al. (Matthew Bender). It's available in virtually all law libraries. *Collier* is both incredibly thorough and meticulously up-to-date; semi-annual supplements, with all the latest developments, are located at the front of each volume. In addition to comments on every aspect of bankruptcy law, *Collier* contains the bankruptcy statutes, rules and exemption lists for every state.

Collier is organized according to the bankruptcy statutes. This means that the quickest way to find information in it is to know what statute you're looking for. If you don't know the governing statute, start with the *Collier* subject matter index. Be warned, however, that the index can be difficult to use; it contains a lot of bankruptcy jargon you may be unfamiliar with.

4. Use Other Background Resources

For general discussions of bankruptcy issues, there are several other good places to start. An excellent all-around resource is called *Consumer Bankruptcy Law and Practice*. This volume, published by the National Consumer Law Center, is updated every year. It contains a complete discussion of Chapter 7 bankruptcy procedures, the official bankruptcy forms and a marvelous bibliography. If your law library has this volume (or will order it), become familiar with it.

Another good treatise is a legal encyclopedia called *American Jurisprudence*, 2nd Series. Almost all law libraries carry it. The article on bankruptcy has an extensive table of contents, and the entire encyclopedia has an index. Between these two tools, you should be able to zero in on helpful material.

Finally, another source of information about specific bankruptcy issues are articles published in law journals—periodicals published by law schools, bar associations and law societies. Most law school and law society articles contain academic, not practical, material. You may, however, find some practical information in bar association journals. Look up your topic in the *Index to Legal Periodicals*.

You can probably find these materials in law school libraries; however, large public law libraries also often keep large collections of law journals.

RESEARCHING BANKRUPTCY PROCEDURE

If you need information on court procedures or the local rules of a specific court, consult the *Collier Bankruptcy Practice Manual*.

---

5. Find and Read Relevant Statutes

After consulting *Collier* or one of the other background resources, you may need to read a statute for yourself.

Statutes passed by Congress rule the bankruptcy courts, and your first step should be to figure out which statute governs the issue you're interested in. Sometimes you'll know this from the references (citations) in this book. For instance, Ch. 2, *Your Property and Bankruptcy*, refers to 11 U.S.C. § 522, which concerns exemptions. The citation means Title 11 of the United States Code, Section 522.

Federal statutes are collected in a multi-volume set of books known as the United States Code (U.S.C.) and organized into 50 numbered titles. Title 11 contains the bankruptcy statutes.

If you need to research a question and don't know what statute to start with, there are two ways to find out. First, use the list below, which tells you what's covered by most of the bankruptcy statutes that might affect your case.

BANKRUPTCY CODE SECTIONS (11 U.S.C.)

§ 109 Who may file for which type of bankruptcy
§ 302 Who qualifies for filing joint cases
§ 341 Meeting of creditors
§ 342 Giving notice of meeting of creditors
§ 343 Examination of debtor at meeting of creditors
§ 347 Property the trustee doesn't want
§ 348 Converting from one type of bankruptcy to another
§ 349 Dismissing a case
§ 350 Closing and reopening a case
§ 362 The automatic stay
§ 366 Continuing or reconnecting utility service
§ 501 Filing of creditors' claims
§ 506 Allowed secured claims & lien avoidance
§ 507 Claims having priority
§ 522 Exemptions
§ 523 Nondischargeable debts
§ 524 Reaffirmation of debts
§ 525 Prohibited postbankruptcy discrimination
§ 541 Property of the estate
§ 547 Preferences
§ 548 Fraudulent transfers
§ 553 Setoffs
§ 554 Trustee's abandonment of property
§ 722 Avoiding lien that impairs exemption; redemption
§ 726 Distribution of the property of the estate
§ 727 Discharge

If the list doesn't help, two different publications of the United States Code contain not only the statutes, but also various types of clarifying information. The two publications are *United States Code Annotated* (U.S.C.A., published by West Publishing Co.) and *United States Code Service* (U.S.C.S., published by Bancroft-Whitney/Lawyer's Coop). The statutes are the same in both publications—for instance, you can find section 506 in Title 11 of either the *U.S.C.A.* or the *U.S.C.S.* The accompanying material, however, varies. Some libraries carry only one of these publications; larger libraries carry both.

To read a statute, find U.S.C.A. or U.S.C.S. in your law library, find the title you need, turn to the section number and begin reading. After you read the statute in the hardcover portion of the book, turn to the very back of the book. There should be an insert pamphlet (called a pocket part) for the current year. Look to see if the statute is in the pocket part as well, to see whether it has been amended since the hardcover volume was published.

When you first read a bankruptcy statute you'll probably be totally confused, if not in tears. Relax. No one understands these statutes as they're written. You can go either to *Collier on Bankruptcy* and read its interpretation (remember, it's organized according to the bankruptcy statutes), or directly to court opinions that have interpreted the statute. You can locate these opinions in the case summaries that directly follow the statute in U.S.C.A. or U.S.C.S. (See Section C.7, below.)

6. Read Procedural Rules

Federal bankruptcy rules govern how bankruptcy courts go about their business. Bankruptcy rules can be found in *Collier* and *Consumer Bankruptcy Law and Practice*. If you have a question about a particular bankruptcy procedure, the rules are a good place to start.

In addition to the federal bankruptcy rules, many bankruptcy courts have their own local rules. You should get a copy of these rules from the court handling your case or read them in the *Collier Bankruptcy Practice Manual*.

7. Find and Read Relevant Cases

To understand bankruptcy statutes and rules, it's usually necessary to read a case (court decision) or two that has dealt with how the particular statute applies to situations like yours. Usually you'll read about two types of cases: those decided by a single bankruptcy judge and those decided by a court of appeal.

A bankruptcy judge who resolves a particular issue in a case may write a statement explaining the decision. If this statement, usually called a "memorandum opinion" or "findings of fact and conclusions of law," appears to be of interest to those who practice bankruptcy law, it will be published. If you want to persuade your bankruptcy judge of a particular point, it's to your advantage to find a supportive case which has been decided by another bankruptcy judge considering similar facts.

Several publications carry bankruptcy cases; the one most commonly found in law libraries is the *Bankruptcy Reports* (West Publishing Co.). You can find references to these cases in the case summaries directly following the

bankruptcy statutes. For example, this case summary appears after 11 U.S.C. § 523:

Refusal of college to provide copies of records to students as a consequence of such students' failure to repay student loans obtained from such college, despite discharge of these loans in bankruptcy, was violation of 11 USCS § 523(a)(8) because college's refusal imposed hardship on debtors and denied debtors a "fresh start"… Lee v. Board of Higher Education *(1979, SD NY) 1 B.R. 781.*

The case name is *Lee v. Board of Higher Education*. It was decided in 1979 by a bankruptcy court in the Southern District of New York. The case is published in the *Bankruptcy Reports* (B.R.). It's found in volume 1 at page 781.

If one of the parties to a bankruptcy dispute appeals the bankruptcy judge's ruling, the appeal is decided by a federal district court or a bankruptcy appellate panel. (Bankruptcy appellate panels have been established in only a few areas of the country.) These decisions are published in the *Bankruptcy Reports*, abbreviated as B.R., or the *Federal Reporter, 2nd Series* (West Publishing Co.), abbreviated as F.2d.

Once you find a relevant case or two, you can find similar cases by using cross-reference tools known as digests and *Shepards*. These are explained in *Legal Research: How to Find and Understand the Law*, by Steve Elias and Susan Levenkind (Nolo Press) and other legal research texts.

ONE-STOP RESEARCH: USING THE CCH *BANKRUPTCY LAW REPORTER*

Most law libraries carry a looseleaf publication known as the Commerce Clearing House (CCH) *Bankruptcy Law Reporter* (BLR). In this publication, you can find all three primary source materials relating to bankruptcy: statutes, rules and cases.

Here is a brief tutorial on using this extremely helpful resource. More complete instructions are at the beginning of BLR Volume 1.

Assume Pamela buys a car from John for $2,000. She pays for the car by check, which bounces two days later. Before John can collect the money, Pamela files for Chapter 7 bankruptcy, listing John as a creditor for $2,000. John asks the bankruptcy court to declare the debt nondischargeable on the ground that writing a bad check is fraud. Pamela wants to know whether or not John is right.

Pamela visits her local law library and finds the *Bankruptcy Law Reporter*. The instructions at the beginning of Volume 1 lead her to the "topical index" which is organized by subject matter. She looks up "debt," "bad check" and "fraud." Under "fraud" she finds an entry for "discharge of debts" and a paragraph reference number: 9228.

Pamela locates paragraph 9228 in Volume 2, which contains:

- the federal bankruptcy statute defining fraud
- an explanation of the statute

- summaries of court decisions interpreting the statute
- a table of contents covering the summaries.

Pamela reads the statute, which states that debts arising from fraud can survive bankruptcy. Then, in the table of contents to paragraph 9228, she locates a reference to cases dealing with bad checks and is referred to subsection 9228.27. There she finds a summary of a possibly relevant case, with a cross-reference to paragraph number 69,195, where the full text of the case is printed. She finds the case and reads it, but it isn't helpful.

Next, Pamela turns to the "cumulative index" in Volume 3 and looks for paragraph 9228 in the left margin. The cumulative index tells her if any newer cases have been decided on this issue. She finds several possibly relevant references, including one that says, "Dishonored check not a false representation without a false statement" and a cross-reference to paragraph number 72,876.

Pamela turns to paragraph 72,876 (located in Volume 3, section "New Developments") and finds two new bankruptcy court cases dealing with when a debt from writing a bad check can survive bankruptcy. She reads the cases and learns that writing a bad check isn't considered fraud without showing an intent to commit fraud. Had Pamela told John that the check was good, the bankruptcy court would probably consider it fraud, and the debt would survive bankruptcy.

D. Online Legal Resources

Every day, a growing number of basic legal resources are available online through the Internet. The Internet is a worldwide network of computers that share rules for collecting and organizing data so that others can use the information easily. There are a number of different ways to use the Internet to search for material, but by far the most important and common tool for doing research on the Internet is the World Wide Web, or the Web. The Web provides links among documents and makes it easy to jump from one resource to another. Each resource is organized graphically like a book, allowing you to skip around by topic.

A wide variety of legal source materials is also available online through large commercial services such as America

Online and Microsoft Network. These services have their own collections of resources and ways of organizing that information. These days, America Online, Microsoft Network and the other commercial services tend to include more information related to popular culture than legal and reference materials. But they also provide links to the Internet, including the Web.

The following resources can help you locate legal materials on the Web.

- *Law on the Net*, by James Evans (Nolo Press), provides basic instructions on how to understand and get into the extensive library of legal information available on the Internet.
- *Government on the Net*, by James Evans (Nolo Press), explains how to find government documents, including federal and state codes, available on the Internet.

- http://www.nolo.com, the Nolo Press online site, includes a vast amount of legal information for consumers. This includes sets of FAQs (frequently asked questions) on a wide variety of legal topics and articles on legal issues.

In addition, a wide variety of secondary sources intended for both lawyers and the general public have been posted on the Net by law schools and firms. If you are on the Web, for example, a good way to find these sources is to visit any of the following Web sites, each of which provides links to legal information by specific subject.

- **http://www.courttv.com**
  This is the site to Court TV's Law Center. You can find links to many federal and state laws.
- **http://www.law.cornell.edu/lii.table.html**
  This site is maintained by Cornell Law School. You can find the text of the U.S. Code and federal court decisions. You can also search for material by topic.
- **http://www.law.indiana.edu/law/v-lib/lawindex.html**
  This site is maintained by Indiana University's School of Law at Bloomington. You can search by organization, including the U.S. government, state governments and law journals, or by topic.

Specific bankruptcy information is available at a few sites, including:

- **http://www.agin.com/lawfind/**
  This site provides an extensive list of online bankruptcy-related materials, such as bankruptcy frequently asked questions (FAQs), important bankruptcy cases, United States Bankruptcy Code, federal bankruptcy rules, background on bankruptcy lawyers and links to other online bankruptcy sites.
- **http://nacba.com**
  This is the site for the National Association of Consumer Bankruptcy Attorneys. In addition to information about the organization and its activities, you can find the text of recent cases and legislative developments. ∎

State and Federal Exemption Tables

Using the Exemption Tables

Every state lets people who file for bankruptcy keep certain property, called exemptions. Ch. 2, *Your Property and Bankruptcy*, Section B.6, discusses exemptions in detail.

1. What This Appendix Contains

- lists of each state's exemptions
- list of the federal bankruptcy exemptions (available as a choice in 14 states and the District of Columbia)
- list of the federal *non-bankruptcy* exemptions (available as additional exemptions when the state exemptions are chosen), and
- glossary defining exemption terms.

Each list is divided into three columns. Column 1 lists the major exemption categories: homestead, insurance, miscellaneous, pensions, personal property, public benefits, tools of the trade, wages and wild card. (These categories differ on the federal *non-bankruptcy* exemptions chart.)

Column 2 gives the specific property that falls into each large category with noted limitations.

For example, bankruptcy laws allow married couples filing jointly to each claim a full set of exemptions (called "doubling"). Some states, however, expressly prohibit the doubling of certain exemptions, usually the homestead exemption. If a court decision or statute clearly says that doubling is prohibited, we've indicated it in Column 2. Also, if a court decision or statute clearly says that doubling is allowed, we've included it. Most of the time the chart doesn't say. In that case, you can double.

Column 3 lists the applicable law, which must be included on Schedule C.

2. Choosing Between State and Federal Exemptions

Each state chart indicates whether the federal exemptions are available for that state. The list of federal exemptions follows Wyoming.

3. Using the Glossary

Many of the terms used in exemption statutes are unfamiliar and can be looked up in the glossary. Even if you think you understand the terms in the chart, at least skim the glossary; some terms have special legal meanings that differ from their everyday meanings.

4. Houses and Pensions

If you own a house, you should also read Ch. 6, *Your House*.

With pensions, some states exempt only the money building up in the pension fund, and a few exempt only payments actually being received. Most exempt both. If the pension listing doesn't indicate otherwise, it means the state exempts both.

5. Wages, Benefits and Other Payments

Many states exempt insurance proceeds, pension payments, alimony and child support payments, public benefits or wages. This means that payments you received before filing are exempt if you haven't mixed them with other money or, if you have mixed them, you can trace the exempt portion back to its source.

If, when you file for bankruptcy, you're entitled to receive an exempt payment but haven't yet received it, you can exempt the payment when it comes in by amending Schedules B (personal property you own or possess) and C (property you claim as exempt).

Alabama

Federal Bankruptcy Exemptions not available. All law references are to Alabama Code.

ASSET	EXEMPTION	LAW
homestead	Real property or mobile home to $5,000; property cannot exceed 160 acres (husband & wife may double)	6-10-2
	Must record homestead declaration before attempted sale of home	6-10-20
insurance	Annuity proceeds or avails to $250 per month	27-14-32
	Disability proceeds or avails to an average of $250 per month	27-14-31
	Fraternal benefit society benefits	27-34-27
	Life insurance proceeds or avails if beneficiary is insured's spouse or child	6-10-8
	Life insurance proceeds or avails if beneficiary is wife of insured	27-14-29
	Life insurance proceeds or avails if clause prohibits proceeds from being used to pay beneficiary's creditors	27-15-26
	Mutual aid association benefits	27-30-25
miscellaneous	Property of business partnership	10-8-72(b)(3)
pensions	Judges (only payments being received)	12-18-10(a), (b)
	Law enforcement officers	36-21-77
	State employees	36-27-28
	Teachers	16-25-23
personal property	Books	6-10-6
	Burial place	6-10-5
	Church pew	6-10-5
	Clothing needed	6-10-6
	Family portraits or pictures	6-10-6
public benefits	Aid to blind, aged, disabled, public assistance	38-4-8
	Coal miners' pneumoconiosis benefits	25-5-179
	Crime victims' compensation	15-23-15(e)
	Southeast Asian War POWs' benefits	31-7-2
	Unemployment compensation	25-4-140
	Workers' compensation	25-5-86(b)
tools of trade	Arms, uniforms, equipment that state military personnel are required to keep	31-2-78
wages	75% of earned but unpaid wages; bankruptcy judge may authorize more for low-income debtors	6-10-7
wild card	$3,000 of any personal property, except life insurance (*In re Morris*, 30 B.R. 392 (N.D. Ala. 1983))	6-10-6

Alaska

Alaska law states that only the items found in Alaska Statutes §§ 9.38.010, 9.38.015(a), 9.38.017, 9.38.020, 9.38.025 and 9.38.030 may be exempted in bankruptcy. In *In re McNutt*, 87 B.R. 84 (9th Cir. 1988), however, an Alaskan debtor used the federal bankruptcy exemptions. All law references are to Alaska Statutes.

ASSET	EXEMPTION	LAW
homestead	$54,000 (joint owners may each claim a portion, but total can't exceed $54,000)	9.38.010
insurance	Disability benefits	9.38.015(b), 9.38.030(e)(1), (5)
	Fraternal benefit society benefits	21.84.240
	Insurance proceeds for personal injury, to extent wages exempt (bankruptcy judge may authorize more—9.38.050(a))	9.38.030(e)(3)
	Insurance proceeds for wrongful death, to extent wages exempt	9.38.030(e)(3)
	Life insurance or annuity contract loan value to $10,000	9.38.017, 9.38.025
	Life insurance proceeds if beneficiary is insured's spouse or dependent, to extent wages exempt	9.38.030(e)(4)
	Medical, surgical or hospital benefits	9.38.015(a)(3)
miscellaneous	Alimony, to extent wages exempt	9.38.030(e)(2)
	Child support payments made by collection agency	9.38.015(b)
	Liquor licenses	9.38.015(a)(7)
	Permits for limited entry into Alaska Fisheries	9.38.015(a)(8)
	Property of business partnership	9.38.100(b)
pensions	Elected public officers (only benefits building up)	9.38.015(b)
	ERISA-qualified benefits deposited more than 120 days before filing bankruptcy	9.38.017
	Judicial employees (only benefits building up)	9.38.015(b)
	Public employees (only benefits building up)	9.38.015(b), 39.35.505
	Teachers (only benefits building up)	9.38.015(b)
	Other pensions, to extent wages exempt (only payments being received)	9.38.030(e)(5)
personal property	Books, musical instruments, clothing, family portraits, household goods & heirlooms to $3,000 total	9.38.020(a)
	Building materials	34.35.105
	Burial plot	9.38.015(a)(1)
	Health aids needed	9.38.015(a)(2)
	Jewelry to $1,000	9.38.020(b)
	Motor vehicle to $3,000; vehicle's market value can't exceed $20,000	9.38.020(e)
	Personal injury recoveries, to extent wages exempt	9.38.030(e)(3)
	Pets to $1,000	9.38.020(d)
	Proceeds for lost, damaged or destroyed exempt property	9.38.060
	Wrongful death recoveries, to extent wages exempt	9.38.030(e)(3)
public benefits	Adult assistance to elderly, blind, disabled	47.25.550
	Alaska longevity bonus	9.38.015(a)(5)
	Crime victims' compensation	9.38.015(a)(4)
	Federally exempt public benefits paid or due	9.38.015(a)(6)
	General relief assistance	47.25.210
	Public assistance	47.25.395
	45% of permanent fund dividends	43.23.065
	Tuition credits under an advance college tuition payment contract	9.38.015(a)(9)
	Unemployment compensation	9.38.015(b), 23.20.405
	Workers' compensation	23.30.160
tools of trade	Implements, books & tools of trade to $2,800	9.38.020(c)
wages	Weekly net earnings to $350; for sole wage earner in a household, $550; if you don't receive weekly, or semi-monthly pay, can claim $1,400 in cash or liquid assets paid any month; for sole wage earner in household, $2,200	9.38.030(a), (b), 9.38.050(b)
wild card	None	

Arizona

Federal Bankruptcy Exemptions not available. All law references are to Arizona Revised Statutes unless otherwise noted.

Note: Doubling is permitted for noted exemptions by Arizona Revised Statutes § 33-1121.01.

ASSET	EXEMPTION	LAW
homestead	Real property, an apartment or mobile home you occupy to $100,000; sale proceeds exempt 18 months after sale or until new home purchased, whichever occurs first (husband & wife may not double)	33-1101
	Must record homestead declaration before attempted sale of home	33-1102
insurance	Fraternal benefit society benefits	20-881
	Group life insurance policy or proceeds	20-1132
	Health, accident or disability benefits	33-1126(A)(4)
	Life insurance cash value to $1,000 per dependent ($25,000 total) (husband & wife may double)	33-1126(A)(6)
	Life insurance cash value to $2,000 per dependent ($25,000 total)	20-1131(D)
	Life insurance proceeds to $20,000 if beneficiary is spouse or child (husband & wife may double)	33-1126(A)(1)
miscellaneous	Alimony, child support needed for support	33-1126(A)(3)
	Minor child's earnings, unless debt is for child	33-1126(A)(2)
	Property of business partnership	29-225
pensions *also see wages*	Board of regents members	15-1628(I)
	ERISA-qualified benefits deposited more than 120 days before filing bankruptcy	33-1126(C)
	IRAs	*In re Herrscher,* 121 B.R. 29 (D. Ariz. 1990)
	Firefighters	9-968
	Police officers	9-931
	Public safety personnel	38-850(C)
	Rangers	41-955
	State employees	38-762
personal property *husband & wife may double all personal property exemptions*	2 beds & living room chair per person; 1 dresser, table, lamp, bedding per bed; kitchen table; dining room table & 4 chairs (1 more per person); living room carpet or rug; couch; 3 lamps; 3 coffee or end tables; pictures, paintings, drawings created by debtor; family portraits; refrigerator; stove; TV, radio or stereo;alarm clock; washer; dryer; vacuum cleaner to $4,000 total	33-1123
	Bank deposit to $150 in one account	33-1126(A)(8)
	Bible; bicycle; sewing machine; typewriter; burial plot; rifle, pistol or shotgun to $500 total	33-1125
	Books to $250; clothing to $500; wedding & engagement rings to $1,000; watch to $100; pets, horses, milk cows & poultry to $500; musical instruments to $250; prostheses, including wheelchair	33-1125
	Food & fuel to last 6 months	33-1124
	Motor vehicle to $1,500 ($4,000, if disabled)	33-1125(8)
	Prepaid rent or security deposit to $1,000 or 1½ times your rent, whichever is less, in lieu of homestead	33-1126(D)
	Proceeds for sold or damaged exempt property	33-1126(A)(5), (7)
public benefits	Unemployment compensation	23-783
	Welfare benefits	46-208
	Workers' compensation	23-1068
tools of trade	Arms, uniforms & accoutrements you're required to keep	33-1130(3)
	Farm machinery, utensils, seed, instruments of husbandry, feed, grain & animals to $2,500 total (husband & wife may double)	33-1130(2)
	Teaching aids of teacher	33-1127
	Tools, equipment, instruments & books (except vehicle driven to work) to $2,500	33-1130(1)
wages	Minimum 75% of earned but unpaid wages, pension payments; bankruptcy judge may authorize more for low-income debtors	33-1131
wild card	None	

Arkansas

Federal Bankruptcy Exemptions available. All law references are to Arkansas Code Annotated unless otherwise noted.

ASSET	EXEMPTION	LAW
homestead *choose option 1or 2, not both*	1. For head of family: real or personal property used as residence, to an unlimited value; property cannot exceed ¼ acre in city, town, village, or 80 acres elsewhere. If property is between ¼ -1 acre in city, town or village, or 80-160 acres elsewhere, to $2,500; no homestead may exceed 1 acre in city, town or village, or 160 acres elsewhere (husband & wife may not double, *In re Stevens,* 829 F.2d 693 (8th Cir. 1987))	Constitution 9-3, 9-4, 9-5; 16-66-210, 16-66-218(b)(3), (4)
	2. Real or personal property used as residence, to $800 if single; $1,250 if married	16-66-218(a)(1)
insurance	Annuity contract	23-79-134
	Disability benefits	23-79-133
	Fraternal benefit society benefits	23-74-403
	Group life insurance	23-79-132
	Life, health, accident or disability cash value or proceeds paid or due (limited to the $500 exemption provided by §§ 9-1 and 9-2 of the Arkansas Constitution, *In re Holt,* 97 B.R. 997 (W.D. Ark. 1988).)	16-66-209
	Life insurance proceeds if clause prohibits proceeds from being used to pay beneficiary's creditors	23-79-131
	Life insurance proceeds or avails if beneficiary isn't the insured	23-79-131
	Mutual assessment life or disability benefits to $1,000	23-72-114
	Stipulated insurance premiums	23-71-112
miscellaneous	Property of business partnership	4-42-502
pensions	Disabled firefighters	24-11-814
	Disabled police officers	24-11-417
	Firefighters	24-10-616
	IRA deposits to $20,000 if deposited over 1 year before filing for bankruptcy	16-66-218(b)(16)
	Police officers	24-10-616
	School employees	24-7-715
	State police officers	24-6-202, 24-6-205, 24-6-223
personal property	Burial plot to 5 acres, in lieu of homestead option 2	16-66-207, 16-66-218(a)(1)
	Clothing	Constitution 9-1, 9-2
	Motor vehicle to $1,200	16-66-218(a)(2)
	Wedding bands; any diamond can't exceed ½ carat	16-66-218(a)(3)
public benefits	Aid to blind, aged, disabled, public assistance	20-76-430
	Crime victims' compensation unless seeking to discharge debt for treatment of injury incurred during the crime	16-90-716(e)
	Unemployment compensation	11-10-109
	Workers' compensation	11-9-110
tools of trade	Implements, books & tools of trade to $750	16-66-218(a)(4)
wages	Earned but unpaid wages due for 60 days; in no event under $25 per week	16-66-208, 16-66-218(b)(6)
wild card	$500 of any personal property if married or head of family; else $200	Constitution 9-1, 9-2; 16-66-218(b)(1), (2)

California—System 1

Federal Bankruptcy Exemptions not available. California has two systems; you must select one or the other. All law references are to California Code of Civil Procedure unless otherwise noted.

ASSET	EXEMPTION	LAW
homestead	Real or personal property you occupy including mobile home, boat, stock cooperative, community apartment, planned development or condo to $50,000 if single & not disabled; $75,000 for families if no other member has a homestead (if only one spouse files, may exempt one-half of amount if home held as community property and all of amount if home held as tenants in common); $100,000 if 65 or older, or physically or mentally disabled; $100,000 if 55 or older, single & earn under $15,000 or married & earn under $20,000 & creditors seek to force the sale of your home; sale proceeds received exempt for 6 months after (husband & wife may not double)	704.710, 704.720, 704.730 *In re McFall,* 112 B.R. 336 (9th Cir. B.A.P. 1990)
	May file homestead declaration	704.920
insurance	Disability or health benefits	704.130
	Fidelity bonds	Labor 404
	Fraternal unemployment benefits	704.120
	Homeowners' insurance proceeds for 6 months after received, to homestead exemption amount	704.720(b)
	Life insurance proceeds if clause prohibits proceeds from being used to pay beneficiary's creditors	Ins. 10132, Ins. 10170, Ins. 10171
	Matured life insurance benefits needed for support	704.100(c)
	Unmatured life insurance policy loan value to $8,000 (husband & wife may double)	704.100(b)
miscellaneous	Business or professional licenses	695.060
	Inmates' trust funds to $1,000 (husband and wife may not double)	704.090
	Property of business partnership	Corp. 15025
pensions	County employees	Gov't 31452
	County firefighters	Gov't 32210
	County peace officers	Gov't 31913
	Private retirement benefits, including IRAs & Keoghs	704.115
	Public employees	Gov't 21201
	Public retirement benefits	704.110
personal property	Appliances, furnishings, clothing & food needed	704.020
	Bank deposits from Social Security Administration to $2,000 ($3,000 for husband and wife)	704.080
	Building materials to $2,000 to repair or improve home (husband and wife may not double)	704.030
	Burial plot	704.200
	Health aids	704.050
	Jewelry, heirlooms & art to $5,000 total (husband and wife may not double)	704.040
	Motor vehicles to $1,900, or $1,900 in auto insurance if vehicle(s) lost, damaged or destroyed (husband and wife may not double)	704.010
	Personal injury & wrongful death causes of action	704.140(a), 704.150(a)
	Personal injury & wrongful death recoveries needed for support; if receiving installments, at least 75%	704.140(b), (c), (d), 704.150(b), (c)

ASSET	EXEMPTION	LAW
public benefits	Aid to blind, aged, disabled, public assistance	704.170
	Financial aid to students	704.190
	Relocation benefits	704.180
	Unemployment benefits	704.120
	Union benefits due to labor dispute	704.120(b)(5)
	Workers' compensation	704.160
tools of trade	Tools, implements, materials, instruments, uniforms, books, furnishings, equipment, vessel, motor vehicle to $5,000 total; to $10,000 total if used by both spouses in same occupation (cannot claim motor vehicle under tools of trade exemption if claimed under motor vehicle exemption)	704.060
wages	Minimum 75% of wages	704.070
	Public employees vacation credits; if receiving installments, at least 75%	704.113
wild card	None	

California—System 2

Federal Bankruptcy Exemptions not available. All law references are to California Code of Civil Procedure unless otherwise noted.

Note: Married couples may not double any exemptions (*In re Talmadge*, 832 F.2d 1120 (9th Cir. 1987); *In re Baldwin*, 70 B.R. 612 (9th Cir. B.A.P. 1987))

ASSET	EXEMPTION	LAW
homestead	Real or personal property, including co-op, used as residence to $15,000; unused portion of homestead may be applied to any property	703.140 (b)(1)
insurance	Disability benefits	703.140 (b)(10)(C)
	Life insurance proceeds needed for support of family	703.140 (b)(11)(C)
	Unmatured life insurance contract accrued avails to $8,000	703.140 (b)(8)
	Unmatured life insurance policy other than credit	703.140 (b)(7)
miscellaneous	Alimony, child support needed for support	703.140 (b)(10)(D)
pensions	ERISA-qualified benefits needed for support	703.140 (b)(10)(E)
personal property	Animals, crops, appliances, furnishings, household goods, books, musical instruments & clothing to $400 per item	703.140 (b)(3)
	Burial plot to $15,000, in lieu of homestead	703.140 (b)(1)
	Health aids	703.140 (b)(9)
	Jewelry to $1,000	703.140 (b)(4)
	Motor vehicle to $2,400	703.140 (b)(2)
	Personal injury recoveries to $15,000 (not to include pain & suffering; pecuniary loss)	703.140 (b)(11)(D, E)
	Wrongful death recoveries needed for support	703.140 (b)(11)(B)
public benefits	Crime victims' compensation	703.140 (b)(11)(A)
	Public assistance	703.140 (b)(10)(A)
	Social Security	703.140 (b)(10)(A)
	Unemployment compensation	703.140 (b)(10)(A)
	Veterans' benefits	703.140 (b)(10)(B)
tools of trade	Implements, books & tools of trade to $1,500	703.140 (b)(6)
wages	None	
wild card	$800 of any property	703.140 (b)(5)
	Unused portion of homestead or burial exemption, of any property	703.140 (b)(5)

Colorado

Federal Bankruptcy Exemptions not available. All law references are to Colorado Revised Statutes.

ASSET	EXEMPTION	LAW
homestead	Real property, mobile home or manufactured home (mobile or manufactured home if loan incurred after 1/1/83) you occupy to $30,000; sale proceeds exempt 1 year after received.	38-41-201, 38-41-201.6, 38-41-203, 38-41-207
	Spouse or child of deceased owner may claim homestead exemption	38-41-204
	House trailer or coach used as residence to $3,500	13-54-102(1)(o)(I)
	Mobile home used as residence to $6,000	13-54-102(1)(o)(II)
insurance	Disability benefits to $200 per month; if receive lump sum, entire amount exempt	10-8-114
	Fraternal benefit society benefits	10-14-122
	Group life insurance policy or proceeds	10-7-205
	Homeowners' insurance proceeds for 1 year after received, to homestead exemption amount	38-41-209
	Life insurance avails to $5,000	13-54-102(1)(l)
	Life insurance proceeds if clause prohibits proceeds from being used to pay beneficiary's creditors	10-7-106
miscellaneous	Child support if recipient does not mix with other money or deposits into separate account for the benefit of the child	13-54-102.5
	Property of business partnership	7-60-125
pensions *also see wages*	ERISA-qualified benefits, including IRAs	13-54-102(1)(s)
	Firefighters	31-30-412, 31-30-518
	Police officers	31-30-313, 31-30-616
	Public employees	24-51-212
	Teachers	22-64-120
	Veterans	13-54-102(1)(h), 13-54-104
personal property	1 burial plot per person	13-54-102(1)(d)
	Clothing to $750	13-54-102(1)(a)
	Food & fuel to $300	13-54-102(1)(f)
	Health aids	13-54-102(1)(p)
	Household goods to $1,500	13-54-102(1)(e)
	Jewelry & articles of adornment to $500 total	13-54-102(1)(b)
	Motor vehicles used for work to $1,000; to $3,000 to get medical care, if elderly or disabled	13-54-102(j)(I), (II)
	Personal injury recoveries, unless debt related to injury	13-54-102(1)(n)
	Pictures & books to $750	13-54-102(1)(c)
	Proceeds for damaged exempt property	13-54-102(1)(m)
	Security deposit	13-54-102(1)(r)
public benefits	Aid to blind, aged, disabled, public assistance	26-2-131
	Crime victims' compensation	13-54-102(1)(q), 24-4.1-114
	Unemployment compensation	8-80-103
	Veterans' benefits for veteran, spouse or child if veteran served in war	13-54-102(1)(h)
	Workers' compensation	8-42-124
tools of trade	Horses, mules, wagons, carts, machinery, harness & tools of farmer to $2,000 total	13-54-102(1)(g)
	Library of professional to $1,500 or stock in trade, supplies, fixtures, machines, tools, maps, equipment & books to $1,500 total	13-54-102(1)(i), (k)
	Livestock & poultry of farmer to $3,000	13-54-102(1)(g)
wages	Minimum 75% of earned but unpaid wages, pension payments	13-54-104
wild card	None	

Connecticut

Federal Bankruptcy Exemptions available. All law references are to Connecticut General Statutes Annotated.

ASSET	EXEMPTION	LAW
homestead	Real property, including mobile or manufactured home, to $75,000	52-352b(t)
insurance	Disability benefits paid by association for its members	52-352b(p)
	Fraternal benefit society benefits	38a-637
	Health or disability benefits	52-352b(e)
	Life insurance proceeds if clause prohibits proceeds from being used to pay beneficiary's creditors	38a-454
	Life insurance proceeds or avails	38a-453
	Unmatured life insurance policy loan value to $4,000	52-352b(s)
miscellaneous	Alimony, to extent wages exempt	52-352b(n)
	Child support	52-352b(h)
	Farm partnership animals and livestock feed reasonably required to run farm where at least 50% of partners are members of same family	52-352d
	Property of business partnership	34-63
pensions	ERISA-qualified benefits, to extent wages exempt (only payments being received)	52-352b(m)
	Municipal employees	7-446
	Probate judges & employees	45-29o
	State employees	5-171, 5-192w
	Teachers	10-183q
personal property	Appliances, food, clothing, furniture & bedding needed	52-352b(a)
	Burial plot	52-352b(c)
	Health aids needed	52-352b(f)
	Motor vehicle to $1,500	52-352b(j)
	Proceeds for damaged exempt property	52-352b(q)
	Residential utility & security deposits for 1 residence	52-352b(l)
	Wedding & engagement rings	52-352b(k)
public benefits	Aid to blind, aged, disabled, public assistance	52-352b(d)
	Crime victims' compensation	52-352b(o), 54-213
	Social Security	52-352b(g)
	Unemployment compensation	31-272(c), 52-352b(g)
	Veterans' benefits	52-352b(g)
	Vietnam veterans' death benefits	27-140i
	Wages from earnings incentive program	52-352b(d)
	Workers' compensation	52-352b(g)
tools of trade	Arms, military equipment, uniforms, musical instruments of military personnel	52-352b(i)
	Tools, books, instruments & farm animals needed	52-352b(b)
wages	Minimum 75% of earned but unpaid wages	52-361a(f)
wild card	$1,000 of any property	52-352b(r)

Delaware

Federal Bankruptcy Exemptions not available. All law references are to Delaware Code Annotated unless otherwise noted.

Note: A single person may exempt no more than $5,000 total in all exemptions; a husband & wife may exempt no more than $10,000 total (10-4914).

ASSET	EXEMPTION	LAW
homestead	None, however, property held as tenancy by the entirety may be exempt against debts owed by only one spouse	*In re Hovatter,* 25 B.R. 123 (D. Del. 1982)
insurance	Annuity contract proceeds to $350 per month	18-2728
	Fraternal benefit society benefits	18-6118
	Group life insurance policy or proceeds	18-2727
	Health or disability benefits	18-2726
	Life insurance proceeds if clause prohibits proceeds from being used to pay beneficiary's creditors	18-2729
	Life insurance proceeds or avails	18-2725
miscellaneous	Property of business partnership	6-1525
pensions	Kent County employees	9-4316
	Police officers	11-8803
	State employees	29-5503
	Volunteer firefighters	16-6653
personal property	Bible, books & family pictures	10-4902(a)
	Burial plot	10-4902(a)
	Church pew or any seat in public place of worship	10-4902(a)
	Clothing, includes jewelry	10-4902(a)
	Pianos and leased organs	10-4902(d)
	Sewing machines	10-4902(c)
public benefits	Aid to blind	31-2309
	Aid to aged, disabled, general assistance	31-513
	Unemployment compensation	19-3374
	Workers' compensation	19-2355
tools of trade	Tools, implements & fixtures to $75 in New Castle & Sussex Counties; to $50 in Kent County	10-4902(b)
wages	85% of earned but unpaid wages	10-4913
wild card	$500 of any personal property, except tools of trade, if head of family	10-4903

District of Columbia

Federal Bankruptcy Exemptions available. All law references are to District of Columbia Code unless otherwise noted.

ASSET	EXEMPTION	LAW
homestead	None, however, property held as tenancy by the entirety may be exempt against debts owed by only one spouse	*Estate of Wall*, 440 F.2d 215 (D.C. Cir. 1971)
insurance	Disability benefits	35-522
	Fraternal benefit society benefits	35-1211
	Group life insurance policy or proceeds	35-523
	Life insurance proceeds if clause prohibits proceeds from being used to pay beneficiary's creditors	35-525
	Life insurance proceeds or avails	35-521
	Other insurance proceeds to $200 per month, maximum 2 months, for head of family; else $60 per month	15-503
miscellaneous	Property of business partnership	41-124
pensions	Judges	11-1570(d)
also see wages	Public school teachers	31-1217, 31-1238
personal property	Beds, bedding, radios, cooking utensils, stoves, furniture, furnishings & sewing machines to $300 total	15-501(a)(2)
	Books to $400	15-501(a)(8)
	Clothing to $300	15-501(a)(1), 15-503(b)
	Cooperative association holdings to $50	29-1128
	Family pictures	15-501(a)(8)
	Food & fuel to last 3 months	15-501(a)(3), (4)
	Residential condominium deposit	45-1869
public benefits	Aid to blind, aged, disabled, general assistance	3-215.1
	Crime victims' compensation	3-407
	Unemployment compensation	46-119
	Workers' compensation	36-317
tools of trade	Library, furniture, tools of professional or artist to $300	15-501(a)(6)
	Mechanic's tools; tools of trade or business to $200	15-501(a)(5), 15-503(b)
	Motor vehicle, cart, wagon or dray, & horse or mule harness to $500	15-501(a)(7)
	Seal & documents of notary public	1-806
	Stock & materials to $200	15-501(a)(5)
wages	Minimum 75% of earned but unpaid wages, pension payments; bankruptcy judge may authorize more for low-income debtors 16-572	
	Non-wage (including pension) earnings for 60 days to $200 per month for head of family; else $60 per month 15-503	
wild card	None	

Florida

Federal Bankruptcy Exemptions not available. All law references are to Florida Statutes Annotated unless otherwise noted.

ASSET	EXEMPTION	LAW
homestead	Real or personal property including mobile or modular home to unlimited value; property cannot exceed 1/2 acre in municipality or 160 contiguous acres elsewhere; spouse or child of deceased owner may claim homestead exemption	222.01, 222.02, 222.03, 222.05, Constitution 10-4
	May file homestead declaration	222.01
	Property held as tenancy by the entirety may be exempt against debts owed by only one spouse	*In re Avins*, 19 B.R. 736 (S.D. Fla. 1982)
insurance	Annuity contract proceeds; does not include lottery winnings	222.14; *In re Pizzi*, 153 B.R. 357 (S.D. Fla. 1993)
	Death benefits payable to a specific beneficiary, not the deceased's estate	222.13
	Disability or illness benefits	222.18
	Fraternal benefit society benefits, if received before 10/1/96	632.619
	Life insurance cash surrender value	222.14
miscellaneous	Alimony, child support needed for support	222.201
	Damages to employees for injuries in hazardous occupations	769.05
	Pre-need funeral contract deposits	497.413(8)
	Property of business partnership	620.68
pensions	County officers, employees	122.15
also see wages	ERISA-qualified benefits	222.21(2)
	Firefighters	175.241
	Highway patrol officers	321.22
	Police officers	185.25
	State officers, employees	121.131
	Teachers	238.15
personal property	Any personal property to $1,000 (Husband & wife may double)	Constitution 10-4; *In re Hawkins*, 51 B.R. 348 (S.D. Fla. 1985)
	Health aids	222.25
	Motor vehicle to $1,000	222.25
public benefits	Crime victims' compensation unless seeking to discharge debt for treatment of injury incurred during the crime	960.14
	Hazardous occupation injury recoveries	769.05
	Public assistance	222.201
	Social Security	222.201
	Unemployment compensation	222.201, 443.051(2), (3)
	Veterans' benefits	222.201, 744.626
	Workers' compensation	440.22
tools of trade	None	
wages	100% of wages for heads of family up to $500 per week either unpaid or paid and deposited into bank account for up to 6 months	222.11
	Federal government employees pension payments needed for support & received 3 months prior	222.21
wild card	See personal property	

Georgia

Federal Bankruptcy Exemptions not available. All law references are to the Official Code of Georgia Annotated, not to the Georgia Code Annotated.

ASSET	EXEMPTION	LAW
homestead	Real or personal property, including co-op, used as residence to $5,000; unused portion of homestead may be applied to any property	44-13-100(a)(1)
insurance	Annuity & endowment contract benefits	33-28-7
	Disability or health benefits to $250 per month	33-29-15
	Fraternal benefit society benefits	33-15-20
	Group insurance	33-30-10
	Industrial life insurance if policy owned by someone you depended on, needed for support	33-26-5
	Life insurance proceeds if policy owned by someone you depended on, needed for support	44-13-100(a)(11)(C)
	Unmatured life insurance contract	44-13-100(a)(8)
	Unmatured life insurance dividends, interest, loan value or cash value to $2,000 if beneficiary is you or someone you depend on	44-13-100(a)(9)
miscellaneous	Alimony, child support needed for support	44-13-100(a)(2)(D)
pensions	Employees of non-profit corporations	44-13-100(a)(2.1)(B)
	ERISA-qualified benefits	18-4-22
	Public employees	44-13-100(a)(2.1)(A), 47-2-332
	Other pensions needed for support	18-4-22, 44-13-100(a)(2)(E), 44-13-100(a)(2.1)(C)
personal property	Animals, crops, clothing, appliances, books, furnishings, household goods, musical instruments to $200 per item, $3,500 total	44-13-100(a)(4)
	Burial plot, in lieu of homestead	44-13-100(a)(1)
	Health aids	44-13-100(a)(10)
	Jewelry to $500	44-13-100(a)(5)
	Lost future earnings needed for support	44-13-100(a)(11)(E)
	Motor vehicles to $1,000	44-13-100(a)(3)
	Personal injury recoveries to $7,500	44-13-100(a)(11)(C)
	Wrongful death recoveries needed for support	44-13-100(a)(11)(B)
public benefits	Aid to blind	49-4-58
	Aid to disabled	49-4-84
	Crime victims' compensation	44-13-100(a)(11)(A)
	Local public assistance	44-13-100(a)(2)(A)
	Old age assistance	49-4-35
	Social Security	44-13-100(a)(2)(A)
	Unemployment compensation	44-13-100(a)(2)(A)
	Veterans' benefits	44-13-100(a)(2)(B)
	Workers' compensation	34-9-84
tools of trade	Implements, books & tools of trade to $500	44-13-100(a)(7)
wages	Minimum 75% of earned but unpaid wages for private & federal workers; bankruptcy judge may authorize more for low-income debtors	18-4-20, 18-4-21
wild card	$400 of any property	44-13-100(a)(6)
	Unused portion of homestead exemption, of any property	44-13-100(a)(6)

Hawaii

Federal Bankruptcy Exemptions available. All law references are to Hawaii Revised Statutes unless otherwise noted.

ASSET	EXEMPTION	LAW
homestead	Head of family or over 65 to $30,000; all others to $20,000; property cannot exceed 1 acre. Sale proceeds exempt for 6 months after sale.	36-651-91, 36-651-92, 36-651-96
	Property held as tenancy by the entirety may be exempt against debts owed by only one spouse	*Security Pacific Bank v. Chang*, 818 F.Supp. 1343 (D. Ha. 1993)
insurance	Annuity contract or endowment policy proceeds if beneficiary is insured's spouse, child or parent	24-431:10-232(b)
	Disability benefits	24-431:10-231
	Fraternal benefit society benefits	24-432:2-403
	Group life insurance policy or proceeds	24-431:10-233
	Life or health insurance policy for spouse or child	24-431:10-234
	Life insurance proceeds if clause prohibits proceeds from being used to pay beneficiary's creditors	24-431:10-D:112
miscellaneous	Property of business partnership	23-425-125
pensions	ERISA-qualified benefits deposited over 3 years before filing bankruptcy	36-651-124
	Firefighters	7-88-169
	Police officers	7-88-169
	Public officers & employees	7-88-91, 36-653-3
personal property	Appliances & furnishings needed	36-651-121(1)
	Books	36-651-121(1)
	Burial plot to 250 square feet plus tombstones, monuments & fencing on site	36-651-121(4)
	Clothing	36-651-121(1)
	Housing down payments for home in state project	20-359-104
	Jewelry & articles of adornment to $1,000	36-651-121(1)
	Motor vehicle to wholesale value of $1,000	36-651-121(2)
	Proceeds for sold or damaged exempt property; sale proceeds exempt only 6 months	36-651-121(5)
public benefits	Public assistance paid by Dept. of Health Services for work done in home or workshop	20-346-33
	Unemployment compensation	21-383-163
	Unemployment work relief funds to $60 per month	36-653-4
	Workers' compensation	21-386-57
tools of trade	Tools, implements, books, instruments, uniforms, furnishings, fishing boat, nets, motor vehicle & other personal property needed for livelihood	36-651-121(3)
wages	Unpaid wages due for services of past 31 days; after 31 days, 95% of 1st $100, 90% of 2nd $100, 80% of rest	36-651-121(6), 36-652-1
	Prisoner's wages held by Dept. of Public Safety	20-353-22
wild card	None	

Idaho

Federal Bankruptcy Exemptions not available. All law references are to Idaho Code.

ASSET	EXEMPTION	LAW
homestead	Real property or mobile home to $50,000; sale proceeds exempt for 6 months	55-1003, 55-1113
	Must record homestead exemption for property that is not yet occupied	55-1004
insurance	Annuity contract proceeds to $350 per month	41-1836
	Death or disability benefits	11-604(1)(a), 41-1834
	Fraternal benefit society benefits	41-3218
	Group life insurance benefits	41-1835
	Homeowners' insurance proceeds to amount of homestead exemption	55-1008
	Life insurance proceeds if clause prohibits proceeds from being used to pay beneficiary's creditors	41-1930
	Life insurance proceeds or avails for beneficiary other than the insured	11-604(d), 41-1833
	Medical, surgical or hospital care benefits	11-603(5)
miscellaneous	Alimony, child support needed for support	11-604(1)(b)
	Liquor licenses	23-514
	Property of business partnership	53-325
pensions *also see wages*	ERISA-qualified benefits	55-1011
	Firefighters	72-1422
	Police officers	50-1517
	Public employees	59-1317
	Other pensions needed for support; payments can't be mixed with other money	11-604(1)(e)
personal property	Appliances, furnishings, books, clothing, pets, musical instruments, 1 firearm, family portraits & sentimental heirlooms to $500 per item, $4,000 total	11-605(1)
	Building materials	45-514
	Burial plot	11-603(1)
	Crops cultivated by debtor on maximum 50 acres, to $1,000; includes water rights of 160 inches	11-605(6)
	Health aids needed	11-603(2)
	Jewelry to $250	11-605(2)
	Motor vehicle to $1,500	11-605(3)
	Personal injury recoveries needed for support	11-604(1)(c)
	Proceeds for damaged exempt property for 3 months after proceeds received	11-606
	Wrongful death recoveries needed for support	11-604(1)(c)
public benefits	Aid to blind, aged, disabled	56-223
	Federal, state & local public assistance	11-603(4)
	General assistance	56-223
	Social Security	11-603(3)
	Unemployment compensation	11-603(6)
	Veterans' benefits	11-603(3)
	Workers' compensation	72-802
tools of trade	Arms, uniforms & accoutrements that peace officer, national guard or military personnel is required to keep	11-605(5)
	Implements, books & tools of trade to $1,000	11-605(3)
wages	Minimum 75% of earned but unpaid wages, pension payments; bankruptcy judge may authorize more for low-income debtors	11-207
wild card	None	

Illinois

Federal Bankruptcy Exemptions not available. All law references are to Illinois Annotated Statutes.

ASSET	EXEMPTION	LAW
homestead	Real or personal property including a farm, lot & buildings, condo, co-op or mobile home to $7,500; sale proceeds exempt 1 year from sale	735-5/12-901, 735-5/12-906
	Spouse or child of deceased owner may claim homestead exemption	735-5/12-902
	Husband & wife may double	*First National Bank v. Mohr*, 515 N.E. 2d 1356 (App. Ct. Ill. 1988)
insurance	Fraternal benefit society benefits	215-5/299.1a
	Health or disability benefits	735-5/12-1001(g)(3)
	Homeowners proceeds if home destroyed, to $7,500	735-5/12-907
	Life insurance, annuity proceeds or cash value if beneficiary is insured's child, parent, spouse or other dependent	215-5/238
	Life insurance policy if beneficiary is insured's spouse or child	735-5/12-1001(f)
	Life insurance proceeds if clause prohibits proceeds from being used to pay beneficiary's creditors	215-5/238
	Life insurance proceeds needed for support	735-5/12-1001(f), (g)(3)
miscellaneous	Alimony, child support needed for support	735-5/12-1001(g)(4)
	Property of business partnership	805-205/25
pensions	Civil service employees	40-5/11-223
	County employees	40-5/9-228
	Disabled firefighters; widows & children of firefighters	40-5/22-230
	ERISA-qualified benefits	735-5/12-1006
	Firefighters	40-5/4-135, 40-5/6-213
	General assembly members	40-5/2-154
	House of correction employees	40-5/19-117
	Judges	40-5/18-161
	Municipal employees	40-5/7-217(a), 40-5/8-244
	Park employees	40-5/12-190
	Police officers	40-5/3-144.1, 40-5/5-218
	Public employees	735-5/12-1006
	Public library employees	40-5/19-218
	Sanitation district employees	40-5/13-808
	State employees	40-5/14-147
	State university employees	40-5/15-185
	Teachers	40-5/16-190, 40-5/17-151
personal property	Bible, family pictures, schoolbooks & needed clothing	735-5/12-1001(a)
	Health aids	735-5/12-1001(e)
	Motor vehicle to $1,200	735-5/12-1001(c)
	Personal injury recoveries to $7,500	735-5/12-1001(g)(4)
	Proceeds of sold exempt property	735-5/12-1001
	Title certificate for boat over 12 feet long	652-45/3A-7
	Wrongful death recoveries needed for support	735-5/12-1001(h)(2)
public benefits	Aid to aged, blind, disabled, public assistance	305-5/11-3
	Crime victims' compensation	735-5/12-1001(h)(1)
	Restitution payments on account of WWII relocation of Aleuts and Japanese Americans	735-5/12-1001(12)(h)(5)
	Social Security	735-5/12-1001(g)(1)
	Unemployment compensation	735-5/12-1001(g) (1), (3)
	Veterans' benefits	735-5/12-1001(g)(2)
	Workers' compensation	820-305/21
	Workers' occupational disease compensation	820-310/21
tools of trade	Implements, books & tools of trade to $750	735-5/12-1001(d)
wages	Minimum 85% of earned but unpaid wages; bankruptcy judge may authorize more for low-income debtors	740-170/4
wild card	$2,000 of any personal property	735-5/12-1001(b)
	Includes wages	*In re Johnson*, 57 B.R. 635 (N.D. Ill. 1986)

Indiana

Federal Bankruptcy Exemptions not available. All law references are to Indiana Statutes Annotated.

ASSET	EXEMPTION	LAW
homestead *also see wild card*	Real or personal property used as residence to $7,500 (homestead plus personal property —except health aids—can't exceed $10,000, 34-28-1(c))	34-2-28-1(a)(1)
	Property held as tenancy by the entirety may be exempt against debts incurred by only one spouse	34-2-28-1(a)(5)
insurance	Fraternal benefit society benefits	27-11-6-3
	Group life insurance policy	27-1-12-29
	Life insurance policy, proceeds, cash value or avails if beneficiary is insured's spouse or dependent	27-1-12-14
	Life insurance proceeds if clause prohibits proceeds to be used to pay beneficiary's creditors	27-2-5-1
	Mutual life or accident proceeds	27-8-3-23
miscellaneous	Property of business partnership	23-4-1-25
pensions	Firefighters	36-8-7-22, 36-8-8-17
	Police officers (only benefits building up)	10-1-2-9, 36-8-8-17
	Public employees	5-10.3-8-9
	Public or private retirement benefits	34-2-28-1(a)(6)
	Sheriffs (only benefits building up)	36-8-10-19
	State teachers	21-6.1-5-17
personal property *also see wild card*	Health aids	34-2-28-1(a)(4)
	$100 of any intangible personal property, except money owed to you	34-2-28-1(a)(3)
public benefits	Crime victims' compensation unless seeking to discharge debt for treatment of injury incurred during the crime	12-18-6-36
	Unemployment compensation	22-4-33-3
	Workers' compensation	22-3-2-17
tools of trade	National guard uniforms, arms & equipment	10-2-6-3
wages	Minimum 75% of earned but unpaid wages; bankruptcy judge may authorize more for low-income debtors	24-4.5-5-105
wild card	$4,000 of any real estate or tangible personal property	34-2-28-1(a)(2)

Iowa

Federal Bankruptcy Exemptions not available. All law references are to Iowa Code Annotated.

ASSET	EXEMPTION	LAW
homestead	Real property or an apartment to an unlimited value; property cannot exceed ¹/₂ acre in town or city, 40 acres elsewhere	499A.18, 561.2, 561.16
	May record homestead declaration	561.4
insurance	Accident, disability, health, illness or life proceeds or avails to $15,000, paid to surviving spouse, child or other dependent	627.6(6)
	Employee group insurance policy or proceeds	509.12
	Life insurance proceeds to $10,000, acquired within 2 years of filing for bankruptcy, paid to spouse, child or other dependent	627.6(6)
	Life insurance proceeds if clause prohibits proceeds from being used to pay beneficiary's creditors	508.32
miscellaneous	Alimony, child support needed for support	627.6(8)(d)
	Liquor licenses	123.38
	Property of business partnership	544.25
pensions *also see wages*	Disabled firefighters, police officers (only payments being received)	410.11
	Federal government pension (only payments being received)	627.8
	Firefighters	411.13
	Peace officers	97A.12
	Police officers	411.13
	Public employees	97B.39
	Other pensions needed for support (only payments being received)	627.6(8)(e)
personal property	Appliances, furnishings & household goods to $2,000 total	627.6(5)
	Bibles, books, portraits, pictures & paintings to $1,000 total	627.6(3)
	Burial plot to 1 acre	627.6(4)
	Clothing to $1,000 plus receptacles to hold clothing	627.6(1)
	Health aids	627.6(7)
	Motor vehicle, musical instruments & tax refund to $5,000 total, no more than $1,000 from tax refund	627.6(9)
	Rifle or musket; shotgun	627.6(2)
	Wedding or engagement rings	627.6(1)
public benefits	Adopted child assistance	627.19
	Local public assistance	627.6(8)(a)
	Social Security	627.6(8)(a)
	Unemployment compensation	627.6(8)(a)
	Veterans' benefits	627.6(8)(b)
	Workers' compensation	627.13
tools of trade	Farming equipment; includes livestock, feed to $10,000 (can't include car, *In re Van Pelt*, 83 B.R. 617 (S.D. Iowa 1987))	627.6(11)
	Non-farming equipment to $10,000 (can't include car, *In re Van Pelt*, 83 B.R. 617 (S.D. Iowa 1987))	627.6(10)
wages	Minimum 75% of earned but unpaid wages, pension payments; bankruptcy judge may authorize more for low-income debtors	642.21
wild card	$100 of any personal property, including cash	627.6(13)

Kansas

Federal Bankruptcy Exemptions not available. All law references are to Kansas Statutes Annotated unless otherwise noted.

ASSET	EXEMPTION	LAW
homestead	Real property or mobile home you occupy or intend to occupy to unlimited value; property cannot exceed 1 acre in town or city, 160 acres on farm	60-2301, Constitution 15-9
insurance	Fraternal life insurance benefits	40-414(a)
	Life insurance forfeiture value if file for bankruptcy over 1 year after policy issued	40-414(b)
	Life insurance proceeds if clause prohibits proceeds from being used to pay beneficiary's creditors	40-414(a)
miscellaneous	Liquor licenses	41-326
	Property of business partnership	56-325
pensions	Elected & appointed officials in cities with populations between 120,000 & 200,000	13-14,102
	ERISA-qualified benefits	60-2308(b)
	Federal government pension needed for support & paid within 3 months of filing for bankruptcy (only payments being received)	60-2308(a)
	Firefighters	12-5005(e), 14-10a10
	Judges	20-2618
	Police officers	12-5005(e), 13-14a10
	Public employees	74-4923, 74-49,105
	State highway patrol officers	74-4978g
	State school employees	72-5526
personal property	Burial plot or crypt	60-2304(d)
	Clothing to last 1 year	60-2304(a)
	Food & fuel to last 1 year	60-2304(a)
	Funeral plan prepayments	16-310(d)
	Furnishings & household equipment	60-2304(a)
	Jewelry & articles of adornment to $1,000	60-2304(b)
	Motor vehicle to $20,000; if designed or equipped for disabled person, no limit	60-2304(c)
public benefits	Crime victims' compensation	74-7313(d)
	General assistance, social welfare	39-717
	Unemployment compensation	44-718(c)
	Workers' compensation	44-514
tools of trade	Books, documents, furniture, instruments, equipment, breeding stock, seed, grain & stock to $7,500 total	60-2304(e)
	National Guard uniforms, arms & equipment	48-245
wages	Minimum 75% of earned but unpaid wages; bankruptcy judge may authorize more for low-income debtors	60-2310
wild card	None	

Kentucky

Federal Bankruptcy Exemptions not available. All law references are to Kentucky Revised Statutes.

ASSET	EXEMPTION	LAW
homestead	Real or personal property used as residence to $5,000; sale proceeds exempt	427.060, 427.090
insurance	Annuity contract proceeds to $350 per month	304.14-330
	Cooperative life or casualty insurance benefits	427.110(1)
	Fraternal benefit society benefits	427.110(2)
	Group life insurance proceeds	304.14-320
	Health or disability benefits	304.14-310
	Life insurance policy if beneficiary is a married woman	304.14-340
	Life insurance proceeds if clause prohibits proceeds from being used to pay beneficiary's creditors	304.14-350
	Life insurance proceeds or cash value if beneficiary is someone other than insured	304.14-300
miscellaneous	Alimony, child support needed for support	427.150(1)
	Property of business partnership	362.270
pensions	Firefighters, police officers	67A.620, 95.878, 427.120, 427.125
	IRAs	In re Worthington, 28 B.R. 736 (W.D. Ky. 1983)
	State employees	61.690
	Teachers	161.700
	Urban county government employees	67A.350
	Other pensions	427.150(2)(e), (f)
personal property	Burial plot to $5,000, in lieu of homestead	427.060
	Clothing, jewelry, articles of adornment & furnishings to $3,000 total	427.010(1)
	Health aids	427.010(1)
	Lost earnings payments needed for support	427.150(2)(d)
	Medical expenses paid & reparation benefits received under motor vehicle reparation law	304.39-260
	Motor vehicle to $2,500	427.010(1)
	Personal injury recoveries to $7,500 (not to include pain & suffering or pecuniary loss)	427.150(2)(c)
	Wrongful death recoveries for person you depended on, needed for support	427.150(2)(b)
public benefits	Aid to blind, aged, disabled, public assistance	205.220
	Crime victims' compensation	427.150(2)(a)
	Unemployment compensation	341.470
	Workers' compensation	342.180
tools of trade	Library, office equipment, instruments & furnishings of minister, attorney, physician, surgeon, chiropractor, veterinarian or dentist to $1,000	427.040
	Motor vehicle of mechanic, mechanical or electrical equipment servicer, minister, attorney, physician, surgeon, chiropractor, veterinarian or dentist to $2,500	427.030
	Tools, equipment, livestock & poultry of farmer to $3,000	427.010(1)
	Tools of non-farmer to $300	427.030
wages	Minimum 75% of earned but unpaid wages; bankruptcy judge may authorize more for low-income debtors	427.010(2), (3)
wild card	$1,000 of any property	427.160

Louisiana

Federal Bankruptcy Exemptions not available. All law references are to Louisiana Revised Statutes Annotated unless otherwise noted.

ASSET	EXEMPTION	LAW
homestead	Property you occupy to $15,000; cannot exceed 160 acres on 1 tract, or on 2 or more tracts if there's a home on 1 tract and field, garden or pasture on others (husband & wife may not double)	20:1
	Spouse or child of deceased owner may claim homestead exemption; spouse given home in divorce gets homestead	
insurance	Fraternal benefit society benefits	22:558
	Group insurance policies or proceeds	22:649
	Health, accident or disability proceeds or avails	22:646
	Life insurance proceeds or avails; if policy issued within 9 months of filing, exempt only to $35,000	22:647
miscellaneous	Property of minor child	13:3881A(3), Civil 223
pensions	Gratuitous payments to employee or heirs whenever paid	20:33(2)
	ERISA-qualified benefits if contributions made over 1 year before filing for bankruptcy	13:3881D(1), 20:33(4)
personal property	Arms, military accoutrements, bedding, linens & bedroom furniture, chinaware, glassware, utensils, silverware (non-sterling), clothing, family portraits, musical instruments, heating & cooling equipment, living room & dining room furniture, poultry, fowl, 1 cow, household pets, pressing irons, sewing machine, refrigerator, freezer, stove, washer & dryer	13:3881A(4)
	Cemetery plot, monuments	8:313
	Engagement & wedding rings to $5,000	13:3881A(5)
public benefits	Aid to blind, aged, disabled, public assistance	46:111
	Crime victims' compensation	46:1811
	Unemployment compensation	23:1693
	Workers' compensation	23:1205
tools of trade	Tools, instruments, books, pickup truck (maximum 3 tons) or non-luxury auto & utility trailer, needed to work	13:3881A(2)
wages	Minimum 75% of earned but unpaid wages; bankruptcy judge may authorize more for low-income debtors	13:3881A(1)
wild card	None	

Maine

Federal Bankruptcy Exemptions not available. All law references are to Maine Revised Statutes Annotated.

ASSET	EXEMPTION	LAW
homestead	Real or personal property (including cooperative) used as residence to $12,500; if debtor over age 60 or physically or mentally disabled, $60,000 (joint debtors may double)	14-4422(1)
insurance	Annuity proceeds to $450 per month	24-A-2431
	Disability or health proceeds, benefits or avails	14-4422(13)A & C24-A-2429
	Fraternal benefit society benefits	24-A-4118
	Group health or life policy or proceeds	24-A-2430
	Life, endowment, annuity or accident policy, proceeds or avails	14-4422(14)C, 24-A-2428
	Life insurance policy, interest, loan value or accrued dividends for policy from person you depended on, to $4,000	14-4422(11)
	Unmatured life insurance policy, except credit insurance policy	14-4422(10)
miscellaneous	Alimony & child support needed for support	14-4422(13)D
	Property of business partnership	31-305
pensions	ERISA-qualified benefits	14-4422(13)E
	Judges	4-1203
	Legislators	3-703
	State employees	5-17054
personal property	Animals, crops, musical instruments, books, clothing, furnishings, household goods, appliances to $200 per item	14-4422(3)
	Balance due on repossessed goods; total amount financed can't exceed $2,000	9-A-5-103
	Burial plot in lieu of homestead exemption	14-4422(1)
	Cooking stove; furnaces & stoves for heat	14-4422(6)A & B
	Food to last 6 months	14-4422(7)A
	Fuel not to exceed 10 cords of wood, 5 tons of coal or 1,000 gallons of petroleum	14-4422(6)C
	Health aids	14-4422(12)
	Jewelry to $750; no limit for 1 wedding & 1 engagement ring	14-4422(4)
	Lost earnings payments needed for support	14-4422(14)E
	Military clothes, arms & equipment	37-B-262
	Motor vehicle to $2,500	14-4422(2)
	Personal injury recoveries to $12,500, not to include pain & suffering	14-4422(14)D
	Seeds, fertilizers & feed to raise & harvest food for 1 season	14-4422(7)B
	Tools & equipment to raise & harvest food	14-4422(7)C
	Wrongful death recoveries needed for support	14-4422(14)B
public benefits	Crime victims' compensation	14-4422(14)A
	Public assistance	22-3753
	Social Security	14-4422(13)A
	Unemployment compensation	14-4422(13)A & C
	Veterans' benefits	14-4422(13)B
	Workers' compensation	39-67
tools of trade *also see personal property*	Boat not exceeding 5 tons used in commercial fishing	14-4422(9)
	Books, materials & stock to $5,000	14-4422(5)
	1 of each type of farm implement needed to harvest & raise crops	14-4422(8)
wages	None	
wild card	Unused portion of homestead exemption to $6,000 of animals, crops, musical instruments, books, clothing, furnishings, household goods, appliances, tools of the trade and personal injury recoveries	14-4422(15)
	$400 of any property	14-4422(15)

Maryland

Federal Bankruptcy Exemptions not available. All law references are to Annotated Code of Maryland unless otherwise noted.

ASSET	EXEMPTION	LAW
homestead	None, however, property held as tenancy by the entirety may be exempt against debts owed by only one spouse	*In re Sefren*, 41 B.R. 747 (D. Md. 1984)
insurance	Disability or health benefits, including court awards, arbitrations & settlements	Courts & Jud. Proceedings 11-504(b)(2)
	Fraternal benefit society benefits	48A-328, Estates & Trusts 8-115
	Life insurance or annuity contract proceeds or avails if beneficiary is insured's dependent, child or spouse	48A-385, Estates & Trusts 8-115
	Medical benefits deducted from wages	Commercial 15-601.1
miscellaneous	Property of business partnership	Corporation 9-502
pensions	Deceased Baltimore police officers (only benefits building up)	73B-49
	ERISA-qualified benefits, except IRAs	Courts & Jud. Proceedings 11-504(h)
	State employees	73B-17, 73B-125
	State police	88B-60
	Teachers	73B-96, 73B-152
personal property	Appliances, furnishings, household goods, books, pets & clothing to $500 total	Courts & Jud. Proceedings 11-504(b)(4)
	Burial plot	23-164
	Health aids	Courts & Jud. Proceedings 11-504(b)(3)
	Lost future earnings recoveries	Courts & Jud. Proceedings 11-504(b)(2)
public benefits	Crime victims' compensation	26A-13
	General assistance	88A-73
	Unemployment compensation	Labor & Employment 8-106
	Workers' compensation	Labor & Employment 9-732
tools of trade	Clothing, books, tools, instruments & appliances to $2,500; can't include car (*In re Chapman*, 68 B.R. 745 (D. Md. 1986))	Courts & Jud. Proceedings 11-504(b)(1)
wages	Earned but unpaid wages, the greater of 75% or $145 per week; in Kent, Caroline, & Queen Anne's of Worcester Counties, the greater of 75% of actual wages or 30% of federal minimumwage	Commercial 15-601.1
wild card	$5,500 of any property	Courts & Jud. Proceedings 11-504(b)(5), (f)

Massachusetts

Federal Bankruptcy Exemptions available. All law references are to Massachusetts General Laws Annotated.

ASSET	EXEMPTION	LAW
homestead	Property you occupy or intend to occupy to $100,000; if over 65 or disabled, $200,000 (joint owners may not double)	188-1, 188-1A
	Must record homestead declaration before filing bankruptcy	188-2
	Spouse or child of deceased owner may claim homestead exemption	188-4
	Property held as tenancy by the entirety may be exempt against non-necessity debts	209-1
insurance	Disability benefits to $400 per week	175-110A
	Fraternal benefit society benefits	176-22
	Group annuity policy or proceeds	175-132C
	Group life insurance policy	175-135
	Life or endowment policy, proceeds or cash value	175-125
	Life insurance annuity contract which says it's exempt	175-125
	Life insurance policy if beneficiary is married woman	175-126
	Life insurance proceeds if clause prohibits proceeds from being used to pay beneficiary's creditors	175-119A
	Medical malpractice self-insurance	175F-15
miscellaneous	Property of business partnership	108A-25
pensions	ERISA-qualified benefits	235-34A, 246-28
	Private retirement benefits	32-41
also see wages	Public employees	32-19
	Savings bank employees	168-41, 168-44
personal property	Bank deposits to $125; food or cash for food to $300	235-34
	Beds, bedding & heating unit; clothing needed	235-34
	Bibles & books to $200 total; sewing machine to $200	235-34
	Burial plots, tombs & church pew	235-34
	Cash for fuel, heat, water or light to $75 per month	235-34
	Cash to $200 per month for rent, in lieu of homestead	235-34
	Cooperative association shares to $100	235-34
	2 cows, 12 sheep, 2 swine, 4 tons of hay	235-34
	Furniture to $3,000; motor vehicle to $750	235-34
	Moving expenses for eminent domain	79-6A
	Trust company, bank or credit union deposits to $500	246-28A
public benefits	Aid to aged, disabled	235-34
	Public assistance	118-10
	Unemployment compensation	151A-36
	Veterans' benefits	115-5
	Workers' compensation	152-47
tools of trade	Arms, accoutrements & uniforms you're required to keep	235-34
	Boats, fishing tackle & nets of fisherman to $500	235-34
	Materials you designed & procured to $500	235-34
	Tools, implements & fixtures to $500 total	235-34
wages	Earned but unpaid wages to $125 per week	246-28
wild card	None	

Michigan

Federal Bankruptcy Exemptions available. All law references are to Michigan Compiled Laws Annotated unless otherwise noted.

ASSET	EXEMPTION	LAW
homestead	Real property including condo to $3,500; property cannot exceed 1 lot in town, village,city, or 40 acres elsewhere	559.214, 600.6023(1)(h), (i), 600.6023(3), 600.6027
	Spouse or child of deceased owner may claim homestead exemption; property held as tenancy by the entirety may be exempt against debts owed by only one spouse	SNB Bank & Trust v. Kensey, 378 N.W. 2d 594 (Ct. App. Mich. 1985)
insurance	Disability, mutual life or health benefits	600.6023(1)(f)
	Fraternal benefit society benefits	500.8181
	Life, endowment or annuity proceeds if clause prohibits proceeds from being used to pay beneficiary's creditors	500.4054
miscellaneous	Property of business partnership	449.25
pensions	Firefighters, police officers	38.559(6)
	ERISA-qualified benefits	600.6023(1)(k)
	IRAs	600.6023(1)(l)
	Judges	38.826
	Legislators	38.1057
	Probate judges	38.927
	Public school employees	38.1346
	State employees	38.40
personal property	Appliances, utensils, books, furniture & household goods to $1,000 total	600.6023(1)(b)
	Building & loan association shares to $1,000 par value, in lieu of homestead	600.6023(1)(g)
	Burial plots, cemeteries; church pew, slip, seat	600.6023(1)(c)
	Clothing; family pictures	600.6023(1)(a)
	2 cows, 100 hens, 5 roosters, 10 sheep, 5 swine; hay & grain to last 6 months if you're a head of household	600.6023(1)(d)
	Food & fuel to last 6 months if you're a head of household	600.6023(1)(a)
public benefits	Crime victims' compensation	18.362
	Social welfare benefits	400.63
	Unemployment compensation	421.30
	Veterans' benefits for Korean War veterans	35.977
	Veterans' benefits for Vietnam veterans	35.1027
	Veterans' benefits for WWII veterans	35.926
	Workers' compensation	418.821
tools of trade	Arms & accoutrements you're required to keep	600.6023(1)(a)
	Tools, implements, materials, stock, apparatus, team, motor vehicle, horse & harness to $1,000 total	600.6023(1)(e)
wages	60% of earned but unpaid wages for head of household; else 40%; head of household may keep at least $15 per week plus $2 per week per non-spouse dependent; others may keep at least $10 per week	600.5311
wild card	None	

Minnesota

Federal Bankruptcy Exemptions available. All law references are to Minnesota Statutes Annotated.Note: Section 550.37(4)(a) requires that certain exemptions be adjusted for inflation on July 1 of even-numbered years. The below exemptions include all changes through July 1, 1994. For additional information, contact the Minnesota Department of Commerce at (612) 296-2297.

ASSET	EXEMPTION	LAW
homestead	Real property, mobile home or manufactured home to $200,000 or, if the homestead is used primarily for agricultural purposes, $500,000; cannot exceed ½ acre in city or 160 acres elsewhere	510.01, 510.02, 550.37 subd. 12
insurance	Accident or disability proceeds	550.39
	Fraternal benefit society benefits	64B.18
	Life insurance proceeds if beneficiary is spouse or child of insured to $32,000, plus $8,000 per dependent	550.37 subd. 10
	Police, fire or beneficiary association benefits	550.37 subd. 11
	Unmatured life insurance contract dividends, interest or loan value to $6,400 if insured is debtor or someone debtor depends on	550.37 subd. 23
miscellaneous	Earnings of minor child	550.37 subd. 15
	Property of business partnership	323.24
pensions	ERISA-qualified benefits needed for support, which do not exceed $48,000 in present value	550.37 subd. 24
	IRAs needed for support, which do not exceed $48,000 in present value	550.37 subd. 24
	Private retirement benefits (only benefits building up)	181B.16
	Public employees	353.15
	State employees	352.96
	State troopers	352B.071
personal property	Appliances, furniture, radio, phonographs & TV to $7,200 total	550.37 subd. 4(b)
	Bible, books & musical instruments	550.37 subd. 2
	Burial plot; church pew or seat	550.37 subd. 3
	Clothing (includes watch), food & utensils	550.37 subd. 4(a)
	Motor vehicle to $3,200 (up to $32,000 if vehicle has been modified for disability)	550.37 subd. 12(a)
	Personal injury recoveries	550.37 subd. 22
	Proceeds for damaged exempt property	550.37 subds. 9, 16
	Wrongful death recoveries	550.37 subd. 22
public benefits	Crime victims' compensation	611A.60
	Supplemental assistance, general assistance, supplemental security income	550.37 subd. 14
	Unemployment compensation	268.17 subd. 2
	Veterans' benefits	550.38
	Workers' compensation	176.175
tools of trade *total tools of trade (except teaching materials) can't exceed $13,000*	Farm machines, implements, livestock, farm produce & crops of farmers to $13,000 total	550.37 subd. 5
	Teaching materials (including books, chemical apparatus) of public school teacher	550.37 subd. 8
	Tools, implements, machines, instruments, furniture, stock in trade & library to $8,000 total	550.37 subd. 6
wages	Earned but unpaid wages, paid within 6 months of returning to work, if you received welfare in past	550.37 subd. 13
	Minimum 75% of earned but unpaid wages	571.922
	Wages deposited into bank accounts for 20 days after depositing	550.37 subd. 13
	Wages of released inmates paid within 6 months of release	550.37 subd. 14
wild card	None	

Note: Some courts have held "unlimited" exemptions (such as fraternal benefit society benefits, musical instruments, personal injury recoveries) unconstitutional under the Minnesota Constitution which allows debtors to exempt only a reasonable amount of property. See *In re Tveten,* 402 N.W. 2d 551 (Minn. 1987) and *In re Medill,* 119 B.R. 685, (D. Minn. 1990).

Mississippi

Federal Bankruptcy Exemptions not available. All law references are to Mississippi Code.

ASSET	EXEMPTION	LAW
homestead	Property you occupy unless over 60 & married or widowed, to $75,000; property cannot exceed 160 acres; sale proceeds exempt	85-3-1(b)(i), 85-3-21, 85-3-23
	May file homestead declaration	85-3-27, 85-3-31
insurance	Disability benefits	85-3-1(b)(ii)
	Fraternal benefit society benefits	83-29-39
	Homeowners' insurance proceeds to $75,000	85-3-23
	Life insurance proceeds if clause prohibits proceeds from being used to pay beneficiary's creditors	83-7-5
miscellaneous	Property of business partnership	79-12-49
pensions	ERISA-qualified benefits deposited over 1 year before filing bankruptcy	85-3-1(b)(iii)
	Firefighters	21-29-257
	Highway patrol officers	25-13-31
	IRAs deposited over 1 year before filing bankruptcy	85-3-1(b)(iii)
	Keoghs deposited over 1 year before filing bankruptcy	85-3-1(b)(iii)
	Private retirement benefits to extent tax-deferred	71-1-43
	Police officers	21-29-257
	Public employees retirement & disability benefits	25-11-129
	State employees	25-14-5
	Teachers	25-11-201(1)(d)
personal property	Tangible personal property of any kind to $10,000	85-3-1(a)
	Personal injury judgments to $10,000	85-3-17
	Proceeds for exempt property	85-3-1(b)(i)
public benefits	Assistance to aged	43-9-19
	Assistance to blind	43-3-71
	Assistance to disabled	43-29-15
	Crime victims' compensation	99-41-23
	Social Security	25-11-129
	Unemployment compensation	71-5-539
	Workers' compensation	71-3-43
tools of trade	See personal property	
wages	Earned but unpaid wages owed for 30 days; after 30 days, minimum 75% (bankruptcy judge may authorize more for low-income debtors)	85-3-4
wild card	See personal property	

Missouri

Federal Bankruptcy Exemptions not available. All law references are to Annotated Missouri Statutes unless otherwise noted.

ASSET	EXEMPTION	LAW
homestead	Real property to $8,000 or mobile home to $1,000 (joint owners may not double)	513.430(6), 513.475
	Property held as tenancy by the entirety may be exempt against debts owed by only one spouse	In re Anderson, 12 B.R. 483 (W.D. Mo. 1981)
insurance	Assessment or insurance premium proceeds	377.090
	Disability or illness benefits	513.430(10)(c)
	Fraternal benefit society benefits to $5,000, bought over 6 months before filing	513.430(8)
	Life insurance dividends, loan value or interest to $5,000, bought over 6 months before filing	513.430(8)
	Life insurance proceeds if policy owned by a woman & insures her husband	376.530
	Life insurance proceeds if policy owned by unmarried woman & insures her father or brother	376.550
	Stipulated insurance premiums	377.330
	Unmatured life insurance policy	513.430(7)
miscellaneous	Alimony, child support to $500 per month	513.430(10)(d)
	Property of business partnership	358.250
pensions	Employees of cities with 100,000 or more people	71.207
	ERISA-qualified benefits needed for support (only payments being received)	513.430(10)(e)
	Firefighters	87.090, 87.365, 87.485
	Highway & transportation employees	104.250
	Police department employees	86.190, 86.353, 86.493, 86.780
	Public officers & employees	70.695
	State employees	104.540
	Teachers	169.090
personal property	Appliances, household goods, furnishings, clothing, books, crops, animals & musical instruments to $1,000 total	513.430(1)
	Burial grounds to 1 acre or $100	214.190
	Health aids	513.430(9)
	Jewelry to $500	513.430(2)
	Motor vehicle to $1,000	513.430(5)
	Personal injury causes of action	In re Mitchell, 73 B.R. 93 (E.D. Mo. 1987)
	Wrongful death recoveries for person you depended on	513.430(11)
public benefits	Public assistance	513.430(10)(a)
	Social Security	513.430(10)(a)
	Unemployment compensation	288.380(10)(l), 513.430(10)(c)
	Veterans' benefits	513.430(10)b)
	Workers' compensation	287.260
tools of trade	Implements, books & tools of trade to $2,000	513.430(4)
wages	Minimum 75% of earned but unpaid wages (90% for head of family); bankruptcy judge may authorize more for low-income debtors	525.030
	Wages of servant or common laborer to $90	513.470
wild card	$1,250 of any property if head of family, else $400; head of family may claim additional $250 per child	513.430(3), 513.440

Montana

Federal Bankruptcy Exemptions not available. All law references are to Montana Code Annotated.

ASSET	EXEMPTION	LAW
homestead	Real property or mobile home you occupy to $60,000; sale, condemnation or insurance proceeds exempt 18 months	70-32-104, 70-32-201, 70-32-216
	Must record homestead declaration before filing for bankruptcy	70-32-105
insurance	Annuity contract proceeds to $350 per month	33-15-514
	Disability or illness proceeds, avails or benefits	25-13-608(1)(d), 33-15-513
	Fraternal benefit society benefits	33-7-522
	Group life insurance policy or proceeds	33-15-512
	Hail insurance benefits	80-2-245
	Life insurance proceeds if clause prohibits proceeds from being used to pay beneficiary's creditors	33-20-120
	Medical, surgical or hospital care benefits	25-13-608(1)(e)
	Unmatured life insurance contracts to $4,000	25-13-609(4)
miscellaneous	Alimony, child support	25-13-608(1)(f)
	Property of business partnership	35-10-502
pensions	ERISA-qualified benefits deposited over 1 year before filing bankruptcy in excess of 15% of debtor's yearly income	31-2-106
	Firefighters	19-11-612(1), 19-13-1004
	Game wardens	19-8-805(2)
	Highway patrol officers	19-6-705(2)
	Judges	19-5-704
	Police officers	19-9-1006, 19-10-504(1)
	Public employees	19-3-105(1)
	Sheriffs	19-7-705(2)
	Teachers	19-4-706(2)
	University system employees	19-21-212
personal property	Appliances, household furnishings, goods, animals with feed, crops, musical instruments, books, firearms, sporting goods, clothing & jewelry to $600 per item, $4,500 total	25-13-609(1)
	Burial plot	25-13-608(1)(g)
	Cooperative association shares to $500 value	35-15-404
	Health aids	25-13-608(1)(a)
	Motor vehicle to $1,200	25-13-609(2)
	Proceeds for damaged or lost exempt property for 6 months after received	25-13-610
public benefits	Aid to aged, disabled	53-2-607
	Crime victims' compensation	53-9-129
	Local public assistance	25-13-608(1)(b)
	Silicosis benefits	39-73-110
	Social Security	25-13-608(1)(b)
	Subsidized adoption payments	53-2-607
	Unemployment compensation	31-2-106(2), 39-51-3105
	Veterans' benefits	25-13-608(1)(c)
	Vocational rehabilitation to the blind	53-2-607
	Workers' compensation	39-71-743
tools of trade	Implements, books & tools of trade to $3,000	25-13-609(3)
	Uniforms, arms, accoutrements needed to carry out government functions	25-13-613(b)
wages	Minimum 75% of earned but unpaid wages; bankruptcy judge may authorize more for low-income debtors	25-13-614
wild card	None	

Nebraska

Federal Bankruptcy Exemptions not available. All law references are to Revised Statutes of Nebraska.

ASSET	EXEMPTION	LAW
homestead	$12,500; cannot exceed 2 lots in city or village, 160 acres elsewhere; sale proceeds exempt 6 months after sale	40-101, 40-111, 40-113
	May record homestead declaration	40-105
insurance	Fraternal benefit society benefits to $10,000 loan value unless beneficiary convicted of a crime related to benefits	44-1089
	Life insurance or annuity contract proceeds to $10,000 loan value	44-371
miscellaneous	Property of business partnership	67-325
pensions	County employees	23-2322
also see wages	ERISA-qualified benefits needed for support	25-1563.01
	Military disability benefits to $2,000	25-1559
	School employees	79-1060, 79-1552
	State employees	84-1324
personal property	Burial plot	12-517
	Clothing needed	25-1556
	Crypts, lots, tombs, niches, vaults	12-605
	Food & fuel to last 6 months	25-1556
	Furniture & kitchen utensils to $1,500	25-1556
	Perpetual care funds	12-511
	Personal injury recoveries	25-1563.02
	Personal possessions	25-1556
public benefits	Aid to disabled, blind, aged, public assistance	68-1013
	Unemployment compensation	48-647
	Workers' compensation	48-149
tools of trade	Equipment or tools including a vehicle used in/or for commuting to principal place of business to $2,400	25-1556
	Husband & wife may double	In re Keller, 50 B.R. 23 (D. Neb. 1985)
wages	Minimum 85% of earned but unpaid wages or pension payments for head of family; 75% for all others; bankruptcy judge may authorize more for low-income debtors	25-1558
wild card	$2,500 of any personal property, except wages, in lieu of homestead	25-1552

Nevada

Federal Bankruptcy Exemptions not available. All law references are to Nevada Revised Statutes Annotated.

ASSET	EXEMPTION	LAW
homestead	Real property or mobile home to $125,000 (husband & wife may not double)	21.090(1)(m), 115.010
	Must record homestead declaration before filing for bankruptcy	115.020
insurance	Annuity contract proceeds to $350 per month	687B.290
	Fraternal benefit society benefits	695A.220
	Group life or health policy or proceeds	687B.280
	Health proceeds or avails	687B.270
	Life insurance policy or proceeds if annual premiums not over $1,000	21.090(1)(k)
	Life insurance proceeds if you're not the insured	687B.260
miscellaneous	Property of business partnership	87.250
pensions	ERISA-qualified benefits to $100,000	21.090(1)(q)
	Public employees	286.670
personal property	Appliances, household goods, furniture, home & yard equipment to $3,000 total	21.090(1)(b)
	Books to $1,500	21.090(1)(a)
	Burial plot purchase money held in trust	452.550
	Funeral service contract money held in trust	689.700
	Health aids	21.090(1)(p)
	Keepsakes & pictures	21.090(1)(a)
	Metal-bearing ores, geological specimens, art curiosities or paleontological remains; must be arranged, classified, catalogued & numbered in reference books	21.100
	Motor vehicle to $4,500; no limit if vehicle equipped to provide mobility for disabled person	21.090(1)(f), (o)
	One gun	21.090(1)(i)
public benefits	Aid to blind, aged, disabled, public assistance	422.291
	Industrial insurance (workers' compensation)	616.550
	Unemployment compensation	612.710
	Vocational rehabilitation benefits	615.270
tools of trade	Arms, uniforms & accoutrements you're required to keep	21.090(1)(j)
	Cabin or dwelling of miner or prospector; cars, implements & appliances for mining & mining claim you work to $4,500 total	21.090(1)(e)
	Farm trucks, stock, tools, equipment & seed to $4,500	21.090(1)(c)
	Library, equipment, supplies, tools & materials to $4,500	21.090(1)(d)
wages	Minimum 75% of earned but unpaid wages; bankruptcy judge may authorize more for low-income debtors	21.090(1)(g)
wild card	None	

New Hampshire

Federal Bankruptcy Exemptions available. All law references are to New Hampshire Revised Statutes Annotated.

ASSET	EXEMPTION	LAW
homestead	Real property or manufactured housing (and the land it's on if you own it) to $30,000	480:1
insurance	Firefighters' aid insurance	402:69
	Fraternal benefit society benefits	418:24
	Homeowners' insurance proceeds to $5,000	512:21(VIII)
miscellaneous	Child support	161-C-11
	Jury, witness fees	512:21(VI)
	Property of business partnership	304A:25
	Wages of minor child	512:21(III)
pensions	Federally created pension (only benefits building up)	512:21(IV)
	Firefighters	102:23
	Police officers	103:18
	Public employees	100A:26
personal property	Automobile to $4,000	511:2(XVI)
	Beds, bedsteads, bedding & cooking utensils needed	511:2(II)
	Bibles & books to $800	511:2(VIII)
	Burial plot, lot	511:2(XIV)
	Church pew	511:2(XV)
	Clothing needed	511:2(I)
	Cooking & heating stoves, refrigerator	511:2(IV)
	Cow, 6 sheep or fleece; 4 tons of hay	511:2(XI), (XII)
	Domestic fowl to $300	511:2(XIII)
	Food & fuel to $400	511:2(VI)
	Furniture to $3,500	511:2(III)
	Hog, pig or pork (if already slaughtered)	511:2(X)
	Jewelry to $500	511:2(XVII)
	Proceeds for lost or destroyed exempt property	512:21(VIII)
	Sewing machine	511:2(V)
public benefits	Aid to blind, aged, disabled, public assistance	167:25
	Unemployment compensation	282A:159
	Workers' compensation	281A:52
tools of trade	Tools of your occupation to $5,000	511:2(IX)
	Uniforms, arms & equipment of military member	511:2(VII)
	Yoke of oxen or horse needed for farming or teaming	511:2(XII)
wages	Earned but unpaid wages; judge decides amount exempt based on a percentage of the federal minimum wage	512:21(II)
	Earned but unpaid wages of spouse	512:21(III)
wild card	$1,000 of any property	511:2(XVIII)
	Unused portion of automobile, bibles & books, food & fuel, furniture, jewelry and tools of occupation exemptions to $7,000 in any property	511:2(XVIII)

New Jersey

Federal Bankruptcy Exemptions available. All law references are to New Jersey Statutes Annotated.

ASSET	EXEMPTION	LAW
homestead	None	
insurance	Annuity contract proceeds to $500 per month	17B:24-7
	Disability or death benefits for military member	38A:4-8
	Disability, death, medical or hospital benefits for civil defense workers	App. A:9-57.6
	Fraternal benefit society benefits	17:44A-19
	Group life or health policy or proceeds	17B:24-9
	Health or disability benefits	17:18-12, 17B:24-8
	Life insurance proceeds if clause prohibits proceeds from being used to pay beneficiary's creditors	17B:24-10
	Life insurance proceeds or avails if you're not the insured	17B:24-6b
miscellaneous	Property of business partnership	42:1-25
pensions	Alcohol beverage control officers	43:8A-20
	City boards of health employees	43:18-12
	Civil defense workers	App. A:9-57.6
	County employees	43:10-57, 43:10-105
	ERISA-qualified benefits	43:13-9
	Firefighters, police officers, traffic officers	43:16-7, 43:16A-17
	IRAs	*In re Yuhas,* No. 96-5146 (3rd Cir. 1/22/97)
	Judges	43:6A-41
	Municipal employees	43:13-44
	Prison employees	43:7-13
	Public employees	43:15A-53
	School district employees	18A:66-116
	State police	53:5A-45
	Street & water department employees	43:19-17
	Teachers	18A:66-51
	Trust containing personal property created pursuant to federal tax law unless conveyance into trust done fraudulently or debt is for child support or alimony	25:2-1
personal property	Goods & chattels, personal property & stock or interest in corporations to $1,000 total	2A:17-19
	Burial plots	8A:5-10
	Clothing	2A:17-19
	Furniture & household goods to $1,000	2A:26-4
public benefits	Crime victims' compensation	52:4B-30
	Old-age, permanent disability assistance	44:7-35
	Unemployment compensation	43:21-53
	Workers' compensation	34:15-29
tools of trade	None	
wages	90% of earned but unpaid wages if income under $7,500; if income over $7,500, judge decides amount that is exempt	2A:17-56
	Wages or allowances received by military personnel	38A:4-8
wild card	None	

New Mexico

Federal Bankruptcy Exemptions available. All law references are to New Mexico Statutes Annotated.

ASSET	EXEMPTION	LAW
homestead	Married, widowed or supporting another may claim real property to $30,000 (joint owners may double)	42-10-9
insurance	Benevolent association benefits to $5,000	42-10-4
	Fraternal benefit society benefits	59A-44-18
	Life, accident, health or annuity benefits, withdrawal or cash value, if beneficiary is a New Mexican citizen	42-10-3
miscellaneous	Ownership interest in unincorporated association	53-10-2
	Property of business partnership	54-1-25
pensions	Pension or retirement benefits	42-10-1, 42-10-2
	Public school employees	22-11-42A
personal property	Books, health equipment & furniture	42-10-1, 42-10-2
	Building materials	48-2-15
	Clothing	42-10-1, 42-10-2
	Cooperative association shares, minimum amount needed to be member	53-4-28
	Jewelry to $2,500	42-10-1, 42-10-2
	Materials, tools & machinery to dig, torpedo, drill, complete, operate or repair oil line, gas well or pipeline	70-4-12
	Motor vehicle to $4,000	42-10-1, 42-10-2
public benefits	Crime victims' compensation paid before 7/1/93	31-22-15
	General assistance	27-2-21
	Occupational disease disablement benefits	52-3-37
	Unemployment compensation	51-1-37
	Workers' compensation	52-1-52
tools of trade	$1,500	42-10-1, 42-10-2
wages	Minimum 75% of earned but unpaid wages; bankruptcy judge may authorize more for low-income debtors	35-12-7
wild card	$500 of any personal property	42-10-1
	$2,000 of any property, in lieu of homestead	42-10-10

New York

Federal Bankruptcy Exemptions not available. All law references are to Consolidated Laws of New York, Civil Practice Law & Rules, unless otherwise noted.

ASSET	EXEMPTION	LAW
homestead	Real property including co-op, condo or mobile home, to $10,000	5206(a)
	Husband & wife may double	*In re Pearl,* 723 F.2d 193 (2nd Cir. 1983)
insurance	Annuity contract benefits due or prospectively due the debtor, who paid for the contract; if purchased within 6 months prior & not tax-deferred, only $5,000	Insurance 3212(d), Debtor & Creditor 283(1)
	Disability or illness benefits to $400 per month	Insurance 3212(c)
	Life insurance proceeds left at death with the insurance company pursuant to agreement, if clause prohibits proceeds from being used to pay beneficiary's creditors	Estates, Powers & Trusts 7-1.5(a)(2)
	Life insurance proceeds and avails if the person effecting the policy is the spouse of the insured	Insurance 3212(b)(2)
miscellaneous	Alimony, child support needed for support	Debtor & Creditor 282(2)(d)
	Property of business partnership	Partnership 51
pensions	ERISA-qualified benefits needed for support	Debtor & Creditor 282(2)(e)
	IRAs	Debtor & Creditor 282(2)(e), 5205(c)
	Keoghs	Debtor & Creditor 282(2)(e), 5205(c)
	Public retirement benefits	Insurance 4607
	State employees	Retirement & Social Security 110
	Village police officers	Unconsolidated 5711-o
personal property	Bible; schoolbooks; books to $50; pictures; clothing; church pew or seat; stoves with fuel to last 60 days; sewing machine; domestic animal with food to last 60 days, to $450; food to last 60 days; furniture; refrigerator; TV; radio; wedding ring; watch to $35; crockery, cooking utensils and tableware needed, to $5,000 total (with farm machinery, etc.)	5205(1)-(6), Debtor & Creditor 283(1)
	Burial plot, without structure to 1/4 acre	5206(f)
	Cash, the lesser of either $2,500, or an amount, that, with annuity, totals $5,000; in lieu of homestead	Debtor & Creditor 283(2)
	Health aids, including animals with food	5205(h)
	Lost earnings recoveries needed for support	Debtor & Creditor 282(3)(iv)
	Motor vehicle to $2,400	Debtor & Creditor 282(1)
	Personal injury recoveries to $7,500 (not to include pain & suffering)	Debtor & Creditor 282(3)(iii)
	Security deposits to landlord, utility company	5205(g)
	Trust fund principal, 90% of income	5205(c), (d)
	Wrongful death recoveries for person you depended on, needed for support	Debtor & Creditor 282(3)(ii)

ASSET	EXEMPTION	LAW
public benefits	Aid to blind, aged, disabled	Debtor & Creditor 282(2)(c)
	Crime victims' compensation	Debtor & Creditor 282(3)(i)
	Home relief, local public assistance	Debtor & Creditor 282(2)(a)
	Social Security	Debtor & Creditor 282(2)(a)
	Unemployment compensation	Debtor & Creditor 282(2)(a)
	Veterans' benefits	Debtor & Creditor 282(2)(b)
	Workers' compensation	Debtor & Creditor 282(2)(c)
tools of trade	Farm machinery, team, food for 60 days, professional furniture, books & instruments to $600 total	5205(b)
	Uniforms, medal, equipments, emblem, horse, arms & sword of military member	5205(e)
wages	90% of earnings from milk sales to milk dealers	5205(f)
	90% of earned but unpaid wages received within 60 days prior (100% for a few militia members)	5205(d), (e)
wild card	None	

North Carolina

Federal Bankruptcy Exemptions not available. All law references are to General Statutes of North Carolina unless otherwise noted.

ASSET	EXEMPTION	LAW
homestead	Real or personal property, including co-op, used as residence to $10,000; up to $3,500 of unused portion of homestead may be applied to any property	1C-1601(a)(1), (2)
	Property held as tenancy by the entirety may be exempt against debts owed by only one spouse	In re Crouch, 33 B.R. 271 (E.D. N.C. 1983)
insurance	Employee group life policy or proceeds	58-58-165
	Fraternal benefit society benefits	58-24-85
miscellaneous	Property of business partnership	59-55
pensions	Firefighters & rescue squad workers	58-86-90
	Law enforcement officers	143-166.30(g)
	Legislators	120-4.29
	Municipal, city & county employees	128-31
	Teachers & state employees	135-9, 135-95
personal property	Animals, crops, musical instrument, books, clothing, appliances, household goods & furnishings to $3,500 total; may add $750 per dependent, up to $3,000 total additional	1C-1601(a)(4)
	Burial plot to $10,000, in lieu of homestead	1C-1601(a)(1)
	Health aids	1C-1601(a)(7)
	Motor vehicle to $1,500	1C-1601(a)(3)
	Personal injury recoveries for person you depended on	1C-1601(a)(8)
	Wrongful death recoveries for person you depended on	1C-1601(a)(8)
public benefits	Aid to blind	111-18
	Crime victims' compensation	15B-17
	Special adult assistance	108A-36
	Unemployment compensation	96-17
	Workers' compensation	97-21
tools of trade	Implements, books & tools of trade to $750	1C-1601(a)(5)
wages	Earned but unpaid wages received 60 days before filing for bankruptcy, needed for support	1-362
wild card	$3,500 less any amount claimed for homestead or burial exemption, of any property	1C-1601(a)(2)

North Dakota

Federal Bankruptcy Exemptions not available. All law references are to North Dakota Century Code.

ASSET	EXEMPTION	LAW
homestead	Real property, house trailer or mobile home to $80,000	28-22-02(10), 47-18-01
insurance	Fraternal benefit society benefits	26.1-15.1-18, 26.1-33-40
	Life insurance proceeds payable to deceased's estate, not to a specific beneficiary	26.1-33-40
	Life insurance surrender value to $100,000 per policy, if beneficiary is insured's relative & owned over 1 year before filing for bankruptcy; no limit if more needed for support; with ERISA-qualified benefits, IRAs and Keoghs exempt under 28-22-03.1 (except pensions for disabled veterans), total cannot exceed $200,000	28-22-03.1(3)
miscellaneous	Property of business partnership	45-08-02
pensions	Disabled veterans' benefits, except military retirement pay	28-22-03.1(4)(d)
	ERISA-qualified benefits to $100,000 per plan; no limit if more needed for support; with insurance exempt under 28-22-03.1, total cannot exceed $200,000	28-22-03.1(3)
	IRAs to $100,000 per plan; no limit if more needed for support; with insurance exempt under 28-22-03.1, total cannot exceed $200,000	28-22-03.1(3)
	Keoghs to $100,000 per plan; no limit if more needed for support; with insurance exempt under 28-22-03.1, total cannot exceed $200,000	28-22-03.1(3)
	Public employees	28-22-19(1)
personal property	1. All debtors may exempt:	
	Bible, books to $100 & pictures; clothing	28-22-02(1), (4), (5)
	Burial plots, church pew	28-22-02(2), (3)
	Cash to $7,500, in lieu of homestead	28-22-03.1(1)
	Crops or grain raised on debtor's tract to 160 acres (64.75 hectares) on 1 tract	28-22-02(8)
	Food & fuel to last 1 year	28-22-02(6)
	Motor vehicle to $1,200	28-22-03.1(2)
	Personal injury recoveries to $7,500 (not to include pain & suffering)	28-22-03.1(4)(b)
	Wrongful death recoveries to $7,500	28-22-03.1(4)(a)
	2. Head of household not claiming crops or grain may claim $5,000 of any personal property or:	28-22-03
	Books & musical instruments to $1,500	28-22-04(1)
	Furniture, including bedsteads & bedding, to $1,000	28-22-04(2)
	Library & tools of professional to $1,000	28-22-04(4)
	Livestock & farm implements to $4,500	28-22-04(3)
	Tools of mechanic & stock in trade to $1,000	28-22-04(4)
	3. Non-head of household not claiming crops or grain, may claim $2,500 of any personal property	28-22-05
public benefits	Crime victims' compensation	28-22-19(2)
	Public assistance	28-22-19(3)
	Social Security	28-22-03.1(4)(c)
	Unemployment compensation	52-06-30
	Vietnam veterans' adjustment compensation	37-25-07
	Workers' compensation	65-05-29
tools of trade	See personal property	
wages	Minimum 75% of earned but unpaid wages; bankruptcy judge may authorize more for low-income debtors	32-09.1-.03
wild card	See personal property	

Ohio

Federal Bankruptcy Exemptions not available. All law references are to Ohio Revised Code unless otherwise noted.

ASSET	EXEMPTION	LAW
homestead	Real or personal property used as residence to $5,000	2329.66(A)(1)(b)
	Property held as tenancy by the entirety may be exempt against debts owed by only one spouse	*In re Thomas*, 14 B.R. 423 (N.D. Ohio 1981)
insurance	Benevolent society benefits to $5,000	2329.63, 2329.66(A)(6)(a)
	Disability benefits to $600 per month	2329.66(A)(6)(e), 3923.19
	Fraternal benefit society benefits	2329.66(A)(6)(d), 3921.18
	Group life insurance policy or proceeds	2329.66(A)(6)(c), 3917.05
	Life, endowment or annuity contract avails for your spouse, child or dependent	2329.66(A)(6)(b), 3911.10
	Life insurance proceeds for a spouse	3911.12
	Life insurance proceeds if clause prohibits proceeds from being used to pay beneficiary's creditors	3911.14
miscellaneous	Alimony, child support needed for support	2329.66(A)(11)
	Property of business partnership	1775.24, 2329.66(A)(14)
pensions	ERISA-qualified benefits needed for support	2329.66(A)(10)(b)
	Firefighters, police officers	742.47
	Firefighters', police officers' death benefits	2329.66(A)(10)(a)
	IRAs needed for support	2329.66(A)(10)(c)
	Keoghs needed for support	2329.66(A)(10)(c)
	Public employees	145.56
	Public school employees	3307.71, 3309.66
	State highway patrol employees	5505.22
	Volunteer firefighters' dependents	146.13
personal property *Note: Jewelry must be counted toward the $1,500/$2,000 totals*	Animals, crops, books, musical instruments, appliances, household goods, furnishings, hunting & fishing equipment & firearms to $200 per item, $1,500 total ($2,000 if no homestead claimed)	2329.66(A)(4)(b), (d)
	Beds, bedding & clothing to $200 per item	2329.66(A)(3)
	Burial plot	517.09, 2329.66(A)(8)
	Cash, money due within 90 days, bank & security deposits & tax refund to $400 total (spouse without income can't exempt tax refund, *In re Smith*, 77 B.R. 633 (N.D. Ohio 1987))	2329.66(A)(4)(a)
	Cooking unit & refrigerator to $300 each	2329.66(A)(3)
	Health aids	2329.66(A)(7)
	Jewelry to $200 per item (1 item may be to $400)	239.66 (A)(4)(c),(d)
	Lost future earnings needed for support, received during 12 months before filing	2329.66(A)(12)(d)
	Motor vehicle to $1,000	2329.66(A)(2)(b)
	Personal injury recoveries to $5,000 (not to include pain & suffering), received during 12 months before filing	2329.66(A)(12)(c)
	Wrongful death recoveries for person debtor depended on, needed for support, received during 12 months before filing	2329.66(A)(12)(b)
public benefits	Crime victim's compensation, received during 12 months before filing	2329.66(A)(12)(a), 2743.66
	Disability assistance payments	2329.66(A)(9)(f), 5113.07
	Public assistance	2329.66(A)(9)(d), 5107.12
	Tuition credit	2329.66(A)(16)
	Unemployment compensation	2329.66(A)(9)(c), 4141.32
	Vocational rehabilitation benefits	2329.66(A)(9)(a), 3304.19
	Workers' compensation	2329.66(A)(9)(b), 4123.67
tools of trade	Implements, books & tools of trade to $750	2329.66(A)(5)
	Seal, official register of notary public	2329.66(A)(15), 147.04
wages	Minimum 75% of earned but unpaid wages due for 30 days; bankruptcy judge may authorize more for low-income debtors	2329.66(A)(13)
wild card	$400 of any property	2329.66(A)(17)

Oklahoma

Federal Bankruptcy Exemptions not available. All law references are to Oklahoma Statutes Annotated.

ASSET	EXEMPTION	LAW
homestead	Real property or manufactured home to unlimited value; property cannot exceed ¼ acre. If property exceeds ¼ acre, may claim $5,000 on 1 acre in city, town or village, or 160 acres elsewhere (need not occupy homestead to claim it exempt as long as you don't acquire another)	31-1(A)(1), 31-1(A)(2), 31-2
insurance	Assessment or mutual benefits	36-2410
	Fraternal benefit society benefits	36-2720
	Funeral benefits prepaid & placed in trust	36-6125
	Group life policy or proceeds	36-3632
	Limited stock insurance benefits	36-2510
miscellaneous	Alimony, child support	31-1(A)(19)
	Property of business partnership	54-225
pensions	County employees	19-959
	Disabled veterans	31-7
	ERISA-qualified benefits	31-1(A)(20)
	Firefighters	11-49-126
	Law enforcement employees	47-2-303.3
	Police officers	11-50-124
	Public employees	74-923
	Tax exempt benefits	60-328
	Teachers	70-17-109
personal property	Books, portraits, pictures & gun	31-1(A)(7), (14)
	2 bridles & 2 saddles	31-1(A)(12)
	Burial plots	31-1(A)(4), 8-7
	100 chickens, 10 hogs, 2 horses, 5 cows & calves under 6 months, 20 sheep; forage for livestock to last 1 year (cows must be able to produce milk for human consumption)	31-1(A)(10), (11), (15), (16)
	Clothing to $4,000	31-1(A)(8)
	Furniture, health aids, food to last 1 year	31-1(A)(3), (9), (17)
	Motor vehicle to $3,000	31-1(A)(13)
	Personal injury, wrongful death & workers' compensation recoveries to $50,000 total; cannot include punitive damages	31-1(A)(21); *In re Luckinbill*, 163 B.R. 856 (W.D. Okla. 1994)
public benefits	Crime victims' compensation	21-142.13
	Public assistance	56-173
	Social Security	56-173
	Unemployment compensation	40-2-303
	Workers' compensation (see personal property)	85-48
tools of trade	Husbandry implements to farm homestead, tools, books & apparatus to $5,000 total	31-1(A)(5), (6), 31-1(C)
wages	75% of wages earned in 90 days before filing bankruptcy; bankruptcy judge may allow more if you show hardship	12-1171.1, 31-1(A)(18)
wild card	None	

Oregon

Federal Bankruptcy Exemptions not available. All law references are to Oregon Revised Statutes.

ASSET	EXEMPTION	LAW
homestead	Real property, mobile home or houseboat you occupy or intend to occupy to $25,000 ($33,000 for joint owners); if you don't own land mobile home is on, to $23,000 ($30,000 for joint owners); property cannot exceed 1 block in town or city or 160 acres elsewhere; sale proceeds exempt 1 year from sale, if you intend to purchase another home	23.164, 23.240, 23.250
insurance	Annuity contract benefits to $500 per month	743.049
	Fraternal benefit society benefits	748.207
	Group life policy or proceeds not payable to insured	743.047
	Health or disability proceeds or avails	743.050
	Life insurance proceeds or cash value if you are not the insured	743.046
miscellaneous	Alimony, child support needed for support	23.160(1)(i)
	Liquor licenses	471.301(1)
	Property of business partnership	68.420
pensions	ERISA-qualified benefits	23.170
	Public officers, employees	237.201
	School district employees	239.261
personal property	Bank deposits to $7,500; cash for sold exempt property	23.166
	Books, pictures & musical instruments to $600 total (husband & wife may double)	23.160(1)(a)
	Burial plot	65.870
	Clothing, jewelry & other personal items to $1,800 total (husband & wife may double)	23.160(1)(b)
	Domestic animals, poultry with food to last 60 days to $1,000	23.160(1)(e)
	Food & fuel to last 60 days if debtor is householder	23.160(1)(f)
	Furniture, household items, utensils, radios & TVs to $3,000 total	23.160(1)(f)
	Health aids	23.160(1)(h)
	Lost earnings payments for debtor or someone debtor depended on, to extent needed (husband & wife may double)	23.160(1)(j)(C)
	Motor vehicle to $1,700 (husband & wife may double)	23.160(1)(d)
	Personal injury recoveries to $10,000, not to include pain & suffering (husband & wife may double)	23.160(1)(j)(B)
	Pistol; rifle or shotgun if owned by person over 16, to $1,000	23.200
public benefits	Aid to blind	412.115
	Aid to disabled	412.610
	Civil defense & disaster relief	401.405
	Crime victims' compensation (husband & wife may double)	23.160(1)(j)(A), 147.325
	General assistance	411.760
	Injured inmates' benefits	655.530
	Medical assistance	414.095
	Old-age assistance	413.130
	Unemployment compensation	657.855
	Vocational rehabilitation	344.580
	Workers' compensation	656.234
tools of trade	Tools, library, team with food to last 60 days, to $3,000 (husband & wife may double)	23.160(1)(c)
wages	Minimum of 75% of earned but unpaid wages; bankruptcy judge may authorize more for low-income debtors	23.185
	Wages withheld in state employee's bond savings accounts	292.070
wild card	$400 of any personal property, however, can't use to increase existing exemption	23.160(1)(k)
	Husband & wife may double	*In re Wilson*, 22 B.R. 146 (D. Or. 1982)

Pennsylvania

Federal Bankruptcy Exemptions available. All law references are to Pennsylvania Consolidated Statutes Annotated unless otherwise noted.

ASSET	EXEMPTION	LAW
homestead	None, however, property held as tenancy by the entirety may be exempt against debts owed by only one spouse	*Keystone Savings Ass'n v. Kitsock*, 633 A.2d 165 (Pa. Super. Ct. 1993)
insurance	Accident or disability benefits	42-8124(c)(7)
	Fraternal benefit society benefits	Annotated Statute 40-1141-403; 42-8124(c)(1), (8)
	Group life policy or proceeds	42-8124(c)(5)
	Insurance policy or annuity contract payments, where insured is the beneficiary, cash value or proceeds to $100 per month	42-8124(c)(3)
	Life insurance annuity policy, cash value or proceeds if beneficiary is insured's dependent, child or spouse	42-8124(c)(6)
	Life insurance proceeds if clause prohibits proceeds from being used to pay beneficiary's creditors	42-8214(c)(4)
	No-fault automobile insurance proceeds	42-8124(c)(9)
miscellaneous	Property of business partnership	15-8341
pensions	City employees	53-13445, 53-23572, 53-39383
	County employees	16-4716
	Municipal employees	53-881.115
	Police officers	53-764, 53-776, 53-23666
	Private retirement benefits if clause prohibits proceeds from being used to pay beneficiary's creditors, to extent tax-deferred; exemption limited to $15,000 per year deposited; no exemption for amount deposited within 1 year of filing	42-8124(b)
	Public school employees	24-8533
	State employees	71-5953
personal property	Bibles, schoolbooks & sewing machines	42-8124(a)(2), (3)
	Clothing	42-8124(a)(1)
	Tangible personal property at an international exhibit sponsored by U.S. government	42-8125
	Uniform & accoutrements	42-8124(a)(4)
public benefits	Crime victims' compensation	71-180-7.10
	Korean conflict veterans' benefits	51-20098
	Unemployment compensation	42-8124(a)(10), 43-863
	Veterans' benefits	51-20012
	Workers' compensation	42-8124(c)(2)
tools of trade	None	
wages	Earned but unpaid wages	42-8127
wild card	$300 of any property	42-8123

Rhode Island

Federal Bankruptcy Exemptions available. All law references are to General Laws of Rhode Island.

ASSET	EXEMPTION	LAW
homestead	None	
insurance	Accident or sickness proceeds, avails or benefits	27-18-24
	Fraternal benefit society benefits	27-25-18
	Life insurance proceeds if clause prohibits proceeds from being used to pay beneficiary's creditors	27-4-12
	Temporary disability insurance	28-41-32
miscellaneous	Earnings of a minor child	9-26-4(9)
	Property of business partnership	7-12-36
pensions	ERISA-qualified benefits	9-26-4(11)
	Firefighters	9-26-5
	IRAs	9-26-4(12)
	Police officers	9-26-5
	Private employees	28-17-4
	State & municipal employees	36-10-34
personal property	Beds, bedding, furniture & family stores of a housekeeper, to $1,000 total	9-26-4(3)
	Bibles & books to $300	9-26-4(4)
	Body of deceased person	9-26-3
	Burial plot	9-26-4(5)
	Clothing needed	9-26-4(1)
	Consumer cooperative association holdings to $50	7-8-25
	Debt secured by promissory note or bill of exchange	9-26-4(7)
public benefits	Aid to blind, aged, disabled, general assistance	40-6-14
	State disability benefits	28-41-32
	Unemployment compensation	28-44-58
	Veterans' disability or survivors' death benefits	30-7-9
	Workers' compensation	28-33-27
tools of trade	Library of professional in practice	9-26-4(2)
	Working tools to $500	9-26-4(2)
wages	Earned but unpaid wages to $50	9-26-4(8)(C)
	Earned but unpaid wages due military member on active duty	30-7-9
	Earned but unpaid wages due seaman	9-26-4(6)
	Earned but unpaid wages if received welfare during year before filing bankruptcy	9-26-4(8)(B)
	Wages of spouse	9-26-4(9)
	Wages paid by charitable organization to the poor	9-26-4(8)(A)
wild card	None	

South Carolina

Federal Bankruptcy Exemptions available. All law references are to Code of Laws of South Carolina.

ASSET	EXEMPTION	LAW
homestead	Real property, including co-op, to $5,000 (joint owners may double)	15-41-30(1)
insurance	Accident & disability benefits	38-63040(D)
	Benefits accruing under life insurance policy after death of insured, where proceeds left with insurance company pursuant to agreement; benefits not exempt from action to recover necessaries if parties so agree	38-63-50
	Disability or illness benefits	15-41-30(10)(C)
	Fraternal benefit society benefits	38-37-870
	Life insurance avails from policy for person you depended on to $4,000	15-41-30(8)
	Life insurance proceeds from policy for person you depended on, needed for support	15-41-30(11)(C)
	Proceeds & cash surrender value of life insurance payable to beneficiary other than insured's estate expressly intended to benefit spouse, children or dependents of insured unless purchased within 2 years of filing	38-63040(A)
	Proceeds of group life insurance	38-63040(C)
	Proceeds of life insurance or annuity contract	38-63040(B)
	Unmatured life insurance contract, except credit insurance policy	15-41-30(7)
miscellaneous	Alimony, child support	15-41-30(10)(D)
	Property of business partnership	33-41-720
pensions	ERISA-qualified benefits	15-41-30(10)(E)
	Firefighters	9-13-230
	General assembly members	9-9-180
	Judges, solicitors	9-8-190
	Police officers	9-11-270
	Public employees	9-1-1680
personal property	Animals, crops, appliances, books, clothing, household goods, furnishings, musical instruments to $2,500 total	15-41-30(3)
	Burial plot to $5,000, in lieu of homestead (joint owners may double)	15-41-30(1)
	Cash & other liquid assets to $1,000, in lieu of burial or homestead exemption	15-41-30(5)
	Health aids	15-41-30(9)
	Jewelry to $500	15-41-30(4)
	Motor vehicle to $1,200	15-41-30(2)
	Personal injury recoveries	15-41-30(11)(B)
	Wrongful death recoveries	15-41-30(11)(B)
public benefits	Crime victims' compensation	15-41-30(11)(A), 16-3-1300
	General relief, aid to aged, blind, disabled	43-5-190
	Local public assistance	15-41-30(10)(A)
	Social Security	15-41-30(10)(A)
	Unemployment compensation	15-41-30(10)(A)
	Veterans' benefits	15-41-30(10)(B)
	Workers' compensation	42-9-360
tools of trade	Implements, books & tools of trade to $750	15-41-30(6)
wages	None	
wild card	None	

South Dakota

Federal Bankruptcy Exemptions not available. All law references are to South Dakota Codified Laws.

ASSET	EXEMPTION	LAW
homestead	Real property (or mobile home larger than 240 square feet at its base and registered in state at least 6 months before filing for bankruptcy) to unlimited value; property cannot exceed 1 acre in town or 160 acres elsewhere; sale proceeds to $30,000 (unlimited if you're over age 70 or an unmarried widow or widower) exempt for 1 year after sale (can't exempt gold or silver mine, mill or smelter, 43-31-5)	43-31-1, 43-31-2, 43-31-3, 43-31-4
	Spouse or child of deceased owner may claim homestead exemption	43-31-13
	May file homestead declaration	43-31-6
insurance	Annuity contract proceeds to $250 per month	58-12-6, 58-12-8
	Endowment, life insurance policy, proceeds or cash value to $20,000 (husband & wife may not double, *In re James,* 31 B.R. 67 (D.S.D. 1983))	58-12-4
	Fraternal benefit society benefits	58-37-68
	Health benefits to $20,000	58-12-4
	Life insurance proceeds, held pursuant to agreement by insurer, if clause prohibits proceeds from being used to pay beneficiary's creditors	58-15-70
	Life insurance proceeds to $10,000, if beneficiary is surviving spouse or child	43-45-6
miscellaneous	Property of business partnership	48-4-14
pensions	City employees	9-16-47
	Public employees	3-12-115
personal property	1. All debtors may exempt bible, books to $200, pictures, burial plots, church pew, food & fuel to last 1 year & clothing	43-45-2
	2. Head of family may claim $4,000 of any personal property or:	43-45-4, 43-45-5
	Books & musical instruments to $200	43-45-5(1)
	2 cows, 5 swine, 25 sheep with lambs under 6 months; wool, cloth or yarn of sheep; food for all to last 1 year	43-45-5(3)
	Farming machinery, utensils, tackle for teams, harrow, 2 plows, sleigh, wagon to $1,250 total	43-45-5(3)
	Furniture, including bedsteads & bedding to $200	43-45-5(2)
	Library & tools of professional to $300	43-45-5(5)
	Tools of mechanic & stock in trade to $200	43-45-5(4)
	2 yoke of oxen, or span of horses or mules	43-45-5(3)
	3. Non-head of family may claim $2,000 of any personal property	43-45-4
public benefits	Public assistance	28-7-16
	Unemployment compensation	61-6-28
	Workers' compensation	62-4-42
tools of trade	See personal property	
wages	Earned wages owed 60 days before filing bankruptcy, needed for support of family	15-20-12
	Wages of prisoners in work programs	24-8-10
wild card	See personal property	

Tennessee

Federal Bankruptcy Exemptions not available. All law references are to Tennessee Code Annotated unless otherwise noted.

ASSET	EXEMPTION	LAW
homestead	$5,000; $7,500 for joint owners	26-2-301
	Life estate	26-2-302
	2-15 year lease	26-2-303
	Spouse or child of deceased owner may claim homestead exemption	26-2-301
	Property held as tenancy by the entirety may be exempt against debts owed by only one spouse	*In re Arango,* 136 B.R. 740, aff'd, 992 F.2d 611 (6th Cir. 1993)
insurance	Accident, health or disability benefits for resident & citizen of Tennessee	26-2-110
	Disability or illness benefits	26-2-111(1)(C)
	Fraternal benefit society benefits	56-25-1403
	Homeowners' insurance proceeds to $5,000	26-2-304
miscellaneous	Alimony owed for 30 days before filing for bankruptcy	26-2-111(1)(E)
	Property of business partnership	61-1-124
pensions	ERISA-qualified benefits	26-2-111(1)(D)
	Public employees	8-36-111
	State & local government employees	26-2-104
	Teachers	49-5-909
personal property	Bible, schoolbooks, pictures, portraits, clothing & storage containers	26-2-103
	Burial plot to 1 acre	26-2-305, 46-2-102
	Health aids	26-2-111(5)
	Lost earnings payments for you or person you depended on	26-2-111(3)
	Personal injury recoveries to $7,500 (not to include pain & suffering); wrongful death recoveries to $10,000 (you can't exempt more than $15,000 total for personal injury, wrongful death & crime victims' compensation)	26-2-111(2)(B), 26-2-111(2)(C)
public benefits	Aid to blind	71-4-117
	Aid to disabled	71-4-1112
	Crime victims' compensation to $5,000 (see personal property)	26-2-111(2)(A), 29-13-111
	Local public assistance	26-2-111(1)(A)
	Old-age assistance	71-2-216
	Social Security	26-2-111(1)(A)
	Unemployment compensation	26-2-111(1)(A)
	Veterans' benefits	26-2-111(1)(B)
	Workers' compensation	50-6-223
tools of trade	Implements, books & tools of trade to $1,900	26-2-111(4)
wages	Minimum 75% of earned but unpaid wages, plus $2.50 per week per child; bankruptcy judge may authorize more for low-income debtors	26-2-106, 26-2-107
wild card	$4,000 of any personal property	26-2-102

Texas

Federal Bankruptcy Exemptions available. All law references are to Texas Revised Civil Statutes Annotated unless otherwise noted.

ASSET	EXEMPTION	LAW
homestead	Unlimited; property cannot exceed 1 acre in town, village, city or 100 acres (200 for families) elsewhere; sale proceeds exempt for 6 months after sale (need not occupy if not acquire another home, Property 41.003)	Property 41.001, 41.002
	May file homestead declaration	Property 41.005
insurance	Church benefit plan benefits	1407a-6
	Fraternal benefit society benefits	Insurance 10.28
	Life, health, accident or annuity benefits or monies, including policy proceeds and cash values to be paid or rendered to beneficiary or insured	Insurance 21.22
	Life insurance present value if beneficiary is debtor or debtor's dependent (see note under personal property)	Property 42.002(a)(12)
	Retired public school employees group insurance	Insurance 3.50-4(11)(a)
	Texas employee uniform group insurance	Insurance 3.50-2(10)(a)
	Texas state college or university employee benefits	Insurance 3.50-3(9)(a)
miscellaneous	Property of business partnership	6132b-25
pensions	County & district employees	Government 811.005
	ERISA-qualified government or church benefits, including Keoghs and IRAs	Property 42.0021
	Firefighters	6243e(5), 6243e.1(12), 6243e.2(12)
	IRAs to extent tax-deferred	Property 42.0021
	Judges	Government 811.005
	Keoghs to extent tax-deferred	Property 42.0021
	Law enforcement officers' survivors	6228f(8)
	Municipal employees	6243g, Government 811.005
	Police officers	6243d-1(17), 6243j(20), 6243g-1(23B)
	Retirement benefits to extent tax-deferred	Property 42.0021
	State employees	Government 811.005
	Teachers	Government 811.005
personal property	Athletic and sporting equipment, including bicycles; 2 firearms; home furnishings, including family heirlooms; food; clothing; jewelry (not to exceed 25% of total exemption); 1 two-, three- or four-wheeled motor vehicle per member of family or single adult who holds a driver's license (or who operates vehicle for someone else who does not have a license); 2 horses, mules or donkeys and a saddle, blanket and bridle for each; 12 head of cattle; 60 head of other types of livestock; 120 fowl; and pets to $30,000 total ($60,000 for head of family)	Property 42.001, 42.002
total includes tools of trade, unpaid commissions, life insurance cash value		
	Burial plots	Property 41.001
	Health aids	Property 42.001(b)(2)
public benefits	Crime victims' compensation	8309-1(7)(f)
	Medical assistance	Hum. Res. 32.036
	Public assistance	Hum. Res. 31.040
	Unemployment compensation	5221b-13
	Workers' compensation	8308-4.07
tools of trade	Farming or ranching vehicles and implements	Property 42.002(a)(3)
see note under personal property	Tools, equipment (includes boat & motor vehicles) & books	Property 42.002(a)(4)
wages	Earned but unpaid wages	Property 42.001(b)(1)
	Unpaid commissions to 75% (see note under personal property)	Property 42.001(d)
wild card	None	

Utah

Federal Bankruptcy Exemptions not available. All law references are to Utah Code.

ASSET	EXEMPTION	LAW
homestead	Real property, mobile home or water rights to $10,000 (joint owners may double)	78-23-3
	Must file homestead declaration before attempted sale of home	78-23-4
insurance	Disability, illness, medical or hospital benefits	78-23-5(1)(c),(d)
	Fraternal benefit society benefits	31A-9-603
	Life insurance policy cash surrender value to $1,500	78-23-7
	Life insurance proceeds if beneficiary is insured's spouse or dependent, as needed for support	78-73-6(2)
miscellaneous	Alimony needed for support	78-23-5(1)(k), 78-23-6(1)
	Child support	78-23-5(1)(f),(k)
	Property of business partnership	48-1-22
pensions	ERISA-qualified benefits	78-23-5(1)(j)
	Public employees	49-1-609
	Other pensions needed for support	78-23-6(3)
personal property	Animals, books & musical instruments to $500 total	78-23-8(1)(b)
	Artwork depicting, or done by, family member	78-23-5(1)(h)
	Bed, bedding, carpets, washer & dryer	78-23-5(1)(g)
	Burial plot	78-23-5(1)(a)
	Clothing (cannot claim furs or jewelry)	78-23-5(1)(g)
	Dining & kitchen tables & chairs to $500	78-23-8(1)(a)
	Food to last 3 months	78-23-5(1)(g)
	Health aids needed	78-23-5(1)(b)
	Heirloom to $500	78-23-8(1)(c)
	Motor vehicle to $2,500	78-23-8(2)
	Personal injury recoveries for you or person you depended on	78-23-5(1)(i)
	Proceeds for damaged exempt property	78-23-9
	Refrigerator, freezer, microwave, stove & sewing machine	78-23-5(1)(g)
	Sofas, chairs & related furnishings to $500	78-23-8(1)(a)
	Wrongful death recoveries for person you depended on	78-23-5(1)(i)
public benefits	Crime victims' compensation	63-63-21
	General assistance	55-15-32
	Occupational disease disability benefits	35-2-35
	Unemployment compensation	35-4-18
	Veterans' benefits	78-23-5(1)(e)
	Workers' compensation	35-1-80
tools of trade	Implements, books & tools of trade to $3,500	78-23-8(2)
	Military property of National Guard member	39-1-47
	Motor vehicle to $2,500	78-23-8(3)
wages	Minimum 75% of earned but unpaid wages; bankruptcy judge may authorize more for low-income debtors	70C-7-103
wild card	None	

Vermont

Federal Bankruptcy Exemptions available. All law references are to Vermont Statutes Annotated unless otherwise noted.

ASSET	EXEMPTION	LAW
homestead	Real property or mobile home to $75,000; may also claim rents, issues, profits & out-buildings	27-101
	Spouse of deceased owner may claim homestead exemption	27-105
	Property held as tenancy by the entirety may be exempt against debts owed by only one spouse	In re McQueen, 21 B.R. 736 (D. Ver. 1982)
insurance	Annuity contract benefits to $350 per month	8-3709
	Disability benefits that supplement life insurance or annuity contract	8-3707
	Disability or illness benefits needed for support	12-2740(19)(C)
	Fraternal benefit society benefits	8-4478
	Group life or health benefits	8-3708
	Health benefits to $200 per month	8-4086
	Life insurance proceeds if beneficiary is not the insured	8-3706
	Life insurance proceeds for person you depended on	12-2740(19)(H)
	Life insurance proceeds if clause prohibits proceeds from being used to pay beneficiary's creditors	8-3705
	Unmatured life insurance contract other than credit	12-2740(18)
miscellaneous	Alimony, child support needed for support	12-2740(19)(D)
	Property of business partnership	11-1282
pensions	Municipal employees	24-5066
	Self-directed accounts (IRAs, Keoghs) to $10,000	12-2740(16)
	State employees	3-476
	Teachers	16-1946
	Other pensions	12-2740(19)(J)
personal property	Appliances, furnishings, goods, clothing, books, crops, animals, musical instruments to $2,500 total	12-2740(5)
	Cow, 2 goats, 10 sheep, 10 chickens; 3 swarms of bees & their honey; feed to last 1 winter; 10 cords of firewood, 5 tons of coal or 500 gallons of oil; 500 gallons of bottled gas; growing crops to $5,000; 2 harnesses, 2 halters, 2 chains, plow & ox yoke; yoke of oxen or steers & 2 horses	12-2740(6), 12-2740(9)-(14)
	Jewelry to $500; wedding ring unlimited	12-2740(3), (4)
	Motor vehicles to $2,500; bank deposits to $700	12-2740(1), (15)
	Personal injury recoveries for person you depended on	12-2740(19)(F)
	Stove, heating unit, refrigerator, freezer, water heater & sewing machines; lost future earnings for you or person you depended on; health aids	12-2740(8), 12-2740(17), 12-2740(19)(I)
	Wrongful death recoveries for person you depended on	12-2740(19)(G)
public benefits	Aid to blind, aged, disabled, general assistance	33-124
	Crime victims' compensation needed for support	12-2740(19)(E)
	Social Security needed for support	12-2740(19)(A)
	Unemployment compensation	21-1367
	Veterans' benefits needed for support	12-2740(19)(B)
	Workers' compensation	21-681
tools of trade	Books & tools of trade to $5,000	12-2740(2)
wages	Minimum 75% of earned but unpaid wages; bankruptcy judge may authorize more for low-income debtors	12-3170
	Wages, if received welfare during 2 months before filing	12-3170
wild card	$7,000 less any amount of appliances, et al, growing crops, jewelry, motor vehicle & tools of trade, of any property	12-2740(7)
	$400 of any property	12-2740(7)

Virginia

Federal Bankruptcy Exemptions not available. All law references are to Code of Virginia unless otherwise noted.

ASSET	EXEMPTION	LAW
homestead	$5,000 plus $500 per dependent; may also claim rents & profits; sale proceeds exempt to $5,000 (husband & wife may double, Cheeseman v. Nachman, 656 F.2d 60 (4th Cir. 1981)); unused portion of homestead may be applied to any personal property	34-4,34-18,34-20
	May include mobile home	In re Goad, 161 B.R. 161 (W.D. Va. 1993)
	Must file homestead declaration before filing for bankruptcy	34-6
	Property held as tenancy by the entirety may be exempt against debts owed by only one spouse	In re Harris, 155 B.R. 948 (E.D. Va. 1993)
insurance	Accident or sickness benefits	38.2-3549
	Burial society benefits	38.2-4021
	Cooperative life insurance benefits	38.2-3811
	Fraternal benefit society benefits	38.2-4118
	Group life or accident insurance for government officials	51.1-510
	Group life insurance policy or proceeds	38.2-3339
	Industrial sick benefits	38.2-3549
miscellaneous	Property of business partnership	50-25
pensions	City, town & county employees	51.1-802
	ERISA-qualified benefits to $17,500 per year	34-34
also see wages	Judges	51.1-102
	State employees	51.1-102
personal property	Bible	34-26(1)
	Burial plot	34-26(3)
	Clothing to $1,000	34-26(4)
you must be a householder to exempt any personal property	Family portraits and heirlooms to $5,000 total	34-26(2)
	Health aids	34-26(6)
	Household furnishings to $5,000	34-26(4)(a)
	Motor vehicle to $2,000	34-26(8)
	Personal injury causes of action	34-28.1
	Personal injury recoveries	34-28.1
	Pets	34-26(5)
	Wedding and engagement rings	34-26(1)(a)
public benefits	Aid to blind, aged, disabled, general relief	63.1-88
	Crime victims' compensation unless seeking to discharge debt for treatment of injury incurred during crime	19.2-368.12
	Unemployment compensation	60.2-600
	Workers' compensation	65.2-531
tools of trade	Horses, mules (pair) with gear, wagon or cart, tractor to $3,000, plows (2), drag, harvest cradle, pitchfork, rake, iron wedges (2), fertilizer to $1,000 of farmer (you must be a householder)	34-27
	Tools, books and instruments of trade, including motor vehicles, to $10,000, needed in your occupation or education (you must be a householder)	34-26
	Uniforms, arms, equipment of military member	44-96
wages	Minimum 75% of earned but unpaid wages, pension payments; bankruptcy judge may authorize more for low-income debtors	34-29
wild card	Unused portion of homestead, of any personal property	34-13
	$2,000 of any property for disabled veterans (you must be a householder)	34-4.1

Washington

Federal Bankruptcy Exemptions available. All law references are to Revised Code of Washington Annotated.

ASSET	EXEMPTION	LAW
homestead	Real property or mobile home to $30,000 (no limit if seeking to discharge debt based on failure to pay a state income tax assessed on retirement benefits received while a resident of Washington, 6.15.030)	6.13.010, 6.13.030
	Must record homestead declaration before sale of home if property unimproved or home unoccupied	6.15.040
insurance	Annuity contract proceeds to $250 per month	48.18.430
	Disability proceeds, avails or benefits	48.18.400
	Fire insurance proceeds for destroyed exemption	6.15.030
	Fraternal benefit society benefits	48.36A.180
	Group life insurance policy or proceeds	48.18.420
	Life insurance proceeds or avails if beneficiary is not the insured	48.18.410
miscellaneous	Property of business partnership	25.04.250
pensions	City employees	41.28.200
	ERISA-qualified benefits	6.15.020
	IRAs	6.15.020
	Public employees	41.40.380
	State patrol officers	43.43.310
	Volunteer firefighters	41.24.240
personal property	Appliances, furniture, household goods, home & yard equipment to $2,700 total (no limit on any property located within Washington if seeking to discharge debt based on failure to pay a state income tax assessed on retirement benefits received while a resident of Washington, 6.15.025)	6.15.010(3)(a)
	Books to $1,500	6.15.010(2)
	Burial plots sold by nonprofit cemetery association	68.20.120
	Clothing, no more than $1,000 in furs, jewelry, ornaments	6.15.010(1)
	Food & fuel for comfortable maintenance	6.15.010(3)(a)
	Keepsakes & pictures	6.15.010(2)
	Two motor vehicles to $2,500 total	6.15.010(3)(c)
public benefits	Child welfare	74.13.070
	Crime victims' compensation	7.68.070, 51.32.040
	General assistance	74.04.280
	Industrial insurance (workers' compensation)	51.32.040
	Old-age assistance	74.08.210
	Unemployment compensation	50.40.020
tools of trade	Farm trucks, stock, tools, seed, equipment & supplies of farmer to $5,000 total	6.15.010(4)(a)
	Library, office furniture, office equipment & supplies of physician, surgeon, attorney, clergy or other professional to $5,000 total	6.15.010(4)(b)
	Tools & materials used in another's trade to $5,000	6.15.010(4)(c)
wages	Minimum 75% of earned but unpaid wages; bankruptcy judge may authorize more for low-income debtors	6.27.150
wild card	$1,000 of any personal property (no more than $100 in cash, bank deposits, bonds, stocks & securities)	6.15.010(3)(b)

West Virginia

Federal Bankruptcy Exemptions not available. All law references are to West Virginia Code.

ASSET	EXEMPTION	LAW
homestead	Real or personal property used as residence to $15,000; unused portion of homestead may be applied to any property	38-10-4(a)
insurance	Fraternal benefit society benefits	33-23-21
	Group life insurance policy or proceeds	33-6-28
	Health or disability benefits	38-10-4(j)(3)
	Life insurance payments from policy for person you depended on, needed for support	38-10-4(k)(3)
	Unmatured life insurance contract, except credit insurance policy	38-10-4(g)
	Unmatured life insurance contract's accrued dividend, interest or loan value to $8,000, if debtor owns contract & insured is either debtor or a person on whom debtor is dependent	38-10-4(h)
miscellaneous	Alimony, child support needed for support	38-10-4(j)(4)
	Property of business partnership	47-8A-25
pensions	ERISA-qualified benefits needed for support	38-10-4(j)(5).
	Public employees	5-10-46
	Teachers	18-7A-30
personal property	Animals, crops, clothing, appliances, books, household goods, furnishings, musical instruments to $400 per item, $8,000 total	38-10-4(c)
	Burial plot to $15,000, in lieu of homestead	38-10-4(a)
	Health aids	38-10-4(i)
	Jewelry to $1,000	38-10-4(d)
	Lost earnings payments needed for support	38-10-4(k)(5)
	Motor vehicle to $2,400	38-10-4(b)
	Personal injury recoveries to $15,000 (not to include pain & suffering)	38-10-4(k)(4)
	Wrongful death recoveries needed for support, for person you depended on	38-10-4(k)(2)
public benefits	Aid to blind, aged, disabled, general assistance	9-5-1
	Crime victims' compensation	14-2A-24, 38-10-4(k)(1)
	Social Security	38-10-4(j)(1)
	Unemployment compensation	38-10-4(j)(1)
	Veterans' benefits	38-10-4(j)(2)
	Workers' compensation	23-4-18
tools of trade	Implements, books & tools of trade to $1,500	38-10-4(f)
wages	80% of earned but unpaid wages; bankruptcy judge may authorize more for low-income debtors	38-5A-3
wild card	$800 of any property	38-10-4(e)
	Unused portion of homestead or burial exemption, of any property	38-10-4(e)

Wisconsin

Federal Bankruptcy Exemptions available. All law references are to Wisconsin Statutes Annotated.

ASSET	EXEMPTION	LAW
homestead	Property you occupy or intend to occupy to $40,000; sale proceeds exempt for 2 years from sale if you plan to obtain another home (husband and wife may not double)	815.20
insurance	Federal disability insurance	815.18(3)(ds)
	Fire proceeds for destroyed exempt property for 2 years from receiving	815.18(3)(e)
	Fraternal benefit society benefits	614.96
	Life insurance policy or proceeds to $5,000, if beneficiary is a married woman	766.09
	Life insurance proceeds held in trust by insurer, if clause prohibits proceeds from being used to pay beneficiary's creditors	632.42
	Life insurance proceeds if beneficiary was dependent of insured, needed for support	815.18(3)(i)(a)
	Unmatured life insurance contract, except credit insurance contract, owned by debtor & insuring debtor, dependent of debtor or someone debtor is dependent on	815.18(3)(f)
	Unmatured life insurance contract's accrued dividends, interest or loan value (to $4,000 total in all contracts), if debtor owns contract & insured is debtor, dependent of debtor or someone debtor is dependent on	815.18(3)(f)
miscellaneous	Alimony, child support needed for support	815.18(3)(c)
	Property of business partnership	178.21
pensions	Certain municipal employees	66.81
	Firefighters, police officers who worked in city with population over 100,000	815.18(3)(ef)
	Military pensions	815.18(3)(n)
	Private or public retirement benefits	815.18(3)(j)
	Public employees	40.08(1)
personal property	Burial provisions	815.18(3)(a)
	Deposit accounts to $1,000	815.18(3)(k)
	Household goods and furnishings, clothing, keepsakes, jewelry, appliances, books, musical instruments, firearms, sporting goods, animals and other tangible property held for personal, family or household use to $5,000 total	815.18(3)(d)
	Lost future earnings recoveries, needed for support	815.18(3)(i)(d)
	Motor vehicles to $1,200	815.18(3)(g)
	Personal injury recoveries to $25,000	815.18(3)(i)(c)
	Tenant's lease or stock interest in housing co-op, to homestead amount	182.004(6)
	Wages used to purchase savings bonds	20.921(1)(e)
	Wrongful death recoveries, needed for support	815.18(3)(i)(b)
public benefits	Crime victims' compensation	949.07
	Social services payments	49.41
	Unemployment compensation	108.13
	Veterans' benefits	45.35(8)(b)
	Workers' compensation	102.27
tools of trade	Equipment, inventory, farm products, books and tools of trade to $7,500 total	815.18(3)(b)
wages	75% of earned but unpaid wages; bankruptcy judge may authorize more for low-income debtors	815.18(3)(h)
wild card	None	

Wyoming

Federal Bankruptcy Exemptions not available. All law references are to Wyoming Statutes Annotated unless otherwise noted.

ASSET	EXEMPTION	LAW
homestead	Real property you occupy to $10,000 or house trailer you occupy to $6,000 (joint owners may double)	1-20-101, 1-20-102, 1-20-104
	Spouse or child of deceased owner may claim homestead exemption	1-20-103
	Property held as tenancy by the entirety may be exempt against debts owed by only one spouse	In re Anselmi, 52 B.R. 479 (D. Wy. 1985)
insurance	Annuity contract proceeds to $350 per month	26-15-132
	Disability benefits if clause prohibits proceeds from being used to pay beneficiary's creditors	26-15-130
	Fraternal benefit society benefits	26-29-218
	Group life or disability policy or proceeds	26-15-131
	Life insurance proceeds held by insurer, if clause prohibits proceeds from being used to pay beneficiary's creditors	26-15-133
miscellaneous	Liquor licenses & malt beverage permits	12-4-604
pensions	Criminal investigators, highway officers	9-3-620
	Firefighters, police officers (only payments being received)	15-5-209
	Game & fish wardens	9-3-620
	Private or public retirement funds and accounts	1-20-110
	Public employees	9-3-426
personal property	Bedding, furniture, household articles & food to $2,000 per person in the home	1-20-106(a)(iii)
	Bible, schoolbooks & pictures	1-20-106(a)(i)
	Burial plot	1-20-106(a)(ii), 35-8-104
	Clothing & wedding rings needed, up to $1,000	1-20-105
	Funeral contracts, pre-paid	26-32-102
	Motor vehicle to $2,400	1-20-106(a)(iv)
public benefits	Crime victims' compensation	1-40-113
	General assistance	42-2-113
	Unemployment compensation	27-3-319
	Workers' compensation	27-14-702
tools of trade	Library & implements of professional to $2,000 or tools, motor vehicle, implements, team & stock in trade to $2,000	1-20-106(b)
wages	Earnings of National Guard members	19-2-501
	Minimum 75% of earned but unpaid wages	1-15-511
	Wages of inmates on work release	7-16-308
wild card	None	

Federal Bankruptcy Exemptions

Married couples may double all exemptions. All references are to 11 U.S.C. § 522. These exemptions were last adjusted in 1994. On April 1, 1998, and at every three-year interval ending on April 1 thereafter, these amounts shall be adjusted to reflect changes in the Consumer Price Index.

Debtors in the following states may select the Federal Bankruptcy Exemptions:

Arkansas	Massachusetts	New Mexico	Texas
Connecticut	Michigan	Pennsylvania	Vermont
District of Columbia	Minnesota	Rhode Island	Washington
Hawaii	New Jersey	South Carolina	Wisconsin

ASSET	EXEMPTION	SUBSECTION
homestead	Real property, including co-op or mobile home, to $15,000; unused portion of homestead to $7,500 may be applied to any property	(d)(1)
insurance	Disability, illness or unemployment benefits	(d)(10)(C)
	Life insurance payments for person you depended on, needed for support	(d)(11)(C)
	Life insurance policy with loan value, in accrued dividends or interest, to $8,000	(d)(8)
	Unmatured life insurance contract, except credit insurance policy	(d)(7)
miscellaneous	Alimony, child support needed for support	(d)(10)(D)
pensions	ERISA-qualified benefits needed for support; may include IRAs	(d)(10)(E); *In re Carmichael,* No. 96-50013 (5th Cir. 11/13/ 96)
personal property	Animals, crops, clothing, appliances, books, furnishings, household goods, musical instruments to $400 per item, $8,000 total	(d)(3)
	Health aids	(d)(9)
	Jewelry to $1,000	(d)(4)
	Lost earnings payments	(d)(11)(E)
	Motor vehicle to $2,400	(d)(2)
	Personal injury recoveries to $15,000 (not to include pain & suffering or pecuniary loss)	(d)(11)(D)
	Wrongful death recoveries for person you depended on	(d)(11)(B)
public benefits	Crime victims' compensation	(d)(11)(A)
	Public assistance	(d)(10)(A)
	Social Security	(d)(10)(A)
	Unemployment compensation	(d)(10)(A)
	Veterans' benefits	(d)(10)(A)
tools of trade	Implements, books & tools of trade to $1,500	(d)(6)
wages	None	
wild card	$800 of any property	(d)(5)
	$7,500 less any amount of homestead exemption claimed, of any property	(d)(5)

Federal Non-Bankruptcy Exemptions

These exemptions are available only if you select your state exemptions; they cannot be claimed if you claim the federal bankruptcy exemptions. All law references are to the United States Code.

ASSET	EXEMPTION	LAW
retirement benefits	CIA employees	50 § 403
	Civil service employees	5 § 8346
	Foreign service employees	22 § 4060
	Military honor roll pensions	38 § 562
	Military service employees	10 § 1440
	Railroad workers	45 § 231m
	Social Security	42 § 407
	Veterans' benefits	38 § 3101
	Veterans' medal of honor benefits	38 § 562
survivor's benefits	Judges, U.S. court directors, judicial center directors, supreme court chief justice administrators	28 § 376
	Lighthouse workers	33 § 775
	Military service	10 § 1450
death & disability benefits	Government employees	5 § 8130
	Longshoremen & harbor workers	33 § 916
	War risk hazard death or injury compensation	42 § 1717
miscellaneous	Klamath Indians tribe benefits for Indians residing in Oregon	25 § 543, 25 § 545
	Military deposits in savings accounts while on permanent duty outside U.S.	10 § 1035
	Military group life insurance	38 § 770(g)
	Railroad workers' unemployment insurance	45 § 352(e)
	Seamen's clothing	46 § 11110
	Seamen's wages (while on a voyage) pursuant to a written contract	46 § 11111
	75% of earned but unpaid wages; bankruptcy judge may authorize more for low-income debtors	15 § 1673

Exemption Glossary

This glossary defines some of the terms that appear in the Appendix 1: *State and Federal Exemption Tables.*

Animals

The "animal" exemption varies among states. In many places, pets or livestock and poultry are specifically exempt. If your state simply allows you to exempt "animals," you may include livestock, poultry or pets. Some states exempt only domestic animals, which are usually considered to be all animals but pets.

Annuity

Insurance that pays out during the life of the insured, unlike life insurance, which pays out at the insured's death. A person who purchases an annuity contract and reaches a specified age, such as 65, gets back monthly payments until death. Thus, an annuity is really a type of retirement plan.

Appliance

Any household apparatus or machine, usually operated by electricity, gas or propane. Examples include refrigerators, stoves, washing machines, dishwashers, vacuum cleaners, air conditioners and toasters.

Arms & accoutrements

Arms are weapons (e.g., pistols, rifles, swords); accoutrements are the furnishings of a soldier's outfit, such as a belt or pack, but not clothes or weapons. A soldier's clothing is his uniform.

Articles of adornment

See Jewelry.

Assessment benefits

See Stipulated insurance.

Avails

Any amount available to the owner of an insurance policy other than the actual proceeds of the policy. Avails include dividend payments, interest, cash or surrender value (the money you'd get if you sold your policy back to the insurance company) and loan value (the amount of cash you can borrow against the policy).

Benefit or benevolent society benefits

See Fraternal benefit society benefits.

Building materials

Items such as lumber, brick, stone, iron, paint and varnish used to build or improve a structure.

Burial plot

Cemetery plot.

Condo

Condominium, a form of housing in which multiple units are constructed on a commonly owned piece of land, but each unit is individually owned. The common areas (lobby, hallways, stairways, etc.) are jointly owned by the unit owners and managed by an owners' association.

Co-op

Cooperative housing. Cooperative housing involves a group of people forming a corporation to own a residential building; stockholders are entitled to live in certain dwelling units.

Cooperative insurance

Compulsory employment benefits provided by a state or federal government, such as Old Age, Survivors, Disability and Health Insurance, to assure a minimum standard of living for lower and middle income people. Also called social insurance.

Credit insurance

Insurance taken to cover a borrower for an outstanding loan. If the borrower dies or becomes disabled before paying off the loan, the policy will pay off the balance due.

Crops

All products of the soil or earth that are grown and raised annually and gathered in a single season. Thus, oranges (on the tree or harvested) are crops; an orange tree isn't.

Disability benefits

Payments made under a disability insurance plan (or a retirement plan) when the insured (or employee) is unable to work (or retires early) because of disability, accident or sickness.

Domestic animals

See Animals.

Endowment insurance

Provides that an insured who lives the specified endowment period receives the face value (the amount paid at death). If the insured dies sooner, the beneficiary named in the policy receives the proceeds.

ERISA qualified-benefits

ERISA (Employee Retirement Income Security Act), a federal law governing pensions, provides benefits to employers and rights to employees. Pensions must meet certain requirements to qualify for ERISA coverage. Many private pensions, including Keoghs and IRAs, qualify.

Farm tools

Tools used by a person whose primary occupation is farming. Some states limit farm tools of the trade to items which can be held in the hand: hoes, axes, pitchforks, shovels, scythes and the like. In other states, farm tools also include plows, harnesses, mowers, reapers, etc. To determine which definition applies in your state, read your state statute, noted in your state exemption chart.

Fraternal benefit society benefits

Benefits, often group life insurance, paid for by fraternal societies, such as the Elks, Masons, Knights of Columbus or the Knights of Maccabees, to their members. Also called benefit society, benevolent society or mutual aid association benefits.

Furnishings

Furniture, fixtures in your home, such as a heating unit, furnace or built-in lighting, and other items with which a home is furnished (e.g., carpets and drapes).

Goods & chattels

Same as Personal property.

Group life or group health insurance

A single policy under which individuals in a group (for example, employees) and their dependents are covered.

Head of family or head of household

A person who supports and maintains, in one household, one or more people who are closely related to him by blood, marriage or adoption.

Health aids

Items needed to maintain their owner's health, such as a wheelchair, crutches and hearing aid.

Health benefits

Benefits paid under health insurance plans, such as Blue Cross/Blue Shield, to cover the costs of health care.

Heirloom

An item with special monetary or sentimental value passed from generation to generation.

Homestead

An exemption that protects up to a specified value (or specified number of acres) in a home from being taken to satisfy creditors. *See* Ch. 6, *Your House.*

Homestead declaration

A form filed with the county recorder's office to put on record your right to a homestead exemption.

Household good

An item of permanent nature (as opposed to items consumed, like food or cosmetics) used in or about the house. It includes linens, dinnerware, utensils, pots and pans and small electronic equipment like radios.

Householder or housekeeper

A person who supports and maintains a household, with or without other people.

Implement

An instrument, tool or utensil used by a person to accomplish her job.

In lieu of homestead (or burial) exemption

This means that the given exemption is available only if you don't claim the homestead (or burial) exemption.

Intangible personal property

See Intangible property.

Intangible property

Property that has no physical existence such as stocks, bonds, notes, franchises, goodwill, trade secrets, patents, copyrights and trademarks. Some intangible items may be represented by a certificate, but it represents the value of the property and isn't the property itself.

Jewelry

Items created for personal adornment; usually includes watches. Also called articles of adornment.

Life estate

The right to live in, but not own, a specific home until your death.

Life insurance

Provides for the payment of money to an individual (called the beneficiary) in the event of the death of another (called the insured). If the insured is alive, the policy is unmatured; when the insured dies, the policy matures.

Life insurance avails

See Avails.

Liquid assets

Cash or an item easily convertible into cash, such as a money market account, stocks, U.S. Treasury bill or bank deposit.

Lost earnings payments or recoveries

See Lost future earnings.

Lost future earnings

The portion of a lawsuit judgment intended to pay an injured person the equivalent of the future earnings lost because of the injury. Also called lost earnings payments or recoveries.

Matured life insurance benefits

Benefits currently payable because of the death of the insured.

Motor vehicle

A self-propelled vehicle suitable for use on a street or road. It includes a car, truck, motorcycle, van and moped.

Musical instrument

An instrument having the capacity, in and of itself, when properly operated, to produce a musical sound. Pianos, guitars, drums, drum machines, synthesizers and harmonicas are musical instruments. Spoons (knocked on knees or into each other) and metal garbage can lids (when banged together like cymbals) aren't.

Mutual aid association benefits

See Fraternal benefit society benefits.

Mutual assessment or mutual life

See Stipulated insurance.

Necessities

Articles needed to sustain life, such as food, clothing, medical care and shelter.

Pain and suffering damages

The portion of a court judgment intended to compensate for past, present and future mental and physical pain, suffering, impairment of ability to work, anxiety about the injury, and mental distress caused by an injury.

Pension

A fund into which payments are made to provide an employee income after retirement.

Personal injury cause of action

The right to seek compensation for physical and mental suffering, including injury to body, reputation or both.

EXAMPLE: Joyce is hit by a car while crossing the street. Her right to sue the driver (and anyone else who might be responsible) for her injuries is a personal injury cause of action.

Personal injury recovery

The amount that comes from a lawsuit or insurance settlement to compensate someone for physical and mental suffering, including injury to body, injury to reputation or both.

Personal property

All property not classified as real property (land, and structures permanently attached to the land). Examples: money, stocks, furniture, cars, bank accounts, pensions, jewelry, oil paintings and patents.

Pets

See Animals.

Proceeds for damaged exempt property

The money collected through insurance, arbitration, mediation, settlement or a lawsuit to pay for exempt property that's no longer exemptible because it has been damaged or destroyed.

EXAMPLE: Hiro, who lives in Hawaii, planned to exempt the equity in his family's home under Hawaii's exemption ($30,000). Right before filing, however, a fire destroyed his house. Rather than claim his home's equity, Hiro now will claim as exempt $30,000 of the insurance proceeds he'll be paid from his insurance company.

Property of business partnership

A partnership's business property having the following characteristics:

- Each partner has a right to possess the property for partnership purposes, but has no right to possess it for any other purpose without consent of the partners.
- At a partner's death, his share of the partnership property passes to the surviving partners.
- The property isn't subject to state non-partnership property laws such as dower, curtesy, spouse's share or inheritance.

Sickness benefits

See Disability benefits.

Stipulated insurance

An insurance policy that allows the insurance company to assess an amount on the insured, above the standard premium payments, if the company experiences losses worse than had been calculated into the standard premium. Also called assessment, mutual assessment or mutual life insurance.

Surrender value

See Avails.

Tangible personal property

See Tangible property and Personal property.

Tangible property

Property that may be felt or touched. Examples: money, furniture, cars, jewelry, artwork and houses. Compare Intangible property.

Tenancy by the entirety

A property ownership form available only to married couples in certain states. Each spouse may possess and enjoy the property, and when one spouse dies, his share goes automatically to the survivor. Most states that exempt tenancy by the entirety property allow the exemption only against debts incurred by one spouse. If a spouse tries to discharge jointly incurred marital debts, the tenancy by the entirety property loses its exempt status.

To ___ acres

The designation "to ___ acres" (for example, "to 160 acres") is a limitation on the size of a homestead that may be exempted.

Tools of the trade

Items needed to perform a line of work. For a mechanic, plumber or carpenter, tools of trade are the implements used to repair, build and install. For a doctor, tools of trade are the items found in the doctor's office and bag. For a clergyperson, tools of trade often consist of no more than books. Traditionally, tools of the trade were limited to items that could be held in the hand. Most states, however, now embrace a broader definition and a debtor may be able to fit many items under a tool of trade exemption. The following list shows examples of what a creative debtor may exempt. This list isn't meant to be a specific guideline, as each state's law differs. At the same time, this list isn't exhaustive; use your imagination.

- Art camera (artist)
- Car (sales manager, insurance adjuster, physician, firewood salesperson, traveling salesperson, real estate salesperson, mechanic)
- Cream separator, dairy cows, animal feed (farmer)
- Drills, saws (carpenter)
- Electric motor & lathe (mechanic)
- Guitar, acoustic amplifier, coronet, violin & bow, organ, speaker cabinet (musician)

- Hair tonic, shampoo, cash register, furniture, dryer, fan, curler, magazine rack (barber, beauty parlor operator)
- Oven & mixer (baker)
- Personal computer & printer (insurance salesperson)
- Photographic lens (photographer)
- Power chain saw (firewood salesperson)
- Safe (physician)
- Sewing machine (tailor)
- Truck (logger, tire retreader, truck driver, farmer, electrician)
- Watch (cabinet maker)
- Word processor (lawyer)

Unmatured life insurance

A policy whose benefits aren't yet payable because the insured is still alive.

Weekly net earnings

The earnings left after mandatory deductions such as income tax, mandatory union dues and social security contributions have been subtracted from an employee's gross income.

Wild card exemption

An exemption that you may apply toward the property of your choice. Some states limit the exemption to personal property; others include any property, real or personal. In nearly all states, you can apply the exemption to nonexempt property (such as expensive jewelry or clothes) or use it to increase the amount for an already partially exempt item. For example, if your state has no specific motor vehicle exemption but does have a wild card exemption, you can use the wild card exemption to exempt the car. If your state has a specific motor vehicle exemption, but the amount is limited, you can use the wild card exemption to increase the exempt amount.

Wrongful death cause of action

The right to seek compensation for having to live without a deceased person. Usually only the spouse and children of the deceased have a wrongful death cause of action. Example: Joyce is killed by a speeding car while crossing the street. Her husband and children's right to sue the driver (and anyone else who might be responsible) for her death is a wrongful death cause of action.

Wrongful death recoveries

The portion of a lawsuit judgment intended to compensate a plaintiff for having to live without a deceased person. The compensation's intended to cover the earnings and the emotional comfort and support the deceased would have provided. ∎

Addresses of Bankruptcy Courts

Alabama	112th & Noble Streets, 122 U.S. Courthouse, **Anniston**, AL 36201, 205-236-6421
	1800 5th Ave. North, Room 120, **Birmingham**, AL 35203, 205-731-0850
	P.O. Box 1289, 222 Federal Courthouse, **Decatur**, AL 35602, 205-353-2817
	201 St. Louis Street, **Mobile**, AL 36602, 334-441-5391
	P.O. Box 1248, Suite 127, One Court Square, **Montgomery**, AL 36102, 334-223-7622
	1118 Greensboro Ave., **Tuscaloosa**, AL 35401, 205-752-0426
Alaska	605 W. 4th Ave., Suite 138, **Anchorage**, AK 99501, 907-271-2655
Arizona	2929 N. Central Ave., 9th Floor, **Phoenix**, AZ 85012, 602-640-5800
	110 South Church Ave., Suite 8112, **Tucson**, AZ 85701, 602-620-7500
	325 West 19th St., **Yuma**, AZ 85364, 520-783-2288
Arkansas	P.O. Drawer 2381, 600 W. Capitol Ave., **Little Rock**, AR 72203, 501-324-6357
California	5301 U.S. Courthouse, 1130 O St., **Fresno**, CA 93721, 209-487-5217
	255 E. Temple, **Los Angeles**, CA 90012, 213-894-6046
	P.O. Box 5276, 1130 - 12th St., **Modesto**, CA 95352, 209-521-5160
	P.O. Box 2070, **Oakland**, CA 94604 (mail) or 1300 Clay St., Suite 300, **Oakland**, CA 94612 (person), 510-879-3600
	8308 U.S. Courthouse, 650 Capitol Mall, **Sacramento**, CA 95814, 916-498-5525
	222 E. Carrillo St., Room 101, **Santa Barbara**, CA 93101, 805-897-3880
	699 N. Arrowhead Ave, Room 105, **San Bernardino**, CA 92401, 909-383-5742
	325 West F Street, **San Diego**, CA 92101, 619-557-5536
	P.O. Box 7341, **San Francisco**, CA 94120 (mail) or 235 Pine Street, **San Francisco**, CA 94104 (person), 415-705-3200
	280 South First St., Room 3035, **San Jose**, CA 95113, 408-535-5118
	506 Federal Building, 34 Civic Center Plaza, **Santa Ana**, CA 92701, 714-836-2993
	99 South E St., **Santa Rosa**, CA 95404, 707-525-8520
Colorado	U.S. Customs House, 721-19th St., **Denver**, CO 80202, 303-844-4045
Connecticut	U.S. Courthouse, 915 Lafayette Blvd., **Bridgeport**, CT 06604, 203-579-5808
	712 U.S. Courthouse, 450 Main St., **Hartford**, CT 06103, 203-240-3675
Delaware	824 Market, **Wilmington**, DE 19801, 302-573-6174

District of Columbia U.S. Courthouse, Room 4400, 3rd & Constitution Aves., NW, **Washington**, DC 20001, 202-273-0042

Florida 299 E. Broward Blvd., Room 206B, **Ft. Lauderdale**, FL 33301, 305-356-7224

P.O. Box 559, U.S. Post Office & Courthouse, **Jacksonville**, FL 32201 (mail) or 311 W. Monroe St., **Jacksonville**, FL 32202 (person), 904-232-2852

51 SW First Ave., **Miami**, FL 33130, 305-536-4320

135 W. Central Ave., Room 950, **Orlando**, FL 32801, 407-648-6364

220 W. Garden St., Room 700, **Pensacola**, FL 32501, 904-435-8475

227 N. Bronough St., Room 3120, **Tallahassee**, FL 32301, 904-942-8933

4921 Memorial Highway, Room 200, **Tampa**, FL 33634, 813-243-5041

701 Clematis St., Room 335, **West Palm Beach**, FL 33401, 407-655-6774

Georgia 1340 R.B. Russell Building, 75 Spring St. SW, **Atlanta**, GA 30303, 404-331-6886

827 Telfaire St., P.O. Box 1487, **Augusta**, GA 30901, 706-724-2421

P.O. Box 2147, 901 Front Ave., One Arsenal Place, Room 310, **Columbus**, GA 31902, 706-649-7837

Federal Building, 126 Washington St., Room 201, **Gainsville**, GA 30501, 404-536-0556

P.O. Box 1957, Old Federal Building, **Macon**, GA 31202, 912-752-3506

P.O. Box 2328, **Newnan**, GA 30264, 404-251-5583

P.O. Box 5231, **Rome**, GA 30161, 706-291-5639

P.O. Box 8347, 212 U.S. Courthouse, **Savannah**, GA 31412, 912-652-4100

Hawaii First Hawaiian Tower, 1132 Bishop St., Suite 250L, **Honolulu**, HI 96813, 808-522-8100

Idaho 550 W. Fort St., Box 042 Federal Building, **Boise**, ID 83724, 208-334-1074

Illinois 301 W. Main St., **Benton**, IL 62812, 618-435-2200

U.S. Courthouse, 219 S. Dearborn St., Room 614, **Chicago**, IL 60604, 312-435-5587

P.O. Box 657, 301 Federal Building, Room 127, 201 N. Vermilion St., **Danville**, IL 61834, 217-431-4817

P.O. Box 309, 750 Missouri Ave., 1st Floor, **East St. Louis**, IL 62202, 618-482-9400

156 Federal Building, 100 NE Monroe St., **Peoria**, IL 61602, 309-671-7035

211 S. Court St., **Rockford**, IL 61101, 815-987-4352

P.O. Box 2438, 226 U.S. Courthouse, 600 E. Monroe St., **Springfield**, IL 62705, 217-431-4820

Indiana 101 NW Martin Luther King Blvd., **Evansville**, IN 47708, 812-465-6440

1188 Federal Building, 1300 S. Harrison St., **Ft. Wayne**, IN 46802, 219-420-5100

221 Federal Building, 610 Connecticut St., **Gary**, IN 46402, 219-881-3335

123 U.S. Courthouse, 46 E. Ohio St., **Indianapolis**, IN 46204, 317-226-6821

102 Federal Building, **New Albany**, IN 47150, 812-948-5254

224 U.S. Courthouse, 204 S. Main St., **South Bend**, IN 46601-2196, 219-236-8247

203 Post Office Building, 30 N. 7th St., **Terre Haute**, IN 47808, 812-238-1550

Iowa   P.O. Box 74890, **Cedar Rapids**, IA 52407 (mail) or 800 The Center, 425 2nd St., S.E., **Cedar Rapids**, IA 52401 (person), 319-362-9696

P.O. Box 9264, **Des Moines**, IA 50309 (mail) or 318 U.S. Courthouse, **Des Moines**, IA 50306 (person), 515-284-6230

U.S. Courthouse, 320 6th St., **Sioux City**, IA 51101, 712-252-3757

Kansas   500 State Ave., **Kansas City**, KS 66101, 913-551-6732

240 U.S. Courthouse, 444 SE Quincy St., **Topeka**, KS 66683, 913-295-2750

167 U.S. Courthouse, 401 N. Market St., **Wichita**, KS 67202, 316-269-6486

Kentucky   P.O. Box 1111, 200 Merrill Lynch Plaza, **Lexington**, KY 40588, 606-233-2608

546 G. Snyder Courthouse and Customs House, 601 W. Broadway, **Louisville**, KY 40202, 502-582-6136

Louisiana   P.O. Box 111, **Alexandria**, LA 71309 (mail) or 300 Jackson St., **Alexandria**, LA 71301, 318-473-7366

412 N. 4th St., Room 301, **Baton Rouge**, LA 70802, 504-389-0211

Hale Boggs Federal Building, 501 Magazine St., Suite 701, **New Orleans**, LA 70130, 504-589-6506

205 Federal Building, Corner of Union & Vine, **Opelousas**, LA 70570, 318-942-2161

300 Fannin St., **Shreveport**, LA 71101, 318-676-4267

Maine   P.O. Box 1109, 331 U.S. Courthouse, 202 Harlow St., **Bangor**, ME 04401, 207-945-0348

U.S. Courthouse, 537 Congress, **Portland**, ME 04101, 207-780-3482

Maryland   U.S. Courthouse, 101 W. Lombard St., Room 919, **Baltimore**, MD 21201, 410-962-2688

6500 Cherry Wood Lane, **Greenbelt**, MD 20770, 301-344-8018

Massachusetts T.P. O'Neill Federal Office Building, 10 Causeway St., Room 1101, **Boston**, MA 02222, 617-565-6051

Edwards Building, 10 Mechanic St., **Worcester**, MA 01608, 508-793-0542

Michigan   111 First St., **Bay City**, MI 48707, 517-894-8850

U.S. Courthouse, 231 W. Lafayette, Room 1060, **Detroit**, MI 48226, 313-226-6395

226 W. Second St., **Flint**, MI 48502, 810-235-3220

P.O. Box 3310, 299 Federal Building, 110 Michigan St. NW, **Grand Rapids**, MI 49503, 616-456-2693

P.O. Box 909, 314 Post Office Bldg., **Marquette**, MI 49855, 906-226-2117

Minnesota   416 U.S. Courthouse, 515 W. 1st St., **Duluth**, MN 55802, 218-720-5253

205 U.S. Courthouse, 118 S. Mills St., **Fergus Falls**, MN 56537, 218-739-4671

600 Towle Building, 330 Second Ave. South, **Minneapolis**, MN 55401, 612-348-1855

200 U.S. Courthouse, 316 N. Robert St., **St. Paul**, MN 55101, 612-290-3184

Mississippi   Biloxi Federal Building, 725 Washington Loop, Room 117, **Biloxi**, MS 39533, 601-432 5542

P.O. Drawer 2448, **Jackson**, MS 39225, 601-965-5301

Missouri	U.S. Courthouse, 811 Grand Ave., Room 913, **Kansas City**, MO 64106, 816-426-3321
	1 Metropolitan Square, 211 N. Broadway, 7th Floor, **St. Louis**, MO 63102, 314-425-4222
Montana	273 Federal Building, 400 N. Main St., P.O. Box 689, **Butte**, MT 59701, 406-782-3354
Nebraska	P.O. Box 428 Downtown Sta., 215 N. 17th St., New Federal Building, **Omaha**, NB 68101, 402-221-4687
	460 Federal Building, 100 Centennial Mall N., **Lincoln**, NB 68508, 402-437-5100
Nevada	300 Las Vegas Blvd. South, **Las Vegas**, NV 89101, 702-388-6257
	4005 Federal Building & Courthouse, 300 Booth St., **Reno**, NV 89509, 702-784-5559
New Hampshire	275 Chestnut St., Room 404, **Manchester**, NH 03101, 603-666-7532
New Jersey	15 N. 7th St., **Camden**, NJ 08102, 609-757-5023
	50 Walnut St., **Newark**, NJ 07102, 201-645-4764
	U.S. Post Office & Courthouse, 402 E. State St., **Trenton**, NJ 08608, 609-989-2198
New Mexico	421 Gold Ave. SW, 3rd Floor, **Albuquerque**, NM 87102, 505-766-8473
New York	327 James T. Foley Courthouse, 445 Broadway, **Albany**, NY 12201, 518-431-0188
	75 Clinton St., **Brooklyn**, NY 11201, 718-330-2188
	310 U.S. Courthouse, 68 Court St., **Buffalo**, NY 14202, 716-551-4130
	601 Veterans Hwy., **Hauppauge**, NY 11788, 516-361-8038
	1 Bowling Green, **New York**, NY 10004, 212-668-2870
	P.O. Box 1000, **Poughkeepsie**, NY 12602, 914-452-4200
	100 State St., Room 2120, **Rochester**, NY 14614, 716-263-3148
	Alexander Pirnie Federal Building, Room 230, **Utica**, NY 13501, 315-793-8101
	1635 Privado Rd., **Westbury**, NY 11590, 516-832-8801
	300 Quarropas St., 5th Floor, **White Plains**, NY 10601, 914-390-4061
North Carolina	401 W. Trade St., **Charlotte**, NC 28202, 704-344-6103
	P.O. Box 26100, 202 S. Elm St., **Greensboro**, NC 27420, 919-333-5647
	P.O. Box 1441, **Raleigh**, NC 27602, 919-856-4752
	P.O. Drawer 2807, 1760 Parkwood Blvd., **Wilson**, NC 27894, 919-237-0248
North Dakota	P.O. Box 1110, 655 1st Ave., **Fargo**, ND 58107, 701-239-5120
Ohio	455 Federal Building, 2 S. Main St., **Akron**, OH 44308, 216-375-5840
	U.S. Bankruptcy Court, 201 Cleveland Ave. SW, **Canton**, OH 44702, 216-489-4426
	Atruim Two, Suite 800, 221 E. 4th St., **Cincinnati**, OH 45202, 513-684-2572
	U.S. Courthouse, 127 Public Square, **Cleveland**, OH 44114, 216-522-4373
	970 N. High St., **Columbus**, OH 43215, 614-469-6638
	120 W. 3rd St., **Dayton**, OH 45402, 513-225-2516
	411 U.S. Courthouse, 1716 Spielbusch Ave., **Toledo**, OH 43624, 419-259-6440
	9 West Front, **Youngstown**, OH 44501, 216-746-7027

Oklahoma
Post Office-Courthouse , 215 D. A. McGee Ave., **Oklahoma City**, OK 73102, 405-231-5642

P.O. Box 1347, U.S. Post Office & Federal Building, **Okmulgee**, OK 74447, 918-756-9248

224 S. Boulder Ave., **Tulsa**, OK 74103, 918-581-7645

Oregon
P.O. Box 1335, **Eugene**, OR 97440 (mail) or 404 Federal Building, 211 E. 7th St., **Eugene**, OR 97401 (person), 503-465-6448

1001 SW 5th Ave., 9th Floor, **Portland**, OR 97204, 503-326-2231

Pennsylvania
P.O. Box 1755, 314 U.S. Courthouse, **Erie**, PA 16507, 814-453-7580

P.O. Box 908, Federal Building, 3rd & Walnut Sts., **Harrisburg**, PA 17108, 717-782-2260

3726 U.S. Courthouse, 601 Market St., **Philadelphia**, PA 19106, 215-597-0926

1602 Federal Building, 1000 Liberty Ave., **Pittsburgh**, PA 15222, 412-644-2700

400 Washington St., The Madison, Room 350, **Reading**, PA 19601, 215-320-5255

217 Federal Building, 197 S. Main St., **Wilkes-Barre**, PA 18701, 717-826-6450

Rhode Island
380 Westminster Mall, Federal Center, **Providence**, RI 02903, 401-528-4477

South Carolina
P.O. Box 1448, 1100 Laurel St., **Columbia**, SC 29202, 803-765-5436

South Dakota
203 Federal Building, 225 S. Pierre St., **Pierre**, SD 57501, 605-224-6013

104 Federal Building & U.S. Courthouse, 400 S. Phillips Ave., P.O. Box 5060, **Sioux Falls**, SD 57117, 605-330-4541

Tennessee
31 E. 11th St., **Chattanooga**, TN 37401, 615-752-5163

P.O. Box 1527, **Jackson**, TN 38302, 901-424-9751

200 Jefferson Ave., Room 413, **Memphis**, TN 38103, 901-544-3202

207 Customs House, 701 Broadway, **Nashville**, TN 37203, 615-736-5590

Texas
624 S. Polk St., **Amarillo**, TX 79101, 806-376-2302

816 Congress, First City Centre, Room 1420, **Austin**, TX 78701, 512-482-5237

300 Willow St., Suite 100, **Beaumont**, TX 77701, 409-839-2617

615 Leopard St., Suite 113, **Corpus Christi**, TX 78476, 512-888-3484

14-A-7 U.S. Courthouse, 1100 Commerce St., **Dallas**, TX 75242, 214-767-0814

111 E. Broadway, Room L100, **Del Rio**, TX 78840, 512-775-2021

8515 Lockheed Dr., **El Paso**, TX 79925, 915-779-7362

501 W. 10th St., Room 310, **Fort Worth**, TX 76102, 817-334-3802

Federal Building, 515 Rusk Ave., 4th Floor, **Houston**, TX 77002, 713-250-5115

102 Federal Building, 1205 Texas Ave., **Lubbock**, TX 79401, 806-743-7336

USPO Annex, Room P-163, 100 F Wall St., 200 Wall St., **Midland**, TX 79701, 915-683-1650

First Interstate Bank Bldg., 660 North Central Expressway, Suite 300B, **Plano**, TX 75074, 214-423-6605

P.O. Box 1439, Old Post Office Building, **San Antonio**, TX 78295 (mail) or 615 E. Houston St., Room 139, **San Antonio**, TX 78205, 512-229-5187

200 E. Ferguson St., 2nd Floor, **Tyler**, TX 75702, 903-592-0904

St. Charles Place, Suite 20, 600 Austin Ave., **Waco**, TX 76701, 817-754-1481

Utah	350 S. Main St., **Salt Lake City**, UT 84101, 801-524-6565
Vermont	P.O. Box 6648, 67 Merchants Row, **Rutland**, VT 05702, 802-747-7629
Virginia	408 Dominion Bank Building, 206 N. Washington St., Room 401, **Alexandria**, VA 22314, 703-557-1716
	P.O. Box 586, 320 Federal Building, **Harrisonburg**, VA 22801, 703-434-6747
	P.O. Box 442, 226 Federal Building, 1100 Main St., **Lynchburg**, VA 24505, 804-845-8880
	222 U.S. Post Office Building 101, 25th Floor, **Newport News**, VA 23612, 804-595-9805
	480 Courthouse, 600 Gramby St., Room 480, **Norfolk**, VA 23510, 804-441-6651
	U.S. Courthouse, Annex Building, **Richmond**, VA 23206, 804-771-2878
	P.O. Box 2390, 200 Old Federal Building, 210 Church Ave., **Roanoke**, VA 24011, 703-857-2391
Washington	315 Park Place Building, 1200 6th Ave., Room 315, **Seattle**, WA 98101, 206-553-7545
	P.O. Box 2164, **Spokane**, WA 92210 (mail) or 904 W. Riverside Ave., Room 321, **Spokane**, WA 99201 (person), 509-353-2404
	1717 Pacific Ave., Room 2100, **Tacoma**, WA 98402, 206-593-6310
West Virginia	P.O. Box 3924, 500 Quarrier St., Room 2201, **Charleston**, WV 25339, 304-347-5114
	P.O. Box 70, 12th & Chapline St., **Wheeling**, WV 26003, 304-233-1655
Wisconsin	P.O. Box 5009, 500 S. Barstow Commons, **Eau Claire**, WI 54702, 715-839-2980
	P.O. Box 548, Room 340, **Madison**, WI 53701 (mail) or 120 N. Henry, Madison, WI 53703 (person), 608-264-5178
	126 U.S. Courthouse, 517 E. Wisconsin Ave., **Milwaukee**, WI 53202, 414-297-3293
Wyoming	111 S. Wolcott St., Room 101, **Casper**, WY 82601, 307-261-5444
	P.O. Box 1107, New Post Office & Courthouse, 2120 Capitol Ave., **Cheyenne**, WY 82003, 307-772-2191 ■

APPENDIX 4

Tear-Out Forms

 Do not complete these forms until you have read the appropriate chapters in this book.

WORKSHEET 1: YOUR DEBTS

1 Description of debt/name of creditor	2 Total amount of debt	3 Is Debt Dischargeable?		4 Is Debt Secured?
If married, indicate if owned by husband (H), wife (W) or jointly (J)		yes/ no	If no, enter amount of debt	If yes, enter amount secured and collateral

Mortgages and home equity loans

_____ _____ _____ _____ _____
_____ _____ _____ _____ _____
_____ _____ _____ _____ _____
_____ _____ _____ _____ _____

Motor vehicle loans

_____ _____ _____ _____ _____
_____ _____ _____ _____ _____
_____ _____ _____ _____ _____

Personal and consolidation loans

_____ _____ _____ _____ _____
_____ _____ _____ _____ _____
_____ _____ _____ _____ _____
_____ _____ _____ _____ _____

Student loans

_____ _____ _____ _____ _____
_____ _____ _____ _____ _____
_____ _____ _____ _____ _____
_____ _____ _____ _____ _____
_____ _____ _____ _____ _____

Medical (doctor, dentist and hospital) bills

_____ _____ _____ _____ _____
_____ _____ _____ _____ _____
_____ _____ _____ _____ _____
_____ _____ _____ _____ _____
_____ _____ _____ _____ _____

Lawyers' and accountants' bills

_____ _____ _____ _____ _____
_____ _____ _____ _____ _____
_____ _____ _____ _____ _____

Totals this page $ _____ $ _____ $ _____

WORKSHEET 1: YOUR DEBTS (CONTINUED)

1 Description of debt/name of creditor	2 Total amount of debt	3 Is Debt Dischargeable?		4 Is Debt Secured?
If married, indicate if owned by husband (H), wife (W) or jointly (J)		yes/ no	If no, enter amount of debt	If yes, enter amount secured and collateral
Totals from previous page	$		$	$
Credit and charge card				
Department store and gasoline credit cards				
Alimony and child support				
Unpaid taxes				
Unpaid utility bills (gas, electric, water, phone, cable)				
Back rent				
Liens (other than tax liens)				
Other debts				
GRAND TOTALS	$		$	$

WORKSHEET 2: YOUR PROPERTY

1 Your property	2 Value of property (actual dollar or garage sale value)	3 Your ownership share (%, $)	4 Amount of liens	5 Amount of your equity	6 Exempt? If not, enter non- exempt amount
1. Real estate					
2. Cash on hand (state source of money)					
3. Deposits of money (indicate sources of money)					
4. Security deposits					
5. Household goods, supplies and furnishings					
6. Books, pictures, art objects; stamp, coin and other collections					

WORKSHEET 2: YOUR PROPERTY (CONTINUED)

1 Your property	2 Value of property (actual dollar or garage sale value)	3 Your ownership share (%, $)	4 Amount of liens	5 Amount of your equity	6 Exempt? If not, enter non- exempt amount
7. Apparel					
8. Jewelry					
9. Firearms, sports equipment and other hobby equipment					
10. Interests in insurance policies					
11. Annuities					
12. Pension or profit-sharing plans					
13. Stocks and interests in incorporated and unincorporated companies					

WORKSHEET 2: YOUR PROPERTY (CONTINUED)

1 Your property	2 Value of property (actual dollar or garage sale value)	3 Your ownership share (%, $)	4 Amount of liens	5 Amount of your equity	6 Exempt? If not, enter non- exempt amount
14. Interests in partnerships					
15. Government and corporate bonds and other investment instruments					
16. Accounts receivable					
17. Family support					
18. Other debts owed you where the amount owed is known and definite					
19. Powers exercisable for your benefit, other than those listed under real estate					
20. Interests due to another person's death					

WORKSHEET 2: YOUR PROPERTY (CONTINUED)

1 Your property	2 Value of property (actual dollar or garage sale value)	3 Your ownership share (%, $)	4 Amount of liens	5 Amount of your equity	6 Exempt? If not, enter non- exempt amount
21. All other contingent claims and claims where the amount owed you is not known					
22. Patents, copyrights and other intellectual property					
23. Licenses, franchises and other general intangibles					
24. Automobiles and other vehicles					
25. Boats, motors and accessories					
26. Aircraft and accessories					
27. Office equipment, furnishings and supplies					
28. Machinery, fixtures, equipment and supplies used in business					

1 Your property	2 Value of property (actual dollar or garage sale value)	3 Your ownership share (%, $)	4 Amount of liens	5 Amount of your equity	6 Exempt? If not, enter non- exempt amount
29. Business inventory					
30. Livestock, poultry and other animals					
31. Crops—growing or harvested					
32. Farming equipment and implements					
33. Farm supplies, chemicals and feed					
34. Other personal property					

Subtotal (column 6):	_____
Wild Card Exemption	− _____
Total Value of NONEXEMPT Property	_____

COURT CLERK
United States Bankruptcy Court

TO THE COURT CLERK:

Please send me the following information:

1. Copies of all local forms required by this court for an individual (not corporation) filing a Chapter 7 bankruptcy and for making amendments.

2. The number of copies or sets required.

3. The order in which forms should be submitted.

4. Complete instructions on this court's emergency filing procedures and deadlines.

I would also appreciate answers to two questions:

1. Do you require a separate creditor mailing list (matrix)? If so, do you have specific requirements for its format?

2. Is the filing fee still $130? Is the administrative fee still $45? If either have changed, please advise.

I've enclosed a self-addressed envelope for your reply. Thank you.

Sincerely,

FORM 1. VOLUNTARY PETITION

UNITED STATES BANKRUPTCY COURT _____ DISTRICT OF _____	**Voluntary Petition**

Name of Debtor (if individual, enter Last, First, Middle):	Name of Joint Debtor (Spouse) (Last, First, Middle):
All Other Names used by the Debtor in the last 6 years (include married, maiden, and trade names):	All Other Names used by the Joint Debtor in the last 6 years (include married, maiden, and trade names):
Soc. Sec./Tax I.D. No. (if more than one, state all):	Soc. Sec./Tax I.D. No. (if more than one, state all):
Street Address of Debtor (No. & Street, City, State & Zip Code):	Street Address of Joint Debtor (No. & Street, City, State & Zip Code):
County of Residence or of the Principal Place of Business:	County of Residence or of the Principal Place of Business:
Mailing Address of Debtor (if different from street address):	Mailing Address of Joint Debtor (if different from street address):

Location of Principal Assets of Business Debtor
(if different from street address above):

Information Regarding the Debtor (Check the Applicable Boxes)

Venue (Check any applicable box)

☐ Debtor has been domiciled or has had a residence, principal place of business, or principal assets in this District for 180 days immediately preceding the date of this petition or for a longer part of such 180 days than in any other District.

☐ There is a bankruptcy case concerning debtor's affiliate, general partner, or partnership pending in this District.

Type of Debtor (Check all boxes that apply)	**Chapter or Section of Bankruptcy Code Under Which the Petition is Filed** (Check one box)
☐ Individual(s) ☐ Railroad ☐ Corporation ☐ Stockbroker ☐ Partnership ☐ Commodity Broker ☐ Other _____	☐ Chapter 7 ☐ Chapter 11 ☐ Chapter 13 ☐ Chapter 9 ☐ Chapter 12 ☐ Sec. 304 – Case ancillary to foreign proceeding

Nature of Debts (Check one box)	**Filing Fee** (Check one box)
☐ Consumer/Non-Business ☐ Business	☐ Full Filing Fee attached
Chapter 11 Small Business (Check all boxes that apply) ☐ Debtor is a small business as defined in 11 U.S.C. § 101 ☐ Debtor is and elects to be considered a small business under 11 U.S.C. §1121(e) (Optional)	☐ Filing Fee to be paid in installments. (Applicable to individuals only.) Must attach signed application for the court's consideration certifying that the debtor is unable to pay fee except in installments. Rule 1006(b). See Official Form No. 3.

Statistical/Administrative Information (Estimates only)	THIS SPACE FOR COURT USE ONLY
☐ Debtor estimates that funds will be available for distribution to unsecured creditors. ☐ Debtor estimates that, after any exempt property is excluded and administrative expenses paid, there will be no funds available for distribution to unsecured creditors.	

Estimated Number of Creditors	1-15	16-49	50-99	100-199	200-999	1000-over
	☐	☐	☐	☐	☐	☐

Estimated Assets							
$0 to $50,000	$50,001 to $100,000	$100,001 to $500,000	$500,001 to $1 million	$1,000,001 to $10 million	$10,000,001 to $50 million	$50,000,001 $100 million	More than $100 million
☐	☐	☐	☐	☐	☐	☐	☐

Estimated Debts							
$0 to $50,000	$50,001 to $100,000	$100,001 to $500,000	$500,001 to $1 million	$1,000,001 to $10 million	$10,000,001 to $50 million	$50,000,001 $100 million	More than $100 million
☐	☐	☐	☐	☐	☐	☐	☐

Voluntary Petition
(This page must be completed and filed in every case.)

Name of Debtor(s):

Form 1, Page 2

Prior Bankruptcy Case Filed Within Last 6 Years (If more than one, attach additional sheet)

Location
Where Filed:

Case Number:

Date Filed:

Pending Bankruptcy Case Filed by any Spouse, Partner or Affiliate of this Debtor (If more than one, attach additional sheet)

Name of Debtor:

Case Number:

Date Filed:

District:

Relationship:

Judge:

Signatures

Signature(s) of Debtor(s) (Individual/Joint)

I declare under penalty of perjury that the information provided in this petition is true and correct.

[If petitioner is an individual whose debts are primarily consumer debts and has chosen to file under chapter 7] I am aware that I may proceed under chapter 7, 11, 12 or 13 of title 11, United States Code, understand the relief available under each such chapter, and choose to proceed under chapter 7.

I request relief in accordance with the chapter of title 11, United States Code, specified in this petition.

X _____
Signature of Debtor

X _____
Signature of Joint Debtor

_____
Telephone Number (If not represented by attorney)

_____
Date

Signature of Debtor (Corporation/Partnership)

I declare under penalty of perjury that the information provided in this petition is true and correct and that I have been authorized to file this petition on behalf of the debtor.

The debtor requests relief in accordance with the chapter of title 11, United States Code, specified in this petition.

X _____
Signature of Authorized Individual

_____
Printed Name of Authorized Individual

_____
Title of Authorized Individual

_____
Date

Signature of Attorney

X _____
Signature of Attorney for Debtor(s)

_____
Printed Name of Attorney for Debtor(s)

_____
Firm Name

_____
Address

_____

_____
Telephone Number

_____
Date

Signature of Non-Attorney Petition Preparer

I certify that I am a bankruptcy petition preparer as defined in 11 U.S.C. § 110, that I prepared this document for compensation, and that I have provided the debtor with a copy of this document.

_____
Printed Name of Bankruptcy Petition Preparer

_____
Social Security Number

_____
Address

_____

Names and Social Security numbers of all other individuals who prepared or assisted in preparing this document:

Exhibit A

(To be completed if debtor is required to file periodic reports (e.g., forms 10K and 10Q) with the Securities and Exchange Commission pursuant to Section 13 or 15(d) of the Securities Exchange Act of 1934 and is requesting relief under chapter 11.)

☐ Exhibit A is attached and made a part of this petition.

If more than one person prepared this document, attach additional sheets conforming to the appropriate official form for each person.

Exhibit B

(To be completed if debtor is an individual whose debts are primarily consumer debts.)

I, the attorney for the petitioner named in the foregoing petition, declare that I have informed the petitioner that [he or she] may proceed under chapter 7, 11, 12, or 13 of title 11, United States Code, and have explained the relief available under each such chapter.

X _____
Signature of Attorney for Debtor(s)   Date

X _____
Signature of Bankruptcy Petition Preparer

_____
Date

A bankruptcy petition preparer's failure to comply with the provisions of title 11 and the Federal Rules of Bankruptcy Procedure may result in fines or imprisonment or both. 11 U.S.C. § 110; 18 U.S.C. § 156.

In re _____, Case No. _____
                    Debtor   (If known)

SCHEDULE A—REAL PROPERTY

Except as directed below, list all real property in which the debtor has any legal, equitable, or future interest, including all property owned as a co-tenant, community property, or in which the debtor has a life estate. Include any property in which the debtor holds rights and powers exercisable for the debtor's own benefit. If the debtor is married, state whether husband, wife, or both own the property by placing an "H," "W," "J," or "C" in the column labeled "Husband, Wife, Joint, or Community." If the debtor holds no interest in real property, write "None" under "Description and Location of Property."

Do not include interests in executory contracts and unexpired leases on this schedule. List them in Schedule G—Executory Contracts and Unexpired Leases.

If an entity claims to have a lien or hold a secured interest in any property, state the amount of the secured claim. See Schedule D. If no entity claims to hold a secured interest in the property, write "None" in the column labeled "Amount of Secured Claim."

If the debtor is an individual or if a joint petition is filed, state the amount of any exception claimed in the property only in Schedule C—Property Claimed as Exempt.

DESCRIPTION AND LOCATION OF PROPERTY	NATURE OF DEBTOR'S INTEREST IN PROPERTY	HUSBAND, WIFE, JOINT, OR COMMUNITY	CURRENT MARKET VALUE OF DEBTOR'S INTEREST IN PROPERTY WITHOUT DEDUCTING ANY SECURED CLAIM OR EXEMPTION	AMOUNT OF SECURED CLAIM

Total ➡ $ _____

(Report also on Summary of Schedules.)

In re _____,   Case No._____

SCHEDULE B—PERSONAL PROPERTY

Except as directed below, list all personal property of the debtor of whatever kind. If the debtor has no property in one or more of the categories, place an "X" in the appropriate position in the column labeled "None." If additional space is needed in any category, attach a separate sheet properly identified with the case name, case number, and the number of the category. If the debtor is married, state whether husband, wife, or both own the property by placing an "H," "W," "J," or "C" in the column labeled "Husband, Wife, Joint, or Community." If the debtor is an individual or a joint petition is filed, state the amount of any exemptions claimed only in Schedule C—Property Claimed as Exempt.

Do not include interests in executory contracts and unexpired leases on this schedule. List them in Schedule G—Executory Contracts and Unexpired Leases.

If the property is being held for the debtor by someone else, state that person's name and address under "Description and Location of Property."

TYPE OF PROPERTY	NONE	DESCRIPTION AND LOCATION OF PROPERTY	HUSBAND, WIFE, JOINT, OR COMMUNITY	CURRENT MARKET VALUE OF DEBTOR'S INTEREST IN PROPERTY, WITHOUT DEDUCTING ANY SECURED CLAIM OR EXEMPTION
1. Cash on hand.				
2. Checking, savings or other financial accounts, certificates of deposit, or shares in banks, savings and loan, thrift, building and loan, and homestead associations, or credit unions, brokerage houses, or cooperatives.				
3. Security deposits with public utilities, telephone companies, landlords, and others.				
4. Household goods and furnishings, including audio, video, and computer equipment.				

In re _____,   Case No._____
          Debtor   (If known)

SCHEDULE B—PERSONAL PROPERTY
(Continuation Sheet)

TYPE OF PROPERTY	NONE	DESCRIPTION AND LOCATION OF PROPERTY	HUSBAND, WIFE, JOINT, OR COMMUNITY	CURRENT MARKET VALUE OF DEBTOR'S INTEREST IN PROPERTY, WITHOUT DEDUCTING ANY SECURED CLAIM OR EXEMPTION
5. Books, pictures and other art objects, antiques, stamp, coin, record, tape, compact disc, and other collections or collectibles.				
6. Wearing apparel.				
7. Furs and jewelry.				
8. Firearms and sports, photographic, and other hobby equipment.				
9. Interests in insurance policies. Name insurance company of each policy and itemize surrender or refund value of each.				
10. Annuities. Itemize and name each issuer.				
11. Interests in IRA, ERISA, Keogh, or other pension or profit sharing plans. Itemize.				
12. Stock and interests in incorporated and unincorporated businesses. Itemize.				
13. Interests in partnerships or joint ventures. Itemize.				

In re _____ ,   Case No. _____
                    Debtor   (If known)

SCHEDULE B—PERSONAL PROPERTY
(Continuation Sheet)

TYPE OF PROPERTY	NONE	DESCRIPTION AND LOCATION OF PROPERTY	HUSBAND, WIFE, JOINT, OR COMMUNITY	CURRENT MARKET VALUE OF DEBTOR'S INTEREST IN PROPERTY, WITHOUT DEDUCTING ANY SECURED CLAIM OR EXEMPTION
14. Government and corporate bonds and other negotiable and non-negotiable instruments.				
15. Accounts receivable.				
16. Alimony, maintenance, support, and property settlements to which the debtor is or may be entitled. Give particulars.				
17. Other liquidated debts owing debtor including tax refunds. Give particulars.				
18. Equitable or future interest, life estates, and rights or powers exercisable for the benefit of the debtor other than those listed in Schedule of Real Property.				
19. Contingent and noncontingent interests in estate of a decedent, death benefit plan, life insurance policy, or trust.				
20. Other contingent and unliquidated claims of every nature, including tax refunds, counterclaims of the debtor, and rights to setoff claims. Give estimated value of each.				
21. Patents, copyrights, and other intellectual property. Give particulars.				
22. Licenses, franchises, and other general intangibles. Give particulars.				

In re _____,   Case No. _____
                          Debtor   (If known)

SCHEDULE B—PERSONAL PROPERTY
(Continuation Sheet)

TYPE OF PROPERTY	NONE	DESCRIPTION AND LOCATION OF PROPERTY	HUSBAND, WIFE, JOINT, OR COMMUNITY	CURRENT MARKET VALUE OF DEBTOR'S INTEREST IN PROPERTY, WITHOUT DEDUCTING ANY SECURED CLAIM OR EXEMPTION
23. Automobiles, trucks, trailers, and other vehicles and accessories.				
24. Boats, motors, and accessories.				
25. Aircraft and accessories.				
26. Office equipment, furnishings, and supplies.				
27. Machinery, fixtures, equipment, and supplies used in business.				
28. Inventory.				
29. Animals.				
30. Crops—growing or harvested. Give particulars.				
31. Farming equipment and implements.				
32. Farm supplies, chemicals, and feed.				
33. Other personal property of any kind not already listed, such as season tickets. Itemize.				
			Total ➡	$

_____ continuation sheets attached

(Include amounts from any continuation sheets attached. Report total also on Summary of Schedules.)

In re _____, Case No._____
                        Debtor   (If known)

SCHEDULE C—PROPERTY CLAIMED AS EXEMPT

Debtor elects the exemptions to which debtor is entitled under:

(Check one box)

☐ 11 U.S.C. § 522(b)(1):   Exemptions provided in 11 U.S.C. § 522(d). **Note: These exemptions are available only in certain states.**

☐ 11 U.S.C. § 522(b)(2):   Exemptions available under applicable nonbankruptcy federal laws, state or local law where the debtor's domicile has been located for the 180 days immediately preceding the filing of the petition, or for a longer portion of the 180-day period than in any other place, and the debtor's interest as a tenant by the entirety or joint tenant to the extent the interest is exempt from process under applicable nonbankruptcy law.

DESCRIPTION OF PROPERTY	SPECIFY LAW PROVIDING EACH EXEMPTION	VALUE OF CLAIMED EXEMPTION	CURRENT MARKET VALUE OF PROPERTY WITHOUT DEDUCTING EXEMPTIONS

In re _____,   Case No._____
                    Debtor   (If known)

SCHEDULE D—CREDITORS HOLDING SECURED CLAIMS

State the name, mailing address, including zip code, and account number, if any, of all entities holding claims secured by property of the debtor as of the date of filing of the petition. List creditors holding all types of secured interest such as judgment liens, garnishments, statutory liens, mortgages, deeds of trust, and other security interests. List creditors in alphabetical order to the extent practicable. If all secured creditors will not fit on this page, use the continuation sheet provided.

If any entity other than a spouse in a joint case may be jointly liable on a claim, place an "X" in the column labeled "Codebtor," include the entity on the appropriate schedule of creditors, and complete Schedule H—Codebtors. If a joint petition is filed, state whether husband, wife, both of them, or the marital community may be liable on each claim by placing an "H," "W," "J," or "C" in the column labeled "Husband, Wife, Joint, or Community."

If the claim is contingent, place an "X" in the column labeled "Contingent." If the claim is unliquidated, place an "X" in the column labeled "Unliquidated." If the claim is disputed, place an "X" in the column labeled "Disputed." (You may need to place an "X" in more than one of these three columns.)

Report the total of all claims listed on this schedule in the box labeled "Total" on the last sheet of the completed schedule. Report this total also on the Summary of Schedules.

☐   Check this box if debtor has no creditors holding secured claims to report on this Schedule D.

CREDITOR'S NAME AND MAILING ADDRESS INCLUDING ZIP CODE	CODEBTOR	HUSBAND, WIFE, JOINT, OR COMMUNITY	DATE CLAIM WAS INCURRED, NATURE OF LIEN, AND DESCRIPTION AND MARKET VALUE OF PROPERTY SUBJECT TO LIEN	CONTINGENT	UNLIQUIDATED	DISPUTED	AMOUNT OF CLAIM WITHOUT DEDUCTING VALUE OF COLLATERAL	UNSECURED PORTION, IF ANY
ACCOUNT NO.								
			VALUE $					
ACCOUNT NO.								
			VALUE $					
ACCOUNT NO.								
			VALUE $					
ACCOUNT NO.								
			VALUE $					

_____ continuation sheets attached

Subtotal ➡ $_____
(Total of this page)

Total ➡ $_____
(Use only on last page)

(Report total also on Summary of Schedules)

In re _____ ,   Case No. _____
                        Debtor   (If known)

SCHEDULE D—CREDITORS HOLDING SECURED CLAIMS
(Continuation Sheet)

CREDITOR'S NAME AND MAILING ADDRESS INCLUDING ZIP CODE	CODEBTOR	HUSBAND, WIFE, JOINT, OR COMUNITY	DATE CLAIM WAS INCURRED, NATURE OF LIEN, AND DESCRIPTION AND MARKET VALUE OF PROPERTY SUBJECT TO LIEN	CONTINGENT	UNLIQUIDATED	DISPUTED	AMOUNT OF CLAIM WITHOUT DEDUCTING VALUE OF COLLATERAL	UNSECURED PORTION, IF ANY
ACCOUNT NO.								
			VALUE $					
ACCOUNT NO.								
			VALUE $					
ACCOUNT NO.								
			VALUE $					
ACCOUNT NO.								
			VALUE $					
ACCOUNT NO.								
			VALUE $					
ACCOUNT NO.								
			VALUE $					

Subtotal ➡ $ _____
(Total of this page)

Total ➡ $ _____
(Use only on last page)

(Report total also on Summary of Schedules)

Sheet no. _____ of _____ continuation sheets attached to
Schedule of Creditors Holding Secured Claims

In re _____,   Case No._____
                     Debtor   (If known)

SCHEDULE E—CREDITORS HOLDING UNSECURED PRIORITY CLAIMS

A complete list of claims entitled to priority, listed separately by type of priority, is to be set forth on the sheets provided. Only holders of unsecured claims entitled to priority should be listed in this schedule. In the boxes provided on the attached sheets, state the name and mailing address, including zip code, and account number, if any, of all entities holding priority claims against the debtor or the property of the debtor, as of the date of the filing of the petition.

If any entity other than a spouse in a joint case may be jointly liable on a claim, place an "X" in the column labeled "Codebtor," include the entity on the appropriate schedule of creditors, and complete Schedule H—Codebtors. If a joint petition is filed, state whether husband, wife, both of them, or the marital community may be liable on each claim by placing an "H," "W," "J," or "C" in the column labeled "Husband, Wife, Joint, or Community."

If the claim is contingent, place an "X" in the column labeled "Contingent." If the claim is unliquidated, place an "X" in the column labeled "Unliquidated." If the claim is disputed, place an "X" in the column labeled "Disputed." (You may need to place an "X" in more than one of these three columns.)

Report the total of all claims listed on each sheet in the box labeled "Subtotal" on each sheet. Report the total of all claims listed on this Schedule E in the box labeled "Total" on the last sheet of the completed schedule. Repeat this total also on the Summary of Schedules.

☐ **Check this box if debtor has no creditors holding unsecured priority claims to report on this Schedule E.**

TYPES OF PRIORITY CLAIMS (Check the appropriate box(es) below if claims in that category are listed on the attached sheets)

☐ **Extensions of credit in an involuntary case**

Claims arising in the ordinary course of the debtor's business or financial affairs after the commencement of the case but before the earlier of the appointment of a trustee or the order for relief. 11 U.S.C. § 507(a)(2).

☐ **Wages, salaries, and commissions**

Wages, salaries, and commissions, including vacation, severance, and sick leave pay owing to employees and commissions owing to qualifying independent sales representatives up to $4,000* per person, earned within 90 days immediately preceding the filing of the original petition, or the cessation of business, whichever occurred first, to the extent provided in 11 U.S.C. § 507(a)(3).

☐ **Contributions to employee benefit plans**

Money owed to employee benefit plans for services rendered within 180 days immediately preceding the filing of the original petition, or the cessation of business, whichever occurred first, to the extent provided in 11 U.S.C. § 507(a)(4).

☐ **Certain farmers and fishermen**

Claims of certain farmers and fishermen, up to a maximum of $4,000* per farmer or fisherman, against the debtor, as provided in 11 U.S.C. § 507(a)(5).

☐ **Deposits by individuals**

Claims of individuals up to a maximum of $1,800* for deposits for the purchase, lease, or rental of property or services for personal, family, or household use, that were not delivered or provided. 11 U.S.C. § 507(a)(6).

☐ **Alimony, Maintenance, or Support**

Claims of a spouse, former spouse, or child of the debtor for alimony, maintenance, or support, to the extent provided in 11 U.S.C. § 507(a)(7).

☐ **Taxes and Certain Other Debts Owed to Governmental Units**

Taxes, customs, duties, and penalties owing to federal, state, and local governmental units as set forth in 11 U.S.C. § 507(a)(8).

☐ **Commitments to Maintain the Capital of an Insured Depository Institution**

Claims based on commitments to the FDIC, RTC, Director of the Office of Thrift Supervision, Comptroller of the Currency, or Board of Governors of the Federal Reserve system, or their predecessors or successors, to maintain the capital of an insured depository institution. 11 U.S.C. § 507 (a)(9).

* Amounts are subject to adjustment on April 1, 1998, and every three years thereafter with respect to cases commenced on or after the date of adjustment.

_____ continuation sheets attached

In re _____,   Case No._____
                    Debtor   (If known)

SCHEDULE E—CREDITORS HOLDING UNSECURED PRIORITY CLAIMS
(Continuation Sheet)

TYPE OF PRIORITY _____

CREDITOR'S NAME AND MAILING ADDRESS INCLUDING ZIP CODE	CODEBTOR	HUSBAND, WIFE, JOINT, OR COMMUNITY	DATE CLAIM WAS INCURRED AND CONSIDERATION FOR CLAIM	CONTINGENT	UNLIQUIDATED	DISPUTED	TOTAL AMOUNT OF CLAIM	AMOUNT ENTITLED TO PRIORITY
ACCOUNT NO.								
ACCOUNT NO.								
ACCOUNT NO.								
ACCOUNT NO.								
ACCOUNT NO.								

Subtotal ➡ $
(Total of this page)

Sheet no. _____ of _____ sheets attached to
Schedule of Creditors Holding Unsecured Priority Claims

Total ➡ $
(Use only on last page)

(Report total also on Summary of Schedules)

In re _____,   Case No._____
                 Debtor   (If known)

SCHEDULE F—CREDITORS HOLDING UNSECURED NONPRIORITY CLAIMS

State the name, mailing address, including zip code, and account number, if any, of all entities holding unsecured claims without priority against the debtor or the property of the debtor as of the date of filing of the petition. Do not include claims listed in Schedules D and E. If all creditors will not fit on this page, use the continuation sheet provided.

If any entity other than a spouse in a joint case may be jointly liable on a claim, place an "X" in the column labeled "Codebtor," include the entity on the appropriate schedule of creditors, and complete Schedule H—Codebtors. If a joint petition is filed, state whether husband, wife, both of them, or the marital community may be liable on each claim by placing an "H," "W," "J," or "C" in the column labeled "Husband, Wife, Joint, or Community."

If the claim is contingent, place an "X" in the column labeled "Contingent." If the claim is unliquidated, place an "X" in the column labeled "Unliquidated." If the claim is disputed, place an "X" in the column labeled "Disputed." (You may need to place an "X" in more than one of these three columns.)

Report the total of all claims listed on this schedule in the box labeled "Total" on the last sheet of the completed schedule. Report this total also on the Summary of Schedules.

☐ Check this box if debtor has no creditors holding unsecured nonpriority claims to report on this Schedule F.

CREDITOR'S NAME AND MAILING ADDRESS INCLUDING ZIP CODE	CODEBTOR	HUSBAND, WIFE, JOINT, OR COMMUNITY	DATE CLAIM WAS INCURRED AND CONSIDERATION FOR CLAIM. IF CLAIM IS SUBJECT TO SETOFF, SO STATE	CONTINGENT	UNLIQUIDATED	DISPUTED	AMOUNT OF CLAIM
ACCOUNT NO.							
ACCOUNT NO.							
ACCOUNT NO.							
ACCOUNT NO.							

_____ continuation sheets attached

Subtotal ➡ $ _____
(Total of this page)

Total ➡ $ _____
(Use only on last page)

(Report total also on Summary of Schedules)

In re _____,   Case No._____
         Debtor   (If known)

SCHEDULE F—CREDITORS HOLDING UNSECURED NONPRIORITY CLAIMS
(Continuation Sheet)

CREDITOR'S NAME AND MAILING ADDRESS INCLUDING ZIP CODE	CODEBTOR	HUSBAND, WIFE, JOINT, OR COMMUNITY	DATE CLAIM WAS INCURRED AND CONSIDERATION FOR CLAIM. IF CLAIM IS SUBJECT TO SETOFF, SO STATE	CONTINGENT	UNLIQUIDATED	DISPUTED	AMOUNT OF CLAIM
ACCOUNT NO.							
ACCOUNT NO.							
ACCOUNT NO.							
ACCOUNT NO.							
ACCOUNT NO.							

Subtotal ➡ $
(Total of this page)

Total ➡ $
(Use only on last page)

Sheet no. _____ of _____ continuation sheets attached to
Schedule of Creditors Holding Unsecured Nonpriorty Claims

(Report total also on Summary of Schedules)

In re _____,   Case No._____
                    Debtor   (If known)

SCHEDULE G—EXECUTORY CONTRACTS AND UNEXPIRED LEASES

Describe all executory contracts of any nature and all unexpired leases of real personal property. Include any timeshare interests.

State nature of debtor's interest in contract, i.e., "Purchaser," "Agent," etc. State whether debtor is the lessor or lessee of a lease.

Provide the names and complete mailing addresses of all other parties to each lease or contract described.

NOTE: A party listed on this schedule will not receive notice of the filing of this case unless the party is also scheduled in the appropriate schedule of creditors.

☐ Check this box if debtor has no executory contracts or unexpired leases.

NAME AND MAILING ADDRESS, INCLUDING ZIP CODE, OF OTHER PARTIES TO LEASE OR CONTRACT	DESCRIPTION OF CONTRACT OR LEASE AND NATURE OF DEBTOR'S INTEREST. STATE WHETHER LEASE IS FOR NONRESIDENTIAL REAL PROPERTY. STATE CONTRACT NUMBER OF ANY GOVERNMENT CONTRACT

In re _____ ,   Case No. _____
                        Debtor   (If known)

SCHEDULE H—CODEBTORS

Provide the information requested concerning any person or entity, other than a spouse in a joint case, that is also liable on any debts listed by debtor in the schedules of creditors. Include all guarantors and co-signers. In community property states, a married debtor not filing a joint case should report the name and address of the nondebtor spouse on this schedule. Include all names used by the nondebtor spouse during the six years immediately preceding the commencement of this case.

☐ Check this box if debtor has no codebtors.

NAME AND ADDRESS OF CODEBTOR	NAME AND ADDRESS OF CREDITOR

In re _____,   Case No. _____
              Debtor   (If known)

SCHEDULE I—CURRENT INCOME OF INDIVIDUAL DEBTOR(S)

The column labled "Spouse" must be completed in all cases filed by joint debtors and by a married debtor in a Chapter 12 or 13 case whether or not a joint petition is filed, unless the spouses are separated and a joint petition is not filed.

DEBTOR'S MARITAL STATUS:	DEPENDENTS OF DEBTOR AND SPOUSE		
	NAMES	AGE	RELATIONSHIP

Employment:	DEBTOR	SPOUSE
Occupation		
Name of Employer		
How long employed		
Address of Employer		

INCOME: (Estimate of average monthly income)	DEBTOR	SPOUSE
Current monthly gross wages, salary, and commissions (pro rate if not paid monthly)	$ _____	$ _____
Estimated monthly overtime	$ _____	$ _____
SUBTOTAL	$ _____	$ _____
LESS PAYROLL DEDUCTIONS		
a. Payroll taxes and Social Security	$ _____	$ _____
b. Insurance	$ _____	$ _____
c. Union dues	$ _____	$ _____
d. Other (Specify: _____)	$ _____	$ _____
SUBTOTAL OF PAYROLL DEDUCTIONS	$ _____	$ _____
TOTAL NET MONTHLY TAKE HOME PAY	$ _____	$ _____
Regular income from operation of business or profession or farm (attach detailed statement)	$ _____	$ _____
Income from real property	$ _____	$ _____
Interest and dividends	$ _____	$ _____
Alimony, maintenance or support payments payable to the debtor for the debtor's use or that of dependents listed above	$ _____	$ _____
Social Security or other government assistance (Specify: _____)	$ _____	$ _____
Pension or retirement income	$ _____	$ _____
Other monthly income	$ _____	$ _____
(Specify: _____)	$ _____	$ _____
_____	$ _____	$ _____
TOTAL MONTHLY INCOME	$ _____	$ _____

TOTAL COMBINED MONTHLY INCOME $ _____   (Report also on Summary of Schedules)

Describe any increase or decrease of more than 10% in any of the above categories anticipated to occur within the year following the filing of this document:

In re _____,   Case No._____
                          Debtor   (If known)

SCHEDULE J—CURRENT EXPENDITURES OF INDIVIDUAL DEBTOR(S)

Complete this schedule by estimating the average monthly expenses of the debtor and the debtor's family. Pro rate any payments made bi-weekly, quarterly, semi-annually, or annually to show monthly rate.

☐ Check this box if a joint petition is filed and debtor's spouse maintains a separate household. Complete a separate schedule of expenditures labeled "Spouse."

Rent or home mortgage payment (include lot rented for mobile home) $ _____

Are real estate taxes included?   Yes _____   No _____

Is property insurance included?   Yes _____   No _____

Utilities: Electricity and heating fuel $ _____

             Water and sewer $ _____

             Telephone $ _____

             Other _____ $ _____

Home maintenance (repairs and upkeep) $ _____

Food $ _____

Clothing $ _____

Laundry and dry cleaning $ _____

Medical and dental expenses $ _____

Transportation (not including car payments) $ _____

Recreation, clubs and entertainment, newspapers, magazines, etc. $ _____

Charitable contributions $ _____

Insurance (not deducted from wages or included in home mortgage payments)

             Homeowner's or renter's $ _____

             Life $ _____

             Health $ _____

             Auto $ _____

             Other _____ $ _____

Taxes (not deducted from wages or included in home mortgage payments)

(Specify: _____) $ _____

Installment payments: (In Chapter 12 and 13 cases, do not list payments to be included in the plan)

             Auto $ _____

             Other _____ $ _____

             Other _____ $ _____

Alimony, maintenance, and support paid to others $ _____

Payments for support of additional dependents not living at your home $ _____

Regular expenses from operation of business, profession, or farm (attach detailed statement) $ _____

Other _____ $ _____

TOTAL MONTHLY EXPENSES (Report also on Summary of Schedules) $ _____

[FOR CHAPTER 12 AND CHAPTER 13 DEBTORS ONLY]
Provide the information requested below, including whether plan payments are to be made bi-weekly, monthly, annually, or at some other regular interval.

A. Total projected monthly income $ _____

B. Total projected monthly expenses $ _____

C. Excess income (A minus B) $ _____

D. Total amount to be paid into plan each _____ $ _____
                                 (interval)

United States Bankruptcy Court

_____ District of _____

In re _____,   Case No._____
  Debtor   (If known)

SUMMARY OF SCHEDULES

Indicate as to each schedule whether that schedule is attached and state the number of pages in each. Report the totals from Schedules A, B, D, E, F, I and J in the boxes provided. Add the amounts from Schedules A and B to determine the total amount of the debtor's assets. Add the amounts from Schedules D, E and F to determine the total amount of the debtor's liabilities.

NAME OF SCHEDULE		ATTACHED (YES/NO)	NUMBER OF SHEETS	AMOUNTS SCHEDULED		
				ASSETS	LIABILITIES	OTHER
A	Real Property			$		
B	Personal Property			$		
C	Property Claimed as Exempt					
D	Creditors Holding Secured Claims				$	
E	Creditors Holding Unsecured Priority Claims				$	
F	Creditors Holding Unsecured Nonpriority Claims				$	
G	Executory Contracts and Unexpired Leases					
H	Codebtors					
I	Current Income of Individual Debtor(s)					$
J	Current Expenditures of Individual Debtor(s)					$

Total Number of Sheets of All Schedules ➡

Total Assets ➡ $

Total Liabilities ➡ $

In re _____,   Case No._____
           Debtor   (If known)

DECLARATION CONCERNING DEBTOR'S SCHEDULES

DECLARATION UNDER PENALTY OF PERJURY BY INDIVIDUAL DEBTOR

I declare under penalty of perjury that I have read the foregoing summary and schedules consisting of _____
sheets, and that they are true and correct to the best of my knowledge, information, and belief.   (Total shown on summary page plus 1)

Date_____   Signature _____
                                                            Debtor

Date_____   Signature _____
                                                     (Joint Debtor, if any)

[If joint case, both spouses must sign.]

CERTIFICATION AND SIGNATURE OF NON-ATTORNEY BANKRUPTCY PETITION PREPARER (See 11 U.S.C. § 110)

I certify that I am a bankruptcy petition preparer as defined in 11 U.S.C. § 110, that I prepared this document for compensation, and that I have provided the debtor with a copy of this document.

_____   _____
Printed or Typed Name of Bankruptcy Petition Preparer   Social Security No.

_____

_____
Address

Names and Social Security numbers of all other individuals who prepared or assisted in preparing this document:

If more than one person prepared this document, attach additional signed sheets conforming to the appropriate Official Form for each person.

X _____   _____
Signature of Bankruptcy Petition Preparer   Date

A bankruptcy petition preparer's failure to comply with the provisions of Title 11 and the Federal Rules of Bankruptcy Procedure may result in fine or imprisonment or both.
11 U.S.C. § 110; 18 U.S.C. § 156.

DECLARATION UNDER PENALTY OF PERJURY ON BEHALF OF CORPORATION OR PARTNERSHIP

I, the _____ [the president or other officer or an authorized agent of the corporation or a member or an authorized agent of the partnership] of the _____ [corporation or partnership] named as debtor in this case, declare under penalty of perjury that I have read the foregoing summary and schedules, consisting of _____ sheets, and that they are true and correct to the best of my knowledge, information, and belief.
(Total shown on summary page plus 1)

Date_____   Signature _____

                                              _____
                                              [Print or type name of individual signing on behalf of debtor]

[An individual signing on behalf of a partnership or corporation must indicate position or relationship to debtor.]

Penalty for making a false statement or concealing property: Fine of up to $500,000, imprisonment for up to 5 years, or both. 18 U.S.C. §§ 152 and 3571.

FORM 7. STATEMENT OF FINANCIAL AFFAIRS

UNITED STATES BANKRUPTCY COURT

_____ DISTRICT OF _____

In re: _____ ,   Case No. _____
(Name)
Debtor   (If known)

STATEMENT OF FINANCIAL AFFAIRS

This statement is to be completed by every debtor. Spouses filing a joint petition may file a single statement on which the information for both spouses is combined. If the case is filed under Chapter 12 or Chapter 13, a married debtor must furnish information for both spouses whether or not a joint petition is filed, unless the spouses are separated and a joint petition is not filed. An individual debtor engaged in business as a sole proprietor, partner, family farmer, or self-employed professional, should provide the information requested on this statement concerning all such activities as well as the individual's personal affairs.

Questions 1–15 are to be completed by all debtors. Debtors that are or have been in business, as defined below, also must complete Questions 16–21. **Each question must be answered. If the answer to any question is "None," or the question is not applicable, mark the box labeled "None."** If additional space is needed for the answer to any question, use and attach a separate sheet properly identified with the case name, case number (if known), and the number of the question.

DEFINITIONS

"*In business.*" A debtor is "in business" for the purpose of this form if the debtor is a corporation or partnership. An individual debtor is "in business" for the purpose of this form if the debtor is or has been, within the two years immediately preceding the filing of this bankruptcy case, any of the following: an officer, director, managing executive, or person in control of a corporation; a partner, other than a limited partner, of a partnership; a sole proprietor or self-employed.

"*Insider.*" The term "insider" includes but is not limited to: relatives of the debtor; general partners of the debtor and their relatives; corporations of which the debtor is an officer, director, or person in control; officers, directors, and any person in control of a corporate debtor and their relatives; affiliates of the debtor and insiders of such affiliates; any managing agent of the debtor. 11 U.S.C. § 101(30).

1. **Income from employment or operation of business**

None   State the gross amount of income the debtor has received from employment, trade, or profession, or from operation of the debtor's
☐   business from the beginning of this calendar year to the date this case was commenced. State also the gross amounts received during the **two years** immediately preceding this calendar year. (A debtor that maintains, or has maintained, financial records on the basis of a fiscal rather than a calendar year may report fiscal year income. Identify the beginning and ending dates of the debtor's fiscal year.) If a joint petition is filed, state income for each spouse separately. (Married debtors filing under Chapter 12 or Chapter 13 must state income of both spouses whether or not a joint petition is filed, unless the spouses are separated and a joint petition is not filed.)

AMOUNT   SOURCE (If more than one)

2. **Income other than from employment or operation of business**

None

☐

State the amount of income received by the debtor other than from employment, trade, profession, or operation of the debtor's business during the **two years** immediately preceding the commencement of this case. Give particulars. If a joint petition is filed, state income for each spouse separately. (Married debtors filing under Chapter 12 or Chapter 13 must state income for each spouse whether or not a joint petition is filed, unless the spouses are separated and a joint petition is not filed.)

AMOUNT	SOURCE

3. **Payments to creditors**

None

☐

a. List all payments on loans, installment purchases of goods or services, and other debts, aggregating more than $600 to any creditor, made within **90 days** immediately preceding the commencement of this case. (Married debtors filing under Chapter 12 or Chapter 13 must include payments by either or both spouses whether or not a joint petition is filed, unless the spouses are separated and a joint petition is not filed.)

NAME AND ADDRESS OF CREDITOR	DATES OF PAYMENTS	AMOUNT PAID	AMOUNT STILL OWING

None

☐

b. List all payments made within **one year** immediately preceding the commencement of this case, to or for the benefit of, creditors who are or were insiders. (Married debtors filing under Chapter 12 or Chapter 13 must include payments by either or both spouses whether or not a joint petition is filed, unless the spouses are separated and a joint petition is not filed.)

NAME AND ADDRESS OF CREDITOR; RELATIONSHIP TO DEBTOR	DATES OF PAYMENTS	AMOUNT PAID	AMOUNT STILL OWING

4. **Suits, executions, garnishments and attachments**

None

☐

a. List all suits to which the debtor is or was a party within **one year** immediately preceding the filing of this bankruptcy case. (Married debtors filing under Chapter 12 or Chapter 13 must include information concerning either or both spouses whether or not a joint petition is filed, unless the spouses are separated and a joint petition is not filed.)

CAPTION OF SUIT AND CASE NUMBER	NATURE OF PROCEEDING	COURT AND LOCATION	STATUS OR DISPOSITION

None   b.   Describe all property that has been attached, garnished or seized under any legal or equitable process within **one year** immediately preceding the commencement of this case. (Married debtors filing under Chapter 12 or Chapter 13 must include information concerning property of either or both spouses whether or not a joint petition is filed, unless the spouses are separated and a joint petition is not filed.)

NAME AND ADDRESS OF PERSON FOR WHOSE BENEFIT PROPERTY WAS SEIZED	DATE OF SEIZURE	DESCRIPTION AND VALUE OF PROPERTY

5. Repossessions, foreclosures and returns

None   List all property that has been repossessed by a creditor, sold at a foreclosure sale, transferred through a deed in lieu of foreclosure or returned to the seller within **one year** immediately preceding the commencement of this case. (Married debtors filing under Chapter 12 or Chapter 13 must include information concerning property of either or both spouses whether or not a joint petition is filed, unless the spouses are separated and a joint petition is not filed.)

NAME AND ADDRESS OF CREDITOR OR SELLER	DATE OF REPOSSESSION, FORECLOSURE SALE, TRANSFER OR RETURN	DESCRIPTION AND VALUE OF PROPERTY

6. Assignments and receiverships

None   a.   Describe any assignment of property for the benefit of creditors made within **120 days** immediately preceding the commencement of this case. (Married debtors filing under Chapter 12 or Chapter 13 must include any assignment by either or both spouses whether or not a joint petition is filed, unless the spouses are separated and a joint petition is not filed.)

NAME AND ADDRESS OF ASSIGNEE	DATE OF ASSIGNMENT	TERMS OF ASSIGNMENT OR SETTLEMENT

None ☐   b.   List all property which has been in the hands of a custodian, receiver, or court-appointed official within **one year** immediately preceding the commencement of this case. (Married debtors filing under Chapter 12 or Chapter 13 must include information concerning property of either or both spouses whether or not a joint petition is filed, unless the spouses are separated and a joint petition is not filed.)

NAME AND ADDRESS OF CUSTODIAN	NAME AND LOCATION OF COURT; CASE TITLE & NUMBER	DATE OF ORDER	DESCRIPTION AND VALUE OF PROPERTY

7. Gifts

None ☐   List all gifts or charitable contributions made within **one year** immediately preceding the commencement of this case except ordinary and usual gifts to family members aggregating less than $200 in value per individual family member and charitable contributions aggregating less than $100 per recipient. (Married debtors filing under Chapter 12 or Chapter 13 must include gifts or contributions by either or both spouses whether or not a joint petition is filed, unless the spouses are separated and a joint petition is not filed.)

NAME AND ADDRESS OF PERSON OR ORGANIZATION	RELATIONSHIP TO DEBTOR, IF ANY	DATE OF GIFT	DESCRIPTION AND VALUE OF GIFT

8. Losses

None ☐   List all losses from fire, theft, other casualty or gambling within **one year** immediately preceding the commencement of this case **or since the commencement of this case.** (Married debtors filing under Chapter 12 or Chapter 13 must include losses by either or both spouses whether or not a joint petition is filed, unless the spouses are separated and a joint petition is not filed.)

DESCRIPTION AND VALUE OF PROPERTY	DESCRIPTION OF CIRCUMSTANCES AND, IF LOSS WAS COVERED IN WHOLE OR IN PART BY INSURANCE, GIVE PARTICULARS	DATE OF LOSS

9. Payments related to debt counseling or bankruptcy

None ☐   List all payments made or property transferred by or on behalf of the debtor to any person, including attorneys, for consultation concerning debt consolidation, relief under the bankruptcy law or preparation of a petition in bankruptcy within **one year** immediately preceding the commencement of this case.

NAME AND ADDRESS OF PAYEE	DATE OF PAYMENT; NAME OF PAYOR IF OTHER THAN DEBTOR	AMOUNT OF MONEY OR DESCRIPTION AND VALUE OF PROPERTY

10. Other transfers

None ☐   a. List all other property, other than property transferred in the ordinary course of the business or financial affairs of the debtor, transferred either absolutely or as security within **one year** immediately preceding the commencement of this case. (Married debtors filing under Chapter 12 or Chapter 13 must include transfers by either or both spouses whether or not a joint petition is filed, unless the spouses are separated and a joint petition is not filed.)

NAME AND ADDRESS OF TRANSFEREE; RELATIONSHIP TO DEBTOR	DATE	DESCRIBE PROPERTY TRANSFERRED AND VALUE RECEIVED

11. Closed financial accounts

None ☐   List all financial accounts and instruments held in the name of the debtor or for the benefit of the debtor which were closed, sold, or otherwise transferred within **one year** immediately preceding the commencement of this case. Include checking, savings, or other financial accounts, certificates of deposit, or other instruments; shares and share accounts held in banks, credit unions, pension funds, cooperatives, associations, brokerage houses and other financial institutions. (Married debtors filing under Chapter 12 or Chapter 13 must include information concerning accounts or instruments held by or for either or both spouses whether or not a joint petition is filed, unless the spouses are separated and a joint petition is not filed.)

NAME AND ADDRESS OF INSTITUTION	TYPE AND NUMBER OF ACCOUNT AND AMOUNT OF FINAL BALANCE	AMOUNT AND DATE OF SALE OR CLOSING

12. Safe deposit boxes

None ☐

List each safe deposit or other box or depository in which the debtor has or had securities, cash, or other valuables within **one year** immediately preceding the commencement of this case. (Married debtors filing under Chapter 12 or Chapter 13 must include boxes or depositories of either or both spouses whether or not a joint petition is filed, unless the spouses are separated and a joint petition is not filed.)

NAME AND ADDRESS OF BANK OR OTHER DEPOSITORY	NAMES AND ADDRESSES OF THOSE WITH ACCESS TO BOX OR DEPOSITORY	DESCRIPTION OF CONTENTS	DATE OF TRANSFER OR SURRENDER, IF ANY

13. Setoffs

None ☐

List all setoffs made by any creditor, including a bank, against a debt or deposit of the debtor within **90 days** preceding the commencement of this case. (Married debtors filing under Chapter 12 or Chapter 13 must include information concerning either or both spouses whether or not a joint petition is filed, unless the spouses are separated and a joint petition is not filed.)

NAME AND ADDRESS OF CREDITOR	DATE OF SETOFF	AMOUNT OF SETOFF

14. Property held for another person

None ☐

List all property owned by another person that the debtor holds or controls.

NAME AND ADDRESS OF OWNER	DESCRIPTION AND VALUE OF PROPERTY	LOCATION OF PROPERTY

15. Prior address of debtor

None ☐

If the debtor has moved within the **two years** immediately preceding the commencement of this case, list all premises which the debtor occupied during that period and vacated prior to the commencement of this case. If a joint petition is filed, report also any separate address of either spouse.

ADDRESS	NAME USED	DATES OF OCCUPANCY

The following questions are to be completed by every debtor that is a corporation or partnership and by any **individual debtor who is or has been, within the two years** immediately preceding the commencement of this case, any of the following: an officer, director, **managing executive**, or owner of more than 5 percent of the voting securities of a corporation; a partner, other than a **limited partner**, of a **partnership**; a sole proprietor or otherwise self-employed.

*(An individual or joint debtor should complete this portion of the statement **only** if the debtor is or has been in business, as defined above, within the two years immediately preceding the commencement of this case.)*

16. Nature, location and name of business

None a. If the debtor is an individual, list the names and addresses of all businesses in which the debtor was an officer, director, partner, or □ managing executive of a corporation, partnership, sole proprietorship, or was a self-employed professional within the **two years** immediately preceding the commencement of this case, or in which the debtor owned 5 percent or more of the voting or equity securities, within the **two years** immediately preceding the commencement of this case.

b. If the debtor is a partnership, list the names and addresses of all businesses in which the debtor was a partner or owned 5 percent or more of the voting securities, within the **two years** immediately preceding the commencement of this case.

c. If the debtor is a corporation, list the names and addresses of all businesses in which the debtor was a partner or owned 5 percent or more of the voting securities, within the **two years** immediately preceding the commencement of this case.

NAME	ADDRESS	NATURE OF BUSINESS	BEGINNING AND ENDING DATES OF OPERATION

17. Books, records and financial statements

None a. List all bookkeepers and accountants who within the **six years** immediately preceding the filing of this bankruptcy case kept or □ supervised the keeping of books of account and records of the debtor.

NAME AND ADDRESS	DATES SERVICES RENDERED

None b. List all firms or individuals who within the **two years** immediately preceding the filing of this bankruptcy case have audited the books of □ account and records, or prepared a financial statement of the debtor.

NAME AND ADDRESS	DATES SERVICES RENDERED

None c. List all firms or individuals who at the time of the commencement of this case were in possession of the books of account and records of the debtor. If any of the books of account and records are not available, explain.

NAME	ADDRESS

None d. List all financial institutions, creditors and other parties, including mercantile and trade agencies, to whom a financial statement was issued within the **two years** immediately preceding the commencement of this case by the debtor.

NAME AND ADDRESS	DATE ISSUED

18. **Inventories**

None a. List the dates of the last two inventories taken of your property, the name of the person who supervised the taking of each inventory, and the dollar amount and basis of each inventory.

DATE OF INVENTORY	INVENTORY SUPERVISOR	DOLLAR AMOUNT OF INVENTORY (Specify cost, market or other basis)

None b. List the name and address of the person having possession of the records of each of the two inventories reported in a., above.

DATE OF INVENTORY	NAME AND ADDRESSES OF CUSTODIAN OF INVENTORY RECORDS

19. **Current partners, officers, directors and shareholders**

None a. If the debtor is a partnership, list the nature and percentage of partnership interest of each member of the partnership.

NAME AND ADDRESS	NATURE OF INTEREST	PERCENTAGE OF INTEREST

None b. If the debtor is a corporation, list all officers and directors of the corporation, and each stockholder who directly or indirectly owns, controls, or holds 5 percent or more of the voting securities of the corporation.

□

NAME AND ADDRESS	TITLE	NATURE AND PERCENTAGE OF STOCK OWNERSHIP

20. Former partners, officers, directors and shareholders

None a. If the debtor is a partnership, list each member who withdrew from the partnership within **one year** immediately preceding the commencement of this case.

□

NAME	ADDRESS	DATE OF WITHDRAWAL

None b. If the debtor is a corporation, list all officers or directors whose relationship with the corporation terminated within **one year** immediately preceding the commencement of this case.

□

NAME AND ADDRESS	TITLE	DATE OF TERMINATION

21. Withdrawals from a partnership or distributions by a corporation

None If the debtor is a partnership or corporation, list all withdrawals or distributions credited or given to an insider, including compensation in any form, bonuses, loans, stock redemptions, options exercised and any other perquisite during **one year** immediately preceding the commencement of this case

□

NAME AND ADDRESS OF RECIPIENT; RELATIONSHIP TO DEBTOR	DATE AND PURPOSE OF WITHDRAWAL	AMOUNT OF MONEY OR DESCRIPTION AND VALUE OF PROPERTY

[If completed by an individual or individual and spouse]

I declare under penalty of perjury that I have read the answers contained in the foregoing statement of financial affairs and any attachments thereto and that they are true and correct.

Date _____   Signature of Debtor _____

Date _____   Signature of Joint Debtor (if any) _____

CERTIFICATION AND SIGNATURE OF NON-ATTORNEY BANKRUPTCY PETITION PREPARER (See 11 U.S.C. § 110)

I certify that I am a bankruptcy petition preparer as defined in 11 U.S.C. § 110, that I prepared this document for compensation, and that I have provided the debtor with a copy of this document.

_____   _____
Printed or Typed Name of Bankruptcy Petition Preparer   Social Security No.

_____

_____
Address

Names and Social Security numbers of all other individuals who prepared or assisted in preparing this document:

If more than one person prepared this document, attach additional signed sheets conforming to the appropriate Official Form for each person.

X_____   _____
Signature of Bankruptcy Petition Preparer   Date

A bankruptcy petition preparer's failure to comply with the provisions of title 11 and the Federal Rules of Bankruptcy Procedure may result in fine or imprisonment or both. 11 U.S.C. § 110; 18 U.S.C. § 156.

[If completed by or on behalf of a partnership or corporation]

I declare under penalty of perjury that I have read the answers contained in the foregoing statement of financial affairs and any attachments thereto and that they are true and correct to the best of my knowledge, information and belief.

Date _____   Signature _____

_____
Print Name and Title

[An individual signing on behalf of a partnership or corporation must indicate position or relationship to debtor.]

_____ continuation sheets attached

Penalty for presenting fraudulent claim: Fine of up to $500,000 or imprisonment for up to 5 years, or both. 18 U.S.C. §§ 152 and 3571.

Form 8. CHAPTER 7 INDIVIDUAL DEBTOR'S STATEMENT OF INTENTION

UNITED STATES BANKRUPTCY COURT

_____ DISTRICT OF _____

In re _____ ,   Case No. _____
          (Name)   (If known)
           Debtor

                                                Chapter _____

1. I have filed a schedule of assets and liabilities which includes consumer debts secured by property of the estate.

2. I intend to do the following with respect to the property of the estate which secures those consumer debts:

    a. *Property to be surrendered.*

Description of Property	Creditor's Name
1. _____	_____
2. _____	_____
3. _____	_____

    b. *Property to be retained.*   *[Check any applicable statement.]*

Description of property	Creditor's name	Property is claimed as exempt	Property will be redeemed pursuant to 11 U.S.C. § 722	Debt will be reaffirmed pursuant to 11 USC.§524(c)
1. _____	_____	_____	_____	_____
2. _____	_____	_____	_____	_____
3. _____	_____	_____	_____	_____
4. _____	_____	_____	_____	_____
5. _____	_____	_____	_____	_____

Date: _____   _____
                                      Signature of Debtor

CERTIFICATION OF NON-ATTORNEY BANKRUPTCY PETITION PREPARER (See 11 U.S.C. § 110)

    I certify that I am a bankruptcy petition preparer as defined in 11 U.S.C. § 110, that I prepared this document for compensation, and that I have provided the debtor with a copy of this document.

_____   _____
Printed or Typed Name of Bankruptcy Petition Preparer   Social Security No.

_____

_____
Address

Names and Social Security numbers of all other individuals who prepared or assisted in preparing this document:

If more than one person prepared this document, attach additional signed sheets conforming to the appropriate Official Form for each person.

X_____   _____
Signature of Bankruptcy Petition Preparer   Date

A bankruptcy petition preparer's failure to comply with the provisions of title 11 and the Federal Rules of Bankruptcy Procedure may result in fine or imprisonment or both. 11 U.S.C. § 110; 18 U.S.C. § 156.

FORM 3. APPLICATION TO PAY FILING FEE IN INSTALLMENTS

UNITED STATES BANKRUPTCY COURT

_____ DISTRICT OF _____

In re _____,   Case No._____
                Debtor   (If known)

                                                 Chapter   _____

APPLICATION TO PAY FILING FEE IN INSTALLMENTS

1.   In accordance with Fed. R. Bankr. P. 1006, I apply for permission to pay the Filing Fee amounting to $_____ in installments.

2.   I certify that I am unable to pay the Filing Fee except in installments.

3.   I further certify that I have not paid any money or transferred any property to an attorney for services in connection with this case and that I will neither make any payment nor transfer any property for services in connection with this case until the filing fee is paid in full.

4.   I propose the following terms for the payment of the Filing Fee*

$ _____   Check one ☐ With the filing of the petition, or
                                                  ☐ On or before _____

$ _____   on or before _____

$ _____   on or before _____

$ _____   on or before _____

* The number of installments proposed shall not exceed four (4), and the final installment shall be payable not later than 120 days after filing the petition. For cause shown, the court may extend the time of any installment, provided the last installment is paid not later than 180 days after filing the petition. Fed. R. Bankr. P. 1006(b)(2).

5.   I understand that if I fail to pay any installment when due my bankruptcy case may be dismissed and I may not receive a discharge of my debts.

_____   _____
Signature of Attorney   Date   Signature of Debtor   Date
                                        (In a joint case, both spouses must sign.)

_____   _____
Name of Attorney   Signature of Joint Debtor (if any)   Date

CERTIFICATION AND SIGNATURE OF NON-ATTORNEY BANKRUPTCY PETITION PREPARER (See 11 U.S.C. § 110)

I certify that I am a bankruptcy petition preparer as defined in 11 U.S.C. § 110, that I prepared this document for compensation, and that I have provided the debtor with a copy of this document. I also certify that I will not accept money or any other property from the debtor before the filing fee is paid in full.

_____   _____
Printed or Typed Name of Bankruptcy Petition Preparer   Social Security No.

_____

Address

Names and Social Security numbers of all other individuals who prepared or assisted in preparing this document:

If more than one person prepared this document, attach additional signed sheets conforming to the appropriate Official Form for each person.

_____   _____
Signature of Bankruptcy Petition Preparer   Date

A bankruptcy petition preparer's failure to comply with the provisions of title 11 and the Federal Rules of Bankruptcy Procedure may result in fine or imprisonment or both. 11 U.S.C. § 110; 18 U.S.C. § 156.

ORDER APPROVING PAYMENT OF FILING FEE IN INSTALLMENTS

IT IS ORDERED that the debtor(s) pay the filing fee in installments on the terms proposed in the foregoing application.

IT IS FURTHER ORDERED that until the filing fee is paid in full the debtor shall not pay any money for services in connection with this case, and the debtor shall not relinquish any property as payment for services in connection with this case.

BY THE COURT

Date: _____   _____

To whom it may concern:

On _____, I filed a voluntary petition under Chapter 7 of the U.S. Bankruptcy Code. The case number is _____. Under 11 U.S.C. § 362(a), you may not:

- take any action against me or my property to collect any debt.

- enforce any lien on my real or personal property.

- repossess any property in my possession.

- discontinue any service or benefit currently being provided to me.

- take any action to evict me from where I live.

A violation of these prohibitions may be considered contempt of court and punished accordingly.

Very truly yours,

Form 20A. Notice of Motion or Objection

UNITED STATES BANKRUPTCY COURT

_____ DISTRICT OF _____

In re _____ ,　　Case No. _____
　　　　　　　　(Name)　　　　　　　　　　　　　　　　　　　　　　　　　　　(If known)
　　　　　　　　　　　　　　Debtor
　　　　　　　　　　　　　　　　　　　　　　　　　　Chapter _____

NOTICE OF [MOTION TO　] [OBJECTION TO　]

_____ has filed papers with the court to [relief sought in motion or objection].

<u>Your rights may be affected</u>. You should read these papers carefully and discuss them with your attorney, if you have one in this bankruptcy case. (If you do not have an attorney, you may wish to consult one.)

If you do not want the court to [relief sought in motion or objection], or if you want the court to consider your views on the [motion] [objection], then on or before <u>(date)</u>, you or your attorney must:

File with the court a written request for a hearing [or, _if the court requires a written response_, an answer, explaining your position] at:

[address of the bankruptcy clerk's office]

If you mail your [request] [response] to the court for filing, you must mail it early enough so the court will **receive** it on or before the date stated above.

You must also mail a copy to:

[movant's attorney's name and address]

[names and addresses of others to be served]

Attend the hearing scheduled to be held on　(date)　, (year)　, at ___ a.m./p.m. in Courtroom _____, United States Bankruptcy Court, [address].

Other steps required to oppose a motion or objection under local rule or court order.

If you or your attorney do not take these steps, the court may decide that you do not oppose the relief sought in the motion or objection and may enter an order granting that relief.

Date: _____　　Signature: _____

　　　　　　　　　　　　　　　　　Name:_____

　　　　　　　　　　　　　　　　　Address: _____

Your Name, Address & Phone Number:

In Pro Per

UNITED STATES BANKRUPTCY COURT FOR THE _____

DISTRICT OF _____

In re _____   )
) Case No. _____
)
) AMENDMENT COVER SHEET
                          Debtor(s)   )
_____

Presented herewith are the original and one copy of the following:

☐ Voluntary Petition (Note: Spouse may not be added or deleted subsequent to initial filing.)

☐ Schedule A—Real Property

☐ Schedule B—Personal Property

☐ Schedule C—Property Claimed as Exempt

☐ Schedule D—Creditors Holding Secured Claims

☐ Schedule E—Creditors Holding Unsecured Priority Claims

☐ Schedule F—Creditors Holding Unsecured Nonpriority Claims

☐ Schedule G—Executory Contracts and Unexpired Leases

☐ Schedule H—Codebtors

☐ Schedule I—Current Income of Individual Debtor(s)

☐ Schedule J—Current Expenditures of Individual Debtor(s)

☐ Summary of Schedules

☐ Statement of Financial Affairs

☐ I have enclosed a $20 fee because I am adding new creditors or changing addresses after original Meeting of
   Creditors Notice has been sent.

_____   _____
Signature of Debtor   Signature of Debtor's Spouse

I (we) _____ and
_____, the debtor(s)

in this case, declare under penalty of perjury that the information set forth in the amendment attached hereto consisting

of _____ pages is true and correct to the best of my (our) information and belief.

Dated: _____, 19_____

_____   _____
Signature of Debtor   Signature of Debtor's Spouse

Your Name, Address & Phone Number:

In Pro Per

UNITED STATES BANKRUPTCY COURT FOR THE _____

DISTRICT OF _____

In re	)	
	)	Case No. _____
	)	
	)	NOTICE OF CHANGE OF ADDRESS
Debtor(s)	)	

Social Security Number (H): _____

Social Security Number (W): _____

MY (OUR) FORMER MAILING ADDRESS AND PHONE NUMBER WAS:

Name: _____

Street: _____

City: _____

State/Zip: _____

Phone: ( ) _____

PLEASE BE ADVISED THAT AS OF_____, 19_____, MY (OUR) NEW
MAILING ADDRESS AND PHONE NUMBER IS:

Name: _____

Street: _____

City: _____

State/Zip: _____

Phone: ( ) _____

_____
Signature of Debtor

_____
Signature of Debtor's Spouse

Your Name, Address & Phone Number:

In Pro Per

UNITED STATES BANKRUPTCY COURT FOR THE _____

DISTRICT OF _____

In re

)   Case No. _____

)

)   SUPPLEMENTAL SCHEDULE FOR

)   PROPERTY ACQUIRED AFTER

      Debtor(s))   BANKRUPTCY DISCHARGE

TO:_____, Trustee.

This is to inform you that I (we) have received the following item of property since my (our) discharge, but within the 180-day period after filing my (our) Bankruptcy Petition under Bankruptcy Rule 1007 (h):

This property was obtained through an inheritance, marital settlement agreement or divorce decree, death benefits or life insurance proceeds, or other (specify):

☐   I (we) claim this property exempt under the following law:

I (we) _____ and

_____, the debtor(s)

in this case, declare under penalty of perjury that the foregoing is true and correct.

Dated: _____, 19_____   _____

                   Signature of Debtor

                 _____

                   Signature of Debtor's Spouse

DAILY EXPENSES

Date:

Item	Cost

Date:

Item	Cost

Date:

Item	Cost

Date:

Item	Cost

1

2

3

4

5

6

7

8

9

10

11

12

13

14

15

16

17

18

19

20

21

22

23

24

25

26

27

28

Your Name, Address & Phone Number:

In Pro Per

UNITED STATES BANKRUPTCY COURT FOR THE _____

DISTRICT OF _____

In re   )
)   Case No. _____
)
)
                          Debtor(s)   )
_____

PROOF OF SERVICE BY MAIL

I, _____, declare that:

I am over the age of 18 years and not a party to the within bankruptcy. I reside in or am employed in the County of

_____. My residence/business address is _____

_____

On _____, I served the within _____

_____ by placing a true and correct copy of it in a sealed envelope with first-class

postage fully prepaid, in the United States mail at _____

_____, addressed as follows:

I declare under penalty of perjury that the foregoing is true and correct. Executed on _____,

19_____ at _____.

_____
Signature

Index

CATALOG

...more from Nolo Press

	PRICE	CODE

BUSINESS

	PRICE	CODE
The California Nonprofit Corporation Handbook	$29.95	NON
The California Professional Corporation Handbook	$34.95	PROF
The Employer's Legal Handbook	$29.95	EMPL
Form Your Own Limited Liability Company	$34.95	LIAB
Hiring Independent Contractors: The Employer's Legal Guide, (Book w/Disk—PC)	$29.95	HICI
How to Form a CA Nonprofit Corp.—w/Corp. Records Binder & PC Disk	$49.95	CNP
How to Form a Nonprofit Corp., Book w/Disk (PC)—National Edition	$39.95	NNP
How to Form Your Own Calif. Corp.—w/Corp. Records Binder & Disk—PC	$39.95	CACI
How to Form Your Own California Corporation	$29.95	CCOR
How to Form Your Own Florida Corporation, (Book w/Disk—PC)	$39.95	FLCO
How to Form Your Own New York Corporation, (Book w/Disk—PC)	$39.95	NYCO
How to Form Your Own Texas Corporation, (Book w/Disk—PC)	$39.95	TCOR
How to Handle Your Workers' Compensation Claim (California Edition)	$29.95	WORK
How to Market a Product for Under $500	$29.95	UN500
How to Mediate Your Dispute	$18.95	MEDI
How to Write a Business Plan	$21.95	SBS
The Independent Paralegal's Handbook	$29.95	PARA
Legal Guide for Starting & Running a Small Business, Vol. 1	$24.95	RUNS
Legal Guide for Starting & Running a Small Business, Vol. 2: Legal Forms	$29.95	RUNS2
Marketing Without Advertising	$19.00	MWAD
The Partnership Book: How to Write a Partnership Agreement, (Book w/Disk—PC)	$34.95	PART
Sexual Harassment on the Job	$18.95	HARS
Starting and Running a Successful Newsletter or Magazine	$24.95	MAG
Taking Care of Your Corporation, Vol. 1, (Book w/Disk—PC)	$29.95	CORK
Taking Care of Your Corporation, Vol. 2, (Book w/Disk—PC)	$39.95	CORK2
Tax Savvy for Small Business	$28.95	SAVVY
Trademark: Legal Care for Your Business and Product Name	$29.95	TRD
Wage Slave No More: The Independent Contractor's Legal Guide	$34.95	WAGE
Your Rights in the Workplace	$19.95	YRW

CONSUMER

	PRICE	CODE
Fed Up With the Legal System: What's Wrong & How to Fix It	$9.95	LEG
How to Win Your Personal Injury Claim	$24.95	PICL
Nolo's Everyday Law Book	$21.95	EVL
Nolo's Pocket Guide to California Law	$11.95	CLAW
Trouble-Free Travel...And What to Do When Things Go Wrong	$14.95	TRAV

▪ Book with disk

● Book with CD-ROM

	PRICE	CODE

ESTATE PLANNING & PROBATE

8 Ways to Avoid Probate (Quick & Legal Series)	$15.95	PRO8
How to Probate an Estate (California Edition)	$34.95	PAE
Make Your Own Living Trust	$21.95	LITR
▣ Nolo's Will Book, (Book w/Disk—PC)	$29.95	SWIL
Plan Your Estate	$24.95	NEST
The Quick and Legal Will Book	$15.95	QUIC
Nolo's Law Form Kit: Wills	$14.95	KWL

FAMILY MATTERS

A Legal Guide for Lesbian and Gay Couples	$24.95	LG
California Marriage Law	$19.95	MARR
Child Custody: Building Parenting Agreements that Work	$24.95	CUST
Divorce & Money: How to Make the Best Financial Decisions During Divorce	$26.95	DIMO
Get A Life: You Don't Need a Million to Retire Well	$18.95	LIFE
The Guardianship Book (California Edition)	$24.95	GB
How to Adopt Your Stepchild in California	$22.95	ADOP
How to Do Your Own Divorce in California	$24.95	CDIV
How to Do Your Own Divorce in Texas	$19.95	TDIV
How to Raise or Lower Child Support in California	$18.95	CHLD
The Living Together Kit	$24.95	LTK
Nolo's Law Form Kit: Hiring Childcare & Household Help	$14.95	KCHLO
Nolo's Pocket Guide to Family Law	$14.95	FLD
Practical Divorce Solutions	$14.95	PDS
Smart Ways to Save Money During and After Divorce	$14.95	SAVMO

GOING TO COURT

Collect Your Court Judgment (California Edition)	$24.95	JUDG
How to Seal Your Juvenile & Criminal Records (California Edition)	$24.95	CRIM
How to Sue For Up to 25,000...and Win!	$29.95	MUNI
Everybody's Guide to Small Claims Court in California	$18.95	CSCC
Everybody's Guide to Small Claims Court (National Edition)	$18.95	NSCC
Fight Your Ticket ... and Win! (California Edition)	$19.95	FYT
How to Change Your Name (California Edition)	$24.95	NAME
Mad at Your Lawyer	$21.95	MAD
Represent Yourself in Court: How to Prepare & Try a Winning Case	$29.95	RYC
The Criminal Law Handbook: Know Your Rights, Survive the System	$24.95	KYR

HOMEOWNERS, LANDLORDS & TENANTS

The Deeds Book (California Edition)	$16.95	DEED
Dog Law	$14.95	DOG
▣ Every Landlord's Legal Guide (National Edition)	$34.95	ELLI
Every Tenant's Legal Guide	$24.95	EVTEN
For Sale by Owner (California Edition)	$24.95	FSBO
Homestead Your House (California Edition)	$9.95	HOME
How to Buy a House in California	$24.95	BHCA
The Landlord's Law Book, Vol. 1: Rights & Responsibilities (California Edition)	$34.95	LBRT
The Landlord's Law Book, Vol. 2: Evictions (California Edition)	$34.95	LBEV
Leases & Rental Agreements (Quick & Legal Series)	$18.95	LEAR
Neighbor Law: Fences, Trees, Boundaries & Noise	$18.95	NEI
Safe Homes, Safe Neighborhoods: Stopping Crime Where You Live	$14.95	SAFE
Tenants' Rights (California Edition)	$19.95	CTEN
Stop Foreclosure Now in California	$29.95	CLOS

HUMOR

29 Reasons Not to Go to Law School	$9.95	29R
Poetic Justice	$9.95	PJ

▣ Book with disk

● Book with CD-ROM

CALL 800-992-6656 OR USE THE ORDER FORM IN THE BACK OF THE BOOK

	PRICE	CODE

IMMIGRATION

How to Get a Green Card: Legal Ways to Stay in the U.S.A.	$24.95	GRN
U.S. Immigration Made Easy	$39.95	IMEZ

MONEY MATTERS

101 Law Forms for Personal Use: Quick and Legal Series (Book with disk)	$24.95	101LAW
Chapter 13 Bankruptcy: Repay Your Debts	$29.95	CH13
Credit Repair (Quick & Legal Series)	$15.95	CREP
The Financial Power of Attorney Workbook	$24.95	FINPOA
How to File for Bankruptcy	$26.95	HFB
Money Troubles: Legal Strategies to Cope With Your Debts	$19.95	MT
Nolo's Law Form Kit: Personal Bankruptcy	$14.95	KBNK
Stand Up to the IRS	$24.95	SIRS

PATENTS AND COPYRIGHTS

The Copyright Handbook: How to Protect and Use Written Works	$29.95	COHA
Copyright Your Software	$39.95	CYS
License Your Invention (Book w/Disk)	$39.95	LICE
The Patent Drawing Book	$29.95	DRAW
Patent, Copyright & Trademark: A Desk Reference to Intellectual Property Law	$24.95	PCTM
Patent It Yourself	$44.95	PAT
Software Development: A Legal Guide (Book with disk—PC)	$44.95	SFT
The Inventor's Notebook	$19.95	INOT

RESEARCH & REFERENCE

Government on the Net, (Book w/CD-ROM—Windows/Macintosh)	$39.95	GONE
Law on the Net, (Book w/CD-ROM—Windows/Macintosh)	$39.95	LAWN
Legal Research: How to Find & Understand the Law	$19.95	LRES
Legal Research Made Easy (Video)	$89.95	LRME

SENIORS

Beat the Nursing Home Trap	$18.95	ELD
Social Security, Medicare & Pensions	$19.95	SOA
The Conservatorship Book (California Edition)	$29.95	CNSV

SOFTWARE
Call or check our website for special discounts on Software!

California Incorporator 2.0—DOS	$79.95	INCI
Living Trust Maker 2.0—Macintosh	$79.95	LTM2
Living Trust Maker 2.0—Windows	$79.95	LTWI2
Small Business Legal Pro Deluxe CD—Windows/Macintosh CD-ROM	$79.95	SBCD
Nolo's Partnership Maker 1.0—DOS	$79.95	PAGI1
Personal RecordKeeper 4.0—Macintosh	$49.95	RKM4
Personal RecordKeeper 4.0—Windows	$49.95	RKP4
Patent It Yourself 1.0—Windows	$229.95	PYP12
WillMaker 6.0	$69.95	WD6

Special Upgrade Offer
Get 25% off the latest edition of your Nolo book

It's important to have the most current legal information. Because laws and legal procedures change often, we update our books regularly. To help keep you up-to-date we are extending this special upgrade offer. Cut out and mail the title portion of the cover of your old Nolo book and we'll give you 25% off the retail price of the NEW EDITION of that book when you purchase directly from us. For more information call us at 1-800-992-6656. This offer is to individuals only.

⌧ Book with disk
● Book with CD-ROM

ORDER FORM

Code	Quantity	Title	Unit price	Total
		Subtotal		
		California residents add Sales Tax		
		Basic Shipping (*$6.00 for 1 item; $7.00 for 2 or more*)		
		UPS RUSH delivery $7.50–any size order*		
		TOTAL		

Name

Address

(UPS to street address, Priority Mail to P.O. boxes)

* Delivered in 3 business days from receipt of order.
S.F. Bay Area use regular shipping.

FOR FASTER SERVICE, USE YOUR CREDIT CARD AND OUR TOLL-FREE NUMBERS

Order 24 hours a day	1-800-992-6656
Fax your order	1-800-645-0895
e-mail	cs@nolo.com
General Information	1-510-549-1976
Customer Service	1-800-728-3555, Mon.-Fri. 9am-5pm, PST

METHOD OF PAYMENT

☐ Check enclosed
☐ VISA   ☐ MasterCard   ☐ Discover Card   ☐ American Express

Account #   Expiration Date

Authorizing Signature

Daytime Phone

PRICES SUBJECT TO CHANGE.

VISIT OUR OUTLET STORES!

VISIT US ONLINE!

You'll find our complete line of books and software, all at a discount.

BERKELEY
950 Parker Street
Berkeley, CA 94710
1-510-704-2248

SAN JOSE
111 N. Market Street, #115
San Jose, CA 95113
1-408-271-7240

on the Internet
www.nolo.com

NOLO PRESS 950 PARKER ST., BERKELEY, CA 94710